Clouds of Glory

Clouds of Glory

The Life and Legend of
ROBERT E. LEE

Michael Korda

HARPER LUXE

An Imprint of HarperCollins*Publishers*

HarperCollins books may be purchased for educational, business, or sales promotional use. For information, please e-mail the Special Markets Department at SPsales@harpercollins.com.

FIRST HARPERLUXE EDITION

HarperLuxe™ is a trademark of HarperCollins Publishers

Library of Congress Cataloging-in-Publication Data is available upon request.

ISBN: 978-0-06-232671-3

14   ID/RRD   10 9 8 7 6 5 4 3 2 1

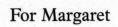

For Margaret

The past is never dead. It's not even past.

—William Faulkner, *Requiem for a Nun*

Our birth is but a sleep and a forgetting:
The soul that rises with us, our life's star,
Hath elsewhere had its setting,
And cometh from afar:
Not in entire forgetfulness,
And not in utter nakedness,
But trailing clouds of glory do we come
From God, who is our home.

—William Wordsworth,
"Ode: Intimations of Immortality from
Recollections of Early Childhood"

Contents

Maps

Preface
The Portent

In October 1859, Brevet Colonel Robert E. Lee,* commanding the Second U.S. Cavalry, in Texas, was home on leave, laboring to untangle the affairs of his late father-in-law's estate. Despite a brilliant military career—many thought him the most capable officer in the U.S. Army—he was a disappointed man. Nobody understood better than Lee how slowly promotion came in this tiny army, or knew more exactly how many officers were ahead of him in the all-important ranking of seniority and stood between him and the seemingly unreachable step of being made a permanent full colonel. He did not suppose, given his age, which was fifty-two, that he would ever wear a brigadier general's

---

* A "brevet" rank was honorary. Lee's actual rank at the time was lieutenant colonel.

single star, still less that fame and military glory awaited him, and although he was not the complaining type, he often expressed regret that he had chosen the army as a career. An engineer of considerable ability—he was credited with making the mighty Mississippi navigable, which among other great benefits turned the sleepy town of Saint Louis into a thriving river port—he could have made his fortune had he resigned from the army to become a civil engineer. Instead, he commanded a cavalry regiment hunting renegade Indians in a dusty corner of the Texas frontier, and not very successfully at that, and was now home, in his wife's mansion across the Potomac from Washington, methodically uncovering the debts and the problems of her father's estate, which seemed likely to plunge the Lees even further into land-poor misery. Indeed, the shamefully run-down state of the Arlington mansion, the discontent of the slaves he and his wife had inherited, and the long neglect of his father-in-law's plantations made it seem only too likely that Lee might have to resign his commission and spend his life as an impoverished country gentleman, trying to put things right for the sake of his wife and children.

He could not have guessed that an event less than seventy miles away was to make him famous— and go far toward bringing about what Lee most feared: the division of his country over the smoldering issues of slavery and states' rights.

Harpers Ferry, Sunday, October 16, 1859

Shortly after eight o'clock at night, having completed his preparations and his prayers, a broad-brimmed hat pulled low over his eyes, his full white beard bristling like that of Moses, the old man led eighteen of his followers, two of them his own sons, down a narrow, rutted, muddy country road toward Harpers Ferry, Virginia. They marched silently in twos behind him as he drove a heavily loaded wagon pulled by one horse.

The members of his "army" had assembled there during the summer and early autumn, hiding away from possibly inquisitive neighbors and learning how to handle their weapons. John Brown had shipped to the farm a formidable arsenal: 198 Sharps rifles, 200 Maynard revolvers, 31,000 percussion caps, an ample supply of gunpowder, and 950 pikes. The pikes Brown had ordered from a blacksmith in Connecticut two years earlier—made to his own design at a dollar apiece, they consisted of a double-edged blade about ten inches long, sharpened at both edges, shaped rather like a large dirk or a broad dagger, and intended to be attached to a six-foot ash pole, a weapon that Brown thought might be more effective and terrifying in the hands of liberated slaves than firearms, with which they were unlikely to be familiar.

Brown's reputation as "the apostle of the sword of Gideon" had been made, for better or for worse, in the widespread guerrilla warfare and anarchy of "bleeding Kansas," where pro-slavery freebooters from Missouri clashed repeatedly with Free Soilers, settlers who were vigorously opposed to the extension of slavery into the territory. Southerners were equally determined to prevent a free state on the border of Missouri, which might render "this species of property"—a current euphemism for slaves—insecure. Violence was widespread and took many forms, from assassination, arson, lynching, skirmishes, and "bushwhacking" to small battles complete with artillery.

Brown had been responsible for the murder of five pro-slavery settlers at Pottawatomie Creek in revenge for the sacking of the antislavery town of Lawrence, Kansas—they had been dragged from their homes in the middle of the night and butchered with broadswords. Brown led the killers, who included two of his sons, and may have given the coup de grâce to one of the victims.

For three years, from 1855 through 1858, a group of Free Soilers under the "command" of "Captain"

Brown (or "Osawatomie Brown," as he was called after his heavily fortified Free Soil settlement) fought pitched battles against "Border Ruffians" (as the pro-slavery forces were known by their enemies), in one of which his son Frederick was killed. Brown achieved fame bordering on idolatry among abolitionists in the North for his exploits as a guerrilla fighter in Kansas, culminating in a daring raid during the course of which he liberated eleven slaves from their masters in Missouri and, evading pursuit despite a price on his head, transported them all the way to freedom across the border in Canada in midwinter.

John Brown was a man of extraordinary courage and persistence, with a grandiose vision and a remarkable gift for organization. Widowed and remarried, he was the father of twenty children by his two wives; a commanding, often intimidating presence even to his enemies; as much at ease in the elegant drawing rooms of the wealthy New England and New York City abolitionists who supported him as he was in the saddle, armed to the teeth, on the plains of Kansas. He was at once a throwback to the undiluted Calvinism and Puritanism of the first New England settlers and far ahead of his time—however opposed they might be to slavery, most abolitionists still shied away from *social* equality with blacks, but Brown had built his home in New Elba, New York, close to Lake

Placid, among freed blacks who ate at the same table as the Browns, and whom he punctiliously addressed as "Mr." or "Mrs." When he redrafted the Declaration of Independence and the Constitution for the benefit of his followers, he included not only racial equality, a revolutionary idea at the time, but what we would now call gender equality, giving women full rights and the vote, promising "secure equal rights, privileges, & justice to all; Irrespective of Sex, or Nation." Brave, unshaken by doubt, willing to shed blood unflinchingly and to die for his cause if necessary, Brown was the perfect man to light the tinder of civil war in America, which was just what he intended to do.

The object of his raid was the U.S. Armory at Harpers Ferry, where 10,000 military rifles a year were manufactured and over 100,000 were stored. Its capture was certain to create a nationwide sensation, and panic in the South; but although Brown was a meticulous planner, his intentions after he captured the armory were uncharacteristically vague. He hoped the act itself would encourage slaves to join his cause, and intended to arm them with rifles if they came in large enough numbers; certainly his intention, once they were armed, was to lead them into the Blue Ridge Mountains, from which they could descend from time to time in larger and larger numbers to liberate more slaves: reenacting the raid into Missouri on a grander and growing scale. When he struck, Brown wrote, "The bees will begin to swarm."

Careful as his preparations had been, Brown had perhaps waited too long before striking, with the result that his usual energy and decisiveness in action seem to have deserted him just when they were most needed. Unlikely as it may seem, he may have come to believe it would be sufficient to "stand at Armageddon and . . . battle for the Lord," and the rest would follow. If so, he was underestimating the anger his raid would cause among the 2,500 people who lived in or near Harpers Ferry, or the alarm it would create in Washington, D.C., less than seventy miles away as the crow flies.

His first moves were sensible enough, given the small number of his force and the sprawling size of the armory. Two of his men cut the telegraph wires, while others secured the bridges over the Potomac and the Shenandoah rivers—Harpers Ferry was on a narrow peninsula, where the rivers joined, and not unlike an island—thus virtually isolating the town. Brown took prisoner the lone night watchman at the armory in the brick fire-engine house, a solid structure that he made his command post, then sent several of his men off into the night to liberate as many slaves as they could from nearby farms and bring their owners in as hostages. The western part of Virginia was not "plantation country" with large numbers of field slaves, but Brown had done his homework—one of his men had been living in Harpers Ferry for over a year, spying out the ground, and even fell in love with a local girl who had borne him a son.

Brown was particularly determined to capture Colonel Lewis W. Washington, a local gentleman farmer and slave owner on a small scale, the great-grandnephew of President Washington, and to have the ceremonial sword that Frederick the Great had presented to George Washington placed in the hands of one of his black followers as a symbol of racial justice. Colonel Washington (his rank was an honorary one) was removed in the middle of the night from his rather modest home, Beall-Air, about five miles from Harpers Ferry, and delivered to Brown in his own carriage, along with a pair of pistols that Lafayette had given George Washington, the sword from Frederick the Great, and three somewhat puzzled slaves.

More slaves were soon brought in, and armed with pikes to guard their former owners in the engine house—most either accepted these weapons reluctantly or refused to touch them. Brown now had thirty-five hostages and possession of the armory, but the slave uprising on which he was counting did not take place, and during the night, one by one, things started to go wrong.

The first problem arose when the night watchman's relief arrived at his post on the Potomac bridge and found it held by armed strangers. He panicked; took a wild punch at Oliver Brown, one of Brown's sons; then ran, at which point one of Oliver's companions shot at him, sending his hat flying and grazing his skull. The night watchman, bleeding profusely, rushed into the Galt House, a saloon opposite the hotel and railway station, and raised the alarm, although the sound of a shot in the middle of the night in a peaceful backwater like Harpers Ferry was by itself enough to arouse the curiosity of those who heard it. Then, at 1:25 a.m., the eastbound Baltimore and Ohio train from Wheeling to Baltimore arrived to encounter the bridge blocked by armed men.

The arrival of the train can hardly have come as a surprise to Brown, since all he had to do was consult a Baltimore and Ohio schedule, but it should have been a signal to him to gather up his hostages, their slaves, and as many rifles as he could pack into the wagon, and get out of town and into the hills with his followers while he could. Given his actions over the next few hours, it is hard not to conclude that somewhere in the back of his mind he had already guessed the effect that a courageous last stand and martyrdom would have on public opinion in the North.

In the meantime, the engineer and the baggage master of the train went forward to see what the problem was on the bridge, and were fired on. Sensibly, they returned and backed the train out of range. The shots attracted the attention of the Harpers Ferry station baggage master, Hayward Shepherd, a freed black man well liked and respected by everybody in town, who went toward the bridge to see what was happening, was told to halt, and was then shot in the back and mortally wounded as he turned away. The irony of the fact that the first victim of the raid was a freed black man holding a responsible job would have been painful news to John Brown, who was, however, too far away from the bridge to know about it.

The shot, and Shepherd's cries of pain, woke Dr. John D. Starry, who lived nearby. He ran to where Shepherd lay to see if he could help the wounded man. Realizing immediately that Shepherd was beyond anything he could do for him, Dr. Starry, an uncommonly courageous man, stayed to give what comfort to Shepherd he could; then, after observing what was going on in town, he went home, saddled his horse, and began to ride around Harpers Ferry in the spirit of

Paul Revere, alerting people to the raid on the armory. He had the presence of mind to send a messenger off to summon the nearest militia, the Jefferson Guard, from Charles Town, the country seat, about eight miles away; he had the church bells rung; and he warned the gathering, puzzled citizens of Harpers Ferry that they had better arm themselves. The bees were beginning to swarm just as John Brown had predicted, but they were not the ones he had in mind.

In the meantime, the train to Baltimore was stuck, since the men holding the bridge refused to let it pass, although they allowed the passengers to walk back and forth. At three in the morning, Brown at last sent word that it could proceed, but the conductor, Phelps, decided it was safer to wait until daybreak before starting. Then Phelps stopped the train at Monocacy, twenty-one miles away, the first stop down the line to the east of Harpers Ferry, to send a telegraph informing W. P. Smith, the B&O's master of transportation in Baltimore, of what had happened. Phelps reported that his train had been fired on, that a B&O employee had been shot, and that at least 150 "insurrectionists" who had "come to free the slaves" were holding both bridges at Harpers Ferry and had told him they would fire on any further train that attempted to cross.

Smith was surprised and, it is possible to guess, irritated by Phelps's message. He telegraphed back, "Your dispatch is evidently exaggerated and written under excitement. Why should our trains be stopped by Abolitionists?" From farther down the line at Elicott's Mills, Phelps replied indignantly that he had not exaggerated, or even "made it half as bad as it is," but by this time the exchange of messages had already reached the desk of John W. Garrett, the president of the Baltimore and Ohio, and he at once took them more seriously than W. P. Smith. Garrett telegraphed the president of the United States, as well as the governor of Virginia and the commander of the Maryland Volunteers, "that an insurrection was in progress . . . in which free negroes and whites were engaged."

In the mid-nineteenth century presidents were by no means as insulated from the communications of ordinary citizens as they are today, and not a few presidents still opened their own mail and read their own telegrams. At the same time, the president of a major railroad was a person of considerable importance, so it is not surprising that Garrett's message to President James Buchanan reached him without delay early in the morning on October 17 or that he acted on it immediately.

Buchanan was not nicknamed "Old Public Functionary" for nothing: he was an American version of "The Vicar of Bray." A Pennsylvania Democrat, he had been a congressman, a senator, U.S. minister to Russia, U.S. minister plenipotentiary to the Court of St. James's, and secretary of state, before winning the presidency in 1856. His service abroad as a diplomat had spared him some of the virulent and passionate political quarrels on the subject of slavery, and he was in any case a "doughboy" (a term of contempt for northerners who were sympathetic to the demands of the slave states), and determined to seek a compromise between southern slave owners and northern abolitionists. Moderation of course gained him no friends on either side of the issue. The only bachelor to have occupied the White House so far, he had lived for fifteen years before his election to the presidency with Senator William Rufus King of Alabama, and it is possible that Buchanan's views on slavery were influenced by his friendship with King—he remarked in his third annual message to Congress that slaves were "treated with kindness and humanity. . . . Both the philanthropy and the self-interest of the master have combined to produce this humane result," a rosy view of the institution of slavery that was common enough in Alabama, but unusual in Buchanan's native Pennsylvania.

Buchanan recognized a crisis when it presented itself, however, and rapidly set in motion as many troops as possible: detachments of regular army infantry and artillery from Fort Monroe, Virginia, and a company of U.S. Marines from the Navy Yard under the command of Lieutenant Israel Green, the only troops available in Washington, were ordered to proceed by train at once to Baltimore and from there to Harpers Ferry, while uniformed companies of the Virginia and Maryland militias (the Hamtramck Guards, the Shepherdstown troop, the Jefferson Guards) had already begun to move into Harpers Ferry and were exchanging fire with John Brown's outnumbered followers, along with a sizable number of armed and angry citizens and "volunteers," or vigilantes.

Buchanan's secretary of war, John B. Floyd, was not efficient, nor would he prove to be loyal—after Harpers Ferry he would be suspected of shipping large numbers of weapons from Federal arsenals in the North to those in the South in anticipation of secession; and in 1862, as a Confederate general, he would abandon his post at Fort Donelson shortly before Grant besieged and took it, for fear he might be tried for treason if he was captured—but he had the good sense to realize that somebody needed to be in command of all these forces converging on Harpers Ferry, and that the right man for the job was at his home in Arlington, just across the Potomac River from Washington.

Robert E. Lee and his wife had inherited the imposing white-pillared mansion that is now the centerpiece of Arlington National Cemetery in 1857 from her father, George Washington Parke Custis, the stepgrandson and adopted son of George Washington. The Arlington property alone comprised 1,100 acres, with a slave population of sixty-three, while two other plantations in Virginia brought the total number of Custis slaves to nearly 200. Custis's management of his plantations, never his first interest—even a sympathetic fellow southerner described him as "a negligent farmer and an easy-going master"—had further slackened with age and infirmity. The Arlington mansion, while it was something of a museum of George Washington's possessions (including the bed he died in), was leaking and in need of major, expensive repairs; the plantations were poorly farmed; and the slaves, who had been given to understand that they would be freed on Custis's death, found instead that their release was contingent on the many other poorly drafted obligations in his will, which looked as if it might drag itself through the courts for years, keeping them in bondage indefinitely.

That this did not make for a happy or willing work-force was only one of the many problems that faced Lee, who, much against his own desire, had taken leave after leave from his post as commander of the recently formed Second U.S. Cavalry at Camp Cooper, Texas, a rough frontier outpost on the Clear Fork of the Brazos River, to devote himself to bringing some kind of order to his father-in-law's estate. Much as Lee might wish he were back in Texas with his troopers chasing bands of Comanche marauders on the frontier, his sense of obligation and duty to his family kept him at Arlington, "trying to get a little work done and to mend up some things," as he wrote to one of his sons, adding, "I succeed very badly."

If so, it was one of the few examples of failure in the life of Robert E. Lee. One of the rare cadets to have been graduated from the U.S. Military Academy with no demerits, he had joined the U.S. Army Corps of Engineers, which in those days got the best and the brightest of cadets, and undertook successfully some of the largest and most difficult public projects of his time, including a safe deepwater channel on the Mississippi that opened up Saint Louis to shipping and caused the mayor of that city to hail him grandly as the man who "brought the Father of the Waters under control." His service in the Mexican War was at once heroic and of vital importance; his "gallantry" won him universal admiration, as well as the confidence and friendship of General Winfield Scott, who singled Lee out for special praise to Congress.

Lee was later appointed superintendent of the U.S. Military Academy; his leadership at West Point won him the confidence and praise of both the cadets and the War Department, as well as giving him an opportunity to take advantage of its library and study in exhaustive detail the campaigns of Napoleon—a scholarly interest that would pay dividends in the most unexpected way only seven years later when he would become celebrated as the greatest tactician in American military history, as well as "a foe without hate, a friend without treachery, a soldier without cruelty, a victor without oppression . . . a Caesar, without his ambition, Frederick, without his tyranny, Napoleon without his selfishness, and Washington, without his reward."

Lee was happy enough to give up the Corps of Engineers for active soldiering, and Jefferson Davis, secretary of war (and future president of the Confederacy), was eager to have him as second in command of the newly formed Second Cavalry, for which Davis had long petitioned Congress to reinforce the American military presence on the frontier. For the next six years Lee's military service was to be of the hardest kind, in places where there was nothing much except lonely space "to attract Indians . . . or to induce them to remain," and from which he wrote to his wife on July 4, 1856, with a burst of sincere patriotism: "the sun was fiery hot. The atmosphere like the blast from a hot-air furnace, the water salt; still my feelings for my country were as ardent, my faith in her future as true, and my hopes for her advancement as unabated, as if called forth under more propitious circumstances." Lee eventually rose to succeed Colonel Albert Sidney Johnston, the future Confederate general who would die of his wound at Shiloh, as commander of the Second Cavalry, and it was from his duties as its commanding officer that he had taken leave to see to the interminable problems of his father-in-law's estate.

Secretary of War Floyd returned from the White House to his office to put in motion the forces that he and President Buchanan had decided to send to Harpers Ferry, and to summon Colonel Lee to the War Department at once. He scrawled a quick note to Colonel Drinkard, chief clerk of the War Department, to write out an order to Lee, which read: "Brvt. Co. R. E. Lee, Lt. Col. 2nd cavalry is assigned to duty according to his Brvt rank & will repair to Harper's

Ferry & take command of the troops ordered to that place. He will direct all the troops from Ft. Monroe to continue their route to that place, Harper's Ferry. [signed] J. B. Floyd, Secretary of War." Finding First Lieutenant J. E. B. ("Jeb") Stuart of the First Cavalry in his waiting room, and since Stuart was actually staying with the Lees at Arlington, Floyd gave him the sealed envelope and asked him to deliver it personally to Lee. Stuart had been a cadet at West Point when Lee became superintendent, and was a close friend of one of Lee's sons, Custis, who had been a classmate. A Virginian, Stuart was already a young officer of great promise, a natural horseman with a reputation for dash and bravery gained in countless clashes with Indians throughout the West, and for steady competence in the pro- and antislavery warfare of Kansas, during which he had briefly met John Brown in the process getting Brown to release a detachment of pro-slavery Missouri militiamen he had taken prisoner. Stuart, who would become a Confederate hero, a major general, and the greatest cavalry leader of the Civil War, was in civilian clothes—he was there on business, having invented and patented "an improved method of attaching sabers to belts," for the use of which the War Department paid him $5,000, plus $2 for every belt hook the army bought, not a bad deal for a junior officer*—and set off immediately to Arlington. Stuart must have overheard enough to know that there was a slave insurrection taking place at Harpers Ferry, and once he reached Arlington and handed Lee the envelope, he asked permission to accompany Lee as his aide. Lee was almost as fond of Stuart as he was of his own sons (two of whom would serve under Stuart in the coming war), and agreed immediately. They set off together at once for the War Department—such was the urgency of the message that Lee did not even pause to change into uniform.

Floyd filled both officers in on what he knew—the president of the Baltimore and Ohio Railroad was already criticizing the small number of troops being sent, and hugely overestimating the number of insurrectionists—then took them over to the White House, to meet with the president. President Buchanan quickly provided Lee with a proclamation of martial law to use

---

*This was a simple but useful innovation. Since the end of the eighteenth century cavalry in North America had fought more often as mounted light infantry than in the traditional cavalry charge of massed horsemen, and by the mid-nineteenth century Yankee ingenuity had provided mounted troops with fast-loading carbines like the Sharps, and even with repeating, cartridge-fed carbines like the Henry. For the dismounted cavalryman fighting as infantry his saber was a cumbersome nuisance that was all too easy to trip over, however effective it was in a mounted charge; Stuart's invention allowed him to remove the saber with one hand and hang it from the pommel of his saddle as he dismounted, then reattach it to his belt as he remounted.

in case he needed it (by now rumor put the number of armed insurrectionists at 3,000), and both officers left for the station, Stuart having borrowed a uniform coat and a sword.

Horror of a slave revolt resonated sharply for Lee—slave rebellion, with the inevitable massacre of white women and children, was a fear of every white southerner, even without the prospect of northern abolitionists and freed blacks seizing possession of a Federal arsenal to arm the slaves. As a young officer, recently married, Lee had been stationed at Fort Monroe, Virginia, less than forty miles from where Nat Turner's rebellion took place over two days in August 1831. Led by Turner, the slaves killed fifty-six whites, including women and children, using knives, hatchets, farm implements, and in the case of a young girl whom Turner himself killed, a fence post. In the wake of that rebellion, fifty-six slaves were executed and at least 200 more killed by the militia, white mobs, and vigilantes, while the state of Virginia passed laws forbidding the education of slaves and freed blacks, and "requiring white ministers to be present at black church services," since the rumor was that Turner had planned his uprising in church between gospel sermons to his fellow slaves. Lee himself felt no great enthusiasm for slavery but he had heard the stories of what Nat

Turner and his followers had done to their owners and the families of their neighbors from those who had seen the results with their own eyes, and so had no illusions about the consequences of a slave rebellion on a much larger scale.

Lee and Stuart took a train for the Relay House, where the spur line to Washington met the main line from Baltimore to the West, but found that the marines had already left there. The president of the Baltimore and Ohio provided them with a locomotive, and Lee telegraphed ahead to order the marines to halt at Sandy Hook, on the Maryland side of the Potomac about a mile to the east of Harpers Ferry, where Lee and Stuart caught up with them around ten o'clock on the night of October 17, after a smoky, noisy ride standing on the fire plate of the locomotive between the engineer and the fireman. By midnight, Lee, Stuart, Lieutenant Green, and the marines (accompanied by Major W. W. Russell, a marine paymaster) were in Harpers Ferry, and Lee had already appraised the situation as being less serious than was feared in Washington. Learning from the militiamen that the insurrectionists and their hostages were in the fire-engine house of the armory, he quickly telegraphed to Baltimore to halt the dispatch of further troops and artillery, ordered the marines into the armory grounds to prevent any insurrectionists from escaping, and decided to assault the fire-engine house "at day-light." He would have attacked at once, but feared that the lives of "some of the gentlemen . . . that were held as prisoners" might be sacrificed in a night assault.

One can sense, even in Lee's brief report after the event, the firm hand of a professional soldier taking over. With exquisite politeness, he offered the honor of forming "the storming party" to the commander of the Maryland Volunteers, who declined it with remarkable candor, saying, "These men of mine have wives and children at home. I will not expose them to such risk. You are paid for doing this kind of work." The commander of the Virginia militia also declined the honor (referring to the marines as "the mercenaries"), as Lee surely guessed he would—a lesson for the future, if Lee needed one, about the value of state militias—and he therefore ordered Lieutenant Green to "take those men out," which is what he probably wanted in the first place, since Green was a professional and the marines were well-trained, reliable regulars. Calmly, Lee surveyed the ground, moved the militiamen back out of the way, and sat down to write a message to the leader of the insurrectionists:

Headquarters Harpers Ferry
October 18, 1859
Colonel Lee, United States Army, commanding
the troops sent by the President of the United

States to suppress the insurrection at this place,
demands the surrender of the persons in the
armory buildings.

If they will peacefully surrender themselves and
restore the pillaged property, they shall be kept in
safety to await the orders of the President. Colonel
Lee represents to them, in all frankness, that it is
impossible for them to escape; that the armory
is surrounded on all sides by troops; and that if he
is compelled to take them by force he cannot
answer for their safety.

> R. E. Lee
> Colonel Commanding
> United States Troops.

The previous twenty-four hours, almost from the
moment he allowed the eastbound train for Baltimore
to proceed, had been a succession of disasters and trag-
edies for John Brown—none of which shook his self-
confidence, his courage, or his command over those
around him. During the night one of Brown's followers shot and killed another citizen of Harpers Ferry,
while Brown busied himself ordering an early breakfast for his men and his prisoners from the hotel across
the street from the gates of the armory, apparently
unaware that the Jefferson Guards from Charles Town
were already on their way—Dr. Starry's alarm that a

slave uprising led by northern abolitionists was taking place in Harpers Ferry was enough to get the local militiamen moving without even bothering to put on their uniform, together with a second, hastily assembled detachment of armed and angry local citizens.

By ten in the morning gunfire could be heard throughout the town, as Brown and his followers were pinned down in the armory, and by noon the militiamen and volunteers had retaken both bridges, cutting off any chance of Brown's escape, and were beginning to kill, one by one, those of Brown's party who were left outside the armory. Brown's men were spared nothing in the way of torture and desecration. One of them, a "mulatto" named Dangerfield Newby, who had been among those trying to hold the Potomac bridge against the militia, had his ears and his genitals cut off for souvenirs, while sharpened sticks were poked into his wounds as he died in agony. His mutilated corpse was left in the street while hogs rooted at his entrails for the rest of the day. Rather than the slave insurrection that Brown had counted on, he had unleashed mob violence instead.

John Brown was a realist in military matters, and although it was not in his nature to surrender, he soon recognized that he was surrounded by superior numbers and that no slave uprising was going to save him.

By noon, the volume of fire had driven him back into the armory's fire-engine house, a stout brick building with oak double doors, and he had already made an attempt to negotiate, proposing to release his prisoners in exchange for the right to take his men across the Potomac into Maryland, from which he no doubt hoped they could reach Pennsylvania. The two men he had sent out under a white flag were taken prisoner—the militia and the volunteers were in no mood to honor a white flag—but he soon sent out three more, with dire consequences: despite the white flag they carried, one of them was shot and wounded, and Brown's son Watson was mortally wounded by a bullet in his guts and dragged back into the fire-engine house.

Brown set his men to work knocking out firing ports to transform the fire-engine house into a makeshift fort, and lashed the big central doors with ropes so as to leave a gap of several inches to fire through. His spirits were undaunted, and his faith in his mission as firm as ever. Even his prisoners, Colonel Washington among them, had come to admire the old man, however strongly they deplored what he was doing. By mid-afternoon, men were falling on both sides—the mayor of Harpers Ferry was shot and killed; Brown's son Oliver, firing through the gap in the doors, was mortally wounded; two more of Brown's men were shot as they tried to swim across the river; and one of the men Brown had sent out under a flag of truce was dragged from the hotel where he was being held to the Potomac bridge by the mob and executed—his body fell into the river and drifted to a shallow pool where people used it as "an attractive target" for the rest of the day. It could still be seen for a day or two "lying at the bottom of the river, with his ghastly face still exhibiting his fearful death agony."

Henry A. Wise, the governor of Virginia, had attempted to reassert some kind of order in Harpers Ferry by appointing Colonel Robert W. Baylor of the militia as commander, and by nightfall Baylor had decided to offer the insurrectionist leader another chance to surrender. He sent an elderly civilian to the fire-engine house with a white handkerchief tied to his umbrella, but this courageous citizen was unable to persuade Brown to agree to an unconditional surrender, and although two more attempts were made, Brown remained defiant—he would not surrender unless he was allowed to leave with those of his men who remained alive, and the bodies of those who had been killed. These were not terms that Colonel Baylor could accept, as Brown must have known.

A final attempt was made to persuade Brown to surrender by Captain Sinn, of the Frederick militia, who hailed the fire-engine house and was invited inside by

Brown. Sinn found him wearing the sword of Frederick the Great, carrying a Sharps carbine, wearing a large bowie knife on his belt, and full of complaints that his men "had been shot down like dogs" while bearing flags of truce. Sinn rather brusquely replied that men who took up arms against their own government "must expect to be shot down like dogs." Brown took no umbrage at this, but merely replied that "he had weighed the responsibility and should not shrink from it." He insisted that his followers "had killed no unarmed men," but Sinn pointed out that the mayor had been unarmed when he was killed. Brown said that if so, he "deeply regretted it." The two men, though opponents, clearly respected each other. Sinn crossed the street to the hotel, and returned with a surgeon to look at the wounds of Brown's son Watson; the surgeon saw at once that the young man was dying, and that nothing more could be done but to make him as comfortable as possible.

With the departure of Captain Sinn and the surgeon, Brown's men and his prisoners settled down for the night as best they could in the total darkness and cold of his tiny "fort." Brown, with all his experience of last-ditch frontier warfare in Kansas, told his men to load all the rifles and stack them by the loopholes so they would not need to reload when the assault came; then he and

Colonel Washington sat down to chat amiably enough together, and Brown reassured Washington that he would return President Washington's sword undamaged, since this appeared to be Washington's chief concern. From time to time Oliver Brown groaned and begged to be put out of his agony, to which his father replied first, "Oh, you will get over it," then later, more sharply, "If you must die, die like a man."

Many of Brown's biographers have commented on the harshness of these remarks to his dying son, and of course to the modern ear they do sound unfeeling, but Brown's love for his sons and grief for their loss were intense beyond any doubt—his spirit was that of the Old Testament, however, not the New, and like Abraham, his submission to God's will was absolute and unquestioning. If the Lord demanded the sacrifice of two more of his sons to bring about the end of slavery, then so be it. It was for his boys and himself to accept God's will with courage, as Isaac had done on Mount Moriah: hence the stern advice to Oliver to "die like a man."

By eleven o'clock Oliver fell silent, and Brown said, "I guess he is dead." Watson Brown's quiet breathing indicated that he was still alive, if only just. Inside the fire-engine house, most of it taken up by two fire engines and their hoses, were the two dead or dying boys; the body of one of Brown's followers, who had been killed while shooting through the gap between the main doors; Brown himself and five of his men, armed with Sharps rifles and revolvers; and Colonel Washington and ten other hostages. It was a small, cramped space, and cannot have been made more cheerful by the unmistakable sound of Lee's marines replacing the militia around one in the morning, boots crashing in unison, orders being given and obeyed crisply—the arrival of regular troops could only mean that an assault was imminent.

Lee made his plans carefully. Now that the fire-engine house was surrounded by the marines, he was certain nobody could escape. He ordered Lieutenant Green to pick a party of twelve men to make the assault, plus three especially robust men to knock in the doors with sledgehammers, and a second party of twelve to go in behind them once the main door was breached, and made it clear that they would all go in with their rifles unloaded—in order to spare the hostages, the assault was to be made with bayonets; no shots were to be fired. Green did not even have a revolver—because his orders had come from the White House, he had assumed that his marines were urgently required for some ceremonial duty. They wore their dress uniforms, and he was armed merely with his officer's dress sword, the marines' famous "Mameluke" commemorating their assault on Tripoli, with its simple ivory grip and slim curved blade, an elaborate, ornamental, but flimsy weapon intended for ceremony rather than combat, instead of the pistol and heavier sword he would normally have worn on his belt going into battle. Major Russell, the paymaster, as a noncombatant officer, carried only a rattan switch, but being marines these officers were not dismayed at the prospect of assaulting the building virtually unarmed.

At first light J. E. B. Stuart was to walk up to the door and read to the leader of the insurrectionists—his name was assumed to be Isaac Smith—Lee's letter. Whoever "Smith" was, Lee took it for granted that the terms of his letter would not be accepted, and he wanted the marines to get to "close quarters" as quickly as possible once that had happened. Speed—and the sheer concentrated violence of the assault—was the best way of ensuring that none of the hostages was harmed. The moment "Smith" had rejected Lee's terms, Stuart was to raise his cap and the marines would go in.

As dawn broke Stuart advanced calmly to the doors carrying a white flag and Lee's message. Through the gap he could see a familiar face, and the muzzle of a Sharps carbine pointed directly at his chest at a distance of a few inches—after being captured John Brown remarked that he could have wiped Stuart out like a mosquito, had he chosen to. "When *Smith* first came to the door," Stuart would later write, as if he had met an old friend, "I recognized old *Osawatomie* Brown, who had given us so much trouble in Kansas."

Lee's message made no great impression on John Brown, who continued to argue, with what Stuart called "admirable tact," that he and his men should be allowed to cross the Potomac and make their way back to a free state. Stuart got along well enough with his old opponent from Kansas—except for their difference of opinion about the legitimacy of slavery, they were the same kind of man: courageous, active, bold, exceedingly polite, and dangerous—and the "parley," as Stuart called it, went on for quite some time, longer almost certainly than Lee, who was standing forty feet away on a slight rise in the ground, had intended. At last Brown said firmly, "No, I prefer to die here," and with something like regret, Stuart took his cap off and waved it, stepping sideways behind the stone pillar that separated the two doors of the building to make way for the marines.

There was a volley of shots from the fire-engine house as the three marines with sledgehammers stepped forward and began to batter away at the heavy oak doors.

Because Brown had used rope to hold the doors slightly open, the sledgehammers made no impression at first, merely driving them back a bit as the rope stretched. Green noticed a heavy ladder nearby, and ordered his men to use it as a battering ram, driving "a ragged hole low down in the right hand door" at the second blow. Colonel Washington, who was inside, standing close to Brown, remarked later that John Brown "was the coolest and firmest man I ever saw in defying danger and death. With one son dead by his side, and another shot through, he felt the pulse of his dying son with one hand and held his rifle with the other, and commanded his men with the utmost composure, encouraging them to be firm and to sell their lives as dearly as they could." This admiration for John Brown as a man was to become a common theme in the South in the next few weeks: he had all the virtues southerners professed to admire, except for his opinion of slavery.

Colonel Washington cried out loudly, "Don't mind us. Fire!" as the door splintered, and Lee, who recognized Washington's voice, exclaimed admiringly, "The old revolutionary blood does tell."

Lieutenant Green was first through the narrow, splintered opening his men had created in the door. The inside of the fire-engine house was already dense with smoke—in the days before the invention of smokeless gunpowder, every shot produced a volume of thick, acrid black smoke—but despite it he at once recognized Colonel Washington, whom he knew. Washington pointed to Brown, who was kneeling beside him reloading his carbine, and said, "This is Osawatomie." Green did not hesitate. He lunged forward and plunged his dress sword into Brown, but the blade struck Brown's belt buckle and was bent almost double by the force of the blow. Green took the bent weapon in both hands and beat Brown around the head with it until the old man collapsed, blood pouring from his wounds. As the marines followed Green in, led by Major Russell with his rattan cane, one of them was shot in the face, and another killed. The rest "rushed in like tigers," in Green's words; stepped "over their fallen comrades"; and bayoneted two of Brown's followers, pinning one of them against the far wall. The others surrendered, and the fight was over in three minutes. Green would later remark that "a storming party is not a play-day sport," which was no doubt true enough, but Lee had achieved his objective: none of the prisoners was harmed in the assault. Colonel Washington refused to leave the fire-engine house until he was provided with a pair of gloves, since he did not want to be seen in public with dirty hands.

Lee "saw to it that the captured survivors were protected and treated with kindliness and consideration."

Indeed, once the fire-engine house was taken, everybody seemed impressed by John Brown, rather than infuriated or vengeful. Lieutenant Green assumed he had killed Brown, but it soon appeared that the old man's wounds were less serious than had been thought, and Lee had him carried to the office of the paymaster of the armory, where Brown soon recovered enough strength to hold what would now be called a "celebrity press conference" combined with some of the attributes of a royal audience. Lee courteously offered to clear the room of visitors if their presence "annoyed or pained" Brown, who, though in considerable pain, replied that "he was glad to make himself and his motives clearly understood," a considerable understatement given what was to come in the next six and a half weeks, during which Brown would be transformed into a national hero and martyr, largely by the skill with which he played on public opinion in the North, and by his natural dignity and courage.

The small room was crowded. Brown and one of his wounded men, both lying on some blood-soaked old bedding on the floor, were surrounded by Lee; Stuart; Governor Wise of Virginia; Brown's former prisoner the indomitable Colonel Washington; Senator Mason of Virginia, who in the near future would become the Confederacy's "commissioner" in the United

Kingdom; Congressman Vallandigham of Ohio and Congressman Faulkner of Virginia, among others; and perhaps more important than all of these, two reporters, one from the *New York Herald* and one from the *Baltimore American,* with their notepads at the ready. To everybody's surprise, Brown allowed himself to be questioned for three hours, never once losing his self-control or the respect of his audience, and giving "no sign of weakness," even though Lieutenant Green's first thrust with his sword had pierced through him almost to his kidneys before striking his belt buckle.

Governor Wise perhaps spoke for everyone when he said of Brown, "He is a man of clear head, of courage, fortitude and simple ingenuousness. . . . He inspired me with a great trust in his integrity as a man of truth. He is a fanatic, vain and garrulous, but firm, truthful and intelligent," unusual words to describe a man who had just stormed and captured a town and a federal arsenal, and was responsible, at least morally, for the death of four townspeople and one marine. Wise added, "He is the gamest man I ever saw," a sentiment everybody seemed to share.

He was also the most eloquent. When Senator Mason asked him how he could justify his acts, Brown replied, "I think, my friend, you are guilty of a great wrong against God and humanity—I say it without wishing to be offensive—and it would be perfectly right in any one to interfere with you so far as to free those you willfully and wickedly hold in bondage. I do not say this insultingly." When Mason asked him if he had paid his men any wages, Brown replied, "None," and when J. E. B. Stuart remarked at this, a trifle sententiously, "The wages of sin is death," Brown turned to him and said reprovingly, "I would not have made such a remark to you, if you had been a prisoner and wounded in my hands."

Again and again Brown trumped his opponents. When asked upon what principle he justified his acts, he replied: "Upon the golden rule. I pity the poor in bondage that have none to help them; that is why I am here; not to gratify any personal animosity, revenge or vindictive spirit. It is my sympathy with the oppressed and the wronged, that are as good as you and as precious in the sight of God."

Lee would later write that the ineptitude of Brown's plan proved he was either "a fanatic or a madman," and from the military point of view he was right: twelve of Brown's eighteen men, including two of his sons, had been killed, and two (including himself) wounded. But in fact Brown's plan had worked out triumphantly, though not in the way he had intended.

Lee ordered Lieutenant Green to deliver Brown to the Charles Town jail to await trial, but Brown was far from being a political prisoner in the modern sense; he was allowed to carry out from the very beginning an uncensored and eloquent correspondence with his admirers and his family. The initial reaction in the North was that he had given abolitionism a bad name by his violent raid, but that quickly changed to admiration—here was a man who did not just *talk* about ending slavery, but *acted*. Although his wounds obliged him to attend his trial lying on a cot and covered with blankets, Brown's behavior during it transformed him into a hero and a martyr throughout the world except in the slave states.

Ralph Waldo Emerson predicted that Brown "will make the gallows glorious like the cross"; Henry David Thoreau would call Brown "a crucified hero"; from France Victor Hugo wrote an open letter pleading for Brown's pardon; and in Concord, Massachusetts, Louisa May Alcott, the author of *Little Women*, defined the widening gulf between North and South over the issue of slavery when she wrote of Brown's coming execution,

No monument of quarried stone
No eloquence of speech,
Can grave the lessons on the land
His martyrdom will teach.

Lee was glad to leave Harpers Ferry and return home, but after a few days there he was ordered back to organize the defense of the armory, since the growing storm of protest over Brown's sentence had made Governor Wise fearful of a new attack on it, or of an attempt by armed abolitionists to free Brown—though Brown himself had discouraged all such attempts, convinced now that his martyrdom was part of God's plan for the destruction of slavery. Lee, who above all things disliked emotional personal confrontations, was obliged to deal as tactfully as he could with the arrival in Harpers Ferry of Mrs. Brown, who wished to see her husband before he was executed. Mrs. Brown had come, accompanied by a few abolitionist friends, "to have a last interview with her husband," as Lee wrote to his wife, explaining, "As it is a matter over which I have no control I referred them to General Taliaferro." (William B. Taliaferro was the commander of the Virginia Militia at Harpers Ferry.)

The day of the execution, December 2, Lee was no more anxious to watch Brown hang than he had been to deal with Mrs. Brown, and took care to station himself with the four companies of federal troops from Fort Monroe, which had been sent by the president to guard the armory at Harpers Ferry at the request of Governor Wise. In his majestic biography of Brown, Oswald Garrison Villard—grandson of

William Lloyd Garrison, the famous abolitionist and supporter of John Brown—mused, "If John Brown's prophetic sight wandered across the hills to the scene of his brief Virginia battle, it must have beheld his generous captor, Robert E. Lee, again in military charge of Harper's Ferry, wholly unwitting that upon his shoulders was soon to rest the fate of a dozen confederated states."

But of course no such "prophetic sight" or "spiritual glance," as Villard also imagined it, carried that far from the scaffold. The old man, who had arrived seated on his own coffin, in a wagon drawn by two horses, was as dignified and commanding a presence as ever—as he reached the scaffold, he remarked, looking at the line of the Blue Ridge Mountains, where he had hoped to shelter with the slaves he had freed and armed, and from which he had intended to raid from time to time to free more until a kind of human chain reaction brought an end to slavery, "This is beautiful country. I never had the pleasure of seeing it before." Erect, serene, calm, he had to wait for twelve minutes with the noose around his neck while the Virginia militia tried clumsily to form up in ranks as a square around the gallows, without showing the slightest sign of trembling in his legs or of fear on his face; the fierce eyes, which countless people who knew him compared to those of an eagle, stared unblinkingly at more than a thousand witnesses to his execution before the hood was placed on his head.

Many in the ranks around the scaffold would die in the war that was coming, some of them rising to fame and high rank, one of them at least to lasting infamy. In command of a detachment of cadet artillerymen from the Virginia Military Institute in their uniforms of gray and red was Thomas J. Jackson, professor of natural and experimental philosophy and instructor of artillery, who was praying fervently for John Brown's soul and who in just nineteen months would receive his nickname, "Stonewall," at First Manassas—First Bull Run, in the North—and would go on to become Lee's most trusted corps commander and lieutenant. Also among the troops drawn up to prevent Brown's being rescued were Edmund Ruffin, a white-haired firebrand secessionist who was determined to see Brown die, had purchased some of the blades from John Brown's pikes in order to send one to the governor of each slave state as a reminder of Yankee hatred of the South, and would fire the first shot on Fort Sumter; and, in the Richmond company of the Virginia militia, a private of dramatic appearance, eyes fixed on the figure on the scaffold and delighted to be part of a historic scene: the actor John Wilkes Booth, who in five years would become Lincoln's assassin, and would himself have stood on a scaffold like Brown's had he not been shot by a Union soldier.

In Philadelphia "a public prayer meeting" was held at just the moment Brown dropped through the trap to hang "between heaven and earth." In Albany, New York, a slow hundred-gun salute was fired, to honor the martyr. In Cleveland, Ohio, Melodeon Hall "was draped in mourning for a meeting attended by fourteen hundred persons." In New York City and in Rochester and Syracuse, New York, huge prayer meetings were held—as they were in Concord, Plymouth, and New Bedford, Massachusetts; and Concord and Manchester, New Hampshire. All over the North bells were tolled mournfully at the moment of Brown's death, and in Boston churches, halls, and temples were filled with mourners—in Tremont Hall, a packed meeting of the American Anti-Slavery Society heard the abolitionist and pacifist William Lloyd Garrison declare: "I am prepared to say: 'Success to every slave insurrection at the South, and in every slave country.' And I do not see how I compromise or stain my peace profession in making that declaration. . . . Give me, as a non-resistant, Bunker Hill and Lexington and Concord, rather than the cowardice and servility of a Southern slave-plantation."

Once it was north of the Mason-Dixon Line the train carrying Brown's body—transferred to a new coffin that was not of southern origin or manufacture—was halted by huge crowds at every station along the way, until he was at last laid to rest before a giant boulder at his home in New Elba, New York, in the shadow of Whiteface Mountain.

Showers of meteors had marked Brown's raid on Harpers Ferry, his trial, and his execution, prompting Walt Whitman, in a poem about Brown, to ask himself, "What am I myself but one of your meteors?" Thoreau too, described Brown's life as "meteorlike, flashing through the darkness in which we live," and Herman Melville, in *The Portent*, described Brown prophetically as the "meteor of the war." It was Melville's phrase that stuck, appropriately, since it would be only seventeen months between John Brown's execution and the firing on Fort Sumter that brought about the war.

Whatever else Brown had done, the reaction to his death effectively severed the country into two opposing parts, making it clear to the South, even to moderates there who were searching for a compromise, that northerners' tolerance for slavery was wearing thin. Until Brown's death, the issues had been whether or not slavery would be extended into the "territories," and the degree to which escaped slaves in the free states could be seized as property and returned to their owners. Now Brown had made the very existence of slavery as an institution an issue—in fact *the* issue.

Southerners were dismayed and angered by the enormous outpouring of sympathy and grief in the northern states for a man who had been convicted of treason, rebellion, first-degree murder, and "conspiring and advising with slaves and others to rebel," while northerners were outraged by the speed with which the Virginia jury had decided Brown's fate—forty-five minutes—in view of the seriousness of the charges against him, and by his execution, when many felt that a pardon or imprisonment would have been more appropriate. "Marvellous old man!" the eloquent abolitionist Wendell Phillips declaimed in a magnificent funeral oration that rivals the Gettysburg Address in simplicity and passion as one of the noblest statements of American history. "He has abolished slavery in Virginia. . . . True the slave is still there. So when the tempest uproots a pine on your hills, it looks green for months—a year or two. Still, it is timber, not a tree. John Brown has loosened the roots of the slave system; it only breathes—it does not live—hereafter."

This was exactly what people throughout the South feared. Assigned temporarily to command the Department of Texas, Lee returned there in February 1860 to resume his pursuit of Mexican bandits and Comanche bands on the frontier. He did not dwell on his face-to-face meeting with John Brown, or on his own role in one of the most striking dramas in American history, but one senses in his correspondence with friends and family a growing alarm, intensified by his experiences at Harpers Ferry, at the speed with which the Union appeared to be unraveling. He was as little pleased with the extravagant demands of what he called, with the natural distaste of a Virginia aristocrat for the noisy and violent nouveaux riches of the great cotton plantations, "the 'Cotton States,' as they term themselves," as with the strident hostility of the abolitionists toward the South. He was appalled at southerners' talk about "the renewal of the slave trade," to which he was "opposed on every ground," and his experience of dealing with his father-in-law's slaves had further soured his view of slavery as an institution. He regarded secession as "revolution," dismissed it as silly, and "could anticipate no greater calamity for our country than a dissolution of our union." He was depressed, lonely, and homesick in San Antonio, deeply conscious of the fact that he was a fifty-two-year-old officer who had spent over thirty years rising slowly from lieutenant to the rank of lieutenant colonel; and at his age he had little hope of ever reaching the rank of brigadier general, since there were twenty-two men senior to him on the promotion list. He had reached an age, in short, to begin to question, now that it was too late, whether his choice of profession had been wise. He had not the slightest inkling of the glory that awaited him.

Never much interested in politics, perhaps because politics had led his father to disgrace and an early grave, Lee was dismayed by the increasing violence of political rhetoric as the country moved toward the election of a new president, and by the threats he heard all around him of secession in the event that Lincoln was elected. "I hope," he wrote, "that the wisdom and patriotism of the country will devise some way of saving it, and that a kind Providence has not yet turned the current of His blessings from us." Robert E. Lee was a Virginian who had lived for over thirty years outside the South, except for brief periods at Arlington and his service in Texas. He was a cosmopolitan, who felt as much at home in New York as he did anywhere in the South; he was opposed to secession; he did not think that preserving slavery was a goal worth fighting for; and his loyalty to his country was intense, sincere, and deeply felt.

He was careful, amid the vociferous enthusiasm for secession in Texas once Lincoln was elected, to keep his opinions to himself, but in one instance, when asked "whether a man's first allegiance was due his state or the nation," he "spoke out, and unequivocally. He had been taught to believe, and he did believe, he said, that his first obligations were due Virginia." This simple, old-fashioned point of view was to guide Lee through the next four years, during which he would become the foremost general, and indeed the figurehead, of a cause in which he did not completely believe. He compared his position to that of Washington, who was not a remote historical figure for Lee, but his wife's step-great-grandfather and his own father's friend and patron. He read Edward Everett's *Life of Washington* as the bad news of secession came flooding in, and although he was too modest ever to have identified himself with the great man, he could hardly have failed to recognize in Washington's dilemma a parallel of his own. "Washington," Everett wrote, "by nature the most loyal of men to order and law, whose rule of social life was obedience to rightful authority, was from the first firmly on the American side; not courting, not contemplating even, till the eve of the explosion, a forcible resistance to the mother country, but not recoiling from it when forced upon the colonies as the inevitable result of their principles."

"Secession," Lee wrote, "is nothing but Revolution. . . . Anarchy would have been established, and not a government by Washington, Hamilton, Jefferson, Madison, and the other patriots of the revolution. . . . Still, a Union that can only be maintained by swords and bayonets, and in which strife and civil war to take the place of brotherly love and kindness, has no charm for me." As a result of the principles he shared with his fellow Virginians, Lee too, however reluctantly, would be obliged to take up arms when "the explosion" came.

He was still in Texas, the great moral decision of his life was still ahead of him, the country he loved was still—just—held together by bonds that were growing more strained with every day that passed, but already Lee was being forced to think about taking the same course as the man he had surrounded and captured at Harpers Ferry. In the short time the two men had spent together in the paymaster's office in the armory at Harpers Ferry, they may not have recognized how much they had in common. The Virginia gentleman and the hardscrabble farmer and cattle dealer from New England were both deeply religious, both courageous, both instinctive warriors, both gravely courteous, both family men, both guided by deep and unquestioning moral beliefs. John Brown may have been, as Robert E. Lee believed, a fanatic and a madman (the first was certainly true, the second not at all), but like him Lee too, despite his firm opinion that "obedience to lawful authority is the foundation of manly character," would himself become, at last, a rebel—perhaps the greatest rebel of all.

Clouds of Glory

Chapter 1
"Not Heedless of the Future"

Ne Incautus Futuri
—The Lee family motto

S tate patriotism in the United States is much diminished in our time in favor of national patriotism, and indeed has been on the decline ever since the end of the Civil War. Today Americans move quickly and easily over great distances, settle in states far from the one in which they were born without giving the matter much thought, and hardly even notice in which state they are traveling except for the change in most of the license plates they see on the highway. Of course this was always a country where tearing up roots and moving farther west to start all over again was a tempting option for those who had failed where they were, or who had greater ambitions, but loyalty to one's "home state" was at one time an important fact of American life. Robert E. Lee's belief that he was first and foremost a Virginian, and owed to Virginia an allegiance stronger than that which he owed to the United States, may seem to some extreme now, but it was by no means so in his lifetime.

Of all the original thirteen states, Virginia had perhaps the strongest claim to the first loyalty of its citizens. It had been the largest, oldest, richest, and most populous of the British colonies in North America, the one where English ideas of class, religion, and social order were the most deeply entrenched, and its role was so central to the creation of the United States of America that the country's capital was built on Virginia's border and four out of America's first five presidents were Virginian.

It was also the colony in which the English ideal of rule by a landed aristocracy took root most deeply. Even as Virginia developed representative forms of government, they were dominated, as in England, by those who possessed wealth and land, or by their sons and other relatives. Since many of the early English settlers were royalists who had fled from Cromwell's Commonwealth, the idea that Virginians were gentlemen—"Cavaliers" who had fought for the king and been defeated, as opposed to New England Puritans who had repudiated the very idea of kingship—took hold early on in the colony's history, and helped to develop Virginia's reputation, or at least its self-image, as a place of elegance, refinement, good manners, and genteel behavior. Certainly it produced, to the astonishment of English visitors, any number of handsome manor houses set on estates that rivaled an English county in size, and a society of a refinement that was perhaps unique in North America. Behind that gracious image, however, it was also a place where huge fortunes were made—and all too often lost—in reckless land speculation on a vast scale; where dueling was not uncommon and often fatal; where going head over heels into debt was commonplace; and where much of the principal crop, tobacco, the mainstay of its commerce with Britain, was grown, picked, and cured by slave labor, with all the moral and practical difficulties of that "peculiar institution." By the time of the Civil War more than a third of the population consisted of black slaves (and a small minority of "freedmen"), in a state that was then 425 miles in width and over 300 miles from south to north at its widest point— bigger than some European countries.

The "First Families of Virginia" formed its aristocracy, and after an initial experiment in marrying the daughters of the more important Indian chiefs, of whom Pocahontas, who became something of a celebrity in Elizabethan England, is the best-known example, the First Families tended to marry within their own rather small social class, quickly producing, as had happened in the English aristocracy, a world in which almost anyone who mattered was related however remotely to everyone else. *"Cousinage—c'est une dangereuse voisinage,"* as Tolstoy wrote in *War and Peace* about a different slave-owning aristocratic society, and certainly in Virginia cousins and vaguely defined "kinsmen" seemed to proliferate to an extraordinary degree, linking all the First Families together in a mesh that was as hard for outsiders to unravel as Penelope's shroud. The Lees would never have boasted of being first in this social order, nor even "first among equals"; they were too well-mannered for that. But they were widely regarded as one of the most respected and best-connected families in Virginia: wealthy, cultured, devoted to public service, patrician in the best sense of that word. Of course, as in every family, there was over time the occasional black sheep or scandal, but for almost 200 years they acquired great estates and plantations, married well, filled major public offices with credit and honor, and when necessary fought for their mother country and colony, and later for their state and country.

The first Lee arrived in Jamestown, Virginia, in 1639, only thirty-two years after the establishment there of the first permanent English colony in North America.

He disembarked not as an impoverished immigrant, but as an ambitious and well-connected one. Colonel Richard Lee ("The Immigrant") was armigerous, bearing the coat of arms of the Lees of Cotton Hall in County Shropshire, England (which oddly enough includes a squirrel eating a golden hazelnut atop an elaborate medieval helmet), who traced their descent back to a Richard Lee, high sheriff of Salop in the mid-fifteenth century, and far beyond him into the misty antiquity of Anglo-Norman genealogy, possibly to a Hugh de Lega who arrived in England with William the Conqueror in 1066, and to a Lionel de Lee who accompanied the ill-fated Richard the Lionhearted on his attempt to take Jerusalem during the Third Crusade in 1183. In short, Richard Lee was a gentleman.

He was also tough, shrewd, fearless, and skillful at climbing the rungs of the colonial political ladder. He arrived with nothing more than the "patronage" of Sir Francis Wyatt, the first governor of Virginia, and soon became attorney general, then secretary of state, then a member of the King's Council, high sheriff, and a colonel of the Virginia Militia. He was also at various times a fur trader, an Indian fighter, a slave trader, and a tobacco planter, and went on to become one of the largest landowners in Virginia, one of the richest men in North America, and the founder of a flourishing dynasty. Two of his descendants would be signers of the Declaration of Independence; two others (Robert E. Lee and his father) generals; and one, Zachary Taylor, not only a general but a president.

Richard Lee was not just a slave trader, in the days when that was still considered a respectable business, but a slave owner on a large scale, and a major employer of "indentured servants," mostly young British men and women who signed up for three to seven years of work without wages to pay for their passage to America, and the chance of a new life once they had completed their indenture; unlike slaves, they could not be bought and sold as chattel property. Thus, almost from the beginning, Virginia had three classes: the landed gentry; impoverished English, Irish, Welsh, and Scots who came over as their indentured servants with the intention of eventually becoming independent farmers or workmen; and black slaves. The idea of a poor man acquiring land of his own was almost impossible to achieve in Britain, or anywhere in Europe—land was the magnet drawing people all the way across the Atlantic to work under conditions not much better than those of the slaves, and forming the basis for the land speculation that so obsessed their betters. Winning "land grants" from the crown, and turning the vast, seemingly endless forest to the west—from which the Native Americans were slowly receding or being driven, or where they were being decimated by disease—into what we would now call developed real estate was an even bigger and more profitable business than growing tobacco, and Richard Lee was as successful at that as he was at all things.

He was as fortunate in his children, ten of them, as he was in business and politics; indeed the family motto might almost have been replaced by Dr. Pangloss's famous remark in Voltaire's *Candide, "Tout est pour le mieux dans le meilleur des mondes possibles."* ("Everything is for the best in the best of all possible worlds.") He had so much land that on his death he was able to leave large parcels of it to his children. They built impressive houses of their own on it and thus created several branches of the Lee family, all of which produced in every generation men of distinction and merit, and women who married well. By the time of the American Revolution John Adams of Massachusetts, by no means an unqualified admirer of the South, was of the opinion that the Lees had "more men of merit . . . than any other family."

One branch of this fast-growing and mighty tree descended from the third of Richard Lee's seven sons, Richard Henry Lee II, known in the family as "Richard the Scholar" because he was educated at

Oxford University, collected one of the largest personal libraries in North America, and wrote fluently in Greek, Hebrew, and Latin. He, like his father, filled numerous colonial offices, serving in the House of Burgesses and the King's Council. He had eight children, one of whom, Captain Henry Lee I, the father of Henry Lee II, who married Lucy Grymes, "the lowland beauty," a distant relative of George Washington—in fact Washington admired her greatly and was widely supposed by the Lees not only to have been in love with her, but to have lost her to Henry Lee II.

Henry Lee II built a handsome manor house for himself, the Lee House, at Leesylvania, and there he and Lucy had eight children together, the first of whom, Henry Lee III, better known as Light-Horse Harry Lee, would grow up to become perhaps the most famous cavalry commander of the Revolutionary War, and a friend, trusted subordinate, and protégé of George Washington's—it was Henry Lee III who gave Washington's funeral oration, calling him, "First in war, first in peace, and first in the hearts of his countrymen," a phrase that is still remembered by millions of people who have no idea who its author was.

Henry Lee III, who despite many disappointments rose eventually to become governor of Virginia and a Virginian representative in Congress, was the father of

Robert E. Lee. The Lee House at Leesylvania was there-fore Robert E. Lee's "ancestral home," which George Washington visited several times, perhaps drawn by the still beautiful Lucy, and which represented for Robert E. Lee, although more in his imagination than in reality, a whole intricately linked, gracious world of stability, wealth, privilege, good manners, and family connections all his life, even though it passed out of his family's ownership while he was still a youth. Other great houses haunted him throughout his life, much of which was spent in modest rented quarters, barracks, and tents: Shirley, built by Robert "King" Carter, then the richest man in Virginia, its roof surmounted by a carved, gilded pineapple, the symbol of hospitality, one of the grandest and most graceful mansions in Virginia, was his mother's home; White House, one of his father-in-law's plantations, would play a significant part in Robert E. Lee's adult life; Stratford, built by Thomas Lee, another son of Richard the Scholar, with an unri-valed view over the Potomac River, set on a plantation of 6,600 acres, a brick mansion of great size and har-monious design, more impressive, perhaps, than beau-tiful, with magnificently proportioned steps sweeping upward to the entrance and one of the most admired formal gardens in America, was where Robert E. Lee was born; and Arlington, in Alexandria, Virginia, with its white columns and its associations with George Washington, was the mansion Lee would inherit by marriage, only to have it occupied by Federal troops at the beginning of the Civil War.

Beyond the Lee family itself, there were two major influences in Lee's life, each of which was to play a major role in forming not only his character, but his tactics and strategy as a general. The first was George Washington himself, for although Washington died ten years before Robert E. Lee was born, the young Robert grew up in his shadow. Everywhere around him in his boyhood there were associations with Washington, to whom he was distantly related (as he was to Thomas Jefferson); his beloved father had been as close to Washington as it was possible to get to that slightly reserved and chilly personality, and the older members of his family had all known Washington well, as a neighbor and fellow Virginian grandee, before, during, and after the war, and in the tumultuous politics of the infant republic. Washington was not ever for Robert E. Lee a remote or distant historical figure; he was an almost living presence, by whose august standards Lee measured himself, as a boy, as a man, and as a general. Washington's strict devotion to duty; his formidable dignity; his firm hold on his own temper; his genius for leadership; his ability to keep a ragtag, poorly supplied army together for years against a foe superior in numbers, weapons, and resources; his courage and resilience in the face of defeat; his magnanimity in victory were all qualities that Robert E. Lee admired and sought successfully to acquire.

Modeling himself upon "the father of his country" would represent a challenge to any young man, but in Lee's case it was complicated by his deeply ambivalent feelings about his own father, whose role in what Freud called "the family romance" was deeply conflicted, an example to be at once copied and avoided at all costs. Light-Horse Harry Lee was one of those men whose good advice to his children was seldom matched by his personal behavior—a courageous and innovative soldier, he was in peacetime an inveterate and increasingly reckless gambler on what we would now call risky investment schemes, mostly land speculation, which invariably failed, saddling him with enormous debts. His status as a Revolutionary War hero; his bluff, hearty good looks, somewhat spoiled in later life by a tendency to put on weight; his charm and the fact that he was a Lee led people to forgive him too easily and too often for his own good—and theirs—the end result being that he was a loving but often absent father, and that he left his large family virtually penniless.

Henry Lee III was born in 1756, and as the eldest son of the wealthy landowner Henry Lee II and the beautiful Lucy Grymes Lee, he must have seemed destined by birth for a brilliant career—a feeling which he clearly shared from earliest boyhood. He attended Princeton (then known as the College of New Jersey), was graduated in 1773, and would have studied law in England if not for the outbreak of war. The years between 1773 and 1776 were as exciting and eventful in Virginia as they were in Massachusetts—prompting Dr. Johnson to ask, "How is it that we hear the loudest yelps for liberty among the drivers of negroes?"—and the young Henry Lee gave up any ambition he may have had to be a lawyer, and joined the army instead, as a captain in a light cavalry regiment raised by one of those many "kinsmen" with which life among the First Families of Virginia was so rich. Although he received no formal military training, he probably needed none—Henry Lee III might have been born to be a soldier. Tall, powerfully built, a natural horseman, he quickly made a name for himself. Though his nickname, Light-Horse Harry, is supposed by some to be a tribute to his horsemanship, it in fact recognized his skill at organizing and leading what was then known as "light horse," that is, cavalry mounted on relatively small, nimble horses—in contrast to dragoons, or "heavy cavalry," big men who rode big horses and wore thigh-high heavy boots, a polished steel cuirass, and a brass helmet and whose purpose was to charge stirrup to stirrup en masse.

"Light horsemen" were intended to carry out daring raids, to move quickly over long distances on missions of reconnaissance, or to dismount and fight as light infantry, for they carried a short musket or pistols as well as a short, curved saber. The idea of light-horse formations had been brought to France early in the eighteenth century by one of those typically charming and ubiquitous Hungarian emigrants, Count Laszlo Bercsenyi, who introduced the French to the *huszár*—the traditional Hungarian light cavalryman with his short, gold-laced, fur-trimmed cape thrown over one shoulder; a fur cap; skintight embroidered riding breeches; short, tight-fitting soft boots; a curved, Turkish-style saber; and a pair of pistols. Bercsenyi's ideas were adopted enthusiastically by the French army, and in the days when France was still the leader in military innovation and fashion they spread rapidly to other countries in the form of countless lancer, hussar, chasseur, and "light dragoon" regiments, with glamorous names and uniforms, and even more glamorous officers, unquestioned as the elite of every army until the charge of the Light Brigade at the Battle of Balaclava brought about increasing skepticism on the subject. Light cavalry was well suited to North America, where there were few opportunities for big, formal European battles. It was cheaper too—big horses consumed more fodder, and heavy cavalry uniforms and equipment were notoriously expensive (the Household Cavalry in Great Britain is the only heavy cavalry still in active service).

Henry Lee's high spirits and taste for taking daring risks made him a perfect light-cavalry leader, and he became the talk of the army when he beat off a surprise British attack at Spread Eagle Tavern in 1778. This earned him the opportunity of becoming one of Washington's aides-de-camp—an honor he turned down because he preferred to fight in the field, gaining himself Washington's lifelong respect, and promotion to major. A year later he stormed Paulus Hook, a British fort at what is now Jersey City, on the lower Hudson River, a daring, if not entirely successful action that won him Washington's "unstinted" praise, and a gold medal awarded by Congress. Washington, recognizing Lee's special skills, then put him in charge of a mixed infantry and light-cavalry formation, something of an innovation at the time, which was "officially known as Lee's partisan corps," and promoted him to lieutenant colonel. He was just twenty-five. Along with Henry Lee's dash and competence there were, however, worrisome signs of a certain lack of judgment, a dangerous side. It was one thing for him to hang a deserter who had gone over to the enemy, but quite another to have the man's head cut off and sent with the noose still around the neck to Washington's headquarters "much to the horror of the commander-in-chief."

Sent south to serve under General Nathanael Greene, Henry Lee quickly proved himself to be a commander of extraordinary talent in the Carolinas, amazing both the enemy and his own superiors by the skill and speed of his raids and forays, and by the distance his men and horses covered in some of the most brutal fighting of the war—though not otherwise resembling either of them, he had many of the qualities that would make Colonel T. E. Lawrence such a gifted leader of "irregular" warriors in World War I, or Major-General Orde Wingate in World War II. His role in General Greene's successful campaign to free the Carolinas and Georgia was a major one, and earned him the honor of carrying dispatches from Greene to Washington in time to be present at the historic moment when Lord Cornwallis surrendered his army to Washington at Yorktown.

This was, in some ways, the high point of Henry Lee's life, or at any rate the moment before things began to go badly wrong for him. He became, in the words of Douglas Southall Freeman, "sensitive, resentful, and imperious," apparently feeling that his services had not been sufficiently appreciated, even though he was one of the recognized heroes of the war, and the only officer below the rank of general to be awarded a gold medal by Congress, and resigned from the army in 1782, determined to win "riches and . . . eminence" in public life. It is possible that he had expected to be promoted to general, and was offended when he was not; in any event, portraits of Henry Lee III do indeed appear to bear out Freeman's description of him, and reveal a certain degree of petulance or dissatisfaction in the downturned corners of his lips. Despite the handsome features, it does not look like the face of a man you would want to buy a horse from.

Henry Lee III seems to have begun as a charming rogue, an eternal optimist, not at first dishonest in the conventional meaning of the word, but he swiftly degenerated into a gifted and persuasive confidence man, careless with facts, convinced of the merit of every harebrained scheme he devoted himself to, always promising more than he could deliver, and apparently neither able to add and subtract nor to learn from his own disastrous experiences—in short, a well-bred crook. Members of his family eventually learned to put codicils in their wills or their financial arrangements to make sure that Henry Lee III could make no decisions regarding their property or their estates, but they do not seem to have been any less fond of him for that. Every family needs a black sheep, and that was the role of Henry Lee III in the Lee family.

At first he seemed to be stepping in the right direction after Yorktown. He married a second cousin, Matilda Lee, known as "the divine Matilda," who had inherited from her father the great mansion of Stratford and its 6,600 acres. Their marriage at Stratford was attended by George Washington, and it appears to have been a happy match. Following in the Lee tradition of public service, he became a member of Congress and then governor of Virginia, and Matilda bore him three children, one of whom, Philip, the eldest, died at the age of ten. Already, however, his business affairs were getting in the way of his other duties, and causing alarm in the widespread Lee family. When Matilda died in 1790 she left Stratford to her children rather than her husband, so she must already have been aware of his poor judgment and unreliability when it came to money—Henry's own father left him only "some of his lesser lands," apparently sharing Matilda's concern. Typically, Henry Lee managed to persuade Matilda's trustees to let him sell off much of the land around

Stratford, and within a year of her death the house was beginning to deteriorate, many of the furnishings were sold off, and tenant farmers were working what remained of the farmland.

A story about him demonstrates the kind of reputation he was developing among his neighbors. He apparently arrived at a friend's home claiming to have lost his horse. "The obliging acquaintance lent Harry a steed and a slave to ride along to lead the horse back. Weeks passed with neither the slave nor the two horses reappearing. When the footsore black came limping back, he told his master that Lee had sold both horses. When the astonished owner asked: 'Why didn't you come home?' the slave replied: 'Cause General Lee sold me too.'"

In a half-baked scheme to restore his fortunes he attempted to secure a commission as a general in the French revolutionary army until Washington gently pointed out to him the impropriety of serving in the French army at the height of the Terror while he was still governor of Virginia, but Washington was soon able to congratulate Henry Lee on exchanging the pursuit of Mars for that of Venus when he learned that Henry was thinking of marrying again. On a visit to Shirley, the home of Charles Carter, then the richest man in Virginia, "he became attached to Ann

Hill Carter, then twenty, Charles Carter's daughter by his second wife." Henry Lee was seventeen years old than Ann, and beginning to put on weight; still, he was a Lee, governor of Virginia, a hero of the Revolutionary War, and a man of expansive charm, and having secured Washington's blessing (and, less easily, that of her father) they were married at Shirley in a lavish ceremony that was the talk of Virginia. Washington's wedding gift to Ann was a miniature of himself mounted in a gold frame as a brooch; it was one of her most cherished possessions, and she wore it attached to her décolleté in the only known portrait of her. In this portrait, she is holding a bouquet of flowers delicately in her right hand, but her eyes and her mouth look a good deal harder and more practical than her husband's, as they would need to be, considering what was in store for her. Her father, who was no fool, made every effort to ensure that Henry Lee would have no access to, or control over, Ann's money, but for all that the marriage seems to have been a love match, although it plunged Ann from the luxuries and elegance of Shirley, where she had been surrounded by servants, into the then tiny and uncomfortable governor's "mansion" in Richmond and the even less congenial surroundings of Stratford, with its vast, drafty, and increasingly bare rooms, and barren fields. They would have six children together, of whom the first died in infancy and the next to last was Robert E. Lee.

Henry Lee may have suffered from *folie de grandeur* as well as a complete lack of business sense and honesty—he gives the constant impression of a man seeking to take on a role much larger than the one he has—and in the next few years of his life he burned up whatever credit he had left with his family, his friends, his fellow Virginians, and even George Washington, transforming himself into an object of commiseration, as well as an object lesson in how to fall from grace. When the Whiskey Rebellion broke out in 1794 in protest over the imposition of a federal excise tax on whiskey, Governor Lee, no doubt hoping to please President Washington, mustered the Virginia militia, and led them into Pennsylvania, where they accomplished nothing. It was an unpopular move; Virginia makers of home-brewed whiskey were just as opposed to the tax as Pennsylvania farmers, and in many places rioted against being drafted into the militia. While Lee was away "in the field," his governorship was declared vacant and he returned to find that he had been replaced. The Lee name was enough to win him a seat in Congress, where he most inopportunely managed to make an enemy of Thomas Jefferson and even briefly offended his patron George Washington by writing him a check that bounced. As usual, he was forgiven, and when Washington was briefly appointed general in chief in 1798—a war with France was expected—he had Henry Lee appointed as a major general. Washington's death in 1799 at last brought to an end the benevolence that he had always shown toward Henry Lee, and marked the start of Lee's steeper descent into debt and other problems.

He involved himself with a plan to purchase part of the Fairfax estate, in which he lost $40,000 and almost bankrupted his old friend Robert Morris, one of the signers of the Declaration of Independence; he speculated unsuccessfully on the sale of "western lands"; he even involved himself in the chimerical and possibly treasonous attempt of Aaron Burr to create a western empire, another folly along a path that his own son Henry would describe as "a course of sanguine and visionary speculations." There was seemingly no investment so unwise that he did not pursue it, or persuade others to invest their money in it. He put chains on the door of Stratford in an attempt to keep his creditors and the sheriffs out, but by 1809 he was effectively ruined, and in April he suffered the disgrace of being arrested and jailed for debt. He remained in debtors' prison for almost a year, keeping himself busy by writing his *Memoirs of the War in the Southern Department of the United States*, a book that he hoped in vain might recoup his fortune, but when he was finally set free it was obvious even to Henry Lee that nothing could save him.

Stratford, which now belonged to his son Henry by his first marriage, had by then been stripped bare, and young Henry could hardly afford to keep his own father's large and growing family there as well as his own, while Ann's trust fund produced an income that was barely sufficient to feed them. Her health had declined sharply—she complained of being "an invalid"—most of the servants had been fired, there was not even enough money to keep the rooms of the great house warm in the winter, so the older Henry was eventually obliged to move his family to a series of rented lodgings in Alexandria, Virginia, and finally to a small brick house rented from yet another "kinsman," William Fitzhugh.

In these modest circumstances, Henry Lee continued to work on his book, and he and Ann conceived another, last child, despite Ann's increasing illness and fragility, which had prompted her to write to a pregnant friend when she was about to give birth to Robert, "I do not envy your *prospects*, nor wish to *share in them*."

There was not much room in the house to add a new-born child, and life cannot have been easy, even for people born in the eighteenth century, when crowded rooms and a complete lack of privacy were commonplace realities, for the gentry as for others, but perhaps in the cramped quarters of the tiny house, Henry Lee had the time and opportunity to become a heroic figure in the eyes of his son Robert, then three years old.

It cannot be said that he seems to have paid much attention to an adoring and hero-worshipping little boy, but then again, in Alexandria Henry Lee *was* a hero, despite his straitened circumstances, and it would have been hard for Robert not to notice. There were many in the small town who had served under his command in "Lee's Legion," and for whom he was now "General Lee," Light-Horse Harry Lee at last promoted to the rank he and they thought he should have had at Yorktown. When he walked down the narrow streets he was greeted with respect, doubly so because of his relationship with George Washington, who had himself been an everyday figure riding in the streets of Alexandria to the post office or the Masonic Hall, and the small house was full of warlike memorabilia attesting to the military triumphs of Henry Lee, as well as the maps and records he needed for his book. It was something that could not fail to make an impression on a boy's mind: the daily evidence, inside the house and outside, that his father was a soldier and a hero.

The older members of the household might have their doubts about Henry Lee's wisdom, and might compare their present circumstances with life at Stratford before he finally slipped into bankruptcy and disgrace, but Robert would have been too young to make such a comparison, and as a result he grew up largely ignorant of the depth of his father's fall, or the fact that Henry Lee had been responsible for his own destruction. On the contrary, the supposed example of General Henry Lee III as a kind of second Washington guided and formed Robert E. Lee as he became a soldier himself, and rose in fame far beyond his father.

However, children often know (or guess) more about their parents than anybody supposes at the time. Throughout his life Robert E. Lee would be scrupulous about money, determined never to get into debt and to pay every bill on time; he was so exactly the opposite of his father that it is difficult to believe he was entirely ignorant of Henry Lee's failings. Even as a child, he cannot have been unaware of the long absences of his father or a certain strain in the family atmosphere, and since he spent a good deal more time with his mother's family, the Carters, than with the extended Lee clan, he may have picked up at Shirley an undercurrent of disapproval toward his father. His mother certainly never breathed a word of criticism about Henry Lee, least of all to her children, but on the other hand she took good care to teach the young Robert the importance of thrift, modesty, truthfulness, economy in all things, unshakable faith in God, and scrupulous accounting of every penny—just the virtues that her husband so conspicuously lacked.

As for Henry Lee, the final act of his life was about to begin, in dramatic, indeed melodramatic circumstances. Having quarreled with President Jefferson, he now proceeded to quarrel with President Madison over the question of war with Britain, to which he was strongly opposed. He wrote a series of violent letters to Madison, with no effect except to disqualify himself from any of the diplomatic posts he had been trying to solicit in order to put some distance between himself and his creditors. When war finally broke out in June 1812, Henry Lee became a lightning rod for those who opposed it, and took up the cause of a young Baltimore newspaper publisher who had been run out of town by an angry mob, which also destroyed the premises of his paper. Whatever Henry Lee lacked in financial judgment, he was never lacking in courage—he not only encouraged the young man to return to Baltimore and resume publishing his pieces against the war, but went there himself to support him. Lee may have underestimated the sanguinary fury of American big-city politics at the time, and unfortunately for him he was in the temporary office of the newspaper when an angry mob assaulted it. Henry Lee helped to barricade the premises and sent for "additional arms," and during the ensuing firefight one man in the street was killed. The militia arrived just in time to separate the two sides, and the publisher, Lee, and their friends were escorted to the Baltimore jail for their own safety, but by this time the entire town was in an uproar and the mob broke into the jail. "Death seemed so certain that Lee proposed to his companions that they should take the few weapons they had and shoot one another rather than let themselves be torn to pieces by the mob." This proposal was not taken up with any enthusiasm by his companions, but perhaps it ought to have been, since the mob tore down the door of their cell and dragged them out into "a confused mêlée," in which one of them was killed, and eleven others were savagely beaten. Eight were thought to have been killed, and their bodies were piled up in the street, and subjected to "continued mutilation." Henry Lee was one of them.

It is difficult to assess how badly he was hurt or the degree to which he was permanently injured, but apparently his tormentors stuck knives into him, poured "hot candle grease" into his eyes, and tried to cut off his nose, as well as subjecting him to vicious kicks. It is some kind of tribute to his strength and courage that he not only survived all this, but refused to react or scream, so eventually they left him for dead. He was, to quote Freeman, "weak, crippled and disfigured," as well as hounded by ever more angry creditors, including his own brother, to whom he had sold a piece of land in Kentucky that he had already sold to someone else eleven years earlier. "Broken in body and spirit," Henry Lee was carried back to his family, but rather than face another term in jail he determined to flee the country, ignoring his debts and the sizable bail bond that had been posted to release him from jail three years before, in the hope of restoring his health in some of the English-speaking Caribbean islands.

There may or may not have been a sorrowful departure. Douglas Southall Freeman, author of a monumental biography of Lee, imagines one in which Robert "shared the final embraces of his father," but given Henry Lee's pattern of behavior it is as likely that Robert simply woke up one morning to find his father gone—after all, he was skipping bail and leaving his wife and his family to pick up the pieces. He wandered from island to island for five years, until a severe illness—it may have been stomach cancer—made him decide to come home to die. He didn't even manage to get all the way to Savannah. "Mortally ill" on the voyage, he was put ashore at Dungeness, Cumberland Island, Georgia, the home of the daughter of his commander in the Revolutionary War, Nathanael Greene. A naval surgeon urged Henry Lee to undergo surgery, but he refused, perhaps with good reason, given the pain and the dangers of surgery in the early nineteenth century. "My dear Sir," Harry Lee said, "were the great Washington alive, and here, and joining you in advocating it, I would still resist." Clearly something of his bold spirit was still present in the old reprobate, but shortly afterward he died in great pain, and was buried in the Greene family graveyard at Dungeness.

Robert E. Lee visited his father's grave for the first time in 1862, and it was noted that he spent only a few brief moments there. Perhaps the boy had known more than the man was willing to admit.

At the very end of Robert E. Lee's life, in 1870, Charles C. Jones published a book about Light-Horse Harry Lee that contained a fairly frank account of his life and death. When it was brought to Robert E. Lee's attention, his wife wrote that he was "painfully" shocked by it, and that his first instinct was "to deny the 'allegations' in it if they were untrue."

Poor health may have prevented Lee from undertaking an effort to defend his father, but it is more likely that he already knew the allegations were true, and was wise enough not to stir up another storm by denying them in public print. That had been tried before—there had already been a considerable fuss in 1822 when a book by Associate Justice William Johnson of the U.S. Supreme Court was published pointing out "errors" and "false claims" in *Memoirs of the War in the Southern Department of the United States,* the book Henry Lee had written in debtors' prison. Johnson's book had prompted Robert E. Lee's older half brother to write and publish an angry 500-page defense of their father, interwoven with a virulent attack on Jefferson, so controversy on the subject of Light-Horse Harry Lee cannot have come as a surprise to any of his children. The likelihood therefore is that Robert E. Lee was aware, both consciously and unconsciously, of the darker side of his father's life, but sensibly chose to remember him instead as a Revolutionary War hero and Washington's friend.* What he did not want to know, he suppressed, as many people suppress

---

*Robert E. Lee may also have thus learned early on the wisdom of not retaliating against attacks on him in print, even when he was deeply pained by them. (See page 356.)

knowledge about a parent. When he grew up and moved away from Virginia and the embrace of the Lee and the Carter families—where there were plenty of victims of Henry Lee's irresponsibility and dishonesty—going first to West Point and then into the army, where most of the people he met were unaware of Light-Horse Harry Lee's long history of troubles and debts in Virginia and regarded him merely as one of the famous names of the American Revolution, he took a more positive view of his father than he may, at some deeper level, have felt.

None of this means of course that Robert E. Lee wasn't influenced by his father, or didn't inherit some of his better characteristics. Like Henry Lee, Robert was tall, physically strong, a born horseman and soldier, and so courageous that even his own soldiers often begged him to get back out of range, in vain of course. He had his father's gift for the sudden and unexpected flank attack that would throw the enemy off balance, and also his father's ability to inspire loyalty—and in Robert's case, virtual worship—in his men. On the other hand, perhaps because of Henry Lee's quarrels with Jefferson and Madison, Robert had an ingrained distrust of politics and politicians, including those of the Confederacy. But the most important trait that influenced Robert was a negative one: his father had been voluble, imprudent, fond of gossip, hot-tempered, and quick to attack anybody who offended or disagreed with him. With Henry Lee, even minor differences of opinion escalated quickly into public feuds. Robert was, or forced himself to be, exactly the opposite. He kept the firmest possible rein on his temper, he avoided personal confrontations of every kind, and he disliked arguments. These characteristics, normally thought of as virtues, became in fact Robert E. Lee's Achilles' heel, the one weak point in his otherwise admirable personality, and a dangerous flaw for a commander, perhaps even a flaw that would, in the end, prove fatal for the Confederacy. Some of the most mistaken military decisions in the short history of the Confederacy can be attributed to Lee's reluctance to confront a subordinate and have it out with him on the spot, face-to-face.

The person who did the most to instill in the young Lee the instincts and the obligations of gentlemanly behavior was his mother—his father had long since stepped over the line that separated a gentleman from a scoundrel. Although Ann Carter Lee seems somewhat overshadowed by the tangled and tragic drama of her husband's life, she was very clearly a much stronger character. She brought up five children in his absence, kept the household going without any financial support from him, and still managed to send one son to Harvard, one to the navy, and another to West Point. The contrast between her childhood at Shirley, with all its luxuries and countless servants, and the straitened circumstances of her life in Alexandria must have been severe and painful, not to speak of the absence of her disgraced husband, who was away so much of the time that she sometimes referred to herself as a "widow" while he was still alive, and whose responsibilities she was obliged to take over herself at a comparatively young age—she was only forty when Henry Lee fled the country. Her health, always a concern, declined steadily into chronic invalidism; the consensus is that she suffered from tuberculosis, then, of course, an incurable and fatal illness, a diagnosis perhaps borne out by the fact that one of her daughters, Anne, was diagnosed with tuberculosis of the bone, and had to have an arm amputated. Invalidism seems to have plagued Ann from an early age. She may have suffered from narcolepsy from childhood on—there are stories that even as a young woman at Shirley she sometimes needed to be helped up and down stairs, and that early on in her marriage she may have slipped into a narcoleptic coma, which lasted so long that she was declared dead, woke up in her coffin, and was only just able to summon help before she was buried. Fear of being buried alive was common in the eighteenth century and the early nineteenth century, in part because medical diagnosis was still so primitive, and in part because embalming had not yet come into vogue,* and examples of people waking up after they had been declared dead by a doctor were by no means infrequent—even so level-headed a man as George Washington left instructions that he was not to be buried for three days after his death, just in case the doctors were wrong.

For somebody whose health was as frail as hers, Ann Carter Lee seems to have had an active and determined spirit and a busy life. Perhaps she was kept going by strong willpower, unquestioning religious faith, "missionary zeal," and a deep sense of responsibility toward her children. Despite her ill health, she moved about a good deal in times when she could afford horses for her carriage, staying with close or distant relatives in their great houses, where she and her children were always welcome: Shirley, where she had grown up; Ravensworth, with its 22,000 acres, and Chatham (both homes of William Fitzhugh, a distant

---

*The embalming of soldiers, particularly officers, and the return of their bodies for burial at home began the widespread use of embalming in the United States, during the Civil War. The railroads would not accept unembalmed bodies, and of course without embalming there was no chance that the body would arrive home in a condition to be "viewed" in an open casket, then a strong social convention.

kinsman who had befriended Ann and made his house in Alexandria available to her); Arlington, the home of William Fitzhugh's sister Mary, who married George Washington Parke Custis, Washington's adopted son; Stratford, now owned by Henry Lee IV, her husband's oldest son from his first marriage—a succession of stately mansions, with innumerable servants and slaves, that must have brought some relief from the crowded house in Alexandria and her constant financial worries, as well as giving her children an opportunity for the rough-and-tumble of country living.

Ann Carter Lee seems to have picked out Robert early on in his childhood as the most responsible and reliable of her children. She entrusted him with the keys to the cupboards and storage rooms, and sent him out to do the shopping with a basket on his arm, and the all-important task of bringing home the right change. She delegated to him the task of overseeing the four Carter family slaves in the household, and of acting as the family nurse in case of illness, of which there was a good deal. His solicitude for her when he was a young boy is remarkable. He accompanied her on drives, which were supposed to be good for her health, and on cold days "he sometimes pulled out his jackknife and pretended to keep out the wind by stuffing paper into the cracks" of the family carriage.

She was determined that Robert would not grow up to be like his father, so she devoted a good deal of her time and energy to his spiritual well-being. For this task she was extraordinarily well suited; her few surviving letters reveal formidable theological knowledge, as well as a precise sense of right and wrong and a deep spiritual belief. "Self-denial, self-control, and the strictest economy in all financial matters were part of the code of honor she taught [him] from infancy," and in his later years Robert E. Lee frequently said that he "owed everything" to his mother. This is not to suggest that she was in any way a religious fanatic; her strong religious enthusiasm and absolute faith in God's will were normal in her day and age, and although in a different form no more out of the ordinary than Abraham Lincoln's or John Brown's. Although her family's religious roots lay in the milder and more formal Protestantism of late-eighteenth-century Virginia, a transplant from the Anglican Church of England, Ann Carter Lee was in many ways a child of the Second Great Awakening that swept through America in the early nineteenth century, creating sometimes startling new religious denominations and laying greater emphasis on the need to be saved and on personal piety rather than simply attending traditional religious services. Her beliefs were what we would now call evangelical, and she had the strength of mind and purpose to impress them on her son Robert for life—indeed the most striking thing about his letters is his lifelong, simple, unshakable belief in the need to accept God's will uncomplainingly, and his deep faith. "It is all in God's hands" is a phrase he used often, not in a spirit of fatalism, but in one of confidence. The intensity of Lee's religious convictions was one of the elements that would make him a formidable warrior, and also one of the reasons why he remains so widely respected not just in the South, but in the North as well—not only as a hero, but as a kind of secular saint and martyr.

That religious intensity, however, did not make him humorless, or less high-spirited than any normal child. When he first went away to school, at the age of seven, he "became a trifle headstrong" and imperious—perhaps this was a natural tendency in a boy with Lee and Carter blood in his veins—and on inquiring into his behavior, his mother was informed that the best advice was "to whip and pray, and pray and whip," so it is likely that he was not free from the occasional naughtiness of childhood, despite the efforts of his biographers to give him, like his idol Washington, an improbable perfection. Throughout his life he had a taste for family jokes, teasing, mild flirtation, and good conversation—it was only the public man who displayed the "marble face" that so impressed those who fought for him.

His extended family was enormous, particularly on the Carter side. His maternal grandfather, Charles Carter, had "eight children by his first marriage, and by his second, thirteen." Charle's grandfather, the fabulously rich "King" Carter, had no fewer than twelve children, and Charles's first cousin Robert had sixteen. Perhaps because Ann Carter Lee was more comfortable with her own family than her husband's, she spent as much time as she could with the Carters, so that Robert E. Lee grew up in a vast and, to the outsider, confusing swarm of first and second cousins, aunts and uncles by marriage, etc.—"kinspeople," as they were called—to whose "journeying and letter-writing and the exchange of family news, the years brought no end," and who would, throughout Robert E. Lee's life, provide a pleasure second only to the company of his own children. Even at the height of the Civil War Lee's letters home are full of mentions of Lee and Carter relatives, however remote, whom he has seen, and inquiries about the health and well-being of countless others.

As a child he was surrounded by relatives, many of them close to his own age, in a family as famous for its "geniality and friendliness" as for its wealth—on Charles

Carter's death one obituary remarked that "his immense wealth flowed like the silent stream, enlivening and refreshing every object around"—and so he never lacked playmates. His home in Alexandria was surrounded by the homes of so many Lee relatives that it almost seems like a Lee family compound, but the Carters were even more numerous, and when he was ready for school he was sent away to one of the two "family schools" the Carters maintained for their own children, "one for girls at Shirley, and one for boys at Eastern View, Fauquier County," the home of Ann's sister Elizabeth. This first experience of being away at school was cushioned, no doubt, by the fact that all the boys attending it were Carter cousins of one degree or another, rather than strangers, and that it was run by his aunt.

His departure for school coincided with what must have been an exciting time for a child. In August 1814 a British naval squadron fought its way up the Potomac and anchored off Alexandria, Virginia; its commander threatened to destroy the town unless all merchant ships and goods were handed over. The mayor of Alexandria was rowed out under a white flag and surrendered the town, and for three days British redcoats and Royal Marines occupied it, seizing tobacco, cotton, wine, spirits, and cigars, while the smoke from the burning capital could be seen rising on the other side of the Potomac.

Whether Robert E. Lee witnessed any of this is uncertain, but as a seven-year-old boy he must certainly have been aware of it, and would have heard tales of the occupation from those who remained in Alexandria. It accentuates the feeling that Robert E. Lee was a man more firmly anchored in the eighteenth century than the one in which he lived, with a father who had fought the British under Washington, a mother who had entertained Lafayette in her modest Alexandria home, relatives on both sides of his family who had signed the Declaration of Independence, and a hometown that had been occupied and looted by the British in his childhood. As a boy, he was surrounded everywhere by reminders of George Washington—Charles W. Peale's famous full-length portrait of Washington hung in the dining room at Shirley, Arlington contained his uniforms and swords and much of his furniture, and there were still slaves in the house old enough to remember serving him. It is not surprising that throughout his life Lee looked toward the past with a combination of nostalgia and reverence, or sought there for the lessons that would teach him how to confront a very new and different America.

At about the age of twelve he entered Alexandria Academy, a day school founded in 1785—of which George Washington had been one of the first trustees, unsurprisingly—where he was introduced to Latin and the classics, acquiring over the next three or four years a taste for the former that he would retain throughout his life; and to mathematics, for which he had a remarkable aptitude, which would stand him in good stead.

It had been hard enough for Ann Carter Lee to send her oldest boy, Charles Carter Lee, to Harvard; there was no way she could afford to send Carter's younger brothers to college as well. The next in age, Sydney Smith Lee, she sent to the navy, seeking from President Monroe a midshipman's commission for him—in those days there was no naval academy; you still learned the profession of being a naval officer by shipping to sea as a midshipman. So it must have seemed natural to send the third, young Robert, to the army; after all, he was healthy, a good horseman, bold, energetic, good at mathematics (the indispensable foundation of military science) and the son of a famous general. At the time the U.S. Military Academy, at West Point, New York, was only fifteen years old, still something of an innovation, and by no means a popular one, since many if not most Americans had no wish to create an "officer class" like that of Great Britain and European countries, and cherished in any case the myth that the Revolutionary War had been won by state militias, and by sturdy farmers like the minutemen, who took a rifle and powder flask down from the wall and went off to fight the redcoats. In fact one of Washington's greatest contributions to victory was the creation of a trained and professional army that could fight alongside the even more professional French army, and nobody recognized more clearly the country's need for a well-trained officer corps. For Ann Carter Lee the most important advantage was that West Point offered the chance of a free college education, as well as a stepping-stone to an honorable, if poorly paid, profession.

It is hard to guess the extent to which Robert's wishes were consulted. In later years he would often regret having taking up the profession of arms, but he may have been more enthusiastic about it when he was sixteen, and had just been graduated from Alexandria Academy. It seems to have been a carefully thought-out family decision about what to do with young Robert, rather than a result of any desire on his part to become a soldier. The difficulty was that West Point was small, and very hard to get into in 1823. At that time there was not as yet any competitive examination for entrance into the U.S. Military Academy; appointment was "at the pleasure of the President, on the nomination of the Secretary of War, who at that time followed no rule regarding geographical distribution." This meant that family reputation and what we would now call political clout played a major part in getting a boy appointed as a cadet. President Monroe was a Virginian, and the name Lee could be counted on to carry great weight with him; after all, he had already made Robert's brother a midshipman. But the secretary of war was John C. Calhoun, the South Carolinian firebrand of states' rights, nullification, and slavery, who was deluged with requests from worthy southern families to nominate a son to the U.S. Military Academy. A strategy had to be found to ensure Robert's nomination, and what is surprising is the degree to which Robert himself, a sixteen-year-old boy, carried out a canny, well-planned, and successful campaign to do so, suggesting that he already possessed excellent organizational skills, good political instincts, and an ability to get beyond the shyness that everybody attributed to him. When something mattered to him, he already went for it boldly, though without ever seeming to show ambition—perhaps another lesson quietly learned from the disastrous fall from grace of his father, whose ambition was only too obvious to everybody.

The choice of his mother's benefactor and adviser William Fitzhugh to write a letter of recommendation to Calhoun was a natural one—Fitzhugh, though hugely rich and well connected, was a distant relation, not a Lee or a Carter, and might seem a little more objective in recommending young Robert than a closer relative. Indeed, perhaps the most important thing about Fitzhugh's letter was its heading: "Ravensworth, Feb 7th 1824." Ravensworth was among the most famous of the great houses of Virginia, and almost guaranteed the close attention of the secretary of war.

In case that was in any doubt, Robert himself called on Calhoun at the War Department and presented the letter to him personally. Whether that was Fitzhugh's idea or Ann Carter Lee's or Robert's is impossible to know, but in any case it would have required a substantial degree of self-confidence and determination on Robert's part, as well as a considerable sense of entitlement. We know that Robert was then about five feet nine inches tall, broad-shouldered, and athletic; in a few years he would be considered the handsomest man in the U.S. Army, and portraits bear this out, so the youth very likely made a good impression on Calhoun. Fitzhugh's letter referred to the late Major General Lee with supreme tact and made the obligatory appeal to southern chivalry on the subject of Ann Carter Lee: "He [Robert] is the son of Genl. Henry Lee, with whose history, you are, of course, acquainted; and who (whatever may have been the misfortune of his latter years) had certainly established, by his revolutionary services, a strong claim to the gratitude of his country. He is the son also of one of the finest women, the State of Virginia has ever produced. Possessed, in a very eminent degree, of all those qualities, which particularly belong to the female character of the South, she is rendered doubly interesting by her meritorious & successful exertions to support, in comfort, a large family, and to give to all her children excellent educations."

Calhoun was sufficiently impressed to tell Robert exactly what he would need in the way of further letters of recommendation, a helpful piece of advice from the man whose ideas about nullification and slavery Lee would be defending thirty-seven years later. He got an endorsement from his teacher at Alexandria Academy, and since it seemed a little too general in nature, basically no more than a character reference, he managed to persuade the teacher to write a second one, emphasizing his knowledge of "arithmetic, Algebra & Euclid." Clearly, Robert knew exactly what was wanted. Acting on Calhoun's suggestion, the boy persuaded two Virginia congressmen to write letters of recommendation, and even managed to get a letter of endorsement circulated around the U.S. Senate and the House of Representatives and signed by five senators and three congressmen, as well as letters from his half brother Henry Lee IV and his oldest brother Carter, now a lawyer practicing in Washington, D.C. Calhoun was so swamped with applications from Virginia that he had to reject twenty-five of them in the year 1824, but it comes as no surprise, given Robert's efforts, that he was accepted into West Point on March 11, although he would have to wait a year before being admitted, owing to the number of successful applicants. Showing a life-long habit of not wasting time, he spent the intervening year being tutored in advanced mathematics—as usual he was a brilliantly successful pupil—and by the spring of 1825 he was collecting the kit he would need to pack in his trunk for the journey to West Point. When he left in June, he was not only going far from home; he was going away for a long time—he would get no leave until he had completed the first two years at West Point successfully.

"How can I live without Robert?" his mother asked plaintively. "He is both son and daughter to me."

Chapter 2
The Education of a Soldier

The journey from Alexandria, Virginia, to West Point, New York, was still an experience for the most part closer to the eighteenth century than the nineteenth. The young Robert E. Lee, together with his regulation leather trunk, traveled overland by stage, just as people had done in his father's time. Currier and Ives lithographs, Christmas cards, and the illustrations in nineteenth-century English novels have given a jolly gloss to travel by stagecoach—"stage" refers to the place where the coach stopped to exchange winded horses for fresh ones—but bumping and swaying on creaking springs along rutted or muddy roads and being confined in a crowded coach with malodorous straw on the floor, freezing cold in the winter and baking hot in the summer, cannot have been a comfortable experience, hence the alacrity and pleasure with which people abandoned it very shortly for the railroad, happy to give up the smell of horse manure for the cinders and smoke of a locomotive. It is worth recalling that among the many innovations that still lay ahead for Robert in June 1825 were railroads, the telegraph, indoor plumbing, and the revolver.

As he left Virginia and Maryland behind and crossed into Pennsylvania Robert cannot have failed to notice one important change. For the first time in his life he was in a part of the country where slavery did not exist. In the South, blacks were omnipresent, and at the same time their presence was hardly even noticed. They toiled in the fields, the barn, and the stable; they did menial labor in the towns; in well-to-do households they were servants in the kitchen and the home; they could be (and were) bought and sold like cattle, or left to one's heirs like any other form of property in one's will, or used to pay debts, but in whatever form they were a constant, familiar presence. Despite her straitened circumstances Robert E. Lee's mother had four slaves who had been given to her by her father, and in the great houses that she visited, most of the servants and all of the field hands were black. In Pennsylvania, blacks were comparatively few, and those few who lived there were free—not necessarily treated as equals, but at the same time nobody's property, able to marry legally, and able to bring up their children without the fear that they might at any time be sold to plantations in the deep South to pay off a debt, and never see their family again. The farther north Robert's journey took him, the fewer black faces he would see, and none of them in bondage.

New York City was then a bewildering and noisy metropolis of over 200,000 people, and from it steamboats departed regularly up the Hudson River to Poughkeepsie and Albany. They did not dock at West Point, just under forty miles upstream, but only paused there long enough for the visitor to be rowed ashore in a small boat. This was a reflection both of the physical isolation of the U.S. Military Academy—it was situated on what amounts to a peninsula, surrounded by farmland and a few small villages, with roads that were poor and in winter often impassible—and of its still ambiguous place in national life. Although presidents Adams and Jefferson had both been in favor of a national military academy, without which the United States might once again have to rely on foreigners as artillery experts and military engineers, as had been the case in the Revolutionary War, neither they nor Congress wished to establish a military elite; and President Jefferson, whose utopian views were well known, wanted to combine the Military Academy with a school of science and what would later be called civil engineering. Placing it in West Point was at once a salute to the then-recent heroic past, when West Point had been the key to the Hudson River, the main link between the New England colonies and their sister colonies farther south, and a prudent fiscal move. There was already a barracks there, and a company of the "Corps of Artillerists and Engineers." The first superintendent of the U. S. Military Academy accepted the post only on the confident assumption that the academy would be moved to Washington, D.C., as soon as it was up and running, but in this he was to be disappointed; congressional parsimony regarding the military obliged the academy to grow slowly and by fits and starts where it was, in the lower Hudson valley, rather than make the move to a grand new campus in the capital, after the example of Les Invalides in Paris. The first years of the academy were marked by political infighting; an uncertain curriculum; open hostility between the superintendent and the faculty; and reports of insubordination, drunkenness, and occasional riots among the cadets. In age, the cadets ranged between boys of ten and married men with children of their own, and the cadets, the faculty, and the superintendent sent frequent letters of complaint about each other to the secretary of war and even to the president. The appointment of Brevet Major (soon to be Colonel) Sylvanus Thayer as superintendent at last brought order, discipline, the famous West Point "honor system," and competitive examinations to the academy, and transformed it gradually into a popular institution resembling its modern form; and the cadets—in their gray coats, starched white trousers, and plumed black patent-leather hats with chinstraps of polished brass scales—became a cherished national attraction.

But the institution toward which Robert E. Lee was rowed in June 1825 was dramatically smaller than it is now, with about 200 students ranging in age from fourteen to twenty-one, and the impressive gray stone buildings rising like cliffs from the river to the chapel had yet to be built. It was, however, together with Bunker Hill and Valley Forge, among the great historic sites of the young republic. Here, Washington had once made his headquarters; Kościuszko had wintered in a cabin overlooking the Hudson; a British squadron of men-of-war had stormed the forts on both sides of the river; everywhere there were monuments, memorials, graves, and the remains of stone fortifications—remnants of the war and of "patriot gore" enough to inspire the soul of all but the dullest of cadets. The academy still consisted of only two four-story stone barracks covered in stucco, a single two-story academic building, and a makeshift "long mess-hall . . . a forlorn place, used as a hotel by the mess contractor . . . who nightly crowded into its ten rooms most of those who came to the Point to visit friends" or a family member. The stone wharf on which visitors landed was guarded only by a sentry box with an artilleryman posted in it, to prevent cadets from receiving guests who were inappropriate, or in excessive numbers. An English visitor with an eye for detail—West Point was already becoming a tourist attraction—noted with some amusement that the academy had ten cannons of different sizes, besides a howitzer, and two mortars, and that among the cannons were "two beautiful brass field-places . . . brought to the United States by the French in the revolutionary war," inscribed, somewhat ironically for a republican institution, with the motto *Ultima ratio regum*, which Louis XIV had ordered to be placed on all French artillery: "The final argument of kings." The same visitor was amazed at the extent and difficulty of the curriculum for cadets, and awestruck "by the natural beauties of the place." Except for the magnificent and much admired view up and down the Hudson, and the steep and wooded landscape, however, the U.S. Military Academy itself was not as yet a place to inspire awe in those who approached it, and still resembled what it was: a fairly shabby, run-down army post, particularly since the cadets were housed during the summer months in tents set up in neat rows on The Plain and called Camp Adams, after John Quincy Adams, who was then president.

After a brief oral examination conducted by Colonel Thayer, so cursory that it can have served only to eliminate idiots and misfits, the cadets were marched off and each was assigned to a tent, which, as for most of the rooms in the barracks, he would share with three other cadets. Tent mates were obliged to purchase together "their joint toilet—a looking glass, a washstand and basin, a pitcher, a tin pail, a broom and a scrubbing brush," spartan equipment that would serve them summer and winter; and each cadet had to buy his uniforms. Most cadets complained bitterly about the food, but Lee did not venture an opinion—then, as later, he was not fussy about food. Meals were ample, but the quality of the ingredients was somewhere between poor and wretched, and the monotony of the menu was described best (though perhaps over-optimistically) by the contractor who owned the hotel and had put in the successful lowest bid for catering the cadets' mess: "Give young men plenty of first-rate bread, butter and potatoes, and they will require little meat, and never complain of that." Cadets who could afford the price sneaked out to nearby Gridley's Tavern to eat (and drink, although alcohol, as well as tobacco in all forms, was forbidden), but since Robert E. Lee was graduated with no demerits we can be certain he was not among them.

Those who have spent a summer in the Hudson valley and experienced its heat, high humidity, and flourishing insect life may feel that living in a tent would be a severe test, but the cadets seemed to prefer it to life in the barracks, and perhaps with reason: the barrack rooms were small, crowded (four cadets to a room in the North Barracks, three to a room in the South), poorly ventilated in warm weather, heated only by a coal fire in the winter months, and furnished only with a study table and four chairs. Each roommate had to unroll his mattress and lay it on the floor in a kind of cubbyhole with curtains, a space better suited for a dog than a human being. Inside or outside there was as yet no plumbing, and cadets filled their own basins with water for shaving and bathing (the latter obligatory once a week). Then, as now, personal cleanliness and the perfection of one's uniform were drummed into the cadets from their first day, as was unquestioning obedience. The new cadets were given four hours a day of drill instruction, and by July 2, less than a month after their arrival, were apparently good enough to be inspected by the aging Marquis de Lafayette, who had visited the Lee household in Alexandria when he was last in the United States. The marquis was greeted by an artillery salute, and he found "the cadets drawn up in military array, the superb band playing national airs, the whole presenting a fine martial appearance." He dined at the mess and met several of the cadets, but there is no knowing if Lee was one of them. It must, however, have been a splendid military event for young Lee to be part of, linking the heroic eighteenth-century past with the nineteenth-century present, and he can hardly not have been moved by the fact that his father and Lafayette had been friends and comrades in arms.

The scholastic year began on August 27, when the cadets moved from their summer tents into the barracks, and it is impossible not to be awed by the curriculum, much of it devised by Thayer, which concentrated on mathematics and French. A knowledge of higher mathematics was of course essential for a military officer, particularly for service in the engineers or the artillery, while French was not only the language of America's oldest—indeed only—ally but, more important, the language of most of the military textbooks the cadets would have to master, few of which had been translated into English. Thayer had himself been sent to France, to study among other things the curriculum at the famous École Polytechnique in Paris, one of France's *grandes écoles* that specialized in science, engineering, and military science, and at the time certainly the most distinguished and advanced institute of its kind in the world. Nothing even remotely comparable existed in America, and insofar as possible Thayer attempted to model West Point intellectually after it; not surprisingly, the rate of failure among the cadets was—and was intended to be—high. For Robert, who had spent a year assiduously cramming in Alexandria, the mathematics courses presented no great difficulty—all his life he had a "head for figures" and a passion for mathematical exactitude, qualities in which his father had been tragically lacking. Even so, the schedule of a West Point first-classman seems to have been designed to test the mind, body, and character of a cadet to the extreme limits, even for one as well prepared as Robert. His day began with reveille at 5:30, following which he rolled up his bedding, washed, dressed, and answered the first of the many roll calls of the day. Cadets then had half an hour to prepare their quarters for inspection, then an hour of study, after which they were marched to breakfast at seven o'clock. Half an hour was all they were allotted for the meal, following which they formed up for inspection and another roll call, and were marched to mathematics class from eight o'clock to eleven o'clock; then they were marched back to their barracks for two hours of study, after which they were marched to lunch, or, as it was then called, dinner, their main meal of the day. At two o'clock they were paraded again and marched to their French class for two hours, after which they performed drill until sundown, ending with a full-dress parade and inspection, followed by half an hour for supper (bread, butter, and molasses); then they were marched back to their quarters to study until 9:30. Another roll call and inspection ended the day at last at ten o'clock.

This was a schedule well calculated to keep cadets out of mischief, though young men being what they are, it often failed. The list of things forbidden to a cadet was long and unambiguous: "No cadet could drink or play cards, or use tobacco"; nor could cadets cook in their quarters, read fiction in any form, or subscribe to more than one periodical, their choice to be approved by the superintendent. Fistfights, hazing of junior cadets, practical jokes, and duels were all strictly prohibited, as was bathing in the river or going beyond the limits of the academy without permission. At chapel, which was compulsory, the sermon sometimes ran for two hours or more. Robert appears, even at this early age, to have been unusually serious, hardworking, and obedient. Unlike third-year cadet Jefferson Davis, the future

U.S. Senator, secretary of war, and president of the Confederacy, Robert would never get himself court-martialed for going off grounds to a tavern and drinking (Davis was found guilty but owing to his previous good record was "allowed to remain at the academy"). Other future Confederate generals among the cadets included Joseph E. Johnston, who would become a lifelong friend of Lee's, and whom Lee succeeded after Johnston was wounded on the second day of the Battle of Seven Pines early in 1862; Albert Sidney Johnston, who was killed toward the end of the first day of the Battle of Shiloh; and Leonidas Polk, who became both bishop of Louisiana and a Confederate lieutenant general. Future Union generals included Napoleon B. Buford, half brother of John Buford, Jr., whose bold decision to hold Seminary Ridge with his dismounted cavalrymen against the Confederate division of Major General Henry Heth early in the morning on the first day of the Battle of Gettysburg made him a northern hero; and Silas Casey, who commanded a brigade against Lee at the Battle of Seven Pines in 1862.

By the end of his first year at West Point, Robert was third in his class, with no demerits and an academic rating of 285¼ points out of a possible 300; he was placed on the list of "distinguished cadets" that was furnished to the secretary of war and published in the Army Register and promoted to staff sergeant, an unusually high rank for a plebe, or first-year cadet. Lee's academic record was and would remain outstanding, although he never managed to beat out his indefatigable rival Charles Mason, who would go on to graduate number one in their class, only to resign from the military, take up law, and die at the age of seventy-seven in comparative obscurity in Iowa. Lee's physical perfection, his erect soldierly posture, and his graceful movement on the drill field had already led his fellow cadets to describe him as the "Marble Model"—ironically, since as a general he would become known as the "Marble Man," after his impassive expression in the face of both victory and defeat: self-control was perhaps the virtue that he sought hardest to achieve, and that he prized most in others. His bearing impressed other cadets, even those senior to himself. One of them later said, "His personal appearance surpassed in manly beauty that of any other cadet in the corps . . . his step was elastic as if he had spurned the ground upon which he trod." Lee's classmate Joseph E. Johnston added: "he was full of sympathy and kindness, genial and fond of gay conversation, and even of fun, while his correctness of demeanor and attention to duties, personal and official, and a dignity as much a part of himself as the elegance of his person, gave him a superiority that everyone acknowledged in his heart." That is pretty much what Grant and the other Union officers thought of Lee at Appomattox Court House in April 1865 when they accepted Lee's surrender of the Army of Northern Virginia—as Lee rode away on Traveller, they all instinctively removed their hats out of respect for him, which he acknowledged with grave courtesy. The boy was father to the man.

In Robert's second year, drawing was added to his list of studies, on the sensible grounds that an officer ought to be able to draw a neat and usable map quickly and without difficulty; and Robert was made a "senior cadet," acting as an "assistant professor of mathematics" to tutor fellow cadets who were having difficulties. He was paid $10 a month for this work—welcome news to him and his mother. He also showed the first signs of a deep and lifelong interest in the campaigns of Napoleon, taking from the library three volumes of General Montholon's memoirs of Napoleon dealing with the early campaigns, and the first volume of General Ségur's *Expédition de Russie*, describing Napoleon's advance to Moscow in 1812. Both of these were comparatively new books—it had been only five years since Napoleon's death—and this fact argues both for the excellence of the West Point library and for Lee's command of French, at least so far as reading is concerned. It would be thirty-four years before Robert E. Lee would have the opportunity of putting into practice Napoleon's battlefield tactics, and at the age of nineteen he can have had no reason to imagine that he would one day lead a large army in a series of brilliant campaigns, but when the time came it was exactly the qualities of the young Napoleon that Lee brought to the battlefield: the restless dynamism; the unwillingness to take up a defensive role for a moment longer than necessary; the constant, fast-paced attacks; the ability to concentrate all his forces rapidly before the enemy realized it; the sudden, unexpected, and risky flank attack against a weak point that caught the enemy by surprise—all the things that made Lee such a formidable commander from 1861 to midsummer 1863 were, whether he knew it consciously or not, Napoleonic. In no sense did he imitate Napoleon, nor did he ever express admiration for Napoleon as a man, but perhaps the most important thing he learned at West Point was not in the curriculum, but in the few hours he had in which to reward himself by reading for his own interest and pleasure, and during which he tucked in the back of his mind the basic lessons of Napoleon's generalship: that with speed, audacity, and élan a well-led army could defeat one twice its size, and that hammer blows repeated at brief intervals could demoralize even the largest and best-equipped armies—that, in the final analysis, numbers counted for nothing. "In war men are nothing; one man is everything. . . . Only the commander understands the importance of certain things, and he alone conquers and surmounts all difficulties. An army is nothing without its head"—these words might have been written to describe Lee's command of the Army of Northern Virginia.

Oddly enough, the assigned reading for Robert's French course included *Gil Blas,* a very long picaresque novel from the early eighteenth century by Alain-René Lesage about an ambitious valet, popular among teachers of French because it combines the maximum of difficulty with an absolute minimum of fictional excitement or pleasure for their pupils; and Voltaire's *Charles XII,* a curious choice for West Point because while the Swedish king was a brilliant tactician, a born soldier and inhumanly indifferent to pain, he failed again and again by taking on larger enemies than he could defeat, and by advancing so far that his supply line was stretched or broken. He might have been chosen, though it seems unlikely, for the very purpose of discouraging cadets from dreams of military glory; in Dr. Johnson's gloomy words,

His fall was destined to a barren strand,
A petty fortress, and a dubious hand;
He left the name, at which the world grew pale,
To point a moral or adorn a tale.

As a commander Lee too would be willing to take great risks with his supply line, and he was never dismayed at being outnumbered; these were certainly characteristics that he shared with Charles XII, along with the charisma and reputation for bravery that still hover around the Swedish warrior-king almost four centuries after his death. If Lee as a youngster was inspired by reading about the exploits of two such famous generals, it is ironic that he was fifty-four years old at the time he first took to the field in full command of an army, an age when most of history's great generals have long since retired or been killed. It had been thirty-six years since he had read Napoleon, or Voltaire on Charles XII, at West Point as a cadet (though he would refresh himself on the former when he became superintendent of West Point), and yet in 1862 he was able overnight to summon up their lessons and experience on the battlefield as if they had been firmly imprinted on his mind, ready and waiting there for the moment they were needed.

The truth is that there was always something going on in Lee's mind that he shared with nobody and that his famous "Marble Face" concealed, whether by a happy accident or by sheer willpower—a cold and calculating brilliance; a mind that could quickly produce an alternative tactical solution to any problem; impatience with men whose minds worked less quickly than his own or who hesitated where he would have plunged ahead; and a ferocity that would, when put to the test in battle, astonish and dismay most of his opponents, except perhaps Ulysses S. Grant, himself a past master at concealing military genius and boldness under an unprepossessing appearance.

Probably no man can truly be called modest or humble who has seen a whole army corps parading before him, regiment after regiment, banners and battle flags unfurled, gleaming bayonets and swords offered in salute, all men's eyes fixed on him, or who has been cheered by men advancing at his orders to their certain death. "It is well that war is so terrible, or else we should grow fond of it," Lee said to General Longstreet as they watched the hapless General Burnside's troops advancing toward them to their death at Fredericksburg in 1862, a remark that is hard to reconcile with the martyr of the "lost cause," or the image of Lee as a man who fought unwillingly and with a troubled conscience. Whether it was what he wanted to be or not, Lee was the perfect warrior: battle stimulated him, and brought out the feelings and qualities that lay behind the carefully cultivated stoic mask. No other American general has ever so clearly or effectively put into action Georges Danton's famous recommendation to the generals of the French Revolution on September 2, 1792: "*Il nous faut de l'audace, et encore de l'audace, et toujours de l'audace.*" Politically conservative as Lee was—his argument against secession was that it was merely a disguised revolution—audacity was always the key factor in his strategy and in his battlefield tactics; his specialty was the sudden, daring exploitation of a momentary opportunity that he alone perceived in the enemy's deployment or position.

At the end of Robert's second year at West Point, his record continued to be enviable, and he was confident enough to apply for a furlough. He had saved enough money to pay for his journey home, and he wrote to his mother for a letter approving his application for leave, though permission would depend on the results of his examination. He had no reason to be apprehensive: in his studies, he was "fourth in his class and earned 286 of a possible 300." This, together with his unblemished record of conduct, placed him second in his class—as usual, Charles Mason was first—and he continued to be a staff sergeant and was placed on the list of "distinguished cadets." He was able to leave for Virginia on June 30 for his first visit home in two years.

"Home" was hard to define. Robert's mother, although only fifty-four, was increasingly weakened by the course of her disease and the cares of bringing up her children on the slenderest of incomes, and was living with Robert's oldest brother, Carter, in Georgetown. Carter, after being graduated from Harvard, was practicing as a lawyer in Washington, but a lack of ambition, a dislike of the law as a profession, and a certain *dolce far niente* were already having an unfortunate effect on his career, although he did not seem to care. He summed himself up accurately enough: "I am amused and amusing," a very different spirit from Robert's, or from that of the middle brother, Sydney Smith, a serious and dedicated naval officer. Robert had always been the one who had taken care of their mother, so it is not surprising that once he was home he managed to get her out on a round of visits to Carter kinfolk, despite her failing health. Everywhere they went, Carter was admired for "his songs and stories, his wit and high good humor," while Robert, considerably shier, and less ambitious to be the life of the party everywhere he went, was admired above all for his good looks, his impeccable manners, and his appearance in uniform. This is not to say that he was a younger version of the solemn and dignified public figure he later became—he had an impish sense of humor; he danced well; he was flirtatious (within the strict bounds of decency); and he attracted a good deal of attention from the young women of the extended Lee and Carter clans, including Mary Anna Randolph Custis, whom Robert addressed as "cousin," the daughter of Martha Washington's grandson George Washington Parke Custis, owner of Arlington, the impressive, columned mansion resembling "an Athenian temple" he had built overlooking Washington. Arlington would come to be like a second home—or even a first, since he had no other.

Robert's enjoyment of his furlough—and his pleasure at being back among his family at the height of the Virginia "visiting season," on display in his tightly fitting gray uniform with its rows of gleaming buttons—may have been overshadowed by the unfolding of another Lee family scandal, of which he can hardly have been unaware, particularly since his Carter kin would have been only too anxious to whisper about it. Light-Horse

Harry Lee's oldest son, Henry Lee IV, owner of Stratford Hall, where Robert had been born, was now being called "Black-Horse Harry," as if he was determined to outdo his father in disgrace and debt. Twenty years older than his half brother Robert, Henry Lee had already managed to make himself a figure of notoriety on a scale dwarfing that of his father, and threatened to bring shame to every member of the Lee family, however remote and respectable. All this, and yet the worst was still to come!

Henry had begun well enough, serving in politics, and commissioned as a major during the War of 1812. By one of those odd ironies of fate, there being no money to send him to Princeton, his father's alma mater, or to Harvard like his half brother Carter, he attended the then-obscure Washington College, in Lexington, Virginia, which his half brother Robert would make famous when he agreed to accept its presidency after surrendering the Army of Northern Virginia in 1865, and where he would spend the last five years of his life as the venerated martyr-hero of the defeated South. Henry inherited Stratford from his mother, but not the money needed to maintain the great house in style. This problem he solved neatly by marrying Ann Robinson McCarty, "a distant cousin" of course, and a wealthy heiress whose lands abutted Henry's.

Blond, beautiful, and spoiled, Ann brought to Stratford not only the money and the furnishings to restore it to elegance, but her equally beautiful younger sister Elizabeth ("Betsy") McCarty to live with them. By a complicated set of legal maneuvers, Henry managed to make himself legal "guardian" of Betsy and her fortune, which was considerable. Ann and Henry had a single child, who was said to have inherited her mother's beauty, but who died at the age of two in 1820 when she slipped on the top step of Stratford's famous, dramatic curved entrance stairway and fell to her death (she was the second Lee to die this way in Stratford's short history).

With this tragedy, Henry's life, like his father's, descended rapidly into melodrama. Unable to forgive herself for her daughter's death, Ann became addicted to morphine and laudanum (liquefied opium, a favorite medicine of the time), while Henry began a passionate affair under the same roof with her sister Betsy. Whether Henry provided Ann with the substances of her addiction to prevent her from noticing that he was having an affair with Betsy is unknown, but in any case morphine and laudanum could be bought at any pharmacy in those days without a prescription; indeed laudanum was the main component, together with alcohol, of all those quaintly named elixirs and patent medicines that were hawked from door to door in the mid-nineteenth century.

Unfortunately for Henry, Betsy became pregnant, or said she was, and wrote to her stepfather and former guardian, who swiftly carried her off to her grandmother's home. Later on, rumors spread that the baby had been disposed of, possibly by Henry and Betsy, but it seems more likely that Betsy had a miscarriage, or that it was merely a hysterical pregnancy. Before then, however, the story was out, both because Henry and Betsy talked of nothing else to anyone who would listen, and because Betsy applied to a court (successfully) to have Henry's guardianship revoked. Even in the days before tabloid newspapers, the testimony of Betsy to the court about how her brother-in-law and guardian had taken advantage of her spread like wildfire, to the mortification of the Lees.

Henry's difficulties were increased by the facts that in Virginia sexual intercourse between in-laws was considered incest, and that by his extravagance and his poor head for business (he was, after all, his father's son) he had frittered away most of his wife's money, and a good deal of Betsy's as well. He waged a vigorous campaign to get Betsy married off to a friend—basically, Henry wanted to sell her to a physician turned writer named Robert Mayo in return for a loan that would allow him to keep

Stratford—but Betsy's grandmother thwarted this plan. With the collapse of this scheme, which far from being secret was the subject of interminable letters in both the Lee and the McCarty families, Henry was forced to sell Stratford to pay off his debts and fulfill the court's order to restore the money he had stolen from Betsy's inheritance. He and Ann, now homeless, entered on a peripatetic life, and were left with no source of income except hiring out the few slaves that remained to her.

To his credit, perhaps, Henry never denied his guilt, but he seems not to have realized that accusations of adultery and incest made him virtually unemployable. In 1825, the year Robert entered West Point, Henry had managed to secure the promise of a "modest" job in the U.S. Post Office from President John Quincy Adams, but even this was withdrawn when the story of his seduction of Betsy was revealed to the president. By the time Robert came home to Virginia on leave Henry and Ann were living in Nashville, Henry attempting to write what would now be called a campaign biography of Andrew Jackson, while Ann sought in vain to overcome her narcotics addiction at a newly opened warm spring, named by its promoter "The Fountain of Health" and reputed to heal almost every disorder.

In a climax worthy of a nineteenth-century romantic novel, a series of events eventually led to Betsy's marriage, and to her husband's purchase of Stratford, the house where Robert E. Lee had been born; where she had been seduced by her brother-in-law, or had seduced him; and where she then proceeded to live, wealthy and respectable, for the next fifty years. Meanwhile Henry and Ann, temporarily reprieved in the aftermath of Andrew Jackson's victory by his appointment of Henry as U.S. consul in Algiers, sailed for North Africa, only to learn that the appointment had been withdrawn when the record of Henry's adultery, incest, and financial depredations was read aloud on the floor of the U.S. Senate, to the horror of the Lee family.

Heredity is not an exact science. Nobody can say, at any rate of human beings, that X plus Y will produce Z. Biographers of Robert E. Lee have contrasted the wildness and irresponsibility of Henry Lee III's son by his first marriage with the respectability of his children by his second marriage, but there is no simple explanation for this. Of course his children by Ann, except for Carter, had never been directly exposed to their father's precipitous decline and fall, but on the other hand they had before them the unavoidable example of their half brother Henry Lee IV to steer them toward the straight and narrow, and keep them there. Certainly Robert E. Lee avoided all his life any kind of excess, scandal, or inappropriate behavior, and so did his siblings, though Carter had a weakness for business schemes that did not meet with Robert's approval, and that Robert almost always managed to talk him out of, with considerable tact and effort. However, wildness comes in different forms. In Robert E. Lee it did not take over his personal life or his business judgment—he was always a paragon of rectitude—but it profoundly affected his judgment and his behavior on the battlefield. He took extreme risks with his own safety: even as the commanding general of the Confederacy he plunged into the fiercest fighting to see for himself what was happening, exposing himself to artillery fire and volleys of musketry at close range, apparently without any hesitation or thought for his own safety even though his aides and his soldiers begged him to retire. And once his blood was up, as General Longstreet complained about Gettysburg, Lee was unsparing of his troops and unshocked by fearful casualties: he would fight it out whatever the odds and whatever his losses. Just as Napoleon depended on the famous *furia francese* to get him out of tight spots, so did Lee depend on the southerners' fury in battle—the rebel yell, the bayonet charge, the sheer élan of his own troops. He did not have, as Grant did, a reputation as a "butcher," but there is not much to choose between Grant's costly frontal assault on Lee at Cold Harbor, Virginia, in 1864, which he acknowledged as being the decision he most regretted in the war, and Lee's determination to attack the center of the Union line on the third day of Gettysburg, Pickett's famous charge—both failed, with casualties that shocked even their closest aides (nearly 7,000 for Lee, and over 10,000 for Grant).

Robert returned to West Point at the end of August 1827 to begin his third year there. This involved, above all, the addition of "natural philosophy," as physics was then called, and chemistry, both subjects that he enjoyed, as well as tactics at the battalion level and an introduction to artillery. He continued to read voraciously for his own pleasure, though for the time being his interest in Napoleon was supplanted by a mixed bag of reading, none of it easy: Machiavelli, Alexander Hamilton, Rousseau (in the original French), a biography of John Paul Jones, a work on navigation, another on astronomy, and another on optics. It is not surprising that throughout his life Lee would surprise people by his knowledge of subjects far removed from military engineering or tactics, or that in the last years of his life he would turn himself, apparently without effort, into an excellent college president. Whatever else he may have been, he was never a narrow soldier—his intellectual curiosity was always intense and well grounded but, like his sense of humor, carefully concealed.

Despite his ambitious reading program, Lee completed his third year at West Point as number two "on the roll of general merit"; Charles Mason always seemed to be just a few points ahead of him in examinations. For his final year Robert was also named adjutant of the corps, the highest rank a cadet could achieve; this added both to his responsibilities and to the need to maintain a constant level of perfection in his person, his drill, and his conduct. The arduous course of studies in the first three years of a cadet at West Point was merely a preparation for the formidable challenge of the fourth year, with more advanced military training and engineering added to an already crowded curriculum.

Perhaps the most intense part of his studies was the course in military science, which covered "field fortification, permanent fortification, the science of artillery, grand tactics, and civil and military architecture," and which was taught from three formidable French textbooks. This course particularly interested Robert, and he excelled at it. His knowledge of "field fortification," gained from the two volumes of S. F. Gay de Vernon's

Traité élémentaire de l'art militaire et de fortification, à l'usage des élèves de l'École polytechnique, et des élèves des écoles militaires, would stand him in good stead in the Civil War. Robert E. Lee would be that rare general who combines two forms of military genius—he was a gifted and experienced engineer, capable of planning and constructing fortifications on a grand scale, and at the same time a master of maneuver, able to move a large army rapidly and to outfox his opponent in the field.

Robert's position as adjutant of the corps eventually gave him the privilege of moving out of the barracks into Cozzen's Hotel, where he could study late into the night, long past the regulation "lights out" at ten o'clock. At last, on June 1, the rigorous final examination began; it continued for two weeks, a grueling experience for both the cadets and the examiners, one would have thought. It is interesting to note that one of the group of visiting examiners was General Pierre Van Cortlandt of the distinguished Dutchess County family, another of those links between the eighteenth and nineteenth centuries, who had studied law under Alexander Hamilton, and as a militia commander "had named [the novelist] James Fenimore Cooper as one of his aides." As was so often the case with Robert E. Lee, his connections with the Revolutionary War were widespread and intensely felt; it can never have seemed like mere history to a son of Light-Horse Harry Lee, and had the effect—along with his natural tendency to identify with the southern past, as well as its standards of gentility and its traditions, which were his own—of making him faintly suspicious of the new and bustling world that was fast emerging in the North: a world of rapid industrialization, immigration on a huge scale, and mass democracy, as opposed to the genteel, agricultural oligarchy in which the Lees had lived, served their country, and prospered.

At the final examinations Robert earned 1,966½ points out of a possible 2,000 in conduct, receiving perfect scores in artillery and tactics, which placed him second in his class, as always a few points behind Charles Mason. Still, this was an extraordinary record, which earned him the right to choose to be commissioned in the Engineer Corps, then the most prestigious and intellectually demanding arm of the U.S. Army, and the one for which his scientific and mathematical abilities best suited him.

On graduation—West Point in those days did not run to a huge, formal event, and no caps were thrown high in the air—Brevet Second Lieutenant Robert E. Lee, U.S.A., took the steamer south to New York City for a two-month furlough, and from there went by stage to Virginia, where a family tragedy awaited him.

Although Douglas Southall Freeman states, "Already his character was formed and his personality was developed," this can hardly have been true on his departure from West Point. Lee was just over twenty-two years old, a handsome, fit young man five feet ten inches tall, broad shouldered and narrow waisted, his figure accentuated by his uniform; but his character was by no means "formed," at this moment of his life, any more than his education as a soldier, which was hardly even begun. Lee had not yet experienced love, nor a profound personal loss, though he was about to experience the latter; nor had a life full of disappointments, glacially slow promotion, and the increasing tension between his own southern way of life and his country made their mark on him. As a soldier, he had not yet experienced being under fire or giving orders that would certainly cost the lives of some of those he commanded, nor the exaltation of triumphing over fear—or at least over self-doubt, for Lee would discover he was one of those fortunate individuals gifted with instinctive courage—and being acclaimed as a hero. As a man, he had not yet experienced the joys and pains of marriage and fatherhood, and as an American he could not yet even begin to imagine the depth of the tragedy to come, in which he would play such a major role. The Lee we tend to think of—weary; solemn; dignified in victory and in defeat; furious in action; bearing on his shoulders responsibility not only for an army but for a nation, as well as for the honor of its cause—did not of course yet exist: he would be formed by accretions and layers of experience good and bad in the three decades to come, as a pearl is inside its shell. The most one can say of young Second Lieutenant Lee as he journeyed home to Virginia with his trunk was that he had the makings of an exceptional soldier, the technical knowledge that would make him an accomplished civil engineer of projects on a grand scale, and the moral character and sense of honor that would sustain him throughout his life. That is already a lot to build on.

By the time Robert arrived home his mother was dying. "My disease is an unconquerable one," she had written to his brother Sydney Smith Lee, two years before Robert's graduation from West Point, and she had long since faced the inevitable with resignation, just as her relatives wisely refrained from encouraging her with false hopes. She was staying at Ravensworth, the palatial home of her cousin William Fitzhugh, in as much comfort as could be provided, and Robert instantly fell back into his role of being her nurse and companion. "When he left her room, her gaze followed him, and she would look steadily at the door until he entered again." She died a couple of weeks after his return, at the age of fifty-six, and was buried at Ravensworth.

Robert no doubt spent some time mourning, and going through the painful business of settling his mother's modest estate. His sister Anne had married William Marshall, a Baltimore clergyman who was a cousin of Chief Justice John Marshall; William soon changed his profession and became a successful lawyer. Robert's brother Sydney Smith Lee was at sea, and his sister Mildred was only nineteen, so the responsibility for carrying out their mother's wishes fell largely upon Carter and Robert. To Anne, her mother left her black maid and the maid's infant, as well as three other slaves, while to Mildred she left the elderly black family coachman and house servant Nat. Slaves, of course, were property, to be left to one's heirs just like the carriage horses, the carriage, the china tea set, the silverware, and the table napkins. Mrs. Lee's trust fund, on the income of which she had scrimped and saved to educate her sons and equip her daughters for marriage, was split between her children: $10,000 to each of the girls, $3,000 to each of the boys.

These are not such small amounts as they seem; $3,000 would be the equivalent in purchasing terms, adjusted for inflation, of somewhere between $75,000 and $100,000 in today's money. The value of Mrs. Lee's slaves is harder to estimate, since except for Nat we do not know their age or health, but "prime field hands" in their late twenties or early thirties sold for between $800 and $1,000 in the 1830s, the equivalent of between $20,000 and $25,000 in today's money, and a well-trained maid with one infant might go for as much, or more if she was still of "breeding age." These considerations must be taken into account in writing about the economic life of the antebellum South, where in Robert E. Lee's time the number of slaves had risen to 4 million, and their total value exceeded $4 billion. Mrs. Lee was hardly a major slave owner, but the value of those slaves she did own cannot be excluded from her estate. To the boys she also left about 20,000 acres in western Virginia; this acreage was then of little value, and heavily burdened by unpaid taxes.

Once freed from these cares, Robert set about visiting one after another the great houses of his relatives and friends, and particularly Arlington, in Alexandria, Virginia, overlooking Washington D.C., the home of George Washington Parke Custis, who was Martha Washington's grandson and the adopted son of George Washington. Custis was a relation of Robert's by marriage—he had married Mary Lee Fitzhugh—and in the small and somewhat incestuous world of the Virginia aristocracy, there were countless connections between Mr. and Mrs. Custis and Ann Carter Lee and her children, enough so that Robert had come to look on Custis as a kind of indulgent surrogate father, and Arlington as a second home. Kind as he was to the Lee boys, Custis was a very different sort of man from their father. He rejoiced in being known as "the child of Mount Vernon," for he had grown up in Washington's home, and therefore tended to think of himself as a kind of national institution. His widespread interests— "hobbies," might be a more appropriate word—which included painting "huge canvases" of historical scenes, composing epic poems, preserving and displaying the belongings of George Washington, serving as his own architect, and breeding sheep, inevitably took a toll on the amount of time he was able to spend looking after his estates, and he was in any case more interested in the magnificent facade he had built for Arlington than in what lay behind it, or how it could be paid for. Like Thomas Jefferson, Custis was self-indulgent and interested in everything, but without Jefferson's universal genius, or Jefferson's perfect taste. In print, Custis comes across as fussy, slightly pompous, and hugely self-important, and a portrait of him with the casual open collar of an artist, in the style of Rodolfo in

La Bohème, suggests a rather pinched face and down-turned mouth, with an expression that conveys in equal amounts a touchy pride and a degree of carefully disguised self-doubt, as well as a morbid fear that people are making fun of him. He does not look like an easy man to deal with.

In fact two of the older Lee boys, Henry and Carter, *did* make fun of Custis, whose nature was very different from that of their own impetuous and heroic father, but there is no evidence that Robert did. On the contrary, Arlington impressed him deeply, with its noble facade, sweeping view, and rooms full of Washington memorabilia, and he felt for Custis some measure of the filial respect and affection that his father had never been home long enough to appreciate. Arlington, with its curious dissonance between the immense columns of the classical porch and the rather poky rooms of the house behind it, was closer to being Robert's home, or at least what he *wanted* as a home, than any other place he would ever live in. Even at the very end of his life he still grieved over the loss of Arlington, and there is no doubt that it inspired in him an even deeper reverence for George Washington than any son of Light-Horse Harry Lee would naturally feel.

His interest in Mr. and Mrs. Custis's only surviving child, Mary Anna Randolph Custis, was formed early on, certainly by the time of his first leave from West Point in 1827, when he had cut such a dashing figure at house parties in his gray cadet's uniform. In accordance with the standards of the time, the friendship between Robert and Mary grew at a glacial pace—there is no evidence of a *coup de foudre* on either side—and only in the most carefully watched and chaperoned circumstances. Still, it escaped nobody's attention that young Lieutenant Lee spent a great deal more of his leave visiting Arlington than anywhere else, and that Mary Custis was always blushingly pleased to see him dismount. They both enjoyed sketching, at which Robert was a fairly accomplished amateur. By the time his leave ended there may have been some sort of understanding between him and Miss Custis: nothing improper or binding—both of them would have understood that Mr. Custis's blessing would have to be sought and given—but enough to give both of them the hope of a closer relationship to come.

They were a curiously ill-matched pair. Robert was enormously handsome—a fellow cadet described him as "beautiful" without any hint of homoeroticism, simply as a statement of fact—while Mary had her father's long, narrow nose and sharp chin, and a hint of the downturned mouth. It is possible that the portrait painted of her in her youth is unskillful, or does not do her justice, and the hairstyle of the day does not do her any favors, but it is not the picture of a great beauty. Their personalities were not perfectly synchronized either. Robert was punctual to a fault, furiously organized, a careful planner; Mary was "scatter-brained," careless, often late, and—despite the attention of her mother and numerous slave maids—frequently "unkempt." Early in life she had become deeply religious, in what we now call an evangelical way, whereas Robert's religious interest was, for the moment, far less intense, and more conventional, as if attending church regularly was merely one of the requirements of an officer and a gentleman. He was amazingly energetic, athletic, and fit; capable of riding many hours a day in all weather. She was an indoor person, already given to fits of dizziness and faintness, and to a need for rest. She was "frail" and tiny, he was nearly six feet tall, and powerfully built. He was poor and used to fending for himself, while she was the spoiled only child of wealthy, indulgent parents, and used to having her own way at all times.

As usual when people are in love they felt themselves ideally suited to each other.

By far the most important letter so far in Robert's life as a soldier was sent to him from Washington on August 11, 1829, ordering him "to report to Major Samuel Babcock of the corps of Engineers for duty in Cockspur Island, in the Savannah River, Georgia" by mid-November, and signed by "C. Gratiot, Brig. Gen. Comndg." If Robert was disappointed, he did not express his feelings to anyone; but as he surely knew, it was a dismal place, not far from the island where his father was buried, a tide-swept coastland island where the Corps of Engineers had been attempting for some years to build a fort to protect the approaches to Savannah, and so plagued by heat, humidity, fever, and mosquitoes that work was not even attempted during the summer months.

The members of the Corps of Engineers were America's busiest soldiers, and its officers by and large the brainiest ones—from the very beginning an elite. That is not to say their work was necessarily glamorous. In war, they built fortifications, bridges, roads, and trench works, and dug in artillery as needed ("batteries"). In peacetime they functioned as civil engineers on projects of vast scale (as of course they still do); they improved and deepened harbors, drew up maps, planned the course of canals, made and kept rivers navigable, built dams and levees and locks—fulfilled, in short, just those functions that Thomas Jefferson had foreseen when he drew up his plans for an American equivalent of France's École Polytechnique, recognizing from the first that America's need for what we would now call an infrastructure was far too big a job for anything but the Federal government to carry out. Their third function was to protect America's ports and harbors from foreign invasion—since the only potential enemy in the eyes of most Americans was Great Britain, this involved building a chain of fortresses guarding the approaches to the principal ports of the East Coast. Such forts had proved useful in the recent past—after all, "The Star-Spangled Banner" still celebrates the inability of a British naval squadron to silence the guns of Fort McHenry and take Baltimore in 1814—and as a result Congress and the Corps of Engineers were committed to a hugely ambitious building program of "coastal defense," much of it in places where the construction of even a modest shack would have presented problems. Cockspur Island was one of these places. Twelve miles downstream from the port of Savannah, in the southern channel of the Savannah River, it was about a mile long and two-thirds of a mile wide, most of it underwater at high tide, and all of it underwater in any serious storm. Its major moment in history was in 1736, when John Wesley, the founder of the Methodist movement, landed on the island and conducted a service on its muddy beach, and today it boasts a unique lighthouse, built in the mid-nineteenth century on a bed of mussel shells and clamshells, with a foundation in the shape of a ship's prow, the better to resist the waves.

Lee journeyed north to New York by stagecoach and sailed from there for Savannah toward the end of October, accompanied by the family's elderly black coachman and house servant Nat, who suffered from "some slow, devitalizing malady" and who, it was hoped, would recover or at least be more comfortable in what Freeman refers to as the "mild" climate of coastal Georgia. Although this is usually cited as an example of Robert E. Lee's care of and for slaves, and it may be, we do not have Nat's side of the story—as in all stories about masters and slaves there is an element of doubt. Did Nat *want* to be torn away from what had been his home and family all his life? Did he have a wife, children, grandchildren whom he was leaving behind? Did he have any say in the matter at all? Is it also possible that Lee simply needed a servant and took an old family retainer for whom his sister Mildred had no use now that the family carriage and carriage horses had been sold? The moral ambiguity of slavery leaves even what appears to have been a benevolent gesture open to doubt.

Whatever Savannah may have done for Nat's health, Lee found it agreeable enough. There was a small garrison of artillery, and he had several friends who were officers in it, one of whom, Jack Mackay, was from an old Savannah family. Lee was made instantly welcome. He was given a room in the Mackay home, and he soon found his place in Savannah society, where he quickly assumed his lifelong habit of innocent flirtation with pretty girls. The Mackays, like the Lees, were a large family—Mrs. Mackay was a well-to-do widow with six children, four of them daughters—and Lee must have felt right at home. All his life he liked nothing better than to be surrounded by a large family, if not his own, then someone else's.

On the other hand, Cockspur Island, when Lee first saw it, presented "a drab and desolate" appearance, which closer examination would not improve, and it must have looked like the most improbable place in the world on which to construct a fort. Major Babcock, to whom Lee was supposed to report, had already been sickened by the climate and the "exertions" involved in trying to find a site for the fort, and was soon to drop out of the picture altogether. Lee seems to have plunged in at once and taken over from his ailing commanding officer, and was soon building embankments to keep back the tide, and a canal to drain the area—in effect his first task was to create enough dry land for a construction site in what amounted to a tidal swamp.

Since this was his first job as an officer in the Corps of Engineers, he labored at it as hard as he could, even digging himself day after day in water up to his armpits.

Work on the island ceased for all practical purposes with the approach of summer, since even a hardened labor force of hired whites and leased or rented black slaves was not expected to excavate there during the summer months, when the combination of heat and mosquitoes made it almost uninhabitable. Taking Nat with him, Lee went home on a long leave—that is, he returned to Virginia and stayed with friends who lived close to Arlington, for by this time he really had no family home, and his brother Carter had moved to New York City. In any case, his attention was fixed on Mary Anna Custis, whom he seems to have wooed gently all summer long. It can hardly have escaped his attention that while Mrs. Custis was pleased by his obvious affection for her daughter—Mrs. Custis was a "kinswoman" of Lee's, a matter of some importance in Virginia, as well as a devoted reader of romantic fiction—Mr. Custis was not. He was fond enough of Lee—who was one of the few young men willing to listen to his interminable recollections of George Washington, and apparently was even *interested* in them, such was his respect for the "father of his country"—but Custis had known Light-Horse Harry Lee well enough to have reservations about his sons, he was au courant on the scandal about Robert's half brother Henry, and in any case he did not see how Robert Lee, on the pay of an army lieutenant, could support Mary in the style she was accustomed to. Behind this concern, which was very natural for the period, lay the problem of Custis's own financial position. Despite Arlington's grand appearance from the outside as one arrived at its famous portico, and despite his ownership of many thousands of acres, several other houses, and 200 slaves, Custis was always desperately short of ready cash. He was neither a prudent nor a careful manager of his own affairs, and liked to live in opulent style as "Washington's adopted son," in his own eyes at least a figure of national importance, without the income to maintain it. It may be that he had hoped Mary would solve his problems by marrying a wealthy young man, or that he feared the cost of the elaborate wedding that she and everyone else would expect her to have, or both, but either way young Lieutenant Lee did not seem to him a suitable husband for her, and he let it be shown.

This did not, of course, deter either Robert or Mary, and there was clearly some understanding between them when Robert returned to Savannah in November to resume work—they regarded themselves as "engaged," probably relying on the fact that Custis would in the end give way to his daughter, who certainly had the stronger will.

On Cockspur Island, Lee was dismayed to find that storms had washed away much of the work that he had done in the previous season. Major Babcock did not reappear, so Lee and the few laborers who had remained on the island set out to redo it all from scratch—not a cheerful prospect. Nat, who had sailed from New York some weeks later than his master, did not arrive until Christmas, and was in even worse health than before because of a nightmare voyage that had taken twenty-five days in stormy seas. Far from being "mild" the winter in Georgia was abnormally cold, and Nat soon sickened and died. Lee's social life in Savannah was busy—so busy that he complained about it—but he cannot have enjoyed the monotony of digging, although the continued absence of Major Babcock gave him a taste of what every young officer wants—responsibility, and an independent command, even if it was merely over a handful of civilians armed with picks and shovels. In January word finally arrived from the War Department that the missing Babcock would be replaced by Lieutenant J. K. F. Mansfield— accounts differ as to whether Babcock resigned or went absent without leave and was arrested, and there were rumors that Mrs. Babcock had fled with their child. No sooner had Mansfield arrived than he decided that Cockspur Island would never bear the weight of the fort the Corps of Engineers wanted to put there, which was estimated at 25 million tons. Mansfield conveyed his doubts to Washington, and in April the Corps of Engineers finally got around to sending a more senior officer, Captain Delafield, to Cockspur Island to survey the site. The two men then set about redrafting the plans for the fort, with Lee's help as draftsman.

This sorry tale of delay and wasted effort was in many ways a good lesson in Army life for Lee. First of all it prepared him for the ponderous slowness of the Corps of Engineers in making any decision, however minor, and for the strain on its officers of carrying out enormous building projects in inhospitable places with insufficient funds, and with promotion that came, when it came at all, at a snail's pace—Major Babcock's sad story was a perfect example of that. Second, it taught him the value of getting things right *before* you started, rather than the reverse. Third, it apparently suggested to him that when you are placed in a hopeless position, the best thing is to get out of it as quickly as you can, a very good lesson indeed. Lee managed to use whatever markers he had in Washington to get himself posted to Old Point, Virginia, where Fort Monroe was under construction and almost complete, and which was only eighty miles distant from Arlington and Mary Custis. Some measure of Lee's strategic sense can be gleaned from the fact that Lieutenant Mansfield, who had been graduated from West Point, like Lee, as number two in his class in 1822, would remain on Cockspur Island for the next fifteen years building what became Fort Pulaski, which was not completed until 1847.

Lee arrived at Old Point on May 7, 1831, and managed to combine a remarkable speed of movement for the day with an innate sense of tactics—a bold frontal attack, in this case—which not only got him off Cockspur Island, where he might have remained until he was old enough to retire as a gray-haired captain or a major, but at last won him Mary Anna Custis as well. Shortly after he arrived back from Georgia, he took the steamboat from Fort Monroe, Virginia, up the Potomac to visit Mary at Arlington, where he was welcomed as a guest by everyone except Mr. Custis, who may have been counting on the Corps of Engineers to keep Lee on Cockspur Island until Mary lost interest in him. Lee laid siege to Mary's mother by reading aloud to her and to Mary from the latest novel by Sir Walter Scott—this seems likely to have been *Anne of Geierstein*—until, as if by prearrangement, Mrs. Custis mentioned to Mary that her guest must be "tired and hungry," and suggested she take him into the dining room and offer him a bite to eat, thus deftly providing a good reason for the two of them to be together without a chaperone. As Mary was slicing a piece of fruitcake for him at the sideboard, Lee popped the question, and she accepted.

Mrs. Custis was delighted (but surely not surprised), and took care of the problem of squaring things with Mary's father at once. It would be wrong to see Mr. Custis as a tyrannical father figure, however. Like Count Rostov in Tolstoy's *War and Peace*, he was putty in the hands of his wife and daughter, and gave in with hardly a protest, and perhaps with relief, to what he must have known was inevitable. Indeed, there is something charmingly Tolstoyan about the whole scene, which in many other ways reminds the reader of Russia in the first half of the nineteenth century—the great estate; the imposing, but badly maintained, mansion; the elegant furnishings, silverware, and china in a rustic, rural setting; the presence of house servants who were slaves, at once indulged and feared; and of course the assumption on the part of the master and his family that slavery was a blessing for them, and that in their simple way they too would share the joy of Miz Custis's engagement to Marse Robert. Unlike Russian serfs, the slaves were black, but in every other respect it all resembles the world of the Russian landed aristocracy: the elegant young officer *sans fortune* who comes as a suitor for the daughter; her loving father, who pretends to be an autocratic authority figure but behind the facade is as soft as jelly and a self-indulgent spendthrift; her mother, who, despite all those romances by Sir Walter Scott, has a more realistic view of the situation than her husband; and outside, stretching to the horizon, the land itself, which is in fact badly farmed by poorly supervised slaves, and burdened with debt.

Once set in motion by his womenfolk, Mr. Custis was an energetic father of the bride, and determined to make a good show of things. The wedding date was set for June 30, only seven weeks after Lee had arrived in Virginia—a brilliant victory on his part—and Mary herself made the decision that she would share her husband's modest quarters at Fort Monroe, and that they would live on his pay, without an allowance from her father. Mary's decision doubtless came as something of a relief to a man with thousands of acres but a constant shortness of ready cash—even paying a bill of $65 a short time before the wedding caused Mr. Custis great and embarrassing problems. Still, he was determined to marry off his only surviving child in great style and with all the trimmings called for by a society wedding. Mary was to have no fewer than six bridesmaids; the great mansion at Arlington, "which usually wore a somewhat neglected look," was painted and, where possible, repaired; and guests from all the First Families of Virginia were invited. Sydney Smith Lee, Robert E. Lee's older brother, splendid in his naval uniform, would be best man; the mansion was so crowded that people were forced to sleep three to a bed; and the house slaves worked day and night to prepare a memorable feast and to decorate the rooms.

This was the boldest and most important decision of Robert E. Lee's life. Nothing except his children was as important to him as Mary Lee; despite her unpunctuality, her carelessness and untidiness, her total lack of every instinct that might be required to look after a well-ordered household, and her tendency to boss around "Mr. Lee," as she always called him, whatever military rank he had achieved, he loved her without reservation, and he came not only to respect her strong religious feelings but to share them. She was not at all the compliant wife of Victorian legend: she took a keen interest in politics; her judgment about Lee's contemporaries and superiors was a good deal sharper and more critical than he was comfortable with, and expressed with a frankness that sometimes mortified him; and, used to getting her own way from childhood on, she did not fall in with his suggestions easily, or conceal her disagreement. He, for his part, was always protective and caring of her, aware that she had given up life on a great estate, surrounded by servants, for a far more modest and confined life as the wife of a junior officer. Neither of them could have foreseen that they would have seven children; or that her health would decline rapidly until she led an invalid life much like his mother's; or that they would be separated for so much of their marriage by Lee's duties; or, finally, that his virtues, in which she had always confidently believed, would carry him to a fame beyond anybody's imagination, and make him the iconic figure of southern rebellion, and of southern manhood, in the North as well as the South.

In marrying Mary, he also acquired a place in Arlington. The house in which he had been born, Stratford Hall, had passed out of the hands of the Lee family in disgraceful circumstances; the great house in which he had spent much of his childhood belonged to his mother's family, the Carters, not to the Lees. In a society in which the ownership of land and a great mansion counted for much, Robert E. Lee possessed neither; he owned only a few thousand worthless and debt-encumbered acres of wilderness in western Virginia, his uniforms, and his sword, but henceforth, Arlington would play that role in his life, with its impressive portico overlooking Washington, D.C., and its vast collection of the furniture, mementos, and personal belongings of George Washington. It was as if by marriage he had acquired, not wealth—Arlington managed by Mr. Custis could never provide that—but physical roots, a place of his own in landowning Virginia society, and a commanding place at that, for however unprofitable Arlington was, no other house except Mount Vernon itself received more respect.

Perhaps nothing is more symbolic of the change in Robert E. Lee's life than the fact that Martha Washington's "Negro maid, Caroline Branham, who had been in the room on the December night when the great spirit of the nation's founder had passed, was among the servants at Arlington at the time of Mary Custis's wedding."

Arlington was to become his home, and with it, as if by adoption, the spirit and the example of George Washington was to guide his life henceforth, and to influence every decision he made.

Chapter 3
The Engineer—1831–1846

I f family history, a West Point education, an intense and personal admiration for George Washington, and a happy marriage formed a significant part of Robert E. Lee's character, hydraulics supplied another.

The science of hydraulics was of course part of the curriculum at West Point, and it was the heart and soul of the Corps of Engineers in peacetime, indeed the engineers' very raison d'être. Their enemy was water: the storms and tides of the sea, the currents and flooding of the great rivers, the navigability of lakes, all these were their responsibility. They deepened and maintained harbors, often where nature had never intended a harbor to be placed; they built canals and locks; they drained marshland; they removed sandbanks and dredged channels to make great rivers navigable for steamboats where not so very long ago the occasional Indian birch bark canoe had been the only vessel; they built levees to prevent rivers from flooding cities and farmland, drew up maps, and constructed massive fortresses to protect the American coastline in places so close to the sea that no sane man would have dared to build a house there. What is more, they did all this with nothing much more than picks, shovels, sledge-hammers, and crowbars as tools, a task bigger than the building of the Pyramids, which were at least on solid ground—the creation of a modern infrastructure for a virgin continent. They had been at it since 1779 in war and in peace, and no project was too ambitious or difficult for them; the engineers proceeded at their own slow, steady pace, although underfunded, poorly paid, and grudgingly promoted, challenging nature and transforming the American landscape.

From 1831 to 1846, when the Mexican War began, Robert E. Lee was an engineer, working in places as far apart as Virginia, Saint Louis, Missouri, and New York City, undertaking enormous responsibilities despite his low rank, obliged to account meticulously for every penny he spent, and reporting back to a bureaucracy in Washington that was as firmly bound in red tape and congressional penny-pinching as it was slow-moving. As for almost every officer in

the Engineer Corps, water was his chief opponent—
he labored to complete a fortress in Virginia (Fort
Monroe, known as the "Gibraltar of Chesapeake Bay,"
was surrounded by water on three sides and connected
to the mainland by only a narrow neck, as well as
being further guarded by a wide moat on its perimeter), and another in New York Harbor; he succeeded in
diverting the current of the mighty Mississippi River,
removing whole islands and rapids and turning the city
of Saint Louis into a thriving port, to the gratitude of
the city fathers. For all Lee's study at West Point of
Napoleon's tactics, he was to all intents and purposes a
successful civil engineer in uniform—no hint of military genius was required of him, nor did he apparently
sense any in himself. Anybody who has ever lived near
the sea, a river, or a large body of water knows its latent
power. If there was one thing the experience taught
Lee it was a determined, patient, almost *serene* state of
mind in facing impossible odds—an attitude that never
failed to amaze and impress his subordinates. He had
learned it in a hard school—the corps did not accept
failure or excuses, however big the task.

The monumental "outworks" of Fort Monroe and
the construction of nearby Fort Calhoun (renamed Fort
Wool when the Civil War broke out) on an island in
Hampton Roads were to occupy Lee for the next three

years. It was one thing to have read about the art of fortification in the French classics on the subject at West
Point, and another to supervise vast work sites, where
the excavation, laying of stone and earth foundations,
and final grading were being carried out in preparation
for the completion of Vauban's complex star-shaped,
perfectly interlocking seventeenth-century defense
works, with their myriad of elaborate and prettily
named architectural details: the bastion, the ravelins,
the glacis, the counterscarp, all made out of smooth
and tightly fitted blocks of stone, just as they were
in the reign of Louis XIV, and scientifically designed
for the purpose of deflecting artillery shots and permitting a small number of men to hold back attacks
by a much larger body of infantry. That the eventual
enemy might consist of Americans attacking other
Americans, rather than the British approaching by sea,
had not as yet occurred to anybody, of course, but even
so Lee did his work well: although they were situated
in Virginia, Fort Monroe and Fort Wool remained in
Union hands throughout the Civil War; indeed Fort
Monroe would serve as the prison for Jefferson Davis
after the Confederacy was defeated.

Lee's work was not made easier by the division of
authority and the acrimony that reigned at the fort.
Fort Monroe was the army's artillery school and neither

its commander nor his gunners liked the presence of the engineers, so there were constant fights between the men, and disputes between Brevet Colonel Eustis, who commanded the fort and the school, and Captain Andrew Talcott, who commanded the engineers and whose large and unruly civilian workforce, white and black, irritated the colonel.

Robert and Mary Lee settled into bare, sparsely furnished quarters in the fort early in August 1831, after a honeymoon of sorts spent visiting their many relatives accompanied by Mrs. Custis. Efforts have been made to read into Lee's correspondence a mild or joshing reference to his sexual relationship with his bride, but this seems far-fetched, since the only comment on which these efforts are based is in a letter to Captain Talcott, written from Ravensworth during his honeymoon: "I would tell you how the time passed, but fear I am too prejudiced to say anything more, but that it went very rapidly & still continues to do so," and apologizing for not writing sooner. "I actually could not find time before I left the district for anything except——." As eroticism, this is pretty tame stuff, even by the standards of the time, but there was no doubt in anybody's mind that Lee was "blissfully happy," though those who saw the new couple were more impressed by his looks than hers, one of them remarking that he already "looked more like a great man than anyone I have ever seen."

The contrast between Lee's appearance—the solemn "great man" even at this early age—and the playfulness and cheeky good humor of his behavior in a private or a social setting was already remarkable. He loved playing with small children and animals (particularly cats), and was deeply sentimental about horses. With pretty young women he was flirtatious—indeed teasing and flirting with them seem to have been a kind of life-long hobby of Lee's. During his honeymoon, for example, he wrote to Eliza Mackay, one of the girls in the family he had stayed with in Savannah, to congratulate her on her wedding: "How I should like to say 'Mr. and Mrs. Lee have the honour to accept Mrs. Mackay's kind invitation. . . .' But this cannot be Miss Eliza (My Sweetheart) because it only arrived here last night, by this token that I have been in tears ever since at the thought of losing you. Oh me! . . . But Miss E. how do you feel about this time? Say 12 o'clock of the day, as you see the shadows commence to fall towards the East and know that at *last* the sun will set? Though you may not be frightened I 'spect you are most marvelously alarmed."

Resuming the letter a few days later, he wrote: "And how did you disport yourself, My child? Did you go

off well, like a torpedo cracker on Christmas morning."
This tone is very typical of Lee's personal correspondence, a lively and endearing mixture of good-humored
taquinerie, as the French call gentle teasing, not in the
least improper, but very intimate and full of lighthearted
charm: no "Marble Man" here! A Freudian might read
a bit more into the reference to the "torpedo cracker,"
and suggest that it could refer to Eliza's wedding night,
but that it was all perfectly innocent is attested to by
the fact that he showed his letter to Mary, who added
a warm, though markedly more formal, note of congratulations of her own. This is a side of Robert E. Lee
that has to be kept in mind—he was a pre- or early-
Victorian sentimentalist, with a passion for domesticity; a fondness for pretty girls and beautiful women;
and a constant deep need for warmth, admiration, and
affection from them, perhaps deeper than Mary could
supply in the long run. Whatever he may have thought,
the tragedy of his life was not so much that he chose a
"military education," but that his service in the army
separated him so often from his own beloved family,
sometimes for long periods of time.

The Lees' "apartment" at the fort consisted of only
two rooms, in a wing that they shared with Captain
Talcott, as well his sister, his brother-in-law Horace
Hale, and the Hales' two children, forming a kind of

makeshift household. Of course in the age before indoor plumbing, there was nothing we would recognize as a bathroom, and a very limited amount of privacy, but people were used to this at the time. There was also nothing in the way of a kitchen. Talcott and the Hales had slaves who lived and cooked for them elsewhere in the fort, and brought meals in, and Mary brought along at least one slave of her own, Cassie, probably to serve as her maid. They seem to have enjoyed a busy, if confined, social life. Lee's friend from West Point, Joseph Johnston, served at the fort, as did several other friends from his cadet days, and Mary seems to have adapted well to life as an army wife for the present, though it must have been a rude change from life at Arlington, where she received constant care from her mother and had a staff of servants to cater to her every whim.

The great French poet and novelist Alfred de Vigny, also a career officer for whom promotion came slowly, wrote *Servitude et grandeur militaires* at about the same time that the Lees were settling into Fort Monroe, and as Mary would soon learn, army life contained a good deal more servitude than glory. Though the fort was large, and only partly occupied, it was still a stone self-enclosed world, devoted entirely to artillery training or military engineering, and for a woman who loved wildflowers and gardening, and had spent all her life on an estate of 1,100 acres overlooking Washington, it cannot have been an easy transition.

It would not have been improved by the shock of Nat Turner's slave revolt, which began about fifty miles away in Southampton County, Virginia, on August 22. Nat Turner, a rare slave who had been taught how to read and write, and who had acquired a reputation as something of a charismatic preacher in the small black churches around his master's plantation, had apparently taken advantage of his Sunday visits to neighboring congregations to plan the revolt. He was not only a student of the Bible, but an inspired prophet, who took a solar eclipse on February 11, 1831, as a sign that he should prepare his revolt and another solar eclipse, perhaps caused by a faraway volcanic eruption, on August 13, as a sign to begin it. (In both cases, the symbolism of a dark cloud blotting out the sun is perhaps significant.) Convinced that "he was ordained for some great purpose in the hands of the Almighty," Turner had fiery, bloody visions in which he carried out God's vengeance on slave owners, and in the early hours of the morning of August 22, he and his four closest confederates set out to murder as many nearby slave owners and their families as they could, gathering up more slaves, freed blacks, and weapons as they proceeded, until the total number of Turner's followers exceeded seventy. In less than two days they killed fifty-six whites, including women, children, infants, and old people, mostly using as weapons the everyday objects that came to hand easily on a farm, axes, picks, spades, and a few old swords—the only person Turner himself killed, a young woman who had befriended him, Margaret Whitehead, he beat to death with a fence post.

That the violence of slavery begat the violence of the revolt is the modern view of the event, and surely the correct one, but of course this did not strike white southerners as the case in 1831. They were not only horrified but indignant and alarmed. Many of Turner's followers, like Nat Turner himself, had been thought of by their masters as "household servants," almost members of the family, and not a few of the white victims, particularly the children, were killed by blacks who had known them, cared for them, and looked after them for years. It was as if Old Nat, the faithful coachman of Robert E. Lee's mother, whom Lee took to Savannah as his servant, and whom he looked after when Nat was ill and dying, had suddenly turned on the Lee family and murdered them.

Turner's revolt was short-lived, but it was the bloodiest in the two-century history of slavery in America.

The local militia put it down quickly and brutally, arresting or killing all of Turner's followers; in addition, vigilantes and groups of angry or frightened armed citizens killed or lynched an additional 200 or so slaves, probably for no other reason than that they were in the wrong place at the wrong time without an explanation, or looked surly, or didn't answer questions with enough respect. In some places the severed heads of slaves who had been killed were placed on posts by the side of the road as a warning to others.

Nat Turner spared the local poor white farmers on the grounds that they were not slave owners and had no more respect for themselves than they had for slaves— like John Brown's raid on Harpers Ferry twenty-eight years later, his was aimed at the *institution* of slavery; he hoped to shake or destroy it by an act of violence that would serve as an example for others and would rapidly metastasize into a more widespread revolt. It was an outburst of rage against a system of laws and social customs that condemned to bondage 4 million people, and their children and descendants from generation to generation, to be owned, bought, and sold as "chattel property" on much the same terms and often with as little sentiment as cattle and horses, and that proposed to go on doing so forever.

Given the size and scope of slavery in the American South it is surprising only that there had not been more or bigger revolts, particularly since the number of slaves in the "near South," in states like Virginia, was by then in excess of their owners' need, while at the same time the opening up of vast tracts of new land in the "deep South" was increasing the temptation to sell slaves south for work in the cane fields, rice paddies, and cotton fields of Louisiana and Mississippi, where the climate and working conditions, as well as the notorious brutality of the overseers, made life expectancy of "that peculiar property" short. Old Massah may have been kind enough (in his own mind) to his house slaves, his butler, his cook, his wife's and daughters' maids, and willing to overlook a certain slackness in his field hands (Lee's father-in-law Mr. Custis was a good example of both attitudes), but once he got into debt, or when he died, his creditors or his heirs seldom hesitated to sell his slaves off to be marched farther south in chains to pick cotton under the whip until they dropped—indeed this is the basic theme of Harriet Beecher's Stowe's novel *Uncle Tom's Cabin*.

By the time of Nat Turner's revolt a huge forced southbound migration had been in progress for decades, leaving in its wake broken slave "marriages" (which of course had no validity in law) and children separated from their mothers, or sold along with them, whichever was more profitable, and the slave dealer had become a familiar figure in southern cities, even riding from door to door in search of likely "slave property" for sale. If you could pick up several hundred dollars in gold coins for the equivalent of Old Nat, who had been with the Lee family since birth and had given a lifetime of faithful service, how many people would resist the chance when it was offered, with slave prices in New Orleans soaring?

Thus, by 1831, the fear of being sent south, away from family, children, friends, and familiar surroundings, with no hope of being reunited and every prospect of being physically abused and worked to death, had hugely exacerbated the misery of being born a slave— it was not only a threat of exile, but in the view of most slaves a sentence of hard labor and death. Only in Russia, where the ancient custom of serfdom produced slavery on a far larger scale (the biggest slave owner in the South possessed just over a thousand slaves, but in Tolstoy's *War and Peace* Pierre Bezukhov's father, the count, is described as owning "40,000 souls"), and where exile to Siberia to clear virgin forests was a virtual sentence of death, could any equivalent to Southern slavery be found in the 1830s.

In the legal proceedings that followed the rising, fifty slaves and freed blacks were tried, of whom nineteen were hanged. Nat Turner himself was not found until nine weeks after the revolt, and was tried, convicted, and hanged on November 11; afterward his body was skinned, beheaded, and quartered. One of the doctors who dissected the body had a "money purse made of his hide," while another apparently kept his skeleton as a souvenir.

At Fort Monroe, Colonel Eustis sent three companies of artillery to Southampton County by steamer the moment he heard news of the revolt, but by the time they arrived, it was all over and their presence was not needed. Fear of further slave insurrections prompted the colonel to request five more companies of artillery and to "put into execution a series of regulations for the exclusion of Negroes from the post." This outraged the engineers: their workforce consisted largely of hired slaves who needed access to the fort for water with which to produce cement and mortar, and their personal servants were also slaves. A brisk objection on Lee's part, in the absence of Captain Talcott, escalated into a "post war," the kind of bad feelings between one branch of the service and another that could quickly render army life in the confined space of a camp or fort poisonous—a good lesson for Lee about the importance of firmly preventing this kind of thing, which, once it started, could rapidly weaken an army, in which cooperation by infantry, cavalry, and engineers was essential. The arrival of five more companies, and the exclusion of slaves, made living conditions in the fort much more crowded and less comfortable, so it is perhaps not surprising that after the Lees went home for Christmas Mary remained at Arlington for several months, while her husband continued his duties at Fort Monroe by himself.

As for the revolt, Lee would have of course heard about the bloody details when the officers who had been sent to Southampton County returned. He reassured his mother-in-law that "much mischief" was prevented by confusion over the date of the uprising—a reference to Nat Turner's misreading of the eclipses and his poor communications with his closest collaborators—and added, "It was ascertained that they used their religious assemblies, which ought to have been devoted to better purposes, for forming and maturing their plans." The same thought also occurred to the Virginia legislature, which quickly passed strict laws against teaching slaves and freed blacks to read and write, and requiring a white clergyman to be present at any black religious meeting.

Notwithstanding his sensible effort to calm any fears Mrs. Custis might have for the safety of her daughter, however, Lee has been described as "profoundly concerned" about it, as every southerner was. Lee was never, by any stretch of the imagination, an enthusiast for slavery, particularly the kind of slavery that was being practiced by the "Cotton Kings" in the "deep South," but his feelings on the subject were firmly held and remained remarkably consistent.

Like many southerners, Lee disliked slavery not so much for its consequences for the slaves as for its effect on whites. He defined his view very precisely in a letter to Mary some twenty years later: "In this enlightened age, there are few I believe, but what will acknowledge, that slavery as institution, is a moral and political evil in any Country. It is useless to expatiate on its disadvantages. I think it however a greater evil to the white man than to the black race, & while my feelings are strongly enlisted in behalf of the latter, my sympathies are more strong for the former. The blacks are immeasurably better off here than in Africa, morally, socially & physically. The painful discipline they are undergoing, is necessary for their instruction as a race, & I hope will prepare & lead them to better things. How long their subjugation may be necessary is known & ordered by a wise and Merciful Providence."

This was not an uncommon view of slavery among moderate southerners, and for that matter among a good many northerners as well before the Civil War. Lee's belief that the end of slavery was a matter for God to bring about in His own good time, rather than something for politicians or white slave owners to deal with, was a little more pessimistic than the more popular and prevailing idea that the problem of slavery might be solved by compensating their owners and deporting the blacks en masse, perhaps to somewhere in South America, or back to Africa—indeed by 1820 three philanthropic Virginians, two of them relatives of Robert E. Lee—Henry Clay, John Randolph, and Richard Bland Lee, cofounders of the American Colonization Society—had already made ambitious plans and raised money to create Liberia (its capital was named Monrovia to honor another Virginian, President James Monroe) and set the process in motion by sending freed blacks there. Even those Americans who were opposed to slavery were not necessarily in favor of free blacks participating in the political process or living as equals with other Americans. Lincoln himself had been a mild but persistent enthusiast for the idea of Liberia, and famously remarked during the Lincoln-Douglas debates, "There is a physical difference between the white and the black races which I believe will forever forbid the two races living together on terms of social and political equality," an opinion not so very different from Lee's.

Lee's opinion in the 1850s was the one that he had always held, and which he retained to his death—it never changed. Indeed, in 1866, a year after the end of the Civil War, when he was called to testify before a Joint Congressional Committee on Reconstruction, far from recanting or softening his opinion, he repeated it in stronger terms: "My own opinion is that they [blacks] cannot vote intelligently, and that giving them the [vote] would lead to a great deal of demagogism, and lead to embarrassments in various ways. . . . I think it would be better for Virginia if she could get rid of them. . . . I think everybody there would be willing to aid it."

To be sure, Lee's feelings about individual blacks differed from his belief that as a race they were better off as slaves. Just as he had shown kindness to Old Nat, his mother's former coachman, he signed a letter in the 1868 presidential campaign that read, "The idea that Southern people are hostile to the negroes and would oppress them, if it were in their power to do so, is entirely unfounded. . . . They have grown up in our midst, and we have been accustomed from childhood to look upon them with kindness."

Even though Lee was still a mere brevet second lieutenant, he appears to have prevailed over Colonel
Eustis at Fort Monroe, possibly because General
Gratiot, the chief of the Corps of Engineers, pulled
more weight in Washington than the chief of artillery. In any case, Lee returned to work, his principal
task being to oversee the transportation and dumping
of large quantities of stone and sand into the Hampton
Roads to extend and reinforce the fifteen-acre
"artificial island" called the Rip-Raps (after riprap, a
grade of loose stone of different sizes and shapes from
which it had been created), where Fort Wool would
eventually be constructed, and, for the work on both
forts, to keep the strict accounting of expenses that
the Corps of Engineers required. The island, on the
south side of the navigation channel, was intended to
support Fort Monroe, and provide cross fire against
enemy vessels entering the Hampton Roads. The work
gave Lee responsibilities but did not excite him, and
he may already have begun to suffer the doubts about
the wisdom of having chosen a military career that
were to plague him before the Mexican War gave
him a chance to experience combat and command—
and sped up his promotion—and which would resume and worsen with peace until the secession of

Virginia unexpectedly made him a general. Strangely, self-doubt and dissatisfaction about his own abilities would haunt this most competent of men most of his life.

He was fortunate in having Talcott as his superior officer, since they became close friends; the presence of the unneeded extra companies of artillery, which had been sent to put down any further slave insurrections, also increased the pace of social life at the fort, though since the newcomers consisted mostly of young officers with time on their hands, it was predominantly masculine and hard-drinking. Lee was tolerant of drinkers, but he seldom drank himself, and found it hard to understand those who drank to excess. Drinking, card playing, and chasing after the few available women being the chief recreations of the younger artillery officers at Fort Monroe, Lee tended to stand apart from them, although he was the same rank, as did his friend Joe Johnston, who was also abstemious. It is worth noting that even at this early stage of his career—among army officers nobody is lowlier than a temporary second lieutenant—Lee was set apart from his fellows both by his physical bearing and by his innate dignity. He was not censorious or stuffy, he was good company, he joined in such fun as there was (provided it did not interfere with duty), but there was a certain reserve to his character that he was to retain all his life, and that made him stand out from the beginning, even though he was too modest for this to have been his intention. He had about him the loneliness of a great commander even when he was still the most junior of officers: it was not something he learned, or assumed; it was something he was born with, accentuated perhaps by his identification since early boyhood with George Washington.

After the Christmas visit to Arlington, Mary Lee did not return to Fort Monroe until June 1832. She then came with her mother and two slaves, so life must have been for a time very crowded indeed in Lee's quarters, particularly since Mrs. Custis brought with her enough furnishings from Arlington to make her daughter's new home more comfortable. By that time, Mary Lee was pregnant, and of course she went home to Arlington to have the baby there in September with the help and support of her mother and the servants. The baby was a healthy boy, George Washington Custis Lee (he was always known as Custis, rather than George), named after his grandfather, George Washington's adopted son; this name was another sign of Lee's instinctive emotional connection with the father of his country.

After the boy's birth, Mary spent almost as much time at Arlington as at Fort Monroe, obliging Lee to be in constant correspondence with "Molly," as he often addressed her in his letters, and sometimes chiding her for not living up to his own high standards. It was not just a question of neatness, orderliness, and perfect housekeeping, about all of which Lee was gently but firmly critical; when Talcott's brother-in-law Horace Hale died while Mary was away in Arlington, for example, she clearly did not come up to her husband's expectations in dealing with the grief of their friend and neighbor at Fort Monroe. "I am sorry," he wrote to her, "it has so happened that you have not been with Mrs. Hale, when in the one case she needed your assistance, & in the other your sympathy." This sounds like a pretty stiff rebuke, coming from a man as devoted to his wife as Lee clearly was, and may also indicate a certain, perhaps subconscious, impatience with the amount of time Mary was beginning to spend away from the fort being cossetted by her mother and father at Arlington. There does not seem to have been any friction between them—his letters to her are affectionate, if sometimes exasperated, although he is sometimes obliged to apologize to others on her behalf: "Tell the ladies that they are aware that Mrs. L. is sometimes addicted to *laziness & forgetfulness* in her housekeeping. But they may be certain that she does her best. Or in her mother's words, 'The spirit is willing but the flesh is weak.'" This is the voice of a loving and forgiving husband, but also one who does not close his eyes to his spouse's defects, and is surprisingly candid about them to their acquaintances—a certain patronizing tone seeps through, making one suspect that although Lee may have been the most understanding of husbands, he may not have been all that easy to live with on a day-to-day basis; perfectionists seldom are.

Mary, it is equally clear, expected to be looked after and protected as she always had been at Arlington, and Lee did his best, though with fewer resources and less time to do so—he was, after all, a busy and ambitious young engineer, whereas Mr. and Mrs. Custis had always been at home and on hand to see to her wants and needs, not to speak of a large number of devoted servants with nothing much else to do. Neither Robert nor Mary Lee could have foreseen the amount of time the army would separate them from each other in the years to come, which was probably just as well, or the way she would become her husband's confidant and sounding board, with strong, and strongly expressed opinions of her own. He held nothing back from her in writing about his political opinions and his career, and she replied with equal frankness and sensible advice. He never hid from her his need for women friends, or his admiration for a pretty face—he was always happiest in domestic surroundings, even if they were not his own, or chatting with women about their lives, their feelings, and their children, although his tone with women was usually avuncular rather than passionate, like that of a graybeard content to sit in their company over a cup of tea, not shy of paying the occasional compliment, or flirting just enough to bring the occasional blush to somebody's cheek. He made no effort to hide this from Mary, and she does not seem to have minded. While she was away the outbreak of the Seminole War in Florida caused many of the artillery officers to be sent south, leaving their wives behind, and for a time Lee luxuriated in being "in the right position to sympathize with them, as Mrs. Lee and her little limb are at Arlington."

When she returned with "Master Custis," as Lee referred jokingly to their infant son, their domestic arrangements at the fort improved. Captain Talcott had married Harriet Randolph Hackley, known to all, including Lee, as "the beautiful Talcott," and his widowed sister and her children had moved out. The Lees were thus able to move upstairs, into larger quarters than the two small rooms they had originally shared, and also gained a greater amount of privacy. However, since Harriet Talcott was soon pregnant and Mary Lee had a small child, there must have been enough domesticity

in the quarters set aside for the engineer officers to satisfy even Robert E. Lee. At that time, Lee owned four
of his mother's slaves, while Mary brought one of her
own from Arlington, so they were not short of help,
though Lee remarked that they were substituting quantity for quality, without being able to suggest a sensible
alternative, beyond saying that Mary might try to hire
one who was better trained. This was, of course, precisely the practical, as opposed to the moral, problem of
slavery—the slaves had no particular incentive to hone
their skills, and the owner was stuck with them for life,
unless he sold them or hired them out.

Harriet Talcott was to play a large—perhaps an
outsize—role in Lee's life. Even so devoted a biographer as Emory M. Thomas refers to their relationship
as "an extended mock love affair," though whether or
not Harriet shared in this fantasy is hard to determine.
Lee certainly did nothing to keep his interest in her
secret—he went so far as to include what amounted to
billets-doux in letters to Harriet's husband when they
were away from the fort, and in the engineers' wing of
Fort Monroe it cannot have escaped Mary's attention
that Lee was enamored of Harriet, or at the very least
chose to play the part of a love-smitten swain for his own
amusement. Whereas the portrait of Mary Custis shows
a rather plain face with thin lips, the portrait of Harriet

Talcott shows by contrast a somewhat luscious beauty: shoulders extravagantly bared; a mouth resembling that of Clara Bow's, the "It girl" of the 1920s with the famous bee-stung lips; a long, graceful neck; and a pile of blond hair. She appears to have been witty and clever as well.

No doubt all this was innocent enough—there is no indication that Lee ever betrayed Mary with Harriet, or anyone else—but it is an odd side of Lee's character, this need to play the whimsical lover, not only with Harriet, but with other women as well. When Harriet gave birth to her first child, a daughter, Lee wrote her a gushing note pressing on her his son "Master Custis Lee" as her daughter's husband-to-be, and even suggesting, in a roundabout way, that he was the father of her girl, and referring to an "Affaire du Coeur" between himself and Harriet, which was largely if not totally imaginary on his part. None of this altered his love for Mary, and indeed he wrote to her often about these fantasies, as if she would share his pleasure at flirting with other women. He wrote to Mary, who was then away in Arlington, of escorting "Miss G," adding, "How I did strut along. . . . How you would have triumphed in my happiness." He wrote to his old friend Mackay in Savannah that pretty girls made his heart "open to them, like a flower to the sun," and again, "As for the daughters of Eve in this country, they are formed in the very poetry of nature, and would make your lips water and your fingers tingle. They are beginning to assemble to put their beautiful limbs into this salt water," a reference to the then fashionable belief in sea bathing, almost fully clothed, as a health measure. The romantic, lyrical side of Lee was fully formed and powerful, was apparently not satisfied by marriage, and would remain a constant throughout his life. It was not so much that he was a roué manqué, though that may be true—he was, after all, the son of a robust eighteenth-century roué and the half brother of a man hopelessly mired in sexual scandal—as that he had a lifelong need for the admiration and girlish chatter of young women, in whose company his normally reserved character expanded and took on a new dimension. Mary, to her credit, seems to have understood that this offered no threat to their marriage. His male friends and contemporaries, like Mackay and Talcott, seem to have understood it as well—after all, Talcott was Lee's superior and close friend, as well as Harriet's husband—but it is a side of Lee that would certainly have surprised those who fought under his command in the Civil War.

Owing to Talcott's frequent absences on "other duty," it fell largely to Lee to defend the position of the engineers at Fort Monroe against the artillerymen.

The feud (no other word will do) had its origin in Colonel Eustis's belief that he did not need two young engineer officers to tell him how to complete a fort that was designed for the purpose of housing artillery in the first place. It was a typical military "turf war," in this case one between the "pioneers" who sited and dug in the guns and the "gunners" who aimed and fired them that had been going on since the fifteenth century.

Lee labored to complete the details of the counterscarp wall and ramparts of Fort Monroe, but his principal task was still to order boatloads of riprap at the best price he could negotiate and have it dumped into the waters of Hampton Roads to create a solid foundation on which Fort Calhoun could be built. Each load of stone simply pushed the preceding one deeper into the soupy bottom, so the visible progress was minimal, no doubt causing the artillerists to question whether the fort there would ever be built, and Lee to wonder whether he would have to spend the rest of his career on this thankless task. The only good news for him was that he ceased to be a brevet second lieutenant in July 1832 and was promoted to the same rank as a regular— a commissioned officer of the army, no longer a temporary and acting one.

Throughout 1833 and much of 1834 Lee fought a lone rearguard action against the artillery in defense of the right of the engineers to complete the work on Fort Monroe and the Rip-Raps. He did so both on the spot and in Washington, at the War Department, where the layers of intrigue were thicker and could have destroyed his career at this early stage, as well as Talcott's. The situation reached a nadir, from Lee's point of view, when Talcott was transferred to the Hudson River and Lee was forced to move to improvised lodgings on the Rip-Raps—a triumph for the artillerymen—but then this order was revoked; the artillery school was broken up and its officers were dispersed to their original units; and Lee was vindicated. He cannot have been pleased at being obliged to live for a time on the equivalent of Elba, instead of enjoying the busy domestic life and admiring ladies of Fort Monroe, but he continued do his job, buying stone and chucking it into the water. That he did his work well is proved by the fact that Fort Wool was still in active service until the end of World War II, after which it was decommissioned and became a modest tourist attraction. Lee's dedication to duty in difficult circumstances was so evident, and so highly appreciated by the chief of engineers, General Gratiot, that in November 1834 he was transferred to Washington as Gratiot's assistant. Since this transfer would have the additional advantage of making it possible for Lee to live at Arlington with Mary, and ride back and forth to work every day, it was something like a complete victory.

The years from 1832 to 1834 were not wasted ones, professionally. Apart from teaching Lee a good deal about how the army worked, they gave him a firm grounding in both artillery and fortification. Napoleon himself was an artilleryman by training, and believed that "God fights on the side with the best artillery." When he took command of the army of Italy in 1796 it had only sixty guns, but sixteen years later at the Battle of Borodino in Russia, the combined artillery of the French and Russian armies was over 1,250 guns, firing over 15,000 rounds an hour on a two-mile front.

The fight between the engineers and the artillerymen had been settled in favor of the former for a time under Louis XIV by the genius of Vauban, whose immense system of fortifications—the military equivalent of Versailles in cost, and also the seventeenth-century equivalent of the Maginot Line—protected France, but Napoleon was always by instinct more interested in attack than defense, and equipped his armies with lighter, faster-moving guns so as to concentrate a mass of artillery fire against the enemy's weak point as quickly as possible. His lack of interest in fortifications cost him dear in 1814, when the Allied armies invaded France, but during the long period when he dominated all Europe, the speed at which his armies moved, his gift for seeking out the decisive battle, and the skill with which he directed the awesome power of French artillery made him almost unbeatable by any combination of enemies until he made the mistake of adding Russia with its vast distances to the list of them.

Like Napoleon, Lee always sought to move quickly, surprise his enemy, and concentrate his artillery—no American general before or since has ever understood how to use artillery to better effect than Lee—but unlike Napoleon, Lee was also able to build formidable defensive positions when he had to. Fort Monroe taught him a lot about the design and construction of defensive works, and he would put it to good use early in 1862 when he made his men dig the elaborate trench system that constituted the defenses of Richmond, despite widespread grumbling among them and criticism in the southern press; and in 1864 and 1865, when his complex, brilliantly improvised defense lines around Petersburg, Virginia, kept the Confederacy alive for nearly a year.

Although skill at playing army politics is not usually something for which Lee is given any credit, it is worth noting that he managed to get out of the thankless task of reinforcing the Rip-Raps just as gracefully as he had managed to get himself clear of Cockspur Island. The first move brought him closer to Arlington and Mary, and the second made it possible for him to move into Arlington, and also gave him a job in Washington at the right hand of the chief of engineers. He could not have done better had he been the most skilled of intriguers! He had at first thought of renting a house in Washington, but with its muddy streets, open sewers, and uncompleted public buildings it was not the attractive city it is now, and we can be sure that Mary Lee was the first to point out to him the advantages of living in Arlington surrounded by more than a thousand acres of land, for a growing family—all seven of their children would be born in Arlington and grow up there, so over time it became, in a real sense, the only home Robert E. Lee had ever known, cherished not just because of its many associations with George Washington but because wherever the army sent him, it remained the stable center of his family and his life. For a man who had been born in Stratford, an imposing mansion, but who grew up in a small, crowded house in Alexandria, and went straight from there to West Point, Arlington was like the home he had never had, and returning every evening to its stately Greek Revival portico with the six gleaming white columns must have given intense pleasure to someone whose extended family, both Lees and Carters, owned so many great houses in Virginia. None of them, though, was more famous than this—indeed, except for Washington's own Mount Vernon and Jefferson's Monticello there was no house in Virginia grander or with more historical associations than Arlington.* It was already a tourist attraction—according to a family joke, carriages full of strangers would turn up from time to time, and finding Mr. Custis near the entrance with his collar open at the neck and his disheveled appearance, tip him a dollar to show them around the house, supposing him to be the caretaker.

What we would now call the commute from Arlington to the War Department, then close by the White House, on horseback was longer than Lee might have wished, and in bad weather tiring and difficult for both horse and rider, but that was more than compensated for by Mary's joy in living at home with her parents and the familiar servants who had looked after her since her birth—Lee could hardly have made any decision that made her happier. With his usual care for

---

*It was no coincidence that in May 1861, after Lee accepted a commission as a general in the Confederate Army, the Union Army occupied Arlington and chopped down the trees he was so fond of. In 1864 the Arlington estate was selected as the site for the new National Cemetery, of which the Lee mansion is still today the most prominent feature. The graves of Union soldiers were dug as close to the mansion as possible, so Lee could never return, and twenty-eight Union dead were buried in Mary Lee's beloved rose garden.

details, Lee sought out a blacksmith in Washington named Schneider whose shop was on his way to the War Department, "on the corner of Twentieth and G Streets," and left his horse there after giving Schneider careful instructions about exactly how he wanted the horse to be shod, remarking with approval when he came back after work to examine the horse's hooves, "You are the first man I have ever come across that could shoe a horse by my directions." As a result Mr. Schneider would become blacksmith for all of Arlington's horses until the Civil War, and even after Lee went south to join the Confederacy in 1861, he still managed somehow to send Mr. Schneider $2 he owed him.

Lee's duties at the War Department were not onerous and he soon became fond of General Gratiot, the chief of engineers, a Louisiana-born hero of the War of 1812 (no fewer than three cities were named after him, in Ohio, Wisconsin, and Michigan) who took a personal interest in all of his officers and their far-flung projects. Despite his admiration for Gratiot, Lee chafed mildly at the dull routine of office work, and struggled with doubts about his self-worth and his future in the Engineer Corps. There was hardly any prospect of promotion, the pay and allowances of a second lieutenant were ridiculously low, and what he saw of the struggle to squeeze a little money out of Congress for even the most necessary and beneficial of projects was enough to sour Lee on politics and politicians for life. Since Gratiot was frequently absent on inspections of the corps' projects, Lee became the equivalent of the general's office manager, assisted by his trusty clerk from Fort Monroe. The amount of correspondence, paperwork, and red tape generated by even the smallest disbursement of the government's money makes his work seem almost Dickensian, so it must have come as a relief when Gratiot sent Lee off to help his old friend Talcott settle a border dispute that had grown into an armed confrontation between the militias of the state of Ohio and the territory of Michigan in the spring of 1835.

The origins of this dispute could be traced all the way back to 1787, and involved a narrow strip of land of nearly 500 square miles, varying in width between 5 and 8 miles. The original boundary line across the Lower Peninsula of Michigan had been defined by Congress before any accurate map of the area existed, indeed before any white man but the occasional trapper had even reached there, and subsequent attempts to survey it more precisely seemed to bear little relationship to what was on the ground. The "Toledo War," as it became known after the major town in the disputed area, ended with nothing more serious than a few shots fired in the air (raised to the status of the "Battle of Phillips Corners" by the participants) and a Michigan deputy sheriff wounded by a boy with a penknife, but from May to October 1835 Talcott and Lee meandered through the forests and lakes of the area attempting to conduct a scientific survey threatened only by dense clouds of "*Moschitoes*," as Lee called them, and the occasional snake. Lee remarked that if there were any inhabitants of this wilderness he never encountered them, and although at one point he reached Pelee Island, Ontario, in the middle of Lake Erie more or less opposite Cleveland, it too appeared to be uninhabited except by one snake in the dilapidated, deserted lighthouse. Evidently, neither the scenery nor the Great Lakes themselves made much impression on him.

Lee's low opinion of the area may have been affected by the duration of the survey, which stretched from the original estimate of one month to five, and by the fact that Mary was pregnant and gave birth to their second child, a daughter, in July while he was absent. The child was healthy, but Mary had a difficult delivery and her recovery was marked by the first of the many illnesses that she would suffer throughout her life, and which eventually made her an invalid. She apparently wrote to Lee and asked him to come home, for he replied to her sternly from Detroit late in August: "But why do you urge my *immediate* return, & tempt one in the strongest manner, to endeavour to get excused from the performance of a duty, imposed on me by my Profession, for the pure gratification of my private feelings?" The apparent harshness of this letter may be a result of Mary's reluctance to tell him frankly how ill she was, for when he returned home at the beginning of October he was alarmed by her condition, which he attributed to her being "too active too soon," although her symptoms seem to have been more serious than any that could have been caused by activity alone, and may have included "a pelvic infection of some sort." In the heroic medical tradition of the day, the doctors bled her, by cutting open a vein, and "cupped" her—a painful treatment that consisted of heating small glass cups with fire and applying them to the skin—without producing any improvement. Eventually two large "abscesses which had formed on her groin broke" (actually the second abscess was cut open by the same surgeon who did the bloodletting and the cupping); this seemed to help, but Mary remained for some time weak and bedridden, while the children came down with "whooping-cough," following which their mother caught mumps. Mary had five more healthy children, but from this point on her own health would always be her husband's major concern, though the only thing he could do for her was to take her at intervals to one or another of Virginia's many warm "mineral springs," which in the nineteenth century were thought to be restorative. It seems likely that she benefited from the social life at these spas as much as from the waters, and they became a regular part of the Lee family's routine. Frequent pregnancies surely took a toll on her, though they were of course considered normal in that day (Queen Victoria set the standard for the English-speaking world with nine children), and she became increasingly crippled by rheumatoid arthritis.

Throughout 1836 Lee was worn down by Mary's illnesses, and by the sheer tedium of his work. The dashing young West Point graduate had become an overworked military bureaucrat and a husband constantly worried by the health of his wife and children. "I have never seen a man so changed and saddened," one of his relatives remarked. Lee seriously considered resigning from the army, and complained to his friend Talcott of his own "procrastination" and poor luck. He was not consoled by his promotion from second to first lieutenant, a modest step up for a man who had been an officer in the army for nearly seven years. Talcott himself had resigned from the army to begin a successful career as a civil engineer, but nobody reached out to tempt Lee into what is now called the private sector, and he seemed unable to take the first step—after all, the army had been his life since 1825, and he had never contemplated anything else. A slow (but temporary) improvement in Mary's health and the natural beauties of Arlington cheered Lee up a bit, and encouraged him to describe to Talcott the Virginia countryside he loved: "The country looks very sweet now," he wrote, almost lyrically in May 1836, "and the hill at Arlington covered with verdure, and perfumed by the blossoms of the trees, the flowers of the garden, Honey-suckles, yellow jasmine, etc." This, like the flirtatious Lee, is a very different person from the dignified "Marble Man" of legend or the stern commander whom he later became and whose grave, gray, bearded face adorns countless statues and paintings. He continued to add flirtatious asides to "Talcott, My Beauty" in his letters to her husband, describing her as "the masterpiece with blue eyes," and speculating on how many children she would have and whether matters could be arranged so that when they grew up they married his.

He was an adoring parent, who rushed home every evening to see his children; he was delighted when Mary presented him with another son in May 1837, and there is no question that Lee's family life consoled him for the fact that he was stuck in a job that offered him no excitement or challenge. He was always happiest in the company of his children, and with Arlington as his home; nevertheless, when General Gratiot finally gave in to his pleas for a major engineering challenge only two months before his second son was born, Lee accepted at once, despite the fact that it would take him away from Arlington for an undetermined length of time, and with no certainty that Mary and the children could join him.

His biographers ascribe this as devotion to duty, and of course with Lee that was always a factor, but it also seems likely that he was simply unable to resist an adventure that would take him out of the office of the chief of engineers and into the field, farther away and with a bigger job and much more independent responsibility than he had enjoyed as Talcott's aide on the survey of the Ohio-Michigan border. Although the element of ambition has been carefully erased from Lee's character (along with every other flaw) over the 144 years since his death—indeed already in his own lifetime he was considered by most people to be almost inhumanly selfless—the fact is that he was hugely motivated by personal advancement, then and later, but chose always to represent to others, and perhaps to himself, that he was only doing his duty, and that although the choice had fallen on him, he was probably not the right man for the job. It was a refrain throughout his life that he wished somebody more able had been chosen for whatever post he was about to assume. In this case, once he had the job he coveted, it was typical of Lee to write in a spirit of good-humored self-deprecation to his old friend from Savannah Jack Mackay that "they wanted a skillful engineer . . . and sent me."

The truth is that he was by far the best man for the job, and knew it, and that the job was an immensely challenging one. This was not a mere survey, but a huge and urgent task: to tame the Mississippi River.

The great river that Indians called the "Father of the Waters" was then America's most important path of trade and communication, linking the grain of the Northwest and the cotton of the upper Mississippi with the thriving port of New Orleans. At the same time, then as now, the Mississippi had a will and a mind of its own—it was not just a river, but a huge natural force of nature, and one by no means always friendly to man. Sometimes the river flooded, inundating hundreds of square miles; at other times its level sank and it filled some stretches with debris, making navigation by steamboat impossible; at still other times the river changed its own course, creating a channel where there had been none before and leaving settlements built along its old course high and dry. To the Indians, who merely fished in it and traveled by canoe, none of these things had mattered; they accepted the river's unpredictability and power, and built no permanent settlements. But to Americans in the first half of the nineteenth century the course of prosperity, trade, commerce, and the development of cities and ports made it necessary to impose some kind of order on the river—a task on which the Corps of Engineers has been working uninterruptedly for the past 200 years, with limited success and not always happy consequences for what we now call the environment. At best, the battle between the Corps of Engineers and the Mississippi River can be said to have resulted in a draw. Ease of navigation has certainly been achieved; levees have been raised; bridges, dams, and locks have been built across it—but the river's ability to counterattack with destruction on a vast scale remains unimpeded, as was proved when Hurricane Katrina hit New Orleans.

The immediate problem facing Lee was the fact that the Mississippi was cutting a new channel for itself that threatened "to destroy the river commerce" of Saint Louis, Missouri. Not by coincidence, General Gratiot was himself a native of Saint Louis, and his family home there overlooked the river. He not only received firsthand but also shared the fears and complaints of the good citizens of the city, some of them his own family—and also those of their representatives in the U.S. Congress, who determined the budget of the Corps of Engineers. The risk that Saint Louis might be cut off from the trade and commerce that had made it (and the Gratiot family) prosperous since 1764 was unacceptable. It was the key "transportation hub" (to use a modern phrase) of the west and the starting point of the California and Oregon trails—at any one time as many as 150 steamboats were moored along its levee on the Mississippi.

Lee's responsibilities included not only saving the port and waterfront of Saint Louis, though that was his first priority, but removing the many snags formed by trees and branches carried downstream by the river's current—these snags severely endangered shipping—and even "cutting a shipway" through the rapids of the Mississippi near the Missouri-Iowa border, thus making him responsible for nearly 200 miles of the river. Here was a multiple task of engineering to test the abilities of any man, not to speak of the tact needed to deal with the more prominent citizens of Saint Louis, the backbone to resist political threats and interference, and the attention to detail to ensure that every penny spent was properly accounted for. Gratiot was absolutely right to pick First Lieutenant Lee over more senior officers—Lee had the technical skills, the self-confidence, and the foresight needed for the task; and his dignity and commanding presence made him a natural figure of authority, despite his low rank, and elicited instant respect even from those who disagreed with him.

Saint Louis did not please Lee at first sight. He described it as "the dearest and dirtiest place I was ever in," though he later came around to a more favorable opinion. His aide and companion on the long trip out to Saint Louis via Philadelphia, New York, and Pittsburgh was Second Lieutenant Montgomery C. Meigs. A Georgian, Meigs was another of those multitalented West Point graduates, who went on to become the quartermaster general of the Union Army in the Civil War, and also supervised the building of the dome over the U.S. Capitol in Washington, D.C. Lee and Meigs paused at Louisville on their journey down the Ohio River by steamboat to examine two "machine boats" for lifting stone, and a small steam launch for towing it. These had been gathered on their behalf by Captain Henry Shreve, a steamboat pioneer who had been laboring on the snags of the Missouri, the Red, and the Mississippi rivers for many years, another engineer apparently stuck in a seemingly endless and thankless task (unless one counts the fact that the city of Shreveport, Louisiana, was named after him). They then proceeded on their way toward Saint Louis.⋆

Lee and Meigs were obliged to wait in Saint Louis in sweltering summer heat for their small fleet to arrive. "They are the greatest people for promising and not fulfilling, that I ever saw," Lee complained of the boatmen, with what was, for him, a rare degree of impatience. Inactivity and unpunctuality then and later on were anathema to Lee; brisk movement suited his temperament best, and would always play a large role in his approach to battle. For the moment, he was obliged to pass his time at what was, for him, the equivalent of cooling his heels: paying social calls on General Gratiot's family and friends, and writing long letters to Mary advising her on how to bring up their children in his absence. "The improved condition of the children, which you mention," he wrote in reply to a letter from her, "was a source of great comfort to me; and as I suppose, by this time, you have all returned to Arlington, you will be able to put them under a proper restraint. . . . Our dear little boy [Custis] seems to

---

⋆ Although they fought on different sides in the Civil War (in which Meigs's son John was killed), Meigs remained an admirer of Lee, and wrote that he was "the model of a soldier and the beau ideal of a Christian man." This did not prevent Meigs from being the one to suggest that the Federal government take over the Lees' Arlington estate as a burial ground for Union soldiers.

have among his friends the reputation of being hard to manage—a distinction not at all desirable, as it indicates self-will and obstinacy." Like many other parents, he sought to inculcate in his children, at any rate in the boys, virtues he did not himself possess. Lee was notably lacking in "self-will," in the sense of selfishness, but "obstinacy" was undoubtedly a strong part of his character, however much he deplored it in his first son. Once Lee tackled something, he was determined to see it through to the end, whatever contrary advice and warnings he received, and however difficult it might appear. The hallmark of Lee's genius as a battlefield commander would be his obstinacy in circumstances that might, to almost anyone else, have urged caution or withdrawal, and he brought this same obstinacy and willpower to bear on the mighty Mississippi River in 1837 as soon as his little flotilla arrived in Saint Louis.

Having been obliged to wait over two weeks, Lee set out 350 miles upstream the moment they arrived, taking with him a group of "rivermen" recruited for their knowledge of the problems of navigation on the Mississippi. The problem to which he gave the most immediate attention was the two rocky rapids that seriously impeded navigation on the Mississippi: the first (from the south) the Des Moines Rapids, just above where the Des Moines River flows into the

Mississippi, near what is now Keokuk, Iowa; and the second the Rock Island Rapids, "where the river was shallow and the riverbed was rock," near present-day Moline, Illinois. These two hazards in the river made navigation dangerous, and expensive. When the river was high and the current was running fast, steamboats could be swept onto rocks at both rapids; and when the river was low, they were obliged to stop at Des Moines and unload their cargo into keelboats, basically large, shallow-draft barges towed by horses on the bank, to be reloaded into other steamboats moored below the rapids—a problem which helped Des Moines to prosper but which slowed down shipping and added to the cost. It is hard to exaggerate the importance of these problems in the age before decent roads or railways existed in what is now the Midwest—goods in bulk moved by river or did not move at all.

The dangers of navigation on the Mississippi were demonstrated only too clearly when Lee's steamboat ran aground on the rocks in the Des Moines Rapids and could not be floated free because of the low water level. He had planned to survey the upper rapids at first, but with his usual ability to change his plans quickly he made the stuck steamboat his headquarters and from it organized a detailed survey of the lower rapids, then moved inland on foot to what he referred to with ironic capitals as "The City of Des Moines," which, he found, consisted of a single log cabin containing "the Proprietor and the entire population." Lee and Meigs bedded down on untrimmed planks (or puncheons) laid on the floor. They then moved on to the upper rapids near Rock Island, where they lodged in cabins on the deck of an old, abandoned steamboat that had been holed by the rocks and from which the engines had been removed—a perfect example of the kind of shipwreck Lee was trying to prevent.

Although previous plans for dealing with the rapids had centered on the idea of avoiding them by digging a canal that would run parallel to them, an immensely expensive project that involved building locks, Lee's survey of the upper rapids convinced him that contrary to popular opinion a safe channel could easily be cut through both rapids—a good example of his preference for simple commonsense solutions and for facing difficulties head-on that would characterize him as a general later on. He and Meigs then journeyed back downstream to where their own steamboat had run aground, and found to their relief that the river had risen high enough to set it free. At Des Moines, Lee also found a large, colorful gathering of Chippewa Indians in their birch bark canoes and tepees "in full costume . . . with scarlet blankets & Buffalo robes and painted faces," although neither then nor later was he as favorably impressed by the Native Americans as some other visitors to the West were. He would report jovially and without a trace of regret a couple of years later, in a letter to his friend Joseph E. Johnston, that a raiding party of Sioux had "fallen on" these Chippewa, taking "one-hundred and thirty-one scalps," and that their chief was planning "ample revenge." Lee was a man of his times, who regarded the Indian tribes on the frontier without sentimentality, as a picturesque and occasionally dangerous nuisance rather than a tragic or romantic people doomed by encroaching progress, white settlement, and widespread contempt for their culture. Because his image is so firmly fixed in people's minds as an elderly general with a gray beard staring toward the horizon from a horse, it is easily forgotten that Lee was well versed in the most advanced technology of his own day; although he was old-fashioned in any number of ways, he was a firm believer in progress, which did not include letting the Mississippi or the Indians run wild.

He was back in Saint Louis by October 11, and rented the second floor of a warehouse on the levee overlooking the Mississippi as his drafting office. His gift for picking the right man was already in evidence when he hired Henry Kayser, a twenty-six-year-old

German-American who had studied architecture and higher mathematics at Wetzlar and Darmstadt, and who was a gifted surveyor and mapmaker. Kayser and Lee quickly developed a great respect for each other, which ripened into trust and friendship. With Kayser's help, Lee quickly produced maps of the upper and lower rapids on the Mississippi, based on his surveys, that were not only precise but works of art, and laid out detailed plans for cutting a channel through both these navigational hazards, then proceeded to produce a beautifully rendered map of the Mississippi's course past the city of Saint Louis.

Kayser, though a civilian, became the equivalent of Lee's second in command and chief staff officer, and their correspondence when Lee was away from Saint Louis is amazing for Lee's grasp of even the smallest detail, from the price of pilings and stone to the construction of floating engines to remove rocks. Modern biographers sometimes treat Lee as if he were inactive or (as one of them puts it) "lethargic," except when called on to do battle in the Mexican War and the Civil War, but this is to misread Lee's character—he was at all times a "body in motion," totally committed to whatever his current job was, whether it was civil engineer, college president, or general; and while the slowness of promotion and the low pay in the army often depressed him and made him question his choice of profession, he approached everything with the same energy, imagination, capacity for detail, and determination to win with which he approached war.

His solution to the problems that were rapidly transforming Saint Louis into a landlocked city was brilliantly conceived, hugely ambitious in scale, and triumphantly successful, so much so that one Missourian later wrote, "Lee mastered the Mississippi; he sent the current back to its old channel, and the river was saved to St. Louis," and went on to point out, as Mark Twain did in 1870, not just the immensity of the task, but the immense consequences of Lee's success, which made possible the commercial development of whole new areas of the country and the creation of a long list of new cities: "The problem of St. Louis was the problem of the whole Mississippi Valley. The improvement of the harbor of St. Louis and the clearing of the channel was by no means of purely local benefit, for the states of Ohio, Kentucky, Indiana, Illinois, Tennessee, Mississippi, Louisiana, Arkansas, and the territories of Iowa and Wisconsin were vitally concerned in the results. . . . Without them the west would have remained a vast wilderness."

Lee altered the course of American history by his vision and by his single-minded determination to bring it about, making possible the building of great cities where there had once been, at best, a few log cabins or an abandoned Indian encampment. Another observer remarked, in 1886, "The commerce thus made available has supplied the wants of the millions who have since made of the upper Mississippi and of the plains of the Red River of the North the granary of North America. Cities have sprung up which, like Minneapolis and Saint Paul, count their inhabitants by the hundreds of thousands." Had Lee never become a hero of the Mexican War or commanding general of the Confederacy he would have deserved fame—and what is more, gratitude—for the two years he spent opening the Mississippi up at last to the hundreds of steamboats that could journey up and down the full length of the river in safety after he completed his work. His own innate modesty prevented Lee from taking pride in his achievement, or indeed from seeking the credit he deserved, but there is no doubt from his letters that it gave him a greater personal satisfaction than winning battles.

Previous attempts to save Saint Louis as a port had consisted of hiring oxcarts to carry away the sand and silt dug up by gangs of laborers, a method that was both expensive and futile—the Mississippi carried so much sediment that it swiftly created shoals and even large islands wherever there was a rock or a tree stump to impede the flow, then changed its own course to adapt to them. In Saint Louis, the river had created two substantial islands—Duncan Island and Bloody Island (the latter so called because it was a well-known place for duels)—and then shifted its main course to the east, so the deep water now ran close to the Illinois bank, while the Missouri side became shallower and shallower. Lee studied the river's currents, and came up with the simple of idea of harnessing its immense force to cut a channel through the silt and eventually to sweep away the islands altogether.

He proposed to accomplish this by building a dam at the head of Bloody Island, and a dike running down its west side, thus moving the full force of the Mississippi's current to the west bank, where it would carry away the silt and eventually the two islands themselves—a simple and very modern approach to the problem, as opposed to the vast program of building levees, locks, and canals that the Corps of Engineers has been pursuing from the late nineteenth century to today in the continuing struggle to make the Mississippi go where man wants it to.

Lee not only plotted out in every detail the exact way he wanted the dam and dike to be constructed, but accounted for the cost exactly: $158,554 for the entire project (about $4 million in contemporary money), a large sum for a mere first lieutenant to request, and an indication of how much trust General Gratiot and the mayor of Saint Louis had in him. To Lee's irritation (but hardly to his surprise, given his opinion of politicians), Congress never appropriated the full sum he had requested, but even so, with $50,000 from Congress and a further $15,000 from the city of Saint Louis, "he accomplished in two years, the return of the channel to the Missouri shore . . . washed out the sand bars and deepened the harbor so that in low stages of the river there was at least 13½ feet of water over the bar." By July 1838, "Lee had pushed Duncan's Island a considerable distance down stream." This, together with surveying and blasting a safe channel for shipping through the upper and lower rapids, would fully earn Lee the grandiose praise he received from the mayor of Saint Louis: "By the rich gift of his genius and scientific knowledge, Lieut. Lee brought the Father of the Waters under control."

He and Meigs returned east in the winter of 1837: Lee to rejoin his family and to submit his report and lobby for the funds to undertake it; Meigs to be transferred elsewhere, in the best military tradition of moving a man the moment he has learned enough to be useful where he is. On the way home Lee encountered a railroad for the first time in his life—the Baltimore and Ohio had extended its tracks as far as Frederick, Maryland, and from there Lee had his first experience of riding on a train, although "the cars [still] had to be drawn by horses for a part of the distance." Steam engines, of course, Lee was already familiar with, but the railway was something of a novelty at that time in America.

About one thing Lee was determined: when he returned to Saint Louis in the spring he would take Mary with him. Judging from her letters to friends after she had arrived there it cannot have been easy for Lee to persuade her to leave Arlington for what was, from the point of view of a Virginian grandee, a raw, primitive town in the wilderness. Even so, the Lees left their daughter Mary behind with her grandparents, and set off with their two sons Custis and William (always referred to as "Rooney"), accompanied by a slave named Kitty to look after them, on a journey of nearly five weeks, which took them from Washington to Baltimore to Philadelphia: then on to Harrisburg, Pennsylvania, by train; from Harrisburg to Pittsburgh by canal boat; then down the Ohio River, pausing in Cincinnati and Louisville; and finally up the Mississippi from Cairo to Saint Louis. Lee boasted that the boys enjoyed the journey, which was probably true—what could be more exciting for small boys than a trip by railway, canal boat, and steamship?—and that Mary spent much of it taking naps; but since he also mentions the "crowding, squeezing and scrambling," it is possible to guess that Mary was not as thrilled as her children, and that napping may have been her way of escaping from the hustle and bustle of travel and the unwelcome company of strangers. Almost a decade later, on his first visit to America, Charles Dickens, an altogether more intrepid traveler than Mary Lee, complained about the poor table manners, tobacco chewing, and constant hawking and spitting of his fellow travelers, as well as the crowding and lack of privacy on trains and river steamboats and the universal western habit of entering into conversation with total strangers as if they were lifelong friends.

Throughout their married life Lee, like many another husband, made a brave effort in letters to emphasize Mary's enjoyment of their travels, although it is perfectly apparent that given an opportunity she preferred to stay at home in the familiar surroundings and comfort of Arlington. Her feelings about Saint Louis cannot have been improved by the discovery, once they arrived there, that the rooms Lee had supposed were rented for them were not available, still less by the news that their furniture and household goods, which were following them, had been destroyed when the steamboat on which they were being shipped had exploded (not an infrequent occurrence with early steamboats, since the American passion for speed and competition often led to overheating the boilers). They spent a month in uncomfortable temporary lodgings before Lee was able to rent part of a large mansion, originally built by William Clark of the Lewis and Clark expedition, which the Lees shared amiably enough with William Beaumont, an army surgeon, and his family.

Saint Louis was by no means a hardship posting, in the army phrase, like a fort on the frontier, but even Lee, who was indifferent to discomfort, complained about the summer heat, and the fact that the streets were choking dust storms when the wind blew in the summer, were ankle-deep mud when it rained, and turned into frozen ruts in the winter, and Mary wrote home about being "devoured alive with moschetas, for they are as thick as a swarm of bees every evening." Fortunately, she enjoyed the company of the Beaumont family, with whom they shared the house, and cozy evenings with guests when " 'Tasy' Beaumont, the doctor's lovely and amusing sixteen-year-old daughter," played the piano while Lee turned the pages for her; but the sight of fur trappers, Indians, and riverboat gamblers in the streets, however exotic and colorful they may have looked, does not seem to have aroused her interest much. Despite its mansions and social pretentions, Saint Louis was at the edge of what was then the frontier, and still a brash, rough-and-ready place.

Although the Lee family eventually adapted to life in Saint Louis, Mary was ill a good deal of the time, or at any rate suffered from what Lee referred to as either "a bilious attack" or "lassitude." One suspects that frequent pregnancies, homesickness, and the prevailing medical ignorance and blundering of the time were probably part of the problem. If one reads between the lines, she seems to have regarded Missouri as a kind of enforced temporary exile from her home in Virginia, and not to have wanted or felt able to look after the boys on the rare occasions when Kitty was absent. Even at home in Arlington surrounded by servants Mary complained of her "brats squalling around," and with only one servant to look after them, they must have been harder to control. Her indifference to what were then considered the "wifely" duties of housekeeping—at least overseeing from a distance the cooking and the disciplined child rearing—was a constant source of annoyance to her husband, though he mostly disguised his disapproval with rather forced good humor.

For Lee himself, "lassitude" was never a possibility; he was always dauntingly energetic. He was frustrated by inadequate funding to accomplish the job, and by the slowness of the workforce, but all the same, he managed to begin blasting the channels through the Des Moines and the Rock Island Rapids and to start work on the dike that would redirect the main current of the river toward Saint Louis. One observer comments on Lee's diligence: "He went in person with the hands every morning about sunrise, and worked day by day in the hot, broiling sun—the heat being greatly increased by the reflection from the river. He shared in the hard task and common fare and rations furnished to the common laborers—eating at the same table . . . but never on any occasion becoming too familiar with the men. He maintained and preserved under all circumstances his dignity and gentlemanly bearing, winning and commanding the respect of every one [sic] under him." Clearly, the sunburned young first lieutenant prefigured the august commanding general.

In July Lee was at last promoted to the rank of captain, ten years after he had been graduated from West Point—a long wait even by the standards of the day, especially considering his responsibilities. To set against this modest achievement, his work obliged him to remain in Saint Louis until winter, so he and Mary missed the traditional Christmas celebration with her parents at Arlington; this cannot have been easy for Mary, who set great store by such things—this was the first time she had ever been away from home at Christmas. She was also pregnant again, and in midwinter ice on the river prevented travel by steamboat, while the overland route was notoriously difficult even for the most hale and hearty of travelers, let alone one who was "in a delicate condition," in the euphemism of the time. It cannot have been easy for Mary to spend Christmas away from her daughter and her parents, and although she would have four more children,* one doubts that she looked forward to another delivery, given her experience at the hands of the doctors, but she was at any rate determined to have the baby at Arlington rather than in Saint Louis.

Although Freeman speculates that Lee feared "his family was increasing more rapidly than his income," in fact Lee seems to have been pleased at the prospect of another child; however much he might complain about the low pay in the army, a large family was what he

---

*Robert and Mary Lee had seven children: George Washington Custis Lee (known as Custis or "Boo"), born 1832; Mary Custis Lee, born 1835; William Fitzhugh Lee ("Rooney"), born 1837; Anne Carter Lee (Annie), born 1839; Eleanor Agnes Lee, born 1841; Robert E. Lee Jr. (Rob), born 1843; and Mildred Childe Lee ("Precious Life"), born 1846. None of Lee's daughters married. All three of his sons served in the Confederate Army.

wanted most, and few fathers have taken more interest in their children, or enjoyed their company more than Lee did—he loved them with an intensity that his own father, who was often absent and seldom showed much interest in his children, had never shown toward him. It was as if the adult Robert E. Lee wanted to make up for what he had not received as a child from Harry Lee by becoming a perfect father himself, a role in which he succeeded remarkably, even when he was swept up by history and became a major figure in great events.

As it turned out, the Lee family would not leave Saint Louis until the spring of 1839, by which time Mary was in her eighth month. They returned home in what may be close to record time for the day: by steamship to Wheeling, Virginia; by private stage to Frederick, Maryland; then by train to Washington—a total of eleven days, the last few of which even Douglas Southall Freeman, who from time to time betrays a certain impatience with Mary Lee's problems, describes as "hard travel."

Lee stayed at Arlington for only two weeks before setting out to return to Saint Louis, so he was not present for Anne Carter Lee's birth on June 18, and did not receive the news of it until around July 1, by which time he was back in Saint Louis. His haste to return was caused in part by the unavoidable fact that his work on the Mississippi could be carried out only in the summer months when the water was low, and in part by the fact that his mentor General Gratiot had been dismissed from command of the Corps of Engineers in December 1838 after a long feud about his accounts, which was finally decided against him by the president. To put the matter in modern terms, it was a question of whether or not Gratiot had been justified in putting certain sums on his expense account and being reimbursed for them; in hindsight, this seems to have been a matter of politics rather than arising from any proof of dishonesty on Gratiot's part, but Lee took the outcome badly, and feared correctly that Gratiot's successor would be less interested in saving Saint Louis as a port—Saint Louis was, after all, Gratiot's hometown. It may be that Gratiot's problem was merely that he did not share Lee's almost obsessive determination to account for everything down to the last penny. Typically, Lee's correspondence with Henry Kayser is incredibly detailed about money: "I paid Mr. Ricket's account for taking care of and caulking the Pearl, which is the amount of check No. 24, $48.22 . . . this, according to my mem. would leave in said Bank to my credit $841.77 in stead of $840.57 as you state" is one example of Lee's lifelong effort to keep perfect control over his finances, however low his pay, and still more so over the public money entrusted to him.

He plunged into Gratiot's defense with a will, and gathered the general's accounts and papers while he was in Washington; but even he was unable to unravel the truth from them, and eventually concluded that Gratiot had been the victim of political intrigue and that the irregularities of which the general was accused had been merely a pretext for removing him. In any event, one consequence of Gratiot's fall was to increase (if that was possible) Lee's exactitude about money and the amount of time he spent balancing his accounts.

The improvements Lee had made by beginning work on the dikes at Bloody Island were already starting to deepen the channel to Saint Louis and wash away some of the sand around Duncan Island just as he had predicted—indeed the fact that Lee was on the right track was strikingly demonstrated when irate citizens of Illinois opened fire with cannons at some of his work crews, fearing that his plans would reduce the depth of the channel on their side of the Mississippi and cut them off from a potentially "lucrative" trade; perhaps this is another example of the rising irritability and turn toward violence of the states against one another that would intensify over the next twenty years. Fortunately, common sense prevailed, and a landowner on the Illinois side of the river—where there were hopes of building a port city to rival or even eclipse Saint

Louis—turned to more peaceful means, and sought for and secured an injunction from the judge of the Second Illinois Circuit to halt the work on Bloody Island. Lee was dismayed—the case would not come before the regular session of the court until February 1840, and in the meantime he could make no further progress at Saint Louis. Instead, he turned his attention to the two rapids upstream, where his workforce had already begun removing huge boulders and slabs of limestone, each weighing over a ton, to start clearing a navigable channel in both the north and the south rapids—a remarkable feat of civil engineering. Still, one detects a growing sense of disappointment in Lee's letters, as if the dismissal of General Gratiot and the injunction had convinced him that his work on the Mississippi as he had planned it would go unfinished, or at least not be completed by him. If so, he was correct.

After an extended journey to suggest improvements that could be made on the Ohio River, and a trip down the Mississippi to Saint Louis to report on the number of snags still remaining, Lee returned home for the winter of 1839, partly on extended leave, partly to serve on "temporary duty" in the office of the new chief engineer while Congress lackadaisically debated whether or not to budget more money for the improvements on the Mississippi River, and then—as was (and remains) so often the case—adjourned without doing anything, effectively halting any further Federal appropriations for the work. In the summer of 1840 Lee returned to Saint Louis, again somewhat reluctantly, mostly to settle his accounts and sell off at public auction the boats and equipment he had acquired; then he returned to Washington in October to await the birth of his fifth child, Eleanor Agnes Lee.

In its frugal way, the Corps of Engineers did not cut him loose from the Mississippi altogether—despite other duties, Lee would continue for years to be responsible for giving advice to the authorities in Missouri who would continue the work he had begun, but his own role in taming the great river was over.

Only three months before Lee's death in 1870 there took place one of the most famous sporting events in American history, one that his work on the river from 1837 to 1840 had made possible—the "Great Steamboat Race," in which two riverboat leviathans competed to steam up the Mississippi from New Orleans to Saint Louis.

"This race found two huge 300 foot plus steamboats racing all out up the Mississippi River . . . at speeds up to 23 mph. . . . The race was our country's first great media event as huge sums of money were wagered, large crowds traveled considerable distances to line the banks of the river, and the new telegraph broadcast the progress of the race to a national audience."* The race was won by an Indiana-made boat that had cost over $200,000 to build in 1866, a fortune for the day. It could carry over 5,000 bales of cotton weighing 1,250 tons, and it had 61 luxury "staterooms" paneled with richly carved, polished rosewood, and a dining salon that seated 240 people under huge, dazzling chandeliers and stained-glass skylights. It was a product of the dawning Gilded Age, with all the lavish appointments and cuisine of a great ocean liner, tall twin stacks belching sparks and smoke as it steamed at full speed day and night—with no risk now of striking a rock, a snag, a sandbar, or a shoal—to reach Saint Louis on July 4, 1870, and beat the *Natchez*: 1,154 miles in three days, eighteen hours, and fourteen minutes, a record that stood unbeaten until 1929. Its name, very fittingly, commemorated to this day in headlines, paintings, photographs, folklore, literature, and song,[†] was the *Robert E. Lee*.

Of course all that—the epic steamboat race between the *Robert E. Lee* and the *Natchez*, the millions of

---

* Quote from Gary R. Lucy, Gary R. Lucy Gallery.

[†] "Waiting for the *Robert E. Lee*" was originally sung in blackface. The most famous recorded versions were those sung by Al Jolson (1912) and later by Mickey Rooney and Judy Garland (1935): "Watch them shufflin' along . . . Hear that music and song! It's simply great, mate, waitin' on the levee, waitin' for the *Robert E. Lee*."

people gathered to watch it, the awe and respect in which his name was held not only in the South but even in the North—was far ahead of him in 1840 when he returned to Washington as a mere captain. In the absence of his old friend General Gratiot, Lee's success in Missouri did not win him much in the way of a new assignment; he was sent off to inspect coastal forts in the Carolinas and draw up plans for badly needed repairs. Not every engineer was as careful a builder as Lee had already proved himself to be at Fort Monroe—it is some measure of the forced economies and makeshift construction of the times that although most of these forts were less than ten years old they had all been badly damaged by the sea and were already in need of major work. It may be true, as Douglas Southall Freeman suggests, that Lee's tour of the Carolinas would prove useful to him twenty years later when he placed Fort Fisher on "a narrow spit" at the mouth of Cape Fear River to safeguard the Confederacy's last unblockaded port, but if so this prescience was the only benefit of his journey. In each case he made practical, economical suggestions for improvements, and detailed drawings to accompany them. Despite his constant doubts about the value of his work, and about his own choice of profession, it is evident that Lee was now a trusted engineer. He returned home for Christmas, and after a protracted leave he was appointed to repair and update the fortresses that guarded New York City, a much larger and more responsible task, though he still remained in charge of the work at Saint Louis and in the Carolinas as well—the Corps of Engineers was undoubtedly getting its money's worth out of Captain Lee.

Today, of course, it is hard to understand the importance of the forts in New York Harbor, which survive mostly as place-names, but in the days when, in anybody's mind, the only potential enemy of the United States was still assumed to be Great Britain, forts Hamilton and Lafayette at the Narrows and the two artillery batteries on Staten Island were of national importance, the major defenses of New York City and its harbor against a raid or landing by the Royal Navy. After all, there were still men alive who could remember the last time, in 1776, when a British fleet lay anchored in New York Harbor, and the Union Jack had flown over the city until 1783. Of course we know in hindsight that by 1841 the defense of New York Harbor against the British was a waste of time and money, but it was a measure of Lee's growing reputation that he was chosen to oversee what was then considered a vital element of national security.

A quick inspection was enough to demonstrate that this was going to be a long job—long enough to make Lee determined to have his family around him, though he could hardly have imagined it would take up nearly five years of his life. Married officers' quarters were available just outside Fort Hamilton, placed in what was then a quiet, leafy Brooklyn neighborhood, but they had been allowed to deteriorate badly, like the fort itself. Apparently everybody else at Fort Hamilton assumed that Mary Lee would hurry north and make quick work of putting things right, but Lee knew his wife better than that, and dealt with the matter in the usual jocular but sharply critical style of so many of his letters to Mary. He took care to praise the countryside around the fort and the healthful effect of the "Sea breezes," which he described, a little optimistically so far as the winter was concerned, as "very cool," but went on to say, of their quarters, "A nice Yankee wife would soon have it in fine order." Clearly he did not expect his Virginian wife to whitewash the walls or polish the floors, although his fellow officers were surprised that he was looking for servants to do work they expected a wife to perform. "I receive poor encouragement about servants & everybody [here] seems to attend to their own matters," he wrote, meaning that wives did their own cooking and housekeeping.

"They seem to be surprised at my inquiring for *help* & have a wife too & appear to have some misgivings as to whether you possess all your faculties." Interestingly, Mary did not bring any of the servants from Arlington north with her; perhaps this is a reflection of the difficulty of preventing slaves from running away once they were in a northern state. In any event, Lee himself shopped for most of their needs in the way of furniture and household goods, though the prices of such items in New York City dismayed him, and he managed to find a cook and a maid for Mary.

In Mary's defense, she had already given birth to five children between 1832 and 1841 (and would go on to have two more), despite poor health and the onset of severe arthritis, and had spent most of her life being looked after by attentive slaves and spoiled by her indulgent parents. Mary was much tougher and shrewder than she is given credit for being, as she would demonstrate during and after the Civil War, but Lee must have known perfectly well that housework and cooking were not among her skills. He pretended to be tolerant of and amused by her failings in this area, but from time to time there is a note of criticism, or perhaps exasperation, that cannot have escaped her notice.

In any event, with whatever difficulties, they settled into life in Brooklyn, which was then a place of rolling

fields and farms, and Lee got on with the task of bringing New York City's defenses up-to-date. Lee was content, as he always was, to have his children around him,
and his work, while time-consuming, soon settled into a
routine—he was basically, in modern terms, the manager
of several large and rather widely separated construction sites. As with a famous later West Pointer, Dwight
D. Eisenhower, Lee's loftiest ambition might have been
to retire from the army having reached the rank of colonel, but even so modest a goal must have seemed out of
reach to him in the summer of 1841. "He seemed to be
weighted down by the very stones of the fort," Freeman
remarks, and Lee cannot have been cheered up by the
fact that his first round of repairs on Fort Hamilton
made it possible to re-garrison the fort, so that he had
to give up the quarters he had gone to such trouble to
refurbish. He sought the chief engineer's permission to
rent a house for his family, at $300 a year (a house in
the same area of Brooklyn, similar in size to the one
Lee describes, was for rent as of this writing at $2,800
a month). As usual, Lee had to scale down his plans for
forts Hamilton and Lafayette because Congress failed to
appropriate enough money, but by the autumn of 1842
he had completed the most essential work on the forts,
and since it was impossible to undertake further repairs
on the sea walls in the Narrows during the winter

months, he returned with his family to Arlington. Mary and the children accompanied him back to New York in the spring, but she soon went home again, pregnant with their sixth child, Robert Edward Lee Jr., while Lee got on with overseeing what must have seemed to him like increasingly routine work: pointing masonry, painting, laying down new drainpipes. Even his warmest admirer, Freeman, calls it "drab labor for a man of action," though in fact Lee had not as yet even been given an opportunity to become a man of action. It was in some ways the low point of Lee's career, comparable to that of another West Pointer and captain whose career reached a low ebb some years later, in 1854, and who could see no future for himself in the army: Ulysses S. Grant. Unlike Grant, of course, Lee was not a drinker; nor had he made a muddle of his accounts; nor did he resign his commission in despair as Grant did—but one recognizes the same sense of midlife futility and failure at a career that seemed to be leading nowhere. Lee, after all, was thirty-five years old, with six children to support, and had been in the army since 1825 (if you include his four years as a West Point cadet) without much to show for it, and with not much likelihood of better things to come.

Perhaps the only bright spot on Lee's professional horizon was that he was named a member of the board of examiners at West Point for 1844, and during the two weeks of the cadets' final examinations he spent a good deal of time with Major General Winfield Scott, the commanding general of the U.S. Army, who formed a good opinion of Captain Lee.

Scott was fifty-eight years old in 1844: an immense, overbearing, towering figure; formidable in appearance; already so huge in girth that he could hardly mount a horse; an authentic hero of the War of 1812; and a national presence who served in uniform under every president from Jefferson to Lincoln. Scott's solemn dignity, his self-importance, his elaborate uniforms bedecked with every possible inch of gold lace and embroidery, his hats with flowing white plumes, his gift for what we would now call self-promotion, his impatience with minds slower than his own, his vanity, and his satisfaction in his role as the nation's longest-surviving and apparently permanent military leader had all contributed to his unaffectionate nickname, "Old Fuss and Feathers," but also managed to partly veil a keen intelligence, strategic skill, ruthless ambition, political shrewdness when it came to the army's interests and his own, and an eye for talent. A Virginian with a voracious appetite for social life and a ponderous, elephantine charm, Scott was in every possible way unlike young Captain Lee, but recognized in him at once a level of competence far above the ordinary. Lee knew better than to flatter the commanding general, who absorbed flattery like a sponge but tended to despise the flatterer; he impressed Scott instead with his intelligence, his sound judgment about men, his physical presence and soldierly bearing—here was a man who looked every inch a soldier—as well as his discreet Virginian charm. That Scott was a prodigious snob is only too clear, but the downturned mouth, the thrusting jaw, and the frowning eagle eyes were easily thawed by a member of the Lee and Carter families whose father had served with honor under Washington and whose father-in-law was the master of Arlington and Washington's adopted son. Lee may not have realized—indeed could hardly have imagined—how far his acquaintanceship with Scott would carry him, once he returned from West Point to his humdrum job of superintending New York City's fortifications against the British, unaware that within two years he would be a national hero himself.

Between 1844 and 1846 Lee alternated between service as a kind of glorified clerk and congressional liaison at the right hand of the chief engineer in Washington, and work on the forts in New York City, with the additional honor of being "appointed as a member of the board of engineers for the Atlantic coast defenses," which added to his responsibilities without any increase to his pay or rank. In Washington he was deluged with paperwork, and expressed his growing "horror at the sight of pen, ink and paper." In New York he oversaw the digging of ditches and the mounting of the few guns that could be spared. It was neither interesting nor demanding work, though he amused himself by riding one of his two horses from Fort Hamilton into New York City on fair days to attend the meetings of the board of engineers, and in the winter by commuting back and forth on the large, crowded horse-drawn sleighs which served as buses, and on which his attention was drawn by the pretty girls returning from school, "held on each others laps with their bags of books and smiling faces." He speculated to his old friend Mackay about whether one of them would sit on his lap if he offered her the opportunity, but chivalrously decided to give up his seat instead. Lee's innocent admiration for a pretty young face was not diminished by his role as a paterfamilias.

The winter of 1845–1846 was marked by a small domestic tragedy that shook Lee badly. Just as Mary Lee was preparing to leave for Arlington, her second son, Rooney, already an "adventuresome young man" at the age of eight, climbed into the hayloft where he had been forbidden to go and cut off "the tips of two of his fingers" while playing with a chopping knife. In a piece of surgery that was advanced for the day, the two severed digits were sewn back on. Aside from the danger of infection in the days before antiseptics were in use, for some days it was doubtful whether they would "reknit," but remarkably they did. Freeman attributes to Lee a horror of deformity, which may have increased his anxiety, and that may be so, but his daughter Anne was born with a large birthmark on her face and Lee seems to have taken it in his stride; he even wrote touchingly about it to Mary: "We must endeavor to assist her to veil if not eradicate it by the purity of and brightness of her mind."

In any event, Lee was the most admirable and concerned of parents, sitting up every night with Rooney to make sure the boy didn't turn over in his sleep and disturb the dressing or pull out the "ligatures." "He may probably lose his fingers and be maimed for life. . . . You cannot conceive what I suffer at the thought," Lee wrote, but that seems like a perfectly natural fear for any father in the circumstances. It is hardly surprising that Rooney was the subject of so many letters of advice and concern from Lee to his wife over the years about how to discipline such a wild and unbroken colt without destroying his spirit. He would describe Rooney as a boy who required a "tight rein," but in fact Rooney and his brothers seem to have been no more than normally troublesome.

When Rooney was well enough to travel, Mary took the family home to Arlington, leaving Lee in New York to the company of the family terrier and her puppy. Early in 1846 Mary gave birth to their last child, Mildred Childe, always referred to by Lee as Milly or "Precious Life," while Lee experienced, as he always did, the agony of being separated from his family, which spurred him to write to Mary, whose slipshod ways he dreaded, endless letters of advice on how to bring up their children, to which she seems to have paid very little attention. He was consumed by small details of construction and repair, a mistake he had made in accounting for his pay, elaborate plans to further improve and extend the fortifications of New York City, and the old worries that his salary would not allow him to provide for his children and that he had chosen the wrong career.

Events far away in Mexico were about to about to render all these concerns nugatory.

Chapter 4
The Perfect Warrior—
Mexico, 1846–1848

War between Mexico and the United States had been simmering since the 1820s, partly as a result of political chaos in Mexico, partly as a consequence of the expanding American settlement in Texas, and partly because the largely unpopulated Mexican territory in North America, stretching from the Louisiana Purchase to California, was an open invitation to a rapidly growing and increasingly self-confident America. Americans looked westward and saw a vast and largely unmapped paradise. The phrase "manifest destiny" was not yet then in common usage, but the idea that America should stretch from the Atlantic to the Pacific Ocean was a powerful if not necessarily a popular one. It was reinforced by the fear that as a consequence of Mexico's weakness Great Britain or Russia might seize

California, and by the belief that America was and must be an exception to monarchical rule and despotism, and therefore by definition could not share the continent with other powers.

Not everybody believed it was God's design for Americans to populate and control the continent. Americans as different as John Quincy Adams and Ulysses S. Grant were dubious about the morality of seizing so much territory from a much weaker Mexico. Even decades after the war between America and Mexico had been fought and won, Grant wrote, "Generally, the officers of the [U.S.] army were indifferent whether the annexation was consummated or not. . . . For myself, I was bitterly opposed to the measure, and to this day regard the war, which resulted, as one of the most unjust ever waged by a stronger against a weaker nation." Many argued that America's claim to worldwide moral authority might be diluted by such an unfair war, and of course some foresaw correctly that the question of whether slavery could be expanded into the new territories won from Mexico by conquest might upset the delicate political balance between slave and free states, and lead to civil war. Here too, Grant expressed it best, though with the wisdom of hindsight: "The Southern rebellion was largely the outgrowth of the Mexican war. Nations, like individuals, are punished for their transgressions. We got our punishment in the most sanguinary and expensive war of modern times." Robert E. Lee himself admitted that he would like to have been "better satisfied with the justice of our cause," an interesting and typical understatement of his feelings.

The most immediate cause of the conflict was the presence of Americans in Tejas, which began in 1810, when Moses Austin was granted "a large tract of land" by the Mexican government—a decision that the Mexicans quickly came to regret, as increasing numbers of Americans crossed the Arkansas River and established "colonies" in the potentially rich farmland of East Texas, where they soon outnumbered native Mexicans. The "Texans," as the Americans quickly became known, were intransigent and insatiable guests, and successive Mexican governments sought in vain to tax them, to limit their number, and to prohibit slavery. If the Mexicans had hoped that the Texans would provide a buffer between themselves and marauding bands of ferocious Comanche Indians in the north of Mexico, they were disappointed. The Texans put down roots, farmed, and brought in slaves. The mercurial General Antonio López de Santa Anna, acclaimed by his supporters as "the Napoleon of the West," rose to power through the violent anarchy of Mexican politics and alternated between threatening the Texans and offering to sell them more land. The result was a war in which a Texan outpost was besieged and its defenders were massacred at the Alamo; this was followed by the Texans' subsequent revenge at the Battle of San Jacinto, which forced Mexico to recognize Texan independence in 1836. Mexicans' acceptance of the Lone Star Republic was grudging, and it soon became apparent that Mexico would regard the annexation of Texas by the United States as a casus belli; furthermore, Mexicans believed the southern border of Texas lay on the Nueces River, rather than 130 miles farther south on the Rio Grande. In 1845, when the lobbying of Texas to join the Union finally succeeded, it alarmed both the Mexicans and American northerners who opposed the expansion of slavery, and ensured that even the slightest provocation would start a war.

Provocation was not long in coming. Though Mexico had broken off diplomatic relations with the United States, President James Polk sent John Slidell as minister plenipotentiary to Mexico City to negotiate the purchase of California and New Mexico from the beleaguered Mexican government. In one year "the [Mexican] presidency changed four times, the ministry of war six times and the finance ministry sixteen times," but if there was one subject on which all Mexicans were united it was their claim to Texas. Outraged that Slidell had not come prepared to discuss compensation for the loss of their territory, they broke off discussions, and he returned to Washington angry and empty-handed. Perhaps anticipating the Mexican reaction, President Polk had ordered Brigadier General Zachary Taylor, a Virginian and a renowned Indian fighter, to occupy the land between the Nueces River and the Rio Grande. Soon afterward a large force of Mexican cavalry attacked an American patrol, killing sixteen of the Americans in what became known as the "Thornton affair" after the patrol's commander. This enabled Polk to inform Congress that "American blood has been shed upon American soil," and to seek a declaration of war, which was passed despite Whig reluctance and widespread skepticism in the North.

General Taylor, who was nicknamed "Old Rough and Ready"—in deliberate contrast to General Winfield Scott's nickname, "Old Fuss and Feathers"—for his slouching indifference to military pomp and his own unprepossessing uniform, moved quickly to defeat the Mexicans twice, at Palo Alto and the next day at Resaca de la Palma. These victories were achieved in part by vastly superior American weapons, which included quickly moved "horse artillery," Colt's famous "revolving pistol," and more modern muskets than the antiquated mid-eighteenth-century weapons of the Mexicans. Nevertheless, an advance south toward Mexico City would involve a march of nearly 500 miles across harsh, difficult terrain, with sparse water, primitive roads, and almost no forage for horses—a formidable undertaking. In addition, the return to power of Santa Anna increased the likelihood that the Mexicans would fight at every opportunity in a rocky, mountainous landscape that favored the defense.

During this time, Lee remained in New York City looking after its fortifications, listening wistfully to what he described as "the Sharpening of Swords, [and] the grinding of bayonets."* In Freeman's words, "If he were left at Fort Hamilton he might as well reconcile himself to the certainty that he would grow old, unregarded in a corps that would assuredly give preference to the engineers who distinguished themselves in war. They would have fame; he would have slippers and old age on the porch at Arlington." This prospect is exactly what Lee feared. The days when he could call on his former mentor and friend General Gratiot for help were long gone, and there was nobody to whom

---

*In those days, it was usual to keep the edge of swords and bayonets dull in peacetime to reduce the possibility of accidents during drill and training. The armorer sharpened them for wartime use, then blunted the edge on weapons again for safety once a unit returned home.

he could appeal for a combat posting; for three months he waited, saying good-bye to officers no more capable than himself who had received orders to proceed to Mexico. At last, on August 19, 1846, Lee received his own orders to proceed at once to San Antonio de Bexar in Texas (as San Antonio was then still known), and report to Brigadier General John E. Wool, whose name would eventually be given to Fort Calhoun (formerly the Rip-Raps), the man-made island that Lee had spent so much time and effort building in Hampton Roads. Lee wrote his will, collected his kit, and sailed for New Orleans on the first available steamer, not even pausing long enough to say good-bye to his family, and he was in San Antonio by September 21, just over a month after his departure from Fort Hamilton—fast traveling for the day. Much of it was hard traveling too. He wrote to Mary the moment he arrived in San Antonio: "I reached here last night, my dear Mary after a journey of six days from Port Sarassa. The first day in consequence of the intolerable heat through the prairie . . . we★ could make but 12 miles where we encamped by a diminutive inlet that furnished some water enough for our horses & selves of a hot and infe-rior quality. I have got such a taste of prairie flies that

---

★The "we" refers to the presence of James Connally, Lee's orderly (see page 185).

I determined to travel by night as long as I was in this region and started the next morn[ing] before 4 a.m."

Lee was approaching forty, still a captain, and after twenty-one years of service in the U.S. Army he had yet to hear a shot fired in anger. He was gratified to be within reach of real service at last, though his initial task was merely to round up the picks and shovels his labor force would need—not an easy task in an impoverished country where even the most basic tools were hard to come by. San Antonio was a quaint little town with a population of around 2,000, most of them Mexican, engulfed by the 3,400 American soldiers who were now encamped there. Lee visited the Alamo, still showing the damage from the twenty-day siege, and spent his brief moments off duty "bathing" in the "clear & rapid" water of the San Antonio River, to which he went either very early or late so as not to be "interrupted by the senoras or senoritas." He admired the landscape, but found the Mexicans "an amiable but weak people . . . primitive in their habits and tastes."

The sheer size of Mexico, coupled with the small number of American troops available, made a quick war unlikely. The distances involved alone were daunting. Brigadier General Stephen Kearny, for example, set off from Fort Leavenworth, just west of Missouri; marched all the way to Santa Fe; and from there continued on to California, over 1,500 miles. Meanwhile a cavalry detachment he sent south from New Mexico under Colonel Alexander Doniphan to Saltillo, in Mexico, made "one of the most remarkable marches in military history," covering a total of 3,500 miles, most of it over rough desert country and despite several Apache and Comanche attacks on his column.

The Mexicans might have been expected to lose heart at the fact that a mere handful of American troops had seized and annexed both New Mexico and California without serious difficulty, but that would have underrated the strength of Mexican outrage about the loss of Texas, and the remarkable determination of Santa Anna, who understood the value in war of trading space for time. The farther American forces marched into the barren vastness of Mexico, the more thinly stretched and vulnerable their supply lines would inevitably become, hampered as they already were by primitive or nonexistent roads, and the more possible it might be to deal them a resounding defeat before they reached Mexico City.

General Taylor had at most 15,000 men at his command, the majority of them southern state militiamen or volunteers, stiffened by a small number of regular units, as well as a number of regular officers and specialists like Lee. Lee's immediate task was to prepare a road so that General Wool could cross the Rio Grande and advance on the "important trading center" of Chihuahua, more than 400 miles west of San Antonio as the crow flies, though Wool was obliged by the absence of any practical direct route through the rugged highlands before him to make a long loop to the south to reach it, nearly doubling the distance he would have to cover.

Lee rode out of San Antonio with Wool's column on September 28, 1846; this was his first opportunity for active service. He was accompanied by his "faithful" orderly James Connally, an Irish-American civilian who had served him in New York. Connally took care of Lee and also looked after the horses Lee had bought on his way out—Lee's favorites were Grace Darling, "a chestnut [mare] of fine size and of great power," which he had purchased in New Orleans; and Creole, "a golden-dun," which today we would call a palomino, which he bought in Texas. Grace Darling and Creole would both perform miracles for him. Throughout his adult life Lee was an excellent judge of horseflesh, and had a keen eye for a bargain too when it came to buying horses for himself and his family. The only one he would ever splurge on was Traveller, perhaps the most beloved horse in American history, who is buried only a few yards from Lee's own grave, under an elaborately engraved stone marker.*

---

*In literature Traveller is not only the subject of a poem by Stephen Vincent Benét but the narrator of *Traveller*, a novel by Richard Adams, the author of *Watership Down*.

Connally must have been a good horseman himself, since he swam Lee's horses to the beach off the ship, there being no barge to take them ashore; but at first Lee found him something less than an ideal traveling companion, complaining that Connally "starves badly & hunger [they were living on hard crackers and warm water at the time] makes him quite savage." Connally's first experience of campaigning in Texas apparently made the New Yorker feel sick and "very low spirited," hardly surprisingly, given the blazing heat, the enveloping dust, the fierce fleas and flies, and the occasional downpour of rain that created instant mud. Because of the amount of "lime in the soil," as Lee, always a precise observer of geographical details, points out, the mud "hardens in like mortar" in the sun, and can be washed off only with considerable difficulty—another unwelcome task for Connally.

General Wool's troops reached the Rio Grande in eleven days, an advance of about eleven miles a day, which was described at the time as "rapid," though Lee would not consider it to be so fifteen years later, during the Civil War. It was made possible only by the engineers' effort to level a road of sorts for the artillery and to bridge whatever small streams were in the column's path. Once at the Rio Grande the column came to a halt and made camp to wait while pontoons were brought up from San Antonio by wagon train. No doubt Lee learned a good deal from this first experience at war— an active reconnaissance by cavalry in advance of the column would have found that the river was running too high and fast to be crossed at most of the fords, and might have led to bringing up the pontoons nearer the head of the column, rather than at the very rear of it. In the rough, semiarid country between San Antonio and the Rio Grande Robert E. Lee got his first practical lesson in the difference between what appears on a map and what the country ahead actually looks like, as well as a lesson in the importance of getting an army's order of march right for whatever problems lay ahead.

Lee led "a party of pioneers" selected unwillingly from "two regiments of Illinois volunteers," who had no great desire to exchange a rifle for a spade, pick, crowbar, or shovel, and eight wagons loaded with material and tools—part of a train of nearly 200 wagons that carried enough food and ammunition for nine months, and for which Lee's pioneers had to smooth out the rocky, makeshift road as they advanced. Even Lee, usually brimming with optimism, complained in his letters that he had too little time and not enough manpower and equipment.

Once the lumbering wagons bearing the pontoons finally caught up with the troops, the river was quickly bridged without opposition, and at General Wool's orders Lee built "field works" at either end of the bridge, digging in artillery to protect it, something at which he soon became an acknowledged expert. This was cautious, but unnecessary: the only enemy to appear once the column of 2,000 men had crossed the Rio Grande was a Mexican officer "under a flag of truce," bearing the news that General Taylor had defeated a Mexican force at Monterey, just under 200 miles away to the southeast, and had accepted "an eight-week armistice in return for [its] surrender," with an armistice line between the opposing armies that could not be crossed during this time. Wool did not consider that the armistice line as explained to him by the Mexican officer prevented him from advancing farther, and marched south to the town of Monclova without meeting any resistance. There he set up his camp and waited three weeks for the armistice to expire. Lee had gained Wool's complete confidence by the calm, efficient way he sounded fords, cut down steep banks, and built bridges. Lee himself was enjoying the landscape, with "spectacular" mountains visible on the horizon (these were the mountains that prevented Wool from making a direct advance on Chihuahua)—"high country," as Lee called it, where "the nights are very cold, but the sun at midday scorching hot." Fortunately, Jim Connally seems to have cheered up, and Lee reports him to be "quite well & sends his remembrances to everybody," while the horses, to Lee's relief, "have improved on the journey." The nights were not only cold but clamorous with a "concert of howling" by "an astonishing number of wolves" which surrounded the camp until dawn.

To Wool's dismay his men were greeted with "hospitality rather than hostility." They had marched hard over dry, dusty country for more than two weeks to reach Monclova, then a small, pleasant old town surrounded by verdant hills, where unfamiliar but potent liquor was easily purchased and where a certain number of the local señoritas were disposed to be friendly to the gringo soldiers. Inevitably the discipline of the militiamen and volunteers, never all that firm to begin with, quickly deteriorated. The troops had eagerly expected a glorious battle and a quick victory, instead of which they found themselves encamped on the outskirts of a town full of temptations. For the moment, the enemy was not the Mexicans, but boredom and bickering between the militiamen and the regulars. Wool attempted to keep his men busy with drill and building projects, but they did not respond well to either, and Wool sensibly decided that if he could not provide them with action, the sooner he got them moving again, the better.

Lee, who had been invited to take his meals with General Wool, feared that "Genl. T[aylor] had been betrayed into a mistake in granting" the Mexicans an armistice, which no doubt reflects General Wool's opinion as well. Lee observed that the mountains to their west were "high, bold & barren . . . bidding defiance to the ascent of man and beast," which pretty much defined Wool's problem with reaching his objective. He could not get over the mountains, and it would take forever to move his army around them. In the meantime, he was stuck at Monclova, while Santa Anna was presumably using the time to "collect his strength" at San Luis Potosí, and Wool's men were consuming their provisions. There was almost no meat available around Monclova, and only a small amount of corn, which the men had to gather for themselves and grind into flour with hand mills. Lee liked the bread this produced, but noted that there was not much of it. "The delay," Lee wrote to Mary, "has been rather irksome to me [rather] than refreshing, for I am one of those silly persons [who] when I have something to do I can't rest satisfied till it has been accomplished and it had appeared to me that we have been losing time important to us & granting [a] season of preparation to the Mexicans." This can hardly have come as news to Mary Lee, who was more familiar than anyone else with Lee's impatience to get on with a job, whatever it might be, and his preference for swift movement, which would come to define his leadership in the Civil War, when he tried at all costs to keep his army moving and to retain the initiative rather than waiting to see what the enemy would do. Any kind of delay was anathema to him.

General Wool and Captain Lee were not the only people who were dismayed by the armistice. Though America rejoiced at Zachary Taylor's victory at Monterey, which immediately made him a presidential contender, President Polk fumed at the armistice and complained that Taylor had exceeded his authority, as well as committing a political and military blunder. Of course nobody in Washington could appreciate how shaken Taylor's army, which consisted largely of volunteers, had been by the unexpected ferocity of the fighting at Monterey, but it certainly seems as if Taylor himself was bluffed by the Mexicans, who were in fact defeated and badly disorganized. The attack on Mexico had been allowed to degenerate into that most fatal and un-Napoleonic of military mistakes: dispersing one's forces rather than concentrating them. Insofar as any single person was responsible for this flawed strategy, Polk was as much to blame as anyone—notoriously stiff and a man for whom political maneuvering was both his lifeblood and his religion, Polk distrusted not only the politically ambitious, folksy Taylor but *all* his generals, and was himself that most dreaded of wartime political figures, an "armchair general" in the White House.

Attacking Mexico from the north was to take the longest and hardest route to Mexico City; and dividing Taylor's forces into two columns—the major one attacking toward Monterey and Saltillo under Taylor while Wool's wandered off in the opposite direction toward Chihuahua for no discernible reason except the belief that it might be a major trading center—made no strategic sense at all. It may be too that Taylor's early victories and low losses at Palo Alto and Resaca de la Palma gave him and his army a false estimate of just how hard the Mexicans could fight under a leader like Santa Anna. Most of the planning for the war had been done under the assumption that after a few battles south of the Rio Grande the Mexicans would sue for peace and settle for a sensible amount of compensation for California and New Mexico. Indeed that was why the administration had ordered the U.S. Navy to allow Santa Anna through the naval blockade to return to Mexico from Cuba, where he had been spending one of his frequent periods of political banishment and exile. This was a huge mistake. Despite his unapologetic greed Santa Anna was at the same time personally courageous, hugely ambitious, a born leader, and an emotional patriot who not only was acclaimed as, but *thought* of himself as, the Napoleon of the West. It was second nature to Santa Anna to first encourage, then betray the hope of President Polk and Polk's advisers that he could be bought cheap. He was as convinced of his own glorious destiny in the endless fight against the hated *yanquis* as Polk was of his subtlety as a strategist. Both were wrong.

Lee remained "at a loss to account for the reasons that induced Genl Taylor to grant a cessation of hostilities." He suspected correctly that Santa Anna would use the time to recruit new forces rather than negotiate a peace, and was pleased when General Wool decided to continue his march south on November 18, a day before the armistice expired, since "he was heartily tired of our present camp," and "Monclova contained nothing of interest" to him. He noted that the residents of Monclova were no longer as friendly as they had been, either—not surprisingly after their three weeks of dealing with an enemy army camped outside their city.

That night a messenger arrived from General Taylor informing Wool that the president had terminated the armistice and that the expedition to Chihuahua was to be abandoned, news which Lee greeted with relief, since he had never been convinced that "any good would come from it except conquering distance." Taylor had "pushed forward" Brigadier General William J. Worth with 3,000 men to take Saltillo, southeast of Monterey, and intended to follow him with the bulk of the army. Worth was a fiery hero of the War of 1812 and had been commandant of cadets when Lee was at West Point; "a splendid horseman, he was physically the ideal soldier," and his fame, though now eclipsed, was such that several places were named after him: Fort Worth and Lake Worth in Texas; Lake Worth in Florida; Worth, Illinois; and Worth County, Georgia.*

Still, General Wool did not move until November 24. His orders were to advance south to Parras, where he would be in a position to support General Worth in Saltillo, a march of over 160 miles, and to abandon his present line of communication for one to Camargo— which was like plunging into the unknown without a lifeline. When Wool's army reached its new destination it would be almost 400 miles deep in enemy territory, marching *toward* the nearest place where it could be resupplied. This was a daring move considering that the men had been living off the contents of their supply train for the best part of a month.

---

*He is also commemorated by a large, elaborate, but seldom noticed monument in New York City, between Fifth Avenue and Broadway at Twenty-Fifth Street.

Lee, with his pioneers, moved ahead of the army, preparing the makeshift road, which in some places was hardly more than a rutted track, for the artillery and the wagon train. Lee roughed it with his pioneers. Two days out of Monclova he wrote to Mary, "We . . . reached Castana in a terrible norther, where we encamped in a cornfield & appeared as if it would be swept away by the fierce wind. I could scarcely get my tent up, & when up, keep it so. . . . We could of course cook nothing, & I was out till dark reconnoitering. We arrived on the ground under a scorching sun. The wind [got] up while they were laying out the camp & became so severe that but a few tents were erected before dark. By the time I got mine up, it was so cold, that when I took to the saddle again I was uncomfortable [even] buttoned up in my greatcoat. So sudden are changes out here. On resuming our march next morn[ing] at sunrise there was plenty of ice in the stream. The thermometer stood at 23: had [to] lead my horse & walk a mile or two to warm my feet. We marched that day 21 miles before reaching water & encamped on a barren plain where there was no wood or grass. . . . We march tomorrow at 5 a.m. Reveille at 3 & have to go 30 miles to reach water. A long march. I have seen all my animals fed & comfortable for the night & men too." Lee also reported that Santa Anna was rumored to be at San Luis Potosí and that "when he received the message from Genl. T[aylor] abrogating the armistice, returned for answer that *he* could never make peace so long as there was an armed American on the soil of Mexico . . . & that we should now have war not only to the *knife,* but to the handle also."

A more important rumor was that the U.S. Navy had taken the fort of San Juan de Ulúa, which commanded the harbor of Vera Cruz, and that, in Lee's words, "our government would push a strong force from Vera Cruz towards the City of Mexico," forcing Santa Anna to give up San Luis Potosí and make peace—or a last stand in the Mexican capital.

Lee was correct, but premature by four months. This was in fact exactly what President Polk intended to do, now that he realized the many obstacles facing General Taylor as he advanced south. What had held Polk up was the enormous task of gathering men, artillery, and equipment for a seaborne invasion of Mexico—the most ambitious American amphibious operation to date. A still more difficult decision was that Polk had to choose who would command it.

The logical choice was General Winfield Scott, the commanding general of the U.S. Army,* not only its

---

*Functionally the equivalent of today's army chief of staff.

most competent and most senior officer, but a national hero, indeed a national institution, and the author of the plan to take Vera Cruz and march directly on Mexico City in the first place.

Unfortunately, the one general in the U.S. Army whom President Polk disliked and mistrusted more than he did Zachary Taylor was Winfield Scott; and Scott had the additional disadvantage from the president's point of view that his headquarters was only a few steps away from the White House. Scott was a huge (at six feet five inches he towered a foot above President Polk) and omnipresent personality in Washington, D.C., overshadowing almost everyone else by his size, his girth, his elaborate uniforms, his taste for military ceremony, and, of course, his legendary reputation—he was greatly admired by that keenest judge of military ability, Field Marshal the Duke of Wellington, the aged victor of Waterloo.

Scott was a larger-than-life figure, the glow of his glory casting into the shadow more ordinary political figures. Like Zachary Taylor, Scott had his eye on the White House—neither general disguised his presidential ambition—but while Scott was a Whig, a member of the party opposing the president's, it was not clear to anyone which party's nomination Taylor would seek. Polk vacillated between the desire to get Scott out of

Washington and into the field, where he might possibly commit a blunder that would tarnish his reputation, and the fear that Scott might win a victory which would make him even more of a national hero than he already was.

Unlike Polk, whose personality has been described as "drab," Scott was capable of a kind of elephantine charm reinforced by military glamour. He loved company and despite his air of lofty superiority enjoyed a certain degree of popularity. He was also apt to make serious gaffes on the subject of the president. Scott would apologize for them later in a grandiose and oleaginous manner that the president found insufferable. The temptation to send him to Vera Cruz and get him out of the way—and, more important, out of Washington—was almost irresistible to Polk. As for Scott, he regarded command of the expedition as no more than his due.

Polk sought for a way out of his dilemma, and found it in his fellow Democrat Senator Thomas Hart Benton of Missouri (known as "Old Bullion" for his opposition to paper money, and a staunch advocate of western expansion). Polk asked the senator to command the Vera Cruz expedition. Senator Benton had served as an aide-de-camp to Andrew Jackson in the War of 1812, but had not worn a uniform since then. He made no claim to being a professional soldier—the highlight of his experience under fire was a duel in which he had killed his opponent—but this did not prevent him from seriously considering the role. As overbearing and arrogant as General Scott, Benton had served five terms as a senator and was one of the most respected figures in national politics—his eminence was such that not even Scott could have objected to Benton's being placed in command. Fortunately for Scott, however, the senator would not consider taking command of the expedition unless he was given the rank of lieutenant general. Since this would have given Benton one more star than Scott, the army's commanding general, and also make Benton the first American since George Washington to hold that rank, even Polk was obliged to throw in the sponge and finally appoint Scott to command one of the most ambitious military operations in the history of the United States.

However reluctant Polk was to put Scott in command—and he made no secret of his reluctance—he had made the right choice. Scott had his failings—arrogance, a taste for political intrigue, and an almost preposterous degree of vanity (he had two large mirrors placed opposite each other, the better to admire himself in uniform). But he was a first-rate professional soldier, his courage had been proved over and over again in battle, and he commanded the respect, even the awe, of his troops. He was not afraid to enforce discipline with a brutal hand, and he had the "battle sense" that is the mark of a great commander: that is, he understood at a glance where the enemy's weak spot was, and how to pierce through von Clausewitz's famous "fog of war." What is more remarkable is that unlike many great generals, and despite his overwhelming egotism, Scott was an unexpectedly good listener who sought the views of those around him, and expected his officers who served on his staff to express their own opinion even when it contradicted his.

Scott was also a gifted planner. For his mission against Mexico he had proposed "the largest amphibious invasion yet attempted in history," and certainly the most risky. He required at least 15,000 men (9,000 of them drawn from Taylor's forces), 50 seagoing transport ships, and 140 "flatboats" to carry a "first wave" of 5,000 men, along with their artillery, supplies, and horses, from the ships to the beaches southwest of Vera Cruz, all of it guarded by U.S. warships. His incredibly detailed plans were based on the assumption that Mexico City could be reached only from Vera Cruz, rather than from the north as Taylor was attempting to do. Once ashore the troops would have to move inland as rapidly as possible to avoid "the seasonal onslaught of the dreaded *vómito* (yellow fever) around Vera Cruz," and the defenses of Vera Cruz, particularly Fort San Juan Ulúa, were so strong that the force would have to land on the open beaches south of the city, then besiege or assault it successfully before moving inland. Scott's plan did not initially anticipate capturing a harbor. The troops would have to secure Vera Cruz, a heavily fortified city, before they could be reinforced and supplied by sea. Giving Scott the number of men he wanted (he would eventually settle for 12,000) could be done only by raising nine regiments of nearly 7,000 volunteers and by stripping Taylor's forces to the bone. The flatboats or, as they sometimes called, "surfboats" had to be made to Scott's design in three different sizes, so they could be stacked to save space on deck. Each of them would weigh more than three tons and cost $795 to make. They were "the first specially built American amphibious craft." Scott even specified the exact dimensions and type of wood to be used—he seemed to think of everything and to consult every expert. This was anything but a hastily improvised attack. Scott took into account everything from medical problems of men and horses to the right choice of beaches and the amount of time it would take to build the flatboats and charter the transport vessels. Given all this, it is a miracle that it took Scott only thirteen weeks from the time he assumed command, the day after Thanksgiving, 1846, to his landing on Collada Beach on March 9, 1847.

As one might expect, the prospect of being stripped of more than half his forces did not please Zachary Taylor, but neither did it reduce him to inactivity. Less than three weeks before Scott left Washington to take command of the Vera Cruz expedition, General Wool was still advancing south toward Parras from Monclova, with Captain Lee and his pioneers in the lead, hoping to place his forces in position to support of General Worth. Lee wrote to Mary on December 1 that he had made "a long hot march," covering over thirty miles in one day before reaching water "& then it was a little saline," over hard ground and through clouds of "lime dust"—a march so severe that 200 men "gave out" from heat prostration, exhaustion, and thirst and "had to be placed in the wagons," and several horses and mules "were left [dead] on the road." Inevitably, the patrician Lee compared the "haciendas" he passed along the way with the mansions at home, and noted that the proprietors had all fled, "leaving nothing but the peones to receive [us], who poor fellows are reduced to a state of slavery worse than our negroes." He arrived at Saltillo two days before Christmas, and commented that with the arrival of General Wool's force, General Worth had now gathered "quite a respectable force," although he was "beginning to have faint hopes of finding any use for them," since Santa Anna's whereabouts were still unknown. Lee was invited by General Worth "to make his house my home," but apparently preferred to camp with his men. He wrote to Mary on Christmas Eve that the countryside around Saltillo was "monotonous and uninteresting," except for the mountains, which were "magnificent." Bird life, always a source of interest to Lee, was scarce in the absence of any trees, except for "the [Mexican] partridge . . . much handsomer than ours," and three blue birds. He was still congratulating himself on his choice of horses. Creole, his palomino, he reported, was "considered the prettiest thing in the army," and Jim Connally had measured "one leap . . . over a gulley & said it was 19 feet."* His second horse, the sorrel mare he had bought in Texas, despite her dainty way of going, did not mind the "weight, blankets & saddle bags, pistols, haversack & [canteen]." (Lee had a strong preference for mares until he acquired Traveller.) Jim rode his

---

*This sounds like an exaggeration on Connally's part, but I am assured by no less an authority than William Steinkraus, noted horseman and former captain and gold medalist of the U.S. Olympic equestrian team, that the Fédération Equestre Internationale record is over twenty-eight feet, so Connally was probably correct.

third horse, a dark bay gelding, "deep chested, sturdy & strong." All three horses were doing fifty to sixty miles a day over hard country with no problems.

One gets a glimpse here of Lee the professional soldier, with his equipment strapped to his saddle, uncomplainingly covering fifty miles a day in blistering heat. On Christmas Day his early breakfast was interrupted by news that the enemy was approaching, and was less than thirty miles away. "The ammunition & provision train was moved to the rear. Our tents were struck, wagons packed & teams hitched ready to move at a moments [sic] warning." Lee moved forward and lay in the grass with his sorrel mare saddled beside him, examining through his telescope "the pass of the mountain through which the road approached," but one senses his disappointment. When Santa Anna's army did not appear, camp was pitched again in the same place and the cooks were set to work preparing a Christmas dinner. "I was surprised myself," he wrote to Mary, continuing his letter, "at the handsome appearance of the feast under the indulgent coloring of candlelight." Lee, always a prolific letter writer even by the standards of the mid-nineteenth century, often reached toward the poetic, giving one a sense of that other person behind the "grim-visaged" soldier. Reading the correspondence one can imagine the talented watercolorist, the man whose finely drawn topographical maps reach the level of art, the flirtatious gentleman with a taste for light badinage with pretty young women, the grown-up who enjoyed childish fun and affectionate teasing. Who knows what it cost Lee to suppress that lighter persona? The trace of him is there in that glorious phrase "the indulgent coloring of candlelight." It was not a phrase that would come to the pen of, say, Stonewall Jackson, still less that master of sternly matter-of-fact prose Ulysses S. Grant. It hints of the romantic personality buried deep within Robert E. Lee.

Dust clouds in the distance constantly caused false alarms about the approach of Santa Anna's army, and a few days after Christmas, following another such report, Lee volunteered "to ascertain the enemy's position" once and for all by making a night reconnaissance in the direction of the dust clouds. Wool gratefully accepted the offer—though it was hardly the job of an engineer to undertake night scouting in enemy territory—and ordered a company of cavalry to meet Lee at "the outer picket line" and act as an escort. Lee picked "the son of a neighboring old Mexican, who knew the country, and . . . prevailed on him to act as his guide." Lee showed the young man his pistols and warned him that "if he played him false he should have the contents of them," though just to make sure, General Wool held the young man's father as a hostage and threatened to hang him if Lee did not return safely.

Lee's cavalry escort failed to meet him in the dark, but rather than waste the hours of darkness he rode on anyway, "with no other companion than the unwilling native"—a courageous decision, since at any moment he might run into an enemy patrol or picket line. In the moonlight Lee was able to see the tracks of numerous wagons in the road, and concluded that a foraging party might have been sent out in this direction, in which case the Mexican encampment must be nearby. Rather than return to General Wool with this rather vague report, Lee pushed forward for several miles, hoping to encounter a picket line or sentries, and after a few miles of hard riding saw campfires "on a hill not far away." At this point his reluctant guide panicked, fearful of being taken prisoner by Mexican soldiers and "hanged as a spy or a traitor," by no means an unreasonable thought in the circumstances. He begged Lee to turn back, but Lee was still not satisfied, and told him to stay put while he continued ahead alone. He could see what looked like tents on the hill, and rode right through a darkened village and beyond it toward a stream without being challenged. He could hear voices ahead, and pulled up his horse at the stream, where he found, to his

surprise, that what he had taken for tents in the darkness was in fact only a large flock of sheep, and that he
had stumbled across a group of Mexican shepherds on
their way to the market in Saltillo. Although startled
by the sudden appearance out of the dark of a *yanqui*
officer in the middle of the night, they greeted him
courteously and told him that the Mexican army was
still on the other side of the mountains. Lee rode back
to where his guide was waiting, and from there back
to camp, where he found that the length of his reconnaissance had put his guide's father in danger of being
hanged. "This Mexican was the most delighted man to
see me," he remarked long afterward. It became one of
the stories Lee enjoyed telling, perhaps because mistaking the sheep for tents resembles the famous scene
of Don Quixote encountering a flock of sheep, with the
Mexican guide as Sancho Panza.

Lee had ridden forty miles during the night, but
after only three hours of sleep, he set off again on a
fresh horse, and rode much farther until he had
acquired definite information about the whereabouts
of the Mexican army. The incident apparently made
an impression on General Wool, who made Lee his
"acting inspector general," and it taught Lee a lesson
he never forgot about the value of pertinacity in reconnaissance, and the importance of not paying too much

attention to exaggerated reports of the strength or the nearness of the enemy until they had been reliably verified. Despite numerous reports that the Mexican army was in sight—as many as 20,000 men were said to have been observed—Santa Anna was in fact still encamped over 100 miles away in San Luis Potosí; the dust storms had been caused by the wind or by patrols of American cavalry.

Wool's forces were ordered to proceed a few miles farther south from the area around Saltillo to Buena Vista, where they supported the troops General Taylor had gathered. Lee busied himself fortifying the new camp in addition to his duties as acting inspector general, but he was ordered on before the climactic battle in northern Mexico on February 23, 1847, when Santa Anna finally advanced with 14,000 men to attack Zachary Taylor's army of 5,000 men at Buena Vista. The Mexicans were crushingly defeated in a battle that assured Taylor of a hero's welcome when he returned home, and nomination as the Whig candidate for the presidency in the 1848 election. Still, his victory did not open up the way to Mexico City from the north.

Lee's departure from Taylor's army was a consequence of the running battle between General in Chief Scott and Major General Taylor in the months before

Buena Vista over Scott's demand for a substantial part of Taylor's forces for the landing at Vera Cruz, to which President Polk had already agreed. Scott needed the regulars serving under Taylor to provide a disciplined core for the volunteers and militiamen, and the moment he reached Brazos Santiago, near the mouth of the Rio Grande, he wrote in detail to Taylor specifying the units and numbers of men he required, and ordering Taylor to take up a "defensive" line on the Rio Grande. Although Scott couched his demand in such ponderous courtesy that it would have read like irony coming from anyone else, he made no secret of the fact that he regarded Taylor as an amateur commander, as well as a subordinate, and that he regarded any attempt to reach " 'the Halls of Montezuma' via Monterey and San Luis Potosi [as a] blunder."

The quarrel between the two generals, each of whom hoped to be the next president, was aggravated by the fact that Scott's "confidential" letter to Taylor, which contained all the details of the planned landing at Vera Cruz, went calamitously astray—the officer carrying it was "inveigled" into a small town near Monterey and killed, so the letter with all Scott's plans was taken by the Mexicans, with the result that Santa Anna read it before Taylor received a second copy. A second problem was that Scott had "appointed a meeting with Taylor" at

Camargo, upstream from Brazos Santiago, but because Taylor had not received the letter informing him of the meeting, he was away when Scott arrived. Scott would describe this later as "a great disappointment," since he had hoped to discuss all this face-to-face and "harmonize operations" with Taylor. In fact, not knowing that his letter had been taken, Scott regarded Taylor's failure to attend the meeting as a deliberate insult from a general of lower seniority, and returned fuming to Brazos, having given the orders to transfer more than half Taylor's army, and offered Taylor a choice between remaining where he was with a smaller force or accepting command of a division under himself. "I had now," Scott wrote in his inimitable style, "without the benefit of the consultation sought, to detach from the army of the Rio Grande such regular troops as I deemed indispensible to lead the heavier masses of volunteers and other green regiments, promised for the descent on Vera Cruz and the conquest of the capital—leaving Taylor a sufficient force to maintain the false* position at Monterey, and discretion to contract his line to the Rio Grande, with the same means of defense." Taylor's reaction, when he was finally informed in full detail of the "stripping" of his forces, Scott described as "gentle

---

* General Scott disagreed with Taylor's advance to Monterey.

regret," but in fact Taylor was furious, and when he returned to the United States after the war he pursued a public feud with Scott that lasted until Taylor's own untimely death in the White House, caused by overindulgence in cherries and cold milk on a hot day. Since Scott survived him by sixteen years, he had plenty of time to get in the last word, and among other things accused Taylor of being "unhinged" by "the gantlet of universal cheers and praise."

Captain Robert E. Lee was one of those officers transferred to the Vera Cruz expedition, once more demonstrating his ability to land on his feet, and to get where he wanted to go without seeming to make an effort. It is not clear whether or not Scott asked for him personally, but they were fellow Virginians and Scott knew and respected Lee—the War Department was a small place in those days, and they would have met frequently while Lee was the right-hand man of the chief engineer. Never one to dawdle when duty called, Lee left on January 17, 1847, for the 250-mile journey to Brazos, riding his mare Creole, and accompanied by Jim and his other horses.

Brazos was an ill-defined and shifting island amid the sandbars that obstructed the mouth of the Rio Grande, and had been transformed into a military supply depot and tented camp for thousands of soldiers arriving by ship from ports from New Orleans to New York. For the moment General Scott was there, "fuming at every wasted hour and writing vigorous letters to all whom he accounted guilty of delaying the start of his expedition." Lee was immediately accepted as a member of Scott's general staff and one of the general in chief's inner council, and assigned to quarters on board the U.S.S. *Massachusetts*, the flagship of the fleet, on which Scott himself would be sailing. He would be sharing a cabin with his friend and classmate from West Point (and a future Confederate general) Joseph E. Johnston. It was a huge and immediate jump up from Lee's previous post as one of General Wool's engineers, and an opportunity to see strategy directed at the highest level, for Scott was not a commanding general who kept his hand close to his vest where his headquarters was concerned, and he expected all the members of his staff to keep themselves fully informed of his intentions and concerns.

To Scott's dismay, the fleet was not assembled and ready to sail until February 15. Not all the surfboats had arrived yet, but Scott was anxious to be under way—it was imperative to take Vera Cruz and advance from the coast to higher ground inland before the yellow fever season began in April. The window of opportunity was narrow, and could not be missed without grave consequences. Three days later they anchored off the Mexican port of Tampico, about halfway between Brazos and Vera Cruz, where most of the army, about 6,000 men, were encamped. Tampico had been taken by the navy as part of the blockade of Mexico's eastern seacoast, and Scott, followed by his staff, came ashore the next day to a thunderous salute and the kind of full-scale, formal military parade he relished, although he prudently avoided mounting the horse that had been provided for him, and chose to review the troops on foot—Scott was already developing the bulk that would eventually preclude his mounting a horse at all. From the sea Tampico looked pleasant, but it was actually a maze of squalid, narrow streets, with "impoverished" inhabitants, few of them pleased at having their city occupied indefinitely by Americans. Lee spent a day examining the town's fortifications, and tried the famous Mexican hot chocolate, which was too bitter for his taste. There appears to have been a lot of drunkenness before the troops boarded the transport ships, but we can be sure that Lee, at any rate, did not try the native tequila, given his prejudice against spirits.

On February 19 the fleet sailed again, this time for the shelter of the Lobos Islands, about 120 miles north of Vera Cruz, where some of Scott's troops were already encamped, and which he had chosen as the "general *rendez vous*" for the remaining supply ships and transports. Scott had been informed by "old shipmasters" he had consulted in New Orleans that his ships might shelter from the dreaded "northers" in the lee of these islands, so he decided to "lay for a few days" until "the greater part of the troops and material of war expected had come up with [him]." What he does not say is that an outbreak of smallpox on board one of the ships prevented him from embarking more troops from this barren and treeless island, or that the voyage from Tampico had run into a fierce storm—exactly the kind of "norther" he was hoping to avoid—that rendered men and beasts seasick for two days, a horror for the horses, and not much better for the troops. Lee was one of the few officers who "possessed sea legs" and remained unaffected, but his cabin mate Joe Johnston was horribly seasick.

The fleet was unable to get away from the Lobos Islands until March 3, and Scott was still short of supplies and had only half the surfboats he required for the landing. This time the weather was favorable, and on March 5 Lee had his first sight of Vera Cruz, and the formidable island fortress of San Juan de Ulúa that guarded the approach to the city from the sea. The next day Lee accompanied Scott on a small steamer, the *Petrita*,* to examine the beaches to the south of the city. The *Petrita* came so close to the fortress that the Mexicans opened fire on it—the first time in the twenty-two years of his army career, as Freeman points out, that Lee had ever been under fire. Scott surveyed the beaches and quickly decided to accept Commodore David Conner's advice that the best choice was Collado Beach, less than three miles south of Vera Cruz, which was somewhat sheltered by two small islands and a coral reef just offshore, and consisted of "a gently curving strip of sand" with "a line of sand hills about 150 yards inland." Although he could see no evidence of Mexican preparations from the *Petrita*, Scott anticipated that the landings would be opposed, that the Mexicans would shelter their artillery behind the sand hills (or sand dunes, to describe them more accurately), and that the first wave of soldiers and Marines would have to rush and carry the dunes.

The landing was scheduled for March 8, but the threat of bad weather, which failed to materialize, obliged Scott to postpone it to March 9, a day of light breezes and bright sunshine. March 9 was also, as it happened, "the thirty-third anniversary of

---

* A virtual constellation of future Confederate generals was aboard the *Petrita*: Lee, Joseph E. Johnston, and Pierre G. T. Beauregard, as well as Lee's opponent at Gettysburg, George G. Meade.

the Commanding General's promotion to the rank of general," apparently a propitious coincidence, since the first wave of 2,595 men went ashore without problems or incidents in the early afternoon, supported by "schooner-gunboats," close inshore in case artillery was needed, thus demonstrating the value of Scott's flatboats and his attention to detail. Lee witnessed the landing from the quarterdeck of the *Massachusetts*, standing beside Scott, and saw "the whole fleet of transports—some eighty vessels, in the presence of many foreign ships of war, flanked by two naval steamers and five gunboats to cover the movement." The men quickly boarded the sixty-seven flatboats, and landed "in the exact order prescribed . . . without the loss of a boat or a man," and virtually without opposition except for a few shells fired from too great a range to be dangerous. On board the ships—even two warships of the Royal Navy were present, attending as observers—crews lined the decks and rigging cheering, and bands played. By the next day, when General Scott landed with his staff, he had about 12,000 men onshore, more than enough to seal Vera Cruz off from the landward side, while the navy blockaded it from the sea. Though Lee could have had no premonition of it, he was about to be transformed from a resourceful military engineer into a daring soldier and a hero.

_____

Immediately after landing, General Scott made a "reconnaissance" of the wall and fortifications surrounding Vera Cruz on the landward side, accompanied by what he referred to as "his inner cabinet," which included Lee. One look was enough to confirm to a professional soldier like Scott that the walled city would not be an easy place to take by attack. The fortifications of Vera Cruz "were considered . . . to be among the strongest, if not the strongest, in North America." The wall around the city's landward side was fifteen feet high, built of solid coral or granite blocks, with nine "bastions" (protruding fortresses that could give covering fire to each other and to the "curtain" or wall), built into it at intervals, "each mounting from eight to ten guns." The Mexicans had lavished a good deal of money and energy on strengthening the city's defenses and those of the formidable fortress of San Juan de Ulúa that guarded it from the sea, since the capture of Vera Cruz by a French expeditionary force in 1838. Scott immediately called his staff together and presented them with his opinion. "A death-bed discussion," he wrote, "could hardly have been more solemn." He saw only two choices: either storming the city and then pushing on as fast as possible into the interior before the yellow fever season set in, or besieging the city. Despite the amount of time a siege would take, Scott himself favored "regular siege approaches," since he feared that taking the city by means of storming parties might cost him as many as 2,000 or 3,000 men, leaving him with not enough troops to march inland and take Mexico City, and also since he wished to limit the "slaughter . . . of non-combatants" that would inevitably accompany an assault. He solicited the opinion of all his officers, including Lee, and to a man all of them expressed a preference for a siege.

"All sieges are much alike," Scott remarked, and he was right. By the mid-nineteenth century formal sieges were becoming rare—although there are exceptions: Grant would besiege Vicksburg in 1863, and the Prussians would besiege Paris in 1870—but the rules of siege warfare were ancient, rigid, and well understood. The attacker must first "invest" the city by digging trench lines around it, effectively isolating it; dig in his artillery; then summon the military commander to surrender the city before opening fire. As "Scott's protégé, prized particularly for his uncanny eye for terrain," Lee was largely responsible for directing the digging of five miles of trenches, extending them closer and closer to the walls, and for the all-important task of siting the artillery and digging it in. Scott raged because the War Department had refused to provide him with "a siege train" of "very heavy artillery," but he had enough heavy mortars in place by March 22 to summon "the Mexican commander to surrender."

General Juan Morales promptly appeared in full uniform under a flag of truce and, after a colorful and formal military ceremony of the kind that was so dear to General Scott's heart, politely declined to surrender the city. The American artillery then opened fire. By nightfall, the effect was spectacular, "a lurid glare, illuminating for one instant the white domes and grim fortresses of Vera Cruz," as each mortar shell landed with a thunderous explosion, but because of their high trajectory and relatively small size the mortars did not lend themselves to battering down thick stone walls and fortresses. Lee had worked hard to accomplish something of a miracle in twelve days, particularly since many of the mules had died during the voyage and the heavy mortars therefore had to be manhandled across the beach and the dunes by the troops. The Mexicans had made full use of dense hedges of chaparral and spiny local cactus, as well as of *trous de loup* (the language of siege warfare was still French, in which most of the textbooks on war were written), conical holes with a sharpened stake at the bottom, intended to impale anybody who fell in. In addition, the besieging Americans suffered from thirst, prodigious numbers of sand fleas, high winds, and dense sandstorms. Lee himself carried out reconnaissance by night so close to the walls that he set the dogs behind them to barking, and was shot at one night by a sentry as he returned to the American lines. The bullet passed so close that it singed his uniform—an unexpected *baptême du feu*, which he passed with flying colors.

Reluctant as Scott was to cede a role in the taking of Vera Cruz to the navy, he was aware that with the artillery at his disposal he had no chance of making a substantial breach in the walls. He swallowed his pride and requested six heavy guns from the warships. This posed a huge challenge for Lee, who had to pick a site for the naval battery close to the city wall, "but hidden from its view by a thick growth of chaparral." Lee built the battery "on a sand ridge about seven hundred yards from Fort Santa Barbara, near the middle of the American line," managing to construct it so that the work was screened from the Mexicans. Each of the eight-inch naval guns weighed over three tons, and had to be lowered from the warship's deck into a cutter and rowed to the beach, then hauled through the dunes to the battery by the sailors. Lee found the sailors as reluctant to dig and fill sandbags as the soldiers were, but he persisted, and by the morning of March 24 he had all six naval guns dug in and ready to fire, one of them under the command of his brother Sydney Smith Lee. As the sailors began to chop down the chaparral and sponge the sand out of their guns, the Mexicans finally noticed the naval battery and opened fire on it. Lee ignored the shells falling around him and directed the return fire, apparently "unconscious of personal danger." His only concern was for his brother. "No matter where I turned," he wrote later, "my eyes reverted to [him]. . . . I am at a loss what I should have done had he been cut down before me. . . . He preserved his usual cheerfulness, and I could see his white teeth through all the smoke and din of fire." (In the days before smokeless powder was invented massed musket fire was accompanied by billowing clouds of thick, dark smoke illuminated from within by orange flashes as weapons were fired. The smoke often made it impossible to tell friend from foe—this was one of the many reasons why British soldiers continued to wear the red coat to the end of the nineteenth century.) The hellish exchange of fire lasted until sunset and resumed early the next day, by which time "a thirty-six-foot breach had been blasted through the city's walls, and its fortresses 'drilled like a colander.' " On March 25 the city's European consuls appealed for "a partial truce to be enable women, children, and neutrals to be evacuated," a sign that enemy's resolve was weakening, but Scott replied "that no truce could be allowed except on the application of the governor (General Morales), and *that* with a view to surrender," and the next day General J. J. Landero—General Morales having prudently "feigned sickness" and turned over command to his deputy—asked formally for terms of surrender. On March 27 Vera Cruz was occupied by the U.S. Army. The garrison of over 4,000 men marched out, laid down their arms, and were sent home as prisoners of war on parole (Scott had no means of feeding them). In just eighteen days Mexico's "principal port of foreign commerce" had been taken, along with more than 400 guns, with the loss of only sixty-four American officers and men.

Scott praised Lee in his dispatch home for his work not just as an engineer, but as an aide. Even more important, Lee had distinguished himself among his fellow officers by the two qualities that count most in war: courage and professional expertise (militarily speaking, neither is of much use without the other). However, he himself was saddened rather than pleased by his first experience of warfare. After he rode around the battered walls of Vera Cruz and surveyed the effect of the 1,800 shells fired from the naval battery as well as 2,500 more from the mortars he had sited so carefully, he wrote home: "It was awful! My heart bled for the inhabitants. The soldiers I did not care so much for, but it was terrible to think of the women and children." Then, as would so often be the case in the future, he expressed no words of triumph, or satisfaction in victory.

As Lee looked at Vera Cruz, with its smashed tenements, its streets "littered with the bloated corpses of dead animals," and its sad rows of civilians waiting to be buried, he might have agreed with the Duke of Wellington's terse comment as he rode over the battlefield of Waterloo in 1815: "Nothing except a battle lost can be half so melancholy as a battle won."

Whatever Lee's failings, a love of glory for its own sake was never among them.

It is 280 miles from Vera Cruz to Mexico City. Scott had two routes before him: one to the south, skirting the barrier of the Sierra Madre range about 90 miles from Vera Cruz, which ran at a right angle across the direction of his advance; the other to the north, slightly longer and steeper, which ran through a mountain pass at Cruz Blanca. The two roads met at the town of Puebla, 100 miles from Mexico City. Of these, the better road was the so-called National Highway, which followed the route used by Cortés in 1519, leading out of the *tierra caliente*, the marshy fever country around Vera Cruz, through Jalapa, Perote, and Puebla; then skirting the famous Mount Popocatépetl and descending into the great Valley of Mexico. This road crossed a number of rivers running west to east, and wound through numerous steep ravines and "narrow passes," any one of which would have provided a perfect place for an ambush, particularly since Scott's army would be strung out along many miles of the National Highway, with the three divisions much too far apart to support one another in case of trouble. Despite the risk, Scott decided to take it. The truth is that Scott was in a race against time. He had been delayed in Vera Cruz longer than he wished by the difficulty of acquiring sufficient mules and horses for his artillery and supply wagons. Two of his men had already died of yellow fever, so he had no choice but to advance deep into enemy territory before he was ready, leaving behind him a lengthening supply line that even a small number of enemy troops or guerrillas could cut at any moment, at the same time cutting off his line of retreat. In Washington, President Polk deplored this "great military error," and far away in London, the Duke of Wellington, who was avidly following Scott's progress on the map from newspaper accounts, decided, "Scott is lost . . . he can't fall back upon his base."

As the march toward Mexico City began, Scott himself seemed to become momentarily slipshod in his planning. One difficulty was that he had no reliable intelligence about where Santa Anna might be; the other was that two of his divisional commanders—the impetuous David E. Twiggs and the sulky and sensitive William J. Worth—were quarrelling, and Scott's old friend Worth blamed Scott bitterly for ordering Twiggs's division to lead the march, instead of Worth's regulars. Worth's behavior, according to a relatively sympathetic fellow officer, was "as arrogant and domineering as pride can make a man." Although Scott did his best to calm his friend down, he was not about to alter his orders. A great deal of time was wasted on what Worth regarded as an insult to his honor. Worth broke off his friendship with General Scott and sulked like Achilles in his tent, with the result that in the end Twiggs left Vera Cruz on April 9, followed shortly by Major General Robert Patterson's division of volunteers, then by Scott and his staff on April 12, and finally by Worth on April 16. The result was that the first division marched out of Vera Cruz a week before the last, not a good plan. Signs of lack of discipline were unmistakable—the volunteers drained their canteens too soon, fell out of the line of march because of the extreme heat, and threw away their excess baggage, leaving the road to take shelter from the sun wherever they could find it.

Scott had ordered Twiggs to advance as far as the town of Jalapa, about forty miles to the northwest, leading the men to conclude that he thought Santa Anna was on the other side of the Sierra Madre. In fact Santa Anna, having returned to Mexico City after his defeat at Buena Vista to reassert his political control and recruit a new army, was already digging into a strong position ahead of Twiggs with something like 12,000 men.* Had Santa Anna truly been the Napoleon of the West, he would have sent out his cavalry and discovered that the American army was strung out along the National Highway in disarray. Instead, he took up a defensive position ahead of them, thus providing Scott with the opportunity to concentrate when he ran into Santa Anna's position. Of course Santa Anna's troops were raw and poorly trained, and he may have been more confident of them in a defensive position on high ground than in a more ambitious fast-moving flank attack, but there is no denying he threw

---

*Numbers where the Mexican army is concerned are uncertain. Freeman puts Santa Anna's forces at Cerro Gordo at 8,000; others put them a good deal higher. Whatever the truth, they outnumbered Scott's forces.

away a chance—perhaps the last chance—of a decisive Mexican victory.

Two days out of Vera Cruz Lee, accompanying General Scott, reached the National Bridge over the Río de la Antigua, "a magnificent structure more than fifty feet high and nearly a quarter of a mile in length, commanding romantic views of the rapid stream winding through towering vistas of luxuriant vegetation." Scott had feared that Santa Anna might make a stand there, since it constituted an obvious "bottleneck," but to his relief he found that it had been neither fortified nor destroyed. Riding a few miles beyond the bridge to the next river—the shallow but wide and swift-moving Río del Plan—they found the first two divisions of the American army roughly encamped on a wide plain under "bowers," rough shelters made of tree branches planted in the ground as uprights, with a covering of grass and leaves. The troops applauded as Scott rode by. "No commander," he later wrote, with a characteristic touch of complacency, "was ever received with heartier cheers."

When he dismounted Scott learned that Santa Anna and his army were entrenched only a few miles away to the west on higher ground that was hard to interpret sensibly from the plain below. The few detailed maps of

Mexico were sketchy and unreliable, so neither General Twiggs nor General Patterson, nor even Scott himself, had a clear idea of what lay ahead. Even the exact route of the National Highway was unknown. Scott had given clear orders that if Twiggs made contact with the enemy he was to wait until Patterson arrived with his volunteers. Scott hoped to restrain Twiggs, who had a well-earned reputation as a hothead. In fact, the day before, when Twiggs realized that the Mexicans were almost directly in front of him, he had given orders to attack, and was prevented from doing so only by the timely arrival of Patterson, who had risen from a sick-bed to take command. This was fortunate, since with Worth's division still in Vera Cruz, Scott had 6,000 men to Santa Anna's 12,000.

1. Sketch map of the Battle of Cerro Gordo.

Clearly, what was needed was a thorough recon-naissance, and Scott chose Lee, "that indefatigable engineer," to lead it. The next day, the morning of

April 15, Lee went forward and observed at once that whatever his other defects as a general, Santa Anna had a good eye for a defensive position. Santa Anna had effectively blocked the highway at a point about a mile and a half from the American camp. To the north of the winding road and overlooking it were two truncated conical hills: Cerro Gordo (also known as "El Telégrafo") and the slightly lower La Atalaya, with a watchtower on its summit. A ridge ran in a northeasterly direction, more or less parallel to the road. On each hill Santa Anna had dug in a battery of guns, well situated to support each other and to flank the road. The ground to the south between the road and the river was broken up by a confusing maze of steep ravines, which were separated by three flattened ridges resembling the extended first three fingers of a hand, extending toward the American camp. At the tip of each Santa Anna had placed a battery of guns in "earthworks" and supported by substantial numbers of infantry. Santa Anna's left was anchored on La Atalaya, and his right on the Río del Plan, the north bank of which rose in a steep cliff, forming an uneven line almost three-quarters of a mile long.

A preliminary reconnaissance by Twiggs's engineers had demonstrated that there was no easy way to out-flank Santa Anna's right along the river, and concluded that the only way to outflank him was therefore to advance against his left by going around La Atalaya, the lower of the two hills. When Lee himself wrote to Mary, allowing himself just the slightest degree of professional condescension about Twiggs's plan of attack—he was, after all, a captain criticizing a major general—the sting at the tail of the paragraph was unmistakable: "The right of the Mexican line rested on the river at a perpendicular rock, unscalable by man or beast, and their left on impassible ravines; the main road was defended by field works containing thirty-five cannon; in their rear was the mountain of Cerro Gordo, surrounded by intrenchments in which were cannon and crowned by a tower overlooking all—it was around this army that it was intended to lead our troops."*

The Napoleonic *coup d'oeil de génie* of Lee's later battles is already clear. At a glance he saw the salient points of what seemed to others merely a confusing landscape, made even more so by the tangled brush, dense thickets, and thorny chaparral. He understood at once the strength of Santa Anna's position and the danger of attacking it frontally, but thought he saw a better way than trying to advance north of La Atalaya in full view of the enemy.

---

*Connoisseurs of military irony will note that the terrain and Santa Anna's use of it somewhat resemble Meade's position on Cemetery Ridge at Gettysburg in 1863 on the second day of the battle, including the two hills on his left.

One of Twiggs's engineers had climbed partway up one of the steep ravines on the Mexican left, where the brush was so thick that Santa Anna believed "not even a jackrabbit could penetrate its fastness." Lee decided to go farther forward himself, convinced that it would lead to the Jalapa road and the lower slopes of the two hills that constituted the strong point of the Mexican line. Although there were Mexican troops on higher ground to either side of him, "he worked his way" slowly through the thickets unseen until he suddenly reached a small clearing with a spring from which led a "well-trampled" path.

As he studied the ground around him he heard voices speaking Spanish approaching, and hid behind a large log lying close to the spring. When the Mexican troops stopped to drink, Lee slipped under the log. He could not move; he could hardly even breathe for fear of revealing his presence. Two of the soldiers sat down on the log not three feet from him, and another stepped over it, almost planting his foot on Lee's back. More soldiers came and went as the day crept by—clearly this was "the water supply for [the left] wing of that army." Lee lay motionless in the heat throughout the day, tormented by biting insects and thirst. Although the zigzag of ravines made it hard to fix his position exactly, he concluded that he was now in fact far *behind* the enemy's left wing and within reach of the road to Jalapa.

When night came, Lee was finally able to make his way back in the dark with great difficulty, descending through the dense thickets hand over hand down to the American campfires. Lee was certain that a working party could cut a trail through the ravines with a good chance of doing so unnoticed by the Mexicans. Scott agreed, and by the end of April 16 "a working party of pioneers" had hacked out a rough trail of sorts, while Lee went even farther behind the Mexican lines than he had gone the previous day. "He did not reach the Jalapa road, which the Americans must occupy if they were to cut off the Mexican retreat," but he had every reason to believe that he had been close to it, and that a determined thrust up the newly cut trail would cut through the center of Santa Anna's line, following which an attack on his left around La Atalaya might then succeed in enveloping half the Mexican army, despite its hold on the high ground and its formidable fieldworks.

Scott ordered Lee to guide Twiggs's division up the trail the next day, and decided that the battle should begin on April 18, when Worth's division had caught up with the rest of the army. The plan was that Twiggs, guided by Lee, would advance his division through the ravines around the extreme left of the Mexican line, flanking La Atalaya and Cerro Gordo, while Brigadier General Gideon Pillow attacked the three Mexican batteries entrenched in front of the American camp. At the same time Worth's division could make a wide, curved flanking attack—an extended "right hook," to use the boxing term—which would bring his men down to the National Highway behind Cerro Gordo, cutting off Santa Anna's retreat. Once all this was set in motion, the remainder of the army would attack the enemy center down the National Highway, driving the Mexicans from their lines with no option but surrender.

As is so often the case in war, little of this tidy plan would take place as it was intended to, except for Lee's role. Part of the problem was that Scott's divisional commanders were still at odds. Worth was still sulking; Twiggs was bullheaded and incautious; Patterson was still ill; and Patterson's deputy, Pillow, was correctly thought to be an indifferent soldier and possibly a spy placed in the army by his old friend President Polk to report on General Scott. All of them resented Scott's seniority, dominant personality, and grandiloquent manner. The spirit of the senior officers was captured best by Scott himself, who would later describe General Pillow as "the only person I have ever known who was wholly indifferent in the choice between truth and falsehood, honesty and dishonesty," and Pillow's own officers "derided him as 'a mass of vanity, conceit, ignorance, ambition and want of truth.'" These were not relationships well calculated to fight a battle, though they are not unfamiliar in military history.

Early in the morning of April 17 Lee guided Twiggs's division slowly up the rough trail his pioneers had cleared. It was a grueling trek—artillery had to be heaved up the steep ravine by hand, along a path "hewed in the roughest way through oaks, mesquite, chaparral, cactus and the like and over almost impassable ground." The intention had been to get the troops up the ravines undetected, as close to La Atalaya as possible, then "lay up" for the night and attack in concert with the other operations planned for the next morning. This plan was frustrated when one soldier slipped on a loose stone, causing "a thud and a rattle." His company commander lunged at him with a drawn sword and shouted, "You infernal scoundrel, I'll run you through if you don't make less noise!" Soldiers burst out laughing, making it clear there were a good number of men scaling the hill. By the time Twiggs sent the leading company of the Seventh Infantry up to the head of the ravine to observe what the Mexicans were doing, they found to their consternation that the enemy was already advancing on them in "greatly superior numbers" from the higher ground ahead. The element of surprise having been lost, Twiggs ordered two regiments forward, to advance on La Atalaya. "I beg pardon, General," one of the regimental commanders asked, "how far shall we charge them?"

"Charge them to hell," Twiggs replied enthusiastically, and his troops took him at his word. They pushed the Mexican line back; stormed La Atalaya and took it; continued to advance down its western slope, despite an effort to recall them; and boldly started up the nearby hill, Cerro Gordo, where they were pinned down by heavy cannon fire. They would have been slaughtered if Lee had not managed to get three pieces of light artillery carried up to the crest of La Atalaya to cover their withdrawal.

Although Freeman comments that Lee "felt thus far that all had gone flawlessly," this can hardly have been the case. Twiggs had sacrificed the element of surprise, then jeopardized Scott's plan by attacking in force before any of the other divisions were in place. In addition, he had lost control over two of his regiments once he had ordered them to charge. Worth was of the opinion that Twiggs not only was a hothead but seldom thought at all. Not for nothing was he nick-named "the Bengal Tiger," and not for nothing was he considered by many good judges of profanity to be the most profane officer in the U.S. Army.

Lee spent a good part of the night supervising the "hauling of heavy [artillery] pieces up the hill," some-thing of a miracle in itself if we consider the terrain. He then had them dug into a well-sited battery on the summit of La Atalaya for the artillery duel that would begin in the morning. Scott had seemingly decided to take advantage of Twiggs's premature attack, order-ing him to assault Cerro Gordo under the cover of the artillery bombardment. At the same time Lee was to lead one of Twiggs's brigades around the "north flank" of the hill, and try to reach the point where his earlier reconnaissance up the ravines indicated that the road to Jalapa could be reached.

In the early morning, Scott himself rode out to watch the assault. Almost immediately the Second Brigade, which Lee was leading, came under flank-ing artillery fire and separated into two columns: one, under Colonel Bennett Riley, took up a position on the southeastern slope of Cerro Gordo, while the other, led by Lee, went around Cerro Gordo to attack a Mexican battery on the Jalapa road. Lee was now approaching the farthest point of his reconnaissance from the opposite direction, and his guess as to the location of the Jalapa road was correct. Although he was under continuous heavy fire, Lee paused to collect the Mexican wounded. He came upon "a Mexican boy, a drummer or a bugler, lying with a shattered arm under a dying soldier. Nearby was a little girl . . . tormented by the plight of the boy, but unable to help him. 'Her large black eyes were streaming with tears,' Lee remembered, 'her hands were crossed over her breast; her hair in one long plait behind reached to her waist, her arms and shoulders bare, and without stockings or shoes. Her plaintive tone of *Mille gracias, Señor,* as I had the dying man lifted off the boy . . . still lingers in my ear.' "

This was not the steely tone of a conquering hero. The authentic voice of Lee comes through in this letter to his son Custis, written just a week after the battle, with its remarkable pathos, its natural sympathy, and its gift for authentic detail. The same day, he wrote to Mary, "You have no idea what a horrible sight a field of battle is," a feeling he would express again and again until the day when he finally "sheathed his sword" for good.

Lee made sure that the Mexican wounded were taken care of, then rejoined the attack on the Mexican battery, which quickly surrendered. By now General

Shields and Colonel Riley had taken both the hills on the Mexican left and crossed the Jalapa road, cutting off any possibility of retreat by the Mexican right. The only part of Scott's plan that had failed was General Pillow's attack on the three "fingers," on the tips of which the Mexicans had dug in batteries of guns overlooking the American camp. Pillow, true to form, got lost in the ravines and attacked the wrong finger, the middle one, thus exposing part of his brigade to a "murderous" cross fire. Taking advantage of a slight wound to his arm, Pillow handed over his command and retired from the field.

Despite the numerous errors in timing and Pillow's failure, Cerro Gordo, as the battle became known, was a major victory for the United States. Over 1,000 Mexican soldiers were killed, and 3,000 were captured, along with five generals, forty guns, and "thousands of small arms."* Santa Anna escaped on a mule, leaving behind his carriage, his horses, his papers, and his "money chest." American losses were 263 dead and 368 wounded. The victory of Cerro Gordo made it possible for Scott to advance along the National Highway on Jalapa, Perote, and Puebla with no significant opposition, almost three-quarters of the way to Mexico City.

---

*Scott released them all "on parole" not to take up arms again, since he could not feed them. The "small arms" were so obsolete that he destroyed them.

Unfortunately, at just that moment the volunteers' one-year enlistment expired, and almost all of them elected to go home, leaving Scott victorious, but stranded in Puebla for four months, waiting for reinforcements to arrive while Santa Anna busied himself with recruiting a new army to defend Mexico City.

Scott's victory at Cerro Gordo was largely due to Lee's courageous reconnaissance. He was promoted to the rank of brevet major. General Shields praised him for his "intrepid coolness and gallantry." General Twiggs gave him a whole paragraph in his report, remarking on Lee's "invaluable services," and "his gallantry and good conduct on both days." However, the highest praise of all came from General Scott, who felt "impelled to make special mention of the services of Captain R. E. Lee, engineers. . . . This officer, greatly distinguished at the siege of Vera Cruz, was again indefatigable during these operations, in reconnaissance as daring as laborious, and of the utmost value. Nor was he less conspicuous in planting batteries, and in conducting columns to their stations under the heavy fire of the enemy."

Lee's reputation as a hero spread throughout the army, and rumors of it soon reached home. He had demonstrated his skill at reconnaissance; his courage, without which no other military virtue has meaning; and his ability to keep his head when all about him were losing theirs, to paraphrase Kipling. All in all, he was the perfect warrior. These were exactly the qualities—together with good manners and a gentlemanly bearing—that had earned his father the trust and respect of George Washington.

Like the rest of the army, Lee was stuck for the moment in Puebla de los Angeles. The landscape delighted Lee, who wrote to Mary that "it was the most beautiful country I have seen in Mexico, and will compare with any I have seen elsewhere, [but] I wish it was in the United States and that I was located with you and the children around me in one of its rich, bright valleys." Even fairly impartial observers were as impressed by the beauty of the countryside as by the dismal poverty of its inhabitants.

To pass the time Lee busied himself by taking an inventory of the Mexican weapons stored in Puebla and, more important, by drawing up as accurate a map as he could of the country between Puebla and Mexico City, with particular attention to the approaches to the capital, which he gleaned from "travellers and natives." All those he talked to confirmed that every approach was "strongly occupied and fortified," a problem made more difficult by the peculiar geography of the place, which had not changed much since the days of Cortés. To the east of the city the National Highway was surrounded on both sides by three shallow but large lakes★ and by extensive areas of marshland, forming a natural causeway that at its narrowest point was less than five miles wide. Clearly any attempt to take Mexico City from the east by advancing down the National Highway was unlikely to succeed—it was a natural bottleneck, easy for the Mexicans to defend. Whether it would be better to advance around Lake Texcoco to the north and approach the city from the rear, or to go around lakes Chalco and Xochimilco to the south, was difficult to determine. The former was by far the longest way around, and everybody whom Lee questioned warned that the road along the eastern shore of Lake Chalco was merely a rough trail. The way around the two southern lakes was shorter and better, but within a few miles of the city it ran alongside an impassable moonscape of jagged, black volcanic rock called the Pedregal, an ancient lava bed whose eastern side formed a corridor less than two miles wide between itself and the westernmost tip of Lake Xochimilco. The Pedregal, with its deep fissures and razor-sharp

★ To the north of the highway lay Lake Texcoco, the largest of the lakes; to its south were lakes Xochimilco and Chalco.

rocks, was a formidable obstacle, difficult and dangerous for a man to cross on foot, impossible for horses
and therefore artillery.

Beautiful as Puebla might be, Scott chafed at the
delay, describing his halt as "protracted and irksome."
Protracted, it certainly was. Scott's army had paused
for nearly a month in Jalapa after the victory at Cerro
Gordo; it had reached Puebla toward the end of May,
and waited there until August 7. Even by mid-nineteenth-century standards this was slow, but Scott was
kept busy by constant wrangling with President Polk
and Congress, and, in any case, could not move forward until he received reinforcements to replace those
who had gone home. These arrived slowly, and in dribs
and drabs—Scott believed that President Polk was
responsible for the delay, and it is hard not to sympathize with him.

By the first week in August he had about
14,000 men, of whom over 2,500 were ill with dysentery (the plague of nineteenth-century armies owing to
inadequate sanitation and poor understanding of even
the most basic standards of hygiene), and another 600
had been wounded. In desperation, Scott determined
to leave Puebla to be garrisoned by the sick, gathered his remaining troops from Vera Cruz and Jalapa,
and all but abandoned his line of "communications

with home." It was one of the most daring exploits in the history of modern warfare—as Scott himself put it with his usual gift for the dramatic phrase, "We had to throw away the scabbard and to advance naked blade in hand."

Captain Lee left Puebla with Scott, accompanied by two engineer lieutenants: P. G. T. Beauregard, the future Confederate general and victor of the First Battle of Bull Run (or First Manassas, as it is known in the South); and George B. McClellan, the future Union commander of the Army of the Potomac who would fight Lee to a bloody draw at Antietam (or Sharpsburg, as it is known in the South). By August 10, since Santa Anna elected to remain in Mexico City to reinforce its defenses, Scott's troops reached "the Rio Frio range of mountains" without serious opposition. They could at last look down on the wide, fertile valley at the center of which lay "the gorgeous seat of the Montezumas, now the capital of a great republic," while the mountain of "Popocatepetl, ten thousand feet higher, apparently near enough to touch with the hand, filled the mind with religious awe." More important, this first view of Mexico City immediately confirmed the accuracy of Lee's map, and decided Scott on "turning the strong eastern defences of the city, by passing around south of Lake Chalco and

Jochimilco,"* just the move that Lee had anticipated as he drew up the map.

After initial doubt that the road could handle the artillery and wagons was resolved by a bold reconnaissance led by Lee, the army proceeded south of the two lakes to San Augustin, a crossroads about ten miles south of Mexico City. Its position was one of extreme danger for the Americans. Reports credited Santa Anna with as many as 35,000 men, and he had had at least four months to build defenses at every approach to the city, and even to cast, from the city's church bells, large-caliber cannons to replace those he had lost. At this point Scott had just over 12,000 men and was cut off from any possibility of retreat or resupply, and forced to live off the land. What is more, Santa Anna now had the advantage of "interior lines." Wherever he was attacked on the periphery of Mexico City he could quickly rush reinforcements there. Although Santa Anna was a competent military leader, he lacked Scott's genius for maneuver and professional skill. He was a formidable organizer and a charismatic figure to his soldiers; indeed his greatest weakness was not in the military sphere: he had no secure footing in

---

*In quoting from nineteenth-century letters and memoirs I have left spellings of Mexican place-names as they were then written. The modern spelling of Jochimilco is Xochimilco, for example.

the treacherous quicksand of Mexican politics. One reason why the war dragged on is that nobody in Mexico wanted to accept the responsibility for negotiating a peace.

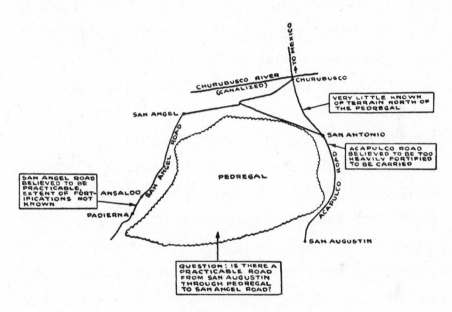

2. *The approach to Churubusco.*

The way ahead from San Augustin was not easily discernible. Scott could not stay there long, since his animals would soon eat up the available forage, and with every hour that went by Santa Anna would further reinforce the city from the south now that he knew the direction from which the American army would attack. A direct advance up the Acapulco road to the hacienda of San Antonio about five miles away from

San Augustin was the shortest way to Mexico City, but it presented great risk. San Antonio was heavily fortified and the Americans could not maneuver off the road. On one side there were the broken, razor-sharp rocks of the Pedregal lava field, and on the other side was soft, marshly ground crisscrossed by ditches, in which the guns would surely sink up to their wheel hubs. Scott decided that if he could circle his army around the Pedregal and advance up its west side, along the San Angel road, he would be in a position to come up behind San Antonio. A reconnaissance across the Pedregal, however hazardous, might find a trail or a road, shortening the distance. He sent Worth's division forward a short way up the Acapulco road to hold the attention of the defenders of San Antonio, and ordered Lee to cross the Pedregal and see what he could find. Lee at once determined that there was a track of sorts around the southern edge of the Pedregal, "passable for infantry and with some work it could be made practicable for artillery." Then Lee pushed on until he reached an "eminence" known as Zacatapec, where he "encountered a strong Mexican force, which exchanged shots, and withdrew." Lee and his escort captured five prisoners, and Lee took the opportunity of climbing to the top of Zacatapec. From there he was able to see that the enemy was in a strong position on the San Angel road, near the village of Padierna. Lee concluded that if the Mexicans could cross the southwestern part of the lava field by a rough "mule path," then the Americans could surely cross it in the opposite direction, and attack the Mexican position from the rear. He returned to San Augustin to report his findings to Scott.

Scott, as was his custom, held a council of war, heard out all his commanders, and then decided in favor of Lee's suggestion: Lee was to lead a force of pioneers with picks and shovels over the Pedregal to make the path suitable for the artillery. By the afternoon of August 19, Lee had extended the track as far as he could—his pioneers were coming under fire from the Mexican position above the village of Padierna on the San Angel road, which was believed to consist of about 5,000 men and over twenty guns, and assumed to be under the command of General Gabriel Valencia, one of Santa Anna's better commanders. Again serving as a kind of trailblazer, Lee crossed the Pedregal; found General Twiggs; with Twiggs's consent, led one regiment of Twiggs's division forward to drive off the enemy; and then picked a site—on rising ground near the edge of a ravine, and less than thirty yards from the Mexicans—for several batteries of American artillery, one of them commanded by Lieutenant Thomas J. Jackson, who would become famous as "Stonewall"

Jackson. Lee stayed with the artillery during a heavy exchange of gunfire, in the course of which the officer standing beside him, the nephew of Lee's old friend Joe Johnston, lost a leg and shortly afterward died of his wound.

This was, in Nelson's famous words, "warm work," in the course of which Lee had plenty of opportunity to demonstrate a steely calmness under fire. Lee's physical bravery and indifference to danger were by no means unusual—indeed these were the basic requirements of military leadership in the age when lying down or taking cover was unthinkable, since troops had to stand upright in their ranks even under the heaviest fire because it was almost impossible to reload a musket with a ramrod nearly four feet long except while standing, while their officers were expected to lead them into attack, sword drawn, on foot or, still more vulnerably, mounted. Throughout Lee's military career his total lack of concern for his own safety—even as a famous general in the Civil War, when mounted on Traveller and wearing his famous pearl-gray hat he was at once instantly recognizable and a perfect target—was remarked on with admiration or horrified concern by very brave men indeed. There are, of course, plenty of men in any army who can "screw [their] courage to the sticking-point," but Lee was not among them—like his father's, his courage was instinctive, unforced, and natural, and it required no effort of will. He seemed to have no fear at all; nor, as was the case with some men, did courage come at the cost of obliterating rational thought. He was among the first to recognize that a frontal attack against the Mexican position would prove impossible because of the ravine in front of it, which could be "swept" by Mexican gunfire, and to suggest instead using a faint track to the north over the Pedregal that would bring American troops down behind Padierna, crossing the San Angel road, and cutting General Valencia off from any retreat to Mexico City.

Unfortunately, as more and more American troops arrived on the scene a confused frontal attack began, which failed just as Lee expected, as a result of old quarrels and rivalries between General Twiggs and General Pillow, neither of whom apparently paid attention to Napoleon's famous maxim, *"Ordre, contre-ordre, désordre."** The attacks against General Valencia's center deteriorated into a bloody stalemate, with small bodies of troops attacking, but no attempt was made to concentrate them for one big attack. Nevertheless, by the afternoon more than 3,000 American troops

---

* "Order, counterorder, disorder."

had crossed the western corner of the Pedregal unseen, thanks to Lee, and were massing half a mile to the north, near the Mexican position around the Indian village of San Geronimo. This area was separated (and concealed) from the left flank of General Valencia's position by a ravine and a hill, covered with corn and thick underbrush.

It was at this point that a large Mexican force, estimated at as many as 8,000 to 12,000 men, was seen descending the San Angel road less than a mile away from San Geronimo—Santa Anna, hearing the noise of battle on his right from the other side of the Pedregal, had marched the bulk of his forces from their position north of San Antonio around the lava field. It was at once clear that the Americans at San Geronimo might be crushed between General Valencia's "earthworks" and Santa Anna's advancing forces. Fortunately night fell, and with it came a violent tropical rainstorm. Even more fortunately for the Americans, Brigadier General Persifor P. Smith, a remarkably steady man, arrived to assume command of the American forces to the west of the Pedregal. Smith was apparently not shaken by the fact that he was surrounded and had fewer than 4,000 troops with which to face the possibility of a combined attack from something between 13,000 and 17,000 men the next day. He summoned Lee, who had scouted the land between San Geronimo and General Valencia's position and "found it unguarded," and decided to ignore the large body of Mexican troops to his north and attack General Valencia's left flank at first light. It would obviously be helpful if the American troops in front of Valencia staged "a strong demonstration in the morning," but Smith had no way of communicating this to them, so Lee volunteered to ride across the Pedregal by night to the hill of Zacatapec, where he expected to find Scott.

Lee set out at eight o'clock, unable "to observe any of the landmarks," and guided only by his excellent sense of direction and by occasional lightning flashes. Before climbing onto the black lava wilderness of the Pedregal, he encountered a large body of American troops searching for the way to reach Smith. He sent one of his escort to show them the quickest route to San Geronimo, then proceeded on across the Pedregal, moving through jagged formations of razor-sharp rocks and waiting for lightning flashes to reveal crevasses, so he could work his way around them. When he finally reached Zacatapec, "drenched and sore," it was only to find that Scott had gone back to San Augustin. Lee did not hesitate—he went on another three miles across the Pedregal; reported to Scott at eleven o'clock; made his way back across the Pedregal in pitch darkness to

Zacatapec; explained Smith's predicament and Scott's orders; guided American troops to the position where he had stood twenty-four hours earlier; and at dawn led with them into heavy enemy fire at the front of General Valencia's position, in a "demonstration" intended to mask Smith's attack. For several minutes men fell all around Lee, as Valencia concentrated his attention on the threat in front of him; then Lee saw Smith's men charging the Mexican force from their undefended rear, bayonets fixed, and in less than seventeen minutes the whole of General Valencia's elaborately dug earthworks was overrun, four Mexican generals and twenty guns were captured, 700 Mexican troops were killed, and 800 were taken prisoner—a victory so quick and unexpected that it shook the confidence of Santa Anna's larger force to the north, which dissolved as the survivors ran back in panic with tales of their defeat.

General Scott hailed Lee's crossing of the Pedregal as "'the greatest feat of physical and moral courage' of the campaign," but Lee's services on the battlefield had hardly begun. Despite Scott's weight and his ponderous manner, the general provided an object lesson in how to follow up a victory quickly. The instant he saw that the Mexicans had been defeated to the west of the Pedregal, Scott withdrew the bulk of his troops to the east and sent them up the Acapulco road to attack San Antonio, while pressing those who remained on the west of the lava field to attack to the north, a well-executed pincer movement carried out despite the exhaustion of the men. He sent Lee on ahead to reconnoiter the road to the north. Lee rode forward and discovered that Santa Anna had abandoned his carefully prepared position at San Antonio and was making a vigorous stand at Churubusco, about two miles north, while most of his disorganized forces retreated into Mexico City. The center of the Mexican position was a heavily fortified convent southwest of the Churubusco canal, protecting a well-planned bridgehead, with a "deep, wet ditch" dug around it, almost like a moat.

Scott decided to attack the Mexican position at once while sending two divisions to attack north of the canal in a flanking movement intended to cut off the enemy's retreat. He instructed Lee, who had ridden ahead and examined the position carefully, to lead the two divisions and select a position for them, despite the fact that Lee was a mere captain of engineers. Lee himself described the action that followed in a letter to Mary: "Discovering a large mass of infantry on the Churubusco bridge, and apprehending a fire from batteries to defend the rear, I drew out towards the City of Mexico until I reached a hamlet on the Mexican road about three fourths of a mile in the rear of the bridge."

There was "a mass" of cavalry on the road, and as the American troops "formed a line" at an oblique angle to the road, the Mexicans pushed their own line farther to their right in order not to be outflanked. "Our troops being now hotly engaged and somewhat pressed," Lee wrote, "I urged forward the Howitzer battery . . . [which] very promptly brought the pieces to bear upon the head of the column with good effect."

Still, the Americans were "greatly outnumbered," so Lee rode back to Scott to ask for reinforcements. He led them back to where the fight was hottest, but owing to the boggy ground they still could not outflank the Mexicans, and there was nothing for it except "a frontal attack on the road," in which Lee took part under constant heavy fire. Just as the Americans reached the road, the troops to the south of the Churubusco canal carried the convent and the bridgehead, and the enemy broke, the survivors retreating to Mexico City. The fight at the fortified convent had been particularly bloody, for it was defended by the 204 remaining members of the "San Patricio (St. Patrick) Battalion," consisting of deserters from the U.S. Army, the bulk of them Irish Catholic immigrants who felt they had been bullied and persecuted because of their religion, and who expected no mercy if they surrendered or were captured. Nor did they receive any: fifty who survived the fierce hand-to-hand fighting inside the convent were hanged, including one who had lost both legs and was carried in a wheelbarrow from his hospital bed to the gallows.

Lee had been on foot or mounted for more than thirty-six hours without rest, had crossed the Pedregal three times, and had fought in three battles. His superiors, in agreement for once about something, joined in praising his "skill . . . and personal daring" (Smith), his "valuable services" (Twiggs), his "skill and judgment" (Shields). Scott added that Lee was "as distinguished for felicitous execution as for science and daring." He would receive a promotion to brevet lieutenant colonel. No other officer in the Mexican War received such universal praise, or won such widespread admiration. The Lee legend began at Churubusco and would carry Lee to the very highest degree of military fame—though not, of course, in a way he could have foretold. In addition, his close relationship with the normally unapproachable general in chief gave him a rare insight into the demands of commanding an army unusual for an officer of his rank.

Despite a succession of victories Scott momentarily hesitated to attack Mexico City. He had lost over 1,000 men, in the past few days of battle, but even though one impetuous American cavalry officer rode all the way to the San Antonio gate, the southernmost of the fortified gatehouses in the city wall (and lost an arm for his pains), Scott did not see how he could take and hold a city of nearly a quarter of a million people with his depleted and exhausted forces. Scott had never believed that the object of his campaign was to take and occupy Mexico City; rather, the object was to force the Mexicans to sign a peace treaty acknowledging the permanent loss of nearly a third of their national territory. When they unexpectedly asked for an armistice a few days after their defeat at Churubusco, Scott was happy enough to agree, believing that it was the first step to peace.

The general made his headquarters at Tacubaya, "a pleasant village where numerous wealthy members of the English colony in Mexico City maintained summer homes," while the negotiators wrangled interminably over the proposed treaty until it became clear after twelve days that no formula could be found that would satisfy President Polk and the Mexican government. Hostilities resumed on September 7. Scott was criticized by many of his own soldiers (and by future historians) for this delay, but they underestimated Scott's losses, as well as the fact that he was now 280 miles from his base, with no reliable means of communication or supply, and above all his belief that his mission was "to conquer a peace."

Lee, who was certainly as close as anyone to the general in chief, did not disagree with him.

The peculiar geography of Mexico City created a unique problem for any attacker. In those days the city itself was "on slightly elevated ground," and surrounded by marshy fields. The only approaches to the capital were along raised, straight, narrow causeways. Advancing along any one of them would put the troops into the position of ducks in a shooting gallery, in addition to exposing them to cross fire from the fortified city gates. The American army was placed so that its most convenient approach to the city was along the three causeways that ran from south to north. The two causeways that approached the city from the southwest and the west posed the further difficulty that they were dominated by a steep hill 220 feet high less than two miles from Scott's headquarters. Once a sacred place for the Aztecs, the hill was topped by a massive "neo-romantic" castle that had been transformed into the Mexican military academy. Approached by a road that zigzagged up a sheer cliff, and surrounded at its base by a high stone wall, Chapultepec looked like a formidable obstacle, which the Mexicans were almost certain to defend with particular zeal because of its symbolic significance.

Before Scott decided on the best way to take Mexico City he determined to attack Molino del Rey, a stout stone building near the base of Chapultepec, where he had been informed that Santa Anna was casting bronze cannons. He wished to have Worth's division make a night attack on it, but after a stormy scene Lee managed to change Scott's mind. The attack began at daylight on September 8, but the result was disappointing. Worth attacked without sufficient artillery preparation; took the building, where there was no evidence of a cannon foundry; and was nearly forced back by a Mexican counterattack, which led to almost 800 American casualties in some of the heaviest fighting of the war. Since the Americans kept the building, they could claim a victory, but it was something of a Pyrrhic one, and a warning that the Mexican army, now that it was literally at the gates of its own capital, could still fight with remarkable bravery.

If nothing else, Molino del Rey underscored the value of Lee's gift for painstaking reconnaissance and his careful siting of artillery before an attack. These gifts were now put to use to find the best way of attacking Mexico City from the south. Accompanied by two other engineering officers, he managed to get "within a mile and a quarter of the city" and observe what the Mexicans were doing to improve defenses. Lee was impressed and became uncharacteristically cautious about the possibility of assaulting Chapultepec, but he was convinced that the city could be taken by well-coordinated attacks from the south. He spent September 9, 10, and 11 in continuous reconnaissance, with almost no rest, looking for the best places to site artillery; but at a "council of war" on the night of September 11 Scott finally decided to attack Chapultepec instead, convinced that a well-conducted artillery bombardment could drive the Mexican defenders out of the fortress, and that once Chapultepec, with its summit overlooking the western wall of the city, was captured, Mexico City would be open to a sustained attack. With American artillery placed on it, the hill would dominate the two western approaches to the city, which was only a mile away. Although all the officers present except Beauregard (and, eventually, Twiggs) supported Lee in arguing against the attack, it is a measure of the respect they had for Scott that they accepted his decision instantly. Here too, Lee learned something: a commanding general should always listen to the opinions of his senior commanders, but once he made up his mind, he had to be obeyed. Like General Scott, whose example he relied on, Lee knew how to cultivate the respect and even the awe of those who disagreed with him. But like Lee's preference for good manners over direct orders, at times this came at a price, as it did for Scott at Molino del Rey, and would for Lee himself at Gettysburg.

Whatever his reservations Lee flung himself into the preparations for the attack on Chapultepec during the next forty-eight hours, exhausting himself in the process. Assisted by Lieutenant George B. McClellan, he placed four batteries of heavy artillery, working so quickly that the first two batteries could open fire in the morning of September 12, less than twenty-four hours after Lee had received his orders. Enormous labor and danger were involved in bringing 8-inch howitzers and 16- and 24-pounder guns across soft, marshy ground and siting them onto platforms that had been dug by pick and shovel to receive them, all of this in full view of the enemy and under constant enemy fire. Once the guns were in place Lee went forward to examine the approaches to Chapultepec more closely. He was so absorbed in his task that General Scott had to send an officer to bring him back to his headquarters in Tacubaya. There, Lee found Scott in a rage. He had not received any reports about the effect the bombardment was having on the Mexicans holding Chapultepec. Scott was determined to attack that evening, and had ordered one division to the west through the dense cypress grove at the foot of Chapultepec, and another to attack from the south, directly up the steep road cut into the cliff face. The volunteers had been formed into two "storming parties," equipped with "scaling" ladders, to lead the assault. It fell to Lee, as the senior engineer officer present, and the one who had ventured closest to Chapultepec, to talk General Scott out of a night attack. Lee was then ordered to brief the commanders who would carry out the attack—one senses the possibility that Scott was under too much nervous strain to do so himself—and during the night the troops moved into their positions west and south of Chapultepec, while others made "an ostentatious demonstration" before the southern gates, intended to fix Santa Anna's attention in the wrong direction.

Lee spent the night inspecting the batteries and making sure that damage caused by Mexican return fire was quickly repaired. By now he had gone forty-eight hours without sleep, but his orders were to guide General Pillow's division in its attack on the western face of Chapultepec. He set out with the leading parties as soon as the bombardment ceased at eight o'clock in the morning on September 13, exposed to artillery fire, musket fire, and—a novelty for the day—buried land mines, most of which fortunately did not go off. He watched while the scaling ladders were brought up, and the storming parties were pushed back with heavy casualties. He regrouped the troops and the second attempt was successful. Lee himself climbed up the steep slope to the terraces at the top, accompanied by Lieutenant James Longstreet, who would be his corps commander on the right on the fatal third day of the battle of Gettysburg; and by Lieutenant George E. Pickett, whose division would make the attack on Cemetery Ridge, the last act in that great, heroic tragedy. At some point in the assault, Lee was "lightly wounded," but he managed to help the wounded General Pillow to safety, then climbed to the summit in time to see the American flag raised. The "fortress" itself turned out not to be as formidable as had been feared. It had been built as a palace, and did not offer much in the way of protection to the Mexican soldiers who took refuge there. The huge building was taken room by room, many of the American soldiers running "wild, looting and hunting down the now defenseless Mexicans in retaliation for the atrocities of Molino del Rey," but knowing what we do about Lee we may be sure that he was among those firmly restoring order and discipline to the troops. Since he never mentioned it, he was probably not a witness to the actions of the fifty to 100 (accounts differ) cadets of the Mexican military academy who became Mexico's famous *Niños Héroes.**

---

* There is a certain degree of skepticism about this story north of the border, but like all patriotic myths it is firmly believed in the country of its origin (think of Barbara Fritchie, for example). There is a huge monument to the six cadets at the entrance to Chapultepec Park, and throughout Mexico there are numerous statues to them and streets named after them.

Six of them fought to their death, and the last boy, Juan Escutia, wrapped himself in the Mexican flag that had flown over Chapultepec and flung himself from the parapet to his death rather than let it fall into the hands of the hated *yanquis*. As Lee watched the Stars and Stripes raised over Chapultepec to replace the Mexican flag, the fifty captured soldiers of the St. Patrick Battalion of deserters who had been condemned to death were hanged, after waiting for two hours in the sun, a noose around each neck, as the battle was fought. Thirty of them were hanged in full view of the battle, each of them standing in the back of a mule-drawn cart, hands tied behind them, the noose already fastened to the immensely long crosspiece of a huge mass gallows built for the purpose on a low hilltop facing the fortress. At the moment when the American flag was raised above a cloud of black smoke around Chapultepec, teamsters whipped the mules, and the deserters dropped to their death amid the sound of cheering from their former comrades in arms.

Despite numerous conventional patriotic paintings of the assault on Chapultepec, there is a certain Goyaesque horror to the entire episode, between the boy soldiers and the hanging of the deserters, not to speak of the bayoneting of Mexican soldiers who were trying to surrender.

It certainly had an effect on the defenders of Mexico City, as Lee, who was by then exhausted and had not even paused to get his wound dressed, instantly realized. With the American victory at Chapultepec, organized Mexican resistance collapsed. He made his way back to Scott, reported the overwhelming success of the attack, carried out yet another reconnaissance of the ground toward the San Cosme gate at the northwestern corner of the city, and returned once more to Scott's side, where, for the first and only time in his life, he fainted. He had been on his feet or in the saddle for three days and nights without rest.

When he came to before dawn, he learned that American troops had already entered the city and seized the citadel, and that Santa Anna had fled. Lee himself entered Mexico City at first light and was watching in the grand plaza as General Scott rode in about eight in the morning in full dress uniform to see the American flag raised over the National Palace. After this Scott reviewed the troops as they presented arms, then dismounted, doffed his plumed hat, and entered the palace.

For two days the American occupiers were forced to fight street battles with armed criminals whom Santa Anna had released from prison. These shots would be the last fired in action that Lee would hear until 1861.

When the Duke of Wellington heard the news of the capture of Mexico City he proclaimed Scott "the greatest living general."

It would take almost a year before the peace was ratified by the American and the Mexican congresses, and celebration of the fact that the United States had been almost doubled in size was muted by endless squabbles between Scott and his generals, and between Scott and President Polk. In the end Polk relieved Scott of his command. Lee never lost confidence in Scott, and complained that the general was "kicked off . . . and turned out as an old horse to die," strong words from Lee. As for Lee's own experiences in Mexico, he remarked that "we bullied [Mexico] . . . for that I ashamed, for she was the weaker party," a point of view shared by many Americans. Indeed, seldom has so great a conquest brought such dire consequences for the victor.

For his part in the assault of Chapultepec, Lee was promoted to brevet colonel, the highest rank he would reach until 1861. More important, he had gained a unique opportunity to learn the art of generalship under the command of an expert, who valued and trusted him at a level far above his rank. Lee had shown himself a master of reconnaissance, and he had learned the value of audacity in warfare and the importance of the bold flank attack, as well as the possibilities of advancing swiftly beyond the conventional lines of communication and "living off the country." Again and again in his "second career" at war, he relied on the lessons he had learned from Scott, and from his own experiences in Mexico.

He also learned much about his own fellow officers that would stand in him in good stead during the Civil War. No fewer than seventy-eight of them would become generals in the Union Army, including Ulysses S. Grant, Winfield Scott Hancock, Joseph Hooker, George Meade, and George McClellan. Fifty-seven of them would become Confederate generals, including Lewis Armistead, P. G. T. Beauregard, Thomas J. ("Stonewall") Jackson, Joseph E. Johnston, James Longstreet, and George Pickett. Hardly any senior officer on either side of the Civil War was a stranger to Lee.

He returned home at last on June 29, 1848, having been away for twenty-two months. With him were his mare Grace Darling and a little white pony he had bought for his youngest boy. He had earned a reputation throughout the army, in the words of General Scott, as "the very best soldier that I ever saw in the field."

It would be thirteen years before Lee could put his reputation to the test again on the battlefield.

Chapter 5
A Long Peace—
1848–1860

"I cannot advise him to enter the army. It is a hard life, and he can never rise to any military eminence by serving in [it]."

—Robert E. Lee to a friend
about his son, May 1856

It is only in fiction that soldiers miss war. Professional soldiers appreciate the fact that the risks of war are balanced out for them by the opportunity for more rapid promotion, but nobody who has made a career of the military relishes being shot at, blown up, or disabled. Lee had the kind of cold courage that every soldier envies, but much as he chafed, over the next thirteen years of peacetime, at his lack of promotion and at the poor pay, he never had any desire to repeat his experience under fire in Mexico City. Far from finding life at home unexciting, Lee was essentially the most domesticated of men, one who hated being separated from his wife, his children, his beloved Virginia, and the great house at Arlington that had become his home. When duty called, he obeyed, but his letters home make it clear that every day away from his family pained him.

It would be hard to find a man less suited to the frequent separations of a military career than Lee, unless it was another West Pointer and Mexican War veteran, Captain Ulysses S. Grant, who reacted to the sheer monotony of life on distant infantry posts far away from his beloved wife Julia by taking to drink, then resigning from the army. Lee, by comparison, had not only the advantage of being a well-connected brevet colonel, but also that of being an engineer, so he was never short of new challenges. The army was still maintaining and enlarging the system of fortresses intended to protect the United States from an unlikely repetition of the War of 1812.

Lee's arrival home at Arlington had been eagerly awaited by his family, but like many another veteran he arrived unexpectedly, having missed the carriage that was sent for him. The family dog Spec, "a black and tan terrier," was the first to recognize him; then Lee plunged into the hallway full of children, and picked up and kissed the wrong one, a friend of his son Robert's. Oddly enough the first memory Robert E. Lee Jr., then five years old, had of his father was this slightly embarrassing event. Years later, he wrote, "After a moment's greeting to those surrounding him, my father pushed through the crowd, exclaiming: 'Where is my little boy?' He then took up in his arms and kissed—not me, his own child in his best frock with clean face and well-arranged curls—but my little playmate Armistead! I remember nothing more of any circumstances connected with that time, save that I was shocked and humiliated." No doubt Robert soon got over it, for a few days later Lee took him to Baltimore on a visit to Mrs. Marshall (Lee's sister), then "down to the wharves" to watch the pony he had bought for the boy in Mexico being unloaded: it was "pure white, five years old and about fourteen hands high," and had been named Santa Anna. Santa Anna and Robert quickly became inseparable companions. The faithful Jim Connally soon arrived with Lee's mare Grace Darling—Lee had taken a longer, slower journey home, up the Mississippi from New Orleans to Wheeling, in order to spare the horse "as much annoyance and fatigue as possible, she already having undergone so much suffering in my service." Lee now began every day that he was home by going to visit Grace Darling in her stall, "always petting her and talking to her in a loving way."

Robert soon came to appreciate that his father was different from other men, and not just in his love of animals. "From that early time," he wrote, "I began to be impressed with my father's character. . . . Every member of the household respected, revered and loved him as a matter of course, but it began to dawn on me that every one else with whom I was thrown held him in high regard. At forty-five years in age he was active, strong, and as handsome as he had ever been. . . . He was always bright and gay with us little folk, romping, playing, and joking with us. Although he was so joyous and familiar with us . . . I always knew it was impossible to disobey my father. I felt it in me, I never thought why, but was perfectly sure that when he gave an order it had to be obeyed. . . . When he and mother went out in the evening . . . we were often allowed to sit up and see them off; my father, as I remember, always in full uniform, always ready and waiting for my mother, who was general late. He would chide her gently, in a playful way and with a bright smile . . . and I would go to sleep with this beautiful picture in my mind, the golden epaulets and all."

Of course it is by no means uncommon for children to idolize their father, but when Robert wrote this he was a middle-aged man and a former Confederate captain, whose father, ironically, had failed to recognize him on a second occasion, this time during the Battle of Antietam (or Sharpsburg) in 1862. Lee, then commanding general of the Army of Northern Virginia, had ridden up to a battery that had been "severely handled, losing many men and horses," and ordered its captain to take the uninjured men and remaining guns back to the front immediately, without realizing that one of the battle-weary artillery privates standing there was his own son Robert.

The picture of family life summoned up by Robert is vouched for by all the other members of the Lee family, as well as by innumerable people who knew the Lees. Lee, punctual to a fault, is always standing there restlessly; Mary, always late and, despite the help of devoted maids, is slightly disheveled and missing some article that will cause a further delay while somebody goes back to find it. Their lives revolved around their children to a degree that seems very modern— for in the late eighteenth century and through most of the nineteenth children, however loved they might be, were not the central focus of family life that they became in America in the twentieth century. On the frontier and among the poor, the rate of death among infants and small children made mothers hesitate to become too attached to them when they were small, and among the wealthy children were kept out of sight in the nursery, in the care of a nanny. (Lee's son Robert mentions his "mammy" Eliza, a Lee family slave, as a major figure in his childhood.) The Lees, to the contrary, seemed to have lived constantly surrounded by their seven children, totally absorbed in their upbringing, their games, and their education.

When Lee returned home after nearly two years away at war his oldest boy, George, known in the family as "Boo," was sixteen; his daughter Mary was thirteen; his son William, "Rooney," was eleven; Anne, "Annie," was nine; Eleanor Agnes was seven; Robert, "Rob," five; and Mildred, usually referred to by her parents as "Milly" or "Precious Life," was two—a large family even by early Victorian standards. Lee, whose need to direct and instruct people was in any case highly developed, took fatherhood more seriously than anything else in his busy life, and his letters to his wife, Mary, when he was away from home are full of detailed good advice about bringing up the children, much of which she ignored. The letters he sent to the children themselves as soon as they could read were also filled with good advice.

Photographic portraits taken of Lee during this period of his life show him looking remarkably young for a man of forty, and as handsome as ever—the white-haired patriarch was over a decade away.

To modern readers Lee's letters to his family may seem exaggeratedly pious—he is constantly thanking God or leaving matters large and small in God's hands—but it is important to recognize the depth, sincerity, and importance of Lee's religious belief. It was not an affectation, or a question of style, or an attempt to enforce piety on his children or others; it was a reality at the very core of his being. When he writes to Mary, "I pray God to watch over and direct our efforts in guarding our dear little son," or to one of his children, "Be true, kind and generous, and pray earnestly to God to enable you to keep His Commandments 'and walk in the same all the days of your life,'" or to his soldiers, "I earnestly pray that a merciful God will extend to you His blessing and protection," these are not mere phrases. They mean exactly what Lee wrote. Although the form of his religious observance changed as he grew older, it remained a constant throughout his life.*

Because of this, Lee is often accused of "fatalism," but that implies a certain lack of control over events, or a lack of effort, or at least indifference to outcomes of things, and these attitudes were entirely foreign to Lee's

---

*The best and most concise analysis that I have read of Lee's religious belief is in Elizabeth Brown Pryor's *Reading the Man,* chap. 14.

character. He was neither passive nor resigned—in everything large or small he demanded of himself the maximum of effort and attention to detail—but as he matured he became more and more convinced that the final arbiter in all matters was the Lord, and this conviction runs like an unself-conscious litany through his letters, and even in his conversations on the battlefield with his generals.

As a boy, and throughout his adult life, he was a devout Episcopalian—Episcopalianism was the "established" church of Virginia—and always punctilious about attending service; but his lifetime almost exactly coincided with the Christian revival movement that began around 1800 and peaked around 1870, the year of his death. Central to this rapidly spreading movement was the individual's personal relationship with God, and his willingness to be "born again." Lee himself moved, by slow and painful steps, toward a form of what we would now call fundamental Christianity, though still within the shelter of the Episcopalian Church, which was undergoing its own revolution.

He was influenced by the prayers and exhortations of his wife and her mother, Mary Fitzhugh Custis, both of whom were passionate converts to evangelical Christianity: Arlington was a house in which "prayers were said morning and evening," and religion was a constant subject of discussion between mother and daughter, despite the old-fashioned deism and world-liness of George Washington Custis, a pleasure-loving and self-indulgent figure straight out of the eighteenth century, for whom piety was never a guiding interest, but who knew better than to interfere with or question the religious enthusiasm of his wife and daughter so long as he was left in peace to follow his own pursuits and interests without criticism or interference. Much as Lee admired his father-in-law—a sentiment that was by no means universally shared—and appreciated the connection to George Washington that Mr. Custis represented, he was much more strongly influenced by his mother-in-law, and of course his wife, for both of whom the saving of Lee's soul by conversion to evangelicalism was a first priority (they had apparently given up on Mr. Custis).

Lee's personality was complex—he was determined to avoid the all too public mistakes of his father, but still strove to equal Light-Horse Harry Lee's military exploits. Coming from a family in which there was no shortage of scandal, he set himself unusually high standards of behavior and almost always met or exceeded them. A perfectionist, obsessed by duty and by the value of obedience, he might been a grim figure, except for the fact that he had another side, charming, funny, and flirtatious. The animal lover, the gifted watercolorist, the talented cartographer—the topographic maps he drew for the Corps of Engineers are works of art, as are the cartoons he drew for his children in Mexico. The father who adored having his children get into bed with him in the morning, and telling them stories, or having them tickle his feet; the adoring husband; the devoted friend—these are all facets of the same man. He was the product of a rationalist education and at the same time a romantic, who sought for a spiritual answer to the problems of life—a man of contradictions, whose natural good manners and courtly bearing disguised his lifelong soul-searching.

Lee's enduring status as a noble, tragic figure, indeed one whose bearing and dignity conferred nobility on the cause for which he fought and still does confer it in the minds of many people, sometimes prevents us from appreciating the degree to which Lee enjoyed life, or from understanding the genuine joy that accompanied his final, wholehearted surrender to the evangelical beliefs of his wife and mother-in-law. In a very real sense he *accepted* the Lord, and that acceptance guided his actions in the years to come. He sought, always, to do his duty, to guide others into doing the same, and to submit humbly to God's will.

Hardly any two things are harder to reconcile than deep Christian belief and skilled generalship. It is even more difficult to combine the role of a heroic leader with deep humility, but Lee did so. It is hard indeed for a man commanding up to 100,000 soldiers in battle to be modest. The massed, obedient, admiring ranks; the battle flags waving in the wind; the knowledge that most if not all of these men are willing, even eager, to follow your orders to their death, has bred vanity, arrogance, pride, and hubris in great generals throughout history, but Lee excluded such feelings entirely. In victory and in defeat alike he retained his composure, his dignity, his self-control, his modesty, and his prayerful hope that he was fulfilling God's will. Throughout the Civil War he did not even have the conviction that slavery and secession were necessarily worth fighting for. To paraphrase Grant, nobody ever fought "so long and so valiantly . . . for a cause"* as Lee—and for one in which he did not totally believe. In that sense he was indeed a martyr to his cause. Lee not only bore this burden uncomplainingly; he struggled mightily throughout his life to remind himself of his own imperfections and shortcomings—he would have had no need

---

* "I felt like anything rather than rejoicing at the downfall of a foe who has fought so long and valiantly, and had suffered so much for a cause, though that cause was, I believe, one of the worst for which a people ever fought, and one for which there is the least excuse" (Ulysses S. Grant on Appomattox, *Memoirs*).

of the slave whose task it was to stand beside a victorious Roman general in his chariot and whisper into his
ear during his triumph: *Sic transit gloria mundi.*

Lee's concern with behaving in a gentlemanly way
to everyone, regardless of rank; his dislike of open
confrontations; and his instinctive tact, which never
deserted him, even in moments of crisis, made him
almost universally admired, but not always an effective commander. He worked best with those who could
guess what he wanted them to do without being told,
and for whom even the slightest frown of displeasure or
the faint flush on Lee's cheeks that signified he was sup-
pressing his anger was recognized instantly as a rebuke.
He could be tough—when the brash young Union cavalry commander George A. Custer proposed to execute
Confederate prisoners Lee simply ordered that a Union
prisoner be hanged for every Confederate who was
executed.* He also had no hesitation in having his own
soldiers executed for disobeying his order to respect
enemy property, or for desertion. But he never used
harsh words, and he went to great lengths to avoid an
angry "scene," so much so that his aides were charged
with keeping those who might stage one away from Lee.

---

* "I have directed Colonel Mosby, through his adjutant, to hang an equal number
of Custer's men in retaliation for those executed by him" (Lee, quoted, in *Southern
Historical Society Papers*, Vol. 27, 317).

This is not to suggest that Lee was perfect, but he aimed at perfection at all times, even under extreme provocation. He *felt* anger, certainly, and those who were close to him recognized the warning signs: "No man," his aide Colonel Venable wrote, "could see the flush come over that grand forehead and the temple veins swell on occasions of great trial of patience and doubt that Lee had the strong, high temper of a Washington." He set himself to control it, however, at whatever cost to himself. His generosity of spirit, undiminished by ideological or political differences, and even by the divisive, bloody Civil War, shines through in every letter he writes, and in every conversation of his that was reported or remembered.

His willingness to take on tasks that did not promise much in the way of a reward and his good nature were both sorely tried by his return home in the summer of 1848. It was one thing to write long letters of advice from Mexico to Mary and the older children, and quite another to resume the role of paterfamilias and husband under the same roof. "Lee not only loved his children, but enjoyed them" is a very true observation, but he was also a tireless fount of advice and religious exhortation who, at least in writing, sounds to the modern ear a bit like a latter-day

Polonius, a failing that Lee himself recognized and occasionally made fun of: "You see I am following my old habit of giving advice, which I daresay you neither need nor require," he wrote to one of his sons, and then went on to add in self-justification, "But you must pardon a fault which proceeds from my great love and burning anxiety for your welfare and happiness. When I think of your youth, impulsiveness, and many temptations, your distance from me, and the ease (and even innocence) with which you might take an erroneous course, my heart quails within me, and my whole frame and being trembles at the possible result. May Almighty God have you in his holy keeping."

"My heart quails within me" is a wonderful phrase; it might seem quaint or forced coming from most other men, but in Lee one senses the depth and sincerity of his concern, a "devoted tenderness" that is unmistakable. Nobody could have worked harder to set his children a good example, or to judge their actions with more unflinching, if tactful, attention, but with never a trace of anger. Lee's boys seem to have benefited from this torrent of advice and care, and far from resenting it, took it as a sign of their father's love for them. About his daughters, it is harder to judge, but Lee's devotion to them and his good humor regarding their occasional failures to live up to his expectations were never in doubt.

As a forty-year-old father of four daughters, with three sons to educate, and without a home to call his own, Lee worried ceaselessly about money, and was enormously careful and exact about it, "frugal and thrifty in the little affairs of daily life," parsimonious in what he spent on himself, but always generous with others. "The necessity I daily have for money," as he put it, haunted him—he had no "family fortune" or estates to draw on, and it cannot have escaped his attention that although his father-in-law possessed three great houses in Virginia—Arlington, White House plantation in New Kent County, and Romancock in King William County—among them adding up to a total of over 13,000 acres of land and almost 200 slaves, Mr. Custis's attention was fixed on his attempts to be a painter and a successful playwright, and on his view of himself as the keeper of George Washington's flame, rather than on managing his estates productively. His life was not unlike that of many of the aristocratic Russian landowners, improvident, pleasure-loving, dreaming about utopian schemes while their serfs mismanaged their estates.* Self-indulgence was Custis's

---

*There is even a word for it in Russian, *khalatnost*, the ability to sit around all day in a dressing gown thinking vaguely about grand schemes while everything falls to wrack and ruin around one's head—named after the lifestyle of the ineffectual, daydreaming hero of Ivan Goncharov's novel *Oblomov*, who fritters away his life and fortune doing exactly that.

besetting sin. Unlike his son-in-law, he was more interested in spending money than earning it; his agricultural interests were more in the nature of a gentleman's
hobby than a business, and he begrudged neither his
wife and daughter nor himself anything in the way of
luxuries and adornments, while the houses went unre-
paired, the land was poorly farmed, and the slaves were
shiftless and—in the opinion of many of Mr. Custis's
neighbors—pampered and overindulged. Lee did not
expect, nor would he have accepted, financial support
from his father-in-law, but he was too shrewd not to be
at least partially aware that when Mary Lee and their
sons eventually inherited the Custis estate it would
bring them problems and debts rather than a fortune.

Lee's duties at the War Department through the
summer of 1848 consisted of completing the maps
he had begun in Mexico, slow, painstaking work.
He was reappointed as a member of the board of
engineers for the Atlantic coast defenses. Later he
would rather dourly say that the work reacquainted
him with "the routine of duty." Still, it had its advantages: he could live at Arlington, and being at the hub
of things he was "in contact with the high officials of
the Government." Lee scrupulously refrained from
any attempt to lobby on his own behalf; most people
meeting him were favorably impressed by his soldierly

bearing and, more important, by his professional competence. In September, he was assigned to oversee the construction of a new fort that was intended to defend Baltimore, as a kind of support to the venerable Fort McHenry. Lee was sent to Boston for a meeting of the board of engineers and then on to Florida with a view to building further fortifications—a long and difficult journey in those days. The Corps of Engineers and Congress were still acting on the assumption that Great Britain would continue to be the enemy to worry about. Whatever Lee thought of that, he was once again involved in building stone-and-mortar fortresses. This expertise, together with the gift he had shown for rapidly building "earthworks"—well-designed trench systems and carefully sited, dug-in artillery batteries—would turn out to be a substantial element of his military genius: his experience as an engineer would save Richmond in 1862 and extend the Civil War by over a year in 1864 and 1865. Lee would prove to be one of the great masters of earthworks in the history of warfare; his experience in Mexico had shown him time and again and that the pick, the shovel, and the sandbag were as important in battle as the musket and the bayonet. Unfortunately, the Corps of Engineers remained wedded to the construction of fortresses, so Lee took up his new position in April 1849, and made preparations to move his family to a rented house in Baltimore while he spent his days examining the shoals and mudflats around Sollers Point and Hawkins Point, halfway between Baltimore and the Patapsco River. He commuted there every morning in a boat rowed by two oarsmen, had his dinner (what we would now call lunch) in a house on Sollers Point, and in the evening was rowed back to the nearby mainland, now an area of hazardous-waste landfills and industrial pollution aptly named Quarantine Road, which was then known chiefly for its thriving mosquito population.

Not surprisingly, Lee "came down with a fever," very likely malaria, and it was not until the autumn that he was back at work. As usual, his work progressed rapidly and efficiently, as piles were purchased and driven and wharves completed in the first stage of construction. Lee's orderly career was briefly interrupted by a most unusual opportunity. "The Cuban revolutionary junta in New York" had been preparing for yet another attempt to free Cuba from Spanish rule, and had been shopping for an experienced American military leader to command it. The Cubans had offered the job to General Worth, but he died before making his decision; they then offered it to Senator Jefferson Davis of Mississippi, a West Point graduate, chairman of the Senate committee on military affairs, and of course the future president of the Confederacy. Senator Davis declined the honor, but recommended Lee.

The cause of Cuban independence from Spain was a popular one in the United States, particularly among southerners, many of whom dreamed of expanding slavery into the Caribbean, and anticipated annexing Cuba as a slave territory, perhaps eventually as a slave state—which in view of its climate, its agricultural wealth, and its mixture of races was by no means an impossible ambition, though not one for which Lee would have had any sympathy. He was not an opponent of slavery, but like many of the founding fathers he hoped to see it gradually removed in God's good time—possibly by God's intervention—and he was firmly opposed to expanding it. Lee's personal experience with slavery was such as to lead him to the conclusion that there were already too many slaves in the South, not that more were needed.

Daily labor overseeing the driving of piles and pouring of tons of concrete may have made the prospect of leading an army of insurgents against the Spanish crown seem attractive, however. He was tempted enough to meet with members of the junta in Baltimore, but in the end, Lee declined on a point of personal honor: whether it was proper for a commissioned officer of the United States to accept an offer of command from the representatives of a foreign power—or in this case, from rebels against a foreign power. Not for the last time in their relationship, Davis and Lee disagreed in a gentlemanly way; Davis felt that Lee should accept the offer, but Lee would not go without full assurance that the army would not object, and that Davis could not give him. Lee was right about army regulations, though it is ironic that when he became a general thirteen years later, the same issue would be raised. He would have to resign his commission in the U.S. Army to accept command of the Virginia state forces. It is hard to imagine Lee leading a colorful army of Cuban insurgents, or playing a role as a kind of freebooting military adventurer, and Freeman speculates that if Lee had gone to Cuba he might have ended his life before a Spanish firing squad as a *yanqui* filibuster, for the expedition eventually failed; of course it is also possible that Lee's expertise might have crowned the expedition with success, but either way his strict sense of duty prevented him from taking part in an exotic, if doomed, uprising, and he does not appear to have had any regrets about it.

Those who write about Lee as a strategist often point out that in the Mexican War he had had no field experience of modern weapons or technology—for example, the replacement of the smoothbore musket by the rifle, which increased the killing range of the standard infantry weapon from 50 yards to 400 or 500 yards; or the huge changes in logistics and tactics brought about by the railway—but to portray him as opposed to or unknowledgeable about what we would now call technology is to underrate him. He helped to design and install on the unpromising Sollers Point flats a steam pile driver, as well as a steam-driven saw, a dredge, a crane, and even a diving bell that permitted his workers to excavate deep underwater. His mastery of modern machines allowed him to complete the first phase of the foundations of what would become Fort Carroll on the site in only a year. (It is useful to remember that Lee's connection with the Revolutionary War made it seem nearer to him than to most men—Charles Carroll of Carrolltown, in whose honor the fortress would be named, not only had known Lee's father, but had been the last surviving signer of the Declaration of Independence.)* Lee's interest in science and mechanics continued throughout his life. There was hardly anybody in the U.S. Army who knew more about artillery, particularly how to site it in the most scientific way, or who had more experience with and enthusiasm for the changes that steamboats and railroads had brought

---

* Carroll died in 1832 at the age of ninety-five.

about. Although his bearing and manner seemed to be of the late eighteenth century, his feet were firmly planted in the nineteenth.

As work on the fort proceeded, the Lee family settled into their new home. As usual, Mary had fought a skillful, but ultimately futile, delaying action against leaving Arlington. Lee, in his gentle, tactful way, won her over by urging on her the need for the children not to start the new school year in Baltimore late. "We must not for our own pleasure lose sight of the interest of our children," he wrote, seizing the moral high ground that was his weapon of choice in persuading Mary to do something she didn't want to. Baltimore was full of Lee and Custis connections, beginning with Lee's sister Anne Marshall; and it was hardly more than fifty miles from Arlington, so this cannot have seemed like a major move, even to Mary. The Lees participated in the busy social life of the city, which may have been some compensation to Mary for the move, and Lee himself was a man who enjoyed good company and was considered a lively guest. Indeed his youngest son, Robert, remembered most of all his father's "bright smile" and "playful way," and remarked on the fact that he was "a great favorite in Baltimore, as he was everywhere, especially with ladies and little children."

The children settled into their new schools with few crises—the only one missing was Custis, the oldest son, who had followed his father's footsteps to become a cadet at West Point, and whose academic career there Lee followed earnestly. Lee had in fact gone to a good deal of trouble to secure Custis "an appointment 'at large' at the Military Academy," demonstrating that he was willing to lobby on behalf of his children, though he would not do so for himself. Here, at last, was an area in which his advice went beyond the moral to the practical. If there was one thing Lee knew about it was life in the "thin gray line," and the temptations and pitfalls facing a cadet. When he detected in Custis a tendency toward indolence, he was at pains to correct it by numerous letters.

Lee had delivered Custis to West Point, and had been relieved that his son did not find it "the dreadful place it had been represented to be." He was pleased that the boy fitted in well and made friends quickly. At first his grades caused concern, but after energetic prodding from his father they improved, and Lee gave a sigh of relief. "Your letter . . . ," he wrote, "has given me more pleasure than any I now recollect having ever received. It has assured me of the confidence you feel in my love and affection, and that with frankness and candor you open to me all your thoughts. . . . I cannot express my pleasure at hearing you declare your determination to shake off the listless fit that has seized you, and arouse all your faculties into activity and exertion. . . . I do not think you lack either energy or ambition. Hitherto you have not felt the incentive to call them forth."

The relief on Lee's part turned out to be premature, for shortly afterward liquor was discovered in Custis's room during an inspection. This was a serious violation of the rules, and although Custis and his roommates denied having any knowledge of how the liquor got there, they were all put under arrest. Lee was, not surprisingly, "deeply humiliated . . . and distressed," but there were apparently strong reasons for supposing that Custis and his roommates were innocent, so much so that their entire class came to their support, leading one to conclude that somebody other than the inhabitants of the room had placed the liquor there and that the cadets knew who it was. The superintendent of the academy contented himself with giving Custis eight demerits, the equivalent of a slap on the wrist.

Lee wrote to his son, "Dearest Mr. Boo," with evident pleasure when he learned the news: "I was delighted at the contradiction in your last letter of that *slanderous* report against the room of those fine cadets Lee, Wood & Turnbull. . . . I trust there will be no cause for even suspicions in future. . . . Your letter also did me good in other respects. It talked of being on the Colour Guard, of being relieved from Post, of taking your ease in your own tent [cadets moved into tents during the summer]. . . . It assured me of your being released from arrest, of being on duty again, of coming right up to the mark, of no discouragement, no abatement in exertion, or relaxation in will. In short, of standing up to the rack, fodder or no fodder. . . .* Think always of your devoted father."

Lee's touching concern for Custis, reawakening as it must have done his own years at West Point and the immense pressures that any first-year cadet must feel bearing down on him—pressure to conform, pressure to compete, pressure to succeed, pressure to resist even the most innocent of temptations—and Lee's belief that he "could meet with calmness and unconcern all else the world may have in store" for him, so long as his children were good and happy, make him seem at once a more vulnerable and more lovable person than the stern, melancholy figure usually portrayed. At times he can seem positively Dickensian,† as when he writes of a family Christmas. He, Mary, and the children always

---

* This was an American expression of the time, meaning "to make a decision to do one thing or another, to stop dithering, to do one's duty" (Jonathan Green, *Cassell's Dictionary of Slang*). It also appears to have been a favorite of Davy Crockett's (*An Account of Col. Davy Crockett's Tour of the North and Down East*, 1835, 137).

† It was only ten years since Dickens's first visit to the United States as a star of the lecture circuit, during which he caused a sensation by openly condemning slavery.

tried to spend Christmas with Mr. and Mrs. Custis at Arlington, and in this case Lee says, "We came home on a Wednesday morning. . . . The children were delighted at getting back [from Baltimore], and passed the evening at devising pleasure for the morrow. They were in upon us before day on Christmas morning, to overhaul their stockings. Mildred thinks she drew a prize in the shape of a beautiful new doll; Angelina's infirmities [Angelina was Mildred's doll] were so great that she was left in Baltimore and this new treasure was entirely unexpected. The cakes, candies, books, etc., were entirely overlooked in the caresses she bestowed upon her. . . . Rooney got among his gifts a new pair of boots, which he particularly wanted, and the girls, I hope, were equally pleased with their presents, books and trinkets. . . . Your mother, Mary, Rooney, and I went into church, and Rooney and the twins [visitors] skated back on the canal, Rooney having taken his skates along for that purpose. . . . I need not describe for you our amusements . . . nor the turkey, cold ham, puddings, mince pies, etc., at dinner."

Lee's joy at being surrounded by his family more than compensates for his constant exhortations and detailed advice to even the youngest members—for he fussed and prodded, and in an age when a girl's education did not seem to most parents as important as a boy's, he urged his girls to excel at their studies with as much firmness as he urged Custis at West Point.

In the meantime, progress on Fort Carroll was slowing. Congress was reluctant to provide the funds, and adjourned in March 1851 without having made any appropriation for continuing the work. As Lee's chief, Brigadier General Totten, commented, "Nothing was needed to assure rapid . . . progress except regular appropriations," but these were not forthcoming, perhaps because Totten's political antennae were not as sensitive as his predecessor's had been, or perhaps because nobody in Congress took seriously the possibility of a renewed British descent on Baltimore. It may have pained Lee, as an engineer, that he was never in a position to see any of the huge projects for which he was responsible fully completed—he had been moved on before his work on Cockspur Island, at Saint Louis, or in New York Harbor was at all near to being finished—but in the spring of 1852, as he was busy driving piles and laying concrete, he received a letter from Brigadier General Totten assigning him to take command as superintendent of the U.S. Military Academy.* On the face of it, there was everything to be said in favor of

---

*In those days superintendents of the U.S. Military Academy were normally chosen from the Corps of Engineers, since so much of the curriculum was technical and scientific, and the highest-ranking cadets invariably chose to serve in the Corps of Engineers after being graduated.

this appointment, except for the problem that it would place Mary Lee at a far greater distance from her parents and her home at Arlington. The superintendency of the academy was a prestigious post, and very much in the public eye; it carried with it a "handsome house," a full staff, and direct access to the War Department; in addition, it would bring Lee's whole family together in one place, since Custis was still a cadet.

Given the care with which Lee oversaw his own children's education, it is surprising that he was not "pleased." Freeman attributes this entirely to Lee's modesty and his belief that "he lacked the experience for the position." True, Lee constantly responded to any form of promotion over the years by protesting that he wished an "abler man" had been chosen for it; this may have been modesty, or simply a polite formula, but it is also possible to guess that Mary Lee's reluctance to exchange Virginia and Maryland for three or four years in the lower Hudson valley may have played a significant part in Lee's attempt to decline the honor. An indication that this was more than a mild, formal protestation is that Lee responded to the letter the same day it was received—there was apparently no soul-searching involved. By Lee's standards, his reply to General Totten was brief and to the point: "I learn with much regret the determination of the Secretary of

War to assign me to that duty, and I fear I cannot realize his expectations in the management of an Institution requiring more skill and experience than I command."

Interestingly, having gone as far as he could in declining the appointment, Lee does not appear to have followed up by going to Washington and paying a call on his old comrade in arms from the Mexican War to argue his case for choosing someone else; after all, Totten admired and liked Lee, and Washington is only thirty-nine miles from Baltimore, even in those days not more than an hour away by train ("the cars" as they were called then). The answer is probably that Lee, with his innate sense of duty and obedience, was willing to write a formal letter objecting to the appointment, but no more willing to lobby to remain in his present post than he was to lobby for a promotion.

Lee had to wait only ten days for a terse reply that "his letter had been received and the chief engineer had to decline to change the assignment," a sign that Totten knew he had picked the best man for the job. Once Lee received the letter, he settled down to the task of drawing up his accounts and passing on to his assistant all his papers regarding Fort Carroll. He continued to point out to friends that he did not feel he was up to the task, but he was resigned to its inevitability. Since the fort was still not completed by the time the Civil War broke out, Lee was perhaps fortunate to be removed from what can only be seen as a dead-end job, and it may well be that he gave it up without regret—certainly he expressed none. On the other hand, he was going from the routine of overseeing a construction project, however ambitious, to what we would now call a high-profile role, in command of several hundred cadets and a large army establishment, for West Point then as now was a hallowed institution. It was also a post that called for an extraordinary degree of tact, both with parents and with politicians, since each cadet had been "sponsored" by a congressman or senator from his home state, and no parents wanted to learn that their boy was falling behind in his studies or was about to be dismissed for accumulating too many demerits.

The West Point to which Lee was returning was much bigger than it had been when he himself was a cadet—West Point's history is one of constant growth and improvement, and the years between 1829 and 1852 were no exception—but at its core it was still governed by the regulations and the inflexible honor code laid down by Colonel Sylvanus Thayer during his years as superintendent. These Lee knew by heart, and—more important—he accepted them without reservations. Hard as it might sometimes be for Lee to enforce Thayer's regulations, he had no doubts about their importance, or about the need for cadets to practice complete and willing obedience to them in every detail.

The duties of the superintendent were equally exacting and inflexible. Even the smallest and least important of decisions required a mountain of correspondence, most of it directed to the chief of the Corps of Engineers, if it involved a cadet; or to the secretary of war, if it involved a matter of policy. Even a cadet's request "to receive a packet of socks from home" had to make its way up the chain of command to Lee's desk, then be sent on to the chief engineer in Washington for his approval or disapproval, with Lee's signed recommendation attached. The sheer volume of paperwork made even Lee sigh.

Lee arrived at West Point in August 1852 alone, and although Mary took her time before joining him there—as every biographer of Lee notes with implied criticism—it does not seem unreasonable for him to have spent some time going over the details of his new command and making sure that everything was in order for her arrival. It was no small move. Mary arrived with four of their children—Mary, Rooney, Rob, and Mildred, respectively seventeen, fifteen, nine, and six years old— while Anne, thirteen, and Agnes, eleven, remained at

Arlington with their grandparents, under the care of a governess. Their daughter Mary was entered in a boarding school in Westchester, while Rooney was placed in one in New York City, but moving the others, together with all their belongings, from Virginia to a new home that Mary Lee had never seen cannot have been an easy undertaking for a woman who was accustomed to being surrounded by familiar servants. The family's horses, as well as all their furniture, soon arrived, and judging from Rob's description, the superintendent's quarters (now known as Quarters 100, on Jefferson Road) were large and comfortable enough to suit Mary. Originally built in 1820 for Colonel Thayer, the house was a substantial two-story brick edifice, painted white, with four chimneys each topped by a chimney cap in the shape of an elaborately worked, ornamental Greek or Roman temple. It provided not only a home for the superintendent but a suitable place to entertain guests. "It was built of stone," Rob wrote, remembering the house years later, "large and roomy, with gardens, stables, and pasture lots. We, the two youngest children, enjoyed it all. 'Grace Darling' and 'Santa Anna' [the pony Lee had bought for Rob in Mexico] were there with us, and many a fine ride did I have with my father in the afternoons, when, released from his office, he would mount his old mare and, with Santa

Anna carrying me by his side, take a five- or ten-mile trot. Though the pony cantered delightfully, he would make me keep him in a trot, saying playfully that the hammering I sustained was good for me. We rode the dragoon-seat,* no posting, and until I became accustomed to it I used to be very tired by the time I got back."

It is typical of Lee to have insisted on a seat that must have been as uncomfortable for the horse as for the rider, and Rob would make the same complaint about having to ride Traveller with a dragoon seat for his father at one point during the Civil War a decade later. There is something endearing in the way that Lee used these father-and-son rides not only to enforce a style of riding that was already old-fashioned but to toughen Rob up.

Lee was a born pedagogue, never happier than when his children were learning to do something the right way. Rob describes how his father went to great trouble to make sure he learned how to skate, to swim, even to sled. When possible he taught the children himself. As soon as each of them was old enough he sent, in his absence, long letters of moral and practical advice.

---

* This is the traditional "heavy cavalry" seat, ridden with long stirrups and straight legs, which can still be observed when the British Household Cavalry (the Life Guards and the Blues & Royals) ride in ceremonies and parades.

A letter he wrote to *"My Precious Annie,"* then four-teen, from West Point, is typical in its combination of jovial good humor and firm instruction: "I am told you are growing very tall, and I hope very straight. I do not know what the cadets will say if the Superintendent's *children* do not practice what he demands of them."

It is a testament to Lee's affection and patience that his children did not rebel; in fact they appear to have thrived. Custis was graduated from the U.S. Military Academy, and Rooney from Harvard; all three of the boys served in the Confederate Army with distinc-tion, two of them as major generals, the youngest rising from the rank of private to that of captain in some of the hardest fighting in the war. Although Lee's biog-raphers tend to avoid Freudian speculation, it is never-theless interesting that none of his four daughters ever married, perhaps because it was hard to find anyone who matched their father's standards, perhaps because he simply remained, by his constant affection, inter-est, and attention in everything they did, the dominant male personality in their lives.

In a perfect world all of this might have made Lee exactly the right man to be superintendent of West Point, but from the beginning he felt himself to be in loco parentis for each of his cadets, and set the same high standards for them that he did for his own children. Every day except Sunday the door to his office was open for one hour from six in the morning until seven, with Lee waiting at his desk in faultless dress uniform for any cadet who had a moral or personal problem to share with him. He may have been unaware that he was an intimidating presence—certainly Lee underestimated the amount of time and emotional energy the problems and tribulations of the cadets would cost a perfectionist like him, and it was about then that his hair started to turn gray, the first step on the path from dashing young officer to careworn patriarch.

The West Point honor code, though it reads simply enough, presented him in real life with a ceaseless stream of baffling moral complexities and seemingly endless hairsplitting that would have tried the patience of a saint. His youngest son, Rob, experienced this on one of his afternoon rides with his father, when they unexpectedly came upon three cadets far beyond where they were allowed to go without permission. The cadets, seeing Lee, leaped over a low wall and vanished into a ravine. "We rode on for a minute in silence," Rob wrote many years later; "then my father said: 'Did you know these young men?'" Before Rob could reply, Lee gently told him not to answer the question: "'But no,'" he said, "'if you did, don't say so.'"

Then, after a moment, " 'I wish boys would do what is right, it would be so much easier for all parties.' "

The code bade cadets not to lie, cheat, or steal, and not to tolerate those who did; but on the other hand it was as firmly ingrained in Lee's mind as in the mind of each of his cadets that a gentleman does not reveal the name of another to the authorities. Lee would of course have to report what he had seen to the commandant of cadets, but since Rob hadn't told him who the cadets were, it would be impossible to punish them. It was, on a small, personal scale, exactly the kind of dilemma that Lee wrestled with every day as superintendent of West Point, with the result that his three years at its head are remembered chiefly because he had to dismiss James McNeill Whistler, who was to become arguably the most important American painter of his time.

"If silicon were a gas I would have been a major general one day," is perhaps one of Whistler's most famous remarks. It refers to the fact that he had failed to answer correctly the first question in a chemistry examination at West Point, and this led to his dismissal by Lee. It is odd that the young Whistler, already a gifted draftsman, a mordant caricaturist, and full-fledged eccentric, should have sought to enter West Point in the first place, or been accepted. Even an admiring commentator describes him as "moody and insolent"—moodiness and insolence are not promising character traits for a cadet—and in addition he was nearsighted, was in poor health, and had a sharp sense of ridicule. He had rejected the idea of becoming a churchman, and apparently faute de mieux decided to become a soldier instead, although he had no interest in military affairs and a poor seat on a horse. It is remarkable that with his long, tousled hair (his nickname at West Point was "Curly") and his sloppy uniform, he managed to survive as a cadet for three years.

Lee's first contact with him was when Whistler requested a special leave to say good-bye to his mother (the model for Whistler's most famous painting),* who was sailing for Europe. Lee seems to have agreed to this request rather reluctantly—possibly Whistler had already attracted negative attention. In any event, Lee felt impelled to write directly to Mrs. Whistler to emphasize the importance of her son's returning to West Point on time. His next contact was after Whistler's mother returned, when the young man was hospitalized with rheumatism, and possibly the symptoms of tuberculosis, and sent home on sick leave. That Lee fussed over each of his cadets like a mother hen is borne out by the number of letters he wrote Mrs. Whistler about

---

* Painted in 1871. The actual title of Whistler's portrait of his mother is *Arrangement in Gray and Black No. 1*, and even today it remains probably the best-known and most popularly admired American painting.

her son's health and the importance of his making up for lost time in his studies—care wasted on Whistler, who returned to the academy after an absence of nearly three months; scraped through with a "1" in drawing but otherwise mediocre grades; and then proceeded to roll up a remarkable quantity of demerits, followed by his famous failure to identify silicon, which resulted in his flunking chemistry and subsequent dismissal.

Whistler appealed to decision, but Lee's letter to General Totten makes it evident that he had made every possible effort to save Whistler, even though he had no reason to expect Whistler's gratitude, or to suppose that anything short of a miracle would turn him into a soldier.

Lee was spared any such trouble from his son Custis, whose record as a cadet, after his initial misstep, was every bit as good as Lee's own. Lee's nephew Fitz Lee, the son of Smith Lee, gave him considerable anxiety, increased of course by Lee's determination to be impartial when it came to his own family. Fitz was a charming, popular, and adventurous young man, and capped a long record of demerits by slipping "out of camp with another cadet about twelve o'clock one night and [not returning] until 2:30." When he was caught and put under arrest, Lee may have wished to spare his brother the disgrace of Fitz's being dismissed, but as usual he was scrupulously fair, and was saved from the necessity of harshness only because Fitz's whole class took the unusual step of offering "a pledge not to commit his offense during the academic year." This, unfortunately, was enough to persuade the secretary of war to pardon Fitz. This somewhat archaic use of the honor code saved young Fitz to serve with credit in the cavalry corps of the Army of Northern Virginia.

All accounts of Lee's three years as superintendent dwell on his constant preoccupation with the moral and academic trials of his cadets—Lee was not a man who would ever fail to get to the bottom of a moral problem, however small or difficult to resolve, and however contradictory the evidence—and of the pain and exhaustion this caused him. But of course as head of the academy he had other concerns: he had to keep a strict accounting of expenses; and he lobbied hard for an appropriation to build a new riding school, drawing up plans for it, based on France's Saumur Cavalry School, founded by Napoleon to perfect French horsemanship,* as well as conducting an army-wide talent search for instructors, improving the officers' housing, building new stables, and acquiring more horses and better saddles.

---

*It still functions today as France's National Equestrian Academy, and it produces the famous Cadre Noir: uniformed dressage riders, similar to those of Vienna's Spanish Riding School.

Lee was fortunate that midway through his command the election to the presidency of Franklin Pierce, who had known Lee in the Mexican War, brought to the War Department as secretary of war Lee's old friend Jefferson Davis, a fellow southerner and West Pointer. General Winfield Scott, as commanding general of the U.S. Army, continued to be Lee's strongest supporter. Scott even paid a surprise visit to West Point with his suite, and put Lee to the trouble of preparing a dinner at the last minute. In a rare burst of sardonic humor, Lee described it in a letter to a friend: "I fear the Genl will again have an opportunity of taking, if not hasty, at least a thin plate of soup, & but for an Arlington ham and some of my Shanghai chickens . . . I should be in doubt whether their hunger could be appeased."

The joke here is that during General Scott's protracted struggle with President Polk at the beginning of the Mexican War in 1846, Scott had been away from his office when then-Secretary of War Marcy called on him bearing a detailed account of President Polk's displeasure. On returning to his desk Scott dashed off a sycophantic letter of apology for his absence to Marcy, lavishing praise on the president's "excellent sense, military comprehension and courtesies," and containing the unfortunate phrase that he had been out his office only "to take a hasty plate of soup." The letter, when

"leaked," as Scott should have known it would be, pro-
voked nationwide ridicule in the press, often accompanied by grossly unflattering cartoons, both for Scott's
abject surrender to Polk and because Scott, already
putting on substantial weight around his middle, was
well known as a hearty and discriminating gourmet,
for whom mealtimes were both lavish and sacred—a
man less likely to take "a hasty plate of soup" for a meal
would be hard to imagine. This led a friend of Scott's
to conclude (correctly) that he had "committed political
suicide." Scott did in fact run for the presidency as the
Whig candidate in 1852 and carried only four states.

Biographers of Lee tend to write about him as if
he had no interest in politics, but this was not entirely true. Although Lee came to mistrust all politicians, whether of the Union or the Confederacy, and
sought to portray himself as a man without politics,
he was actually a shrewd if discreet observer of political events, and since a good part of his military career
until 1861 was spent dealing with congressional com-
mittees on behalf of the chief engineer or the secretary
of war, he had a highly developed knowledge of politics for a comparatively junior officer.

The period during which Lee served as superintendent
of the U.S. Military Academy was one of intense political

turmoil and increasing anger between the northern and the southern states over the burning issue of whether— or how far—slavery could be extended into the vast area seized from Mexico in 1848. The level of political acrimony was rising sharply. Although most "moderate" people in the North were still resigned to the existence of slavery south of the so-called Mason-Dixon Line, that is to say in those states where slavery had been an established institution before the American Revolution, they were to varying degrees opposed to its extension in the new territories. Abolitionists were still a small, fringe group of extremists in the North. Even those who favored the eventual elimination of slavery were for the most part in favor of accomplishing it slowly, perhaps with some form of compensation for the slave owners, but without any thought that the former slaves might someday become fellow citizens with full voting rights. Except for wealthy slave owners in the plantations of the deep South and those who worked in the slave trade, most Americans treated slavery as a kind of tragic national mistake. Lee's own attitude toward slavery was typical of "moderate" southerners—they owned slaves, they depended on slave labor, and they made some effort to treat slaves well within the reality of the master-slave relationship; but they hoped that in the far future slavery might eventually be eliminated, with the majority of the slaves moved elsewhere, perhaps to Liberia, in a benevolent fashion. In the meantime, life for slaves on the Lee farms continued unchanged, as it did everywhere else in the South: long, numbing toil from generation to generation, with little or no hope of advancement.

During Lee's years at West Point the subject of slavery was already becoming the flash point of American politics, and although succeeding presidents and Congress struggled mightily at increasingly short intervals to find a new compromise that would replace the previous one, each accession of territory, every new proposition for statehood for former territories, and even so farsighted and benevolent a proposal as the building of a transcontinental railroad sparked off bitterly acrimonious sectional argument at the heart of which was slavery. As if it were a portent, Harriet Beecher Stowe's *Uncle Tom's Cabin,* the second best-selling book of the nineteenth century in the United States (after the Bible), was published in 1852, further inflaming passions on both sides of the divide.

Tension rose rapidly during the presidency of Franklin Pierce, a northerner who sympathized with the southern states. He hoped to replace the old Missouri Compromise of 1820–1821—in which Missouri was allowed into the Union as a slave state, in return for the prohibition of slavery north of the parallel 36 degrees

30 minutes N in the former Louisiana Territory. In 1845 the compromise was extended farther west as part of the Texas Annexation Resolution. Also in 1845, the hugely controversial Kansas-Nebraska Act allowed settlers in the two territories to determine "by popular sovereignty" whether they wished to allow slavery there. Senator Thomas Hart Benton of Missouri summed up the feeling of many when he said, "What is the excuse for all this turmoil and mischief? We are told it is to keep the question of slavery out of Congress! Great God! It was out of Congress, completely, entirely, and forever . . . unless Congress dragged it in by breaking down the sacred laws which settled it!" The two senators from Ohio attacked the bill "as a gross violation of a sacred pledge . . . a criminal betrayal of precious rights," intended to transform the new territories to the west "into a dreary region of despotism, inhabited by masters and slaves."

This rhetoric is calm and modest compared with most of the flood of angry debate and raging editorials that accompanied the lengthy and stormy passage of the legislation through both houses of Congress, and in the process fatally eroded the reputation of President Pierce. The policies that he followed as president might as well have been designed for the specific purpose of dividing the United States into two warring camps.

No sooner had the legislation passed than the Kansas Territory descended into political turmoil, murder, and finally open warfare, as pro-slavery "Border Ruffians" and free-soil "Jayhawkers" fought out the question of slavery. "Bleeding Kansas" soon acquired a pro-slavery and an antislavery, or "free state," capital,★ and became an awful example of just where the dispute over slavery was heading. Not more than a year after the Kansas-Nebraska Act John Brown, the "meteor of war," arrived in Kansas, marking the beginning of a new and more bloody conflict, as the state filled with outsiders who wanted to abolish or to extend slavery, a situation apparently beyond the control of the Federal government.

During this time Lee's interest in slavery was luke-warm at best, and his personal involvement with the day-to-day realities of slave ownership on any substantial scale had not yet begun. Of course he had spent all of his life, except when he was in the North or at war in Mexico, surrounded by slaves—they were, if nothing more, part of the background of genteel southern life, a constant presence.

Then his beloved mother-in-law, Mary Lee Fitzhugh Custis, died in April 1853. Lee had long

---

★ The former was Lecompton, the latter Topeka.

since come to think of her as a second mother, and as his spiritual mentor, and to think of Arlington as his home. His wife, Mary, managed to reach home shortly after her mother died, but Lee was unable to return for the funeral because of his duties at West Point. He had called Mrs. Custis "Mother," and had depended on her as a kind and stabilizing element of family life, unlike her mercurial husband; he described her death with no exaggeration as a "sudden and crushing" blow, and writing to Mary he expressed the fundamental Christian belief that Mrs. Custis had been at such pains to inspire in him, and which would sustain him in the years ahead and make him seem to almost everyone who met him, friend or foe, a noble and almost saintly figure, even on the battlefield: "May God give you strength to enable you to bear and say 'His will be done.' She has gone from all trouble, care and sorrow to a holy immortality, there to rejoice and praise forever the God and Saviour she so long and truly served. Let that be our comfort and consolation. May our death be like hers, and may we meet in happiness in Heaven." Of course people strive to write consoling phrases to those who have just lost a loved one, and in Victorian times they were more apt to use religious terms than they are today, but Lee's letter to Mary is nothing like that; it clearly expresses his own basic faith, a firm belief in the goodness of God's purpose, the need to submit to it and the certainty for those who did so of a place in heaven. Lee's religious belief, in part thanks to Mary and her mother, was unshakable, and surely the most important part of his character—he *believed* absolutely. There was no pose about it, no doubt in his mind, no need for outward show; figuratively, it lit him from within, and it helps to explain his extraordinary appeal, the respect given him as a leader during the war to come, and the unique place he came to fill in American life in the century and a half after his death—a strange combination of martyr, secular saint, southern gentleman, and perfect warrior. It is surely no accident that Mrs. Custis left him a ring "with General Washington's hair and pearl initials," since she understood perfectly the degree to which Robert E. Lee's code of behavior was anchored in the previous century, and the strength of the "mystic bonds" that tied him to George Washington.

These qualities made Lee a daunting example to his cadets, all of whom seem to have recognized in him the virtues he was trying to instill in them. Classes were small then, by comparison with today (forty-three cadets in the class of 1852, thirty-four in the class of 1853),* and their spiritual welfare troubled

---

* Almost 1,000 now.

him as much as or more than their academic standing. Only one West Point graduate managed to combine the seemingly contradictory careers of general and
clergyman—Leonidas Polk, who attended the academy
at the same time as Lee but two classes behind him and
would become the Episcopalian bishop of Louisiana
and a Confederate lieutenant general—still, Lee's constant concern was for "inculcating those principles of
manliness and honour which are the only safeguard
of a soldier." Much of his correspondence with the
War Department has the tone of a sermon. It was not
the demerits of cadets that caused Lee grief so much as
the wayward spirit behind them. "You must not infer,"
Lee wrote in a polite letter of warning to the parents
of one cadet who was in danger of dismissal, "that his
conduct has been in the least disgraceful or calculated
to affect his moral character. . . . His amount of demerit
has arisen from acts of carelessness [and] inattention
to his duties." Lee considered discharging cadets "the
most unpleasant office I am called upon to perform."
His pride in inspecting the first graduating class of his
superintendency, in 1853, was appropriate: it included
four future Civil War generals. One of them was Philip
Sheridan, who would rise to become commander of
Grant's Cavalry Corps in 1864, and was the first Union
general to institute a scorched-earth policy, in the

Shenandoah Valley; and another was John Bell Hood, a bold, reckless Texan who rose to become a Confederate lieutenant general and led the attack against the Union left on the second day of Gettysburg. The following year Lee had the pleasure of seeing his son Custis graduated first in his class of forty-six, of whom no fewer than seven would become Confederate generals. The most famous of these was a dashing young horseman named J. E. B. Stuart, of whom Lee was almost as fond as he was of his own sons.

Lee's tenure at West Point was one of the most peaceful and satisfying periods of his life. Most of his family was with him, and Mary, however much she missed the South and the visits to the warm springs that were her only relief from the rheumatism that was slowly crippling her, seems to have enjoyed life as the wife of the superintendent, which involved a good deal of entertaining, both of cadets and of visiting "celebrities," although she found the Hudson valley winters hard to bear. She brought several of the familiar Arlington servants north with her, including "a cook, a waiter, and Eliza, Rob's childhood 'mammy,' now a fully-fledged housemaid." Bringing one's household slaves to northern states did not yet present the difficulties it soon would as the issue of slavery heated up, and as abolitionists became more numerous and daring.

The grounds and gardens at West Point were beautiful and well cared for, and although the atmosphere was inevitably more martial and disciplined than that of drowsy Arlington, with the sounds of marching, drilling, bands, and trumpets in the background, Mary Lee seems to have settled in, and even made use of the greenhouse "to propagate cuttings from the Arlington gardens."

How content Lee was is harder to say. He felt that he had improved the discipline and the moral condition of the cadets, and set in motion a number of improvements in the academy, ranging from the introduction of gaslight to the beginning of work—at last—on the new riding school he had designed; but he may have also feared that he was slipping into a backwater of the army. The board of visitors praised his conduct "in the exalted position he so worthily fills," and this was gratifying, but Lee himself was constantly aware that however "exalted" his position might be in the eyes of others, he was growing older without any realistic hope of promotion or higher command, and with two sons remaining to be educated and four daughters to marry. (Rooney would disappoint his father by failing to obtain an appointment to West Point, but then succeeded in winning a place at Harvard University. Rob, the youngest boy, would attend the University of Virginia.)

Lee used his spare time to read prodigious numbers of books from the West Point library, a significant number of them about Napoleon, including O'Meara's two-volume *Napoleon at Saint Helena;* no fewer than eight volumes of memoirs about the emperor; and Napoleon's own *Considérations sur l'Art de la Guerre,* in which, as Freeman points out, Lee would have read the emperor's recommendations for protecting a capital city against an enemy army of greater numbers, a situation that Lee himself faced in 1864 and 1865.

But steps were being taken in Washington that would radically change the direction of Lee's career, and send his family back to Arlington. Secretary of War Jefferson Davis was dismayed by the small number of American troops available to defend settlers in the West—the entire U.S. Army consisted of fewer than 15,000 men, approximately the size of a division. Fewer than 10,000 were combat troops and perhaps half were available to guard and protect the entire western frontier against something like 40,000 hostile Indian warriors. Again and again small detachments of American troops were besieged in their fort or cut down when they journeyed outside it by superior numbers of Indians. The culmination was the notorious Grattan Massacre of 1854, in which twenty-nine American soldiers; their, commander

Lieutenant Grattan; and an interpreter were killed by over 1,000 angry Lakota Sioux braves in what is now Wyoming. Davis was determined to impose what we would now call law and order on the frontier. He asked Congress for two new regiments of infantry, and two of cavalry specially trained and equipped for frontier service, the First and Second Cavalry. For once, the legislators listened and appropriated the money, though not without complaints. Davis immediately appointed Albert Sidney Johnston, a Texan who had been two classes behind Davis at West Point, as colonel of the Second Cavalry; and Robert E. Lee as lieutenant colonel, or second in command. Johnston was a distinguished soldier who would serve in three armies: that of the Republic of Texas, the U.S. Army, and the Confederate Army. He had won the admiration of Jefferson Davis, who rated his military skills above those of Lee. A good many of the officers of both new cavalry regiments were southern: in the Second Cavalry, as well as Albert Sidney Johnston and Robert E. Lee, both E. Kirby Smith and John Bell Hood would become generals in the Confederate Army; and the lieutenant colonel of the First Cavalry was Lee's best friend at West Point, Joseph E. Johnston, who would become not only a Confederate general but codesigner of the Confederate battle flag.

Lee's mother, Ann Carter Lee, wearing the brooch George Washington gave her as a wedding present, an enameled portrait of himself in an oval gold frame; and Lee's father, Henry Lee III, "Light-Horse Harry" Lee.

George Washington's family with Lee's father-in-law George Washington Parke Custis on Washington's left.

Mrs. Robert E. Lee; and her husband, Robert E. Lee, as a lieutenant.

The Spring of the Confederacy, a mural by Charles Hoffbauer, showing Lee on Traveller at the center, flanked by some of the principal generals of the Confederacy. From left to right: John Bell Hood, Wade Hampton, R. S. Ewell, John Brown Gordon, T. J. Jackson, Fitzhugh Lee, A. P. Hill, R. E. Lee, James Longstreet, J. E. Johnston, George Pickett, P. G. T. Beauregard, and J. E. B. Stuart.

The Eve of the Storm by Don Troiani, depicting Lee the night before the Battle of Chancellorsville. On Lee's right is the cartographer Major Jedediah Hotchkiss; seated to his left is Stonewall Jackson; seated in front of him on the log is his aide, Colonel Marshall, transcribing Lee's orders.

The last meeting
of Lee and Jackson.

Decision at Dawn by Don Troiani, showing Lee standing before ordering the attack on the second day of the Battle of Gettysburg. Seated on the log whittling are Generals Longstreet and A. P. Hill. In the tree is Lieutenant-Colonel Fremantle, wearing a gray top hat and pointing, and the Austro-Hungarian observer, with field glasses; in uniform at the bottom of the tree is the Prussian observer, talking to a journalist.

View of Little Round Top as the Confederate line advances toward it, July 2, 1862.

Winslow Homer's painting of Confederate prisoners
being addressed by a Union officer at Gettysburg.

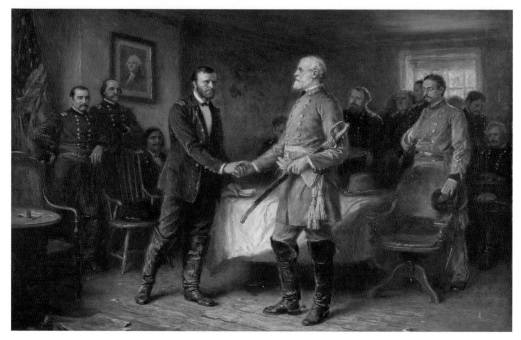

General Ulysses S. Grant and General Robert E. Lee in the parlor of
the McLean house, Appomattox Court House, Virginia, shaking hands
after Lee has signed the surrender of his army, April 9, 1865.

The sword Lee wore to meet Grant.

The uniform frock coat
that Lee wore the day
of the surrender.

The Virginia Memorial at Gettysburg, with Lee on Traveller gazing up toward Cemetery Ridge in the direction of Pickett's Charge.

Lee on Traveller, Richmond, Virginia.

Stone Mountain, Georgia: Jefferson Davis, Lee, and Stonewall Jackson.

Scott was at odds with Davis, and would have preferred Lee as colonel of the Second Cavalry, with Johnston as his second in command; he reaffirmed his belief that if the United States were ever to be faced with a war in which the existence of the country was at stake, even on his deathbed he would tell the president "with his dying breath" that Lee should command the army, but in the end he accepted the secretary of war's decision after several bitter exchanges of letters.

Lee gained nothing in terms of compensation, since he was already being paid as a brevet colonel. Always prudent with money, not only did he manage to live on his salary, but by the time he reached West Point he had put aside $64,500, most of it invested in state and municipal bonds at 6 or 7 percent,★ not an inconsiderable amount of capital for the time, and the equivalent of about $1.68 million today. It is understandable that Lee *felt* poor—he had seven children, and although Custis attended West Point at government expense, the cost of sending the other boys to college no doubt seemed just as appalling to him as it would seem to parents today. Also, he had before him the prospect of four girls to marry in a style acceptable to the Lee, Carter, and

---

★Emory M. Thomas lists Lee's most important investments as "bonds from the states of Virginia and Missouri, the cities of Pittsburgh and St. Louis, the New York & Erie and the Hudson River Railroads." These would seem to represent a cautious but sound financial strategy on Lee's part.

Custis families. He was certainly pained at leaving the Corps of Engineers after twenty-seven years of service, as well as "bitter in the extreme" at the necessity of being parted from his children, but it is also possible that getting out from behind a desk held a certain appeal for him. He would be leading troops in the field, he would have direct military responsibilities, and given the rising tension along the frontier he was almost certain to see action. Then too, the cavalry was still seen as an elite, and Lee was a born horseman. That he gave the matter some consideration, possibly to discuss the ramifications with Mary Lee, is demonstrated by the fact that it took him twelve days to reply—a long delay for Lee, but his acceptance was never in doubt.

Lee had about a month in which to move his family back to Arlington and prepare his affairs for his departure. It was already clear that the Second Cavalry was unlikely to be stationed anyplace where Mary and the children would be able to follow him. On April 12, 1855, he left for Louisville, Kentucky, where the regiment was being formed. For reasons that remain unclear, the War Department was unable to locate Colonel Johnston, so for the time being Lee was in command. Even before his men's uniforms and equipment had arrived, he was ordered to proceed with them to Saint Louis, Missouri, where he set about drilling his troopers. Lee would later say that he could make a soldier out of any man—he was referring to the daring proposal to arm Negroes to fight in the Confederate Army in 1864—and he does indeed seem to have had a gift for turning reluctant men into proper soldiers. In fact, a good many of the recruits for the Second Cavalry were regular soldiers from lesser regiments, who may have needed almost as much whipping into shape as civilians to come up to Lee's standards. The Second Cavalry would eventually become so perfectly drilled, uniformed, and equipped that they became known throughout the rest of the army as "Davis's pets," a reflection of the secretary of war's personal interest in the regiment.

Lee himself was not to enjoy the comforts of Jefferson Barracks, on the Mississippi River, since the army decided he should use his time attending courts-martial as far afield as Kansas, Texas, and Pennsylvania, one of the wearisome duties of line officers which he had been spared as an engineer and superintendent of West Point. He was on the move from the beginning of September 1855 to March 1856, when he finally rejoined the regiment at Fort Mason, 100 miles north of San Antonio. It was one of a chain of small, crudely built, isolated forts intended to protect settlers from raids by Comanche, Kiowa, and Apache Indians, or by marauding Mexican bandits. The sheer tedium of travel between army posts, much of it on horseback, not to speak of the tedium of the cases being tried, was enough to make Lee write a warning to his daughter Agnes that she "must expect discomforts and annoyances all through life," a prediction that was to prove more accurate than her father can have foreseen.

At the end of March, Colonel Albert Sidney Johnston, who had finally appeared to take command of the regiment, put Lee in command of two advance squadrons of the Second Cavalry encamped under canvas on the Brazos River, in the heart of Comanche country, at a site named Camp Cooper, really no more than a couple of lines of tents, about 170 miles north of Fort Mason, an isolated encampment in the middle of a largely unexplored and forbidding wilderness of brush and thorny mesquite inhabited by wolves, coyotes, and snakes, and sparsely populated by bands of hostile Comanche. Lee's orders were to overawe the Indians and prevent them from following their proud tradition of tribal warfare, murderous raids on exposed Anglo settlements, cattle and horse theft, and the scalping of their enemies. Lee had a tent of his own, a few chickens to supplement the army rations with eggs, and for a time a pet rattlesnake, since no cat or dog could survive the bold depredations of the wolves. He was to spend nineteen months in this unpromising place, his only pastime the search for a site to build a new fort, accompanied by Lieutenant John Bell Hood.

The nearby Comanche encampment downstream of Fort Cooper held little interest for Lee. The Native Americans did not seem to most Americans of the mid-nineteenth century either romantic or worth studying, and Lee was no exception. In the post–Civil War effort to turn Lee into a kind of secular saint, his views on race have been almost altogether eliminated from his portrait. He believed that Negroes were better off as slaves than they had been in Africa, and after the Civil War he opposed giving them the vote; he thought that Mexicans were only slightly better (and lived more poorly) than slaves in the South; and he did not think that the government's efforts to "humanize" the Indians, as he put it, were worth the trouble or likely to succeed. His attitude can be summed up by his comment to Mary on the Comanche after he got to know them: "These people give a world of trouble to man and horse, and, poor creatures, they are not worth it."

Lee was no anthropologist, and he had scant patience with the troublesome Comanche, or with the squalor of their village. Soon after Lee's arrival at Camp Cooper the local chief, Catumse, paid him a ceremonial visit, which he felt obliged to return, and which he described shortly afterward in a letter to Mary: "Yesterday I returned his [Catumse's] visit, and remained a short time at his Lodge. He informed me that he had six wives. They [the Indians] are riding in and out of camp all day, their paint and 'ornaments' rendering them more hideous than nature made them, and the whole tribe is extremely uninteresting." Lee was polite to the chief but minced no words: "I hailed him as a friend, as long as his conduct and that of his tribe deserved it, but would meet him as an enemy the first moment he failed to keep his word." That Chief Catumse might have his own standards of behavior, and a code of honor as rigid in its own way as Lee's, was not a thought that ever crossed Lee's mind.

The dullness of life on the frontier eventually brought Lee back to his old regrets about his choice of profession. Clearly there was not much gain or glory to be had in fighting the Comanche, and still less in pursuing them, since they left few traces of their passage and knew every square mile of their barren territory like the back of their hand. Lee was now a forty-eight-year-old brevet colonel, 1,000 miles from his beloved wife and children, accomplishing nothing. "Monotony of the darkest and dullest descended again," Freeman writes, and it is a fair description of Lee's state of mind—like many another soldier on the frontier, he felt that his life was being wasted, and that his military career was drawing to its end with no hope of further promotion.

His boredom was relieved when he was placed in command of an expedition to subdue a rogue band of Comanche under the leadership of a warrior called Sanaco—or possibly the more famous Buffalo Hump—which had been raiding in the vicinity of Fort Chadbourne, more or less equidistant from modern Fort Worth and Midland, and about eleven miles northeast of what is now Bronte.* This was some of the roughest and most barren country on the Texas frontier, and the chance that Lee's troopers could locate Sanaco or Buffalo Hump† in it was about zero, but the prospect of action seem to have cheered Lee up. He was given four squadrons of cavalry drawn from several forts, perhaps 400 to 500 men, plus supply wagons, guides, and an interpreter—not much with which to cover a huge area whose only features were ravines and dry riverbeds. To the west, stretching for hundreds of miles, was the Llano Estacado, or Staked Plain, featureless grassland virtually the size of New England into which the Indians could (and did) simply

---

*Although this town name honors the novelist Charlotte Brontë, author of *Jane Eyre*, it is pronounced "Brahnt."

† Buffalo Hump is a major character in Larry McMurtry's *Dead Man's Walk* and *Comanche Moon.*

disappear without leaving a trace. Lee and his men covered many miles and rode for days without seeing anything more than smoke on the horizon—smoke that turned out on closer examination to be a prairie fire. He commented that the grass was poor and what little water could be found was salty, but he managed to get close to the source of the Wichita River, probably the first white man to do so, or at any rate the first white man since the conquistador Coronado. One of his squadrons actually succeeded in killing two Indians, though whether they were part of the raiding party seems doubtful. After a thirty-mile ride he spent Independence Day, July 4, 1856, camped on a branch of the Brazos River under the shade of a blanket suspended from four sticks sunk in the ground. From this barren campsite he wrote a description of his whereabouts to Mary: "the sun was fiery hot. The atmosphere like the blast from a hot-air furnace, the water salt." He wrote, movingly, that "my feelings for my country were as ardent, my faith in her future as true, and my hopes for her advancement as unabated, as if called forth under more propitious circumstances."

In the end, despite his exertions—he covered 1,600 miles in forty days—he found no trace of the Indian raiders. "I saw nothing," he would report bitingly of the land around the Brazos, "to attract Indians to the country, or to induce them to remain."

Eventually the troopers returned to their forts, and Lee returned to Camp Cooper, where the searing heat had dried up the river and killed Lee's vegetable garden. There he learned that his sister Mildred—Mrs. Edward Vernon Childe—had died unexpectedly in Paris. Mildred, who was four years younger than Robert, had bravely determined to marry a stranger and a northerner when she was only nineteen, despite the doubts of her brothers, who were not convinced by a letter of recommendation from Daniel Webster himself. That Edward Childe was a wealthy Boston lawyer with literary ambitions did not immediately mollify them, but Mildred stood up for herself, married Edward, and went with her husband to live in Paris, from where she "thereafter resisted all efforts to coax her into returning" to the United States. Lee's grief over her death was increased by his loneliness and sense of failure at Camp Cooper. "The news came to me very unexpectedly," he wrote to Mary, "and in the course of nature I might never have anticipated it, as indeed I had never realized that she might precede me on the unexplored journey upon which we are hastening. . . . It has put to an end all hope of our meeting in this world. . . . I trust that our merciful God only so suddenly and early snatched her away because he saw that it was the fittest moment to take her to himself." The letter perfectly expresses Lee's literal and heartfelt belief in the evangelical Christianity of his wife and late mother-in-law, and this religious tone would enter all of Lee's correspondence, even correspondence of military or political significance. It is no accident that in so many popular portraits of him, although mounted and in uniform, he is shown in an attitude of prayer.

It was perhaps fortunate that the army, which like all armies was reluctant not to make full use of a soldier's time, removed Lee from Camp Cooper and sent him off on a seemingly endless round of courts-martial. Officers of field grade were in short supply on the frontier, and Lee was a punctilious and careful member of any court-martial. He paid the same strict attention to the papers and evidence as he had to the work of the cadets at West Point. Merely assembling the witnesses, the documents, the lawyers, and the required number of officers as members of the court-martial in one place might take weeks or months, and often the charges do not seem to have been of great importance in the first place. It took Lee twenty-seven days to cover the 700 miles from Camp Cooper to Ringgold Barracks in Rio Grande City, about as far south as you can go in Texas, and from there he rode on to Fort Brown, San

Antonio, and Indianola, a circuit that took him from September 1856 to April 1857, before he returned to Camp Cooper. Luckily for Lee, the forts and camps he visited were full of officers he knew, sometimes with their wives, and he was able to enjoy a small taste of domesticity and to catch up on the news of the day.

Military gossip was that the First and Second Cavalry might be disbanded because of northerners' fears that Jefferson Davis had staffed them with too many southern officers—a dispute which began on the pages of the New York Times, but which in the end came to nothing. Lee was distressed by the possibility of disbandment, and to his further annoyance he discovered that his friends in Virginia had been circulating a petition to the president to have him promoted to a vacant brigadier generalship for "his brilliant and pre-eminent distinctions," an effort which he gently but firmly discouraged.

Political news was concentrated on the issue of Kansas, where something approaching open civil war was now raging; and on the entire issue of slavery, which was beginning to subsume all other matters. The incumbent president, Franklin Pierce, managed to lose his fight for renomination by his own party, a unique event in American political history for an elected president. The Democratic Party was now sharply divided between northern Democrats and southern Democrats, and in danger of collapsing as the Whig Party had done in the previous election, and Pierce was too much of a "doughboy" to satisfy those who were opposed to slavery. Instead, the party nominated James Buchanan, American minister to the Court of St. James's, after fifteen ballots, and chose Senator John Breckinridge of Kentucky, a future Confederate major general, as the vice presidential candidate. Buchanan had actually been "born in a log cabin"—this was then considered an advantage for a presidential candidate— and he was popular in his home state, Pennsylvania; but his determination to keep an even balance between the slave states and the North made him the butt of ridicule on both sides of the issue. The threat of secession by the slave-owning southern states was sharply increased by events in Kansas, by the steady rise of abolitionist feeling in the North, and by the division of the Democratic Party into two warring factions, as well as by the collapse of the old Whig Party and the rise of the new Republican Party from its ashes. Although the vast majority of southerners were not slave owners, and although abolitionists were a small minority in the North, the issue of slavery was effectively dividing the country and revolutionizing its political institutions. Buchanan was a man of considerable charm and an experienced diplomat, but he fancied himself as a skillful compromiser at a moment in American history when compromise was rapidly becoming unacceptable.

Lee was opposed to secession, dismissing it as "silly" and the equivalent of revolution. He was, in fact, rather like Buchanan, a man who would certainly have been open to compromise if it would keep the Union together. He was no enthusiast for extending slavery in the territories, or for resuming the slave trade, which he abhorred; still less did he favor the annexation of new slave territory in Cuba.

President Pierce's defense of his controversial and ill-starred repeal of the Missouri Compromise and his arguments against the wisdom of northerners' attempts to interfere with slavery in the South were the main subject of his message to Congress in December 1856. Unlike the president, Lee saw slavery as a *spiritual* issue, not a political one. He was not himself the owner of more than a few slaves, whom he had determined should be liberated on his death, and most of his contact with slaves had been with familiar and sometimes beloved house servants, rather than with field hands, but in general he had found the responsibilities of owning them more onerous than any benefit that could be derived from their labor. So far as can be ascertained, he had never actually purchased a slave; he had either inherited his slaves or received them as a gift from Mr. Custis. He shared the interest of several members of the Lee family in sending freed slaves to Liberia, a cause still eliciting cautious if somewhat skeptical support on both sides of the Mason-Dixon Line, but very little from those whom it was proposed to send there. The last place freed blacks wanted to go was back across the Atlantic to Africa as part of a large-scale social experiment intended to expiate the guilt of white Americans. Lee put most of his thoughts in a letter to Mary. After a few line of cautious optimism about the president's message to Congress, a sense of an approaching crisis over northerners' growing determination to limit slavery pervades his letter to Mary.

"I was much pleased with the President's message & the report of the SecY of War, the only two documents that have reached us entire. Of the others synopsis [sic] have only arrived. The views of the Pres: of the Systematic & progressive efforts of certain people of the North, to interfere with & change the domestic institutions of the South, are truthfully & faithfully expressed. The Consequences of their plans & purposes are also clearly set forth, & they must also be aware, that their object is both unlawful & entirely foreign to them & their duty; for which they are irresponsible & unaccountable; & Can only be accomplished by them through the agency of a Civil & Servile war. In this enlightened age, there are few I believe, but what will acknowledge, that slavery as an institution, is a moral & political evil in any Country. It is useless to expatiate on its disadvantages. I think it however a greater evil to the white than to the black race, & while my feelings are strongly enlisted in behalf of the latter, my sympathies are more strong for the former. The blacks are immeasurably better off here than in Africa, morally, socially & physically. The painful discipline they are undergoing, is necessary for their instruction as a race, & I hope will prepare & lead them to better things. How long their subjugation may be necessary is known & ordered by a wise Merciful Providence. Their emancipation will sooner result from the mild & melting influence of Christianity, than the storms & tempests of fiery Controversy. This influence though slow, is sure. . . . While we see the Course of the final abolition of human Slavery is onward, & we give it the aid of our prayers & all justifiable means in our power, we must leave the progress as well as the result in his hands who sees the end; who Chooses to work by slow influences; & with whom two thousand years are but as a Single day. Although the Abolitionist must know this, & must See that he has neither the right or power of operating except by moral means & suasion, & if he means well to the slave, he must not Create angry feelings in the Master; that although he may not approve the mode by which it pleases Providence to accomplish its purposes, the result will nevertheless be the same; that the reasons he gives for interference in what he has no Concern, holds good for every kind of interference with our neighbours when we disapprove their Conduct; Still I fear he will persevere in his evil Course. Is it not strange that the descendants of those pilgrim fathers who Crossed the Atlantic to preserve their own freedom of opinion, have always proved themselves intolerant of the Spiritual liberty of others?"

Lee was of course not wrong about the religious intolerance of the Pilgrim fathers toward faiths other than their own, but it may seem strange at a first reading of his letter to link that to northerners' intolerance for slavery in the mid-nineteenth century. Until one reads the letter carefully to the end, one does not see that Lee's belief is that slavery is God's will, and can be ended only by allowing "Merciful Providence" to work at its own pace. In the course of the later metamorphosis of Lee from a southern into a national hero, his opinion about slavery has been very largely swept under the rug, all the more easily because his distaste for the institution was genuine. His firm belief on the issue helps to explain his eventual decision to resign from the army and take up arms for the Confederacy. Despite his dislike of slavery, he was fighting for what he held to be right and moral. He would not have fought for less.

He regarded slavery as a *moral* and *religious* issue, not one that could be solved by politics. It is difficult for us, more than a century and a half later, to understand that something we regard as immoral and unjust could have been thought of as part of God's plan, but such was the fact, and to ignore it is to underestimate both the strength of Lee's religious beliefs and the fact that he saw *all* events as a demonstration of God's will.

By Easter Lee was at last in Fort Mason, on his way back to Camp Cooper where he learned for the first time that during his absence there had been several clashes with the Comanche, in which two of his troopers and twelve "hostiles" had been killed. Two weeks later James Buchanan was inaugurated as the fifteenth president of the United States. In his fatally optimistic inauguration speech, he counseled the nation to be calm on the subject of Kansas, since the matter would shortly be settled by the Supreme Court, leaving people to suppose that a soothing decision would be handed down. Instead, only two days later, the unobliging Chief Justice Roger B. Taney announced the court's bombshell decision in the case of *Dred Scott v. Sanford.* It held that "persons of African descent cannot be, nor were ever intended to be, citizens of the United States," and that Congress had no power to "ban slavery in the territories," thus undermining both the Missouri Compromise and the Kansas-Nebraska Act. Taney further declared that the "Due Process Clause" of the Fifth Amendment "prohibits the federal government from freeing slaves brought into federal territories." The Court thus removed in one stroke every ground on which President Buchanan might have hoped to negotiate a settlement satisfactory to the North. As if to rub salt in the wound, Taney added, "Negroes had no rights which the white man was obliged to respect."

Apart from threats of impending Indian raids, which did not materialize, life at Camp Cooper was uncomfortable and tedious: the temperature exceeded 112 degrees in the shade, and the wind was so hot that it brought no relief, just sand and dust. "I have been out four days the past week reconnoitering the country & looking for springs," Lee wrote to Mary, "in which I have not had much success. We have also had an alarm that a large body of Indians were coming down from the North to attack our camp. . . . I confess I was incredulous & went to bed with no expectation of being aroused." Lee continued to suffer patiently through his duty on the frontier until July 1857, when he was recalled to Fort Mason to serve on yet another court-martial, only to find that Albert Sidney Johnston had been ordered back to Washington by the War Department and that he was now commanding officer of the Second Cavalry in Johnston's place.

Lee rode 113 miles across the prairie from Fort Mason to San Antonio to take up his new command. San Antonio was a pleasant town with tree-shaded walks along the San Antonio River, and handsome Spanish houses, one of which Lee took over from his predecessor as his headquarters, a huge improvement over a windblown tent on the Brazos. "The weather here is excessively hot," he wrote to his daughter Annie, then eighteen. "In the day, the houses afford more protection from the sun than the tents I have been living in. But having been accustomed to sleeping in the open air for so long, the nights are oppressive to me & are wretchedly long." He quickly found a surrogate family, with the two young daughters of the paymaster, but there was little to stimulate his professional interest; it was the dullest and most routine peacetime garrison soldiering, with none of the intellectual challenge of engineering. Not surprisingly he still expressed his regret at having chosen the profession of soldier, and longed for the company of his own children. He was particularly concerned about Rooney, who after failing to get into West Point had succeeded in gaining admission to Harvard—where, his father complained, he was "running around amusing himself." Rooney caused further consternation by leaving Harvard without taking a degree; with the help of General Scott his father obtained a commission for him in the army. Nothing could be more troublesome to Lee, however, than a lack of direction or a lack of purpose in one of his sons—Rooney, Lee complained sadly, "adds more than years to the gray hairs on my head"; and to make matters worse, the young man had run up debts, had fallen in love, and was determined to get married. Young Rob was still in school and would soon be attending the University of Virginia, and seems to have been sufficiently pious and well behaved to suit his father; but between Rooney's debts at Harvard and Rob's tuition, Lee must have felt hard pressed. He was further troubled by Mary's health, which seemed to be failing—she was increasingly crippled with what we would now call rheumatoid arthritis, for which the only treatment in those days was frequent visits to hot springs; and with an aging father, four daughters to look after, and three spirited sons she was finally obliged to address a few sharp words to her husband. "I will do my best," she wrote to Lee, "but you can do so much better . . . it is time now you were with your family." Nothing could have been more painful for Lee than to be faced with deciding between two opposing duties—one to the army, the other to Mary and his family—and he seemed unable to resolve the conflict.

Then, in October 1857, the dilemma was suddenly solved for him. He received the news that his father-in-law, George Washington Custis, had died of pneumonia at the age of seventy-six, leaving a grief-stricken Mary with no male relative at home to help her deal with Mr. Custis's considerable estate. Whatever others might think of Mr. Custis and his numerous eccentricities, Lee had always cherished his father-in-law, perhaps as his last living link with George Washington. Mr. Custis, after all, had been born in 1781, only seven days after Lord Cornwallis surrendered to Washington at Yorktown—an event that was the effective end of the American Revolutionary War, and at which Lee's own father had been present.

In the 1850s, when communications and travel were so slow, it was understood that for an officer of Lee's rank and social class a death in the family required time off, and he had no difficulty in obtaining two months' leave. He summed up his position in a letter to his friend Albert Sidney Johnston: "I can see that I have at last to decide the question, which I have staved off for 20 years. Whether I am to continue in the Army all my life, or to leave it. . . . My preferences which have clung to me from boyhood impel me to adopt the former course, but yet I feel that a mans [*sic*] family has claims too."

The family's problems nearly overwhelmed Lee the moment he arrived back at Arlington on November 11. His first shock was the extent to which Mary Lee had become an invalid—nothing in her letters had prepared Lee for the pain she was in, or for the fact that at the age of forty-nine she could hardly even move around the house without assistance. The second shock was Mr. Custis's will. As anyone who knew him might have guessed, Mr. Custis had written his own will rather than relying on a lawyer, and the result was hodgepodge of good intentions and self-contradictory stipulations. Mr. Custis was generous in his bequests to his heirs, but had given little or no thought to how to produce the cash to pay them.

Resolving matters would have been a full-time job for a skilled lawyer, but since Lee's wife and his children were the principal beneficiaries, Lee felt obliged to take on the duty of trying to straighten out the mess—a task which would occupy him almost entirely over the next two years, and which would continue to haunt him for the rest of his life. He had already had the thankless task of trying to unravel a dispute between Mr. Custis and the manager of the White House and Romancock estates, each of about 4,000 acres. During the course of his investigations Lee discovered that Mr. Custis had neither visited the estates nor scrutinized the manager's accounts for at least ten years. Lee can hardly have been unaware of what was in store for him, but he was nevertheless dismayed at his father-in-law's negligence. At once Lee began to look into things in the same patient, methodical way he had administered West Point or any of the projects he had undertaken for the Corps of Engineers.

In theory Mr. Custis's estate should have been a prize to his heirs. He was rich in land, stately homes, and possessions of extraordinary historical value. But in reality everything was burdened by debt and years of mismanagement. Mr. Custis had attempted to divide up his estate as fairly as he could. He left Mary Lee a "life interest" in Arlington, which after her death would pass on to the Lees' eldest son, Custis. He left White House to Rooney and Romancock to Rob, while each daughter was to receive $10,000 (no small amount for a girl in those days, perhaps equivalent to $200,000 today) from the sale of other, smaller properties and the income from White House and Romancock. Each of these places was of course a proverbial white elephant, with a badly run-down house,★ land producing no income, and an unwilling, disgruntled slave labor force.

The slaves, in fact, constituted the largest problem Mr. Custis had left to his executors, of whom Lee quickly became the chief and most active. At the time of his death there were 196 slaves on the three major properties, and Mr. Custis stipulated that once the estate had been settled—that is, when the necessary sales of land were completed to raise cash, all debts were paid, and the distributions to his heirs were made in full—they were all to be "emancipated" no later than five years from his death.

However well-intentioned Mr. Custis's decision to free his slaves had been, it was almost impossibly difficult to do. In the first place, in Virginia the law held that freed Negroes must leave the state, but in order for the Custis slaves to lead an independent life with any hope of gainful employment away from Virginia, they would need at least the rudiments of reading and

---

★An indication of how run-down the houses were is that twenty years earlier an English visitor had already commented that from a distance Arlington "had the appearance of a superior English country residence beyond any place I had seen in the states, but as I came close to it, I was woefully disappointed." Things had not improved since then, and White House and Romancock were in an even more advanced state of dilapidation.

writing. And in Virginia it was a crime to teach a black person to read or write.

There were further problems as well. Even a cursory examination of Mr. Custis's affairs was enough to make Lee doubt that the land sales which could be made within five years would be sufficient to settle his father-in-law's debts, let alone provide money for the distributions to his heirs to take place and for undertaking, as well, some kind of responsible preparation for the emancipation of the slaves. "I can see little prospect of fulfilling the provisions of your Grd father's will within the space of five years, within which he expected it to be accomplished & his people liberated," he wrote to his oldest son, Custis, although Robert and Mary Lee did in the end succeed in accomplishing Mr. Custis's wishes in respect to his slaves—something of a miracle in the circumstances. An inventory of the Arlington slaves made after the death of Mr. Custis gives a hint of the difficulties facing Lee: there, in neat columns, in the elegant penmanship of the time, Lee enumerated the slave families (a matter of convenience, since neither slave "families," nor slave "marriages" had any legal standing in Virginia), although some individuals are listed only by a single name—"Fanny," for instance, or in one case "Baby." Lee no doubt knew the household servants, but did he know the field hands, or recognize who "Obadiah

Gray" was? He was deluged with statistics about the taxable Custis property, from the twelve "working oxen" (down from twenty-six the previous year, a bad sign) to the 2,500 bushels of Indian corn, all of which had to be meticulously accounted for, and of course examined, to ensure, for example, that the sixty "swine" were actually there and alive and healthy. The slaves were certainly more troublesome property than the elegant Custis carriage and the carriage horses or Mr. Custis's gold watch, but all of it was now Lee's responsibility. He had often dreamed about taking up a life of farming, but not on this scale, or with so many problems.

To Lee's great embarrassment he was obliged to apply for one leave after another, as he applied himself to the Augean task of making the Custis properties self-sustaining and profitable in the interest of his wife and children. In the end, he would be separated from his regiment from November 1858 to February 1860, with a few interruptions to attend courts-martial and once to take command of the troops sent by the government to restore order in Harpers Ferry. Lee's friend and mentor General Winfield Scott raised no objections to this extended period of leave, and did his best to ensure that Lee's career did not suffer, but Lee chafed as men less able than himself were promoted to the rank of brigadier general.

An inspection of the White House and the Romancock properties further depressed him—houses and land were in a dreadful state—and the only thing he could accomplish quickly was to change the name of the latter to the less offensive Romancoke. Both his older boys were serving in the army—Custis was in the West; Rooney was about to join an expedition to Utah to subdue the Mormons (the fact that it was called "Buchanan's Blunder" is enough to describe its place in American history)—and Lee thought it proper to give both boys the opportunity to resign from the army and take over their inheritance immediately, but both declined. Custis generously sent his father "a deed to Arlington and all the other property inherited under his grandfather's will," reasoning that his father should certainly own Arlington if he was obliged to spend so much time and effort restoring it. Lee returned the deed with an affectionate letter of thanks, adding characteristically that he regretted "the expense you incurred [in having the deed drawn up], which I fear in that country is considerable, as I wish you to *save all* your money. . . . The necessity I daily have for money has, I fear, made me parsimonious."

The slight parental bite is uncharacteristic of Lee's correspondence with his children, but although he was an unfailingly generous father, if there was one subject he was sharp about it was the waste of small amounts of money. No doubt his irritation with his late father-in-law made the subject all the more painful to him.

However difficult it might be to deal with the numerous problems of the Custis estate, nothing caused Lee more suffering or singed his reputation as much as his father-in-law's slaves.

Of course at that time no subject was more apt to produce moral dilemmas than slavery. Lee, who had owned only a few slaves, mostly family servants of one kind or another, had little or no experience in dealing with a disgruntled workforce of almost 200 people, who represented among them a considerable portion of the value of the Custis estate. As a military man Lee was no martinet, but when he gave an order, however courteously conveyed, he expected it to be obeyed. Unfortunately for Lee, the Custis slaves were not West Point cadets—they had long since grown accustomed to their late master's unwillingness to pay close attention to their work, and they resented Lee's eagle-eyed attention and his schemes for making the Custis lands profitable, which of course depended on their labor. Neighbors complained that the Custis slaves were indolent, spoiled, and impudent, and it is certainly true that apart from taking a sporadic interest in his various agricultural hobbies, like breeding sheep, Mr. Custis allowed his slaves to do pretty much as they pleased. They farmed their own gardens, rather than looking after his lands; they were free to fish as they pleased; in the eyes of most observers they ruled Mr. Custis rather than the other way around.

This was not a situation Lee could accept, if only because he was dealing with the inheritance of his wife and children. To put matters in perspective, two young women were sold by the Alexandria, Virginia, slave dealer Joseph Bruin for $2,250, the equivalent of at least $40,000 in today's money. If Lee could have sold half a dozen of the Custis slaves in nearby Alexandria he would have been able to pay off all the estate's debts and provide the cash for his daughters' legacies at one stroke. But neither the terms of the will nor his own honorable character would permit him to consider this. Instead, in the five years before the Custis slaves were to be emancipated Lee hired some of them out to work elsewhere. This was quite a usual practice, particularly in northern Virginia, where many plantations had a bigger slave force than was needed, but it was bitterly resented by the slaves. The Custis slaves, after all, had been at Arlington for two generations under one master. Some of the older ones had helped build the house; they had formed families and friendships; they were a *community*. Slaves who were hired out were suddenly separated from parents, from spouse and children, from friends—sent away to a strange place at the mercy of what might be a brutal overseer, or at the very least a taskmaster determined to get his money's worth out of them. Most of them could not read or write, and even had they been able to, nobody would mail a letter home for them, or deliver one.

This was a sensitive subject, because in the years between 1800 and 1860 a huge *involuntary* migration took place. Between 800,000 and 1 million slaves were moved westward: some were taken along as their owners moved toward new land opening up on what was then the frontier in Kentucky or Tennessee, and then farther south to Mississippi and Alabama; others were sold by their owner or their owner's heirs to the great cotton and rice plantations in the deep South. Slaves were no longer needed in large numbers in Virginia, but to the west their price rose as the need for slave labor soared. Exporting slaves became an industry—male slaves were marched in coffles of forty or fifty, handcuffed to each other in pairs, with a long chain through the handcuffs passing down the column to keep it together, closely guarded by mounted slave traders and followed by an equal number of female slaves and their children.

Most of them were taken to Wheeling, Virginia, the "busiest slave port" in the United States, and from there they were transported by steamboat to New Orleans, Natchez, and Memphis.* Some were sent by sea from Virginia ports to New Orleans, where there was also a lively trade in the notorious fancy girls, a source of increasing indignation among northern abolitionists, and a strong theme running through *Uncle Tom's Cabin*—one which Harriet Beecher Stowe faced unflinchingly, by nineteenth-century standards. Even if only half the slaves who traveled west were merely following their owners, like the livestock, the sale of the remaining half represents a profit of at least $500 million in mid-nineteenth-century money, or about $10 *billion* in today's money. The slave trade was a hugely profitable business, and the labor of the slaves created enormous wealth.

This did not help solve Lee's problem. He was in no way tempted to sell his father-in-law's slaves; nor could he have done so—on the contrary, he and Mary went to great effort to fulfill the terms of the will. Still, the effect of this great forced migration on the slaves themselves cannot be underestimated. Ignorant and illiterate some of them might be, but they knew what was

---

*By the 1850s the railways were replacing the old coffles of slaves on foot, and speeding up the transport of slaves westward.

happening, and it frightened them—rightly so, since if they were sold south to the new plantations they would not only be separated from everything and everyone they knew, but very likely worked to death under brutal conditions. Lee simply failed to understand the enormous sense of fragility in slave communities like those of Arlington, and the fear of being sent away. When slaves were hired out, they did not know where they were going, or for how long, and feared that instead they might end up on the auction block. In fact it was common practice to hire out the more troublesome slaves and send them somewhere farther away from the temptation of escaping than northern Virginia.

This was a practical factor of slave ownership with which Lee was familiar, and he does not seem to have ignored it in choosing which of the Custis slaves to hire out. However, it was only one of the causes of growing resentment among the slaves, who had "the general impression" they would be freed on Mr. Custis's death—an impression for which Mr. Custis himself was no doubt to blame, since he probably could not be bothered to explain that their emancipation would not in fact take place until his estate had been settled. It cannot have helped that Lee was the proverbial new broom that sweeps clean. His goal was worthy—to restore his late father-in-law's properties and make them profitable for his own wife and children—but this could be done only by working the slaves harder and by eliminating the slackness, the lack of supervision, and the small privileges that Mr. Custis had permitted for many years. The fact that Lee was a former superintendent of West Point, accustomed to having his orders obeyed crisply and without question, probably did not help either—the Custis slaves were not cadets.

From the very beginning Lee had problems with runaways who believed they should have been freed, and who resented his strictness. Each one required Lee to advertise for his or her return, and pay a reward when the slave was brought back. Whether Lee punished the runaways except by hiring them out to someone farther south or west, who might take harsher measures to prevent their escape, is unknown. Elizabeth Brown Pryor, in her book on Lee's letters, *Reading the Man,* speculates that "a whipping post [still] stood" at Arlington, as it did outside the slave quarters on many other plantations, but if so it may have been merely symbolic—although nothing is more powerful than a certain kind of symbol.

The Lees themselves complained that abolitionists were "lurking" around Arlington, urging the slaves to demand their freedom. Arlington and Alexandria were only a stone's throw from Washington, D.C., where there was a substantial community of freed blacks and intense abolitionist activity, so much so that slave owners in the area hesitated to send their slaves there on errands, or to hire them out in the city. One of the major routes of the Underground Railroad involved smuggling fugitive slaves out of the District of Columbia and on to the free states of Pennsylvania and New Jersey.

If the Lees, living so close to Washington, felt besieged, it was not without cause. Lee was not yet famous, but as the last living link to George Washington Mr. Custis had been; it was widely supposed by abolitionists that he had freed his slaves, and that Lee was nevertheless keeping them in bondage. Lee was chagrined, although certain he was not only acting within his rights but, more important, doing the right thing. He and Mary set up a school (against state law, which forbade teaching slaves to read and write) to better prepare the slaves for emancipation, and Lee struggled to pay off the debts and put the widespread Custis plantations on a sound business footing, without which he could not free the slaves within the five-year period stipulated in the will; but the only result was an increasingly sullen and uncooperative workforce and a buzz of scurrilous stories about the Lees, which reached their peak in the spring of 1859 with the escape of three Arlington slaves: Wesley Norris, his sister Mary, and a cousin.

With or without the help of abolitionists, the three made it as far as Maryland, where they "were apprehended and thrown into prison," and after two weeks in a "slave jail" they were returned to Arlington. According to Norris's account, when they were brought before Lee, "he told us he would teach us a lesson we would never forget." What happened then is a matter of dispute. Norris would later claim that Lee ordered all three to be tied to posts in the barn and stripped; that the two men were then whipped fifty times, the woman twenty; and that afterward their backs were washed with brine to intensify the pain of the lacerations—all this in Lee's presence. The two men were then sent to jail for a week and thereafter hired out as farmworkers farther south; the woman was hired out to Richmond.

Allegations about Lee's treatment of his slaves reached New York City quickly, in the form of two anonymous "letters to the editor" published on the same day.

To the Editor of the N.Y. Tribune.

Sir: It is known that the venerable George Washington Parke Custis died some two years ago; and the same papers that announced his death announced also the fact that on his deathbed he liberated his slaves. The will, for some reason, was never allowed any publicity, and the slaves themselves were cajoled along with the idea that some slight necessary arrangements were to be made, when they would all have their free papers. Finally they were told five years must elapse before they could go. Meantime they have been deprived of all means of making a little now and then for themselves, as they were allowed to do during Mr. Custis's life, have been kept harder at work than ever, and part of the time have been cut down to half a peck of unsifted meal a week for each person, without even their fish allowance. . . .

Some three or four weeks ago, three, more courageous than the rest, thinking their five years would never come to an end, came to the conclusion to leave for the North. They were most valuable servants, but they were never advertised, and there was no effort made to regain them which looks exceedingly as though Mr. Lee, the present proprietor, knew he had no lawful claim to them. They had not proceeded far before their progress was intercepted by some brute in human form, who suspected them to be fugitives, and probably wished a reward. They were lodged in jail, and frightened into telling where they started from. Mr. Lee was forthwith acquainted with their whereabouts, when they were transported back, taken into a barn, stripped, and the men received thirty and nine lashes each, from the hands of the slave-whipper, when he refused to whip the girl, and Mr. Lee himself administered the thirty and nine lashes to her. They were then sent to Richmond jail, where they are now lodged. . . .

The second letter, rather shorter, read:

To the Editor of The N.Y. Tribune.

Sir: I live one mile from the plantation of George Washington P. Custis, now Col. Lee's, as Custis willed it to Lee. All the slaves on this estate, as I understand, were set free at the death of Custis, but are now held in bondage by Lee. . . . Custis had fifteen children by his slave women. I see his grandchildren every day; they are of a dark yellow. Last week three of the slaves ran away; an officer was sent after them, overtook them nine miles this side of Pennsylvania, and brought them back. Col. Lee ordered them whipped. They were two men and one woman. The officer whipped the two men, and said he would not whip the woman, and Col. Lee stripped her and whipped her himself. These are facts as I learn from near relatives of the men whipped. . . .

Yours,

A Citizen

Although these letters are dismissed by most of Lee's biographers as exaggerated, or simply as unfounded abolitionist propaganda, it is hard to ignore them. The second one, from "A Citizen," reads as if it might have been written by an envious or malicious neighbor—one who claims to live only "one mile" away from Arlington and to see the slaves "every day"—rather than by an abolitionist propagandist. The reference to the late Mr. Custis having fathered fifteen "dark yellow" children by his slave women must have been mortifying to Mrs. Lee, and scarcely less so to Lee, but the longer letter, which was signed "A," is actually more damaging to Lee's reputation, and also full of small details that can have been obtained only from the Arlington slaves themselves. In any case, Lee decided not to reply, and that was surely the right decision. As he wrote to his oldest son Custis, "*The New York Tribune* has attacked me for my treatment of your grandfather's slaves, but I shall not reply. He has left me an unpleasant legacy."

It seems incongruously out of character for Lee to have whipped a woman slave himself, particularly one stripped to the waist, and that charge may have been a flourish added by the two correspondents; interestingly enough, it was not repeated by Wesley Norris when his account of the incident was published in 1866. After Norris's account appeared Lee wrote to an acquaintance, "No servant, soldier or citizen . . . can with truth charge me with bad treatment," which is as close he ever came to denying the accusations. Brown speculates with some reason that the definition of "bad treatment" is elastic and must take into account the difference in attitude toward corporal punishment in our day and the mid-nineteenth century. The whipping of disobedient or runaway slaves was not necessarily considered "cruel or unusual punishment" in most of the South—this was still, after all, an age when children were often whipped in school and at home. "Spare the road and spoil the child," remained a widespread belief about child rearing. Lee did not use corporal punishment on any of his children—he was the most benign of parents, who relied on moral suasion and setting a good example to instruct his children— but in the mid-nineteenth century people were not squeamish about corporal punishment, and Lee may very well have been infuriated by the way the Custis slaves were resisting his reforms and running away. It was humiliating and expensive for him to search them down and get them back, and he may have felt it was time to set a stern example. Whipping was far from being unusual: Virginia law actually *stipulated* whipping slaves for certain offenses. So Lee was well within his rights, whatever we may think of the incident, and although it seems unlikely that he would have done any of the whipping himself, he may not have flinched from observing it to make sure his orders were carried out exactly.

Lee was never an enthusiast of slavery, and his experience with the Custis slaves further soured him on the institution. He and Mary quietly went on with their plan to educate the Custis slaves, until, one after the other, the Custis properties were overrun by Union troops. The Lees met their obligation to free the Custis slaves within the five years stipulated by Mr. Custis on December 29, 1862, only three months after President Lincoln had announced that he would sign the Emancipation Proclamation, by which time most of the Custis slaves were behind Union lines.

It is hard to know what to make of this incident, or of the slightly different accounts it generated, except to conclude that it was a good example of the moral ambiguities and dilemmas slavery produced for those who

owned slaves, even those who, like Lee, were among
the noblest and most chivalrous citizens in the South.
Wesley Norris's account appears too specific to be a
total invention, and although he differs from the two
letters to the *Tribune* in details—the number of lashes
administered and Lee's personally whipping Mary
Norris—it remains possible that something like this
took place in Arlington in the spring of 1859. Ironically,
Norris ended up working at Arlington in the National
Cemetery after the war, and his sister found employment "by the French Minister at Washington," a happy
outcome for two of the Arlington slaves. As to the final
judgment of the episode, one must look to the choice of
verdicts in the old Scottish courts, where juries could
choose one of three verdicts, "Guilty," "Not guilty,"
and "Not proven," the last meaning that the jury had
its doubts about the accused, but was not convinced by
the facts presented to it by the prosecution.

Lee continued to devote his time to repairing
Arlington and trying to make the Custis properties
self-supporting, if not profitable, with a short break
to sit on a court-martial in New York. His military
career was more or less suspended at his own request,
although General Scott offered him an appointment
as his own "military secretary," a significant sign of

the trust and confidence Scott had in Lee. Lee declined the post because "he did not wish to return to staff duty," and perhaps also because he thought that promotion would be even slower there than as commander of a cavalry regiment in the West. In mid-October, he had the good fortune to be the only officer of the appropriate rank and experience to be placed in command of the forces sent to Harpers Ferry. Then, to his dismay, he was obliged to remain in Arlington until mid-February 1860, in order to testify before the Senate investigation of the Harpers Ferry incident, though he was not asked any questions of real importance.

He was impatient to resume command of the Second Cavalry, but he can hardly have been unaware of the growing discord in the country. His numerous relatives in Virginia would have discussed the southerners' rising resentment against northern abolitionist sentiment, and Lee's fellow officers can hardly have failed to bring the subject up in his presence—indeed it was almost the only subject of conversation in the months that separated John Brown's raid on Harpers Ferry and the firing on Fort Sumter. Talk of secession was widespread, and Lee, though he was wise enough to keep his opinions about the politics of the day to himself, was only too conscious of the difficulties that would face him as an officer of the U.S. Army if he was forced to chose between his country and his state.

He left Arlington on February 10 and arrived in San Antonio on February 19, fast traveling for the day. In addition to command of his regiment, he was "assigned temporary command of the Department of Texas," since he was for the moment the highest-ranking officer in the state, and settled down, perhaps with some relief, to the problems of Indian raids and Mexican bandits.

Chapter 6

1861—"The Thunder of the Captains and the Shouting"

Douglas Southall Freeman, perhaps preeminent among Lee's many biographers, whose four-volume biography, published in 1934 and 1935, was for many years the gold standard on the subject, goes a lot further in expressing enthusiasm for secession than Lee himself ever seems to have done. Freeman writes of Lee at the beginning of 1860: "Like the fated victim of a Greek tragedy, he was coming under forces that he could not control, forces against which it was futile for him even to struggle. . . . The development of the concept of a nation had eclipsed in their minds the older principle that a man's first duty was to his state. It had never been so with Lee. . . . The spirit of Virginia had been alive in his heart every hour of his life. . . . Having ploughed her fields, he had a new sense of oneness with her. He was a United States officer who loved the Army and had pride in the Union, but something very deep in his heart kept him mindful that he had been a Virginian before he had been a soldier."

There is an element of truth in Freeman's moving description of Lee's predicament, but it needs to be taken with a grain of salt. We know that Lee would eventually conclude his first loyalty was to his family, his neighbors, and the state of his birth—he would refuse "to raise his sword" against them when the time came to make a choice—but having taken an oath "to support and defend the Constitution of the United States, against all enemies foreign and domestic" when he entered West Point, he had not yet permanently defined himself as "a Virginian before he had been a soldier," and he still condemned secession as "revolution."

He had an intense loyalty toward Virginia, certainly, intensified by pride in Virginia's role as the "cradle of the Revolution,"* and a dislike of abolitionism that went back to the horrors of Nat Turner's uprising in 1831, and which can only have been increased by his recent problems with the Custis slaves and by his clash with John Brown at Harpers Ferry. But although Lee might

---

*Even in the eighteenth century, while the Revolution was still in progress, many citizens of the Commonwealth of Massachusetts would have contested this, however.

have been reluctant to go to war to defend an institution that he disliked and thought the South would be better off without, like most southerners he also believed that the Federal government had no business imposing northerners' views on the "slave states." His opinions, in short, were moderate by the southern standards of his time. As for having his loyalty to Virginia rekindled by plowing her fields, this, while it is a touching turn of phrase, is without foundation. Lee had worked hard to restore Arlington to its former glory and to make the farms profitable in the two years since the death of Mr. Custis, and he was not afraid of physical labor, but the plow was guided by the callused hands of the Custis slaves, not by Lee's—he was a gentleman farmer, not a farm laborer.

Having won his father's blessing after some hesitation on Lee's part, Rooney, the Lees' second son, had resigned from the army to wed the young woman he loved and had moved to White House, the plantation on the Pamunkey River in New Kent County, Virginia, where George Washington first courted the widowed Martha Dandridge Custis. Here too there was a decrepit manor house and a disgruntled slave workforce. Lee, learning of a fire at a neighboring farm, wrote a pessmisstic warning to Rooney to "gain the affection of your people, that they will not wish to do you any harm." It was a sign of Lee's growing anxiety that he leaped to the conclusion that arson committed by slaves had been the cause of the fire.

From San Antonio Lee continued to worry about the state of his late father-in-law's properties, but at least he was spared a daily struggle with the people who worked there, and the constant discovery of still more items on the endless list of things that needed to be cleaned, repaired, painted, or replaced. Nobody would deny Lee's fondness for Virginia, or his sense of himself and the many branches of his family as Virginian, but his experience with managing a farm in Virginia had given him little pleasure, nor was he content with what he had been able to achieve. He wrote to Custis to sum up his displeasure with his own efforts: "I have been able to do nothing to the grounds around the house, except to clean up on the hill. . . . You will find things, therefore, I fear rough and unsightly, as much as I desire to polish up your mother's habitation, and to prepare for you an acceptable home."

The old sense of failure, which haunted him whenever he thought about his military career, returned to him stronger than ever. He was a fifty-three-year-old man who had been in the army for thirty-five years and felt he had little to show for it, and small hope of promotion. His old friend and classmate Albert Sidney

Johnston had been promoted to quartermaster general, a post which carried with it the rank of brigadier general, making Lee feel even more of a failure, and his stay in San Antonio was not calculated to raise his spirits. Since he did not know how long his command would continue, he lodged in a boardinghouse rather than go to the expense of setting up his own headquarters. He enjoyed neither the food nor the company of strangers. His chief concern was Comanche raids, which carried off cattle, horses, and mules, but his troop strength had dropped to such low numbers and the state of his horses was so poor that he was eventually reduced to sending the members of the band out on whatever mounts they could find to search for Indian raiders.

Another of Lee's concerns was the Mexican bandit Juan Cortinas, who raided American settlements along the Rio Grande. The Mexican authorities did little or nothing to discourage him. Lee himself rode in pursuit of Cortinas accompanied by a company of cavalry, only to discover that Cortinas had fled across the river into Mexico. Lee was perfectly willing to pursue him across the border into Mexico if necessary, but not before writing a notably stiff letter to the closest Mexican authority, "His Excy. Andres Trevino, Govr. Of State of Tamulipas, etc.," bringing to his attention that Lee had been "instructed by the Sec'y of War of the U.S. to notify the authorities of Mexico on the Rio Grande frontier, that they must break up and disperse the bands of banditti which have been concerned in these depredations and have sought protection in Mexican territory."

This did not halt the problem, and ten days later Lee received a protest from General G. Garcia about some Texas Rangers who had crossed the river frontier in pursuit of the elusive Cortinas. His reply to Garcia was even sharper than his first message to the governor. "For the attainment of this object," he wrote, "I shall employ, if necessary, all the force in this Department." Though Lee eventually made good on his warnings by sending two companies of U.S. cavalry across the Rio Grande into Mexico, the wily Cortinas continued to evade those sent in pursuit of him. This can only have added to Lee's gloom. One might have supposed that getting away from his desk and back into the saddle with saber and pistol by his side, in pursuit of armed bandits, would have cheered Lee up, but it does not seem to have done so.

Even the birth of a child to Rooney and his wife, Charlotte, did not shake Lee from his melancholy. He looked on the future with the grim realism of a professional soldier who knows the army—with twenty-two men ahead of him in rank and seniority, he would very likely never reach the rank of brigadier general before he retired. He shared his thoughts with his cousin Anna Fitzhugh: "A divided heart I have too long had, and a divided life I have too long led. . . . Success is not always attained by a single undivided effort, [but] it rarely follows a halting vacillating course. . . . And thus I live and am unable to advance either. But while I live I must toil and trust." He complained to her not only of his "slow progress," but of "a thousand anxieties," presumably about Mary's declining health and the future of Arlington, and added that he was "worn and racked to pieces," strong words for a man who exhibited in every way an extraordinary degree of dignity and self control, and no self-pity. To his twenty-one-year-old daughter Annie he wrote that, lonely as he was, and much as he missed her and the rest of his family, they were perhaps better off without him. "You know I was very much in the way of everybody," he wrote, "and my tastes and pursuits did not coincide with the rest of the household. Now I hope everybody is happier." It is an odd confession, and may have had its origin in Lee's difficulty in relating to his daughters now that they were no longer girls but grown-up young women. Benevolent as Lee was as a father, he was no more tolerant than any other father of his time toward his daughters' romantic yearnings and their choice of beaux. To the ailing Mary he complained about his own health, problems that ranged from a stubborn cold to painful rheumatism in his right arm (Emory M. Thomas in his biography of Lee speculates that this pain may already have been the first symptom of cardiovascular disease). This was not exactly a midlife crisis (a phrase that did not yet exist) even though Lee was fifty-three, but rather the first sign of aging in a man who felt that he had not only failed in his career and lost his chance of a place in history, but also failed his family.

Much as Lee disliked San Antonio, he was no more pleased when he was ordered to return to his regiment in Fort Mason, and replaced as commander of the Department of Texas by David Twiggs, who was now a brevet major general. Lee had been in command, after all, of 1,000 miles of border between the United States and Mexico for almost ten months, and was now merely commander of a much reduced cavalry regiment in one of the remote, dusty, jerry-built "forts" that were supposed to discourage the Comanche and the Kiowas from raiding the new settlements in eastern and central Texas.

Although it may have been Lee's nature to "leave politics to the politicians," he still paid close attention to events in Washington; it is hard to imagine how he could do otherwise, as the nation seemed about to tear itself in two. Many of Lee's own officers "were talking of secession if the 'Black Republicans,' as the new party was called in the South, carried the presidential election." Although Lee deplored such talk, he also deplored any attempt to coerce Virginia; and the Republican ticket of Abraham Lincoln and Hannibal Hamlin can hardly have pleased him. Nor was he impressed by Stephen A. Douglas and Herschel Johnson, who were the choice of the northern wing of the Democratic Party, for that party too, like the Whigs in the previous election, was dividing itself terminally into a northern and southern wing. As early as July Lee had expressed his opinion that Senator Douglas should "withdraw" from the race and join or support John C. Breckinridge, the candidate of the southern, pro-slavery Democrats. "Politicians," Lee concluded, "I fear are too selfish to become martyrs."

The split among the Democrats virtually guaranteed a Republican victory in the North, and with it enough electoral votes to bring Lincoln to the White House. Though Lee did not dwell on the subject, his views were not very far from Lincoln's at this time. Both men disliked slavery as an institution, and hoped it would be allowed to dwindle away peacefully. Neither man believed that Negroes and white men could or should live together as equals. Lee was no more enthusiastic than Lincoln on the issue of extending slavery to the new territories, although the two men might have differed on the subject of returning fugitive slaves to their masters from the "free" states. Lee had already showed his willingness to pursue his slave "property" and have it returned to him, a right reinforced by the Dred Scott decision, but one that Lincoln would certainly have opposed. The southerners' rising passion for states' rights was a subject that Lee approached cautiously, as did Lincoln, since apart from economic issues the only rights actually under dispute were the recovery of fugitive slaves and the extension of slavery into the new territories to the west. Virtually all the other complaints of the southern states against the Federal government might have been negotiated, given a minimum of goodwill on both sides, but the subject of slavery polarized the country on both sides of the issue to the point where talk of secession would swiftly become a reality. This was as alarming a prospect to Lee as it was to Lincoln—both wanted to preserve the Union, but Lee stopped short of any threat of force to coerce the southern states. This was a small chink in the solidity of his loyalty to the Union, but one that was to have enormous consequences, both for him and for the United States.

It is important to realize that Lee moved toward secession reluctantly, with infinite doubt and sadness, but with a firm line in mind that he would not or could not cross. He was not in sympathy with the cheering crowds calling for secession when it became clear that Lincoln had won the presidency on November 6, 1860; nor was he eager to give up the rank in the U.S. Army that had taken him so long to achieve. Then too, he was a Virginian, born in a manor house which George Washington had often visited; he grew up in a town where George Washington had worshipped and attended the Masonic Lodge; his son owned the home in which George Washington had courted his wife, Martha. The Federal government was not a faraway abstraction for Lee; it was only a short ride from his house to the War Department. It would not be easy for Lee to think of that government as the enemy.

Four days after Lincoln's election, the South Carolina state legislature "issued a call for a convention to withdraw the state from the Union." In Texas Lee saw the Lone Star flag of the Texas Republic replacing the Stars and Stripes—the Union flag. It was, he wrote to Custis, "a convulsion," and one of which he could not approve. It was already clear that Texas would secede, despite the opposition of Governor Sam Houston, who, when evicted from office, said to an angry crowd: "Let me tell you, what is coming. After the sacrifice of countless millions of treasure and hundred of thousands of lives, you may win Southern independence if God not be against you, but I doubt it. . . . The North is determined to preserve this Union. They are not a fiery, impulsive people as you are, for they live in colder climates. But when they begin to move in a given direction, they move with the steady momentum and perseverance of a mighty avalanche." Houston expressed what Lee already feared. Long before Houston's eviction from office, Lee wrote Custis: "I hope, however, the wisdom and patriotism of the country will devise some way of saving it. . . . The three propositions of [the outgoing] President Buchanan are eminently just." He doubted that Buchanan's plan would prevail, but he added, "It is, however, my only hope for the preservation of the Union, and I will cling to it to the last. . . . While I wish to do what is right, I am unwilling to do what is wrong, either at the bidding of the South or the North. One of their plans seems to be for a renewal of the slave trade. That I am opposed to on every ground."

Although there has been an immense effort to dissociate Lee from the subject of slavery, it is notable that the three "propositions" of Buchanan's to which he referred as his "only hope for the preservation of the Union" all relate to slavery—(1) the recognition of the "right of property in slaves" in the states where it then existed "or may hereafter exist," the last four words being something that many northerners would regard an as invitation to extend slavery; (2) the "duty" of "protecting this right in the territories," exactly what abolitionists were fighting against in Kansas; and (3) "the enforcement of the fugitive-slave laws, with a declaration of the unconstitutionality of state laws modifying them," which amounted to having the Federal government enforce slavery on the northern states. Lee did not think "that the Northern and Western states [would] agree" to these propositions, and he was absolutely correct, but those who suppose that his only concern was the armed coercion of southern states by the Federal government should consider that he wrote to Custis, who was then serving in the War Department, as early as December 14, 1860, of his belief that national acceptance of Buchanan's three propositions about slavery was the only way to save the Union.

Since Lee would never have dissembled—least of all to his own son—the conventional description of him as being indifferent or opposed to slavery is not altogether correct. He may have disliked it—his personal experience of slavery on a large scale had been for the most part unhappy—but he recognized that the *institution* of slavery was the central political issue for all southerners, and that to allow any interference by northerners would make all southerners second-class citizens, and uproot the social structure and conventions of the South.

Lee also rejected for himself any automatic support of "southern nationalism," describing the "Cotton States" in terms that are, for him, very strong indeed, and objecting to their attempts to coerce the "Border States" in the same terms as he objected to northerners' attempts to coerce Virginia. That he was against renewing the slave trade (he meant the slave trade across the Atlantic from Africa, not internal slave trading in the United States) is hardly surprising. Almost everybody was against it, and in any case Britain's Royal Navy had been taking vigorous action against slave ships since 1807, treating their captains and their crews as pirates.

Ultimately, Lee was opposed to *any* attempt to dictate radical alterations to the status quo in the South. His position was, not surprisingly, that of a landed Virginian social conservative, similar to that of most of his family,* although unlike many of the radical southern firebrands, he preferred to keep the Union intact, both out of self-interest as an officer in the U.S. Army

---

*Notable exceptions were Lee's sister Anne Lee Marshall and her husband, who would be firm Unionists, and whose son Louis, Lee's nephew, served with distinction in the Union Army, was decorated for bravery, and rose to the rank of colonel.

and out of patriotism. Still, he was no longer optimistic that it would not be torn apart, and he had some presentiment of what the future was likely to bring, since he told Custis to "hold on to specie," that is, United States currency—sound advice given the rapid descent into worthlessness of Confederate currency once it appeared, and the difficulties southern banks would face once they were cut off from the national banking system. Lee's advice, both to his wife and to his children, was always objective, practical, and sensible, and the steps he took regarding his own career were equally careful and well thought out. America might be descending into chaos, but Lee remained determined not to be swept along by the tide himself.

A good example of this is a "confidential pamphlet"* that General Scott sent at about this time to a number of officers, summarizing his opinions about what might be done to prevent the outbreak of war, and the strategy he intended to follow if it should break out, written in his inimitable style. This was a fairly rash act on Scott's part—the new president would not be inaugurated for another four months, and Scott had no idea as yet what his views might be on the subject. If the pamphlet was

---

* *Views Suggested by the Imminent Danger, Oct. 29, 1860, of a Disruption of the Union by the Secession of One or More of the Southern States,* by General Winfield Scott (Freeman, *Robert E. Lee,* 418).

"leaked" to the press it could only inflame the feelings of southerners, as well as give them a broad outline of Scott's plans to defeat them. Lee successfully urged his fellow officers in San Antonio not "to suffer these *Views* to get in the newspapers," rightly concerned that Scott's opinions would infuriate Texans and convince doubters that the Federal government intended to attack them. When Dr. Willis G. Edwards, who had read Scott's *Views,* asked him whether "a man's first allegiance was due his state or the nation," Lee, perhaps resenting the fact that he had been put on the spot about the opinion he most wanted for the time being to keep to himself, replied abruptly "that he had been taught to believe, and he did believe that his first obligations were towards Virginia." If that is truly what Lee believed in December 1860, then it is hardly surprising that he prayed for the Union to be preserved. Armed conflict between the Federal government and Virginia would place him in a painful situation, in which his sense of duty and his loyalty to his roots would inevitably clash.

Back in direct command of the Second Cavalry at Fort Mason, Lee found his officers and troopers bewildered by events. On December 20 South Carolina seceded from the United States, and six days later Major Robert Anderson moved his troops from Fort

Moultrie, where he feared they could be surrounded, to Fort Sumter in Charleston harbor, thus unintentionally providing both the Federal government and the South Carolina secessionists with the means to turn a political crisis into a war. On January 9, 1861, the Union steamer *Star of the West* was fired on as it attempted to land reinforcements and supplies at Fort Sumter, and within a few days Mississippi, Florida, Alabama, and Georgia joined South Carolina in seceding from the Union.

Many of Lee's men were divided in their loyalty, as he himself increasingly was, and supplies, pay, and mail to a remote outpost like Fort Mason were now long delayed, as were any sensible orders. Lee passed the time reading Edward Everett's *Life of George Washington,* sent to him from home, as if seeking answers to his dilemma from the past.* He found little there to console him. "How his great spirit would be grieved if he could see the wreck of his mighty labors," he lamented in a letter home on January 23. "I will not, however, permit myself to believe till all ground of hope is gone that the work of his noble deeds will be destroyed, and that his precious advice and virtuous example will so soon be forgotten by his countrymen."

---

*Ironically, Edward Everett would give the two-hour speech that preceded Lincoln's Gettysburg Address on November 19, 1863, at the site of Lee's greatest defeat. Everett's speech, a real nineteenth-century stem-winder, was thought by most people at the time to have far outshone Lincoln's short one.

To Custis, he wrote almost in despair: "I can anticipate no greater calamity for the country than the dissolution of the Union. . . . I am willing to sacrifice everything but honor for its preservation. . . . Secession is nothing but revolution." Lee went on to further describe secession as "anarchy," but also defined as clearly as he could his own position: "A Union that can only be maintained by swords and bayonets . . . has no charms for me. . . . If the Union is dissolved, and the Government disrupted, I shall return to my native State and share the miseries of my people, and save in defence will draw my sword on none."

Clearly, between December 14, 1860, and January 23, 1861, however much Lee desired to see the Union preserved intact, he had made up his mind about what it would take to make that possible: the Federal government must not tamper with the institution of slavery or give in to the demands of abolitionists in the North or attempt to use force against the southern states. Custis would have known his father well enough to recognize the significant reservation (or, as we might call it today, escape clause) in the phrases *"save in defence"* and *"my native State."* With anyone else but Lee these words might have been a rhetorical flourish, but Lee always wrote exactly what he meant, and meant what he wrote. Much as he wished to preserve "a government by Washington, Hamilton, Jefferson, Madison, and the other patriots of the Revolution," if the United States used armed force against Virginia he would join in its defense, whatever the cost or the personal anguish.

Events were moving quickly. On January 26 Louisiana seceded, and on February 1 Texas followed, turning the U.S. Army forces in the state into the enemy overnight in the view of many secessionists. General Twiggs,* who had replaced Lee as commander of the Department of Texas, believed that it was his duty to surrender his troops, a position that Lee did not share, but Lee was spared the embarrassment of deciding what to do with his regiment by an urgent message for him to return to Washington, D.C., immediately and "report in person to the general-in-chief by April 1st."

Rightly assuming that he would not be returning to Texas, Lee traveled to San Antonio in a horse-drawn "ambulance," probably the only closed vehicle in a cavalry regiment that could carry all his kit and belongings. These were "bulky and somewhat valuable," the home away from home of a professional soldier, and would serve Lee throughout the Civil War. He described it to his daughter Agnes: "On the right of the entrance of the tent, stands an iron camp bed.

---

*Twiggs would surrender his entire command "to avoid bloodshed," and would himself become a Confederate major general.

On the left a camp table and chair. At the far end a trunk. On the side near the entrance a water bucket basin & broom, clothes hung around within easy reach of all points, & a sword & pistol very convenient. A saddle & bridle at the foot of the bed on a wooden horse." Of course there was more to it than that—but Lee's needs were Spartan: writing desk, books, his Bible, his bedclothes, his uniforms, and his boots were all the kit he needed.

No sooner had Lee arrived at the hotel in San Antonio than he was surrounded by armed men in civilian clothes. The wife of a friend who happened to be passing by informed him that General Twiggs had only that morning surrendered his command, and that all Federal troops were now "prisoners of war." Lee was shocked, and outraged at the possibility that he might be treated as a prisoner of war. He prudently changed into civilian clothes and made his way to headquarters, where he found that the secessionists were already in charge, and not disposed to treat him with the courtesy he expected. He explained that his allegiance was to Virginia and the Union, in that order, and that he was returning home, but the "Texas commissioners," as they called themselves, were not mollified. If Lee agreed to resign his commission and accept one in the Confederate Army, he was told, he would be free to travel home with his belongings, but if not he would have to leave them behind.

This seems like an odd decision. If the Texas commissioners were willing to let him go home, why hold on to his luggage? Lee was infuriated, and went immediately to the home of a friend, Charles Anderson, a lawyer and an outspoken Unionist and abolitionist, who would become colonel of the Ninety-Third Ohio Volunteer Infantry and eventually governor of Ohio. It speaks volumes for Lee that he was a friend of a man like Anderson who disagreed vehemently with him, although at this stage, at any rate, he and Anderson were of one mind about the Texas secessionists. Perhaps because he was angry, Lee was franker about his position than he had been with anybody else except his family. "I cannot be moved by the conduct of those people [the "Texas commissioners"] from my sense of duty. I still think . . . that my loyalty to Virginia ought to take precedence over that which is due the Federal Government. And I shall so report myself at Washington. If Virginia stands by the Union, so will I. But if she secedes, then I will follow my native state with my sword, and if need be with my life." Though he told another friend that he planned to go home and plant corn, and that the world would have "one soldier less," he cannot have imagined that Virginia would be neutral, or that he would be left alone to cultivate his garden. Lee asked Anderson to hold on to his belongings and have them shipped to Arlington, which Anderson agreed to do. That problem solved, Lee set off for home by way of Indianola (then a thriving Texas seaport, though it became a ghost town after the Civil War) and New Orleans.

He arrived at Arlington on March 1, three days before the inauguration of Abraham Lincoln—the first presidential inauguration in Washington since Thomas Jefferson's that no member of the Lee or the Custis family attended.

Although Mary Lee was badly handicapped by rheumatoid arthritis and occasionally gave the impression of being a helpless southern belle, she was in fact a dauntless and outspoken woman, who did not share her husband's dislike of confrontations or his relatively moderate opinions about the growing divide between North and South. Medical knowledge being what it was in the mid-nineteenth century, the only treatment doctors could prescribe for her condition was "taking the waters," that is to say bathing in or drinking the water of mineral springs, of which there were and still remain a great number in Virginia, including Hot Springs, Warm Springs, White Sulphur

Springs, and Rockbridge Baths. Jones Springs was just over the border in North Carolina. Mary visited them all in search of relief. Though travel was excruciatingly difficult for her, she managed to make the journey to an amazing number of spas; and while Lee was in San Antonio she even managed to get as far as Canada, to Saint Catherine's Well, just north of Niagara Falls, a "long journey via Baltimore, New York City, and Elmira," which she made in the company of her son Custis, her daughter Agnes, and her cousin Markie Williams, leaving her daughter Annie to supervise the servants at Arlington and get Millie (the Lees' youngest child) off to boarding school. Even with three relatives to help Mary, it cannot have been an easy journey, but she seems to have enjoyed the principal scenic attractions—Niagara Falls and Lake Ontario—though even more than a century and a half ago she complained about the many buildings close to the falls, and the commercialism. She was struck by the large number of runaway slaves living in Canada, just across the border from the United States, and the terrible conditions in which they lived. "I am told," she wrote to Annie, "that they suffer a great deal here in the long cold winters." Perhaps fortunately, she did not recognize any familiar faces among them.

Leaving Agnes and Markie behind in New York City, she returned at the end of the summer, despite the "increasingly polarized atmosphere" of the North. It seems unlikely that Mary concealed her own feelings on the subject. She was appalled at southerners' threats of secession—she was not George Washington's step-great-granddaughter for nothing—but was equally affronted by the growing abolitionist sentiments of northerners she met. Even when Mary Lee returned home to Virginia, it was to discover that feelings there too had risen very high. In consequence, when Custis "had to be away for several days," he asked a fellow officer at the War Department, Orton Williams, Markie's brother, to stay at Arlington "to look after us lone feminines," as Mrs. Lee put it.

As state after state seceded, both Custis Lee and Orton Williams were eager to resign from the U.S. Army and take commissions in the Confederate Army then being formed. This produced an anguished letter from Lee—it was exactly the kind of thing that he would not do himself, and did not want any of his family to do; and it may have contributed to his opinion that Orton Williams was a hothead, which would later have serious consequences both for Williams and for the Lee family. He was determined to remain loyal to the United States until, or unless, Virginia seceded, and once he arrived

home he firmly discouraged any loose talk or speculation on the subject. This, however, did not prevent
Mary from expressing her strong opinion that having
won the election, Lincoln should have resigned before
taking office, "if he had been a true or disinterested
patriot," as a gesture of conciliation toward the South:
"Nothing he can do now," she continued firmly, "can
meet with any favor from the South."

Even if Lee agreed with her—and there is no indication that he did—this was just the kind of extreme opinion that he most wanted to avoid. He was acutely aware
of the importance of exact language at this point, when
he was walking a fine line between his duty to the U.S.
government and his loyalty to Virginia. He was not alone.
Mary Chesnut, the sharp-witted and indefatigable South
Carolinian diarist, whose comments are full of good gossip
and formidable common sense, and who seems to have
known everybody of any consequence in the Confederate
government, noted that Lee's elder brother Commander
Sydney Smith Lee wished "South Carolina could be
blown out of [the] water . . . for disrupting his beloved"
U.S. Navy, a feeling that Robert E. Lee might well have
shared on the subject of the U.S. Army.

Apart from a "long interview" with General in Chief
Winfield Scott shortly after he arrived home, in which
Lee presumably made his position clear to Scott, while

Scott urged him to do nothing hasty, he did nothing except enjoy the company of his family and wait for news, which was not long in coming. On March 16 he was at last promoted to the rank of full colonel (he had previously been a lieutenant colonel with the brevet rank of colonel). His new commission was signed by President Lincoln. Under normal circumstances this would have gratified Lee, but it is hard not to see in it the hand of General Scott. Had Scott already revealed to the president that he considered Colonel Lee the best-qualified man in the U.S. Army to command an army in the field in case of war? Was the new commission, signed by the president, a discreet hint of much higher promotions to come, not so much a quid pro quo—Lee was above that kind of thing, as Scott knew very well— as a test to see if Lee would accept it? In any case, he did so on March 28, ironically about a week after he had received a courteous letter from the Confederate secretary of war, L. P. Walker, offering him a commission as a brigadier general in the Confederate Army. Lee ignored Walker's letter; he clung to his formula, which was that he would do nothing until Virginia decided its own fate.

On April 4 a "test vote" by the members of the Virginia Convention, which had been called to decide whether or not the state would secede, "showed a majority of two-for-one against secession," which essentially left Lee in limbo. Virginia having declined to join the other southern states in secession, the convention appointed a three-man delegation to ask Lincoln what his intentions were toward Fort Sumter, one of the forts commanding the harbor of Charleston, South Carolina, which had become the potential flash point of civil war. Major Robert Anderson was sharply criticized on both sides of the conflict for having moved his garrison into such an exposed position with insufficient food or ammunition, turning the fort into a highly visible casus belli: "Why did that green goose Anderson go into Fort Sumter?" Mary Chesnut moaned in her diary. "Now they have intercepted a letter from him, urging them [the Federal government] to let him surrender. He paints the horrors likely to ensue if they do not. He ought have thought of all that before he put his head in the hole." Though he may well have shared Mary Chesnut's feelings, Lincoln made it clear to the Virginia delegation that he felt entitled to defend any Federal installation that was threatened—something that Buchanan had notably failed to attempt. The president specifically warned against the consequences if "an unprovoked assault on Fort Sumter" was made. "I shall," he said firmly, "to the best of my ability, repel force with force."

Events were now moving so rapidly that no message from the president, however carefully written, could halt them. On April 7 Confederate Brigadier General P. G. T. Beauregard, believing that Fort Sumter was about to be reinforced by sea, ordered all supplies of fresh food to the island from the mainland stopped. The next day, in response to this, Lincoln ordered U.S. ships to resupply the garrison, and five days later, at daylight on April 12, 1861, massed Confederate artillery opened fire on the fort. The first rounds were fired by the young cadets of The Citadel and by the vehement secessionist Edmund Ruffin, who, with his unmistakable shock of shoulder-length white hair, had been a prominent figure at John Brown's hanging. The next morning the *Charleston Mercury* hailed the opening bombardment as a "Splendid Pyrotechnic Exhibition," as if it were a fireworks display, and described the beauty of the first shot, "which, making a beautiful curve, burst immediately above Fort Sumter." The *New York Times*, with passionate fury, declared, "Whatever the leaders of this conspiracy may believe, the civilized world will have but one opinion of their conduct; they will be greeted with the indignant scorn and execration of the world."

Two days later Fort Sumter surrendered and President Lincoln called for the raising of 75,000 men to suppress the rebellion and "cause the laws to be duly executed." During the night of April 16–17 the Virginia convention went into a "secret session." The next morning, Lee received an urgent note from General Scott, who asked Lee to call on him at the War Department the following day. Lee also received a message that Francis Preston Blair (Sr.) wished to see him.

The note from General Scott would not have surprised Lee, but the message about Francis Preston Blair certainly would. Blair was a wealthy journalist and publicist from Kentucky, a longtime Washington insider and former member of President Andrew Jackson's "Kitchen Cabinet" who still exerted considerable political power and was a friend and confidant of President Lincoln. One of Blair's sons, Montgomery, who had been a friend of Lee's in Saint Louis, was now the postmaster general, and an influential adviser, political "fixer," and dispenser of patronage on behalf of the president.* Francis P. Blair had already discussed with both Lincoln and Secretary of War Simon Cameron the possibility of making Colonel Lee the commander of the Union Army that was being raised, and Lincoln had authorized Blair "to ascertain Lee's intentions and feelings." Lincoln, a consummate politician, wanted

---

* Blair House, at 1651 Pennsylvania Avenue, has been the official state guesthouse of the president of the United States since 1942. Francis P. Blair's daughter Elizabeth married a member of the Lee family. Blair was, among many other things, a great-great-grandfather of the actor Montgomery Clift.

to make sure, before making the offer, that it would be accepted, and chose somebody he trusted who was *not* a member of the cabinet to sound Lee out privately. Appointing a southern officer to command a northern army was a risky political move, but having him decline the offer publicly was riskier still, and would look like a humiliation for the new president. It was Blair's task to prevent this.

Early in the morning on April 18 Lee rode from Arlington to Montgomery Blair's home at 1651 Pennsylvania Avenue, where Francis P. Blair was waiting for him, and the two men sat down "behind closed doors" for a talk. There were no witnesses and both men were reticent on the subject afterward, but Blair almost certainly told Lee that an army was being raised "to enforce Federal law," and offered Lee the command with the rank of major general. For a man who only a few weeks earlier had been lamenting the failure of his military career, it must have been an ironic moment. Already promoted to colonel by Lincoln, Lee had been offered the rank of brigadier general by the Confederacy. Now Lincoln was prepared to make him a major general in command of the largest army in American history. Could he possibly have been tempted, or at least felt a momentary pang of regret? It seems doubtful. Lee had already made up his mind, about what he would *not* do, and his integrity was unshakable. Blair spoke at great length, and no doubt with persuasive effect, but Lee stuck to his guns. "I declined the offer he made me to take command of the army that was to be brought into the field," he wrote much later, "stating as clearly as candidly and as courteously as I could, that though opposed to secession and deprecating war, I could take no part in an invasion of the Southern States." He had no idea what the Virginia Convention was deciding, and of course no way of knowing that on the night of April 17 it had already voted to secede. Given the number of his Lee, Carter, and Custis relatives who were involved in Virginia politics, it seems unlikely that Lee didn't have a good idea of what was going on in Richmond, but he had already decided that he could not agree to lead an army "in an invasion of the Southern States," whatever Virginia decided. Now Lee was unwilling to participate in military action against *any* of the southern states. Once he announced his position to Francis Blair, he was anxious to move on quickly. He realized he could not honorably remain an officer in the U.S. Army knowing that he might have to disobey an order from his superiors. He went directly from Blair House to see General Scott.

"There are times," Scott is reported to have told Lee, "when every officer in the United States service should fully determine what course he will pursue and frankly declare it. No one should continue in government employ without being actively employed. . . . I suppose you will go with the rest. If you purpose to resign, it is proper that you should do so at once; your present attitude is equivocal."

There is some question whether these were Scott's exact words, but they certainly sound like him. In any case, Lee had already reached the same conclusion. He went immediately to see his elder brother Commander Sydney Smith Lee, who was serving in Washington at the time. Neither of them knew that Virginia had already made the critical decision. Lee rode home to Arlington, still under the impression that he and Smith had some time to spare, but when he went into Alexandria the next morning the news of the Virginia Convention's decision to secede was in the newspapers. "I must say that I am one of those dull creatures that cannot see the good of secession," Lee is reported to have said to the druggist as he was paying his bill, expressing an opinion that he was not to change, though increasingly he would keep it to himself.

Cheering crowds had greeted the news of secession, but Lee still thought of the government across the Potomac River as *his* government, one that his own father had fought to establish. "I am unable to realize," he had written Mary Lee's cousin Markie Williams, only four months ago, "that our people will destroy a government inaugurated by the blood & wisdom of our patriot fathers, that has given us peace and prosperity at home, power & security abroad, & under which we have acquired a colossal strength unequalled in the history of mankind. I wish to live under no other government, & there is no sacrifice I am not ready to make for the preservation of the Union, save that of honour. . . . I wish for no other flag than *The Star Spangled Banner,* & no other air than *Hail Columbia.*" Honor and duty had brought him to a decision that he did not welcome, and to a future that must have seemed deeply uncertain for an Army officer of fifty-four whose whole adult life had been spent obeying the orders of his superiors and urging obedience on those under his command, and whose role model since childhood had been George Washington.

What would Lee have done if Virginia had not seceded? It is hard to imagine him sitting at home as a retired colonel while war raged between the Union and the other southern states, but he had already made his mind up that he would not participate in *any* Union attack against the South, and once Lee reached a decision, he did not retreat from it. His stubbornness and inflexibility of purpose were remarkable. They were qualities that he shared with the retired Captain

Ulysses S. Grant, then still humbly wrapping parcels in his father's harness shop in Galena, Illinois, and they would make Lee a formidable opponent on the battlefield.

He sat down late that night and wrote his brief, formal letter of resignation to Secretary of War Cameron: "I have the honor to tender the resignation of my commission as Colonel of the 1st Regt. of Cavalry." It is easy to imagine with what pain Lee wrote those few lines bringing to an end a thirty-six-year career. Perhaps more painful still was his longer letter to General Scott, in which he wrote that to "no one, General, have I been as much indebted as to yourself for uniform kindness and consideration, and it has always been my ardent desire to earn your approbation"—adding what had become part of his formula: "Save in defense of my native State, I never desire again to draw my sword." These were not empty words. Lee would not take up arms against the Union until the Union took up arms against Virginia, whatever the other southern states did. When he was done, he brought the letters down to show them to Mary—she had heard him upstairs fall to his knees in prayer. Having received her approval Lee sent them off by messenger first thing in the morning. Rooney and Custis were at home at the time, both of them appalled by Virginia's decision to secede, as well as by their father's decision to resign from the army, which, as one of his daughters put it, "Was to him home and country."

Lee then went back to his desk to write what was, no doubt, the most difficult letter of all, to his beloved sister Anne Marshall in Baltimore, knowing that she and her husband were staunch Unionists and would not approve of what he had done. "I know you will blame me," he wrote, "but you must think as kindly of me as you can, and believe that I have endeavored to do what I thought right." He then wrote to his brother Sydney Smith Lee, informing him of the decision, without suggesting that Smith follow his example.

Having informed those he wanted to inform of his decision, Lee patiently waited on events. Patience was another of those qualities that would make him a great general. His self-control was unshakable and inspired confidence even in men who might otherwise have lost heart. He had only to appear at any critical point on the battlefield to infuse men with his own courage. It was not a pose, Lee's calmness, his "marble image," and his refusal to reveal his emotions were all reflections of the man himself. He had no wish and no ability to create an image; he was, quite simply, what he appeared to be. He would shortly become the major military and political asset of the Confederacy.

He showed no emotion when he discovered in the morning that his own daily newspaper, the *Alexandria Gazette,* called for his appointment to a high-ranking command if he resigned his commission in the U.S. Army: "There is no man who would command more of the confidence of the people of Virginia, than this distinguished officer." Lee, the most modest of men, must certainly have been embarrassed by this un-called-for effusion, but by lunchtime he received a letter from Judge John Robertson of Richmond, asking for an interview with him the next day. He was left for the moment with nothing to do, and it surely occurred to him, as it did to Custis, that if hostilities began the town of Alexandria, and with it Mary Lee's beloved Arlington, which commanded the south bank of the Potomac River from high ground within sight of Washington, would be occupied by the Union Army. Indeed, Custis remarked that if he were in command of the Union forces in Washington this would be his first move, and he was not wrong.

The next day, a Sunday, Lee attended service at Christ Church in Alexandria, and was dismayed by the enthusiasm of the people for war and perhaps even more so by the hope they placed in him. He learned, after church, that Judge Robertson would not be able to meet him as planned, since the Federal authorities had seized the mail steamboats on the Potomac River—a sign that would not have surprised Lee. At least some people in the U.S. government knew what they were doing. Virginia's many difficulties in communication, supply, finance, and transportation soon followed. That evening Lee received a message from the judge apologizing for his inability to reach Alexandria earlier in the day, and inviting Lee to accompany him to Richmond to meet with the governor of Virginia, John Letcher. Never one to waste a minute, Lee departed by train for Richmond early the next morning, wearing civilian clothes and a silk top hat, and accompanied by Judge Robertson.

Lee would never see Arlington again.

Richmond was abuzz with excitement. Alexander Stephens, the vice president of the Confederate States of America, had arrived to negotiate Virginia's union with the Confederacy, a major but inevitable step. Lee checked into the Spotswood Hotel, and after a meal made his way to the capitol through the boisterous crowds in the street, apparently unrecognized by them. Like many military officers Lee had an ingrained distrust for politicians, both southern and northern, and John Letcher may have seemed to him at first glance exactly the kind of politician he didn't like. Although some describe Letcher as "bald-headed, florid, and bottle-nosed," in photographs he looks thin, stern, and intelligent—not at all a southern version of a Tammany Hall type. Certainly Letcher had the delicate skill of the born politician when it came to altering his principles to take advantage of events. He was a longtime foe of secession and had wanted to bring slavery to an end in Virginia, but once elected to the governorship he adroitly put all that behind him, and rather like Lee, he went to work with considerable efficiency for two causes in which he did not believe.* He seems to have won Lee's trust at their first meeting, and kept it throughout most of the war. His letter to Lee having gone astray, he explained that Virginia needed "a commander of [its] military and naval forces," carrying with it the rank of major general. He offered the post to Lee, who instantly accepted. If Lee felt any doubts, he did not express them. Governor Letcher informed the convention of Lee's nomination, which was unanimously approved. By the time Lee got back to his hotel, he was, at last, a major general, though without the uniform.

---

*Letcher was rather unfairly punished by both sides; he was defeated in his attempt to win a seat in the Second Confederate Congress, and briefly imprisoned after the Civil War ended, as well as having his house burned to the ground by Union troops.

Photographs of him published around the time of his appointment are all old ones altered for the occasion, showing him in the pre–Civil War full dress uniform of a U.S. Army colonel, but with the badge of the U.S. Army and the letters "U.S." clumsily changed into those of the Virginia Militia. In these photographs he looks remarkably young and dashing for his age, now fifty-four, with penetrating dark eyes, a thick black mustache, and a full head of Byronic dark hair—the noble, careworn face with the silver hair and the full white beard had yet to appear.

Before he could get to bed he was politely summoned to meet the vice president of the Confederate states at Ballard House. A Georgian, Alexander Stephens was tiny, frail, ill, wizened—he weighed less than 100 pounds—but his skeletal hands, pitted face, and high voice were offset by fierce intelligence and great courage. Although a friend described him as "highly sensitive," with "poverty-fed pride" and "morbid" self-preoccupation, he had risen high in the ranks of the U.S. Congress until 1858; his greatest achievement was the passing of the Kansas-Nebraska Act, which infuriated northerners. His bravery was legendary—despite being repeatedly stabbed by an opponent during an argument about the Wilmot Proviso, preventing the extension of slavery into the territories, Stephens vocally held to his opinion even when he was seriously wounded. In 1861, just two months before his meeting with Lee, he had defined the Confederate government's policy firmly: "Its foundations are laid, its cornerstone rests, upon the great truth that the Negro is not equal to the white man; that slavery, subordination to a superior race, is his natural and normal condition."

Lee and Stephens did not discuss slavery, but Stephen's position on the subject was exactly the same as the one Lee had described in a letter to Mary on December 27, 1856, and would state under oath to a committee of the U.S. Senate in 1868.

Stephens immediately got to the point of the meeting. He was concerned that Lee's new rank of major general might become an obstacle to Virginia's joining the Confederacy. With some embarrassment, Stephens explained that the Confederate Army had no higher rank than brigadier general. If Virginia were, as he hoped, to merge its military forces with those of the new nation, Lee might have to lose a star, or become a subordinate of an officer of lower rank than his own. Lee replied that he did not wish "his official rank or *personal* position" to stand in the way of the "alliance" between Virginia and the Confederacy.

Behind this polite exchange was a serious political issue: Virginians had not yet voted on the Virginia

Convention's decision to secede, and of all the southern states Virginia had the longest border with the northern states—over 425 miles—and was therefore the most exposed to immediate attack from the North. It was also the largest, richest, and most populous of the slave states, with more than 1.5 million people, 500,000 of them slaves. Virginians saw their state as a *country*, bigger indeed than some European nations, and their institutions, history, and major figures of the Revolution as having been instrumental in shaping the U.S. government. Many Virginians, including Lee, had already guessed that if war came, much of it would be fought in the narrow space between Richmond and Washington; it would not be easy for Virginia to cede control of its armed forces to the new Confederate nation, or to allow Georgians or Mississippians to dictate Virginia's strategy or command its troops. Virginians had a natural reluctance to give up one form of subordination for another—hence the delicate negotiations Stephens was in Richmond to undertake. Lee himself, though he accepted the logic of joining the Confederacy, would remain a Virginian throughout the war, and would often be criticized for focusing so much of the Confederacy's limited strength on the great battles in northern Virginia.

Already, it was obvious that given its resources, the Confederacy was too big to defend at every point—its coastline alone was nearly 3,000 miles long, from the Potomac to the mouth of the Rio Grande, and its frontier stretched even farther, including eleven states and contested areas of Arizona, New Mexico, Missouri, and Kentucky, as well as long stretches of the nation's biggest river systems. Lee knew better than most the harsh maxim of Frederick the Great: "He who attempts to defend everything, defends nothing." What people wanted Lee to do was to attack the North as soon as possible, and attempt to win a single, decisive victory in the field, one big enough to shatter northerners' self-confidence and confirm the South's independence in the eyes of the world. On the other hand, as a professional officer who had served under General Winfield Scott in Mexico, Lee knew that the Confederacy was unprepared to take the offensive. The South lacked men, arms, horses, and mules, and above all it lacked a well-trained, efficient command and logistic structure. It was symbolic of Lee's problems that many weeks would pass before he could improvise any kind of uniform for himself—not until late in the year would he first appear in Confederate gray, with what was to become his trademark headgear, a silvery gray, modestly broad-brimmed hat. Producing a real army would take longer.

From the beginning, Lee was plagued by enthusiasts who believed the war could be won in thirty days, or

at worst in ninety, and that some combination of southerners' zeal, courage, spirit, and breeding would overwhelm the forces of the "money-grubbing Yankees."
He was also plagued by legions of wide-eyed visionar-
ies each of whom had a surefire plan for winning the
war at one stroke. Lee's imposing dignity and remote
courtesy provided a kind of natural protective barrier
between him and people like this until such time as he
had formed a loyal staff whose primary responsibility
was to shield him from as many interruptions as they
could.

Lee was given a small office in "the Virginia
Mechanics Institute at Ninth and Franklin Streets,"*
which was soon enlarged until it filled the building.
He had barely settled in when four members of the
Virginia Convention arrived to escort him to the capitol
to confirm his new commission.

If there was one thing that Lee disliked almost as
much as Grant did, it was formal ceremonies at which
he was obliged to speak, but he submitted to the ordeal
with his usual grace. The convention was in session
behind locked doors when he arrived, and he was
obliged to wait several minutes in the rotunda, which

---

*Emory M. Thomas is probably correct; but in fairness it should be noted that
Freeman places this temporary office either at the Richmond Post Office or "in the
old state General Court building" (Freeman, *Robert E. Lee,* 464).

had been designed by Thomas Jefferson. In its center stands Jean-Antoine Houdon's life-size marble stature of Washington, dressed in his simple uniform, resting his arm against a fasces, or bundle of rods, the Roman symbol for political power, with a plow behind him, emphasizing his roles as general, president, and gentleman farmer. One of Lee's escorts, watching him contemplate Washington, heard him say, oddly enough, "I hope we have heard the last of secession." Did he mean that now that Virginia had seceded it was time to think about defense, or was he reflecting again, now that it was too late, on his dislike of the whole idea of secession? Might he have been thinking about how difficult it would have been to explain to his idol George Washington that his own state had seceded from the Union, which the founding fathers had fought so hard and so long to establish and which had lasted only eighty-four years before unraveling into civil war?

Finally, the doors were opened, he was ushered into the crowded room, and "the convention rose to receive him." He stood a few paces from the entrance, in the central aisle of the chamber, while the nineteenth-century taste for fulsome oratory ran its course.

In contrast, his reply, though gracious, was hardly more than fifty words long, including his disclaimer, that he "would much have preferred had your choice fallen upon an abler man." It was not so much that Lee felt inadequate to the task before him—in fact, thanks to his position on General Scott's staff in Mexico few officers could have been better prepared—as that he would have happily yielded his place to a more competent soldier had such a person existed. But the truth was that there was nobody abler than Robert E. Lee, and nobody who commanded such universal respect. After Lee had spoken, the delegates left their seats to crowd around him, as if seeking confidence from his presence: he was, from the beginning, the totem of the southern cause, the person who seemed to embody its highest aspirations and lend nobility to them. It was not a role he enjoyed, though in the end he grew so used to it that it became part of his personality.

As soon as he decently could, he left and returned to his office to get on with the task of defending Virginia.

The two immediate problems facing him had already been met, with mixed results. The Federal arsenal at Harpers Ferry, the target of John Brown's raid, was occupied by Virginia "volunteers," many of them militiamen, but not before the small detachment of departing Union troops had set fire to the workshops and storage buildings, destroying most of the muskets kept there, but leaving the machinery for producing them intact. The Virginia officer commanding the forces now holding Harpers Ferry was a then little known and mildly eccentric former brevet major of the U.S. Army, Thomas J. Jackson, professor of natural and experimental philosophy and instructor of artillery at the Virginia Military Institute in Lexington. He had distinguished himself in the Mexican War, and would soon earn the nickname "Stonewall," becoming Lee's most valued corps commander, and indeed ranking as a southern hero second only to Lee himself. Although Lee had seen and admired Jackson fighting in Mexico, he may not at first have realized that the loss of thousands of desperately needed rifles was less important than the fact that Major Jackson had joined the cause.

The second incident involved the Norfolk Navy Yard. It had been seized by Confederate troops, then swiftly recaptured in a daring raid from the sea during which Union troops set fire to most of the ships and the yards, then steamed off with one of the naval vessels in tow—an early and embarrassing demonstration of Union naval strength. On the positive side over 1,000 stored naval guns and nearly 3,000 barrels of gunpowder were saved, and many of the guns could be mounted on carriages and used as artillery on land—but the loss of the ships was a grave blow. Several of them would be rebuilt from the waterline up, and the hulk of one of them, the steam frigate U.S.S. *Merrimack,* would eventually be converted into the Confederate ironclad *Virginia,* and do battle against the Union ironclad *Monitor* in March 1862.

Lincoln's reaction to the firing on Fort Sumter had been to issue "A Proclamation" on April 15, calling forth "the militia of the several States of the Union, to the aggregate total of seventy-five thousand . . . to cause the laws to be duly executed." This was the army whose command Lee had been offered on April 18. Describing "the present condition of public affairs" as "an extraordinary occasion," the president commanded the rebels "to disperse, and retire peaceably to their respective abodes within twenty days of this date." By design Lincoln's proclamation was something less than a declaration of war, but it seemed to suggest that on, or shortly after, May 5 the Federal government would take military action against those states which had seceded. This gave Lee less than two weeks to prepare for the defense of Virginia against what he supposed would be overwhelming forces. Events were moving at a dizzying pace. The bombardment of Fort Sumter began on April 12, three days later, on April 15, Lincoln released his proclamation calling up 75,000 men; on April 18 Lee was offered command of the new Union Army that was being called up; early on April 19 he resigned from the U.S. Army; on April 22 he left Arlington forever and took the train for Richmond with Judge Robertson; and on April 23 he was already in command of the armed forces of Virginia, with just twelve days to go before the deadline in the president's proclamation took effect.

Lee immediately set about transforming chaos into the makings of an effective military machine. He quickly put together a personal staff (perhaps its most important member would be young Walter Herron Taylor, a graduate of Virginia Military Institute who would remain with Lee throughout the war) and to dexterously replace inept or elderly senior militia officers (most of them possessed of varying degrees of local political clout) with experienced officers. He drew up plans to gather arms from wherever he could, and to designate railway junctions throughout the state where militia companies could be mustered and armed under the command of an experienced officer and instructed in drill by cadets chosen from VMI. He made a personal inspection of the defenses at Harpers Ferry and Norfolk, and set everyone to digging the fieldworks at which he was the acknowledged expert. He soon established a training depot near Richmond, nicknamed Camp Lee, to turn civilian volunteers into soldiers. Lee amazed everyone by his energy and professional skill, putting together in a matter of weeks an army of "40,000 troops [and] one-hundred fifteen field artillery pieces," as well as a group of officers many of whom would be among the South's leading generals—including Thomas J. ("Stonewall") Jackson; John Bell Hood, Lee's companion from Camp Cooper, Texas; and John B. Magruder.

Lee was always aware that only a few miles north, in the Union, his friend and mentor General in Chief Winfield Scott was doing the same thing on a much larger scale, and with much greater resources to command. Despite his impeccable courtesy Lee did not accomplish all this without ruffling some feathers in the process, mostly because he did not appear to many people sufficiently enthusiastic about secession, or about the ability of the South to win the war. Part of this was the realism of a professional military man, not given to the easy optimism of amateur soldiers; part of it was the fact that whoever won the war, the world he knew and loved would be destroyed. Armies would march back and forth across Virginia, uprooting families, destroying farms and crops, threatening the established order that was so dear to Lee, and disrupting the grace, formality, and traditions of 200 years.

This foreboding of loss touched Lee deeply, and came true more quickly than he had anticipated. Although both he and Custis had gently—perhaps too gently—warned Mrs. Lee that she might be forced to leave her beloved Arlington, she remained at home, writing to him in Richmond that she had never seen "the country more beautiful, perfectly *radiant.* The yellow jasmine [is] in full bloom & perfuming all the air."

"You *have to move,*" he wrote to her sharply on April 26. When she didn't, a week later he urged her "to prepare all things for removal . . . & be prepared to move at any moment," again to no effect. In the end it was her cousin Orton Williams who rode over from the War Department to warn Mary that Union troops would be taking over the house the next day. In the morning he rode over again to say that the occupation of Arlington had been delayed, but would not be canceled—she *must* move, and quickly. Her daughter Mildred was at school, and Annie was away at the Pamunkey River plantation with her brother Rooney and his wife, so it was left to Mary and her daughter Agnes to oversee the monumental task of packing up the contents of Arlington. The silver of the Lee and Custis families was placed in two heavy chests, together with Lee's personal papers and the "irreplaceable Washington and Custis documents," and shipped by rail to Richmond. The family portraits and Mr. Custis's paintings were carefully removed from their frames, to be transported by wagon to Ravensworth for safekeeping. The carpets, rugs, draperies, and books were removed and stored, along with George Washington's 302-piece set of the blue-white-and gold Society of the Cincinnati china. Finally, his famous punch bowl,★ with a pen-and-ink drawing of an American frigate inside, "the hull resting on the bottom, mast[s] projecting to the rim," so that drinkers could empty it from the mastheads down to the waterline, was packed into one of the wooden boxes which were nailed shut and put away in the cellar under lock and key, the latter entrusted to one of the Arlington slaves: Selina Grey, Mrs. Lee's "personal maid."

The dashing Lieutenant Orton Williams's visits to warn Mrs. Lee at Arlington were part of his pattern of reckless, if sometimes chivalric behavior, which together with his undisguised southern sympathy was to lead to his arrest and brief detention on Governors Island in New York. As an officer serving in General Scott's headquarters, he had access to Scott's war plans, which it was feared he would disclose to General Lee. Always the true romantic, "he was reported to have

---

★This bowl survived the occupation and partial looting of the house by Federal troops, and is now privately owned but on exhibit at Mount Vernon.

fallen in love with his jailer's daughter." In June he was paroled on the condition that he agree not to go south for a month, after which time he promptly turned up in Richmond to be commissioned as a Confederate officer, though Lee, who was wary of Orton's volatility, was careful not to place him on his personal staff.

There is no question that the Lee family owed a debt to Orton Williams for persuading Mary to do what her husband had not been able to—on May 8 Mary Lee and Agnes left Arlington in the Lee carriage for the ten-mile journey to Ravensworth, home of her widowed aunt Anna Fitzhugh, followed by wagons carrying many of the family's possessions, including the piano, and as much as they could pack in the way of food supplies and wine. Emotionally wrenching as it must have been for Mary to leave her home, the physical challenges she faced were harder. Lee did not consider her to be safe even at Ravensworth, and he urged her to "retire further from the scene of war [which] may burst upon you at any time." He worried too that Mary's presence at Ravensworth might "provoke annoyance [from the Federal authorities] to Cousin Anna," adding, "I really am afraid that you may prove more harm than comfort to her," concerned that Federal troops might punish Anna for sheltering a member of the Lee family. As usual, Mary stuck to her guns and did not listen.

On May 23 she heard that 13,000 Federal troops had occupied Arlington, pitching their tents on the lawns and chopping down the trees around the mansion for firewood. Her oldest son, Custis, who had resigned from the U.S. Army and was waiting for his assignment as an officer in the Confederate Army, joined her and Agnes at Ravensworth, apparently annoying his mother by his uncomplaining calm. No such attitude could be attributed to his mother, who dashed off a furious letter to Major General Charles W. Sanford, a New York City lawyer and businessman now commanding the occupying militia forces on Arlington Heights: "It never occurred to me, . . ." she wrote, "that *I* could be forced to sue for permission to enter *my own* house & that such an outrage as its military occupation to the exclusion of me & my children could ever have been perpetrated. . . . I implore you by the courtesy due to any woman & which no brave soldier could deny, to allow my old coachman by whom I send this letter to get his clothes, to give some letters to my manager relative to the farm etc. to give my market man a pass to go & return from Washington as usual where his family resides." She went on at some length to demand permission for her gardener Ephraim to visit Washington as well, for "my boy Billy" to be sent to her with his clothes, and for her maids Selina and Marcellina to send her some "small articles" she had not remembered to pack. Sanford was sensible enough to pass this letter on to his superior across the Potomac in Washington, Brigadier General Irvin McDowell, who perhaps not coincidentally would shortly become the first Union general of the war to endure a major defeat, at the First Battle of Bull Run (or First Manassas, as it was known in the South). McDowell swiftly retreated before Mary Lee's indignant onslaught, and capitulated with gentlemanly courtesy on every point.

Any notion that this gesture would pacify Mrs. Lee was wishful thinking. Her capacity for anger far exceeded the comfort level of her husband. For the mistress of Arlington to be dependent on the generosity of her many kinfolk brought constant reminders of what the Union had taken from her. All homes would henceforth seem to her temporary stopping places pending the restoration of Arlington, which did not take place within her lifetime. She refused to see in this painful pilgrimage, as Lee gently suggested to her, an expression of "God's will," still less the proof that "we have not been grateful enough for the happiness there within our reach [at Arlington], and our heavenly Father has found it necessary to deprive us of what he has given us." Deep and sincere as Mary Lee's evangelical religious belief was, she was not consoled by any of this, and remained convinced that her heavenly

Father wanted to see her returned to Arlington, even as she journeyed on to Chantilly, the home of her Stuart relations; then to Eastern View, home of her Randolph kinfolk; and eventually from there to Kinloch, home of Edward Turner—the last at Lee's suggestion, since he was aware that northeastern Virginia would soon be the site of fierce fighting. The Lee family was now scattered: Custis and Rooney were serving as officers in the Confederate Army; their brother Rob would soon join them as a private in the artillery; Lee himself was constantly in motion from Richmond to all the places under his command; Mildred was away at school; and the other girls were moving from house to house, to their father's displeasure. "I wish they were all at some quiet & safe place," he wrote, rather than enjoying what seemed to be an endless round of family house parties, but he had no suggestion of where such a place might be found. It was one of the ironies of history that the man who was to become the commanding figure of southern leadership in the Civil War was among its first victims, his property occupied, he and his family rendered homeless, the land on which he had spent so much time and effort to make it productive now barren and wasted, the great trees which he had thought would shade him in his old age chopped down by the enemy for their cookstoves.

Lee also knew the war would not soon be over. Shortly after he arrived in Richmond, he told Mary Lee that the war might "last ten years." He made no secret of his belief that it would be a lengthy, bitter, "fratricidal" war, but this was a message that not everyone wanted to hear. A flurry of complaints about Lee reached President Jefferson Davis, in Montgomery, Alabama, then still the capital of the Confederacy, warning that Lee was "too despondent," and that "his remarks are calculated to dispirit our people." Some even accused him of "treachery." In the North the newspapers predicted that his name would be "remembered with scorn" and branded him a "traitor." Even Mary Chesnut confided to her diary such comments by her acquaintances as "At heart Robert E. Lee is against us—that I know"; and, from another, "General Lee will be hanged as a traitor [to the Confederate cause]. . . . He is blazing out a path behind them, in case of a retreat. To talk of retreat is treason—disheartens soldiers." The firebrand of secession Edmund Ruffin, who had witnessed John Brown's hanging and fired one of the first shots on Fort Sumter, arrived in Richmond to see for himself what General Lee was up to, and reported back by telegraph to Jefferson Davis: "FOR SALVATION OF OUR CAUSE COME IMMEDIATELY AND ASSUME MILITARY COMMAND." No suggestion could have been more harmful to the Confederacy. The mistaken belief that President Davis was a military genius or had a gift for command on the battlefield was shared by many people, including Davis himself, though interestingly enough not by his second wife, Varina.* As secretary of war, Davis had recognized and rewarded Lee's great qualities, so he was not as moved by these complaints as Lee's critics had hoped. Indeed when he and Varina arrived in Richmond on May 20 Davis, who was staying at the same hotel as Lee, immediately co-opted him as a military adviser. Although its secession was ratified by the voters on May 23, Virginia remained an independent republic until June 17, when it at last officially joined the Confederacy. The presence of President and Mrs. Jefferson Davis was intended to speed up this decision, and one way to ensure it was to cater to Virginians' pride by placing the capital of the Confederacy in Richmond. This was a military mistake. The distance from Washington, D.C., to Richmond, Virginia, is only 106 miles. The symbolic importance of Richmond as the Confederate capital more or less ensured that great battles would take place there, thus pinning down a large proportion of the limited strength of the Confederacy in northern Virginia, and ensuring

---

* Davis's first wife, who died only three months after their marriage, was a daughter of Zachary Taylor, the victor of Buena Vista, elected to the presidency in 1848.

that there were never enough troops to hold large parts of Missouri, Kentucky, and Tennessee. The choice of Richmond inevitably meant that the "back door" of the Confederacy in the West was open to attack.

Of course the vulnerability of Richmond was true of Washington, D.C., as well—President Lincoln was equally concerned that the Confederate Army might take Washington, dealing what might have been a fatal blow to the Union in the eyes of the world, and at least three times during the Civil War it seemed possible. The concentration of so much of the Confederacy's manpower in the narrow area between the two capitals was a major strategic error made before the fighting had even begun. To Lee too, however, this seemed like a natural decision. Though shortly after Davis's arrival in Richmond, Virginia's forces were joined with those of the Confederacy, still leaving Lee's position and rank uncertain, he and Davis would have agreed about the importance of Virginia—even as the war spread across half the continent, Lee's attention remained fixed on that portion of his native state which he knew and loved, and was determined to defend at any cost.

Not everyone who saw him was an instant convert. Mary Chesnut was at first ecstatic at the news that Lee had been made "general in chief in Virginia," but later decided that she preferred his brother Sydney Smith

Lee, who had resigned from the U.S. Navy and was now serving in the Confederate Navy: "I like Smith Lee better," she wrote, "and I like his looks too. I know Smith Lee well. Can anybody say they know his brother? I doubt it. He looks so cold and quiet and grand."

Cold, quiet, and grand is exactly how Lee looked to many people, but this was, in fact, one of his strengths. There were plenty of other leaders in the Confederacy who looked ferocious, or were full of "passionate intensity," to quote W. B. Yeats, but Lee rose above them all by his refusal to pander to other people's emotions. Once, when he was returning from an inspection trip to Manassas Junction, a critical point for the defense of Virginia as well as for any attack on Washington, to meet President and Mrs. Davis, Lee's train was briefly halted at Orange Court House, where a large crowd gathered and demanded to hear him speak, anticipating a hefty dose of patriotic southern oratory. At first Lee refused to leave his railway carriage at all; then, when he was finally persuaded to appear, he merely told the audience that "he had much more important matters on his mind than speech-making." This was true, but not exactly the way to win "hearts and minds"; moreover it must be put within the context of the mid-nineteenth century, when listening to speeches was a form of entertainment.

Lee, however, had no wish to inspire the good people of Orange Court House. His father would certainly have made a rip-roaring stem-winder of a speech, then worked his way through the crowd shaking hands, accepting toasts, and kissing pretty girls, but Lee's main object in life, whether unconscious or not, was to avoid so far as possible all those things that had made Light-Horse Harry Lee one of the most popular heroes of the American Revolutionary War. Like Washington, Lee had an instinctive dislike of "mobs," or anything that smacked of "democracy," which to the generation of the founding fathers implied rule by the mob. Within less than a year his aristocratic reserve, the perfection of his appearance, his calm and collected expression, and his apparent indifference to danger would turn him into a kind of demigod. The Confederacy would have no shortage of popular generals: Stonewall Jackson, with his ferocity in battle and his numerous eccentricities, was one; J. E. B. Stuart, the perfect Cavalier, was another; P. G. T. Beauregard seemed for a time to convey an image of military flamboyance that Lee neither possessed nor required; and many people (though not Jefferson Davis) supposed until 1862 that Lee's old friend Joseph E. Johnston was the better general. But after the Seven Days battles in the summer of 1862 Lee, impenetrable and unreadable, was revered like no other general, and remained so to his death and indeed for 150 years after it.

In the spring of 1861 Lee performed something of a miracle. In the twelve days between his assuming command of Virginia's armed forces and May 5, Lincoln's deadline when those in arms against the United States must "retire peaceably to their respective abodes," Lee created the rudiments of an army to be reckoned with, not yet strong enough to take the offensive, but perhaps strong enough to defend Virginia at all but a few exposed points. Young Lieutenant Walter H. Taylor, who joined Lee's staff on May 3, was perhaps the most accurate chronicler of Lee's generalship and his grasp of logistics, and the closest of his aides to him, throughout the war. Taylor was not immune to Lee's charisma—"I was at once attracted and greatly impressed by his appearance . . . he appeared every inch a soldier and a man born to command," he wrote—but seeing beyond Lee's natural gift for projecting gravitas, Taylor rapidly formed a clear understanding of his new commander's remarkable power of concentration, his patience, and his extraordinary professional skill. Taylor also realized at once that Lee hated the endless, time-wasting correspondence he was forced to deal with, despite being a prompt and tireless letter writer himself to family and friends. The young man quickly transformed himself into his commander's amanuensis, sparing Lee hours of thankless toil. Lee, Taylor commented, was "not satisfied unless at the close of his office hours every matter requiring prompt attention had been disposed of," echoing the judgment of that ultimate soldier and administrator the Duke of Wellington, "The business of the day must be done within the day."

Nobody was in a better position to understand the problems Lee faced than Taylor, who saw almost all Lee's correspondence. There was no shortage of manpower as such—Virginians were so eager to volunteer to defend their state that Lee had to turn away those he could not arm—but there was very little in the way of organized training or of the military staff and structure needed to turn them into a real army. Former Governor Wise's offer to form companies of sharpshooters, each man armed with his own rifle, from the rural areas of western Virginia, though warmly supported by President Davis and Governor Letcher, was typical of the kind of amateur military thinking that Lee felt obliged to discourage. However skilled the riflemen of western Virginia might be at putting meat on the table at home, their rifles were of different calibers, complicating Lee's logistic problems, and were not fitted with any means of attaching a bayonet, in an age when the massed bayonet charge was still considered to be the deciding factor in battle.

Lee struggled with shortages of everything his army would need. Muskets were in such short supply that many volunteers were issued with smooth-bored flintlocks, like those of the Revolutionary War, rather than the more modern percussion weapons. Soldiers who received the older weapons often felt humiliated and enraged. Almost everything else was also in short supply, including uniforms, shoes, cavalry sabers, and pistols, as well as tents, blankets, horses, mules, and wagons— the last three to remain critical problems throughout the war. Taylor's admiration for Lee never failed— to a friend who had worked with him at the Bank of Virginia before the outbreak of war Taylor wrote, "Oh! Mr. Barrot, he's a trump, a soldier, a gentleman & above all a Christian." Taylor quickly adapted himself to Lee's working day, which began after an early breakfast and continued until well past eleven at night, as well as to Lee's abstemious habits. But despite Taylor's premature hero worship of his boss, whether Lee knew it or not, his role had become that of a skilled military bureaucrat, the mid-nineteenth-century southern equivalent of Dwight D. Eisenhower eighty years later, before Ike got out from behind his desk and took over active command of Operation Torch, the Allied invasion of North Africa.

Lee was deluged with problems. It was one thing to call up the militia and volunteers, and another to decide how long they would serve. On this crucial point Lee and the Virginia Convention differed widely. Governor Letcher and the convention wanted to limit the term of enlistment—many of the members believed that the war would be over quickly, perhaps after a single victory, while Lee, whose opinion on the length of the war was far more pessimistic (and as it turned out, more realistic), wanted the men enlisted "for the duration of the war." In the end Lee was obliged to settle for an enlistment of one year, with predictable problems in the spring of 1862, as men's enlistment expired at just the moment when they were most needed.

His problems were further complicated by the move of the capital of the Confederacy from Montgomery to Richmond. The armed forces of Virginia would shortly become part of the Confederate Army, and Confederate troops from other states would inevitably be ordered to take up positions in Virginia. Although Lee and Jefferson Davis had great respect for each other—the stiffness of Davis's personality and Lee's dislike of politics make it seem unlikely that they were "friends" in any conventional sense of the word—the integration of Virginia's government and armed forces into the Confederacy was neither easy nor universally popular. Virginians were apt to presume that they were primus inter pares* and that the defense of Virginia should be under the command of Virginian generals, while troops from other states thought that they were coming to Virginia's rescue, and in some cases that there was more important fighting to be done nearer home. To read Lee's correspondence in May and June 1861 is to marvel at both his strategic ability and his tact. However pressed for time he was, and however critical the circumstances, Lee never failed to phrase his commands as suggestions, or to praise even the most recalcitrant of his senior officers.

He grasped at once the strategic reality of Virginia's position, which can be explained by a simple analogy. If you place your left hand flat before you, fingers and thumb widely separated, and imagine the thumbnail as Richmond, then each of the outstretched fingers represents a point at which the enemy can enter Virginia, and where the geography, the course of a river and its valley, or the direction of mountain

---

* "First among equals."

ranges might favor an attacker, and offer him natural "access points." Moving from east to west, the index finger represents the long peninsula between the York and the James rivers, which was easily accessible to the enemy because of Union naval power, and which if seized boldly could cut Richmond off from the rest of Virginia and the South in one blow. The middle finger represents Alexandria and the path of the Orange and Alexandria Railroad, by which the enemy might reach the vital railway junction at Manassas, and again isolate the capital. The ring finger represents the Shenandoah Valley, from Harpers Ferry south to Waynesboro and Lynchburg, where the enemy could not only cut Virginia in two but also cut the Richmond and Danville Railroad connecting Richmond to the West, and allow an army to follow the path of the James River eastward with few natural obstacles toward Richmond. The little finger represents the possibility of advancing into Virginia from Pennsylvania and Ohio along the Monongahela and Cheat rivers, and then through gaps in the Blue Ridge Mountains to flank Richmond. The first (index) finger was of particular concern. Washington's preponderance of naval power would make a landing on the peninsula an attractive strategic move—Fort Monroe, which Lee had helped build, was still in Union hands. A Union army could be landed at Newport News and indefinitely supplied from there by sea. The last of these possibilities (the little finger) was also of immediate concern—mountainous northwestern Virginia was not slave-owning country; it was largely populated by settlers from Pennsylvania who were instinctively pro-Union and deeply opposed to secession. A vigorous thrust there by Union forces toward Grafton might generate considerable local support. In addition one of the major railway lines to the area ran there from the north, in Pennsylvania, making it easy to supply any Union advance. Strung out along a border of at least 400 miles, these four vulnerable points were widely separated, all the more so since they were not directly linked to one another or to Richmond by railway; Harpers Ferry and Grafton were also separated by a daunting chain of mountains running from north to south. The east-west orientation of railway routes to the north of Virginia gave the Union the equivalent of "interior lines" of communication, allowing for quicker movement of troops from one point of attack to another. Lee also had to contend with the strong possibility that Union forces would attack two or more points simultaneously, dangerously stretching Confederate troop strength, as well as his overburdened and inconveniently linked supply routes—if there was one thing the builders of railway lines in Virginia had not anticipated it was supplying armies defending the state's northern border.

Lee endeavored, with some success, to provide each of the points that concerned him with a strong commander and an adequate supply of arms. He attached great importance to Harpers Ferry, not only because of its position but also because of the Federal arms factory that was located there. One of his first letters on taking command of the armed forces of Virginia was to the former VMI professor he had assigned there to defend it.

HEADQUARTERS VIRGINIA FORCES
Richmond, Va., May 1, 1861

Col. T. J. Jackson, *commanding Harper's* [sic]
Ferry, Va.:

COLONEL: Under authority of the governor of the State, you are directed to call out volunteer companies from the counties adjacent to Harper's Ferry . . . including five regiments of infantry, one regiment of cavalry, and two batteries of light artillery, of four pieces each. The average number of enlisted men in each company will be eighty-two, and the troops will be directed to rendezvous at Harper's Ferry. You will select, as far as possible, uniformed companies with arms, organize them into regiments under the senior captains, until proper field officers can be appointed. You will report the number of companies accepted in the service of the State under this authority, their description, arms, &c. Five hundred Louisiana troops, said to be en route for this place, will be directed to report to you, and you will make provisions accordingly.

You are desired to urge the transfer of all the machinery, materials, &c., from Harper's Ferry, as fast as possible, and have it prepared in Winchester for removal to Strasburg, whence it will be ordered to a place of safety. . . . Should it become necessary to the defense of your position, you will destroy the bridge across the Potomac. . . .

I am, sir, &c.

R. E. LEE,

Major-General, Commanding

This is typical of Lee's orders; methodical, detailed, practical, and containing not a hint of ambiguity. Anybody receiving such an order knew exactly what was expected of him. The warning to destroy the bridge across the Potomac was sound practical advice from a man who had been there and crossed it. Lee's grasp of geographical realities was that of an experienced military engineer and mapmaker; he could see at a glance which points had to be taken or defended, and how to take advantage of the terrain. In the course of May and June his letters are strewn with sound military advice—he requested a spur line to be laid to connect Richmond and Petersburg, explained exactly how to build a fortified artillery battery to protect "the land approaches to Yorktown," advised how to prepare coarse-grained gunpowder intended for artillery for use in muskets, and warned (correctly) against trying to call up volunteers from what would soon become West Virginia, "as it might irritate, instead of conciliating the population of that region." He hunted up tents, muskets, haversacks, percussion caps, and mules from every corner of Virginia; questioned whether "the revetment at Fort Norfolk [is] sufficiently protected by earthen-covered ways"; and asked the commander there whether "the parapets of all your redoubts are sufficiently thick and high to resist heavy shot and protect the men within?" He recommended setting steel rails into the ground at a thirty-degree angle to deflect long-range shots from Union ships and explained exactly how to do it; he wisely advised Jackson at Harpers Ferry "not to intrude upon the soil of Maryland," lest it make the citizens of that state turn away from the Confederacy. He also never failed to take the time to console officers who had to step down in rank as they were transferred from the Virginia armed forces to the Confederate Army: "Recognizing as fully as I do your merit, patriotism and devotion to the State" he wrote to a disappointed Colonel St. George Cocke, "I do not consider that either rank or position are necessary to bestow on you honor, but believe that you will confer honor upon the position." Even his sharpest rebukes were couched in terms carefully calculated not to offend: "The General regrets to have to remind an officer of your experience of the propriety of adhering to the usages of the military service in relation to official communications. . . . He feels constrained to call your attention also to the necessity of economizing the ammunition issued to the troops. . . . As understood by him, the recent exchange of shots between your batteries on the Potomac and the enemy's vessels could have no other result than to waste ammunition and to expose our conditions and the strength of the batteries, which was probably the object of his visit." Lee was a one-man general staff, dealing deftly with major strategic issues and the smallest details of logistics and bruised egos at every level, while all the time making sure that President Davis was kept fully informed and that his ideas about military affairs were taken seriously. It was as if the jobs of General George C. Marshall and General Dwight D. Eisenhower were combined in one man, a remarkable achievement.

Lee recognized at once the need to place an experienced general officer in command at every vulnerable point of danger on the Virginia border, and in making his choices he suppressed entirely his own desire to command in the field and any sign of resentment at the often outsize egos of the generals chosen. Lee wisely placed his friend and West Point classmate Joseph E. Johnston in command at Harpers Ferry, confident that Johnston and Colonel Thomas J. Jackson would work well together. For the forces assembling near Manassas, President Davis and Lee gave the mercurial and flamboyant Creole P. G. T. Beauregard, a member of a wealthy New Orleans family, the command—Beauregard, who had led the attack on Fort Sumter, had been given a hero's welcome at every stop on the railway from Charleston to Richmond, and had ambitious plans for attacking the Union forces around Washington—plans that Lee was determined to delay. Keeping a firm rein on Beauregard would become one of Lee's major concerns. The defense of Richmond from the sea was in the hands of Benjamin Huger and John B. Magruder "on opposite sides of Hampton

Roads": Huger on the southern shore of the James River, in Norfolk; Magruder of the northern shore on the peninsula itself, between the James and the York rivers. Neither general was to prove a happy choice— Huger would prove to be slow to advance and too hasty to retreat, while Magruder had the misfortune to interpret Lee's orders to him too literally at the Battle of Malvern Hill in 1862. Splitting the command between them was probably also a mistake, but both Davis and Lee supposed that since the area was only eighty miles from Richmond they could exercise direct control of any battle that took place there. In western Virginia, confusion reigned. Most of the population remained strongly pro-Union, and after the Confederates suffered a serious defeat at Philippi, south of Grafton, Lee feared that Union forces might march on to Staunton, turning Johnston's position at Harpers Ferry and cutting off Richmond from the west. Lee reacted quickly by promoting his adjutant general Colonel R. B. Garnett to brigadier general and sending him off to hold a line in the Alleghenies with whatever militiamen could be summoned up. From Richmond, Garnett's job seemed easy enough; the Alleghenies stretched from north to south in a series of "long parallel ridges," separated by deep valleys and fast-running rivers, with few roads or towns. Most of the roads, such as they were, followed the valleys; those crossing the mountains from west to east were poor, few, and far between. Union troops advancing from Ohio into northwestern Virginia would need to cross ridge after ridge of wild and heavily forested country, and on any one of these ridges a relatively small number of men, if properly led, ought to be able to hold back an army.

The question of when and where the Union would strike first was answered on May 27, when Lee received an alarming message from General Huger, in Norfolk: "Seven steamers, with troops, have been and are now landing troops at Newport News. Other steamers, with troops, arrived at Old Point this morning." This was familiar territory to Lee, who had helped to build Fort Monroe and Fort Wool opposite it in Hampton Roads. He knew the shoreline and the bay like the back of his hand. Fort Monroe was (and would remain for the duration of the war) in Union hands, but Lee prudently ordered General Magruder to dig in on a line from Jamestown to Williamsburg to Yorktown, at the narrowest "neck" of the peninsula, about fifteen miles west of Fort Monroe. There was nothing Lee could do to prevent the Union from assembling a large force around Newport News and supplying it by sea while waiting to see whether the Union commander, General Benjamin Butler, would advance up the peninsula, or cross the James River and invest Norfolk, or divide his forces by attempting to do both. Magruder complained that the Virginian troops sent to him were unready to take the field for want of shoes "and other necessaries" and that Butler's position at Newport News was too strong to assault. He also reported—a typical complaint of the period—that there was some dispute between himself and Colonel Hill, commander of a North Carolina regiment, over which of them outranked the other. Lee had to waste a good deal of time soothing ruffled feelings.

As control of the armed forces assembling in Virginia gradually passed from the state to the Confederate Department of War, a period of confusion reigned, until Lee's steady hand could sort things out. In less than a month he had collected over 40,000 armed men, equipped them with 115 field guns, and produced over 100,000 cartridges and 1 million percussion caps, as well as creating formidable artillery batteries and fieldworks to protect Richmond. It was an enormous achievement, and having completed it he was content, as he wrote Mary Lee, to leave the outcome in other, more powerful hands: "God's will be done," he wrote to her on May 11.

With the completion of preparations for the defense of Virginia and the transfer of its armed forces to the Confederacy on June 7, Lee's position became anomalous. Since the Confederate Army had, for the moment, no higher rank than that of brigadier general, he dropped one step down from his rank of major general. This did not trouble him. He would be made one of five full generals soon after the Confederacy created that rank, but Lee never wore a general's insignia on his uniform, content to wear on his collar the three small stars of a full colonel in the Confederate Army, his old rank in the U.S. Army, and made it clear that he would not wear a Confederate general's insignia until the South was victorious. Having no army to command, and living in the same hotel as the Davises, Lee became, for the moment, a kind of unofficial chief of staff and military adviser to the president. "I should like to retire to private life," he wrote to Mary, but at the same time he was anxious to prevent any "antagonism" from developing between the Confederate government and that of Virginia.

Lee may also have known that he was still needed, and that there was not the slightest chance of his being allowed to retire to private life. He constantly expressed the wish that there was "an abler man" to take his place, but no such person existed: the Confederacy desperately needed a realistic professional commander who could both train and prepare the army for the long war to come, and at the same time tactfully restrain President Davis from trying to lead the army in the field as if he were a general in chief. Only Lee fitted this description. It was, after all, similar to the role that General Winfield Scott had played during the Mexican War.

Lee already guessed that the major attacks on Virginia would come simultaneously in the west, where it was weakest, and on the peninsula, from which, once the Union Army had accumulated enough troops and equipment, an attempt to take Richmond, only eighty-one miles away, would certainly be made. It did not escape his attention that once Union troops were placed in force to attack from the west and from the east, the two forces separated by almost 400 miles, their center would inevitably be weak. A Confederate counterattack launched from Manassas might therefore catch them unprepared, and perhaps even threaten Washington.

Some generals are good at defense, some at offense, but very few in the history of warfare have been good at both. Grant and Sherman, for example, were brilliant at offense, but were never put to the test of waging a defensive campaign, given the superiority of the North in manpower, equipment, and supplies. Lee was an exception to the rule. As a trained engineer with great experience in building fortifications and fieldworks, he was a master at defense, but at the same time he was a genius in offense, a master of maneuver and of the unexpected flank movement, undaunted by adverse odds and always bold, even to a fault. He was that rarest of generals, a formidable opponent both attacking and defending; there is nobody else quite like him in American military history. Even in full retreat Lee would prove to be a dangerous opponent—even though the Army of Northern Virginia was reduced to hardly more than 28,000 men in April 1865, most of them starving and low on ammunition, Lee was still able to maneuver with the small force remaining to him, and to put up a stiff defense against overwhelming odds.

In June 1861 Lee found himself in the unenviable position of trying to shore up Confederate positions in three places—western Virginia, Manassas, and the peninsula—without any formal authority to give orders, and always having to tread carefully lest he offend President Davis, who was at once sensitive to any perceived slight and determined to cling to his prerogatives as commander in chief. Although Davis held Lee in "esteem," and respected his advice, his patience, and his organizational skill, he had yet to see any evidence of Lee's genius on the battlefield. It would be some time before Davis reluctantly accepted that the proper place for the president of the Confederacy was not in the front line, exposed to enemy fire, urging the troops forward.

In the meantime, Lee's predictions about the enemy's operations came true, and he was thrust into the role of what we might now call a fireman, sent to cope with whatever emergencies arose as the widely separated Union armies began to attack in force. At dawn on June 10, only two days after Virginia's forces (Lee with them) formally became part of the Confederate Army, Major General Benjamin Butler attacked Magruder in the peninsula at Big Bethel, and was stopped by the trenches and earthworks Lee had insisted on digging, as well as by an incident of what is now called friendly fire when two New York regiments opened fire on each other, perhaps because the Third New York Volunteer Regiment wore gray uniforms exactly like those of the Confederates. Union troops attempted several assaults against the Confederate lines, and soon learned the futility of attacking well-entrenched infantry with a bayonet charge. They eventually retreated back to the safety of Fort Monroe, leaving much of their equipment scattered on the road behind them because of the heat. Butler had achieved nothing except the satisfaction of burning down the houses of several supposed secessionists at Little Bethel and taking some of their slaves back to Fort Monroe, white Lee took the opportunity of sending more artillery to Magruder and digging in some batteries of heavy guns.

Whether at the suggestion of President Davis or on his own responsibility, Lee quickly became de facto commander of the Confederate far right in Virginia, on the peninsula and across the James River at Norfolk; and of the Confederate far left, to the west in the Alleghenies, where his former adjutant general Brigadier General R. B. Garnett was in command facing an extremely competent Union major general, George B. McClellan. Neither Lee's rank nor any formal authority accompanied these weighty responsibilities—he simply took control of Virginia's flanks, while allowing President Davis and General Joseph E. Johnston to concentrate on the vital center, at Harpers Ferry and Manassas, either one of which seemed likely to be the objective of the large Union forces being collected in Washington. His role was still limited to hastening supplies and reinforcements, when he could find them, and to overseeing matters from a distance—a kind of watching brief rather than direct command. There has been conjecture among historians that President Davis did not like Lee, but it seems more likely that Davis simply did not wish to share the limelight with him. General Johnston, then thought to be the Confederacy's most competent commander, made it clear enough that while he wanted

Lee's logistic support, he did not want to receive orders from him, or even advice. For that matter, neither Magruder nor Garnett was under any obligation to obey Lee's orders, though Magruder soon learned the wisdom of paying attention to what Lee had to suggest. Garnett, being Lee's former subordinate, would probably have accepted his advice willingly, but he was far away from Richmond, in the mountains of what is now West Virginia, so there was very little chance that any advice from Lee would reach him in time to make a difference.

Unfortunately Garnett had inherited a calamitous situation. On his arrival he found that Grafton and Philippi were both in Federal hands, leaving the way to Staunton open; that the ragtag Confederate army gathered around Huttonsville was "in a miserable condition"; and that the inhabitants of northwestern Virginia were for the most part strongly pro-Union. Garnett had fewer than 5,000 men, woefully lacking in arms, clothing, discipline, food, and enthusiasm, and was heavily outnumbered. A vigorous attack on Staunton by the Union forces, followed by a bold "hook" to the southeast, might have brought McClellan's army into the Shenandoah Valley in the rear of the Confederate forces at Harpers Ferry and Manassas; and this, if coordinated with an attack from Alexandria by the Union brigadier general Irvin McDowell, might have cut Virginia in two and ended the war with a decisive Union victory in 1861. Fortunately for the Confederacy, while McClellan had many of the attributes of a great general, they did not include boldness. His manner was grandly self-confident, but this was a mask. He constantly overestimated the enemy's strength, sometimes by a factor of two or three, and while he was efficient at training an army, he seemed reluctant to spoil it by use. Though he was personally courageous, he had no appetite for risk—a perfectionist, he wanted a perfect record of victories, with the result that he would attack only when he thought there was no chance of losing.

There was no chance of his losing in the beginning of July 1861. He carried out a textbook attack on Garnett's positions, securing "the passes on Rich Mountain and Laurel Hill," which commanded what were then the major roads to Ohio and Pennsylvania. Garnett had unwisely divided his forces to guard both passes, and the two parts were not close enough to support each other; thus McClellan was enabled to take both positions *en série,* attacking the 2,500 Confederates on Rich Mountain with over 10,000 men. Once that position had been taken, Garnett was forced to abandon his position on Laurel Hill. Most of Garnett's defeated, discouraged troops either disbanded or surrendered—McClellan took over 1,000 prisoners. Garnett himself was killed at Corrick's Ford, on the Cheat River, bravely trying to rally a few of his remaining men. He was the first general officer of the war to meet his death in battle.

McClellan's victory brought him a torrent of praise in the northern press—his reports of the battle, "magnified by [his] rhetorical congratulations to his troops," made him an instant hero, the first of the war. The *New York Herald* hailed him as "the Napoleon of the Present War," and both reporters and his own men took to referring to him as the "young Napoleon," a comparison that would stick to him, at first without irony, and which he encouraged, perhaps unconsciously, by his habit of placing his right hand between the buttons of his coat at stomach level like the emperor. All this inspired a misplaced confidence in him among the northern public and in the White House. More dangerously, McClellan himself took all this praise seriously; he came to the conclusion that his already high opinion of his own military genius had been confirmed. In the meantime, General in Chief Scott, fearing that McClellan's supply line was stretched too far and that he was vulnerable to attacks on his extended flanks, ordered McClellan to stay put at Monterey, although at that point he was only forty miles away from Staunton, from which he could have reached the Shenandoah Valley and cut the Virginia Central Railroad line. Fortunately for Lee, McClellan lacked the "Nelson touch." Admiral Nelson, when he received Admiral Sir Hyde Parker's signal to withdraw at the Battle of Copenhagen in 1801, had put his telescope to his blind eye, and said, "Really, I do not see the signal," and sailed on to win one of his greatest victories. But McClellan was no Nelson. He obeyed Scott's order and stayed put, throwing away the opportunity for what might have been a decisive Union victory—or at least his men stayed put, for on the strength of his victory in western Virginia McClellan himself would shortly be recalled to Washington to oversee the defense of the capital and to command the Army of the Potomac.

To many this seemed like an early low point of Confederate fortunes. True, Butler's attempt to break out of Newport News and the protection of Fort Monroe had been stopped, largely owing to Lee's foresight in improvising a fortified line in the peninsula; but the defeat in northwestern Virginia was a calamity, and despite the importance attached to Harpers Ferry, it had for the moment fallen (the town was to change hands fourteen times during the Civil War, and would be reduced to a ruin). The Union major general Robert Patterson had forded the Potomac River at

Williamsport, Maryland, and by dint of superior num-bers and better-handled artillery Falling Waters* suc-ceeded in pushing the forces of two future Confederate heroes—Colonel Thomas J. Jackson and Colonel J. E. B. Stuart—almost back to Winchester, Virginia. At that point Patterson, like McClellan, halted his advance; he returned to Martinsburg, his resolve apparently shaken by the ferocity of the Confederates' fighting retreat.

Lee followed these events, from Richmond, where his first priority was to find men and arms to send on to General Johnston in Winchester and to General Beauregard, who was camped around Manassas Junction, about twenty-five miles southwest of Washington.

Lee wrote to Mary, "My movements are very uncertain, and I wish to take the field as soon as certain arrangements can be made. I may go at any moment." But this was optimistic. Eighteen days later he wrote that despite his anxiety "to get into the field," he was "detained by matters beyond my control," and told her to disregard the rumor that he was about to be cre-ated "Commander-in-Chief of the Confederate States Army," a title which, he reminded her, belonged to President Davis. He "had been labouring to prepare and

---

* Also known as the Battle of Hoke's Run.

get into the field the Virginia troops, and to strengthen, by those of the other States, the threatened commands of Johnston, Beauregard . . . &c." The combination of overwork and inaction led to a mild breakdown in his health that confined him briefly to bed. Still, he was responsible for both the reinforcements and the strategy that would produce the Confederate victory at First Manassas (or the First Battle of Bull Run, as it is known in the North). For the first time, Lee used the railway to swiftly transfer Johnston's troops from Winchester to Beauregard's position at Manassas Junction once battle had been joined—an ambitious and daring plan, since it would leave Winchester and the Shenandoah Valley briefly uncovered. But Lee already knew he would not take part in the battle. For the moment he was relegated to a role at headquarters.

From Kinloch, Edward Turner's home in Thoroughfare Gap, Fauquier County, where Mary Lee was staying "in [the] cooler hill country" of the Bull Run, she wrote to ask Lee to buy her the sheet music of "Dixie," which, though it was an old minstrel song usually performed in blackface, had become the unofficial national anthem of the Confederacy.* One music

---

*There were three Confederate anthems—"God Save the South," "The Bonnie Blue Flag," and "Dixie," but none of them was officially authorized. "Dixie" was by far the most popular of them.

publisher reported that sales were "altogether unprecedented"; indeed it was so popular that President Davis
had a music box that played it. Lee sent a young man
out to buy a copy, but had to report that he had visited
everyplace in Richmond without finding it: "I suppose
it is exhausted," he wrote to her. "The booksellers say
Dixie is not to be had in Virginia."

Mary continued moving from place to place, pushed
westward by her husband's anxiety for her safety, so
it is ironic that, for once obedient to his wishes, she
ended up no more than thirty miles from where First
Manassas would be fought, and more or less in the
direct path General Johnston would take to bring his
army to join that of General Beauregard at Bull Run.
Her daughter Mildred, or Precious Life, as her father
called her, had joined her mother and her sister Mary
Custis at Kinloch, bringing with her at her mother's
advice "all her winter and summer clothes." As Mary
Lee observed, "it is best to be prepared for any emergency." At Kinloch they received a letter from Mary's
cousin Markie, who had just visited Arlington: "The
poor house looked so desolate," she wrote. "Oh! Who
in their wildest dreams could have conjured all this last
summer? It was but one year ago that we were all there,
so happy & so peaceful." Mary's maid Selina showed
her around the house, and Markie passed on greetings

from many of the Lee family's servants, including Ephraim, the gardener, and reported that Tom Titta, the family cat, about whom Mildred had been deeply concerned, had appeared and "rubbed his little head against my dress in the most affectionate way."

Lee was no happier in Richmond than Mary was as a guest at Kinloch. In the few hours when he was away from his desk, he was living along with President and Mrs. Davis at Spotswood Hotel—which meant that Lee was in effect part of Davis's household, a kind of general-in-waiting to the president. This was uncomfortably close quarters for Lee, who did not much like to explain himself or his plans to anyone, let alone his chief executive. Lee's strategy was to remain on the defensive until the South had a better supply of men and weapons, so he was constantly discouraging President Davis's zeal for a big battle that would establish at one blow the Confederacy's credibility with foreign governments and, more important, with the North.

Lee had no patience with spectacular and unrealistic plans. His own instinct was that McDowell, the Union general, would attack in the direction of Manassas Junction. It was not so much that Lee was clairvoyant, or even benefited from a good intelligence service, as that he knew how General Scott's mind worked as well as he knew his own—and that a bold attack on his right by General

Johnston would defeat him. As skeptical as Lee was about the flamboyant Beauregard, he respected his old friend Joe Johnston's professional ability. On paper, McDowell was superior in numbers to Beauregard—McDowell had 35,000 men in and around Centreville and Alexandria to Beauregard's 20,000 around Manassas Junction, but Lee had noticed the fact that General Patterson had halted at Martinsburg with his 18,000 men, instead of continuing to advance toward Winchester, and guessed that the first priority was to keep Johnston's army of 12,000 bottled up in the Shenandoah Valley. And true to form, Patterson advanced only ten miles from Martinsburg to Bunker Hill, before "taking counsel of his fears," then retreated back to Charlestown, worried about the length of his supply line and the constant presence of J. E. B. Stuart's cavalry in front of him. None of these generals, not even Scott, had ever commanded more than 5,000 men in battle, so they were in some ways as raw as their troops, most of whom lacked the veteran infantryman's ability to put one foot in front of the other for hours on end, then stand his ground calmly when facing an attack.

Although since the 1820s, railways had revolutionized transportation in the eastern half of the United States, the railway as a factor in military strategy lagged far behind. It might take four days or more for Joe Johnston to march his army over the Blue Ridge Mountains from Winchester to Manassas, even in good weather—infantry could cover fifteen miles a day, but artillery and cumbersome supply wagons moved at the speed of horses and mules at the walk. Lee believed that if J. E. B. Stuart's cavalry could successfully mask Johnston's movements. Johnston could march his army ten miles south and entrain it on the cars and wagons of the Manassas Gap Railroad at Piedmont, and then it could be in Manassas overnight. It might be a day or more before Patterson realized that the Shenandoah Valley lay before him undefended. Lee thought that at the first sign of a Union advance the Confederate army could be reinforced to 32,000, plus 5,000 men under Brigadier General Theophilus Holmes marching northwest from Aquia Landing, on the Potomac. This would give the Confederates more troops than McDowell had by a narrow margin, with a substantial portion of them well positioned for a flanking attack. Not only had Lee integrated the railway into his plans; he foresaw how to make the best use of Johnston's army—unlike General Scott, who despite his long experience in warfare, allowed Patterson and his 18,000 men to sit out the coming battle in Charlestown.

The great difficulty on the Confederate side was command. The missing element was precisely what Lee was best suited to provide, but neither Johnston nor Beauregard was prepared to serve under anyone but President Davis.

It is fascinating to speculate what might have been gained had Lee been in a position to carry out his own plan, and had command not been divided between two rival generals, and with President Davis, who rushed to the scene. As it was, there would be a victory, and a stunning upset to the North, but not the decisive one it might have been had Lee been present and in command.

McDowell's plans were an open secret, as was his reluctance to put them into effect. He complained to President Lincoln—and to anyone else in Washington who would listen—that his men were not ready to take the offensive, but Lincoln was under considerable pressure to do something before Congress reconvened, and before the ninety-day enlistments of McDowell's volunteers expired. "You are green, it is true," the president told McDowell, "but they are green also; you are all green alike." This was true enough, but it ignored the fact that McDowell had a far higher proportion of ill-prepared "political" officers than did Johnston and Beauregard. McDowell himself had never commanded men in battle. Tall, bulky,* and incommunicative, a West Point classmate of Beauregard, he protested that he was a supply

---

*In the only photograph I have seen of generals McDowell and McClellan (the "young Napoleon") standing together they look like Laurel and Hardy. McDowell, like Hardy, towers over his companion, his expansive paunch thrust forward, while McClellan, dwarfed like Stan Laurel, looks as if he would give anything to be elsewhere.

officer, not "a field commander." He owed his command of the Union's "Army of Northeastern Virginia" to "his mentor" Salmon P. Chase, Lincoln's treasury secretary, and to his friendship with General in Chief Scott, both of whom admired his imperturbability. True, McDowell had the look of a man who would be unlikely to panic, but he made no claim to being a skilled tactician. His plans for attacking the Confederate Army at Manassas were too complicated for inexperienced troops to carry out—and seemingly made without any thought of concentrating, rather than dissipating his forces, thus breaking the first and most important rule of battle. It was not so much the Union troops who would fail at Bull Run as their officers and their commanding general. McDowell seems to have been under the impression that if he marched south and made a demonstration in sufficient force, the Confederates might retreat. In fact they were well positioned on good ground on the southern bank of the meandering Bull Run, and determined to fight.

Even the date of McDowell's advance was no secret. The well-placed socialite and Confederate spy Rose O'Neal "Wild Rose" Greenhow had no difficulty in finding it out and passing it on to General Beauregard in Manassas. After the war she became such a celebrated heroine that she was received by Queen

Victoria and Emperor Napoleon III, but since all the officers in Washington were talking about the coming attack, and toasting each other on their certain victory in barrooms and salons all over the city, it must have been common knowledge, so it seems overgenerous to give Mrs. Greenhow all the credit for the Confederate victory. Apart from that, as McDowell's troops began to march southwest through what are now the Virginia suburbs of Washington, D.C., toward Centreville on July 16, many of them collapsing from heat exhaustion within the first few miles, the news that the Union army was on the move traveled faster than the army itself. The men were unfit, ill disciplined, and poorly led. Even on a good day they could march only six miles, less than half what a veteran infantryman was expected to do. In any case an army of 35,000 men (the largest army so far assembled in North America), together with their supply wagons, artillery, and cavalry, threw up dust clouds that could be seen for miles, in what amounted to enemy territory once they were across the Potomac. Even without the help of Wild Rose Greenhow, Beauregard would have had to be blind not to know they were coming.

Lee, stuck in Richmond, had ample time to order General Johnston's army toward Manassas Junction and to start General Holmes's brigade marching to the northwest. They would cover over twenty-five miles in just two days' march, moving at twice the speed of McDowell's infantry.

Carl von Clausewitz's comment on the "fog of war"★ has seldom been better illustrated than at the First Battle of Manassas. McDowell intended to divide his army into three columns, two of which would attack and hold the Confederate army deployed in the area of Bull Run, while the third made a wide swing around the Confederate right and advanced south to cut the line of the Richmond, Fredericksburg, and Potomac Railroad, separating Beauregard's army from Richmond. McDowell's first mistake, perhaps made through overcaution, was that although he had almost 35,000 men, he kept two divisions in reserve: one around Centreville, three miles from the battle; the other spread out from Fairfax back to the Potomac, to guard the roads leading to Washington. Thus he would go into action with fewer than 19,000 men, giving up any hope of superiority in numbers.

His second mistake was that although his attack on the Confederate left was meant to be diversionary—that

---

★ The phrase has been squeezed from Von Clausewitz. What he actually wrote was: "War is an area of uncertainty; three quarters of the things on which all action in war is based are lying in a fog of uncertainty" (*Von Kriege,* Book I, chap. 3). But the "fog of war" is real and is a factor in every battle, big or small; and the term distills his meaning well enough (Wikipedia, "Fog of War," 1).

is, intended to pin down the bulk of Beauregard's troops while he went behind them to sever their line of communications—McDowell allowed it to bog down into his main thrust, and then, instead of concentrating his forces in a single powerful attack, threw his units into the battle in what, in a later war, Britain's Field Marshal Sir Bernard Montgomery would dismiss scornfully as "penny packets."

Flowing from west to east, with many bends, Bull Run itself was not a serious military obstacle, since it could be forded in many places; but the ground immediately behind its southern bank was defined by a series of modest, gently sloping hills that gave the Confederates the advantage of higher ground on which to form their line. Despite the fact that McDowell had an innovative secret weapon, in the form of a reconnaissance balloon, he does not seem to have grasped that the bends in Bull Run gave Beauregard the advantage of interior lines, by means of which to move reinforcements quickly to any point that was threatened. McDowell's third mistake was showing his cards too soon, by ordering Brigadier General Daniel Tyler to probe the Confederate right at Mitchell's Ford and Blackburn's Ford on July 18 with one division; the engagement degenerated into a prolonged skirmish and artillery duel and then petered out, giving Beauregard three days' warning to prepare his positions.

Beauregard, who had been warned to fall back behind the Rappahannock River if attacked, fortunately took this as advice rather than an order and ignored it, even though he supposed that the Federal army advancing on him had 50,000 men. As Confederate reinforcements arrived he placed them on his right, where Tyler had made his demonstration, hoping to make a flanking attack from there against McDowell's left when he advanced. Beauregard was thus badly balanced when McDowell finally attacked his left in the early morning of July 21, and had to rush General Johnston's army, which was detraining at Manassas Junction piecemeal over to his own left, where the Union troops were pushing back the Confederates in some of the hardest fighting yet seen in the war.

It took some time before Beauregard—who had now been joined on the field by Johnston—realized from the intensity of gunfire on his left that a disaster was taking place there, but to his credit as soon as it was apparent, he abandoned his own plan of attack; he and Johnston moved "all their available forces" to the left, and quickly rode there themselves, in time to see Brigadier General Barnard E. Bee Jr.'s brigade retreating in panic and confusion. Bee and the two commanding generals tried in vain to rally the men, and Bee finally rode over to where Brigadier General Thomas J. Jackson was seated on his horse, his face grim and the brim of his crushed gray kepi cap pulled low over his eyes as he watched the men of his brigade trying to hold their place in line under withering artillery and musket fire. "General," one of his men cried out, "they are beating us back!" Jackson, whose determination and calm under fire were always an example to his men, replied: "Then we will give them the bayonet."

Bee, impressed by Jackson's firm control of his men, his "soldierly bearing," and his ferocious intensity, rode back to where his own men were milling about trying to find someplace to shelter from the Union artillery, and pointing to his left cried out: "Form! Form! Look, there stands Jackson like a stone wall! Rally behind the Virginians! Let us determine to die here, and we will conquer! Follow me!"* It was the moment of crisis in the battle. Enough of Bee's men rallied, managed to form into two lines, and followed him in a charge that stopped the Union advance. Bee himself was killed as he led them, but Jackson rode out in front of his men, apparently indifferent to enemy fire, and shouted: "Reserve your fire until they come within fifty yards!

---

* There is a theory that Bee was reproaching Jackson for standing there "like a stone wall" instead of coming to Bee's help, rather than pointing him out as an example to follow, but the logic of the battle is against this interpretation. It was Jackson's job to keep his men formed up and in line, not to abandon his position and try to move them to the left in support of Bee's brigade while under fire.

Then fire and give them the bayonet! And when you charge, yell like furies!" They did so, giving birth to the rebel yell, a high-pitched, savage scream partly inspired by the cries of fox hunters, partly of Scottish and Irish tradition in warfare, that would continue to chill the blood of men who had heard it until the last veterans of the Civil War died. General Beauregard, in the thick of the fighting himself, took advantage of the moment to order the colors of all the regiments of his left wing to be advanced forty yards in front of the mass of Confederate infantry. It was a grand gesture, and it was enough. The shaken Confederate line re-formed, and the men advanced toward their own standards. The battle, which had been as good as lost in the morning, was won by the late afternoon, as regiment after regiment of Union troops broke and ran before repeated Confederate charges.

President Jefferson Davis, unable to remain in Richmond while the battle was raging, left Lee behind "to mind the shop,"* and arrived at Manassas Junction by special train in the late afternoon (one guesses how much Lee must have disapproved of this dramatic

---

*Winston Churchill's phrase when he went off to confer with Franklin D. Roosevelt and the American chiefs of staff in Washington, D.C., leaving General Sir Alan Brooke, the new chief of the Imperial General Staff, behind in London. Brooke's feelings about being left behind in London mirrored those of Lee left behind in Richmond.

rush to the front by the president, whose job after all was to remain calmly at his desk). Seeing the number of Confederate stragglers on the road to Bull Run, Davis concluded that Beauregard had been defeated. A Confederate surgeon who was dressing a wound in Jackson's hand at a field hospital watched Davis as he rode among the stragglers. "He stopped his horse . . . stood up in his stirrups, the palest, sternest face I ever saw, and cried to the great crowd of soldiers, 'I am President Davis, follow me back to the field.'" Jackson, who was hard of hearing—a natural physical defect for an artillery instructor—did not know who it was until the surgeon told him, but then he stood up, took off his cap, and cried out to Davis, "We have whipped them—they ran like sheep. Give me 10,000 men and I will take Washington tomorrow."

Jackson, who from that day forth would be known as "Stonewall" Jackson, was right. Major General McClellan, arriving in Washington from northwestern Virginia, would find "no preparations whatever for defense, not even to the extent of putting troops in military positions. Not a regiment was properly encamped, not a single avenue of approach guarded. All was chaos, and the streets, hotels and bar-rooms were filled with drunken officers and men . . . a perfect pandemonium." Even Secretary of War Edwin

M. Stanton remarked that Washington "might have been taken without resistance. The rout, overthrow and demoralization of the whole army were complete." But the Confederate Army was as exhausted and disorganized by victory as the Union army was by defeat. There was no one to take command, form the force of 10,000 men that Jackson wanted, and order an immediate advance to the Potomac. Many of the retreating Union troops were throwing away their muskets or cutting horses loose from their harness to ride them back to Washington along roads blocked by panicked politicians who had driven out in their carriages. Sometimes a politician was even accompanied by his wife and her friends in all their finery to watch the anticipated Union victory. From Fairfax Court House the unfortunate General McDowell telegraphed to General Scott that his troops were "pouring through this place in a state of utter disorganization. They could not be prepared for action by tomorrow morning even if they were willing. . . . There is no alternative but to fall back on the Potomac."

But President Davis, General Johnston, and General Beauregard were too dazed by the magnitude of the Confederate victory, as well as by the bloodshed in the aftermath of what was then the biggest and most costly battle fought on American soil, to seize the moment. Brigadier General James Longstreet, who would become Lee's "Old War-Horse," lived into the twentieth century still arguing, as he did that evening at Bull Run, that the supplies and ammunition abandoned by the Union forces at Centreville were "ample to carry the Confederate army to Washington," and that his brigade, together with those of Holmes, Ewell, and Early, all of which had been on the Confederate right and were "quite fresh," could have reached Washington the next day.

Instead, the Confederate army stayed put and missed the opportunity of ending the war in 1861. As night fell, President Davis telegraphed to the one man who, had he been present on the battlefield, might have seen the good sense of Stonewall Jackson's promise. "We have won a glorious though dear-bought victory," was Davis's message to Lee. "Night closed on the enemy in full flight and closely pursued."

Indeed, the indefatigable Colonel J. E. B. Stuart had pushed his cavalry as far as Fairfax Court House, hard on the heels of General McDowell, within ten miles of the Potomac. Stuart reported that "there was no [Union] force this side of Alexandria," but it was too late. All that was missing was, in the words of one historian, "a general who grasped the full meaning of victory," but that man was in Richmond.

For the moment, Beauregard was the hero of the hour throughout the South, with Johnston taking an honorable but secondary role. Despite his pivotal role in the battle, Stonewall Jackson's turn in the limelight was yet to come. The fact that the victory had been orchestrated by Lee was not appreciated by the general public. It must have galled Lee to realize that J. E. B. Stuart's vedettes had been less than ten miles from Arlington, the Lee home, on the night of July 21.

At Kinloch, Mary Lee and her girls were close enough to Manassas that they "could hear faintly but distinctly, the sound of cannonading" in the distance, carried on the hot, still summer air, all through all day and the evening of July 21. The next day, in the pouring rain, they saw ambulances carrying badly wounded Confederate soldiers to a nearby estate, which had been turned into an improvised hospital. Mildred and Mary Custis volunteered to work there as nurses, stifling their horror at the stench and the dreadful wounds—for battlefield wounds and surgery were not for the faint of heart in the days before doctors had any knowledge of germ theory, and surgeons had no treatment to offer but the scalpel and the saw. Wounds to the head or torso were considered fatal, and usually were. Infection, if it set in, was often fatal too. For the girls this was a rude awakening to the realities of war.

They were not alone. Though the casualties at Bull Run were light compared with those of the great battles to come—just under 3,000 on the Union side, just under 2,000 on the Confederate side*—the report that the "dead and dying cover the field," as Mary Chesnut recorded in her diary, swept through the South as quickly as the news that the Confederate army was victorious. In the Spotswood hotel in Richmond, where Mrs. Chesnut was staying, alongside President and Mrs. Davis and Robert E. Lee, there was grief aplenty among the guests. Mrs. Chesnut described how Mrs. Davis herself woke up the wife of Colonel Francis Barstow. "Poor thing! [Mrs. Barstow] was lying in her bed. Mrs. Davis knocked. 'Come in.' When she saw it was Mrs. Davis, she sat up ready to spring to her feet—but then there was something in Mrs. Davis's pale face that took the life out of her. She stared at Mrs. Davis—and then sank back. She covered her face. 'Is it bad news for me?' Mrs. Davis did not speak. 'Is he killed?' . . . As soon as she saw Mrs. Davis's face—she knew it all in an instant—she knew it before she wrapped the shawl around her head." The next

---

* The military term "casualties" does not mean deaths; it refers to the total number of men put hors de combat. The figures break down as follows for First Manassas. Confederates: 387 killed; 1,582 wounded; 13 missing. Union: 460 killed; 1,124 wounded; 1,312 missing. In the age before high explosives, which are capable of volatizing people, "missing" usually connoted deserters.

day Mrs. Barstow fainted at the funeral ceremony. "The empty saddle—and the led war horse—we saw and heard it all," Mrs. Chesnut wrote. "And now we are never out of the Dead March in *Saul.* It comes and comes until I feel inclined to close my ears and scream."

Lee was well aware of the suffering all around him, and also of the fact that this was only the beginning. In the North, the defeat produced a new determination to increase the number of troops, and to train them better. General McClellan would soon be brought to Washington to replace McDowell, and shortly to replace the aged and increasingly infirm Scott too. In the South, jubilation over the victory was tempered by the realization that it had not ended the war. "Do not grieve for the brave dead," Lee wrote to Mary from Richmond. "Sorrow for those they left behind. The former are at rest. The latter must suffer." Writing about the victory at Bull Run, he told her that he had wished "to partake in the former struggle, and am mortified at my absence, but the President thought it more important that I should be here." He also broke the news that he was taking a field command at last: "I leave tomorrow for the Northwest Army. . . . I cannot say for how long, but will write you."

Pleased as Lee was to be out of Richmond and in command of troops, his appointment to oversee military operations in what is now West Virginia was not an enviable one. The military situation was "deteriorating steadily." The Confederate forces were divided into three mutually antagonistic commands, the principal one led by Brigadier General William Loring, a doughty and experienced professional soldier who had lost an arm in the Mexican War.★ He had only just arrived to replace the late General Garnett. The other two consisted of locally recruited "legions," one led by former governor Henry A. Wise, the other by former U.S. secretary of war John B. Floyd. Rival politicians, Floyd and Wise detested each other, and both were reluctant to obey orders from Loring, who at least understood his business—neither Floyd nor Wise had any significant military experience, unless one counts the fact that Floyd was suspected of using his position as secretary of war to move over 150,000 rifles and muskets and many tons of heavy ordnance to arsenals in the South after John Brown's raid in 1859. Floyd was an out-and-out liability in military terms, and Wise scarcely less so. Lee's own position was ambiguous—"he had no written instructions"; he was to advise on strategy, and attempt to make the three generals cooperate with one another long enough to carry out an attack; but he still

---

★ Loring had studied military tactics in Europe between the Mexican and the Civil wars, and after the Confederate defeat in 1865 he went to Egypt to modernize the army of Khedive Ismail Pasha, attaining the rank of *fareek pasha*, or major general.

did not have the full authority of a commander in chief, possibly because Floyd and Wise still had the political clout to prevent it. President Davis did not understand the importance of placing command unambiguously and firmly in the hands of one person, or perhaps he still thought of that person as himself. In any event, Lee arrived in Staunton as a peacemaker between contentious generals, a role for which he was in fact better suited than that of knocking heads together. If Lee had one weakness, it was his dislike of open confrontation. Good manners and the gentle handling of people who disagreed with him were instinctive with Lee, but not always effective.

What Lee found at Staunton when he arrived on July 28 dismayed him. The men were hungry, ragged, insubordinate, sick. Desertion had thinned their ranks, and some regiments had simply disbanded or had dwindled to the point where only a few officers and men remained. An epidemic of measles, as well as typhoid fever and what was probably a form of flu had sickened much of the army, which was living in miserable conditions. Even in midsummer the nights were cold in the mountains, and the men lacked both overcoats and blankets. A day was enough to tell Lee all he needed to know about the state of the army. He left early the next morning for a ten-mile ride to Monterey, with the two aides who had accompanied him from Richmond: Colonel John A. Washington, a great-grandnephew of George Washington; and Captain John H. Taylor, who would remain with Lee throughout the war. He would write to Mary a few days later with considerable enthusiasm about the scenery: "I enjoyed the mountains as I rode along. The views are magnificent—the valleys so beautiful, the scenery so peaceful. What a glorious world Almighty God has given us. How thankless and ungrateful we are, and how we labour to mar his gifts." He did not mention that it was pouring rain and the roads were so mired in mud that wagons sank up the hubs of their wheels. Five days later, it was still raining. Colonel Washington and Captain Taylor were sharing a tent at the camp of Brigadier General Henry R. Jackson—a Georgian, as well as a "Yale graduate, an art lover, a poet, an ex-judge and former United States minister to Austria," another of those odd, talented civilians whom the war pushed into uniform. Jackson pointed out to Lee that the rain had been falling steadily since July 22, that his men were without tents or camp equipment, and that his horses were "jaded and galled" and unfit for use.

Lee wrote to Mary that their second son, Fitzhugh ("Rooney"), now a major in the cavalry, had visited him for dinner and still—a touch of Lee's taste for gentle teasing—"preserves his fine appetite." He did not add that the boy had no overcoat. The Union troops facing Jackson were commanded by Brigadier General J. J. Reynolds, whom Mary Lee would remember as an assistant professor of philosophy at West Point. A few days later Lee wrote to two of his *"Precious Daughters,"* Mary and Mildred, to complain that it was still raining and so cold that he was writing in his overcoat. His servant Perry, who had been one of the slaves who waited on the Lees in the dining room at Arlington, was unable to dry any of Lee's socks or towels.* The health of Richmond, Lee's horse, he reported, was fine, although the animal was not accustomed to such meager rations and poor shelter. Lee describes a cozy domestic scene under canvas, with Colonel Washington seated on a folded blanket doing his own sewing. To reassure his wife and daughters, Lee preferred to make light of the discomforts of camp life. It is also possible that despite those discomforts he was glad to be back in the field, but one gets from his letters home a sense of the extreme misery of the troops, as well as the difficulty of holding the Confederate positions in northwestern Virginia against the superior strength of the Union forces, and the hostility of the local population. Lee is always very

---

*Lee took two slaves with him on this campaign: Perry and Meredith, the latter a cook from White House, the estate on the Pamunkey River, which G. W. P. Custis had left to Lee's second son, Fitzhugh (Thomas, *Robert E. Lee*, 201–2).

frank about the war in his letters to Mary and to his daughters, and makes no attempt to varnish the truth.

The difficulties Lee faced in northwestern Virginia would probably have been insurmountable by any general, however gifted, but it must also be said that the Lee of legend had not yet been forged. Some generals ascend to fame and glory in one quick leap, but Lee was a fifty-four-year-old man who had never commanded an army in the field, and whose last experience of war had been nearly fifteen years ago. He had much to learn, first of all about himself.

He could see the military situation clearly enough—the parallel chains of mountains running diagonally northeast from the Great Kanawha River to the Cheat River were like a series of natural barriers preventing the Union Army from advancing to Staunton and cutting the Virginia Central Railroad, thus splitting Virginia in two, and at the same time cutting Richmond off from Tennessee and the Shenandoah Valley. The "front," if it could be called that, was over seventy-five miles, and the mountains were not easily crossed except by three passes.* Lee saw no great dif-

---

* These were, from north to south the Parkersburg-Staunton Turnpike, which was dominated by Cheat Mountain, taken by the Federals during the battle in which Garnett had been killed; then a very rough and difficult road from Huttonsville to Millsboro, just west of Cheat Mountain; and finally the James River and Kanawha Turnpike from Charleston to Covington.

ficulty at first in holding this line—despite McClellan's superiority in numbers, supplies, and equipment, but that was before he had fully measured the enmity between the Confederate commanders. He could see at once that the strongpoint of the Union line was Cheat Mountain, on top of which McClellan had built a substantial earthwork fortress, well equipped with artillery, and had felled enough trees to give the defenders a clear field of fire. If Lee could take Cheat Mountain before winter set in, then the whole Union line would have to fall back toward the Ohio River.

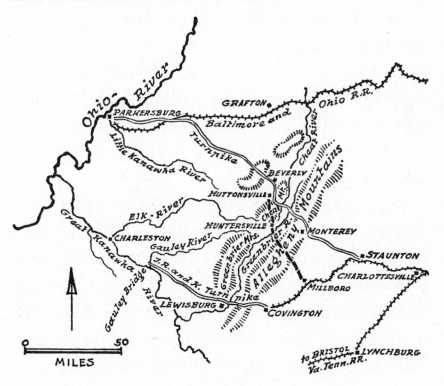

3. Cheat Mountain.

On August 3 Lee rode up to Huntersville, from which any attack on Cheat Mountain would have to begin; found it crowded with sick and miserable troops; and called on General Loring, who to Lee's dismay greeted him in a cold, surly manner. Loring, it transpired, had been senior to Lee as a colonel in "the old Army," and resented both Lee's rank and his presence. An experienced professional soldier, Loring saw no reason why he needed Lee's supervision, still less his tactical advice.

It is possible that Lee underrated how swiftly winter came to the mountains—it was already cold at night, and on the night of August 14–15 an ice storm would freeze mules to death and would be followed by an early snowfall that covered their bodies so only their ears showed. Certainly he underrated the sheer, bloody-minded refusal of the generals to cooperate with each other, or with him.

Lee had already learned that there was a rough road or track along which it was possible to advance unseen less than eighteen miles to the Tygart River valley, then turn eastward in a sharp "fishhook" to climb Cheat Mountain and attack the Union battery on its summit from behind. This uncannily resembled the flanking route around a supposedly impregnable enemy position on a mountaintop that Lee had discovered in

April 1847, and which had led to Scott's victory at the Battle of Cerro Gordo.

Loring, although he understood what Lee had in mind, was slow to move; and Lee certainly should have overruled him but chose not to. The problem was that Loring was unwilling to advance anywhere until he had built up a base of supplies at Huntersville. Days went by, the rain continued making the roads almost impassable, and the moment passed. There was after all no point in a flanking attack if it was not made in conjunction with a bold advance from the rest of Loring's forces. The attack that should have been made on August 4 did not in the end take place until September 12, by which time Loring's attempt to build up his base had been more or less canceled out by the rapidly spreading sickness of his troops, due partly to the increasingly cold, wet weather and partly to carelessness about even the most elementary rules of hygiene. Lee lamented the sickness of the troops. "Our troops, I know, suffer much." he wrote to Mary. "They bring it on themselves by not doing what they are told." This was probably true; but still, Lee, who had just been confirmed as a full general by the Confederate Congress, had only to give an order that sanitary precautions must be taken, latrines dug, and men forbidden to foul the streams or to drink downstream from where horses were watered—elementary rules for an army since Roman times—but he did not do so. A show of temper or a well-placed threat might have helped, but Lee waited patiently for Loring to get ready, and put up with what he knew perfectly well was a total lack of professionalism on the part of Loring's officers, while seventy miles to the south the jealousy and spiteful lack of cooperation between Wise and Floyd threatened to open the Kanawha Valley to the Federals. That would expose Loring's left flank and his line of communications, and bring about a debacle in northwestern Virginia.

Douglas Freeman, Lee's loyal admirer, blames all this entirely on the fact that until now Lee "had lived with gentle people, where kindly sentiments and consideration for the feelings of others were part of *noblesse oblige*," and that this rendered him unable to deal with people who were "sour or self-opinionated." Certainly there is some truth to this, but Lee at this point was a man in his mid-fifties who had been in the army since his youth, and fought in a war—a small one, by later standards, but still nasty enough. Brigadier General Loring, whom Lee himself had chosen to replace Garnett, cannot have been the first ungentle person with whom he was obliged to cope!

It is true that Lee did not wish to instill fear in people, and there was nothing in his character that resembled the frightening intensity of, for instance, Stonewall Jackson. Lee preferred to lead by example, and to inspire those who served with him rather than shout them down or threaten them. He held himself under strict self-control, and expected others to do the same, but this still does not explain his inability to deal with Loring, Floyd, and Wise, or to demand that Loring carry out an attack that might have succeeded in early August, but was becoming problematic as the winter approached and the Federals on Cheat Mountain began to patrol and secure the complicated tangle of trails to the west of the mountain. The answer, perhaps, is that Lee was still in the process of inventing himself as the "Marble Man," whom everybody sought to please, and whose slight frown of disappointment was all it took to chasten a subordinate. These elements of his character were always present, but they required an effort of will on Lee's part, and they needed to be confirmed by victory in battle.

Despite the torrential rain, the misery of the troops, and the continuing resentment of General Loring, Lee saw another chance to attack Cheat Mountain. A civilian engineer approached Colonel Albert Rust of the Third Arkansas Regiment with the information that there was another rough trail through the dense brush and steep ravines to the south and west of Cheat Mountain, by which it was possible to climb unseen to a position west of the Union lines on the summit and overlooking them, at a point where they were poorly defended by merely a few trenches and an improvised wooden blockhouse. If this movement was coordinated with a frontal assault from the east that Loring had been putting off for weeks, and if an attack from the west could be launched at the same time to sever the road from the summit to Huttonsville by which the Union forces were supplied, there seemed to be a good chance of dislodging the Federals from Cheat Mountain. Since very few people in this part of Virginia were secessionists, the civilian engineer's story about the existence of the trail had been cause for some doubt, so Rust himself had accompanied the man on a second trip to the summit, and vouched for the truth of it. In return for this good news, Rust asked to be given command of the assault from the position he had reconnoitered. Lee agreed. By this time Major General McClellan had been recalled to Washington to replace McDowell, and Brigadier General W. S. Rosecrans was in command of what would become the Department of Western Virginia.

Lee and Loring came up with a plan that had every virtue except simplicity, since it depended on perfect timing and the element of surprise, neither of which would prove easy to achieve. One of the difficulties was topographical. From a distance Cheat Mountain and its neighbors looked like gently rolling hills covered in autumn foliage, but they were in fact much steeper than they seemed, and separated by deep ravines. The ground was broken by many ridges, and all of it was heavily wooded and covered in dense thickets of shrub, except for the summit of Cheat Mountain itself, which had been cleared by the Federals to offer a good field of fire. This would not only make it difficult for Lee's troops to attack but also make it difficult for Lee to see or communicate with the three different elements of the attack.

Lee chose to oversee the battle from the left, which was probably the appropriate place for him to be in terms of its importance, but it still didn't give him real control over the battle. His plan called for the left wing, under Loring, to approach Cheat Mountain along both sides of the Tygart River valley. When they were directly west of the summit, the rest of his force would arc left to cross Elkwater Ford, where the bulk of Reynold's forces were encamped. This would block any Union reinforcements from coming to the support of the troops on the summit. Meanwhile, the rest of Loring's troops would attack the summit from behind. This attack, along with Brigadier General Henry Jackson's frontal attack from the east, would begin the moment they heard Rust's small force of 2,000 men commence fire at the trenches and blockhouse. This effectively ceded control of the battle to Rust, who had previously estimated that there were between 2,000 and 3,000 Union troops on the summit after his personal reconnaissance.

On paper, seen as a plan, it looks excellent, particularly since Lee had about 15,000 men, approximately the same number as his Union opponent, Brigadier J. J. Reynolds, the former assistant professor of philosophy at West Point. In Lee's case, however, at least half his men were disabled by sickness, and the effect of his plan was to divide what remained of his forces in four, thereby giving up the principle of concentration in favor of dispersal, never a sound policy in war. Then too, drawn up as a neat map, the plan fails to convey the difficulties of the terrain, which were considerable. The attack was set for September 12, but troops were on the move from September 9 on, mostly over muddy roads or worse trails, on which the men and even the mules slipped and slid, and where in some places men had to climb or descend by grasping the branches of trees. The troops soon ran out of rations, and although it was cold at night, fires were forbidden, so the men were forced to huddle together in the mud and torrential rain for a miserable two days and nights to get into position.

The morning of September 12 began inauspiciously with a heavy fog. When it lifted, Lee could look down the Tygart valley and see Reynolds's encampment clearly, although the summit of Cheat Mountain was still shrouded. He waited for the sound of Rust's men opening fire, but instead he heard the irregular crackle of musket shots from ahead on his right, near Becky's Ford. The explanation was, as he discovered only later, that some of Brigadier General Joseph Reid Anderson's men, concerned that the rain may have dampened the powder in their muskets, were firing into the air to clear and dry the chambers—the lazy man's way of preparing a weapon for use, rather than the one prescribed by the army. The result was that Lee's plan to surprise the enemy was immediately eliminated. Lee galloped ahead to see what was happening, and he and his party nearly collided with a Union cavalry charge. For a moment they actually found themselves behind Reynolds's lines, but they managed to retire unnoticed in the confusion.

The next element of the plan to go wrong involved Rust's column, from which no firing had been heard. The reason was that Rust had captured a few Union pickets and teamsters, who managed to persuade him that there were at least 4,000 or 5,000 Union troops facing him on the crest, when the real number was only between 200 and 300. Rust held a brief council of war with his senior officers and decided to follow their advice and withdraw. In the absence of any firing from Rust's men, Lee's planned frontal attack never took place, and he was unable to persuade Loring and his officers to carry out the attack on the left—the morale of the men had plummeted as the resolve of their commanders dissolved. Still another Confederate loss was the death of Lee's aide Colonel Washington, when he and Rooney Lee blundered into the Federal picket line on "the right branch of the Elkwater Fork," looking for another way of attacking Reynolds's forces. It was a tragic end to a battle that had failed dismally before it began.

In pouring rain, the dispirited, starving Confederate troops made their way back slowly to where they had started from. A week of exhaustion and misery had accomplished nothing, and it was clear that with winter coming on, nothing else could be attempted here. Lee paused in camp long enough to inform one of Colonel Washington's two daughters about their father's death and to write a rather bland letter to Governor Letcher about the failure of the "expedition," laying the blame on the weather, and carefully avoiding any criticism of the men or their officers. Curiously enough, except for the usual expressions of humility and unworthiness, Lee is notably reticent about his own failings in his letter to Letcher. He should have imposed his authority on Loring from the very beginning; he should have chosen an officer more experienced than Rust to lead the attack on the summit; and when Rust didn't attack, Lee should have concentrated his own forces and pushed them forward to attack anyhow. Above all, Lee should have taken firm control of the battle himself. His expressions of regret were mild indeed compared with the opprobrium that soon descended on his head from the southern press; it was from this time on that he would be called "Granny Lee" by a public that thought he was too cautious to command in battle. The truth is that Lee did not seek praise for things that went right for him, nor did he blame others or himself when things went wrong. He saw in everything God's will, and patiently endured the criticism. This is saintly behavior, but very rare among generals, and it explains a certain opaque quality in Lee's character, even as described by his admirers. Even his devoted aide Walter Taylor seems baffled by it, and no man was closer to Lee.

On September 19 Lee rode south to the Kanawha valley, where yet another potential Confederate disaster seemed to be unfolding. An enemy advance there would threaten both the Virginia Central and the Orange and

Alexandria railroads. Generals Wise and Floyd not only were contemptuous of each other, but now refused to cooperate at all; as a result, Floyd had fallen back with "his little army" under modest Union pressure, while General Wise refused to retreat from his position at Sewell Mountain, maintaining that he was determined to fight it out and was under no obligation to obey an order from General Floyd. Lee, finally aware that the missing element in the defense of northwestern Virginia was his own failure to impose his will on recalcitrant or incompetent generals, managed to get Floyd to move forward; but here too, as at Cheat Mountain, bad weather, scanty rations, and poor morale made it impossible to launch a convincing attack. For nearly four weeks Lee tried to sort out the mess that Wise and Floyd had made on their own in a key area, the loss of which would endanger two vital railways. Wise and Floyd were perfect examples of the danger of giving politicians not only the rank of general, but actual active command in the field. Wise was the more aggressive and courageous of the two; Floyd would bring disgrace on himself in a few months' time by fleeing from Fort Donelson when Ulysses S. Grant surrounded and attacked it, abandoning his command to General Buckner—an episode about which Grant later wrote, "[Floyd] was no soldier, and possibly, did not possess the elements of one," calling him "unfitted for command," a judgment that seems moderate and was shared by both armies.

Oddly enough, it was the cautious Floyd whom Lee favored over the more impetuous Wise. On his advice President Davis had Wise recalled to Richmond, leaving Floyd in command. Fortunately for the Confederacy bad weather and timid generalship prevented the Federals from taking advantage of the situation, and with winter coming on Lee was able to stabilize a kind of front. This was something of a triumph for Lee, who had overcome chaos and a broken chain of command, and in the end he prevented a disaster by his presence.

The press gave Lee no credit. Floyd, a career politician, had a surer sense of public relations, as we now call it, than Lee, and managed to get his side of the story into print before Lee was back in Richmond again. Even Lee, who was seldom critical of anyone, took note of the fact that Floyd had "three editors" on his staff, grinding out praise for their general and blame for everyone else. The *Richmond Examiner* dismissed Lee as "outwitted, outmaneuvered, and outgeneraled," and suggested that Floyd had been eager to fight but that Lee overruled him and allowed General Rosecrans to get away "unmolested," pretty much the opposite of what had happened. The same newspaper also criticized Lee for devoting too much time to studying maps and planning, and complained that since Lee's strategy had failed, "it will be useless to discuss its merits," then went on to blame Lee for his "excess of caution." The *Charleston* (South Carolina) *Mercury* accused him of being "a great General, who can never get up to the enemy," and went on to ask, "Are the roads any worse for Lee than Rosecrans? The people are getting mighty sick of this dilly-dally dirt digging, scientific warfare, so much so, that they will demand that the Great Entrencher be brought back and permitted to pay court to the ladies." One of Lee's officers was quoted as saying that the army would never move forward "unless somebody puts a coal of fire on the back of that old terrapin Lee." "Granny Lee," "the King of Spades," "the Great Entrencher"—Lee's stock had plunged throughout the South, and he was now pitied and laughed at more than he was admired. He wrote to Mary, who was in Hot Springs "seeking treatment," with just a touch of asperity: "I am sorry, as you say, that the movements of the armies cannot keep with the expectations of the editors of papers. I know they can regulate matters satisfactorily to themselves on paper. I wish they could do so in the field." Lee would have agreed with Stephen Vincent Benét's line about him, in the poem "Army of Northern Virginia," "But God is the giver of victory and defeat."

He had little to show for his four months in the field, but it was not time wasted. Given the sad state of the troops and their commanders in northwestern Virginia, he had managed to at least hold the line there, and stave off a Union advance. More important, he had learned a great deal. He was still unwilling to knock heads together, but this does not mean that he failed to recognize a fool or a mediocrity when he met one, and he succeeded in getting anyone who fell into either category adroitly moved to some other command, out of the way, as he did first with Wise and then with Floyd. It was one of Lee's gifts—the ability to get rid of people he didn't trust without a confrontation, so they often didn't even realize what had happened until it was too late. He had also relearned the value of digging earthworks, much as the men hated doing it (for southern soldiers, it was "nigger work") and despite the fact that people made fun of him over it. Earthworks had given Reynolds's men on the crest of Cheat Mountain the ability to hold back a force many times their size, and earthworks had prevented Rosecrans from advancing in the Kanawha valley.

The war in the harsh terrain and bad weather of Virginia had changed Lee in many ways. He now understood the effect his presence had on the men, if not always on their officers. Naturally abstemious, he shared their hardships, lived on the same rations as they did, ate off a battered tin plate, lived under canvas even when a house was available, and when necessary slept in the open, wrapped in his overcoat. Although he was not a man who thought in those terms, his image was formed here, indelibly, for the ages. He had let his beard grow—a full, silvery gray beard that soon turned white and replaced all previous images of him. The man with the trim, dark mustache and the flowing Byronic locks was simply erased, so completely that earlier pictures of him seem those of another man altogether. He wore a simple Confederate uniform of his own design: a gray frock coat and waistcoat without braid or ornamentation; the polished leather leggings of a dragoon over boots and spurs when he was in the field, or gray trousers when he was not mounted. It was the plainest of uniforms, as much like that of his soldiers as he could devise. He was already famous for his superb calmness, his self-control, and the way he spoke to everyone from privates to generals in the same gentle voice, as if good manners meant more to him than anything else, which was indeed the case.

All the elements in Lee's personality came together during those four grueling and disappointing months when he commanded an army in the field, even including the horse that would soon share his fame, for it was in what is now West Virginia that Lee first saw and determined to purchase Traveller, possibly the most famous and beloved horse in history:

> ... Why,
> You're weeping! What, then? What more did
> you see?
> A gray man on a gray horse rode by.*

On few horses has so much praise been showered, and not only by Lee himself. In the words of Stephen Vincent Benét:

> And now at last
> Comes Traveller and his master. Look at
>   them well.
> The horse is an iron-grey, sixteen hands high,
> Short back, deep chest, strong haunch, flat legs,
>   small head
> Delicate ear, quick eye, black mane and tail,
> Wise brain, obedient mouth. Such horses are
> The jewels of the horseman's hands and thighs,
> They go by the word and hardly need the rein.
> They bred such horses in Virginia then,

---

*Richard Adams, "Traveller."

Horses that were remembered after death
And buried not so far from Christian ground
That if their sleeping riders should arise
They could not witch them from the earth again
And ride a printless course along the grass
*With the old manage and light ease of hand.**

Traveller was born near the Blue Sulphur Springs in Greenbrier County, Virginia (now West Virginia), and raised by Andrew Johnston. His original name was, of all things, Jeff Davis, and he was "of the Gray Eagle stock, and as a colt took first prize at the Lewisburg, Virginia, fairs in 1859 and 1860." Years later, Major Thomas L. Broun recollected that he had placed the horse in Lee's hands. Broun had authorized his brother, Captain Joseph M. Broun, "to purchase a good serviceable horse of the best Greenbrier stock." After a lengthy search Captain Broun bought the four-year-old Jeff Davis for "$175 (gold value) . . . from Captain James W. Johnston, son of the Mr. Johnston first above mentioned." Major Broun was serving, like his brother, in the Third Virginia Infantry in the "Wise Legion" encamped near Meadow Bluff, where he often rode the horse, "which was then greatly admired for his rapid, springy walk, his high

---

*Stephen Vincent Benét, "Army of Northern Virginia."

spirit, bold carriage, and muscular strength." When Lee took command of the Floyd and Wise "legions" he saw the horse "and took a great fancy to it." Perhaps Lee was dissatisfied with his present horse Richmond, or perhaps he simply saw in Jeff Davis something he liked, but he made it clear to both Brouns that he was interested in the horse, though they were in no hurry to sell it. It was not until February 1862, when Lee, Captain Broun, and Traveller met up again in South Carolina, that Lee actually acquired the horse. Captain Broun, knowing how strong Lee's interest in Jeff Davis was, offered "to give him the horse as a gift," but Lee would not hear of that, although he agreed to take the horse for a week on trial to see how they got on together. The trial was successful. The Broun brothers then offered to sell the horse to Lee for what they had paid, but Lee insisted on adding $25, "to make up for the depreciation in our currency from September, 1861, to February, 1862"* (a first warning sign of the disastrous economic and financial consequences of secession).

Lee had several horses during the war, including Richmond; Ajax; an unnamed "brown roan"; and Lucy Long, who was purchased for him by J. E. B. Stuart (one of the great cavalry commanders of all time,

---

* This would be about $5,500 in today's money.

and also a fine judge of horseflesh) and lived on to a remarkably old age, dying in 1891. But it was Traveller Lee loved most and rode most often, though others who rode him from time to time were less enthusiastic. Lee's youngest son, Rob, complained of the difficulty of sitting to Traveller's bouncy, "short, high trot" and remarked that he "was glad when the journey ended"— not surprisingly, since it was thirty miles long. In any event, the horse suited Lee, and his greatest pleasure after the war was to take Traveller out for a ride. Horse and rider are fixed together now in history and legend as they were in life. When Traveller died, he was, after some delay, buried where he belongs, a few feet from his master.

Even Jefferson Davis would later say that Lee "came back, carrying the heavy weight of defeat," but Lee showed no sign of it. He quietly slipped back into his position as Davis's chief military adviser, and on November 5 wrote to Mary that he hoped to meet her at Shirley, the Carter plantation on the James River, where she had gone after her "cure" in Hot Springs, on her way to the White House. But the next day he was ordered to take immediate command of the newly formed Department of the South, which had been created to protect the coastline of South

Carolina, Georgia, and Florida. When news came that a large fleet of Federal warships and transports was at sea and bound for Port Royal, South Carolina, it was natural for Lee to be chosen, given his experience with fortifications, and his familiarity with the area itself. On the other hand, it is also possible that Davis, despite his professed admiration for Lee, was relieved to get him out of Richmond, where Lee remained a very visible object of criticism for what was widely viewed as his mishandling of the northwestern Virginia campaign. If Davis thought sending Lee south would solve this problem, he was wrong. Fear that Lee would lose the three southeastern states, as he had lost northwestern Virginia, led to protests that included a "round-robin" from South Carolina officers, and Davis was forced to remind the governors of Georgia and South Carolina that Lee was not only a full general but "the best man available." This time, however, Lee insisted on being in undisputed command. His arrival in Charleston soon stilled any further protests. If, since the South still lacked a navy, he could not prevent the U.S. Navy from blockading the southeastern ports or from attacking Confederate fortifications from the sea, he at least prevented what might easily have been a catastrophe involving the loss of three states.

He established his headquarters at Coosawhatchie, near Port Royal Sound, where the Union fleet was already bombarding two Confederate forts. This time he quickly established his authority. It was at once clear to him that he could not defend the entire coastline of three states from attack, or even from small-scale landings. The U.S. Navy was able to sail anywhere without interference, and the shoreline, over 8,000 miles long, contained endless inlets, islands, and bays, any one of which might serve as a landing place. Only by the most arduous pressure on the three governors was Lee able to put together a force of of some 6,800 men—he would have had no arms for most of them had not a Confederate blockade-runner appeared in Savannah with a cargo of Enfield rifles.

Lee quickly set about inspecting his vast department. The fact that he covered 115 miles in one day, 35 of them on Traveller, gives some idea of his "grueling" pace. He came to the conclusion that he must withdraw troops and guns from the myriad of islands and waterways, which it was impossible to defend, and instead concentrate all his strength on the defense of Charleston and Savannah. He set about constructing an "inner line" of earthwork fortifications to protect the two ports and the railway that connected them, "an unromantic routine of duty, dirt and drudgery" for those doing the digging. This was a sensible strategy, though it did not please the owners of rice plantations or those who produced "sea island cotton," many of whom had to abandon their homes, lands, and slaves to the enemy. Not only had Lee made the right decision militarily; his presence this time seemed to calm even those who wanted a full-scale battle rather than a careful defense scheme. It did not hurt that his father had been a dazzling hero as a cavalry commander in the Carolinas during the Revolutionary War. One South Carolinian, Paul Hamilton Hayne, described Lee in semireligious terms: "In the midst of the group, topping the tallest by half a head was the most striking figure we had ever encountered, the figure of a man seemingly about 56 or 58 years of age, erect as a poplar, yet lithe and graceful, with broad shoulders well thrown back, a fine justly-proportioned head posed in unconscious dignity, clear, deep, thoughtful eyes, and the quiet, dauntless step of one every inch the gentleman and soldier. Had some old English cathedral crypt or monumental stone in Westminster Abbey been smitten by a magician's wand and made to yield up its knightly tenant restored to his manly vigor . . . we thought that thus would he have appeared, unchanged in aught but costume and surroundings." Lee's venerable appearance—he was in fact fifty-four, not fifty-six or fifty-eight—may have been due to his cares as the man responsible for the protection of three states and the Confederacy's two major remaining ports, but the rest of Hayne's somewhat overwrought description is notable for being the first to compare Lee to a knight of olden times, and even to a knight of the Round Table, for "a magician's wand" is a clear reference to Merlin's role at King Arthur's court. In any case Lee is cast in the noble, heroic mold of mythic heroes of the past, the image that he would assume in the eyes of all southerners (and many northerners) early in 1862 and which has remained his to this day. Clearly, the image preceded the victories that would justify it, and it was not just the way his countrymen wanted to see Lee, but to some degree the way they wanted to see *themselves*. The North was viewed by many southerners as money-grubbing and corrupt, a place of rampant industrialism, big banks, mass immigration of foreigners, and disregard for the traditions of America, and in favor of blind "progress," while the South was a bucolic paradise of small farms, stout yeomen, and courtly aristocrats, all hewing to the untarnished ideals of Washington and Jefferson—a simplified, romantic vision in which the reality of slavery played no part. It was a contest of Camelot versus the "dark Satanic mills," and it would be Lee's fate to play the role of Sir Galahad.

It must be said at once that Lee had no part in creating this legend, nor would his modesty have enabled him to accept it, but it was to become a major weapon of the Confederacy—in its final days its *only* weapon. So it is interesting to see the web of myth already being drawn around Lee, as it would be drawn around even his new horse: for Traveller, only just purchased and renamed, would also play his part in the legend, as Lee's "noble steed."

In the meantime, his biggest challenge was to overcome his soldiers' reluctance to dig. Despite this, he created a series of fortifications that daunted even Brigadier General William Tecumseh Sherman. Lee was enraged that the U.S. Navy sank "half a dozen old ships" to block the main channel to Charleston, an "achievement . . . unworthy of any civilized nation," as Lee described it in a rare burst of anger. He was relieved that Mary Lee had finally settled at White House, and he paused to pluck some violets from the garden of the deserted house he occupied in Coosawhatchie to send his daughter Annie. Lee's concern for his family was magnified by his anger at the behavior of Union forces, which he feared would be extended to them in the form of "ruin and pillage," if not worse, though in fact Mary and their daughters were treated with considerable courtesy when they fell briefly into the hands of the enemy. He wrote to Mary again on Christmas day, urging her to put Arlington out of her mind. "As to our old home, if not destroyed, it will be difficult ever to be recognised. . . . With the number of troops encamped around it, the change of officers, etc., the want of fuel, shelter, etc., and all the dire necessities of war, it is vain to think of its being in habitable condition. I fear, too, books, furniture, and the relics of Mount Vernon will be gone. It is better to make up our minds to a general loss. They cannot take away the remembrances of the spot, and the memories of those that to us rendered it sacred." This was sensible, if not welcome, advice. With bleak realism, he urged her not to believe rumors that Great Britain would recognize and support the Confederacy: "We must make up our minds to fight our battles and win our independence alone. No one will help us."

In mid-January 1862, he paused in his travels long enough to visit Cumberland Island and see his father's grave for the first time, dwelling only on the beauty of the garden and hedges around the grave. As late as early March he was still laboring mightily to complete the fortifications protecting Savannah, and complaining about his "slow workmen."

Although Lee was successful in preventing any major Federal incursion into the Department of the South, the outlook for the Confederacy was bleak everywhere else. In the west, a new and amazingly efficient new general, Ulysses S. Grant, captured Fort Henry on the Tennessee River, and shortly afterward demanded and received the surrender of Fort Donelson, capturing over 15,000 Confederate soldiers, endangering the Confederacy's hold on Tennessee, and forcing General Floyd to abandon his command and flee, fearful of being tried for treason if he was captured. In the east, there were rumors that General McClellan, who had replaced not only General McDowell but also Lee's old mentor General in Chief Winfield Scott, had assembled a force of as many as 130,000 men and might at any moment land his army on the peninsula between the York and the James rivers and attempt to take Richmond. Meanwhile Henry Wise, another of Lee's vexations from the failed campaign in northwestern Virginia, was driven from the island he was supposed to defend in North Carolina, losing two-thirds of his men. Lee did not gloat, much as he had reason to dislike both these politicians turned generals, but wrote to Mary: "The news is . . . not favorable, but we must make up our minds to meet with reverses and overcome them."

On March 2 he received an unexpected telegram from Richmond that would call him from worthy but somewhat humdrum service to glory:

General Robert E. Lee,
Savannah:
If circumstances will, in your judgment, warrant your leaving, I wish to see you here with the least delay.

Jefferson Davis

The moment of crisis, for the Confederacy and for Lee, had arrived.

Chapter 7
The Seven Days

"The Power of the Sword"

In March 1862 the outlook for the Confederacy seemed bleak from Richmond: politics as usual; retreat; shortages of everything that mattered, even gunpowder; and dissension rife among the generals, as well as between President Davis and almost everybody else. If Lee had expected to be greeted with a command in the field, he was disappointed. There was a movement in the Confederate Congress to appoint him secretary of war, but Davis saw this as an attempt to diminish his own power as commander in chief, and vetoed the suggestion, causing the *Charleston Mercury*, hitherto Lee's sharpest critic, to complain that he was being demoted "from a commanding general to an orderly sergeant." Lee's official position was described by Davis as "the conduct of military operations in the armies of the Confederacy," but apart from its vagueness, the definition of his duties was further curtailed by placing him "under the direction of the President." Short of the vice presidency of the United States, it would be hard to find a position more anomalous, and with as little direct authority. It was a weak, muddled response to an emergency. Davis had ordered Lee home because the war was going badly and he hoped that Lee's presence in Richmond would reassure the public, but he withheld from Lee the authority that any commanding general needs to form a coherent strategy.

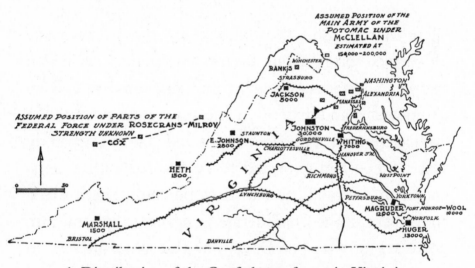

4. Distribution of the Confederate forces in Virginia,
as of the morning of March 24, 1862, and the
assumed positions of the opposing United States forces.

Lee had been away from Richmond since November 1861, and his return gave him his first opportunity since then to examine the files, the maps, and the disposition of the Confederate armies. What he found certainly required every bit of his stoic belief that the outcome of events was in the end determined by the will of God, and not by man. Defeat at Fort Henry and Fort Donelson had placed Kentucky and Tennessee at jeopardy, and it was already possible to see that Union control of the Mississippi River and its tributaries was a realistic danger, while in Virginia General Joseph E. Johnston had persuaded Davis to agree to the withdrawal of his army from Centreville, where it threatened Washington, to the line of the Rappahannock, in anticipation of a major attack by the Army of the Potomac. Retreating from the line established by Beauregard's and Johnston's armies after the First Battle of Manassas was huge step backward, and would certainly have a bad effect on southerners' morale. Davis had agreed to it reluctantly, and Lee would certainly have been opposed to it, had he been consulted. He never forgot Napoleon's answer to his own question: whether a capital should be "defended by covering it directly?" The correct answer, Napoleon wrote, was instead: "To maneuver incessantly, without submitting to be driven back to the capital." Apparently, when Johnston and President Davis were at West Point they had been dozing during that lesson on the tactics of Napoleon, but Lee remembered it well and would put it to brilliant use himself over the next two years.

The ostensible reason for Johnston's caution was that if he was attacked in overwhelming force, as he expected to be, his line might be turned on the right by a simultaneous landing in his rear on the Potomac. Since retreating twenty-five miles did not solve that problem for him, he was giving up ground for no real gain in security.

Of course what nobody in Richmond could guess was that General McClellan was not about to launch a bold frontal attack, still less to combine such an attack with a daring landing on the Potomac. On the contrary he was infuriating and puzzling President Lincoln by his procrastination and his refusal to attack in *any* direction, convinced that he was vastly outnumbered by the Confederate forces around Manassas—which he estimated at 180,000, when in fact they consisted of less than 60,000 ragged, hungry, poorly equipped men, less than a third the number of McClellan's own well-fed, well-supplied forces. "McClellan is one of the great mysteries of the war," Grant would later write, and this was as true in Richmond as in Washington. Johnston and Davis consistently overestimated not only the strength of McClellan's army but, more important, his eagerness to fight, while Lee, perhaps because he knew McClellan better or had better intuition, thought him too cautious for his own good. As for McClellan, he badly misjudged Lee, describing him in a letter to President Lincoln as "cautious and weak . . . & is likely to be timid & irresolute in action."

This was a singularly poor reading of Lee's character, in keeping with McClellan's description of Lincoln as "nothing more than a well-meaning baboon." McClellan, who had served under Lee as a first lieutenant in the assault on Chapultepec in 1847, had every reason to know better. And most people would disagree. "There was no hesitation or vacillation about him," Colonel A. L. Long, who knew him well, wrote of Lee: "When he had once formed a plan the orders for its execution were positive, decisive and final." Major-General J. F. C. Fuller, the British military historian, wrote: "In audacity, which is the mainspring of strategy as it is of tactics, Lee has few equals."

Lee himself found some consolation in being closer to his family. His oldest daughter, Mary Custis, was in Richmond, and he permitted her to exercise Traveller (an accomplished horsewoman, she was the only person except Lee himself who found the horse's gaits comfortable). His daughter Mildred had courageously made her own way alone from her school in Winchester after the Federals took the city, to join her mother, who was at White House with Agnes and Annie. Lee could not see his sons, since all three were now in the army, Rob having left the university to engage as a private in the Rockbridge Artillery despite the fact that university students were exempted.

In this brief lull in the war, Mrs. Lee and her daughters did their best to lead a normal family life. Even though White House was her son Rooney's home and had belonged to her father and mother, it could not console Mrs. Lee for the loss of Arlington. Her arthritis had by now made her a permanent invalid, though she was still spirited. The girls seem to have settled down comfortably, sharing from time to time the romantic, chivalric side of Confederate life, epitomized by such daring exploits as J. E. B. Stuart's recovery of Mary Custis's "copybook" (or what we would now call a scrapbook), in which she had pasted poems, songs, and newspaper clippings that caught her attention during her girlhood at Arlington. Stuart, already a "dashing hero" and a brigadier general, the principal leader of the cavalry of what would soon be renamed the Army of Northern Virginia, had been out on a reconnaissance behind enemy lines with Mary's cousin Lieutenant Colonel Fitzhugh Lee. The two paused at

Kinloch, not more than a few miles from Arlington, where Mrs. Lee and the girls had taken refuge after the Federals occupied Alexandria. There Stuart found Mary's scrapbook, which he sent back to Richmond for her. In two of the blank pages remaining at the back of the book, Stuart and Fitzhugh Lee both wrote poems to Mary in mock-romantic style, Fitzhugh "gently mocking" her "bossy ways," while Stuart, always the Cavalier in spirit, wrote:

> *It chanced tonight on outpost duty—*
> *I found an album with thy name in:*
> *So full of gems of love and beauty*
> *I looked it o'er till lo' there came in—*
> *My muse—so long forgot—neglected—*
> *A form I least of all expected . . .*

He signed his poem "Jeb," a reminder of the more carefree days when he had so often visited Lee's home at West Point and flirted gently with his daughters. Like Lee, Stuart was, although a devoted and faithful husband, an inveterate flirter.*

Lee would surely have enjoyed knowing that his favorite cavalryman and his nephew were writing

---

*I am indebted to Mary P. Coulling's *The Lee Girls* for this material, and for her excellent account of the lives of Lee's daughters.

poetry to his daughter Mary around their campfire, but he had much else to keep him occupied in Richmond, even though White House was only twenty-five miles away, no more than a good day's ride for Traveller. His chief concern was that the Confederate Army would simply disintegrate as men came to the end of their twelve-month enlistment. He became the moving force in persuading President Davis and the Congress to pass a Conscription Act, though it was heavily watered down by those politicians whose first concern was states' rights, and by those who felt that conscription would undermine patriotism. In his former capacity as commander of the military and naval forces of Virginia, Lee had persuaded Governor Letcher to adopt similar legislation, so the arguments for and against it were familiar. The act as it eventually passed contained much that Lee did not like, particularly the election of officers, but it at least ensured that the Confederate Army would not simply evaporate. It also demonstrated how Lee, loath as he was to involve himself in politics, could skillfully lobby behind the scenes when it was necessary.

Lee also was good in getting what he wanted without open confrontation between himself and the rival Confederate commanders in the field. His broader plans depended to a great degree on his faith in the military genius of that most difficult and secretive of generals, Thomas J. ("Stonewall") Jackson. Lee's faith in J. E. B. Stuart as a cavalry leader was that of an indulgent father toward a son; his faith in Stonewall Jackson was more complex: he perceived in Jackson the distillation of his own belief in maneuver and sudden, unexpected flank attacks as the way to overcome Union superiority in numbers and equipment. It did not hurt that both Stuart and Jackson were, though in different ways, deeply religious men, for whom God's presence in human affairs was always a first consideration, and that both of them, like Lee, were instinctively courageous and absolutely indifferent to personal danger. With rare exceptions, Lee did not need to explain his intentions at length to Jackson, or persuade him to do what he didn't want to do—Lee hated both explaining and persuading. Jackson developed a remarkable ability to read Lee's mind and deduce what Lee wanted him to do from only the barest of suggestions. Not only would he become Lee's strong right arm, but he almost always did what Lee himself would have wanted done in any situation on the battlefield.

At first sight, it seems unlikely that the two men would forge such a close relationship. They were both graduates of West Point, but apart from that they had little in common. Lee was the descendant of generations of landed Virginia aristocrats on both sides of his family, while Jackson was born in the hardscrabble hills of what is now West Virginia, a rawboned, awkward, and ungraceful figure. Two of Jackson's great-grandparents had arrived in Virginia as a consequence of the English penal laws of the mid-eighteenth century—both of them had been convicted of theft at a time when the sentence for even the most minor of crimes was usually hanging or transportation to work for seven years in he plantations of the southern colonies as "indentured servants."

The military side of Stonewall Jackson's personality may have owed something to his great-grandfather, an Indian-fighter who was commissioned as a captain in the Revolutionary War, but it owed a lot more to his remarkable great-grandmother, who was over six feet tall, blond, muscular, determined, and a formidably good shot. Their descendants spread throughout northwestern Virginia, some of them prosperous, some not, but very different in spirit and upbringing from First Families of "Tidewater" Virginia, with their substantial slaveholdings, enormous tracts of land, and imposing mansions. Brought up in poverty, and orphaned at an early age, Thomas Jackson had a rough edge, a touch of the frontier, which he never lost. His seat on his favorite horse, Little Sorrel—the animal was to become almost as famous as Traveller in Confederate mythology—was awkward enough to draw attention during the Civil War. A tall man on a small horse, he rode with long stirrups, his upper body canted forward so that it seemed his nose might touch the horse's neck—a great contrast to the supremely graceful horsemanship of Robert E. Lee, in an age when horsemanship still mattered.

The young Jackson worked as a schoolteacher and as a constable before deciding to take the examination for West Point, and got in only because the boy who won the appointment took one look at the Military Academy and decided to return home. At West Point Jackson overcame his many handicaps to graduate seventeenth in a class of fifty-nine cadets, and win the place he coveted as a second lieutenant in the Artillery Corps, graduating just in time to be sent to Mexico, where his courage and his gifted handling of artillery against overwhelming odds earned him one of the most brilliant records of the war.

Throughout his life Jackson suffered from a wide variety of ailments, possibly magnified by intense hypochondria. Only on the subject of religion was his interest more intense than in his own health: dyspepsia, weak eyesight, deafness, rheumatic and neuralgic pains, poor digestion—reading Jackson's correspondence with his loved ones is like reading a prolonged and deeply pessimistic medical report. He was a devotee of quack cures, homeopathic medicine, hot water spas, and strange diets, all to no effect. When invited to dinner, he invariably brought his own food with him, neatly wrapped in a napkin, and avoided alcohol and all stimulants. Despite all this he appeared to most people strong, physically fit, and in ruddy good health.

This strange and awkward man, ill at ease among strangers and tongue-tied when asked to speak, did not do well in the peacetime army. His firm Presbyterian conscience, his inability to distinguish any shades of gray between right and wrong, and a strong dose of primness brought him into conflict with his commanding officer in Florida, whom Jackson accused of carrying on an affair with a servant girl. Hardly anything is more certain to destroy an officer's career than accusing a superior of immoral conduct, and in the end Jackson was obliged to resign and become "Professor of Natural & Experimental Philosophy" and artillery instructor at the Virginia Military Institute, in Lexington, in 1851. Though many of the cadets ridiculed and caricatured their professor, who relied entirely on rote learning, did not seem to know very much more about science than themselves, and lacked any gift for making the subject seem interesting to his students, Jackson might have gone on to spend the rest of his life as a fierce, uniformed version of Mr. Chips. But history drew him and his students to witness John Brown's execution in 1859, and with Virginia's decision to secede from the Union in 1861 he marched his students to Staunton and embarked on a new military career that would take him to the rank of brigadier general within less than six months and to the rank of lieutenant general and the status of legendary hero before his death in May 1863 at the battle of Chancellorsville.

Lee was among the first to recognize the merits and the potential of this eccentric, silent genius, whose swift march to the field of First Manassas and whose boldness there had earned him the nickname Stonewall, and made him famous and admired throughout the South—indeed far more famous and admired than Lee himself was at the time.

As Lee looked at the map, it was clear to him that wherever McClellan eventually attacked, the key to stopping him was control of the Shenandoah Valley. Running southwest to northeast from Staunton to Harpers Ferry, "the Valley" could be held only by a general whose swift movements and sudden, fierce attacks would force the Union keep a large number of men defending its northern (or lower)* end against the possibility of a Confederate attack through Maryland on Washington, and thereby prevent McClellan from achieving a concentration of Union forces sufficient to overwhelm the Confederate forces defending Richmond. Too much has probably been made of Lincoln's concern for the protection of the capital, but it certainly preyed on his mind and made him all the more suspicious of McClellan's constant complaints that he was outnumbered and of his occasionally underhanded attempts to transfer to his own command Federal units that the president supposed were guarding Washington. This cat-and-mouse game between President Lincoln and the commander of the Army of the Potomac was something that no general with Lee's keen ability to judge character on the battlefield was likely to ignore. Keeping the enemy guessing about what was happening in the Valley was essential now that the northwestern corner of Virginia was in Union hands, in part because of Lee's own failure there in the autumn of 1861, and would become even more

---

*I owe Robert K. Krick, former historian of the Fredericksburg and Spotsylvania battlefield parks and a distinguished expert on the Army of Northern Virginia, many thanks for the following illuminating explanation: "The southern (or southwestern, if you will) reach of the Valley is the 'upper Valley' because of how the rivers flow. The Shenandoah and its tributaries . . . flow nominally from south to north, so the farther south you go, the farther *up*stream, or *up* the Valley, and vice versa."

important as strategic defeat after defeat struck the Confederacy in the west.

During much of this time Stonewall Jackson was maneuvering his small force in the Shenandoah Valley. At first it consisted of no more than the 5,000 men of the "Stonewall Brigade," which he had led at First Manassas, reinforced by a few militia units. Jackson's headquarters were at Winchester, and he came under the nominal command of General Joseph E. Johnston. Jackson had, along with his other military virtues, a certain gift for what we would now call guerrilla warfare, in the style of T. E. Lawrence, and understood the value of tearing up enemy railway lines and destroying railway bridges. Jackson's cavalry ranged far enough north to harass the Baltimore and Ohio railroad, and interrupt traffic on the Chesapeake and Ohio Canal, while he himself fought small actions at Hancock, Maryland; and Bath, Virginia. These were more in the nature of nuisance attacks than for any major strategic purpose, his mission being to prevent the Union's Major General Nathaniel P. Banks, with much larger forces centered on Harpers Ferry, from ascending up the Valley toward Strasburg and Staunton and threatening the vital railway lines linking Richmond with the west. The sudden arrival of Jackson's forces in places where they were unexpected—and the indignation of pro-Union residents at being subjected, however briefly, to Confederate occupation—kept Banks's attention (as well as Lincoln's) fixed on Jackson, who seemed able to appear and disappear at will. This has been attributed to the fact that he was a local boy and knew the countryside, but in truth Jackson simply had the good sense to ask local secessionists to sort out the tangled back roads and twisty creeks of the Valley for him. He also put to work a supremely gifted topographer and mapmaker, Captain Jedediah Hotchkiss, a native of New York who had settled in the South and whose maps are works of art, some of them sketched in the saddle with a pad and colored crayons. The map he made of the Valley at Jackson's request would eventually consist of three pieces of "linen tracing paper," glued together and nearly nine by four feet when unfolded.

Lee's interest in Jackson was in part a reflection of an underlying difference of opinion between Lee, as President Davis's military adviser, and Joseph E. Johnston, field commander of the Confederate forces in northern Virginia. Lee was studiously careful not to second-guess Johnston, who was prickly about any kind of interference; but, conscious of how slender the resources of the Confederate Army were and how inferior in numbers it was to the Union Army, Lee had grave doubts about Johnston's wish to concentrate all of the Confederacy's forces for one decisive battle to defeat McClellan before Richmond. Lee believed in the importance of concentration of forces as much as Johnston did, but he understood that there were advantages to keeping McClellan off balance with smaller attacks elsewhere that would delay or prevent him from achieving an overwhelming concentration of Union forces against Richmond. In any case the Confederacy could not afford the risk of losing a major battle at the gates of its own capital. Lee feared that Johnston was, in other words, prepared to play all or nothing, while he himself was not.

This was not really caution on Lee's part, as many historians have suggested, so much as ordinary common sense. Lee's objective was to keep the approaches to Richmond covered until such time as it was clear from which direction McClellan attacked, even if it meant the dispersal of Confederate forces in relatively small numbers at key points—exactly what Johnston most wanted to avoid. Although Confederate knowledge of the size of the Army of the Potomac was reliable enough—it was estimated at 155,000 men, almost three times the number of all Confederate troops in Virginia, plus at least 45,000 "garrison troops" to defend Washington—intelligence about the direction in which McClellan would attack was merely conjectural. It did not occur

to Lee (nor to Davis or Johnston) that McClellan himself, like Hamlet, would be unable to decide; still less
could Lee have guessed that McClellan supposed the
Confederate forces facing him consisted of at least
200,000 men.

What Lee devised in his thankless role as the military
éminence grise of President Davis was a daring strategic solution to the problem of McClellan's inevitable
attack on Richmond. He did this without any authority to give orders and with almost no friction between
himself and the other senior Confederate generals.
He saw at once that allowing Johnston to put all the
Confederacy's eggs in one basket on the Rappahannock
would be fatal. McClellan could march south on
Culpeper; cut the Virginia Central Railroad, at the same
time flanking Johnston; then turn east at Gordonsville
and march on Richmond. Or he could march south on
Fredericksburg and attack Richmond from the north,
the shortest route. Or he could make use of the Union's
overwhelming resources in shipping and move his army
down the Potomac, landing it on the peninsula, close to
Fort Monroe, only thirty-five miles from Richmond.
Or—the worst case scenario for the Confederacy—he
could order Banks (and later McDowell) to march on
Fredericksburg from the west and simultaneously land
on the peninsula himself, thus applying force on both

sides of Richmond, like a nutcracker. Less probable, but still possible, McClellan could land his army at Norfolk *and* at Hampton Roads, advancing toward Richmond up both sides of the James River.

While keeping in mind Frederick the Great's dictum, "He who attempts to defend everything, defends nothing," Lee ensured that the key points on a rough semicircle drawn around Richmond were sufficiently well manned to slow down any enemy advance for long enough to carry out the concentration of Confederate forces in the right place. Timing would of course be a crucial factor, but with proper planning Lee would have the advantage of interior lines, and he understood the importance the railways would play in the defense of Richmond. He placed 3,000 men under Brigadier General Edward Johnson near McDowell (about twenty miles from Staunton and the Virginia Central Railroad) in case Major General John C. Frémont advanced through the Alleghenies to threaten Johnston's left. At the same time he placed Jackson at Winchester to discourage General Banks from advancing up the Valley, while the main part of Johnston's force, 40,000 men, remained at Centreville, behind stout earthworks and what McClellan assumed were substantial quantities of guns dug in. Closer to Richmond, Lee had Major General Theophilus Holmes at Fredericksburg

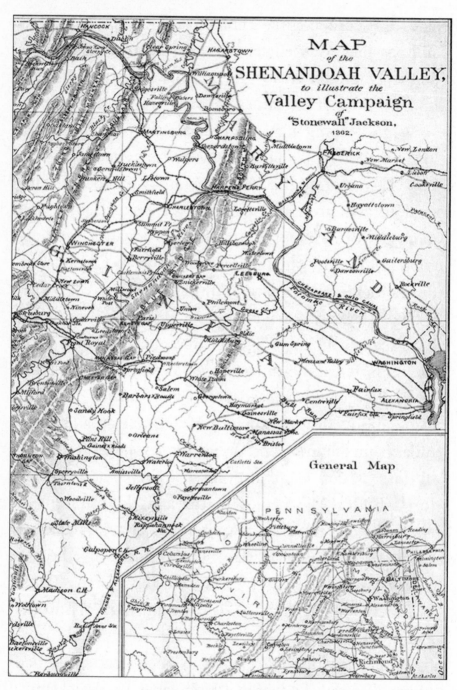

5. *The Shenandoah Valley.*

with 6,000 men, Major General John B. Magruder with 3,000 men manning the line that crossed the peninsula, and Major General Benjamin Huger holding Norfolk and the vital navy yard with 9,000 men.

Lee quietly resisted Johnston's desire to add some if not all of these troops to his force of 40,000, and set about the task of reinforcing Jackson in the Valley, first of all because he had absolute confidence in Jackson's tactical skill and fighting spirit, and second because the Valley was the ideal place for a force as small as Jackson's to tie up the 23,000 men of Banks's army, and discourage any thought in Washington of moving those men toward the Rappahannock to support McClellan. He understood at once what seemed to be a mystery to everybody else except Jackson: the Valley contained one of the finest macadamized roads in the country, the famed Valley Pike, a commercial enterprise begun in 1834 and completed in 1841, which ran down the middle of the Valley and by the outbreak of the Civil War connected Staunton to Winchester, a distance of ninety-four miles. To the west there were five gaps in the Alleghenies, known as "river gaps" because they dropped to the floor of the Valley. To the east in the Blue Ridge Mountains, there were at least seven "wind gaps," so called because they were merely depressions in the skyline. If one thinks of the Valley Pike as the spine of a fish skeleton, and the river gaps and wind gaps as its ribs, one can understand how Jackson, once Hotchkiss had drawn the map, could move his troops through one of the gaps, reach the Valley Pike, and once on it advance them at an astonishing speed. They could attack, then move through another of the gaps to regroup and attack somewhere else within a few days. Jackson had been born and bred in what is now West Virginia, so the landscape was familiar to him, and Hotchkiss's map of the Valley enabled him to take full advantage of it. Even Mary Chesnut, the diarist, remarked that she slept more securely "with the serenest faith that Jackson is to flank everybody and never to be flanked himself," a faith that Lee shared.

What is so striking about the Civil War is the rapid pace of events. We are used to thinking of the past as more leisurely, as of course it was in terms of transportation and communication by our standards, but considering the distances involved, the pressure and pace of events must have seemed dizzying, all the more so because of the new effect of railways and the telegraph on war.

Lee returned to Richmond in the first week of March 1862, only to discover that on March 9 Johnston had abandoned his line on Centreville and withdrawn his army twenty-five miles farther south to the Rappahannock, with his center at Culpeper Court House. Johnston abandoned many of his stores, revealing that many of the batteries that had aroused McClellan's fears were armed with "Quaker guns," logs painted black to give the impression of a mass of artillery.

On March 14 Lee paused long enough to write to Mary, suggesting that she might want to consider moving from White House, on the Pamunkey River, which was outside Magruder's lines and right in the path of any Union advance up the peninsula, to Richmond (advice which as usual she did not take). This suggests that Lee was already outthinking Johnston, and possibly even McClellan.

On March 23, having marched his troops forty miles in two days, Jackson attacked the Union forces of Brigadier General James Shields at Kernstown, and suffered his only defeat (though it was a strategic victory for Lee, since it kept the Union forces bottled up in the Valley). The next day General Magruder reported that startling news that 35,000 Union troops had been landed from steamers at Old Point, sheltered by Fort Monroe, raising the possibility of a Federal advance up the peninsula on Richmond. Among his other attributes, Lee had nerves of steel: momentous events and bad news at short intervals never shook him, he remained calm, calmed others, and searched for a solution. Now, Lee cannily responded by moving small units of troops toward the peninsula and sought everywhere for weapons with which to arm them, including ancient smoothbore flintlocks. He was even forced to set in motion, as an emergency measure, the manufacture of pikes like those John Brown had taken to Harpers Ferry.

Everywhere he looked, from the Mississippi to the peninsula, he was besieged by pleas from governors and from generals for troops, weapons, and ammunition, which he dealt with in his usual polite and efficient way. In Walter H. Taylor's words, Lee exercised "a constant supervision over the condition of affairs at each important point, thoroughly informed as to the resources and the necessities of the several commanders of the armies in the field, as well as the dangers which respectively threatened them, [and] was able to give them wise counsel, to offer them valuable suggestions, and to respond to their demands for assistance and support to such extent as the limited resources of the Government would permit." This was not a role Lee enjoyed, but nobody else could have fulfilled it with such objectivity and care.

In the meantime, blow after blow struck the Confederacy. Johnston, anticipating a crushing attack by McClellan in northern Virginia, resisted sending reinforcements to support Magruder in the peninsula, while Jackson appealed for reinforcements in the Valley. The worst news came from southwest Tennessee, regarding the two-day battle of Shiloh on April 6 and 7, the bloodiest battle in the history of American warfare to that date,* in which General Ulysses S. Grant won a precarious victory and another Johnston—the Confederacy's General Albert Sidney Johnston—was killed. By April 9 it became clear that the Army of the Potomac, instead of advancing on Fredericksburg (as Joseph E. Johnston had supposed), was landing on the peninsula in full force. General McClellan had already reached there, feeling "very glad to get away from that sink of iniquity," by which he meant Washington and the White House. This was an unparalleled military achievement—over the next few weeks "121,500 men, 44 artillery batteries, 1,150 wagons, nearly 15,600 horses and mules," and a vast amount of equipment, ammunition, tents, food, and fodder would be shipped to Hampton Roads. It was the biggest amphibious landing in the history of warfare, indeed one which would not be bettered until D-day in June 1944. It should have been a triumph for McClellan, but although he had

---

* 13,047 Union casualties, 10,699 Confederate.

succeeded in surprising the Confederates, he remained troubled. In the first place he was not aware that his 50,000 troops were facing only 11,000 Confederate troops under Magruder; second, he was still smarting over the fact that Lincoln had insisted on retaining some of his troops to reinforce McDowell's army defending Washington and the Valley; and finally, the U.S. Navy, alarmed by the prospect of fighting the Confederate ironclad *Merrimack,* was unable to promise support by its gunboats up the James and York rivers to protect McClellan's flanks as he advanced, something he should have ascertained before leaving Alexandria. As Stephen W. Sears points out in his biography of McClellan, the general was already developing excuses and planning to throw the blame on Lincoln and the navy if he failed. Despite bad maps and miserable weather, which turned the roads into rivers of mud, McClellan still outnumbered the enemy almost five to one, and could surely have broken Magruder's line, which at this point was something less than formidable, had he boldly attacked at once. But he did not. "No one but McClellan could have hesitated to attack," General Johnston would later remark uncharitably but correctly.

Instead, McClellan made elaborate plans for laying siege to Yorktown, and began the long, expensive task of bringing up his siege train, which included thirteen-inch mortars each weighing over eight tons. Little in warfare is as time consuming and slow moving as a siege, but this suited McClellan, whose strongest gift was for logistics and planning. As for Johnston, he was called back to Richmond to deal with the threat. He arrived there on April 13 and set off on April 14 to inspect Magruder's lines, only to return, to everyone's surprise, the very next day with "a disheartening report." To the consternation of President Davis and Lee, Johnston told them that Magruder's line at Yorktown was too long to defend. He proposed to abandon Norfolk and the peninsula altogether, and either concentrate all the Confederacy's troops before Richmond to fight a decisive battle there or, alternatively, allow Richmond to be besieged and concentrate all Confederate forces elsewhere for a major advance into enemy territory. (The first of these alternatives would actually take place in the winter of 1864–1865, with dire consequences, and the second would lead to Lee's unsuccessful invasion of Maryland in 1862 and of Pennsylvania in 1863.) Lee was strongly opposed to the idea of abandoning the peninsula and Norfolk, and persuaded President Davis of the value of gaining time by slowing down McClellan's advance for as long as possible, rather than risking everything on a single throw of the dice before the Confederate forces in Virginia were adequately armed and equipped.

This was more than an argument about strategy. Johnston was willing to take the risk of losing Richmond in order to strike a blow that might win the war, while Davis and Lee both recognized that like it or not Richmond symbolized the Confederacy's existence, and that to lose it was to lose everything. In the end the irascible, impatient Johnston, although still unconvinced of the wisdom of what he had been ordered to do, set off reluctantly to assume command in the lower peninsula, while Lee scoured the Confederacy for men, arms, and ammunition to supply him. In addition, Lee set as many men as he could to digging defensive works around Richmond, gaining for himself once more the derisive nickname "King of Spades." Little as Lee wished to allow the defense of Richmond to degenerate into "a War of posts," as his idol George Washington put it in 1776 during the effort to defend New York City, like Washington, who was proud to say that he had "never spared the Spade and the Pick Ax," Lee was determined to make Richmond defensible in case Johnston had to fall back before McClellan. Lee had no compunctions about making his soldiers dig like laborers, despite their protests.

Having worked on Fort Monroe as a young lieutenant in the Corps of Engineers, Lee probably had a better sense than Johnston—or, for that matter, than

McClellan—of just how difficult the terrain in front
of McClellan was. The peninsula was not only poorly
mapped but also muddy, swampy in places, and crisscrossed by unmarked narrow lanes and a maze of meandering creeks with steep banks. Such roads as existed
were poor and dissolved into thick mud with even the
slightest rain. Johnston's concern that any defensive
line on the peninsula could be quickly outflanked by
gunboats operating on the James and York rivers was
well founded, but he ignored the fact that both rivers
offered numerous places from which Confederate batteries could shell any boat steaming upstream.* In any
case, from Lee's point of view, the longer McClellan
could be delayed, the more time there was to build up
the Confederate forces in front of him. The last thing
Lee wanted was to denude the Confederacy of troops in
order to fight a much larger and better-supplied army
within earshot of the Confederate capital.

The wisdom of his more cautious approach was
borne out on April 25, only eight days after Johnston
assumed command, with the news that New Orleans
had been taken by the enemy. Lee could not withdraw

---

*The tactical problem was not unlike what the British faced in 1941 in Malaya, a
much longer and very narrow peninsula, where every time they tried to form and
hold a line the Japanese simply outflanked them by landing behind them on both
sides. Eventually the British were forced to retreat all the way back to Singapore,
where they were besieged and obliged to surrender.

troops in any significant number from the Carolinas and take the risk of losing Savannah or Charleston, and after Grant's victory at Shiloh, he could not afford to do so in the west.

It was a measure of Lee's skill at staff work, and of his tact, that by carefully sifting every unit of the Confederate Army he had been able to increase the number of Magruder's troops to just over 30,000 by April 11. That was almost three times his strength when McClellan's force had landed, though still less than a third of what McClellan thought was facing him at Yorktown. These transfers were made with such attention to detail that even General Johnston—a man of extreme sensitivity, with an eagle's eye for any sign of interference with his army from Lee—was not moved to protest.

Lee also had to be careful in transferring General Johnston's four divisions (approximately 28,000 men) from Fredericksburg down to the peninsula, since he was uncovering the approach to Richmond from Alexandria and Manassas. In the words of Douglas Southall Freeman, Lee "exhibited . . . a patient persistence in attaining his object." He advised Magruder to march his men back and forth in circles through the trees in columns to make the Federals believe he had far more troops than he did, and he kept the few men remaining on the Rapidan-Rappahannock line busy demonstrating their presence, as Johnston's divisions were moved "in piecemeal reconcentrations" back to Richmond and on to the peninsula. He knew that a simultaneous Union attack on Magruder's line on the peninsula and toward Fredericksburg in northern Virginia could overwhelm the Confederate forces defending Richmond, particularly in the crucial period when Johnston's divisions were on the march and the northwestern flank of the city was exposed. Lee never expected that McClellan would give him nearly a month's time to perfect Richmond's defenses. Meanwhile McClellan continued to believe that Johnston's army, which he estimated at over 120,000 men when it was in fact less than half of that, was still holding the line in northern Virginia. Considering the stakes, Lee played a poor hand with a combination of brilliance and coolness that has seldom been equaled in warfare.

On April 21 Lee wrote his "historic" message to Jackson outlining his strategy for the Valley. He stressed that Jackson's paramount goal must be to prevent McDowell and McClellan from uniting to attack Richmond simultaneously, and that Jackson should do this by inflicting a serious defeat on Banks in the Valley that would threaten Washington. If Jackson thought he could drive Banks's army down the Valley toward the Potomac, he should do so at once. If he was not strong enough to do that, he should place Major General Richard Stoddert Ewell's division in a position to support him. If on the other hand he thought that he "could hold Banks in check" with his own forces, Jackson was to send Ewell to join with Brigadier General Charles W. Field's small force on the Richmond, Fredericksburg, and Potomac Railroad line fourteen miles below Fredericksburg, which Field had just abandoned, burning the bridges over the Rappahannock behind him. In either event, Jackson was to take the initiative with enough speed and imagination to stun Banks and to prevent McDowell from marching on Richmond.

This was a task for which Jackson, with his emphasis on speed and secrecy, and his instinctive feel for the geography of the Valley, was eminently well suited. It is also a striking example of the way Lee clearly established his goals at the beginning of a campaign, allowing his subordinate commanders the maximum leeway in moving their own troops. Lee's job, as he saw it, was to concentrate his forces in the right position to attack where he wanted them to, and leave their commanders to get there in their own way. Few commanding generals have ever given their subordinates more freedom than Lee. Lee wrote Jackson a longer letter on April 25, emphasizing, "The blow, wherever struck, must, to be successful, be sudden

and heavy." Characteristically, he added, "I cannot pretend at this distance to direct operations depending on
circumstances unknown to me and requiring the exercise of discretion and judgment as to time and execution,
but submit these suggestions for your consideration."
This was a commonsensical point of view—Lee would
often qualify his orders with the phrase "if practicable,"
which was merely a shorthand version of his words to
Jackson. He felt that the man on the spot, knowing Lee's
intentions, should make up his own mind as to how to
put them into effect. Luckily for Lee, Jackson was at his
best when given such discretion.

Jackson replied that he wanted 5,000 more men,
but Lee could not provide them. He wrote to Jackson
explaining this, and further defining his plans, on
April 29:

HEADQUARTERS, RICHMOND, VIRGINIA,
April 29, 1862.

Major-General T. J. JACKSON, commanding, etc.,
Swift Run Gap, Virginia:

GENERAL: I have had the honor to receive your
letter of yesterday's date. From the reports that
reach me that are entitled to credit, the force of

the enemy opposite Fredericksburg is represented
as too large to admit of any diminution whatever of
our army in that vicinity at present, as it might not
only invite an attack on Richmond, but jeopard[ize]
the safety of the army in the Peninsula. I regret,
therefore, that your request, to have five thousand
men sent from that army to reënforce you, cannot
be complied with. Can you draw enough from the
command of General Edward Johnson to warrant
you in attacking Banks? The last return received
from that army shows a present force of upward of
thirty-five hundred, which, it is hoped, has been
since increased by recruits and returned furloughs.
As he does not appear to be pressed, it is suggested
that a portion of his force might be temporarily
removed from its present position, and made
available for the movement in question. A decisive
and successful blow at Banks's column would be
fraught with the happiest results, and I deeply
regret my inability to send you the reenforcements
you ask. If, however, you think the combined
forces of Generals Ewell and Johnson, with your
own, inadequate for the move, General Ewell
might, with the assistance of General Anderson's
army near Fredericksburg, strike at McDowell's
army between that city and Aquia, with much

promise of success; provided you feel sufficiently strong alone to hold Banks in check.

Very truly yours,

R. E. Lee.

Major General Edward Johnson with 3,000 men was covering Staunton against a possible Union attack on the Virginia Central Railroad by General R. H. Milroy with the advance guard of General Frémont's army, and Stonewall Jackson's instinct was identical to Lee's—an early example of the way their minds worked in harmony. On May 1, informing no one of his intentions, Jackson disengaged his men and marched them through a gap in the Blue Ridge Mountains, and then on to Staunton to join Johnson. Instead of following Lee's suggestion to "draw" Johnson north toward him, Jackson moved swiftly south to join him. This was typical of Jackson. He simply disappeared with his army, his whereabouts a mystery both to Lee in Richmond and to Banks in Harpers Ferry. This was the opening move in Jackson's famous "Valley campaign," a series of swift marches, countermarches, and attacks, carried out so successfully that it has been a staple on the curriculum of every major staff college in the world. The British military historian Major-General J. F. C. Fuller, in his enormously influential book *The Foundation of the Science of War,* published in 1926, complained—although he was a fervent admirer of Jackson—that students at the British Staff College learned everything about the Valley campaign by rote until they could recite what Jackson ate for breakfast on every morning of it, whereas in Germany's staff college Jackson's Valley campaign was studied with much greater intellectual curiosity and imagination, and would become the basis for blitzkrieg, the lightning-fast use of armor, mechanized artillery, and mobile infantry to break through the enemy's line, strike a devastating blow, then vanish overnight to strike again elsewhere unexpectedly.

Jackson's weary, footsore infantrymen were proud to call themselves his "foot cavalry," because of the speed with which they covered the roads, good and bad, of the Valley. They created, as Lee had foreseen, a new kind of warfare, one which Fuller described very aptly as "an electric campaign," and which still stands today as an example for every general who wants to avoid the dangers of being forced into fixed positions. Jackson's solution was to fight a war in which speed is more important than superiority of numbers.

A week after he vanished into the Blue Ridge Mountains, Jackson reappeared to join General Johnson's small force of 3,000 before Staunton, giving himself a total of nearly 10,000 men. He then went on to defeat General Milroy at the village of McDowell on May 8, a day's battle that began with a Union attack and ended in a Confederate victory. Afterward, Jackson marched nearly sixty miles to the north. His plans were temporarily delayed by General Johnston's attempt to order Ewell to fall back toward Richmond with his 8,000 men, which Jackson quickly thwarted by a direct plea to Robert E. Lee, who intervened in his favor. With a combined force of 17,000 he won a major victory at Front Royal on May 23 and retook Winchester on May 25, sending Banks's army reeling back across the Potomac in chaos. By the end of the month Jackson's cavalry was threatening Harpers Ferry. It was an extraordinary achievement: "In a classic military campaign of surprise and maneuver, he pressed his army to march 646 miles . . . in forty-eight days . . . and [won] five significant victories with a force of about 17,000 against a combined force of over 50,000." Even when outnumbered three to one, Jackson managed time and again to avoid being surrounded by marching his army through the gaps in the mountains and then up or down the Valley roads to fight again, always on ground of his own choosing. Jackson also prevented 40,000 men from joining McClellan's forces on the peninsula—exactly what Lee had intended from the beginning.

Though the Valley campaign was a military miracle, it had produced no corresponding victory on the peninsula, where General Johnston warned Lee constantly that he wanted to abandon Yorktown and move his forces closer to Richmond. This was, perhaps, the most serious crisis of the Confederacy to date—Johnston was as convinced that Yorktown could not be held as McClellan was that it could not be turned, and had reverted to his earlier idea, rejected by Lee and President Davis, of concentrating all Confederate forces for an attack across the Potomac and into the North, even at the risk of leaving Richmond virtually defenseless. Lee understood Johnston's reasoning. The Army of the Potomac was encamped on the lower peninsula, and McDowell and Banks were preoccupied with Stonewall Jackson. If Johnston could move his army quickly enough he might be able to march north between the two Union armies. It was a bold concept, but it risked losing the capital and abandoning large supplies of ammunition and equipment at Norfolk. Lee used every effort to slow Johnston down, but Johnston thwarted these attempts by simply not reporting his movements to Lee. Although Lee did not mention the matter in his messages to Johnston, which went unanswered, he was of course aware that a retreat down the peninsula, if McClellan pursued Johnston, as he surely must, would soon place White House plantation, where his wife Mary, his daughters, and his grandchild were living, directly in Federal hands. He had warned Mary of this as early as April 4, and added that if she were caught up in a Federal advance, the consequences would be "extremely annoying & embarrassing." Lee's phrasing, characteristically, politely conceals anxiety, but "she wanted to remain on the property to protect it," and as usual ignored her husband's advice when she did not agree with it.

Worry about his family was nothing compared with Lee's conviction that Johnston was wrong. The two men admired and respected each other, they were friends of long standing, and neither doubted the other's courage or skill, but Johnston's character was marked by a troubling combination of stubborness and sensitivity. He could not brook interference and, unlike Lee, he did not have the full confidence of Jefferson Davis and knew—and resented—that fact.

Johnston abandoned Yorktown on May 4, but did not inform Lee of this until May 7. From Lee's point of view, Johnston had simply vanished for three days with 55,000 men, the largest army in the Confederacy. A determined advance by the Federals might have caught Johnston's rear guard, but Johnston had surprised McClellan, who was still preparing for a siege of Yorktown, as much as he had Lee.

Captain the Comte de Paris—the Orléans pre-
tender to the French throne and a grandson of King
Louis-Philippe*—who was one of McClellan's aides,
reported the astonishment of the Union Army outside
Yorktown on finding that "the Confederate army had
disappeared." The count, like the troops, was "stu-
pefied" and "disappointed" by Johnston's decision.
Much as he admired McClellan, he reported in detail
the extreme slowness of the Army of the Potomac to
pursue the Confederates, whose retreat was being carried out "in the greatest order." Everything, the count
complained, "had to be organized for an advance,
which had not been contemplated," with the result that
the Confederacy's Major General James Longstreet was
able to occupy and hold Williamsburg, though unable
to hold it for long under the weight of the Federal
advance. The leisurely quality of the Union advance was
in part a consequence of the weather, but even more of
poor maps and inadequate reconnaissance. McClellan
needed multiple roads—his large army could not move
effectively on a single narrow, muddy lane—but again
and again his generals took a wrong turning and got
hopelessly lost. Still, numbers eventually told, and
Longstreet was forced to abandon Williamsburg after

---

*McClellan had a *penchant* for surrounding himself with French aristocrats—the
comte de Paris's brother, the duc de Chartres, was one of his cavalry commanders.

bitter fighting. Johnston withdrew his army across the last remaining natural barrier protecting Richmond, the Chickahominy River. He had preserved his army, which was now concentrated around Richmond, but in every other respect he brought about just the events Lee had feared: Norfolk had to be abandoned to the enemy, and facilities there had to be destroyed and ships burned; Union control of the James and the York rivers allowed McClellan to move his troops quickly up the York to West Point; and Union gunships steamed up the James River close to Richmond, where the government archives were "being packed for removal."

Johnston chose this, of all moments, to threaten to resign his command on May 8. In a sharply worded letter of complaint to Lee about the limitation of his authority—which, he wrote, "does not extend beyond the troops immediately around me," a complaint obviously directed at Lee—he requested to be "relieved of a merely nominal geographic command." He actually began his letter with a sarcastic complaint against Lee's aide W. H. Taylor: "I have just received three letters from your office signed 'R. E. Lee, gen'l, by W. H. Taylor, A. A. G.,'* written in the first person, all dated yesterday. . . . One of these informs me

---

* Assistant Adjutant General.

that certain supposed orders of mine had been countermanded by you or 'W. H. Taylor, A. A. G.'" Lee
tactfully deflected Johnston's anger and ignored his
resignation, pointing out that Major Taylor, whom
Johnston knew, had only been doing his job: "Those
[letters] to which you allude as having received yesterday were prepared for my signature and being unexpectedly called away, and not wishing to detain the
messenger, I directed Major Taylor to affix my signature and send to you." However much he may have
disliked having to explain and justify the perfectly ordinary procedures in his office, Lee refused to be drawn
into an angry correspondence. By May 9, Johnston
had calmed down somewhat and dropped the threat to
resign, but he still took the time to write Lee a bristling 400-plus-word letter, complaining first about his
troops ("Stragglers cover the country, and Richmond
is no doubt filled with the absent without leave."), then
returning to his original theme that *all* the troops in
and around Richmond should be under his command.
("If this command [mine] includes the Department
of Northern Virginia still this Army of the North is a
part of it; if not, my position should be defined anew.
Nothing is more necessary to us than a distinct understanding of every officer's authority.") This was a
point that Lee was unwilling to concede, not because

he doubted Johnston's ability but because he disagreed with his strategy.

These were anxious moments for Lee on a personal level as well. On May 11 Mary Lee and two of her daughters, Annie and Mildred, were obliged to leave her son Rooney's home and take shelter in a neighbor's smaller and less conspicuous house on White House plantation. They were still less than ten miles from West Point, where the Pamunkey River joins the York, the landing point for those of McClellan's divisions that were being shipped partway toward Richmond rather than slogging slowly up the peninsula. Before leaving White House Mary pinned a defiant parting note on the door:

> *Northern soldiers who profess to reverence*
> *Washington,*
> *forebear to desecrate the home of his first*
> *married life,*
> *the property of his wife, now owned by her*
> *descendants.*
> *A GRAND-DAUGHTER OF*
> *MRS. WASHINGTON.*

On May 18 a party of Union troops led by two officers entered the house that she had moved to, and demanded to know who she was. Mrs. Lee had no hesitation about letting them know, and forcefully expressed to the officers her indignation at being confined to the house and guarded by sentries. These two Union officers were aides of Brigadier General Fitz John Porter, who, she complained, had been "a favored guest" at Arlington before the war. They patiently explained that the sentries were intended by General Porter for her own protection, and that she was in no sense a prisoner. Porter eventually allowed Mary to move farther up the river to the home of Edmund Ruffin, the famous secessionist who had fired the first gun at Fort Sumter. Lee managed to send two aides under a flag of truce to meet with General McClellan and request that his wife and daughters be allowed to join him, but it was not until June 10 that arrangements were finally completed to send a carriage across the lines and bring them back to Richmond. Outraged as Mrs. Lee was at having been "in the hands" of Federal troops, one can only be impressed at the courtesy shown to her by generals Porter and McClellan, and at the equal courtesy shown by General Lee toward General McClellan in securing her release. Lee also seems to have refrained from pointing out to Mary that this was exactly what he had warned her might happen if she stayed at White House. Still, Mary Lee's feelings are easy enough to understand: she had now been forced to abandon two of her father's homes: Arlington, which would soon be turned into a Union military cemetery; and White House, which Union soldiers would shortly burn to the ground, "against General McClellan's orders," though that can hardly have consoled her.

It is worth noting that while Lee himself never regretted his decision to side with his native state in a cause about which he had many reservations, his choice was not without cost or sacrifice. His three sons were all in the army and exposed to danger; his two major properties had been seized, damaged, or destroyed; the comfortable fortune he had amassed with such care was diminished by the collapse in the value of the Confederate dollar; his army pension was almost certainly lost to him, since he had taken up arms against the United States; the Lees' personal possessions had been looted or vandalized; and the precious relics of George Washington had been removed into Federal custody. He and Mrs. Lee had never contemplated selling the slaves she had received from her father, despite the fact that they represented a considerable part of the value of her inheritance. On the contrary the Lees went ahead as they had promised and freed their slaves legally in 1862, although since most of them were by then in territory occupied by the enemy, they were, for all practical purposes, already emancipated. Lee had gone from being a well-to-do man and property owner in 1861 to having no home of his own in 1862, uprooted like his whole family by the war that had swept over Virginia, and in no position to protect his own wife and children—a curious fate for a man who had always been so careful with his investments, and so protective of his family.

One thing that was clear about General Johnston's retreat in the first weeks of May was that he was doing so without serious losses or a major battle. His burst of letter writing on the subject of his bruised ego had relapsed into sullen silence, while Lee anxiously waited to learn where the army would make its stand. Always a master of earthworks, Lee flung himself into the task of preparing a line behind which the army, if it reached there intact, might defend Richmond. He dug in whatever heavy artillery he could salvage from the loss of Norfolk on Drewry's Bluff, overlooking the James River on its west bank about six miles from Richmond; and on Chaffin's Bluff, facing the water on the east bank. If Johnston retreated across the Chickahominy River this would be the logical place for him to anchor his right, with the bulk of the army forming a half circle around the city, extending to Mechanicsville on the left.

Mechanicsville was where the all-important bridge of the Virginia Central Railroad crossed the Chickahominy, connecting Richmond with the Shenandoah Valley, and Johnston's army with that of General Jackson in the Valley—a connection on which the fate of the Confederacy might depend. With this in mind Lee set every hand to digging, preparing for a literal last-ditch defense. He would have preferred to fight on the Chickahominy, a sluggish stream except when rains filled it to overflowing; but it was already clear from advance units of Johnston's army arriving near Richmond that he was conceding the Chickahominy south of Mechanicsville to McClellan, perhaps following the maxim that it always best to give battle when your opponent's lines of communication are stretched to the limit—although given a general as cautious and slow-moving as McClellan this was unlikely to happen.

On May 15, unable to sit at his desk in Richmond any longer, Lee rode out to inspect the works at Drewry's Bluff, just in time to see four Federal gunships, including the famous U.S.S. *Monitor* and the ironclad U.S.S. *Galena* steam up the James River to within a few miles from Richmond. For over three hours they fought a gun battle with the Confederate artillery on Drewry's Bluff.

In the end, the Federal ships withdrew, the *Galena* badly damaged. Lee's insistence on the importance of fortifying Drewry's Bluff and Chaffin's Bluff was thus proved correct, but at the same time the ability of the U.S. Navy to come within a few miles of the Confederate capital demonstrated its vulnerability. Lee also understood the danger that Union troops might outflank Johnston's army by carrying out a landing from the James River.

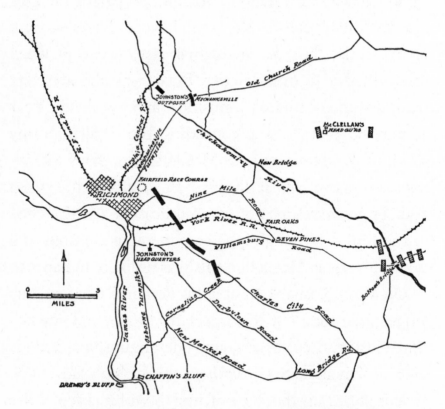

6. *Approximate situation in front of Richmond, about May 22, 1862, showing defensive disposition of Johnston's army and the approach of McClellan.*

About that date—the record is unclear—Lee was asked to attend a cabinet meeting to advise the government where Johnston's army should fall back to, if it became necessary to abandon Richmond. Lee apparently answered without hesitation that the next defensible line would be the Staunton River, 108 miles to the southwest. This was the correct military answer, but the Staunton was not a formidable obstacle by any stretch of the imagination. It was a robust river and a line could be formed behind it, and supplied from North Carolina—but as Lee was surely aware, that would mean giving up not only Richmond but Petersburg, the junction of four different railway lines, and ceding all but a fragment of Virginia to the enemy. If that happened Jackson, unsupported on his left and right, would be obliged to withdraw from the Shenandoah Valley. The Confederacy would not survive for long, since wherever Johnston placed his line the Federals could always outflank him by landing an army behind him. Lee, to whom displays of emotion were anathema, carefully refrained from expressing any opinion of his own at cabinet meetings, unless in answer to direct questions about military affairs; but now he suddenly burst out, as "tears ran down his cheeks," to the amazement of all present: "But Richmond must not be given up; it shall not be given up!"

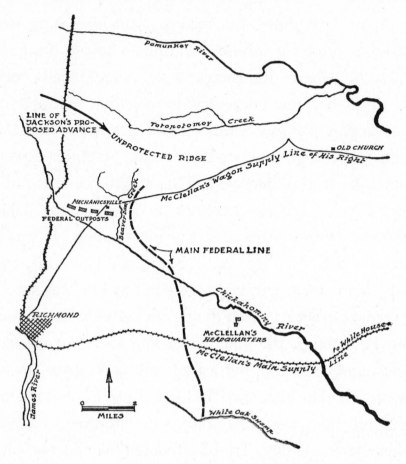

7. Area between Chickahominy and Pamunkey rivers, showing
watershed (unprotected, according to Stuart's report) down
which Jackson was to advance.

Although "the fate of the Confederacy hung in the
balance," Johnston remained as silent as the Sphinx
about his plans, and more difficult to approach. He did
not respond to letters, nor even to a personal attempt
on the part of President Davis and General Lee to find
him. Even when he at last consented to ride in from

the field to meet with Davis, he did not divulge his plans to the president. Davis may have said to Johnston that "if he was not going to give battle, he would appoint some one to the command who would," but if so it made no impression on the general, who remained as uncommunicative as ever. At last Lee, for once out of patience, rode out alone to confront Johnston, and returned to Richmond with the welcome news that Johnston planned to attack on May 29.

McClellan was advancing "cautiously," as usual—the sheer size of his army was enough to slow down his advance along the narrow, boggy roads. By May 24 he had 105,000 men along the Chickahominy, facing Johnston's army of 60,000. He still believed that Johnston had at least 200,000 men, and although he predicted to his wife, Ellen, that he was anticipating "one of the great historical battles of the world," and worried whether his men could be restrained from pillaging when they took Richmond, he was in no hurry to begin the battle. It never occurred to him that Johnston might beat him to the punch. Just as he had at Yorktown, McClellan toyed with the idea of a siege, the kind of warfare he understood best, and set his engineers to the formidable (and time-consuming) task of transporting his siege train to the Chickahominy and building new bridges across the river. McClellan had in mind that McDowell, with 40,000 men, would march from Fredericksburg southeast to Mechanicsville, a distance of just fifty-five miles, to support him. With that in mind, he began to move a portion of his army across the Chickahominy, while keeping the bulk of it to the north of that river in order to protect his line of communications with White House and the vital railway line to his base at West Point. His idea was to shift the bulk of his army across the Chickahominy as McDowell's men took their place to the north of the river, but in doing so he made the cardinal error of splitting his forces in two. His left was on the Richmond side of the Chickahominy, stretching from White Oak Swamp Creek to Fair Oaks; his right was on the opposite side of the Chickahominy, stretched out nearly ten miles along the river. The two halves of his army formed a kind of a V lying on its side (like this >) with the lower end pointing at Richmond and the upper toward Mechanicsville. There was no way one half could support the other if it came to a battle, and McClellan would probably have seen this clearly had he come forward to examine the situation himself. Unfortunately, he was in bed with a fever, and far from expecting an enemy attack, he left his corps commanders to handle things.

Johnston understood the situation clearly, although he was reluctant to share his views with President Davis and Lee, and had decided to attack that portion of McClellan's army that was north of the Chickahominy before McDowell could get there from Fredericksburg. This was sound enough reasoning, but at the very last moment fate in the shape of torrential rain intervened, along with the news that McDowell, alarmed that Jackson had taken Winchester and that Banks was in full retreat, was now marching toward Harpers Ferry rather than Richmond.

Not only did the downpour wash away the work of McClellan's engineers; it isolated the smaller portion of his army on his left in a salient extending from the river to within six miles of Richmond, the point of the salient reaching Fair Oaks and Seven Pines (the ensuing battle is known as Fair Oaks in the North and as Seven Pines in the South). Like a good boxer, Johnston switched from his left to his right, reversing his preparations. Still without having informed Lee or Davis of his intentions, he attacked McClellan's left south of the Chickahominy in full force with most of his army in the early afternoon of May 31, two days later than he had told Lee. The sound of his cannons was heard clearly in Richmond (and in McClellan's tent, four miles away at New Bridge, where he was still bed-ridden).

There was now no question of McClellan's receiving McDowell's support, even though McDowell's troops had been less than twenty-five miles away from joining with those of McClellan when he turned back, as a daring reconnaissance by J. E. B. Stuart's cavalry scouts had revealed. Johnston was offered the opportunity to attack just over a third of McClellan's army with his full strength, thanks to Lee's patient and careful support of Jackson's Valley campaign. Lee's letter of April 29 to Jackson had borne fruit exactly as he had anticipated, though even Lee must have held his breath as McDowell approached within two or three days' march of a junction with McClellan. The bond of trust between Lee and Jackson, forged at a distance, was to become one of the most important weapons in the arsenal of the Confederacy. "If Lee was the Jove of the war, Stonewall Jackson was his thunderbolt. For the execution of the hazardous plans of Lee, just such a lieutenant was indispensable."

On May 30, impatient with being kept out of the coming fray, and still believing the attack would be to the north of the Chickahominy, Lee sent an aide to find Johnston. The aide was to tell him that Lee could not be absent from the coming battle and would be happy to command a brigade or even a regiment, or to serve in any capacity regardless of his rank. As usual, Johnston had made himself unfindable, and Lee, seized with impatience, finally rode in the direction of Mechanicsville, where he still supposed Johnston's attack would take place. Finding nothing happening there, he rode back to Richmond to receive a polite but uninformative message from Johnston that he would welcome Lee's presence in the field in any capacity. That night rain turned the roads to mud and the Chickahominy flooded its banks, but there was still no news from Johnston.

On May 31, Lee rode forward again in search of Johnston, and at last learned that he was now on Nine Mile Road, somewhere near Old Tavern, south of the Chickahominy. This was Lee's first indication that Johnston had decided to attack the left of the Union line, rather than the right. At the junction of Nine Mile Road and the road leading directly to New Bridge, Lee saw troops forming up in line of battle. There, in a modest house where the two roads joined, he finally found General Magruder and General Johnston himself, who, incredibly, was still reluctant to reveal his plans. Shortly after noon, Lee heard cannon and musket fire to the south. The troops in front of the house marched toward it, and General Johnston followed them with Magruder and their staffs. The postmaster general of the Confederacy, John H. Reagan—a Texan, who had ridden out from Richmond as a kind of cheerleader for Brigadier General John Bell Hood's Texas Brigade— was there, and "witnessed the advance" of the troops "on the Federal earthworks, bristling with cannon."

He noted that they "marched into the jaws of death . . . with the steadiness of regulars."

Still in the dark as to Johnston's intentions, Lee was surprised to see an equally mystified President Davis ride up and dismount. Together, they walked to the rear of the house and listened to the sound of a growing battle. Without hesitation the two men mounted and rode down the road toward the gunfire. Within minutes they came under heavy fire from a Union artillery battery on their left, and found themselves in the middle of fierce fighting in the dense bush and woods on both sides of the road. Smoke and thick foliage obscured their view of the battle. To Lee's dismay President Davis rode right into the fighting, determined to warn Magruder that he must silence the Union battery, acting as if he were one of Magruder's aides-de-camp rather than the head of state. Whatever the extent of Davis's political wisdom there was never any doubt of his courage. He succeeded in passing the message along, but as the afternoon wore on and the light began to fail, he and Lee found themselves under constant fire in a battle over which they had no control. Indeed they could not even be sure how big the battle was, still less how it was progressing.

At this point, Postmaster General Reagan appeared out of the clouds of gun smoke in the gathering gloom

and attempted to draw Davis out of danger. "I protested," he wrote, "against the President's unnecessary
exposure and said to them that I had just left General
Johnston where he was in great danger, exposed as he
was to the enemy's fire." Johnston had replied to Reagan
that "this was no time to look for safe places," and
President Davis apparently felt the same, so they all sat
their horses under brisk small-arms fire, and watched
as the last Confederate attack against the Union battery
failed. As night fell they learned from a courier that
both Brigadier General Wade Hampton and—a more
serious problem—General Johnston himself, had been
severely wounded.

Shortly after this news, Johnston appeared "apparently in a lifeless condition," carried on a stretcher, in
such terrible pain that he had been unable to bear the
jolting of an ambulance. He was in no position to give
a report on the battle. Major General G. W. Smith,
now the ranking officer on the field, appeared to
explain that the attack had miscarried. Major General
Longstreet, not yet Lee's trusty "Old War Horse," had
taken the wrong road with his division. In the ensuing confusion many of the Confederate units did not
arrive on the battlefield, and General Johnston had
forfeited his superiority in numbers. The only question
remaining was whether he should move the army back

toward Richmond or attempt to hold its present position. Davis, with Lee's blessing, ordered Smith to hold his present line. All three men thought that the battle would be renewed in the morning. For the moment, "Darkness [had] ended the battle, which had been fought in violent weather and seas of mud." Indeed the fighting on both sides over the next few weeks would be in large part shaped by the weather, with constant references to flooding creeks, constant rain, and mud. There was "as much mud . . . as if the waters had but newly retired from the face of the earth." With it the temperature rose, and there was a growing danger of malaria, dysentery, and yellow fever, particularly for those troops who were not used to the climate.

McClellan would claim that Fair Oaks had been "a glorious victory," but in fact it was a draw, and a fairly bloody one at that: approximately 5,000 Union casualties to 6,000 Confederate. The fighting had been desperate, and on both sides the tactical handling of troops had been poor. Lee realized that the opportunity of delivering a crushing blow to the Union left wing had been lost.

Davis and Lee rode back to Richmond in silence. It must have been apparent to both of them that General Smith, sensible though he was, was not senior enough to be left in command. At long last Davis ordered Lee to assume command of the army immediately. He may have done so reluctantly, or for want of a better option. Joe Johnston was widely admired throughout the South as the victor of First Manassas, while Lee was seen as an able administrator, a "desk man," rather than a battlefield commander. In the judgment of J. F. C. Fuller, Davis had made the right choice: "From June 1, 1862, until his surrender to Grant at Appomattox Court House, Lee was the central military figure in the South, and never did this great soldier show his worth more than at this moment."

His appointment did not create any immediate enthusiasm. Stonewall Jackson was the hero of the hour; Johnston and Beauregard were regarded as the South's most competent "fighting generals." Lee was considered the trusted, white-haired military bureaucrat, a "preeminent staff officer." He was fifty-five years old, three years older than Napoleon at his death; he had never commanded an army in the field; and he had not seen combat since 1847.

That night Lee closed down his office in Richmond, assembled his small staff, and wrote out his first orders, addressing his army for the first time under the name with which it would become as immortally famous as its commander: the Army of Northern Virginia.

Some great generals begin with a stunning success, knowing—or finding within themselves—everything they need to know to win a victory, like the young Bonaparte; but Lee started with a series of stumbles. He had much to learn, although his aggressiveness in battle—in sharp contrast to his gentle manner, courtesy, and unshakable dignity—would startle both northerners and his own countrymen alike. His military experience in Mexico had been in the age of the smoothbore musket, when aimed fire of thirty to fifty yards was the norm, but the rifled percussion muskets* with which both sides were increasingly armed, though slower to reload because the ball had to be pushed down hard against the rifling, were deadly at 300 yards in the hand of a competent marksman. The rifled cannons, although rarer, were also making artillery far more accurate over greater distances. In the North cavalry troopers were armed with breech-loading Sharps carbines that gave a far higher rate of fire than anything previously known, and toward the end of the war some of them were even armed with cartridge-loading Spencer repeating carbines[†]—indeed, Lee's son Rooney would be wounded by a shot from one.

---

[*] In both armies there was at first a hodgepodge of weapons (which remained the case in the Confederate Army throughout the war), some smoothbore, some rifled, and of different calibers, from .54 caliber to an astounding .69 caliber. At closer ranges the lethality of such big-bore balls or conical minié bullets was remarkably high, as was that of the "buck and ball," a .65-caliber round ball and three .31-caliber buckshot—a formidable load (Joseph G. Bilby, "Opening Shots," *American Rifleman*, July 2011, 43).

[†] Even the Gatling gun, the first crude machine gun, was used in the Civil War, though only in a "demonstration."

Six-shot revolvers had been mechanical novelties in the 1840s, but by now, thanks to the genius for mass production of Sam Colt, all officers and many cavalry troopers were armed with them. The firepower of armies had increased dramatically, while their tactics remained for the moment unchanged.

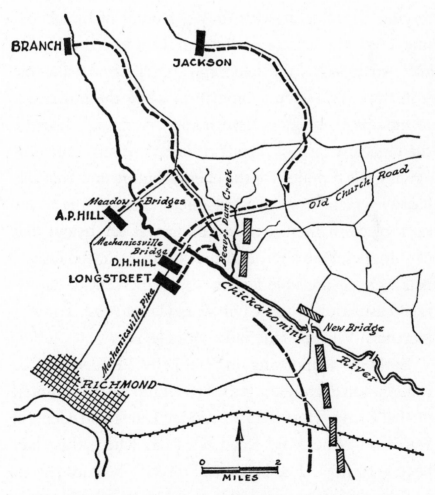

8. *Plan of battle north of the Chickahominy River, as announced by General Lee at the council of war, June 23, 1862.*

Although Lee's favorite tactic was the swift-moving flank attack, he soon came to realize that these improvements in infantry weapons favored the defense, and he put that understanding to good use in what was certainly one of his most striking victories, at Fredericksburg in December 1862, and also during the winter of 1864–1865 as he retreated again and again, forcing Grant to attack him on ground of his choosing. Over the course of the war Lee would adapt to such novelties as the telegraph, observation balloons, iron ships, and even submarines, while the intricacies of moving men, guns, and horses by railway became the chief concern of a staff officer. Lee still talked of "giving the bayonet" to the enemy, but by now this was largely a metaphor for a last-ditch defense—the bayonet's place in the order of killing was far below that of shrapnel, case shot, and musket fire; indeed, bayonets were responsible for less than 1 percent of battlefield casualties in the Civil War. He and the Army of Northern Virginia still had a lot to learn.

Early in the morning on June 1, 1862 Robert E. Lee rode out of Richmond into the field to take command of that army. He found President Davis and General Smith on Nine Mile Road, close to where they had been yesterday. The battle had already been renewed, at first with intense fighting, but then petering out.

On the Union side General McClellan finally rose from his sickbed to survey the battle "in a state of utter exhaustion." Many of his generals hoped that if he could bring enough reinforcements over from the north side of the Chickahominy to the south, a victory on the second day of the battle would still enable them to take Richmond. McClellan remained unconvinced; he thought the river was rising too fast and would make it difficult to reinforce his artillery, and worried about reducing the number of troops guarding "his communications and the immense park of artillery." In short, he dithered away the chance of a decisive victory.

Still intent on a siege, McClellan wanted to move his heavy guns forward along the Richmond and York River Railroad, which ran from West Point (Virginia) and White House to Richmond, north of the Chickahominy. McClellan was loath to risk losing the railway by reinforcing his left at the expense of his right, or perhaps he simply did not feel well enough to make such a decision. In the end, he left things as they were, and went back to his bed, where he was to remain off and on for the next ten days, unable to mount a horse. To the disappointment of some of his generals, Lee ordered "the whole army back to the lines back to the lines it had occupied before the battle of the previous day."

General Longstreet, whose failure to take the correct road the day before had cost Johnston a decisive victory, now wanted to commit the whole army to a new attack, even though the forces on his flanks were scattered and disorganized. His own attack that morning had been "feeble and accomplished nothing," in the judgment of that final arbiter of Civil War history *The West Point Atlas of the American Wars.* As a professional soldier Lee was always unwilling "to reinforce failure."

Despite his troops' disorder Lee understood that falling farther back on Richmond would eventually allow McClellan to bring up his heavy artillery and begin a siege—a recipe for disaster. He decided to stay put. He had worked hard, despite ridicule and criticism, to build a defensive line around Richmond, and he would now expand and improve it so that he could defend the city with as few men as possible, relying on earthworks and batteries to secure the capital in the last resort. Then the bulk of the army could be used to drive McClellan back down the peninsula, while Lee waited for the right moment to move Jackson's army from the Shenandoah Valley to Richmond to join him. There were serious risks involved—lightly defended, Richmond might be taken by the enemy; bringing Jackson from the Valley to the peninsula might allow Banks to regain all that he had lost. But whereas Johnston had been waging a defensive fight, hoping to lure McClellan forward into a position where he could be defeated in one grand battle, Lee intended to take the initiative and attack McClellan boldly, every day and everyplace where McClellan attempted to draw a line.

Fortunately for Lee, McClellan gave him breathing space in which to perfect his strategy. Lee had more than three weeks, during much of which heavy rain poured down, to take the measure of his own generals, all the way down to brigade commanders. He also used the time to drill his troops hard and impose stricter discipline. He had been unpleasantly surprised by the amount of drunkenness, desertion, and insubordination in Johnston's army. Only four days after he assumed command of the Army of Northern Virginia, he wrote a long letter to President Davis, suggesting a bold new strategy. "After much reflection I think if it was possible to reinforce Jackson strongly, it would change the character of the war. This can only be done by the troops in Georgia, South Carolina & North Carolina. Jackson could in that event cross Maryland into Pennsylvania. It would call all the enemy from our Southern coast & liberate those states."

This was radical thinking—too radical, as it happened, for Davis. It is interesting to note that Jackson had already acquired Lee's confidence, and ironic to realize that Lee was already considering the advances into Maryland and Pennsylvania that would lead him to Antietam in 1862 and to Gettysburg in 1863. The letter provides a clear indication of Lee's broad strategic intention, which was remarkably consistent from the very beginning, as well as of its limitation, which is that he always saw the focal point of the war as threatening Washington, and the crucial area in which it would be decided as northern Virginia. He was not indifferent to the war in the West, but just as being a Virginian had trumped his being an American, driving the enemy out of Virginia was his dearest goal. If his ambitious original plan been carried out, it would have forced McClellan to abandon the peninsula and come to the defense of Washington, opening the possibility that Lee might be able to destroy him with a flanking attack carried out as he retreated. Such an attack, if carried out simultaneously with Jackson's advance into Maryland and Pennsylvania, and reinforced with 40,000 men from Georgia and the Carolinas, might well have brought the war to an end in 1862 with a decisive Confederate victory. But not even President Davis could persuade the governors of those states to strip their own defenses for the benefit of such a risky operation—the Confederacy was an alliance of equals, not a single country like the Union.

"States' rights," ostensibly the reason for the war, was always a factor limiting the powers of the Confederate government. Lee's strategic vision was amazingly clear-sighted, and Napoleonic in scope, but in the end Davis did not have the political authority to impose it on all the Confederate states, or the will to do so.

Lee seems to have accepted this decision calmly—he may even have been relieved—and instead turned his attention to a new and promising form of attack. The mud and the overflowing rivers and creeks were slowing McClellan's effort to bring his siege artillery far enough forward to bombard Richmond. Instead of waiting passively, Lee decided to use the pause to bring a bombardment to McClellan. He had a heavy gun placed on a railway flatcar, with improvised armor protection; sent it down the length of the Richmond and York railway line that was still in Confederate hands; and began shelling McClellan's artillery park and supply dumps.

Lee has a certain reputation as an old-fashioned soldier, perhaps because of his dignified Old Testament appearance, but the Civil War was in fact the first *modern* war: a war of masses, railways, conscription, industrial power, and new technology.

In fact, the Civil War should be seen not as a continuation of eighteenth-century warfare in the tradition of

Lee's father, but as the first in a series of vastly greater and progressively more destructive modern wars. Some Civil War generals were throwbacks to an earlier and more romantic view of war, like J. E. B. Stuart, who unself-consciously played the role of a Cavalier. Others, like General William Tecumseh Sherman,★ were precursors of the late-twentieth-century military doctrine of total war, the belief that the indiscriminate destruction on a vast scale of the enemy's cities, crops, infrastructure, and civilian population is the fastest way to end a war—"War *as* hell," to paraphrase Sherman. Lee was neither of these. Unlike Stuart, he found little romantic appeal in war. He was not nostalgic for the imagined glories of the past. Unlike Sherman, Lee did not encourage his troops to burn and pillage in enemy territory; indeed he had them punished severely for even minor theft, whenever it was brought to his attention. He did not attempt to wage war against civilians; he regarded that as uncivilized. Some military historians have criticized him for not having a "siege train" of heavy artillery ready to employ against northern cities like Washington or Baltimore; but in the first place the Confederacy had no means by which to procure

---

★ The burning of Atlanta in 1865 and the firebombing of Dresden by the R.A.F. in 1945 are analogous to Sherman's march; Arthur Harris, chief of Britain's Bomber Command, simply had more sophisticated technology than Sherman did, but the intention was the same.

or produce the equivalent of McClellan's heavy artillery, and—more important—Lee was reluctant to subject enemy civilians to bombardment. In many ways Lee was a man more of the eighteenth century than the nineteenth in his thinking, even though he was of his own century professionally. A trained engineer, he understood technology far better than he is given credit for, and when he could, he employed it—Lee's innovative use of artillery mounted on a flatcar is a good example of his willingness to embrace new ideas. Still, it is worth noting that Lee used the railway gun to strike at McClellan's supply dumps, whereas McClellan's "siege train" was intended to level Richmond and kill those civilians who did not flee their homes.

Despite his foray into grand strategy, Lee's principal concern in the first two weeks of June 1862 was to develop a strategy that would drive McClellan back from Richmond, and if possible expel him from the peninsula altogether. He was correct in assuming that the Confederacy could not expect foreign support or recognition so long as its capital was in danger from an army with superior numbers dug in only a few miles away. The fact that the Confederacy might have been better off had its capital not been moved from Montgomery, Alabama, was not Lee's responsibility, but the preservation of Richmond was.

Even before assuming command of the Army of Northern Virginia Lee recognized that the key to defeating McClellan on the peninsula was a swift, secret transfer of Jackson's forces in the Shenandoah Valley for just long enough for the combined troops to strike a crushing blow at McClellan's right. It was with this in mind that Lee maintained a general oversight of Jackson's operations even though Jackson still came under Johnston's command. Lee sought to understand Jackson's difficult, secretive, and sometimes impenetrable character by means of an exchange of letters, which not only revealed Lee's own thoughts and plans but gently drew out Jackson's. Seldom have two generals corresponded with such frankness and mutual admiration—or with such fruitful results. By June 1862 Lee did not have to spell matters out in detail for Jackson; he merely had to hint at what he wanted, and leave it to Jackson to develop a detailed plan and timetable.

On June 8 Lee wrote to Jackson, congratulating him on his march to Winchester, which, he wrote, had been "conducted with your usual skill and boldness," and warning him to be ready to move his entire command at a moment's notice. "Should there be nothing requiring your attention in the valley so as to prevent your leaving it for a few days, and you can make arrangements to deceive the enemy and impress him with the idea of your presence, please let me know, that you may unite at the decisive moment with the army near Richmond."

On June 11 Lee managed to scrape up fourteen more regiments to reinforce Jackson, "the object [being] to crush the forces opposed to you," and made his own plans somewhat clearer. "Leave your enfeebled troops to watch the country and guard the passes covered by your cavalry and artillery, and with your main body . . . move rapidly to Ashland by rail . . . and sweep down between the Chickahominy and Pamunkey, cutting up the enemy's communications, &c., while this army attacks General McClellan in front. He will thus, I think, be forced out of his intrenchments, where he is strongly posted on the Chickahominy, and apparently preparing to move by gradual approaches on Richmond."

This was the critical letter: in it, Lee's intentions are made crystal clear, as is his concern for security. Military intelligence in the Civil War was poorly organized on both sides—the Union spy chief Allan Pinkerton, while effective at foiling plots on Lincoln's life, consistently overestimated the strength of the Confederate forces, contributing to McClellan's belief that he was facing numbers two or three times greater than his own—but the fact that there were no "foreigners" in the war made security hard to achieve in moving large numbers of men. Fortunately, no commander was more obsessed with security than Jackson, who seldom shared his plans even with his own senior officers. He took care to make sure that Union ambulances were not permitted to cross the lines to pick up their wounded, and that "bearers of the flag of truce" were impressed "as much as possible with the idea of a heavy advance [to the north] on our part, and let them return under such impression." Jackson also put a stop to the practice of allowing local civilians "to drive their cattle on this side of the lines." As far as possible he sought to "cut off communication across the lines between us and the enemy," and did so very effectively—quite an achievement in the Valley, where there was no easy way to distinguish a Union supporter from a Confederate sympathizer.

In Richmond Lee's staff set about preparing rail transportation for men and horses, together with forage for horses, while Lee continued to urge upon Jackson the need for speed and secrecy. "In moving your troops," he wrote to Jackson on June 16, "you could let it be understood that it was to pursue the enemy in front. . . . To be efficacious, the movement must be secret. . . . Be careful to guard from friends and foes your purpose and your intention of personally leaving the valley." For his part, Jackson met even with his own cavalry commander in secrecy, writing from "Near Wyeth's Cave": "If you can meet me in Staunton by 5 o'clock tomorrow morning I hope you will do so. . . . I will be on my horse at the north end of the town so you need not inquire after me. I do not desire it to be known that I am absent from this point."

Lee had been in command of the Army of Northern Virginia for only two weeks, but his energy and sense of purpose had already touched every man, from general to private. He had quickly seized the initiative, no longer merely reacting to McClellan's moves, as Johnston had done, but completing a large and complicated plan to destroy him before his artillery could threaten Richmond. He put J. E. B. Stuart* on notice "to send some cavalry at least as far north as Hanover Junction . . . to watch the movements of the enemy and give protection to the railroad," characteristically adding, "Endeavor to spare your horses as much as possible, and charge your officers to look to their comfort." Lee is sometimes charged by military historians, Major General Fuller for one, with giving insufficient attention to detail, but his correspondence with his own commanders is full of practical details, as well as sound

---

*Lee's second son, Fitzhugh (Rooney) Lee, was then serving as a lieutenant colonel under Stuart's command.

advice. For example, he advised Jackson that if he was short of rations, "Beef cattle could at least be driven, and if necessary we can subsist on meat alone." This is not the voice of a general lost in grand strategy; despite his dislike of paperwork, Lee seems to have had a firm grasp of the details, right down to rations for the men and the transportation of artillery batteries. Aware of how much weaker in numbers he was than the enemy, he kept his cards close to his chest and played his hand very shrewdly indeed.

Before he could transfer Jackson's army from the Valley to attack McClellan there was still much that Lee needed to know. McClellan's left was anchored less than seven miles east of Richmond, and protected by White Oak Swamp, his center ran "northward" to the Chickahominy, and his army was strongly entrenched. What Lee did *not* know was how far McClellan's right ran north of the Chickahominy, and whether there was a wagon trail from White House in addition to the railroad to carry McClellan's supplies forward. So on June 11, he risked the best part of his cavalry, and ordered the twenty-nine-year-old Brigadier General J. E. B. Stuart to ride behind the enemy's line and bring back a clear report of McClellan's dispositions to the north of the Chickahominy. Stuart set off the next day with 1,200 men, including Lee's son Rooney and a colorful group of adventuresome young officers—among them Lieutenant John S. Mosby, the future Confederate partisan leader, who would be known as the "Gray Ghost"; and Captain Johann August Heinrick Heros von Borcke, a mighty six-foot-two Prussian who weighed between 200 and 300 pounds and carried a whole arsenal of weapons, including a sword of medieval weight and length and three pistols. Borcke was almost fanatically devoted to Stuart.

Stuart set off in his trademark finery—a plumed hat, a scarlet-lined cape, "a tasseled yellow sash," and buckskin gauntlets. He led his troopers north at a brisk pace, then crossed the Richmond, Fredericksburg, and Potomac railway line in the direction of Louisa Court House, fifty-eight miles away. He hoped that Federal spies would think he was riding to join Jackson in the Valley. The fine, sandy roads were dry, and the sun was shining—another worry for Lee, who feared that good weather and drying roads would enable McClellan to bring his heavy guns forward and start shelling Richmond. They bivouacked for the night on the farm of a Confederate supporter, giving Stuart and Rooney Lee a chance to spend a few hours at Hickory Hill and visit Rooney's wife, Charlotte. Then the next day they turned east and made a circle around Hanover Court House.

By now the Federal cavalry had spotted Stuart's group and were in hot pursuit, and much of June 13 was spent in fierce hand-to-hand clashes with Union cavalry units. The following morning Stuart pressed on to Old Church, seventeen miles from Hanover Court House, at which point he could, with honor, have turned back. He had already learned what Lee most wanted to know: McClellan had no fortified line north of Beaver Dam Creek toward Hanover Court House, the direction in which Jackson's army would attack, and only small numbers of troops. It seems amazing that the presence of 1,200 Confederate cavalry troopers well behind his own lines did not arouse McClellan's suspicion that Lee might be about to attack him there, but given Stuart's flamboyant reputation, he may have considered it just a stunt.

Stuart had broached the idea of riding around the Union army to Lee, who had cautioned against it, but now that he was east of Old Church Stuart decided it would be safer and more interesting to go on than to return the way he had come, which was now swarming with Union cavalry. He pressed on to Tunstall's Station, not five miles from the house from which Mary Lee had been evicted by the arrival of the Federal army; shot up a train; destroyed the tracks; pulled down telegraph poles; and rode on to Talleysville, where his men rested for a few hours, then saddled their horses and rode south toward the Chickahominy. After covering forty miles that day his men were so exhausted that they fell asleep in the saddle, but they rode on by moonlight to the Chickahominy, only to find that the bridge there had been destroyed. Stuart paused to build a plank bridge using an upturned skiff as a pontoon—another demonstration of his genius for mounted warfare. Once across the river, they burned the bridge they had jerry-rigged behind them; they were safe now from the pursuing Federal cavalry, which, typically of the Civil War, was led by Stuart's own father-in-law. Stuart then rode on himself from Charles City Court House and covered the thirty miles from there to Richmond in less than nine hours. Afterward, he rode out to meet the main body of his men as they entered the city. By midmorning Stuart's exploit had already made him a southern hero second only to Stonewall Jackson. As they paraded through the city he and his men were greeted by girls throwing flowers—even Stuart's horse was decorated with a garland of flowers around its neck. Stuart not only had relieved the city's inhabitants of the fear that they were cut off but also had covered nearly 100 miles in three days, burned stores of supplies valued at over $7 million, and brought home 165 prisoners and 260 horses and mules. The fact that his men had ridden right around 100,000 Union soldiers made the Federal army on the peninsula look foolish as well as inept.*

More important, he had brought exactly the information Lee wanted. There was nothing north of McClellan's right to stop Jackson from flanking him there, at the same time cutting off his two supply lines, the railway, and the wagon trail from West Point and White House. Though Jackson was still asking for his strength to be increased to 40,000 men so he could invade the North, Lee had already decided against this. When he met with Colonel Boteler of Jackson's staff on June 14, having learned from Stuart that there was nothing to stop an attack to the north of Beaver Dam Creek, he hinted that Jackson would have to march east, not north. When the colonel pointed out that Jackson's men were used to mountain air and would die of disease in the pestilential swamps around the Chickahominy, Lee replied, "That will depend on the time they will have to stay here."

Clearly, what Lee had in mind was for Jackson to make a crushing blow against McClellan's right, followed by a swift return to the Valley. Boteler sounds a mite skeptical in his conversation with Lee—or as

---

*I am indebted to Jeffry D. Wert for his painstaking account of Stuart's ride in *Cavalryman of the Lost Cause: A Biography of J. E. B. Stuart,* which succeeds in making sense of an often confused and overdramatized feat of arms.

skeptical as a colonel can be when talking to a full general—but then he knew Jackson better than Lee did. General Longstreet, when Lee discussed his plans with him, seems to have been even more skeptical. It would be Longstreet's fate to play the role of a doubting Thomas for three years, but Lee did not hold it against him. Despite his calm demeanor, Lee approached all his battles with the utmost zeal and conviction. A slow, stubborn, grumbling skeptic, provided exactly the balance that Lee needed to temper his own natural optimism. He recognized that "Old Pete," as Longstreet was known, was a first-rate professional soldier. Today Lee's defenders are generally more critical of Longstreet than Lee himself ever was.

On June 16, having learned from Stuart what the ground was like north of the Chickahominy, and how muddy the roads still were, Lee rode out to view the Union lines for himself. Turning to A. L. Long, the aide who accompanied him, he said, "Now, Colonel Long, how are we to get at those people?" Probably, Lee was speaking to himself rhetorically and neither wanted nor expected to hear Colonel Long's opinion, but it is interesting to note that he was already in the habit of calling the enemy "those people." Some writers have assumed that this was a sign of contempt, but it would have been unlike Lee to harbor any such feeling. It seems far more probable that he simply could not bring himself to call the enemy "the United States Army." The men in front of him were wearing the blue uniform that had been his for thirty-five years, even though he now wore the gray uniform of the Confederate Army. Despite Lee's rhetorical question to Long, he had already decided exactly what he was going to do. He explained his plans in detail to President Davis, who was concerned that Richmond would be virtually uncovered as Lee concentrated his forces. It was a risk Lee was willing to take. Jackson, following Lee's instructions, was disengaging his troops in the Valley and dropped out of sight himself. Once Jackson arrived north of the Chickahominy, Major General D. H. Hill and Major General Longstreet would cross the Chickahominy and join him at Mechanicsville. This would give Lee 65,500 men against approximately 30,000 Federal troops of Brigadier General Fitz John Porter, while Major General A. P. Hill held the Union forces entrenched behind Beaver Dam Creek in place until they had been turned by Jackson's advance. In the meantime, 21,000 Confederate troops would hold the entrenchments around Richmond against the remaining 60,000 Federal troops dug in facing that city. Lee anticipated that Jackson, Longstreet, and D. H. Hill would then sweep forward, driving Porter's troops back and threatening to cut McClellan's lines of communication to White House and West Point, taking New Bridge, about six miles east of Mechanicsville, on the way. Lee could then move his troops north or south of the Chickahominy depending on how the situation developed. Cut off from their supply lines, McClellan's forces would have no option but to retreat. It might even be possible to attack them in the flank as they did so, bringing about the disintegration, if not the destruction, of the Army of the Potomac.

A glance at the map will show that this was an ambitious concept. Beyond the risks that Davis and Longstreet had pointed out to Lee, there was the question of how he could command a coordinated action over a front that extended almost fifteen miles from just south of Seven Pines (where the Federal left ended) to Totopotomoy Creek, just north of Mechanicsville, which was where Jackson's columns were to deploy.

For a man who had never commanded an army of this size in the field, Lee was taking on a formidable task. Granted, he knew McClellan well enough to guess that his reaction would be slow and cautious. But Lee could still have had no idea that McClellan believed he was facing an army more than twice the size of his own, when in fact Lee had just over half the number of troops McClellan had. In fact McClellan was still accusing the president of betraying him by withholding reinforcements: "Honest A has again fallen into the hands of my enemies," he wrote to his wife, Ellen, and he predicted to her that he would pin Lee down "in his lines around Richmond." He promised her, "I will then have them in the hollow of my hand," and he was even confident enough to write to Lincoln, offering "to send the president his views 'as to the present state of military affairs throughout the whole country,'" adding his opinion that a negotiated peace with the Confederacy might be obtained by guaranteeing the right of slave owners to their property.

Lee was by now anxious to meet with Jackson "at some point on [his] approach to the Chickahominy." On June 19, having set his army in motion, Jackson made haste to Gordonsville, which he reached on Sunday, June 22, with his 18,500 troops and his artillery spread out behind him, on foot, in relays of freight trains, and in wagons. Jackson spent that day and evening in the village of Fredericks Hall—he would not travel or transact business on the Sabbath—and left at one o'clock in the morning on the first of a series of "commandeered" horses, accompanied by three of his staff. He wore no badges indicating his rank, and traveled with a pass made out "for an unidentified colonel." He covered the fifty-two miles between Fredericks

Hall and Richmond in just fourteen hours, changing horses at intervals, but taking no rest himself. In the mid-afternoon on Monday, June 23, members of Lee's staff were surprised to see a dusty, shabby, visibly exhausted horseman, the peak of his crushed, battered kepi pulled low over his face, dismount "stiffly" in the yard of the Widow Dabbs's house just off Nine Mile Road, near Richmond, where Lee had established his headquarters. On being told that General Lee was at work, the dusty horseman, who had declined to identify himself, slouched against the fence until General D. H. Hill, rode up and to his surprise recognized his brother-in-law Jackson, who he had supposed was still in the Valley. Hill shepherded Jackson into the house, where Lee at once appeared and offered him "refreshment," though Jackson accepted only a glass of milk.

Lee had called together his commanders for the forthcoming attack against McClellan: Jackson, D. H. Hill, Longstreet, and A. P. Hill. The oldest were Longstreet and D. H. Hill, both forty-one; Jackson was thirty-eight; A. P. Hill was thirty-seven—all four comparatively young for their rank and responsibilities. It was a "historic" meeting, not only because of the battle to come, but because it was a significant turning point in the war. Up until now, the South had for the most part fought a *defensive* war, reacting to Federal attacks on southern soil. Now, although Lee was not yet ready to "invade" the North, he was determined to fight an *offensive* war, subjecting a larger army to continual attack. Even Lee could not have imagined he would fight ten battles in just one week.

As for his four major generals, they were very different personalities, and not without some trace of the usual human flaws, among them competitiveness, rivalry, personal ambition, and a stubborn belief on the part of each that he knew best. Like Lee, Longstreet, A. P. Hill, and D. H. Hill admired Jackson, who was the hero of the hour owing to his victories in the Valley, but found him awkward, uncommunicative, and showing no apparent "mark of genius."

It may be that Jackson was already exhausted by the effort of moving his army east, but it is also possible that his personality simply did not lend itself to a council of war of equals. Only a month earlier, he had decided, in disgust, never to hold another council of war in his own army, and he probably did not like this one any better. He was willing to subordinate himself to Lee, but he was not a team player. By nature a loner, Jackson did not share his plans even with his closest subordinates—a habit that could sometimes backfire on him. He could be very kind, and he had a certain grim sense of humor, but he was an exceptionally harsh disciplinarian, and his soldiers were awed by him rather than fond of him. When one of his officers remarked, of a doomed Federal charge, what a pity it had been to shoot down so many brave men, Jackson replied, "I don't want them brave, I want them dead." When another protested that if he followed Jackson's order his men would be annihilated, Jackson replied sternly, "I always endeavor to take care of my wounded and bury my dead. Obey that order, sir."

Jackson's admiration for Lee was such that he would say, "So great is my confidence in General Lee that I am willing to follow him blindfolded." Unlike Longstreet, who would, to the end, resist following Lee blindfolded, Jackson was never troubled by any doubts about Lee's judgment.

Lee then did a curious thing. Having described his battle plan he left the room—we do not know for how long—so that the four generals could discuss it without his presence. He may have felt that they could speak more frankly in his absence, or that as experienced professional soldiers they could work out the details for themselves. Whatever he intended, it was a mistake, certainly so far as Jackson was concerned. Lee's plan hinged on Jackson's prompt arrival and attack, but whether Jackson understood that is open to question. Jackson's troops had the farthest distance to travel, so it was logical that the moment he arrived to flank

General Porter's lines on Beaver Dam Creek would be the signal for the other three generals to advance. Exact timing was therefore crucial. When asked when his army would be in position to attack, Jackson is said to have "mumbled" June 25: that is, in two days' time. Typically, it was Longstreet, always the pessimist, who questioned this date and suggested that Jackson give himself an extra twenty-four hours. At that, the conference drew to a close and Lee returned: the attack would begin at three in the afternoon on June 26.

It seems a pity that Jackson had left his gifted cartographer Captain Jedediah Hotchkiss behind in the Valley. Nobody at the conference in the parlor of the Dabbs house appears to have had an altogether clear picture of the ground ahead—and no two of those present had the same picture—while Jackson seriously underestimated the difficulties crossing the country between Fredericks Hall and Totopotomoy Creek even though he had just ridden over it himself.

Jackson then set off—without a rest—to the vanguard of his army, a thirty-mile ride, much of it in the dark and in pouring rain. What he found when he got there should have alarmed him. His inability to delegate or share his plans had led to delay and to large numbers of stragglers, that is to say, men who fell far behind their units (always a serious problem in the Civil War on both sides). Some of his regiments were moving by train, others slogging along muddy roads. Nobody seemed to be in command, and the army was spread out over fifteen miles with no one person urging it forward. The presence of Jackson, with his grim Old Testament face, by the side of the road mounted on Little Sorrel, urging his men to "Press on, press on," was one element that had made it possible for his army to perform miracles, but he was apparently in no mood, or shape, to perform a miracle on June 24. Hardly anything in warfare is more important or demanding than a general's ability to keep his men together and moving to a demanding schedule under difficult conditions, and by this test Jackson failed between June 24 and 26. Jackson's biographers ascribe this to exhaustion, and that was surely a factor; but it is one of a general's duties to keep himself alert and rested, even at the risk of appearing self-indulgent to his critics, and another, scarcely less important, is to delegate authority so that he is not always obliged to be sorting out traffic jams, or searching for the right road.*

---

*The British general Bernard Montgomery was often ridiculed during World War II for going to bed promptly at nine o'clock—he did not even make an exception for Winston Churchill and King George VI when they visited his headquarters—but he was not entirely wrong. A general should take care of himself, and be woken only in case of dire emergencies, requiring what Napoleon called the rarest kind of courage, "Le courage de deux heures du matin," i.e., the ability to make a critical decision when woken suddenly at two in the morning.

Military historians also criticize Lee for not drawing up his plans clearly enough, for tolerating poor staff work, and for overrelying on his corps commanders. In short, Jackson did not delegate enough and Lee delegated too much. There is some truth to this, but the reality is that the first of the "Seven Days" of battle on the peninsula was a painful learning experience—Lee had never commanded an army of this size before, and Jackson had never served as a critical part of a much larger army. What matters more is that when the first day of battle began General McClellan was within seven miles of Richmond, waiting for the roads to dry to bring up his siege train and start the bombardment of the city, and a week later he and his army had been driven into a small "pocket" on the James River under the protection of Union gunboats, twenty-five miles away from Richmond, which would not be threatened closely again for two more years. That, by any standards, is a victory—Lee's victory.

Mechanicsville, June 25 and 26, 1862

Perhaps the mo st unexpected moment of the battle that came to be called Mechanicsville took place the day before it. Sharply prodded by Washington, McClellan finally began to test the Confederate strength in front of him, though in a halfhearted and cautious way.

He ordered General Samuel P. Heintzelman, commander of his Third Corps, a grizzled veteran of Mexico and First Manassas, who belying his appearance was if anything even more cautious than McClellan, to advance the picket line of one of his brigades "in front of Seven Pines" almost a mile forward in preparation to support an attack planned for the next day toward Old Tavern crossroads by Major General William B. Franklin's corps. Old Tavern was one of the places where McClellan planned to put his siege guns for the bombardment of Richmond, and since it was less than a mile a way it seemed like a reasonable objective. On June 25, just a day before Lee's own attack was to begin, this move on Heintzelman's part sparked a small but increasingly sharp battle at Oak Grove. The battle was marked by fatal indecision on the part of McClellan, who from the rear first ordered Heintzelman to advance one of his brigades, then sent an order to withdraw it from the ground the men had gained (somewhere between 600 and 800 yards). Then, when McClellan rode from his headquarters to see what was happening, he ordered them to regain the ground they had just abandoned.

It is a sound military maxim (sometimes attributed to George Patton)* never to pay twice for the same

---

*Probably wrongly—the words may have been placed in his mouth, or rather George C. Scott's, by the screenwriter of the film *Patton*.

piece of real estate, but it may be that McClellan's nerves were rattled—he had not seen combat up close since the Mexican war and had a kind of gloomy premonition that Lee was preparing to attack him. In any case McClellan might have done better to leave matters at Oak Grove in Heintzelman's hands. Though not a particularly gifted commander, Heintzelman was the man on the spot and perfectly competent to command three brigades without the help of the commander in chief of the army. Federal artillery north and south of the Chickahominy began a fierce bombardment to support Heintzelman, and the sound could be heard clearly seven miles away in Richmond.

Puzzled and anxious, Lee rode forward in the midafternoon to see for himself what was happening, and concluded at once that the Federal attack was being held and, more important, that it remained "local" for the moment—that is, it was not going to be supported by McClellan's other corps south of the Chickahominy this afternoon.

Lee made the "audacious" decision not to postpone his own attack, scheduled for the next day. One of President Davis's aides, who had served briefly with Lee, when asked what the new commander of the Army of Northern Virginia was like, replied, "If there is one man in either army, Federal or Confederate, who is head & shoulders, far above every other one in either army in audacity that man is Gen. Lee. . . . Lee is audacity personified. His name is audacity." This was not how Lee was viewed by most people at the time, but it was correct. Almost any other commander would have postponed his attack at least long enough to see what the enemy was doing and prepare for what might, after all, become a general assault against the Confederate right toward Richmond the next day, of which Heintzelman's attack at Oak Grove was merely the first move; but Lee decided that his own attack would shake McClellan's nerve, so long as he kept his own.

Lee's instincts served him well. By early evening the Union attacks and the volume of Union gunfire began to peter out. Though Lee could not have known it, McClellan had received reports throughout the day that Jackson's army had vanished from the Valley and might be on the move toward him, and about the same time that Lee reached Nine Mile Road to observe the battle at Oak Grove, McClellan left it to hurry back to his headquarters, where an urgent message from Major General Fitz John Porter, commanding the Union line north of the Chickahominy, stated that his cavalry pickets were being pushed back, and that "a fugitive slave" from Richmond had described the arrival of fresh troops in the city, who had been greeted by cheering crowds. McClellan "took counsel of his fears" and drew the wildly incorrect conclusion that he was now facing between 150,000 and 200,000 Confederate troops, though in fact, even including Jackson's 18,500 men still on their way and the 21,000 men holding the lines that Lee had dug around Richmond, the Confederates had a total of only 85,000. He also drew the correct conclusion that Jackson intended to turn his right north of Beaver Dam Creek. By that time the transfer of Jackson's army from the Valley to Richmond was an open secret. On June 25 Mrs. Chesnut, always well informed, noted it in her diary, having learned about it far away in Columbia, South Carolina: "Stonewall is coming up behind McClellan—and then comes the tug of war," she wrote. In the circumstances, McClellan decided to break off the fight before Seven Pines, just as Lee had guessed he would.

Lee's audacity had paid off. Had McClellan chosen to take advantage of Heintzelman's attack to push the corps on either side of him forward, he might indeed have been in Richmond the next day, as President Davis had always feared—there was nothing in front of him but two divisions. Instead he returned to his headquarters to write a blistering letter to Secretary of War Edwin M. Stanton: "I regret my great inferiority in numbers, but feel I am in no way responsible for it. . . . I will do all a general can do with the splendid Army I have the honor to command & if it is destroyed by overwhelming numbers I can at least die with it & share its fate." Since he had observed the Battle of Oak Grove in perfect safety from a redoubt in Heintzelman's lines the last sentence quoted is not only overwrought but also a useful indication of McClellan's incredible narcissism, and hints of a persecution complex bordering on paranoia.

For all that, he was a very capable soldier—even Lee, when asked after the war who was the ablest Union general, replied, "McClellan, by all odds." Nobody was better at training an army, or keeping it deployed, or anticipating the enemy's intentions than McClellan. Even before he wrote his letter to Stanton with the operatic suggestion that he expected to die at the head of his troops, he was already giving orders to start moving his base of supply by ship from the York River to the James River, anticipating that Lee intended to cut his lines of communication to White House and West Point. McClellan's problem was not that he lacked courage or skill; it was that he excelled at building up an army that was neat, tidy, disciplined, and equipped in every detail, and having done so he could not bear to see it destroyed.

As for Lee, he rode back to Richmond as the sun began to set. It had been raining all day, but just as the rain stopped, the clouds parted, and behind him there appeared a rainbow, an omen celebrated in a poem by John R. Thompson:

There our army—awaiting the terrible fight
Of the morrow—lay hopeful, and watching, and still;
Where their tents all the region had sprinkled with
*   white.*
From river to river, o'er meadow and hill . . .

When lo! On the cloud, a miraculous thing!
Broke in beauty the rainbow our host to enfold!
The centre o'erspread by its arch, and each wing
Suffused with its azure and crimson and gold.

Blest omen of victory, symbol divine
Of peace after tumult, repose after pain;
How sweet and how glowing with promise the sign,
To eyes that should never behold it again!

A tired gray man on a gray horse, riding thoughtfully back to the Dabbs house in the glow of a rainbow: this paints a dramatic picture, but whether or not Lee was aware of the augury in the sky behind him is

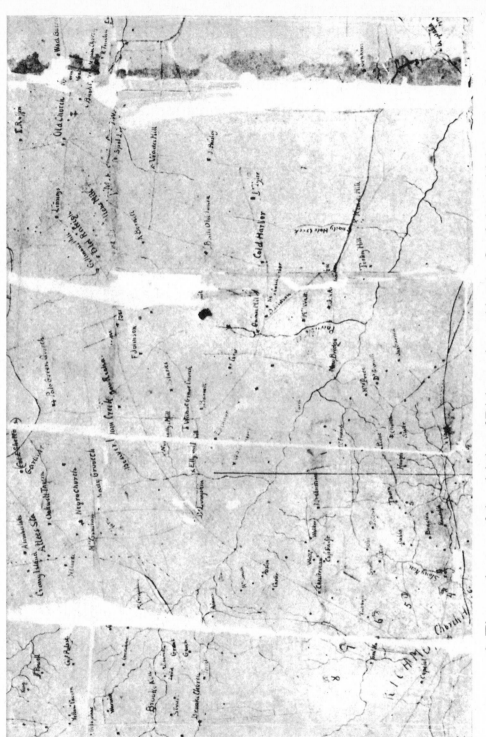

9. *The crude map of the vicinity of Richmond, used by the Confederate high command during the Seven Days of battles of 1862.*

unrecorded. He had a lot on his mind. He had willed himself to put aside any personal concerns in view of the task before him, but his family was scattered, homeless, and in grief—his daughter-in-law Charlotte, driven from her home at the White House plantation and five months pregnant, had traveled to Jones Springs, North Carolina, together with three of Lee's daughters, hoping that the "healing springs" would restore health to Lee's only grandchild, Rob. But despite the "nice clean comfortable" surroundings the sickly infant died of what seems to have been pneumonia. Mary Lee was in Richmond, suffering more than ever from arthritis and the brutal summer heat, but Lee had not yet been able to take time off from his duties to see her.

Lee was also concerned, with good reason, that his plan for tomorrow was too complicated. His written order had been drafted with care, but on rereading it seems very hard to follow. Jackson's copy was followed by an additional and even more confusing letter about the approaches to Beaver Dam Creek: "The four divisions," his order ran, "keeping in communication with each other and moving en echelon on separate roads, if practicable, the left division in advance, with skirmishers and sharpshooters extending their front, will sweep down the Chickahominy and endeavor to drive the enemy from his position above New Bridge, General Jackson bearing well to his left, turning Beaver Dam Creek and taking the direction toward Cold Harbor."

The phrase "if practicable" was to become familiar in Lee's orders, and it led to many unfortunate consequences, since it provided subordinate commanders with a kind of escape clause, allowing them to argue after the event that what they had been ordered to do was not, in their view, "practicable." The phrase "separate roads" also raised all sorts of problems, particularly for Jackson, to whom this part of Virginia was unfamiliar, and who had unwisely left the indispensable Hotchkiss, his mapmaker, behind in the Valley. Lee's attempt to further clarify matters for Jackson only compounds the confusion: "In your march tomorrow on reaching the Merry Oaks, the roads divide. By the map before me the right hand, called the Ash Cake road, intersects, near Mrs. McKenzies, a road leading to Shady Grove Church." In the days when roads were largely unmarked by signposts, and when, as Walter H. Taylor remarks, "country people who were relied on as guides seemed to have no knowledge of such matters beyond the immediate vicinity of their homes," this was an invitation to disaster.

Even the faithful Walter Taylor notes that the Confederate generals were hampered by "their

ignorance of the country and lack of adequate maps."
This was a puzzling statement, since they were after
all going to be fighting less than ten miles from their
own capital, and one would have supposed that in
the months since McClellan landed on the peninsula
there had been ample time to prepare maps showing at the very least "the location of the roads."
Brigadier General Richard Taylor, in *Destruction
and Reconstruction,* wrote somewhat waspishly of his
fellow generals around Richmond, "The Confederate
commanders knew no more about the topography
of the country than they did about Central Africa."
He was not wrong. In fact McClellan had better maps
of Richmond than Lee did.

Still, in the four weeks since Lee took command
of the Army of Northern Virginia, he had performed
miracles in preparing it for battle, while at the same
time developing a complex, and ultimately successful,
strategic plan for its use. Since much of what he had
done was invisible to the general public, he was still a
target of doubt and ridicule, but Davis understood it,
and so did the generals who served under Lee—though
even they, and for that matter even Lee himself, might
not have believed that a man of his age was about to
fight ten major battles in a single week, surely a record
unequaled in military history.

The only way to understand the "Seven Days" is to regard it as one long battle, in which Lee constantly attacked the enemy. Some days he lost; other days he won; sometimes the two armies fought to a brief, bloody draw; but inexorably and untiringly Lee pushed McClellan's larger army back until he had lifted the threat from Richmond.

On June 26 when Lee woke at dawn the weather was promising; but from first light on he was confronted by bad news from the field, beginning with a message from Jackson to say that his march had been delayed.

Jackson had given himself "less than forty-eight hours to get his divisions into position more than thirty miles away," but after two nights without sleep he had lost the crisp power of command that compelled his men to march beyond their limits. On June 24 he waited for the rear units of his army to catch up "with the main body," and seems to have been dazed with fatigue himself. That night he was found sitting up reading a novel while his uniform dried, apparently oblivious to the state of "confusion" of his army. His assistant adjutant general* was Major Robert L. Dabney, whom he had plucked from civilian life because of "his dis-

---

* We would now refer to Dabney as a chief of staff.

tinguished theological career," an eccentric and unfortunate choice. Dabney had no military experience, let alone any enthusiasm for his job. Putting him in charge of moving 18,500 men merely because he was a "stimulating preacher and brilliant professor of theology" was placing altogether too much faith in God's ability or willingness to perform miracles. Without Jackson's constant presence and fierce concentration to back him up, Dabney dithered and failed: Soldiers straggled, the supply and commissary wagons lagged miles behind the troops; even sensible plans for watering the horses and giving the men a chance to fill their canteens were ignored.

By the end of the day Jackson's army had marched twenty-two miles, an impressive feat considering that the roads were meandering muddy tracks rather than the straight macadamized surface of Valley Pike, and that the weather was hot, sultry, and humid, with occasional showers, hard marching for men who were used to the cooler air and higher ground of the Shenandoah Valley. The army encamped for the night six miles short of Ashland to the *west* of where Lee expected it to be at that point, and almost twelve miles from the Virginia Central railway that it should have crossed by now; and Jackson's increasing irritability and short temper with his own officers were not helping matters. This was a bad beginning. In a note to Lee, Jackson drew his attention to the fact that enemy cavalry scouts had been driven back from Ashland and the telegraph wires near there had been cut, a sure sign that McClellan already knew Jackson was coming and what his route would be. The element of secrecy had been lost—in fact, the story the "fugitive slave" had told was now confirmed by a deserter from Jackson's own army.

Jackson spent the night in a farmhouse and close to the railway line, just where his army should have been. During the evening he heard cheering as some of his men greeted the arrival of Brigadier General J. E. B. Stuart, whose 2,000 troopers were to guard Jackson's left flank as he advanced the next morning. Their ride around McClellan's army had made Stuart almost as great a military celebrity as Jackson, but he and Jackson must have made a striking contrast—Jackson in his threadbare, dusty, uniform and enormous muddy boots; Stuart with his plumed hat, impeccable gold-braided uniform, yellow sash, gauntlets, and gleaming top boots. The two men knew and admired each other despite the difference in their appearance: Stuart, underneath his Cavalier pose, was a deeply religious man, and religion was always a matter of importance to Jackson. But now Jackson was too tired for a long conversation, regrettably; since Stuart had found his way to Ashland easily enough, one would think he could have given Jackson useful advice about the way ahead. He does not seem to have pressed his assistance on Jackson, nor does Jackson seem to have asked for it. Stuart was a first-rate professional soldier; he knew exactly where Lee expected Jackson to be the next day and how to get there. He could surely have shed a good deal of light on Lee's somewhat opaque letter, which Jackson was puzzling over. It may have been that Jackson did not think a major general should ask a brigadier general for advice, though that does not sound like Jackson, who always listened carefully to Hotchkiss, a mere captain. When two of his own brigadier generals—Richard Ewell and William Whiting—appeared at the farmhouse around midnight to urge that the army advance on two parallel roads once it crossed the Virginia Central railway track, in order to cut in half the time it would take to approach Hundley's Corner, about two miles above the right of Porter's lines on Beaver Dam Creek, Jackson nodded politely but did not commit himself. James L. Robertson Jr., author of a meticulous biography of Stonewall Jackson, states that when Ewell went back to the house to retrieve his sword, which he had left there, he found Jackson kneeling in prayer. Since Jackson had promised Lee the army would be "underway" by 2:30 a.m., and since he always rose before his soldiers and appeared fully uniformed and mounted as they formed up, he cannot have had more than an hour's sleep that night. This was not good for a man of thirty-eight who had been on the move and without a decent night's sleep since June 20.

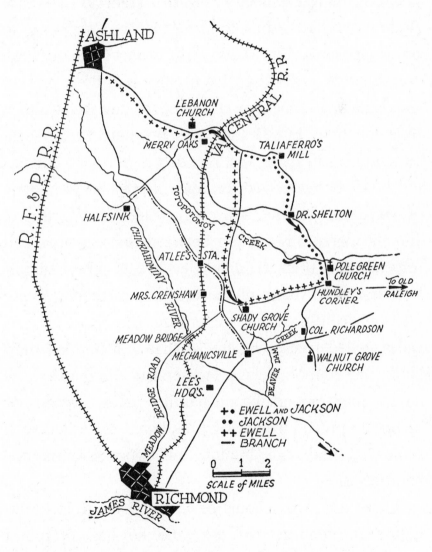

10. *Route of Jackson, Ewell, and Branch, June 26, 1862.*

Despite Jackson's order, his troops were not in fact on the move until 8 a.m. on the morning of Thursday, June 26, and the vanguard did not cross the railway until 9 a.m., six hours behind schedule, at which point Jackson sent a message to Brigadier General Lawrence Branch, who according to Lee's plan was supposed to cover Jackson's right flank while Stuart's cavalry covered his left. Stuart and his cavalry had been present since dawn, and for a good deal of the day the two men rode together, but Branch was nowhere to be seen, although his brigade was intended to be the "connecting link" between Jackson and the rest of the Army of Northern Virginia. The countryside was oppressive, and the narrow roads ran between dense woods and impenetrable thickets of tangled brush. The Federals had destroyed many of the bridges, further delaying Jackson's columns, and sniper fire, improvised barricades, felled trees, and creeks that had flooded their banks caused more delays. Jackson had accepted Ewell's advice about advancing on parallel roads, though not before he prayed over it first, as Ewell remarked with somewhat malicious humor, but progress remained painfully slow.

There are two schools of thought about Jackson's failure to keep to the schedule he had promised Lee. Supporters argue that Jackson was addled by exhaustion, and delayed by Major Dabney's inability to get the men fed, provided with water, and moving on time. In addition, Jackson was hampered by his choice of Dabney's brother, who claimed to know the area well, as his chief guide; and finally, fatally by the incompetence of Lee's staff and the obscurity of Lee's orders. Jackson, his supporters claim, tried to follow those orders to the letter but did not even understand that his attack was intended to be the signal for the other corps commanders to begin theirs. In short Jackson did not realize that the battle would not begin until he had passed Mechanicsville and turned Porter's lines on Beaver Dam Creek.

Supporters of Lee admit that his staff was too small for a commander in the field, but point out that its competence—certainly that of those closest to Lee like Walter Taylor, A. L. Long, and Charles Marshall—was unquestioned. As for Lee's orders, although they are possibly too detailed and specific, he had made his plan clear enough to everyone who attended the meeting on June 23. Unless Jackson was dozing during it, he must have been aware that Lee's intention was to launch the entire attack as Jackson's army appeared. The other generals at the meeting certainly understood exactly what Lee intended—hence Longstreet's concern that Jackson was not giving himself enough time.

Captain Dabney would later claim to have been confused by the new paths the Federals had cut through the woods, producing crossroads that were unfamiliar to him; but leaving to one side the wisdom of choosing him as the pathfinder (once again, the absence of Hotchkiss was a detriment), it seems odd that Stuart, with 2,000 troopers at his disposal, did not send a few ahead to reconnoiter the roads and make contact with General Branch. Stuart and Jackson never complained, then or later, about any ambiguities in Lee's orders or in his letter giving additional directions. If Jackson's columns were having "a fit of the slows," as Lincoln once complained about McClellan, it can only have been a result of poor discipline and organization on the march. Jackson would have been better off riding up and down the columns exerting his formidable will on his men, or at least on poor Major Dabney, rather than riding ahead of it with Jeb Stuart.

By noon it was clear to Jackson that something was wrong. He was advancing slowly south toward Totopotomoy Creek, the only serious natural obstacle between his troops and their objective, while Ewell, invisible to him, marched his column on a parallel though longer route about two miles distant, but Branch's brigade was still nowhere to be seen. A vigorous reconnaissance could easily have ended

the confusion, and perhaps even have reached Lee himself, who was only a few miles away, on high ground
overlooking Mechanicsville, but the three elements of
Jackson's force continued on their separate ways as if
unaware that Longstreet, D. H. Hill, and A. P. Hill
were anxiously waiting to hear the sound of Jackson's
guns in order to launch their attack.

It is only seven miles from the Virginia Central
railway, which Jackson had crossed at 9 a.m., to
Totopotomoy Creek, but Jackson took until 3 p.m. to
reach it, which means that his infantry did not cover
more than about a mile an hour—a sure sign of straggling and unauthorized halts. Stuart had sent some of
his troops ahead to secure the bridge across the creek,
and they skirmished briefly with an outpost of Federal
cavalry holding the bridge, driving them away, although
not before the Federals had set fire to it. Jackson's engineers immediately set to work repairing it, but not
until 4:30 p.m. was his column able to begin crossing
it—an hour and a half after Lee's timetable called for
Jackson to have begun his attack. Jackson deployed a
battery of artillery to shell the woods on the opposite
bank to flush out any Union troops before the bulk of
his own troops finally crossed the bridge and advanced
to Hundley's Corner, on the road to Old Raleigh, about
a mile to the southeast. It was not until after 5 p.m.

that Ewell, who had finally made contact with General Branch, reached Hundley's Corner and took up his position on Jackson's right. As Jackson understood his orders, he was to advance with A. P. Hill on his right and D. H. Hill "in support," but neither formation was in sight. After a certain amount of soul-searching, Jackson decided to wait for further orders and "bivouacked for the night," although he could clearly hear the sound of heavy fighting to his right.

Lee had received Jackson's message from the night before that his column was delayed, but during the course of the day he had no reason to suppose that Jackson would not make up the lost time and be in place by 3 p.m. Lee waited with no apparent sign of impatience or anxiety through much of the long, hot day, at last taking up a position in the mid-afternoon on a ridge overlooking the Chickahominy River, less than a mile south of Mechanicsville. From here, he could see a broad, lushly green "panorama" of the intended battlefield: in front of him was the Chickahominy River, to his left the parallel Meadow Bridges, across which A. P. Hill would advance the moment General Branch made contact with Jackson. Directly ahead of Lee was the apparently deserted village of Mechanicsville; to his right, hidden by scattered brush and woods, meandered Beaver Dam Creek, on the far side of which

General Porter had dug in his artillery batteries and his infantry; and still farther to Lee's right, on the horizon, General McClellan's observation balloons—still something of an innovation at the time—gleamed in the hot, clear sky. Like the increasingly impatient A. P. Hill, Lee saw smoke on the horizon ahead of him and shortly afterward heard the sound of guns. He very likely supposed, as A. P. Hill did, that Jackson was in place and already turning Porter's line, since he had no way to know that the smoke was from the burning bridge, or that the gunfire was from Jackson's attempt to clear the woods in front of him. Certainly Lee had no reason to think that General Branch was not yet even in contact with Jackson, or that Jackson's 18,500 men were strung out behind the burning bridge for miles. In any event, A. P. Hill, already impatient since nothing had been heard from Jackson all day, leaped to the conclusion that he had begun his attack, and thus given the signal for Lee's plan to be put in motion.

If Lee felt any anxiety at all—the face of the famous "Marble Man" was, after all, intended to hide any such emotion—it can only have been increased by the presence on the hilltop around him of President Jefferson Davis, as well as "the Secretary of State, and a number of public men," who had ridden out from Richmond to watch the battle.

Shortly after three o'clock there were loud volleys of musket fire from the woods on the far side of the river. A. P. Hill had crossed the Meadows Bridges over the Chickahominy about two miles away and, turning right, parallel to the river, his troops were advancing toward Mechanicsville, driving Federal troops before them, while his artillery deployed behind them in the woods and opened fire. Lee, and his spectators from Richmond, could see the fighting as if on a stage before them.

When Hill's troops approached the tiny hamlet of Mechanicsville, however, they began to come under heavy fire from the Federal batteries on Beaver Dam Creek, less than a few hundred yards away. There was still no sign of General Branch's brigade approaching Mechanicsville, or of the Federal troops starting to withdraw from their lines on Beaver Dam Creek as Jackson turned their right with 18,500 men. On the contrary, the fire from the Union lines was hot, heavy, and steady, with no sign of panic or retreat on the part of the Federals. A. P. Hill was, in fact, attempting the impossible: a frontal assault of 11,000 men across almost a mile of open ground against 14,000 men and thirty-two guns in well-prepared positions.

Even before then Lee must have had his first strong intuition that something had gone badly wrong.

Around 4 p.m., he sent a young lieutenant, Thomas W. Sydnor, who knew the local country well, to warn A. P. Hill, whose men were already in Mechanicsville, to "suspend all movement until further orders." As the Federals retreated from Mechanicsville, a few planks were hastily thrown across the broken bridge over the Chickahominy in front of Lee, and the first of D. H. Hill's brigades crossed. It was one thing for infantry to cross the river on planks, but another for artillery, and no pioneers had been provided for the purpose— certainly a mistake in planning—so Lee rode down to take charge of things while the president and his entourage crossed over the river in front of him. It was after 5 p.m. when Lee got to Mechanicsville and discovered that A. P. Hill had "disregarded his orders, and . . . moved on his own responsibility," in effect starting the battle before he had any idea where or how far away Jackson might be. By this time the battle was effectively out of Lee's control. Much of A. P. Hill's division was pinned down along Beaver Dam Creek, and taking heavy casualties; the divisions of D. H. Hill and Longstreet were crossing the river and forming up behind his. Even General Branch's brigade appeared at last, still with no sign of Jackson.

Lee's attention was momentarily distracted by the presence of President Davis and his entourage, now exposed to heavy artillery fire and surrounded by wounded, dead, or dying men and horses. Politely, but firmly, he shooed Davis back, saying, "Mr. President, who is all this army and what is it doing here?" He gestured to the members of the cabinet and the politicians. Davis, apparently embarrassed, disclaimed any knowledge of why so many civilians had accompanied him. "It is not my army, General," he said. Lee sternly told him that this was "no place for it," and Davis, no doubt impressed by Lee's "frigid" tone, added, "Well, General, if I withdraw, perhaps they will follow me," and rode down the hill until he was out of Lee's sight, though he remained on the battlefield. One can understand that Lee wanted a moment to study his predicament without being surrounded by a gallery of civilian spectators. The sun was beginning to go down; he already knew from A. P. Hill's experience that a direct frontal attack on Porter's line would almost certainly be a bloody failure; and he was concerned that McClellan, when he realized that the Confederate attack north of the Chickahominy had failed, might use the opportunity to attack Richmond—just the result that Davis had feared.

Lee acted with the decisiveness that would always mark his command. He dictated an order to General Huger telling him that the trenches around Richmond

CLOUDS OF GLORY · 611

must be held, in Freeman's words, "at the point of the bayonet, if need be," an old-fashioned euphemism for "to the last man"; and, realizing that Porter could be driven back only by turning his right flank, ordered two brigades—Brigadier General William Dorsey Pender's and Brigadier General Roswell S. Ripley's—to try to do so while there was still enough light. A successful turning movement followed by a frontal attack might yet save the day, but it was not to be. Pender's and Ripley's brigades took heavy casualties and were unable to make their way around Porter's left; and the first day of battle ended in a bloody but futile artillery duel that went on into the night.

Very fortunately for Lee, General McClellan, who had arrived to join Porter in the late afternoon, neither ordered an attack on Richmond nor reinforced Porter. Instead, McClellan set in motion exactly what Lee had been trying to accomplish—he ordered Porter to abandon the lines he had defended so successfully along Beaver Dam Creek and withdraw to "a more defensible position" at Gaines's Mill. McClellan also gave orders to begin the transfer the contents of his supply bases by ship from White House and West Point to the James River, thus abandoning his supply lines north of the Chickahominy, which it had been Lee's intention to cut.

It is rare in history for a victorious general, with forces and artillery that greatly outnumber his foe's, to give up his own bases, abandon a strong position he has successfully defended, and order a retreat of his whole army over difficult terrain to a new base, at the same time exposing his army to repeated flank attacks while it is on the move, but that is exactly what McClellan did. Lee had nothing for which to congratulate himself. Jackson's failure to appear, whatever the reasons for it, undercut his entire plan for the battle, and the Confederates had 1,484 casualties to only 361 of the enemy's. Still more seriously, of Lee's 56,000 men he had been able to get only 14,000 into action. The rest were either lost, late, or delayed by crowded roads and damaged bridges. Nor of course had he any way of knowing that McClellan had already reached the extraordinary conclusion that Lee "was falling into a trap." McClellan reassured his wife, Ellen, that he planned to "allow the enemy to cut off our communications in order to ensure success," a very strange comment for a general in full retreat. McClellan even sent a self-congratulatory telegram to Secretary of War Stanton informing him of a "complete" victory, and adding that he had almost begun "to think we are invincible," without mentioning that once he had given up his supply lines and bases north of the Chickahominy, he had as good as given up any hope of laying siege to Richmond, never mind taking it. Lee had already accomplished his first priority: McClellan, who on June 25 had been within seven miles of Richmond, was now moving his army farther away from it.

Gaines's Mill—June 27, 1862

Perhaps the most important decision Lee made during the night of June 26 was to attack again early in the morning. He did not brood on what had gone wrong at Mechanicsville, or consider retreating to defend Richmond. Lee, like Wellington, indeed like all great generals, had the ability to look on the misery of a battlefield, absorb its horrors—he never turned away from them—and then move on calmly to his next decision.* During the whole "Seven Days" Lee continued to attack, despite whatever had gone wrong the day before. He, his staff, and his generals were, in effect, *learning* how to fight as a single army, and perhaps the most important thing they now understood was that Lee did not waste time consolidating or reorganizing his army,

---

* Total indifference to suffering, however, is a bad sign in a general. Talleyrand remarked that the moment he knew Napoleon was lost was when they rode over the battlefield of Eylau together—Talleyrand remarked on the number of dead and dying, and the emperor merely replied in a tone of surprise and mild irritation, *"Mais ce sont de la petite espèce."* ("But they are people of no importance.") Lee's admiration for his soldiers and empathy for their suffering, by contrast, never wavered.

or waiting to see what the enemy would do. He simply attacked, determined to keep the enemy off balance and to drive him farther and farther away from Richmond. McClellan thought that the farther Lee advanced, the more likely he was to make a mistake, and of course he was right—Lee committed mistake after mistake in the week ahead, but he never gave McClellan a chance to exploit his errors. Day by day he pushed McClellan's army back toward the James River.

Lee's plan was to turn both ends of Porter's line at Beaver Dam Creek. At the same time, he sent Walter Taylor off to find Jackson—something he should have done the day before. It was brutally hot, promising dry roads, and therefore an opportunity for a rapid advance. But by the time Lee was ready to begin the assault to the north and south of Beaver Dam Creek, Porter had abandoned the positions he had fought so hard for the previous day, and was in full, but orderly retreat toward New Cold Harbor, about five miles to the east. There, the high ground behind Powhite Creek would enable Porter to make a vigorous stand, with his left resting firmly on the bulk of McClellan's forces facing Richmond to the south of the Chickahominy, and connected to them by two bridges over the river, so that he could receive substantial reinforcements if needed. It was a naturally strong position. When Porter had been at Beaver Dam

Creek he was, in effect, isolated in a salient, ahead of the bulk of McClellan's army. Now that Union army was concentrated in an arc almost ten miles long with good interior lines, a formidable force of nearly 100,000 men in total, 57,000 of them north of the river.

Lee had only 35,000, still spread out on the move in a haphazard way, but he was relying on General Magruder, south of the Chickahominy, to distract McClellan and keep his attention focused in the wrong direction. From early morning, Magruder marched his division back and forth through the woods, creating the impression of a much larger force preparing to attack. He reinforced this pantomime by raising what was at the time the Confederacy's only hot air balloon over Richmond,* to give the impression that McClellan's army was about to be attacked both south and north of the Chickahominy.

Porter was too busy digging in behind Powhite Creek on his left and Boatswain's Swamp on his front to pay much attention to what was going on facing McClellan's other four corps, which were five miles

---

* The Confederate balloons were of the old-fashioned "hot air" kind, like those of the eighteenth century, since unlike the North the Confederacy had no means of producing hydrogen in the field. The balloons were made out of "dress silk," though not out of women's silk dresses contributed for the purpose, as legend has it (Richard Billies, *Civil War Observation Balloons*, November 28, 2011; and *Balloons in the American Civil War*, Web site).

away and on the south side of the river; but Magruder's charade made a substantial impression on McClellan, who convinced himself that Lee had 100,000 men in and around Richmond, and that he himself was "out-numbered . . . every where." He had already sent his engineers out "to bridge White Oak Swamp" behind him—the most direct path for his army to retreat south to the James River.

By 9 a.m. Lee had four columns moving eastward along separate roads in the direction of New Cold Harbor and Gaines's Mill to engage Porter. The problem of inadequate maps continued to plague Lee, who was still working from a large hand-drawn map that was almost devoid of topographical details and failed to show Boatswain's Swamp, a significant natural obstacle directly in the path of Jackson and D. H. Hill.

Lee himself followed the path of Longstreet's division to the house of William Gaines, whose mill would give the forthcoming battle its name, and from whose peach orchard a Federal battery was firing. There, he learned that Jackson and A. P. Hill had at last made contact, and that the head of Jackson's column had reached Walnut Grove Church, about three miles northwest of the Gaines house. Lee rode there at once and found Jackson and A. P. Hill talking to each other. Hill withdrew tactfully, Lee and Jackson dismounted, and Lee seated himself on a tree stump while Jackson stood, with, in the words of his latest biographer, "the seedy appearance of a farmer who had been plowing all day." It is unfortunate that neither of them gave an account of their conversation—it is hard to imagine that even a man as tactful as Lee would not have at least mentioned Jackson's failure to get his 18,500 men to the battlefield the previous day—but Lee's confidence in Jackson had not been shaken. The two men talked for the best part of an hour as Lee explained his plan for the next day, confirmed that D. H. Hill would continue to support Jackson, and urged Jackson to make haste toward Cold Harbor.

Lee's concept of the battle was once again flawed by the inadequacies of his map. He supposed that Porter, having withdrawn his forces from Beaver Dam Creek, would take up a similar position, running from north to south, along Powhite Creek, where the rising ground provided a natural defensive position. Lee's parting instruction to Jackson was to turn the Federal line along Powhite Creek—in short, to repeat what ought to have been his role the previous day.

By the time Jackson was on his way back to alert D. H. Hill, Lee had already become aware that Powhite Creek was virtually undefended, and that McClellan instead had ordered Porter to take up a position facing north, rather than west, about a mile farther on from Powhite Creek, on a hill the approach to which was made difficult by the marshy course of the sluggish Boatswain's Creek, which did not appear on any of the Confederate maps. The acerbic Confederate general Richard Taylor complained, "We had much praying at various headquarters, and large reliance on special providence; but none were vouchsafed, by a pillar of cloud or a fire to supplement our ignorance." This was a none too subtle dig at his commander Stonewall Jackson. Taylor later described Porter's new line with the accuracy of a man who has fought over it: "McClellan had chosen an excellent position, covering his military bridges over the Chickahominy. His left, resting on the river, and his center, were covered by a small stream, one of its affluents, boggy and of difficult passage. His right was on high ground, near Cold Harbor, in a dense thicket of pine-scrub, with artillery massed. This position, three miles in extent, and enfiladed in front by heavy guns on the south side of the Chickahominy, was held by three lines of infantry, one above the other on the rising ground, which was crowned with numerous batteries, concealed by timber." This naturally strong position was held by nearly 40,000 men, and Porter had been given enough time to dig shallow trenches and rifle pits, and to erect abatis, felled trees and branches with the sharpened ends pointed toward the enemy, making it even more formidable.

Moreover, at this point in time Jackson and D. H. Hill would have to march at least five or six miles farther than they expected to reach Porter's right flank, a task made more difficult by the fact that although everybody on the Confederate side referred to "Cold Harbor," there were in fact two tiny hamlets—Old Cold Harbor and New Cold Harbor—separated by nearly a mile and a half and approached by different roads. Lee's plan was that Jackson and D. H. Hill should turn the enemy's right flank, and that A. P. Hill, supported by Longstreet as soon as he came up, should then attack Porter's front and drive the enemy back "into the very mouth of Jackson's artillery."

It was 11 a.m. when Jackson remounted Little Sorrel after his talk with Lee. By noon, A. P. Hill's skirmishers were exchanging fire with Union skirmishers in the marshy ground to the left of Porter's position, which was far more formidable than Lee had supposed. It was not until after 1 p.m. that the sound of heavy firing from A. P. Hill's division as it crossed Powhite Creek on the way past Gaines's Mill toward New Cold Harbor drew Lee down Cold Harbor Road, where he instantly surmised that Porter's line was drawn up not from north to south, but in a semicircle from the south and east.

At that moment a number of men from Brigadier General Maxey Gregg's South Carolinian Brigade began to retreat before it. " 'Gentlemen,' Lee said to his staff and to the officers of [a nearby] battery, 'we must rally those men.' He spurred his horse into a gallop and soon was in the midst of the fleeing infantry, calling them to stop and for the honor of their state go back and meet the enemy.' " His appearance was sufficient to rally the troops, and Gregg soon appeared to lead his own men back into the woods. Over the next three years Lee would never hesitate to rally his troops and lead them forward toward the thick of the heaviest firing, serenely indifferent to danger. The troops of the Army of Northern Virginia soon realized that Lee would never ask them to do what he was not willing to do himself, and that he cared more for their lives than he did for his own.

As the day's battle progressed thick woods, tangled undergrowth, and drifting gun smoke prevented Lee from getting a clear view of Porter's position. There were two parallel roads—paths or farm tracks would describe them better—that led southeast to Despatch Station on the Richmond and York River railway line, and to the bridges over the Chickahominy River. Reasoning that Jackson's advance would threaten Porter's lines of retreat, and that Porter would then have to shift forces from his left and center to his right to forestall this, Lee decided on an immediate attack on the Union center by A. P. Hill, followed by an attack on the Union left by Longstreet's division, to catch Porter at just the moment when he was moving his forces.

At 2:30 p.m. A. P. Hill attacked from "the Gaines's Mill–Cold Harbor road," advancing south, with his center at New Cold Harbor, in the direction of the road to the McGee house toward the woods which were less than half a mile away, his line extending just over a mile. What nobody seems to have accounted for was the existence of Boatswain's Creek in front of them. It was screened from view by a low, thickly wooded ridge, which circled the higher ground in front of Hill like a boggy moat. Dense with greenery in the summer, in some places it was just a shallow, muddy trench or ditch, easily forded; in others it ran sluggishly between steep, slick banks that made it difficult to cross.

As Hill's division approached Boatswain's Creek over cleared farmland, a tangled line of brush and undergrowth concealed the low ridge in front of it until the last moment. When they crossed it they were momentarily silhouetted against the sky. The Federals opened fire with devastating effect.

Porter had placed his troops on the higher ground to the south and east of the creek. It was merely a broad, low, uneven series of hills and ridges, perhaps a mile in diameter, consisting of cleared farmland alternating with bands of thick woods, and sloping gently down toward the creek, but in warfare the importance of holding "higher ground" is absolute; it need not be a mountain, or steep sided—even a few feet of elevation is enough to give the defenders the advantage. Although Fitz John Porter was not popular with his fellow Union generals (he had a reputation for gossiping), he was a professional who knew his business. He had deployed his men and his artillery to give them as much protection as he could, placing them behind felled logs, knapsacks piled against post-and-rail fencing, and long lines of brush and timber, with a clear field of fire down the slope of the hill, which was so insignificant that it has no clear name, although the locals called the flat summit, about 150 feet high, facing west toward Powhite Creek, "Turkey Hill."

The Confederate soldiers from A. P. Hill's division who stumbled into the thick mud and swampy vegetation of Boatswain's Creek were subjected to withering musket fire. For the Federal pickets and sharpshooters (as snipers were then called) it was like shooting fish in a barrel. Even if Hill's men made it the other side, they were met with volleys of shrapnel from massed batteries less than 500 yards away. Regiment after regiment of his division struggled out of the creek bed and up the gentle slope and tried to form a line, but by 3 p.m. the entire hill was shrouded in thick, black smoke, and the sound of artillery fire was so strong that men who survived the Battle of Gaines's Mill (as it came to be known) would remember it with particular horror to the very end of the war.

A Union war correspondent describes A. P. Hill's attack from the other side as "a tornado of musketry," driving the Union pickets back "into that dense wood where now corpses [were] as thick as the trees." Despite repeated assaults the Confederate troops never got more than halfway up the sloping hill. In some places the Union troops confronting them were three lines deep—and the Confederates were "brutally repulsed." Soon the survivors reappeared from the smoke, first in small numbers, then in whatever remained of whole units, the men retreating back to Cold Harbor Road, from where they had started. By 4 p.m. it was apparent to Lee that A. P. Hill's attack had failed and that Porter was not weakening his left and his center to defend his right, as Lee had expected him to. Lee correctly concluded that Jackson was not yet in contact with the enemy.

Once again bad luck dogged Jackson. His wits may still have been dulled by exhaustion, and many historians have speculated that he may also have had an unconscious unwillingness to cooperate with Lee's other major generals and give up what had been his largely independent role in the Valley. All of these things, or some combination of them, may well have been affecting Jackson, but his respect for Lee was only a little short of idolatrous.

It may be that nothing more was involved than yet another consequence of poor maps and general ignorance of the countryside around Richmond by the Confederate high command. To ensure that he arrived where Lee wanted him this time, Jackson had himself chosen a guide from among Stuart's cavalry troopers who were native to the area, Private John Henry Timberlake. The Timberlake family's farm "was midway between Ashland and Gaines's Mill," so there can have been no question that Timberlake knew his way, but Jackson himself may have been a victim of the confusion between "Cold Harbor Road," "Old Cold Harbor" and "New Cold Harbor." (New Cold Harbor was the place from which A. P. Hill had launched his unsuccessful attack against Porter's center; Old Cold Harbor, from which Jackson was supposed to launch his attack on Porter's right, was about a mile and a half farther north and east; and Cold Harbor Road was the most direct route linking them. Because of the rolling hills and the midsummer foliage, none of these places was instantly identifiable.)

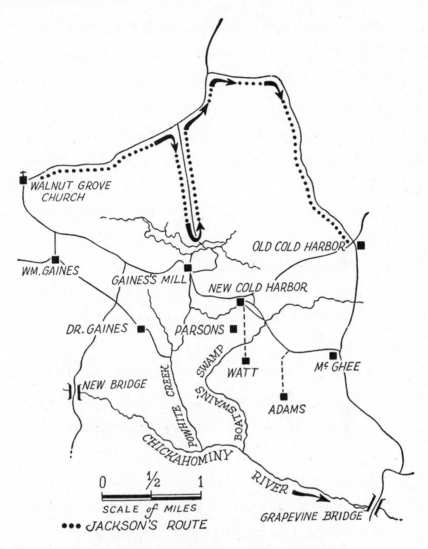

*11. Battlefield of Gaines's Mill, June 27, 1862,
with sketch of Jackson's line of advance.*

Jackson ordered the twenty-six-year old Private
Timberlake to take him to Old Cold Harbor, and the
two of them rode together silently—one of Jackson's
biographers, James L. Robertson Jr., comments that

the general was "both very tired and very ill humored," and if this was true, it cannot have helped matters between them. They rode two miles from Walnut Grove Church to a fork in the road, then took the right fork, leading directly south toward Cold Harbor Road, which links, from west to east, Gaines's Mill, New Cold Harbor, and Old Cold Harbor. They had not gone more than a mile and a half when Jackson heard the sound of a battle in front of him. "Where is that firing?" he asked Timberlake.

Timberlake replied that it seemed to be coming from Gaines's Mill. Jackson was dismayed. "Does this road lead there?"

Private Timberlake began to explain that the road they were approaching went past Gaines's Mill to Old Cold Harbor, but Jackson clearly feared that he was being led to the wrong place. He was determined not to repeat the mistake he had made the day before, and not to disappoint Lee again. "But I do not wish to go to Gaines's Mill," he said sharply, "I wish to go to Cold Harbor, leaving that place on my right."

One can guess that Jackson made a forbidding figure, with his grim expression and the peak of his dusty old cap pulled low over his piercing eyes. When displeased, Jackson struck terror into soldiers of far higher rank than his young guide, and Timberlake can hardly have failed to realize that the major general riding beside him was furious. What Timberlake should have done was take a deep breath and explain that the road they were on would bring them out onto the Gaines's Mill–New Cold Harbor–Old Cold Harbor road in less than half a mile, and that it was the fastest, most direct route to where Jackson wanted to go. Jackson may have made it clear, however, that he was in no mood to listen to explanations, and it is never easy for a mere private to argue with a major general.*

Timberlake was a young man of exceptional courage, and he seems to have felt insulted by Jackson's tone, and perhaps by the fact that Jackson doubted his ability as a guide. At any rate he took refuge in what the British armed services call "dumb insolence," and gave Jackson what sounds like a flip reply. "Then the left-hand road was the one which should have been taken," Timberlake said, "and had you let me know what you desired, I could have directed you aright at first."

This sounds as if Timberlake's grammar has been tidied up for posterity, very likely by Major Dabney,† the theologian and preacher whom Jackson had put

---

*I try to relate this to my own experience in the armed forces and imagine what it would have been like if, as an Aircraftman Second Class (AC2) in the Royal Air Force, I had been obliged to argue with an Air Vice Marshal.

† The source for this incident is Dabney's *The Life and Campaigns of Lieut. Gen. Thomas J. Jackson.*

in charge of the army's march from the Valley to the peninsula with such unfortunate results; but there is no mistaking the tone of a man who is washing his hands of the whole affair. If Jackson had continued to follow Timberlake's route he would have reached Old Cold Harbor at the same time as D. H. Hill, making it possible for Jackson to attack the Union right while A. P. Hill's men were still fighting—exactly what Lee had planned.

Though Private Timberlake could not have known it, one of Jackson's few weaknesses as a general was his unwillingness to explain his orders, or to pay attention to other people's opinion of them. Even so great an admirer as Major Dabney, who was within earshot at the time, remarks that the misunderstanding with Timberlake may have been caused because Jackson's "habitual reticence, in this instance too stringent, withheld all explanation of his strategic designs." A few words of explanation to young Timberlake might have saved a lot of time and lives, and hearing him out patiently even more.

At this point Jackson was riding at the head of a column of men that filled the road from Walnut Grove Church to the Gaines's Mill pond. It was basically a narrow, rutted country lane with thick woods and tangled bush on either side. Thousands of men, not to speak of horses and horse-drawn artillery, had to turn around and march back in the direction from which they had laboriously come. This was not something that could be done quickly, or without confusion and long delays as the men tried to pass the word back down the column and sort themselves out.

Jackson not only had to back up and reverse his troops, but had to march them over four miles to reach Old Cold Harbor, and all this in brutal heat and suffocating dust, and to the noise of a major battle going on less than three miles away, in which they should have been taking part. Those who remember from their schooldays that the hypotenuse of a right triangle is shorter than the sum of the other two sides, and who look at the map, will instantly perceive the position in which Jackson had placed himself—he would now be marching *away* from the battle on the longest route to his place in it.

By retracing his route Jackson had also effectively vanished from sight. Lee sent several couriers to find him and tell him to attack at once, including his trusted staff officer Major Walter H. Taylor, but to no effect. Jackson had no option now but to continue the way he was going, however long it took him to get there. Dabny reports that "Jackson bore the same calm and assured countenance" as usual, and when someone suggested that "irreparable" harm might be caused by the delay, he replied, "No, let us trust that the providence of our God will so overrule it, that no mischief shall result."

In the absence of Jackson, Lee was obliged to move on to a new plan. The Federals were not retreating; they were staying put—indeed there was some danger they might advance and overwhelm A. P. Hill's "shattered division." Consequently, Lee ordered Longstreet "to make a diversion" on the far right, until he had enough troops in position for "a general assault." It was now about four o'clock in the afternoon, and Lee hoped to avoid another "draw," like that of the day before, with the Federals remaining in possession of the field. Besides all the usual problems of the "fog of war," estimates of the number of men on both sides were wildly mistaken. Porter had about 40,000 men on the field and assumed he was facing up to 75,000 Confederates. Lee had about 56,000 men, but so far more than half of them were not yet in action, and their whereabouts were uncertain. On the right, Longstreet decided that the "diversion" he was supposed to make would merely waste lives, and brought his troops forward to attack instead. In the center, where A. P. Hill's exhausted troops had fallen back, the first elements of Jackson's corps, under Richard Ewell and D. H. Hill, were gradually coming through the woods behind Telegraph

Road and forming up on A. P. Hill's left. There was no time to form a neat line of battle; Jackson's straggling units simply took up positions as they reached them, under steady and increasing fire from the far side of Boatswain's Creek. "D. H. Hill and Ewell were speedily engaged . . . and suffered heavily," mostly from well-placed, effective Federal artillery, to which there was for the moment little or no reply, since Jackson's guns were still behind him on the roads to Old Cold Harbor. General Richard Taylor, always hypercritical, notes, "Ignorance of the ground, densely wooded, and want of guides, occasioned confusion and delay." Still, there is no question that having finally arrived where he wanted to go, Jackson took his time about deploying his men, and was at first still under the impression that he was to hold ground while A. P. Hill and Longstreet drove the Federals toward him. This tends to be taken as a criticism of Lee's staff work, but it seems unlikely that Major Walter Taylor, who managed to find Jackson twice during the afternoon and urge him on, would not have shared Lee's change of plan with him.

Just before six o'clock Lee, aware that the battle hung in the balance, rode out along Telegraph Road to meet Jackson, whom Freeman describes as "dust-covered, with his dingy cadet cap pulled down over his weak eyes, sitting awkwardly on an ugly horse, and sucking a lemon." "Ah, General," Lee said, "I am very glad to see you. I had hoped to see you before."

Various interpretations of this greeting are given. James L. Robertson Jr., one of Jackson's biographers, describes it as "warm," whereas Freeman, Lee's partisan, merely describes it as "tactful," but with a nuance of reproach. Knowing what we do about Lee, it seems safe to assume that this was as close to criticism of a subordinate as he was likely to come. One senses behind Lee's icy politeness a certain deft gift for irony. In any case, quite apart from Lee's dislike of emotional scenes and confrontations, the last thing he would have wanted to do was dress Jackson down in front of his own troops, who were cheering wildly at the sight of the two men greeting each other from horseback.

The sound of firing from the woods to the south had become "deafening," and Lee wisely chose to ask a practical question. "That fire is very heavy," he said. "Do you think your men can stand it?"

That seemed to arouse Jackson's combative instincts. He glanced at the rising clouds of gun smoke and said gruffly, "They can stand almost anything. They can stand that."

Lee's presence seemed to wipe away Jackson's fatigue. He quickly got his divisions into a semblance of order, and sent messengers from his staff to all his division commanders. "Tell them this affair must hang in suspense no longer! Sweep the field with the bayonet!" There was certainly no ambiguity about *this* order.

It was growing darker, shadows were lengthening, and the battle seemed to be hanging fire. After having left Jackson, Lee rode back down Telegraph Road toward New Cold Harbor, where he saw Brigadier General John B. Hood, at the head of the Texas Brigade—Hood had been his young companion back in the days when he had been searching for Indian tracks on the frontier in Texas. He quickly explained to Hood that the Union line must be broken in the center, whatever the cost. "This must be done," he said urgently. "Can you break his line?" Hood stared at the woods on both sides of Boatswain's Creek, and the high ground behind it, bristling with guns and bayonets and veiled in smoke. "I will try," he said. "May God be with you," Lee replied, and sent a messenger off to tell Longstreet on the far right to attack at once.

For almost half an hour, as the woods grew dark except for the bright orange flashes of the guns, the noise of artillery drowned out every other sound. Then, from both sides of the field, Lee heard the shrill rebel yell, as the entire Confederate line moved forward. Charles Page, the *New York Tribune* correspondent, stood on the slope directly behind those woods while "a spatter of Rebel lead lifted little puffs of dust" all around him. He described how the sound of the fierce rebel yell rose above the "the incessant roar of musketry," and, being a northerner, added, "There are cheers and yells, for our men *cheer,* while they, like other savages, *yell.*"

Page described what it was like to be on the other side of that charge, and the "awful firing that resounded from that smoke-clouded valley" as Jackson on the Confederate left and Longstreet on the right attempted to turn both Porter's flanks, while Hood's brigade, yelling ferociously, led the assault on the center of the Union line. "The fire grew faster. So did the pace of the men. By the hundred they fell, but without a break in their alignment . . . they were plunging down the grade to the swamp. A thousand had fallen now, but scarcely a musket had been fired from the attacking division. The men were within twenty yards of the Federal front line—within ten—and then suddenly, as if the same fear had seized every heart, the Federals were leaving their works, were running, were throwing their arms away. . . . Up the hill and over the second line they rushed, and then, as the bluecoats spread in a confused mass, the Confederates loosed their volley, where every bullet reached its mark." Lee's aide Major Taylor, not a man given to overstatement, rode over the field where Hood's men had made their charge, and remarked that he "had to take great care in guiding my horse not to strike a dead or wounded Federal soldier."

The Federals fought a good deal better than Page's words would suggest, but Longstreet's attack on the Federal far left effectively turned Porter's flank, at which point the Union line began to crumble. By 7 p.m. "our officers judiciously ordered their men to fall back; the order was not obeyed so judiciously, for they ran back, broken, disordered, routed. Simultaneously the wounded and skulkers about the buildings used as hospitals caught a panic, whether from a few riderless horses plunging madly across the field, or from instantaneously scenting the rout, does not appear. A motley mob started pell-mell for the bridges." Still, some Federal units fought on amid the chaos. A battery of twenty guns "opened a terrifying fire of canister★ at short range. The enemy recoiled. The bridge at Lodi [where the twenty-seven-year-old general Napoleon Bonaparte had rallied his troops in circumstances of great difficulty in 1796] was not half so terrible." As darkness fell, the battlefield was a place of confusion and slaughter and headlong panic. Page described "Scores of riderless, terrified horses dashing in every

---

★ "Canister" or "case shot" is a round made of tin containing a large number of iron balls, which spread out in a wide pattern when fired, rather like a giant shotgun shell.

direction; thick-flying bullets singing by, admonishing of danger; every minute a man struck down; wagons and ambulances and cannon blockading the way; wounded men limping and groaning and bleeding amid the throng."

The crush of Porter's retreating army was so great that Page himself did not manage to get across a bridge to the south shore of the Chickahominy until after 11 p.m. He remarked that "few of the dead were brought from the field, and not one half of the wounded."*

The Confederates spent the night on the field. Those who could slept, but most of them were kept awake by the cries of the wounded and the silent presence of so many dead.

Lee had won his first victory.

Gaines's Mill made Lee overnight not only *a* southern hero, but *the* southern hero. Hitherto, he had been overshadowed by Joseph E. Johnston and by Jackson. Now, in two battles fought in just forty-eight hours, he had broken the siege of Richmond and forced McClellan to retreat with an army more than twice the size of his own. Everyone overlooked the fact that both these battles were poorly planned and executed, and

---

*Union casualties were 6,837; Confederate, 7,992.

that at Mechanicsville he had scarcely managed to get a third of his army into action. In the South Lee could do no wrong, and in the North, by his dignity and gentlemanly bearing as much as by his victories, he also acquired a miraculous reputation, sustained because no Union general managed to beat him decisively on the battlefield until the third day of Gettysburg in July 1863, despite the numerous deficiencies of the Confederate Army in manpower, supplies, and material.

McClellan had been slow and reluctant to recognize the danger facing Porter at Gaines's Mill—he did not even approach the battlefield; he remained at his headquarters south of the Chickahominy listening to the sound of the battle and arranging the vast and tedious movement of his army's supplies and artillery from the York River to the James River. He confined himself to sending cheerful, supportive messages to Porter, but did not attempt to transfer any significant reinforcements to him, although this would have been easy to do. That night he wrote a dispatch to Secretary of War Stanton that laid all the blame for his defeat on Stanton and Lincoln. "I have lost this battle because my force was too small. I again repeat that I am not responsible for this & say it with the earnestness of a General who feels in his heart the loss of every brave man who has been needlessly sacrificed. . . . I have seen too many dead & wounded comrades to feel otherwise than that the Govt has not sustained this Army. If you do not do so now the game is lost. If I save this Army now I tell you plainly that I owe no thanks to you or any other persons in Washington—you have done your best to sacrifice this Army." McClellan was so vitriolic that his last sentence was expurgated before the letter was shown to Stanton and Lincoln. McClellan guessed this might happen and leaked it to the press intact the next day. The tone of the rest of the letter was enough to alert the secretary of war and the president to a major crisis for the Army of the Potomac, and perhaps to lead them to question its commander's sanity as well. With commendable restraint Lincoln attempted to calm McClellan the next day with a dose of common sense, advising him to "Save your army at all events." Having predicted only a few days before that he would be in Richmond at any moment, McClellan was now no longer even certain he could still save his army, and clung to the illusion that he was outnumbered by two to one. Apparently he was convinced by reports from Allan Pinkerton, the Union spymaster, that there were at least 180,000 Confederate troops in Richmond, and that "Jackson's whole force [is] estimated at two hundred and twenty thousand to two hundred and sixty thousand," when in fact Lee had only 37,000 men at

Gaines's Mill, and the lines around Richmond were held by a mere two understrength divisions.

Early in the morning on June 28 Lee sent J. E. B. Stuart off in the direction of White House and West Point to seize the bases McClellan had placed in these towns, but McClellan was already carrying out the transfer or destruction of his supplies there, without having informed Washington of the fact. The Confederate general Richard Taylor gives a graphic description of the scale of the destruction: "A train was heard approaching. . . . Gathering speed, it came rushing on, and quickly emerged from the forest, two engines drawing a long string of carriages. Reaching the bridge the engine exploded with terrific noise, followed in succession by explosions of the carriages, laden with ammunition. Shells burst in all directions, the river was lashed into foam, trees were torn for acres around. . . . The enemy had taken this means of destroying surplus ammunition."

The day after Gaines's Mill Lee's youngest son, Robbie, who had left the university to enlist in the Confederate Army despite his father's reservations, and who was serving as an artillery private in Jackson's army, was "rudely awakened by a comrade, prodding me with his sponge-staff," as he slumbered under a caisson. He staggered out, face and hands blackened with powder stains, and stood, "face to face with General Lee and his staff. Their fresh uniforms, bright equipments and well-groomed horses contrasted so forcibly with the war-worn appearance of our command that I was completely dazed . . . but when I saw my father's loving eyes and smile it became clear to me that he had ridden over to see if I was safe and to ask how I was getting along."

Apart from this brief but charming scene, Lee's primary concern on June 28 was to ascertain where McClellan was going. His own army was occupied with gathering up prisoners and safeguarding the thousands of muskets the Federal soldiers had discarded during their retreat. The Confederates were also burying the dead of both sides in common mass graves. Across the Chickahominy columns of smoke rose from where the Union quartermasters were burning their supplies, rather than let them fall into the hands of the enemy, and from time to time huge explosions erupted as ammunition dumps were destroyed. There was no doubt that McClellan was in retreat, but in what direction? Lee at first thought that McClellan would probably move east toward Yorktown and Fort Monroe; but to retrace his steps all the way back to the tip of the peninsula would be a tremendous admission of defeat, so he might instead be moving directly south to the James River, where he could be supplied by the U.S. Navy and still remain a threat to Richmond. If McClellan moved eastward, the configuration of the Chickahominy River would give him the opportunity of crossing by a number of bridges farther downstream. If Lee moved his army to the south of the Chickahominy in pursuit he might have to fight his way back across it against considerable opposition. Lee decided not to move his army until he was sure where McClellan was going, and in the opinion of several military historians thereby missed his last opportunity to engage the Union army while it was still widely spread out and destroy it. On the other hand, there was now a Union army of 100,000 men on the south side of the Chickahominy within eight miles of Richmond, which was defended only by the two divisions of Huger and Magruder, about 23,000 men at most. Might McClellan make a bold move to take advantage of his defeat and seize the capital while Lee was on the wrong side of the river? Lee's men were exhausted and most of the bridges in front of them had been destroyed or badly damaged. Could he move the army quickly enough to join Huger and Magruder and save Richmond if he had to? Uncharacteristic as it was of Lee to wait, he had no choice—for the moment it was more dangerous to move his army in the wrong direction than to stay put.

Battle of Savage's Station—June 29, 1862

Late in the morning a message arrived from Stuart saying that he had ridden all the way to Despatch Station without serious opposition. The Federals had retreated across the Chickahominy and burned the railway bridge behind them. Not until mid-afternoon would further reports make Lee believe that McClellan was moving south, not east, though that would not preclude his making a bold dash for Richmond. Magruder was anxious as only a general with 13,000 men can be who is facing an enemy army of 100,000 men just a mile or so away from him; and Lee was equally anxious *for* him, urging on him "utmost vigilance," though it is hard to imagine that Magruder was not already peering into the woods in front of him with all the vigilance he could muster.

Toward the end of the day Lee came to a decision—he would cross the Chickahominy in pursuit of McClellan, with the intention of destroying the Federal Army before it reached the James River. The priority now was to restore the bridges the Federals had destroyed. Jackson had already been wrestling with the task of making "Grapevine Bridge," so called because it was a ramshackle construction of untrimmed logs and timber, usable. He also sent engineers to the more important "Alexander's Bridge," named after the U.S. Army engineer officer who had constructed it. Unwisely, Jackson had placed both these projects in the hands of the unfortunate Major Dabney, and it was not until June 29 that another officer, a former civilian contrator with a more practical hands-on approach, appeared to take charge. Photographs of the restored Grapevine Bridge, which acquired a certain historical glamour, make it look precarious indeed,* but Alexander's Bridge was more important because once rebuilt it could take horses, artillery, and wagons, as well as men. Both jobs were difficult in the absence of several companies of well-trained military engineers with the proper tools and equipment. The Chickahominy itself was not particularly wide—about fifteen yards at this point—or fast moving, but its banks on both sides were so marshy and swampy that they might almost have been extensions of the river. The rough-and-ready reconstruction of the two bridges is best described by the former contractor, who, when Jackson asked him whether he had followed the drawings prepared for

---

* A pretty good description of the bridge as it was originally built by the Federals appeared in the June 13, 1862, *New York Times:* "It is about three-quarters of a mile long [including its approaches]. . . . Large trees had first to be cut down and made into piles, which were driven down into the swamp. . . . Others were then lashed on to these piles, forming a support for logs thrown across the road." In photographs its approaches are surrounded on both sides by dense vegetation. Rebuilt, it resembled the original but perhaps was even more makeshift.

him, replied: "Gineral Jackson, I ain't seen no sketch, and don't know nothing about no pictures . . . but that bridge is done, sir, and is ready, and you can right now send your folks across in to it."

"Done" the bridges might be, but Jackson would not begin moving his four divisions over them until dawn on June 30, despite the noise of battle from across the river, where Magruder had begun an attack toward Savage's Station, the main supply base for the Federal forces facing Richmond, in the expectation that Jackson would be crossing the river to support him. Lee's orders to Jackson were ambiguous, however, and Jackson obeyed them literally, believing that he was to stay on the north side of the Chickahominy until ordered otherwise.

Lee was determined not to let the Federal army slip away to safety on the James. He understood that the only way the Confederacy could win its independence was by inflicting on a Federal army a defeat costly enough to bring the Union to the negotiating table—"annihilation," in fact, like Napoleon's victory at Austerlitz. He launched a number of attacks in the hope of provoking a major battle while the bulk of McClellan's army was spread out and still north of White Oak Swamp Creek. But these attacks were widely separated and ill coordinated—Lee was still learning the art of high command by experience in the field. He told Magruder to move east along the York River Railroad and Williamsburg Road, and attack the Union lines around Savage's Station in cooperation with Jackson, but he seems to have ignored the fact that Jackson was still on the other side of the river waiting for his bridges to be repaired. In the absence of Jackson, Magruder called on Lee for reinforcements, but Lee was able to give him only two of Huger's brigades, which were to be returned to Huger if they were not in action by 2 p.m. Lee may have hoped this would make Magruder move swiftly, but if so it had no effect.

Magruder, who was suffering from a stomach ailment, probably severe dysentery, that required treatment by either opium or alcohol,★ was in no shape to carry out an attack against a larger force than his own. He delayed his assault until the late afternoon, by which time he had lost Huger's brigades, and had still seen no sign of Jackson. The result was a bloody draw, despite the use of Lee's famous "armored railroad battery," with its enormous 32-pound rifled naval cannon. Neither Magruder nor his opponent Major General Edwin V. Sumner managed to get even half his troops

---

★ Laudanum, or tincture of opium, was then still a popular (and effective) treatment for diarrhea, and there are still people today who believe alcohol relieves the symptoms. Side effects of laudanum can include euphoria, sleepiness, and anxiety.

into action, and despite a considerable number of casualties on both sides, the day ended inconclusively, in pouring rain and violent thunderstorms. Sumner's aim, after all, was not to win a victory but to get his men away and moving toward the James River more or less intact. In that he succeeded, though he got scant thanks from McClellan for it. The degree of misery on the sodden battlefield was no doubt increased by the fact that the Federals had retreated from Savage's Station taking their field hospital with them, leaving over 2,500 Union wounded behind to be captured by the Confederates, who had little means of caring for them.

Nobody comes out of Savage's Station with much credit, Lee least of all. His orders to Jackson were unclear, and Magruder was certainly entitled to expect Jackson's support; the only map available to Lee was poorly drawn; and his staff officers passed on changes to Lee's original orders in ways that only increased Magruder's confusion and Jackson's delay.

By the time Jackson finally crossed the Chickahominy early on June 30, the battle for Savage's Station was over and the Union forces defending it had gone. Magruder may not have handled things effectively, but considering his own befuddled state and the disparity between the strength of his forces and those of General Sumner, he does not seemed to have merited Lee's uncharacteristically sharp rebuke: "I regret much that you have made so little progress today in the pursuit of the enemy." It is hard to see how Magruder could have pursued Sumner's corps with any effect; besides, the Federals had abandoned a virtual treasure trove of supplies and equipment at Savage's Station—to ragged, poorly fed Confederate soldiers the temptation to stop and loot was irresistible, and the number of muskets Federal soldiers had dropped was so great that it required work parties to gather them up and load them into wagons. All of these things would have slowed down any "pursuit," even had Magruder intended one.

During the night, the confusion about which side of the Chickahominy Jackson's divisions should be on was straightened out, but twenty-four hours had been lost because of Lee's doubts about McClellan's intentions. Sometime in the middle of the night it became evident at last to Lee that McClellan would probably not turn east, and that his own object must now be to crush McClellan's army before it reached the safety of the James River.

This presented Lee with a number of tactical problems. Just as the peninsula was divided laterally by the Chickahominy River, so the country between that river and the James below Savage's Station was divided by White Oak Swamp Creek, which was directly in

McClellan's path as he moved south. The swamp was a significant military obstacle, broad, boggy, and with few bridges spanning it. If McClellan found it hard to cross with his artillery and wagon train, as he surely would, Lee calculated that it might be possible to trap him. If the divisions of Huger and Magruder attacked from the west, and Jackson's four divisions attacked him from the north and east, the Army of the Potomac—virtually immobilized by the swamp in front of it and surrounded on three sides, with its lines of communication cut off—could then be annihilated despite its superior numbers.*

Time was now the critical element—time, and weather, and neither of them was working in Lee's favor. During the night of June 29 rain poured down, making such roads as there were scarcely usable. "Darkness fell as we bivouacked on the low ground south of the river," wrote one of Jackson's brigade commanders, Richard Taylor. "A heavy rain came down, converting the ground into a lake." A "half-drowned courier" was brought to the small ambulance in which Taylor was resting (suffering from "severe pain in the head and loins" and unable to mount his horse); he proved to carrying an outdated dispatch

---

* This is the famous and classic "nutcracker" tactic used so effectively by the German army from 1939 through 1941.

from Magruder asking for reinforcements, not surprisingly, since Magruder had used his division to attack an entire corps. By this time Lee had gotten the divisions of A. P. Hill and Longstreet across the Chickahominy farther upstream and was pressing them hard down the Central (Barrytown) Road in pursuit of McClellan. As for McClellan himself, he neither sought to control the fighting nor appointed anyone to do it for him. He had already ordered his headquarters to be set up at Haxall's Landing, on the James River, and was pressing his quartermasters hard to get over 100 guns, "supply trains [consisting] of something over 3,000 wagons and ambulances, drawn by nearly 14,750 horses and mules," as well as "a lumbering herd of 2,500 beef cattle" along the one road across White Oak Swamp. His major concern was that his retreat should be seen as a "change of base" to the James River, rather than as a defeat. He had abandoned his carefully prepared entrenchments on the outskirts of Richmond around Fair Oaks and Seven Pines, and his whole army was now moving across or around White Oak Swamp in the direction of Malvern Hill, the most prominent high ground between Richmond and Harrison's Landing, which was as far up the James as Federal gunboats could get without coming under fire from Confederate batteries on the shore.

Frayser's Farm (or Glendale)—June 30, 1862★

Jackson reached Magruder's headquarters at about 3:30 a.m. on June 30, and managed to get an excited Magruder calmed down and off to bed. Magruder was still indignant that Jackson had not arrived in time to support his attack on Savage's Station the day before, so Jackson may not have been the ideal person to attempt to calm him; in any case Magruder can hardly have had time to sleep off his "nervous anxiety," before Lee himself arrived at dawn.

Lee's impatience seems to have communicated itself to most of those around him. He was aware that this day was his best chance—possibly his only chance—to destroy McClellan's army, and here was a clearly distraught Magruder trying to justify the botched attack he had made the previous day. Lee does not seem to have reproached Jackson, who had left most of his troops on the wrong side of the Chickahominy. His faith in Jackson was, and would remain, unshakable. Officers standing around the two men at a respectful distance remember Jackson nodding in agreement as he listened to Lee's plans for the day and drawing a triangle

---

★Also known as the Battle of Glendale, Frazier's Farm, Nelson's Farm, Charles City Crossroads, New Market Road, and Riddell's Shop (a blacksmith's shop), all of which were nearby (Wikipedia).

in the dust with the toe of his boot—presumably the route he would take to attack McClellan's army from the northeast as it retreated.

There is some doubt about the verisimilitude of this scene: Jackson's uniform is described by one witness as dusty, when in fact it would have been soaking wet; and the ground he was standing on in front of Magruder's headquarters would have been a muddy quagmire, not easy to draw a map in with the toe of a boot. Jackson may or may not have said to Lee, "We've got him," before calling for his horse, but if he did say it he was optimistic. Also, if Lee's order to Jackson was to continue "to pursue the enemy on the road he [has] taken," it might have been helpful for Lee to be more precise. It was not a pursuit Lee wanted, but a decisive battle.

Lee cut short Magruder's attempts to explain himself and ordered him to move his men to Derbytown Road—this involved a long loop curling back toward Richmond—to reinforce Longstreet's division as it advanced eastward, a "countermarch" of nearly ten miles for men who had fought the previous day. Lee then provided Magruder with a guide, remounted, and rode there himself.

But Lee seems to have misjudged the amount of time it would take to get everyone in position for a decisive blow against McClellan's retreating army, or perhaps he failed to convey his own sense of urgency. There was no word from Magruder and Huger, and it was 2:30 p.m. before Longstreet made contact with the Federal troops. More disturbingly still, there was no word from Jackson that he had crossed White Oak Swamp.

For the third time in four days Jackson was stalled. The retreating Federals had burned the one bridge over the White Oak Swamp Creek, and its charred debris made crossing even more difficult. Major Dabney describes the ground before Jackson as "soft and miry from recent rains," and the far side as "covered by a belt of tall forest, in full leaf," which effectively screened a Federal artillery battery and several "long lines" of infantry. Jackson "halted his army" and waited until twenty-eight guns had been brought forward, but the ensuing artillery duel did not inflict much damage on either side.

Jackson's cavalry used the time to discover two practicable fords, but it was clear that he was facing an opposed crossing, during which his infantry would be exposed to heavy fire. Even the loyal Dabney seems surprised that Jackson "came short of that efficiency in action for which he was everywhere else noted." He adds that "the remainder of the afternoon" was spent in failed attempts to rebuild the bridge, which were hampered by heavy fire, and regrets "the temporary eclipse of Jackson's genius," attributing it to fatigue and sleeplessness. Indeed, Jackson was so exhausted that on June 30 he fell asleep while eating his evening meal, "his supper between his teeth." When he woke, he remarked that everybody should "rise with the dawn, and see if tomorrow we cannot *do* something!" Reams have been written to explain or justify Jackson's curious failure to live up to his reputation during the Seven Days campaign, and it is in fact hard to imagine how any human being could have functioned on so little food and sleep from June 22 to the night of June 30. Still, Jackson was notably unforgiving of others who failed to comply with his own exacting orders, so there seems no reason why he should not be judged by the same standard he set for his own officers and men. By that standard, he failed.

More mysterious is why Lee, who was only three miles away, did not at least send somebody to find out what Jackson was doing, and to deliver a written message to get on with it. Even Dabney, who was there at White Oak Swamp Creek by Jackson's side, thought Jackson could have crossed the swamp had he tried, and should have tried, given "the vast interests dependent on [his] co-operation with the proposed attack upon the centre [*sic*]." For once Major Dabney had it right: any hope Lee had on June 30 of crushing McClellan's army like a nut in the jaws of a nutcracker was dependent on Jackson, whose men made up one of the jaws.

At this point, Lee was with Longstreet, overlooking the Union center from "a little clearing of broom straw and small pines," when they were joined by President Davis. Longstreet had ordered one of his batteries to fire a few rounds in reply to what he supposed was Huger's signal that he was in place. The Federals took this as the opening of an attack, and began to shell the clearing vigorously. As explosions went off all around them, Davis warned Lee that this was "no place for the commander of our army," to which Lee replied courteously that it was also no place for "the commander-in-chief of *all* our armies." At that point A. P. Hill rode up and ordered both men to retire, though he had to repeat his order before they obeyed him.

Having ridden away from the front line, Lee now learned that the Federals were retreating across Malvern Hill, which was about three miles to the south and was the most prominent feature of the landscape. It is a low, broad, irregularly shaped hill, then partly cleared, partly woodlands, rising gently from its base to a rather steeper ridge around a plateau on the summit. The southern slope dips down more steeply, almost directly to the James River. Lee recognized immediately that once the bulk of the Federal army had crossed over the hill it would be beyond his reach. There was no time to waste.

Over President Davis's objections, Lee rode forward to see for himself what was happening at the southwest salient of Malvern Hill; there, it extended within half a mile of the James River, from which Federal gunboats could give covering fire to the Union army. By now Lee had three divisions ready to attack, facing the extreme left and the center of the Union line; that of General Theophilus H. Holmes, which was deploying on New Market (or River) Road; and those of A. P. Hill and Longstreet, beginning to deploy about one and a half miles to the northeast, along Long Bridge Road. Of Magruder, who had been ordered to support Holmes, there was no word; nor was there word from Huger or Jackson.

The afternoon wore on and Lee, watching the enemy columns moving toward Malvern Hill, decided that he had no choice but to attack. Despite his sense of urgency the attack did not begin until after 4 p.m., under the overall command of Longstreet, who fed in brigade after brigade instead of concentrating his forces to split the enemy forces in two. Lee's plan, which had called for a simultaneous assault on the left, center, and right of the improvised salient formed by the Federal forces as they halted their retreat and faced the enemy, never materialized. Lee did not know that Huger's division was blocked by trees felled industriously in front of him by Union pioneers, or that Magruder's division "spent the day countermarching" fruitlessly, while Jackson remained stuck behind White Oak Swamp. The battle itself degenerated into brutal hand-to-hand combat on the Federal left, in which soldiers clubbed each other with their musket butts and officers thrust at each other with their swords. At best only half of Lee's forces got into action, and the chance to cut off and destroy the bulk of the Federal army was lost. The Federals were able to spend the night preparing well-thought-out defenses on Malvern Hill, a naturally strong position.

Casualties were about the same on both sides (3,797 Federals; 3,673 Confederates), although the number of Confederate dead and wounded was 40 percent higher than that of the Federals. The number of Federals "missing," that is to say those who were captured or had deserted under fire, was an astounding 1,804, six times the number of those killed. Lee's disappointment at being deprived of a decisive battle was intense and long-lived, but brought out his most impressive quality as a commander. He would give neither his troops nor the enemy an opportunity to rest—he would attack again next day.

It was not until ten o'clock at night that the sounds of battle ceased, to be replaced by the moans of the wounded and the dying. Jackson, who had at last retired on "a pallet" that had been prepared for him on the ground, was woken around one o'clock in the morning by his division commanders, who were concerned that McClellan might order his army to advance in the morning. Jackson heard them out politely; replied realistically, "No, I think he will clear out in the morning"; and then went back to sleep.

He was absolutely right. McClellan, who had spent the entire day safely on board the U.S.S. *Galena* in the James River—from which he nevertheless wired dramatically to the War Department, "If none of us escape we shall at least have done honor to the country"—had the good sense to order Fitz John Porter to dig his artillery in on Malvern Hill and let Lee attack him there.

Malvern Hill—July 1, 1862

At first light Jackson saw that the Federals in front of him were gone, and was able to cross White Oak Swamp unimpeded. Lee now had the concentration he had been seeking the day before—Magruder's troops had arrived after an eighteen-mile march, much of it unnecessary; Huger's troops had appeared at last; Jackson would soon be in position on the far left. As the sun rose and the early-morning mist dissipated, however, an ominous sight was revealed: "the enemy [was] most advantageously posted upon an elevated ridge in front of Malvern Hill, which was occupied by several lines of infantry partially fortified, and by a powerful artillery. In short, the whole army of McClellan, with three hundred pieces of field artillery,★ was now, for the first time, assembled on one field, determined to stand at bay, and contend for its existence; while the whole Confederate army was also converging around it, under the immediate eye of the Commander-in-Chief and the President."

To his credit Fitz John Porter had managed to extricate the bulk of the Union army, and its artillery from yesterday's battlefield shambles, and place them overnight on high ground under the protection of a powerful force of artillery, as well as the powerful long-range cannons of the gunboats. The opportunity of catching the enemy on the move had slipped through Lee's fingers on June 30, and he was now facing the most difficult of military situations, an attack against an enemy in a formidably concentrated position on higher ground

---

★ The actual number of Federal guns was more like 250, plus those of the gunboats on the James River, an advantage of at least two to one over the number of Confederate guns. Since batteries were rotated into and out of line throughout the battle, there was never anything like this number firing at one time.

with an excellent field of fire. The Federal infantry was drawn up, in some places as deep as three lines, in a semicircle about three-quarters of the way up the hill, facing several hundred yards of gently sloping open ground, at the base of which was a dense thicket of woods, brush, and marshland that would inevitably slow down the Confederates' approach, and make it difficult, perhaps impossible, for them to deploy in line for an attack until they were in the open ground on the fields beyond it, where they would be heavily shelled. Porter had chosen "a natural fortress," in Freeman's words: "Had the Union engineers searched the whole countryside below Richmond, they could not have ground more ideally set for the slaughter of an attacking army." The far left of the Union line was protected by a small stream, Turkey Run, as well as by the gunboats* in the James River, and the far right by Western Run, which meandered through marshy ground toward the James.

Once again, getting the Confederate troops into position for the assault was a slow and faltering process, consuming most of the day. Lee met with his principal commanders shortly after dawn. A good night's sleep

---

* The gunboats would prove a mixed blessing to the Union. Their fire was directed by relays of Union soldiers with semaphore flags, but the fire direction was so erratic that the 100-pound explosive missiles dropped on friend and foe alike.

had apparently restored Jackson's vigor. It was now Lee, despite his usual calm demeanor, who showed the effects of fatigue, nervous strain, and an unspecified illness—none of it surprising in a man of fifty-five who had been fighting without interruption for a week. "His temper," Freeman notes, "was not of the best," an occurrence rare enough to be noticed. He was sufficiently aware of his state of mind to ask General Longstreet to accompany him as a kind of ad hoc second in command and chief of staff. Longstreet was bluffly optimistic, but except for him the general feeling was that an attack would be "well nigh hopeless." D. H. Hill had discovered a chaplain in his command whose home was in the vicinity. The chaplain's opinion on the wisdom of attacking Malvern Hill was: "If General McClellan is there in strength, we had better leave him alone." But this opinion carried no weight with Lee, who was determined to destroy the Federal army before it was out of his reach, let alone with Longstreet, who told D. H. Hill, "Don't get scared, now that we have got him whipped," a daring thing to have said to a fellow general (and brother-in-law of Stonewall Jackson).

When Brigadier General Jubal A. Early "expressed his concern lest McClellan escape, Lee answered grimly, 'Yes, he will get away because I cannot have my orders carried out!'" Although Early himself was famous for his bad temper, so much so that Lee called him "my bad old man," this morning he was tactful enough not to point out that Lee's orders of the day before had been contradictory.

Lee's temper remained frayed all day, perhaps because the more closely he looked at Malvern Hill, the greater the difficulties of carrying it seemed to be. Not only was it a textbook example of a strong defensive position; there were only two halfway decent roads toward it, which joined about three miles from the summit—the rest were all rough farm tracks. This meant that he would have to push most of his divisions down a single narrow road to approach in full view of the enemy on the summit.

The issue of incorrect or misleading maps arose again almost at once. Lee had ordered Magruder to proceed down what he called "the Quaker road," by which he meant Willis Church Road, which was sometimes known as the Quaker road to locals,* but Magruder's guide had chosen another road known by the name "Willis" farther to the right—where Longstreet at last found him moving in the wrong direction. Magruder's division now had to countermarch, a problem similar to the one that had faced Jackson at Gaines's Mill.

---

*For the reason that Willis Church was a Quaker meetinghouse.

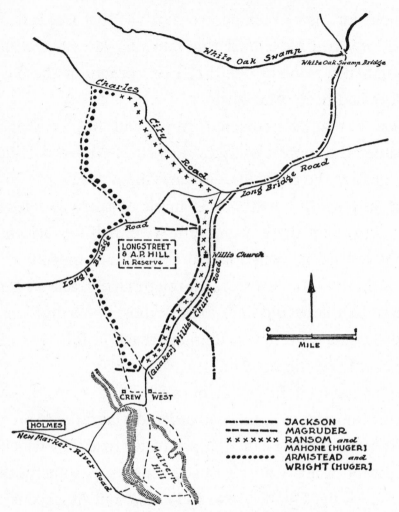

12. *Lines of advance by the Army of Northern Virginia,*
morning of July 1, 1862.

While searching for Magruder, Longstreet discovered a bare ridge on the extreme Confederate
right, with an open field of fire, from which massed
Confederate artillery could rake the Union artillery.
If advantage could be taken of a similar position on

the far left, Confederate fire would be converged from two directions against the Federal guns. "Converging fire" is the beau ideal of gunnery, rarely achieved, in which artillery fire from separate points comes together against a single point of the enemy's line with devastating effect. To accomplish this at Malvern Hill would take time, however. On the right, pioneers had to be deployed to fell trees and "cut a road," while on the left, heavy woods and swampy ground had slowed down the arrival of the guns. It is a well-known fact of war that "the speed of deployment by artillery . . . decides the outcome of the battle," and by this standard, Lee's deployment was slow; nor was he able to assemble the number of guns needed to produce the effect he wanted. The idea of "neutralizing" the enemy's superior artillery power by carefully aimed cross fire was brilliant, but it needed at least fifty guns on each side, and in the end not more than twenty were pushed, pulled, and hauled into place.

Magruder's division still had to be brought forward, and the Confederate line had to be formed up across a front stretching nearly 2,400 yards from Crewe's Run to the wooded hills overlooking Western Run, where Jackson's left flank—consisting of Hood's predominantly Texan brigade and Isaac

Trimble's brigade of Georgian, Mississippian, Alabaman, and North Carolinian regiments—overlapped and flanked the Union line, but they still faced nearly 400 yards of heavy woods and boggy marshland.

In the nineteenth century, signaling the exact moment to attack was a significant military problem—the relatively open, carefully cultivated fields of eighteenth-century European warfare were not present here. Lee's intention was that his entire army should advance together when the converging bombardment from Confederate artillery had destroyed the line of Union guns; but who was to decide when that moment had arrived, and how was he to signal it to the rest of the army? From the summit of Malvern Hill Fitz John Porter (and briefly in the early morning, George McClellan) could look down with a good view of the Confederate army, but from Willis Church Road to Crewe's Run the ground was broken by wooded hills and ridges—most of Lee's troops as they formed could see neither the slope of Malvern Hill nor the brigade or regiment on either side of them. They would not be able to form a cohesive line of battle until they emerged from the woods onto open ground, at which point they would be within 300 yards of the Federal guns.

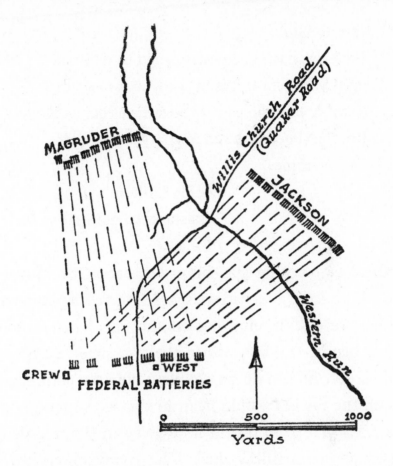

13. Longstreet's plan for "converging fire" at Malvern Hill.

Since Brigadier General Lewis Armistead's brigade was at the far right of the Confederate line, close to the open ground where the guns on the right were being placed, Lee decided that Armistead would be the first to judge the effect of the bombardment on the Federal gunners. At 1:30 p.m. Lee sent a written order to his divisional commanders to inform them of his decision.

July 1, 1862

Batteries have been established to rake the
enemy's lines. If it is broken, as is probable,
Armistead, who can witness the effect of the
fire, has been ordered to charge with a yell.
Do the same.

> R. H. Chilton,
> Assistant Adjutant-General

It is worth noting that this order is at once optimistic
and misleading. The batteries were not yet in place, and
in fact were still being hauled through felled woods,
heavy brush, and swamps to the two sites Longstreet
had chosen. It also doesn't explain how the commanders on the far left would hear Armistead's men giving
the rebel yell from over a mile away in the middle of
a thunderous artillery duel. The Army of Northern
Virginia was a formidable fighting force, but it was still
being commanded in a relatively amateurish fashion
by officers many of whom were not yet accustomed to
Lee's ways, while Lee himself was trying to command
an army of 55,000 men with the same small staff he had
brought with him from his headquarters in Richmond.
By comparison, command and control in McClellan's
army were tighter, more professional, and better organized. Indeed, this was the major factor in keeping

the Army of the Potomac from destruction, and saving
its artillery and its wagon trains during its retreat.

It was not until two o'clock that the first of the
Confederate guns were in place, and then the results
were disappointing. Volume—that is, the sheer *number*
of guns firing simultaneously from different points at
the same target—is an integral part of "converging
fire," but no sooner were the first few Confederate
guns unlimbered than the Union artillery opened fire
on them. The neat lines of converging fire shown in
the drawing on page 665 were never achieved, but Lee
could not simply disengage and allow the Federals to
retreat to safety. His entire army was poised to attack,
and Lee was confident that if pushed home hard
enough, the attack would break the Union line, bringing about a headlong, panicked flight, a rout. He was
certain that his men's spirit, dash, and bravery would
achieve what his artillery could not, and if he believed
it, his men would too. This is the side of Lee's character that makes him a great general: his bold and ruthless determination to attack even in the face of greatly
adverse odds, as well as his mystic bond with his troops
that carried the South to the very end of the war. If
"Marse Robert" believed they could break the Union
line, *they* believed it. "When the hunt was up, Lee's
combativeness was overriding," Longstreet wrote long

after the war, though by then he no longer meant it as praise. Still, it was the most remarkable part of the character of this calm, reserved, and gentle man—that once committed to battle he would fight with the utmost ferocity and would never back off.

At first Lee sought a way to outflank Porter's formidable position. He rode to the left and decided to shift two reserve divisions, those of Longstreet and A. P. Hill, to that side, for an attack aimed at cutting off Porter's line of retreat. This was a bold move that might have succeeded—Longstreet certainly thought so—but about 4 p.m., while the two divisions were still in motion, Lee received a report that Federal supply and ammunition wagons were on the move, an indication that Porter might be retreating. At the same time Magruder, who had been delayed by his guide's choice of the wrong road, arrived to take up his position on the far right, where he found that Armistead had already advanced his brigade and was heavily engaged. Lee feared that "the enemy was getting away from us," as Longstreet put it. Trusting that all his commanders had received and were still prepared to carry out his order of 1:30 p.m., Lee changed his mind about the "turning movement" on the left, and quickly dictated a second order, calling on all his commanders "to advance rapidly," that is, for a general assault on the

Union center and right, hoping to catch the Federals as they retreated.

But they were not retreating. Magruder, who had received Lee's 1:30 p.m. order while he was still on the road, saw that Armistead's brigade was fighting, and in keeping with that order took it as the signal to advance immediately, even though his artillery was still far behind. Soon the entire center and right of Lee's army, reacting to the noise of heavy fighting on the right, moved forward to assault the Union positions despite the unbroken line of Federal artillery facing them.

The result was a protracted catastrophe, one that continued well into the evening. D. H. Hill later wrote, "It was not war—it was murder." The repeated charges of Confederate regiments against an unbroken line of guns, though "grandly heroic," horrified even the Union gunners. A Union soldier wrote home that a gunner had told him "it was horrible to see the rebels advancing in a line of ten deep. . . . He said that it made his heart sick to see how it cut roads through them some places ten feet wide." Malvern Hill was remembered by those who survived it as the most terrible battle the Army of Northern Virginia ever fought, worse even than Antietam and Gettysburg. Once the assault began it was a battle out of Lee's control, continuing on until night fell on the "heart-breaking calls from agonizing boys on the hillside." Descriptions of the battle and the gory aftermath, whether by reporters or from the soldiers in letters home, are invariably horrifying. Years later a cooler judgment was written by Longstreet, who had been in favor of the attack, but afterward changed his mind: "The result of the battle was a repulse of the Confederates along the entire line and the sacrifice of several thousand brave officers and men." Confederate casualties were three times higher than those of the Federals,⋆ and Porter managed to move his men and artillery to safety on the James River during the night.

Lee was well aware he had failed. When he came to write his report on the campaign, he noted, "Under ordinary circumstances, the Federal army should have been destroyed," which was true enough—both at Gaines's Mill and at Frayser's Farm there was an opportunity for a decisive victory, which slipped through his fingers. Most historians and biographers, particularly southerners, are loath to saddle Lee with the blame. They tend to attribute blame to larger and better-supplied Federal forces, and the peninsula campaign is no exception—even Malvern Hill is seen through the filter of southern heroism (ragged infantry charging Northern artillery again and again), but

---

⋆ Union casualties were 2,100; Confederate 5,880.

the defeat there was very clearly the result of muddled and contradictory orders from Lee, the almost complete absence of coordination between divisions and brigades, poor maps, and the lack of a clear plan to concentrate all of Lee's forces in a single, powerful thrust. Once again, Jackson's men, all 18,500 of them, virtually sat out the battle as observers, placed facing the far right of the Union line where they could do no good, almost as if, having placed them there, Lee simply forgot all about them. Rather typically, General Richard Taylor, who was there, later wrote that the morning found McClellan's army "in an impregnable position" at Harrison's Landing, on the James River, and then goes on to say, "The strategy displayed on the Confederate side was magnificent," without noting the contradiction.

It is often alleged that Lee learned from General Winfield Scott that a commander's job was merely to get his army in the right place at the right time to fight, after which it was up to the corps commanders on the spot to decide what to do, but Scott was a good deal more involved in making decisions on the battlefield than Lee at Malvern Hill, and his orders were a lot more specific once the battle had begun. Lee had been Scott's most daring and gifted scout, and his talent for carrying out reconnaissance behind the enemy's lines was what first brought him to Scott's attention; but now he had no such person to rely upon himself. It is Lee's tragedy that while his staff was loyal, admiring, even worshipful, it contained no such person as the young Captain Robert E. Lee.

That night, when Lee rode through the Confederate lines, he passed General Magruder, just preparing to "lie down on the blankets that had been spread for him."

Lee reined in his horse and asked, "General Magruder, why did you attack?"

Magruder replied: "In obedience to your orders, twice repeated."

Lee is not reported to have said anything more. What, indeed, could he say? Magruder had his faults, and had forfeited any confidence Lee may have had in him, but he was not wrong. A wiser or more prudent general might have questioned whether Lee wanted him to assault an unbroken Union line with its artillery still intact, but since Magruder was already late in arriving on the field—thanks to Lee's change of orders—he would hardly have wanted to add to the delay by sending an aide to find Lee and ask whether he still wanted an assault made.

Despite Lee's flawed attempt to destroy the Army of the Potomac, the South still considered that he had achieved a triumph. In just one week he had lifted the threat against Richmond; captured 10,000 Federal prisoners, 52 guns, and over 30,000 small arms; and driven the Army of the Potomac back to a spit of marshy ground where, to be sure, it was safe from attack, but from which it could no longer threaten Richmond. This was an extraordinary achievement, but it was not the victory that Lee wanted, or that the Confederacy needed.

The *New York Times* noted that despite the fact that McClellan had been fighting continuously for six days, he had managed to save his "grand army, with its immense artillery and wagon train . . . his ammunition; its cattle-drove of 2,540 head; in fact, the entire matériel, horse, foot and dragoons, bag and baggage, have been transferred. This maneuver, however—one of the most difficult and dangerous for a commander to execute in the face of the enemy—has been accomplished safely, though under circumstances of difficulty and trial which would have taxed the genius of Napoleon."

Although in the South headlines proclaimed "A Great Victory," the *New York Times*' "Special Correspondent" on the James River echoed Lee's own view exactly. Lee had become a southern hero, in fact *the* southern hero, eclipsing every other general, including Stonewall Jackson (whose performance in the campaign had been problematic, to put it very mildly indeed), but he been unable to strike the blow that would end the war.

In just five weeks—hardly any time to rest himself, let alone his battered army—Lee would try again, with a series of brilliant marches and assaults that would have astonished even Napoleon.

Chapter 8

Triumph and Tragedy— Second Manassas and Sharpsburg

"You must consider that no wars may be made without danger."

> —Sir Roger Williams★ to the
> Earl of Leicester, Siege of Sluys,
> 1557

N apoleon observed, "The most dangerous moment comes with victory," and history bears him out. With victory come a natural slackening of effort and a period of self-congratulation, but Lee was immune to all such temptations. He had freed Richmond, a seemingly impossible feat, but he had failed to destroy McClellan's army.

★ Sir Roger is thought by many people to have been the model for that prickly Welsh professional soldier Captain Fluellen in Shakespeare's *Henry V.*

J. E. B. Stuart, with his gift for the grand gesture even when it was inappropriate, had reached the high ground that circled the Union encampment at Harrison's Landing on July 2, but instead of riding back to let Lee know that it was still unoccupied, he had fired a single contemptuous howitzer shot into the Union camp. The Federals, alerted to his presence, drove him off, and rushed to fortify Evelington Heights with artillery and infantry, effectively preventing Lee from attacking them. He could not reach McClellan and McClellan could not reach him. By July 9 Lee was back at his headquarters in Richmond, and his army was marching back to its camps there. Only a brigade of Stuart's cavalry was left to watch over the Army of the Potomac.

Lee had to reflect on his losses. He had begun the campaign with 85,500 men. A week later over 20,000 of them were dead, wounded, or missing, a little less than a quarter of the total, with a disproportionately high number of officers among the dead—in the age when officers led their own troops into action, sword drawn, this was inevitable—who would be increasingly difficult to replace. But Lee did little to reorganize his army and nothing to expand or change his own staff. He continued to act as his own chief of staff, laboring over reports and orders whose drafting should have been left to someone else. When a senior officer had clearly failed him, like Huger or Magruder, Lee moved the man—always with infinite courtesy—either to a routine staff job or to someplace where there was no immediate prospect of serious fighting. Lee's faith in the man who had failed him the most in the campaign, Stonewall Jackson, remained undiminished. This was a "mystic bond" of personality, although in the future he would take care to give Jackson the greatest possible independence.

That Lee made little attempt to reorganize his army was not because he ignored its faults, or indeed his own or those of his staff, but because he recognized that time was his enemy. The North could quickly replace men, small arms, artillery, horses, locomotives; the South could not. Having struck a blow against McClellan, Lee had to take advantage of the fact that his adversary was for the moment stuck at Harrison's Landing to strike a blow elsewhere.

The Union divisions that Jackson had defeated in the Valley had been reinforced and formed into a new army, the Army of Virginia, under the command of Major General John Pope, who was one of the few officers of what Confederate West Pointers referred to as the "old army" and for whom Lee expressed scant regard, soon to be turned into outright contempt.

A further Federal "column" of around 18,000 men was centered on Fredericksburg under Major General Irvin McDowell, and another of 14,000 waited "on transports" off Fort Monroe, under Major General Ambrose Burnside. Lee had to consider that McDowell and Burnside could move to join McClellan and renew the attempt to take Richmond, but he seems to have concluded that McClellan was in no condition personally to launch such an ambitious scheme. Once again, Lee chose an audacious strategy. Instead of concentrating his own forces, as Johnston had always advocated, Lee warily kept his options open, waiting for Pope to show his hand. If Pope moved toward the Valley, Lee would send Jackson there; if Pope moved toward Richmond, Lee could send the rest of the Army of Northern Virginia to defend it; if Burnside attempted to join McClellan, Lee would move to prevent that. In the meantime he devoted a good deal of effort to improving and strengthening the defenses of Richmond and of Petersburg, the crucial railway junction twenty miles south of Richmond. Jackson, his health and optimism restored, wanted to advance into the north while Pope's forces were still scattered, but Lee was not tempted. There was danger in every direction he looked, and he preferred to let Pope make the first move.

Pope preceded that move by a volley of ill-chosen words, which became the source of much ridicule in the South, and confirmed Lee's personal contempt for him. Pope liked to head his orders dramatically, "Headquarters in the Saddle," which inevitably led southerners to suggest that his headquarters were where his hindquarters ought to be. His fellow Union general Fitz John Porter dismissed Pope as "an ass." Pope took command of his army with an address that offended all his officers and men, declaring that he had come to them "from the West, where we have always seen the backs of our enemies, from an army whose business it has been to seek the adversary and to beat him where he was found; whose policy has been attack and not defense," and urged them to forget about "lines of retreat," "bases of supplies," and "taking strong positions," advice which "one of his own brigadiers called . . . 'windy and insolent.'" He also infuriated Confederates with a series of draconic orders. His army was to "live off the country," seizing crops, supplies, and cattle in "secessionist territory," and he threatened to take hostages, to arrest "all male non-combatants" within the Federal lines, and to shoot anybody who communicated with the enemy—which, as somebody pointed out, could be construed to include a mother who wrote to her son. Even the usually placid Lee referred to Pope as a "miscreant."

The appointment of Major General Henry Halleck as general in chief on July 11 did not particularly concern Lee—Halleck was a competent military bureaucrat whose chief accomplishment in the West had been a sustained but in the end unsuccessful campaign to undermine the reputation of Major General Ulysses S. Grant, and whose chief gift was for backstairs intrigue against his fellow generals. Lincoln, who had appointed him in the hope that Halleck could control his generals, referred to him as "little more than a first-rate clerk." Halleck arrived in Washington on July 22, apparently in no hurry to take up his new position, but the news of his appointment was enough to further demoralize McClellan, who held Halleck in contempt and had expected to be reinstated as general in chief himself. "The President . . . has not shown the slightest gentlemanly or friendly feeling," he wrote to his wife, on learning of Halleck's promotion in the newspapers, "and I cannot regard him in any respect as my friend."

If McClellan hoped that Pope would support him in a new attack on Richmond, he would be disappointed. Pope's eyes were fixed on the Virginia Central Railroad, which ran through Gordonsville, Charlottesville, and Staunton, linking Richmond to the West. If he were successful, he would isolate Richmond and severely increase the problem of supplying Lee's

Army of Northern Virginia. Lee worried about this, especially since McDowell's line was less than thirty miles from Gordonsville, on the northernmost bend of the Virginia Central Railroad. Lee had already understood a basic fact about protecting railways: that scattering small pockets of infantry along the tracks was both ineffective and wasteful of troops.* Instead, Lee ordered Jackson to advance from Richmond to Gordonsville, to be in a position to strike hard against the flank of any force sent south to cut the railway.

Pope himself had been ordered to remain in Washington until Halleck arrived, and his army was still widely spread out. Perhaps under the circumstances it was impossible for Pope to move with any speed. He sent a cavalry brigade to cut the Virginia Central Railroad, but it was so "encumbered" with artillery and a wagon train that it was still ten miles from Gordonsville when its commander learned that Jackson had occupied the town "in considerable strength." The initial movements of the rest of Pope's army all seem to have been similarly slow and uncoordinated, as if Pope had not yet made up his mind what he intended to do with it. Through no fault

---

*This was still being ignored as late as World War I, when the Turks attempted to defend the hundreds of miles of railway that linked Damascus with Medina across the desert in exactly this way by scattering troops along it. That made it possible for T. E. Lawrence and his bedouin to ride out of the desert in 1917–1918, blow up a section of line, destroy a train, and vanish back into the desert again. As Lawrence said of the Turks guarding the railway, "They are all flanks and no front."

of his own Pope was obliged to remain in Washington while Halleck made his way slowly east.

Lee was left in an uncomfortable position. To his east McClellan's army was encamped only eighteen miles away, with 101,691 men and an enormous mass of artillery. As Lee looked toward the northwest, Pope had at least 49,000 men, spread out in a rough arc from Strasburg to Fredericksburg, and was being swiftly reinforced. Lee was thus caught between two armies. He had 69,559 men in and around Richmond, once Jackson brought two divisions, about 12,000 men, to Gordonsville. Lee might be able to count on some delay while Pope sought to reorganize his scattered army and to decide in what direction to aim, and as always Lee counted on the unlikelihood that McClellan would make a rash move. Had Lee but known it, McClellan continued to believe that he had at least 200,000 men, and to the intense annoyance of President Lincoln, did not contemplate making any move with his army until he was reinforced by 10,000 to 20,000 more men. Halleck's first job once he reached Washington was to go to Harrison's Landing and talk some sense into McClellan. On his return to Washington he told Lincoln that the Army of the Potomac should be evacuated from the peninsula and joined with Pope's. It apparently did not occur to Halleck to leave the army where it was, a mere two days' march from Richmond, and replace McClellan.

It was not in Lee's nature to adopt a defensive position and wait on events. Though the future Marshal Ferdinand Foch was only eleven years old in 1862, his famous comment on what to do when surrounded by superior forces could have served as Lee's motto: *"Mon centre cède, ma droite recule, situation excellente, j'attaque."** Lee knew that his best option was a forceful rapid attack, to exploit the gap between the two principal Union armies in Virginia. Lee would hold Richmond with the bare minimum of men needed and reinforce Jackson, in whose appetite for a daring attack he continued to believe; shatter Pope's army before it was concentrated; then bring Jackson back to join with the forces around Richmond and renew the attack on McClellan. This was bold strategic thinking, a one-two punch in which time was of the essence—only by speed and constant, unexpected maneuvering could Lee hope to defeat forces that were bigger, better equipped, and better supplied than his own. Delay would expose Richmond to attack; defeat in the field might cost the Confederacy Virginia. Lee did not hesitate.

---

* "My center is giving way, my right is retreating, situation excellent, I am attacking." Message of September 8, 1914, from General Foch to General Joffre, the French commander in chief, during a crucial day in the Battle of the Marne.

It is important to remember the pace of events: Lee had taken command of the Army of Northern Virginia on June 1, 1862; he fought his first major battle at Mechanicsville on June 26, then fought nine more battles over the next week, ending in the bloody stalemate of Malvern Hill on July 1; on July 12 he ordered Jackson with two divisions to advance on Gordonsville. There was hardly a day between June 26 and July 1 when Lee was not in the saddle, in blazing heat or pouring rain, leading what must have seemed like an endless series of attacks against a much larger foe. He gave himself ten days in which to reorganize his army, combing the eastern part of the Confederacy for reinforcements. Then on July 27 he made up his mind to stake everything on Jackson, and sent him A. P. Hill's division, masking his intention by a well-planned series of "diversion operations" aimed at Harrison's Landing. Lee did this so successfully that McClellan ordered troops and artillery back to Malvern Hill anticipating a major battle there, while all the time the bulk of Lee's strength was being quietly shifted sixty miles to the northwest, in the shadow of the Blue Ridge Mountains. No poker player could have played a cooler hand.

He incorporated two brigades from North Carolina into his own army, and took the risk of sending A. P. Hill and his division to join Jackson. This was a considerable gamble. It stripped Lee of a first-rate, battle-tested division, and he knew that A. P. Hill and Jackson were like oil and water. Hill "was high spirited, impetuous and proud," an aristocrat who brought out the worst in Jackson, who could be surly, impatient, and stern. The two men had disliked each other since they were West Point cadets, when Hill had been something of a rake and had made fun of Jackson's backwoods ways. Jackson's repeated failure to reach the battlefield on time during the Seven Days campaign had further inflamed Hill's dislike, so putting him under Jackson's command was a calculated risk on Lee's part, and came about only because Lee could not at first part with Longstreet.

He did, however, write tactfully to Jackson, suggesting how to handle A. P. Hill, but in fact it is a good example of his reluctance to knock heads together where his generals were concerned. He still had not confronted Jackson over the latter's repeated failures during the Seven Days campaign, and he did not now order him to put aside whatever animosity he might feel toward Hill. "A. P. Hill you will find a good officer," Lee wrote hopefully, as if the two had never met, "with whom you can consult, and by advising your division commanders as to your movements much trouble will be saved you in arranging details, as they can act more intelligently. I wish to save you trouble from my increasing your command." This was at once sensible advice and wishful thinking. Jackson was a genius, but a moody and erratic one, and secrecy was a part of his nature. He despised "councils of war," expected his orders to be instantly obeyed without questions, and seldom consulted anyone except Lee himself. "None of his Division commanders were informed of his intentions." General William B. Taliaferro would later complain, "and it was a source of much annoyance to them to be ordered blindly to move without knowing whither, or to what purpose." Lee's attempt to correct this problem was so politely phrased as to be worthless, and had no effect on Jackson, whose suspicion of A. P. Hill remained as strong as ever.

Just as Lee's grand strategy depended on keeping the Union armies separated, advancing between them, and attacking whichever seemed the weakest, so his plan for Jackson depended on the latter's ability to maneuver and defeat parts of Pope's army before Pope could concentrate them. Lee comes in for criticism from military historians for not enlarging his staff, for not providing an adequate supply of up-to-date maps, and for many of the other deficiencies in the Army of Northern Virginia, but these failings must be placed in the context of his realistic appreciation of the situation facing the Confederacy.

His greatest enemy was time. The Union's armies could be reinforced, enlarged, and supplied almost at will, but the armies of the Confederacy were already stretched to the limit. The only way Lee could win—even if "winning" merely meant forcing the North to sit down at the negotiation table—was to strike hard again and again, before he was overwhelmed by sheer numbers. "We cannot afford to be idle," he wrote. There was no time to perfect his army, even had there existed the resources with which to do it. From mid-July on he would set the Army of Northern Virginia in motion to fight a whirlwind succession of major battles one after the other, with little or no time for rest. Because the distances involved were not enormous—Lee's battles all took place in a relatively small half circle with a radius of less than 100 miles drawn from the northeast to the southwest around Washington, most of them close to each other, several of them fought in the same place—Lee had admittedly none of the long-distance logistical problems that Napoleon had to contend with (one thinks of the Egyptian or the Russian campaign, for instance). Also, most of Lee's battles were fought in places where the local population was all or partly Confederate in sympathy (Gettysburg is the notable exception); but as one looks at the dates it is still an extraordinary achievement.

The problem of maps would soon be soon be helped by Jackson's gifted topographer Jedediah Hotchkiss; the greater problem of finding food and forage would be solved by keeping the army on the move before it laid waste to the area around it—a partial explanation for Lee's forays into Maryland and Pennsylvania. Although Lee deplored the "miscreant" Pope's order to seize food and forage from civilians in Confederate territory, and insisted that his own quartermasters pay for supplies, it is only fair to note that they paid in Confederate dollars, which were declining in value inside the Confederacy and worthless outside it.

Lee's grasp of the strategic opportunities (and the dangers) of his position was immediate. With a Union army of over 90,000 men only a few miles from Richmond, he could make no move until he was certain that McClellan would not take the initiative. At the same time, to remain on the defensive was to invite attack. He shrewdly realized that the Federals suffered from one major weakness—Lincoln's fear of a Confederate attack on Washington. Even a successful "raid" on Washington would constitute a political disaster. Any Confederate move in the direction of Washington would cause Lincoln to reinforce the Union forces south of the Potomac immediately. As if in a chess game, Lee could rely on Lincoln's instinctive countermove to any move he made in force toward Washington. This would remain the core of Lee's strategy until May 1864, when Grant crossed the Rapidan and at last put him on the defensive.* Lee did not expect to take Washington— only a disaster of unimaginable proportions to the Union armies could make that possible—but he understood that the best way of protecting Richmond and northern Virginia was to threaten the Federal capital. Lee had not the troops to defend Richmond and the Valley, and in any case he always remained conscious of Frederick the Great's famous maxim. "He who attempts to defend everything, defends nothing"; but he had enough men to mount a serious attack toward Washington, and could count on the fact that much of McClellan's army would be shifted to its defense the moment Confederate forces advanced to cross the Rappahannock and threaten Pope's lines of communication. Lee's dislike of Pope was visceral—his order to Jackson of July 27, along with his decision to send him A. P. Hill's division plus a brigade of Louisiana Volunteers, comprising all told more than 18,000 men, contains the interesting (and for Lee, unusual) instruc-

---

*As late as July 1864 the rough-hewn, irrepressible Lieutenant General Jubal A. Early managed to attack the outskirts of Washington, and Lincoln came out to see the fighting, exposing himself to Confederate fire. Early himself commented to an aide as he withdrew back into the Valley, "Well, Major, we haven't taken Washington, but we scared Abe Lincoln like hell," which just about sums up Lee's strategy.

tion, "I want Pope to be suppressed." It was rare for Lee to refer to an enemy general and fellow West Pointer as if he were vermin, but Pope's bullying orders about the treatment of Confederate civilians offended all that was most chivalrous in Lee's nature. He not only wanted Pope "suppressed"; he knew that Jackson was exactly the right man to do it.

At the same time Lee simplified the composition of the Army of Northern Virginia by dividing it effectively into two "wings": the "right wing" under the command of Longstreet, the "left wing" under the command of Jackson. Longstreet's sparring with McClellan's army around Harrison's Landing persuaded Lee that he had less to fear there than he had initially assumed, although he continued to worry that McClellan might take advantage of Union naval strength to cross to the southern bank of the James and advance toward Richmond via Petersburg. He also worried that Burnside might succeed in joining his force to that already at Harrison's Landing, giving McClellan more than enough men to resume his siege of Richmond. Despite these concerns, Lee moved quickly and boldy with his plan for Jackson to "strike [his] blow."

Major Walter Taylor, Lee's "indispensable" aide, was perhaps closest to the mind and thoughts of the man he sometimes referred to as "the Tycoon" during the two weeks when Lee prepared for a campaign that would at once "suppress Pope" and remove McClellan's army from the peninsula altogether. "It required great confidence in his own judgment," Taylor wrote, "to carry out a campaign apparently so bold and fraught with such possibilities to the enemy, should events prove that the estimate put upon their sagacity was at fault. It required, also, great confidence in his lieutenants and his troops to place them where the odds would be greatly against them, and where courage and endurance of the highest order would be required to assure success." Lee had at his back over 100,000 Union troops and faced an adversary with over 43,000 men, against both of which he had only 65,000 men to secure Richmond and threaten Washington; but he still seized the initiative. On July 13 he ordered Jackson to advance twenty miles northwest following roughly the path of the Virginia Central Railroad to Louisa Court House and "if practicable to Gordonsville, there to oppose the reported advance of the enemy from the direction of Orange Court-House."

On July 18 Lee ordered J. E. B. Stuart "to send some cavalry at least as far north as Hanover Junction," and to send scouts close enough to Fredericksburg to ascertain Pope's "intention, strength, &c." Typically, Lee urged Stuart: "Endeavor to spare your horses as much as possible, and charge your officers to look to their comfort and that of the men."

He could not have picked two generals better suited to what he had in mind than Jackson and Stuart, both of whom were aggressive and fearless and had an intuitive grasp of Lee's intentions. By July 25 it was clear to Jackson that Pope's army was still divided into two parts: the right wing advancing south toward Gordonsville and the left, under McDowell, preparing to cross the Rappahannock. Jackson knew that he had to strike Pope's right before McDowell could join it.

He paused briefly at his new "headquarters in the grove of an old church in Louisa County" to integrate the reinforcements Lee had sent him into his small army—Lee's good advice had not changed Jackson's mind about A. P. Hill, or Hill's about Jackson—which now had a total of almost 24,000 men (variously overestimated by Pope as somewhere between 35,000 and 60,000). On August 2 Jackson's cavalry fought an unsuccessful engagement with Federal troopers in the normally quiet streets of Orange Court House, as a result of which Jackson vigorously campaigned to replace his cavalry commander, but Lee was not convinced. Jackson's unforgiving nature created what seems to have been an inordinate number of personnel problems and courts-martial that increased the amount of paperwork with which Lee had to deal.

Perhaps because of the great importance of "honor," and the Cavalier self-image prevalent among the senior officers of the Army of Northern Virginia Lee had an unusual number of such headaches to deal with. As Jackson prepared to attack Pope, he was busy with two courts-martial of senior officers. One of them, Brigadier General Richard S. Garnett survived the proceeding only to be killed leading his brigade in Pickett's Charge at Gettysburg. Jackson would probably have started court-martial proceedings against his cavalry commander had Lee let him. For that matter General A. P. Hill had been under arrest after a quarrel with General Longstreet when Lee sent him and his division off to join Jackson. Courts-martial, arrests, and threats of duels were a constant distraction to Lee, but he usually handled them deftly and with great, though weary, patience.

On August 7 General Garnett's court-martial was interrupted by the news that one of Pope's divisions—that of Major General Nathaniel P. Banks— had advanced to Culpeper Court House, less than twenty miles away. This was exactly the news for which Lee and Jackson had been waiting. It was Jackson's intention to attack Pope's army before it was concentrated, and here a part of it was moving straight toward him unsupported, commanded by the man he had defeated less than four months ago at Winchester.

Lee wrote to Jackson expressing his confidence—"Being on the spot you must determine what force to operate against," he wrote on August 7, and urged him to "turn the enemy's position" rather than attack frontally. Lee finished by writing, "I must now leave the matter to your reflection and good judgment. Make up your mind what is best to be done under all the circumstances which surround us." It is very clear that Lee's mind had already moved beyond the immediate possibilities of an attack by Jackson on Pope's right. He had already been warned by an exchanged Confederate prisoner of war—none other than the future (and notorious) guerrilla leader John S. Mosby—that Burnside's men were being moved from Fort Monroe to Fredericksburg to reinforce Pope's army. Lee concluded from this, and from Stuart's vigilant cavalry scouts around Fredericksburg, that far from ordering McClellan to attack Richmond, Lincoln and Halleck had decided to unite his army with Pope's and attempt to take Richmond from the northwest. The threat was no longer from Harrison's Landing but from the direction of Fredericksburg. Lee decided that the focus of the war was shifting from the peninsula to northern Virginia, and from the James River to the Rappahannock. He not only saw an opportunity for Jackson to carry out a series of bold flank attacks against the right of Pope's army as it advanced, but also the more dramatic opportunity to shift Longstreet's forces from the peninsula to join with Jackson before McClellan's army could unite with Pope's, and to deliver an unexpected and annihilating blow at the Union army.

On August 5 Stuart fought a brilliant little cavalry action at Massaponax Church, less than five miles south of Fredericksburg—in the course of which he cut off the baggage train of two Union brigades and captured enough prisoners to complain to Lee that they were "already thronging in my presence." Some of the Union prisoners seem to have been more than willing to tell Stuart that General Burnside's 14,000 men had already reached Fredericksburg; this gave Lee the final confirmation he needed. If he moved swiftly and boldly he might not only stop Pope in his tracks, but also put the Army of Northern Virginia between Pope and Washington, forcing Pope to fight a battle on ground of Lee's own choosing, and relieving the threat to Richmond at the same time. Bit by bit, he began the process of preparing to move his army to the other side of Richmond. D. H. Hill was told to be ready to move quickly. John Bell Hood, Lee's young riding companion in Texas, now a brigadier general, was ordered to Hanover Junction, where he could protect both the Virginia Central and the

Richmond, Fredericksburg, and Potomac railroads, and join Jackson if need be. The Army of Northern Virginia was being shifted westward in steps too small to attract Pope's attention.

In the meantime, Jackson was marching his army north to meet the enemy—it was not so much a well-thought-out plan on either side as a collision. Jackson's 24,000 men were marching in brutal, pitiless heat and dust. As usual he had not shared his intentions with any of his senior officers, nor did he have any fancy maneuvering in mind this time. Word had reached him that Pope had ordered General Banks to advance south toward Gordonsville, and Jackson planned to meet him on the way and fight him when he encountered him, and that was that.

Pope, who seems to have misjudged Jackson's character, assumed that he was retreating. In fact, Jackson was moving as fast as he could, hoping to overwhelm a portion of Pope's army while it was isolated and exposed. Despite his secretive and sometimes difficult character, Jackson had one great advantage—when he wanted, he could read Lee's mind. Just over fifty years later, when General Joffre was asked how he proposed to defeat the larger and rapidly advancing German army at the Marne in 1914, he replied, *"Je les grignote."* ("I am nibbling away at them.") In this way

Joffre succeeded in stopping the Germans virtually at the gates of Paris by inflicting on them a constant rate of loss they could not support, and depriving them of the opportunity to concentrate their forces. This was Lee's idea too: that Jackson should attack isolated parts of Pope's army with superior numbers, rather than risk a single decisive battle.

This time Jackson once again had the services of his cartographer Captain Hotchkiss, who managed to find routes for the march along obscure, unnamed country roads. Under a blazing sun—the temperature during the day never dropped below ninety degrees—and amid clouds of choking dust Jackson's troops managed to cover only eight miles on the first day. Neither the soldiers nor their senior commanders had any idea where they were going except toward the next low, rolling hill in front of them.

They reached Orange Court House by nightfall, and at "earliest dawn" resumed their march, on a day that would reach ninety-six degrees. During the night Jackson had changed his mind about the order of march, sending Ewell, whose division had been in the lead, to a different route via Liberty Mills without informing A. P. Hill. The resulting confusion (and vivid resentment on A. P. Hill's part) and the intense heat caused a lot of straggling, and immense suffering for the animals, and slowed the progress of the army to a crawl. Worse still, while a seething Hill struggled to make sense of his orders, Jackson's old division, meant to be the last in line, got ahead of him, with the result that "nightfall found the Confederate army spread out over parts of three counties," only fifteen miles from Culpeper, but hopelessly unconcentrated. From the standpoint of military orthodoxy, it made sense to advance the army by parallel routes, rather than trying to cram them along one narrow road—but by neglecting to inform A. P. Hill of his decision Jackson almost ensured that his three divisions would all meet the enemy at different times and places, with no way of communicating with each other. By now the element of surprise had been lost. Banks knew perfectly well that Jackson was advancing toward him, and was preparing to meet him on a line almost a mile and a half long drawn perpendicularly across the main road just a mile and a half northwest of Cedar Mountain, the most prominent feature of the landscape ahead of Jackson. Cedar Mountain (also called, less promisingly, Slaughter's Mountain by the locals, after the family who lived closest to it) was not really a mountain, but a broad, kidney-shaped wooded hill, less than 300 feet high. It was girdled to the north by a fordable stream, the south fork of Cedar Run, and overlooked the main road to Culpeper. Hotchkiss's map of the area is wonderfully clear, but it was made a year after the battle, allowing for twenty-twenty hindsight. At the time, it was much less clear to Jackson what the countryside ahead of him looked like, and the one man who could tell him was A. P. Hill, a Culpeper boy, with whom Jackson had already had harsh words that day, and whose advice Jackson was unlikely to seek.

The Reverend Major Dabney, Stonewall Jackson's faithful former chief of staff, describes the area between Orange and Culpeper as "a region of pleasant farms, of hills and dales, and of forests interspersed," which is no doubt accurate enough, but fails to mention the phenomenal heat. On August 9 Jackson had his army moving north toward Culpeper well before dawn on a day "that must have been one hundred degrees in the shade," according to one soldier. Around eleven o'clock in the morning Federal cavalry were seen on a long, low ridge to the west of Cedar Mountain, shimmering in the heat haze, and signaling the presence nearby of General Banks's corps. Jackson saw at once the importance of getting some of his artillery onto higher ground on the northern slope of Cedar Mountain, which turned out to be steeper and more difficult to approach than it had looked from a distance, but by 1:00 p.m. his gunners had succeeded, and a fierce artillery duel was under way. Confederate troops began to form a rough-and-ready crescent-shaped line to the left of Cedar Mountain, on the open ground of a cornfield and an adjoining a field of stubble, although Hill's division was still miles away thanks to Jackson's decision to change the order of march.

At this moment Jackson paused to play with some children in the yard of a nearby farmhouse and then stretch out on its porch for a nap. Even his admiring biographer James I. Robertson Jr. finds this odd, but the truth is that Jackson seems to have shared Napoleon's gift for taking a catnap in the middle of a battle. Mrs. Petty's modest farmhouse was a mile away from the traffic jam of wagons and artillery that was holding up the arrival of Hill's division, and less than two miles from where those of his infantry brigades which had arrived on the field were deploying, and until something happened Jackson was as well off dozing on her porch as else-where.

By early afternoon the artillery duel had become one of the most intense of the war so far, audible as far away as Richmond, according to some; and Jackson rode to the center of it to watch calmly, binoculars in hand, one leg out of the stirrup and thrown across the pommel of his saddle as if he were sitting in a chair, until a Federal infantry charge threatened to engulf him. As with most great commanders, Jackson's calm in the middle of chaos and carnage set a stern example for his troops. After an afternoon of hard fighting and constant shelling, it seemed only too likely that by six o'clock Jackson's left would be overwhelmed, and his forces driven from the field. Jackson knew that there was a moment in battle when calmness will no longer suffice—he put his spurs to Little Sorrel and galloped straight to the left, where the fighting was fiercest and the Confederate line was collapsing, the fields and woodland "filled with clamor and horrid rout," as Dabney puts it. He reached for his saber to rally the men, only to find he had drawn it so seldom that it was rusted firmly into the scabbard. Undeterred, Jackson unfastened sword and scabbard from his belt, and brandishing both over his head with one hand, he grabbed a Confederate battle flag with the other and charged into the thick of the fight shouting at his troops to follow him, "in a voice which pealed higher than the roar of battle. 'Rally, brave men, and press forward! Your general will lead you. Jackson will lead you. Follow me!'" These may not have been his exact words—Dabney was not present at the battle and was writing a year after Jackson's death—but whatever Jackson shouted, the sight of him capless (his stained old VMI cap had caught on a low branch) and looking like an Old Testament prophet, "his face flaming with the inspiration of battle," charging directly toward the Federal line, was enough to make his troops follow him at a run. They deployed quickly behind a fence and fired a volley at point-blank range into the oncoming Federal ranks with withering effect.

Even Jackson's flamboyant charge might not have saved the day, if it had not coincided with A. P. Hill's arrival with his division. From that point on until darkness the battle continued, but Jackson by now had all his troops on the field—"his blood was up; and he delivered blow after blow from his insulted left wing, with stunning rapidity and regulated fury"—while Hill's division advanced on the right, close to Cedar Mountain, to turn the Federal left.

The fighting went on into the night until eleven o'clock. Jackson was determined to reach Culpeper, seize Pope's supplies, and interrupt his major line of communication, the Orange and Alexandria Railroad. But the troops were too exhausted to continue the pursuit, and information from prisoners and Jackson's own cavalry soon made it evident that Major General Franz Siegel's Union corps was close behind Banks. With two Federal corps uniting in front of him Jackson's opportunity for isolating and destroying them one by one was gone. He halted his army along a line just a mile or two north of the battlefield. Impulsive as Jackson could be, he was a thoroughly professional soldier, willing to fight when the odds were against him, but realistic when they appeared overwhelming. He consolidated his line and on August 11, two days after the battle, agreed to a truce to allow the Federals to bury their dead. Jackson took advantage of the lull to start moving the bulk of his army back in an orderly fashion toward Gordonsville. Employing an old ruse, he lit campfires in the dark "as if the troops were preparing their evening meal." Jackson had inflicted 2,353 casualties on Banks, for a total of 1,338 himself,* a victory if one counted the numbers, but not the victory he had wanted.

All the same, it was a vital turning point. From Washington, Halleck urged caution on Pope—who one would have thought was exceeded in that respect only by McClellan. Pope's full attention remained fixed on Jackson. Perhaps even more important, Jackson's victory at Cedar Mountain raised southerners' spirits, and undermined Pope's fragile self-confidence. Like McClellan, he thought himself outnumbered and clamored for reinforcements. Burnside was dispatched to join Pope, and the process of moving McClellan's army from Harrison's Landing to northern Virginia

---

*Banks had 314 killed, 1,445 wounded, and 594 missing; Jackson, 231 killed and 1,107 wounded. Jackson also took over 5,000 Federal muskets, abandoned on the field.

was accelerated. No one in Washington looked toward the Blue Ridge Mountains, where Lee quietly began to move Longstreet's forces to join with Jackson. He was determined to concentrate the Army of Northern Virginia before McClellan arrived to join his army to Pope's.

On August 15, the most significant military movement of all took place. Robert E. Lee arrived by train in Gordonsville to confer with Jackson, Longstreet, and Stuart, and to take personal command of the army.

The flurry of orders Lee sent from Richmond between hearing of Jackson's victory at Cedar Mountain on August 10 and departing with his staff for Gordonsville demonstrates his single-minded grasp of the strategic situation, and his determination to move with all possible speed, before the addition of McClellan's army to Pope's made the Federal forces outside Washington too numerous for him to be able to defeat. His "window of opportunity" was narrow, and he knew it.

We do not know if Lee left Richmond with relief at returning "to the field." He and his staff had been quartered at the Dabbs house on Nine Mile Road again since the Battle of Malvern Hill, far enough from the center of Richmond to be spared the epidemic of illness that the heat and the large number of wounded inevitably produced. Malaria, typhoid fever, and dysentery were rampant, and almost every house and public building had its quota of sick and wounded. In her book about the Lee daughters, *The Lee Girls,* Mary Coulling quotes a vivid description of Richmond as "one immense hospital' where citizens 'breathed the vapors of the charnel house," which was surely no exaggeration. The "Seven Days" battles had produced nearly 16,000 Confederate wounded alone. Ignoring her husband's sensible advice as usual, Mary Lee had returned from the North Carolina spa where her little grandson Rob had died of pneumonia. Both Mrs. Lee and her daughter Mary, like most of the ladies of Richmond, devoted themselves to nursing, which in the days before antiseptics and modern plumbing was almost as dangerous as the battlefield. In addition to looking after Rooney's grief-stricken wife, Charlotte, who had lost both her infant son and her home, which had been burned to the ground by Union troops, Mary looked after her oldest son, Custis, who lay dangerously ill in Richmond. For a man whose chief joy lay in his family, Lee found himself in 1862 without a home to call his own, and with most of his children scattered and many of them exposed to danger. Custis was serving as an aide-de-camp to President Jefferson Davis; Rooney was a colonel, who would soon be promoted to command his own brigade of cavalry under J. E. B. Stuart; young Rob was serving as a gunner in Stonewall Jackson's army; Annie, Agnes, and Mildred remained for the moment in North Carolina. "He was the same loving father to us all, as kind and thoughtful of my mother, who was an invalid, and of us, his children, as if our comfort and happiness were all he had to care for," Rob notes, adding that his father's victories "did not elate him"—hardly surprisingly, since Lee still reproached himself for not destroying McClellan's army at Malvern Hill.

Mrs. Lee cannot have been cheered by a letter her cousin Markie Williams managed to send "through the lines" about another "sad" visit Markie had paid to Arlington. She told Mrs. Lee that the wife of the Union general occupying the mansion was using her room downstairs as the parlor, and enclosed a pressed leaf from the garden, cut for Mary by one of her own slaves. As soon as Mary Lee could leave Custis, she traveled to Hickory Hill, the 3,000-acre plantation of the Wickham family, in Ashland, about twenty miles north of Richmond, remaining there despite the urgings of her husband to move farther south, away from the fighting. No doubt the plantation life appealed to her; its rhythms would have been familiar and soothing. War had scarcely touched Hickory Hill, though

Stonewall Jackson had marched his army close to it on his way to Mechanicsville, and all around it lay the charred remains of other great houses she had known and visited so often before the war: her father's own White House, where George Washington had once decorously wooed Martha Washington, had been burned to the ground by Federal troops, and only the chimneys were still standing; the Carter family home, the "Great House," at Shirley, where Robert E. Lee's mother had been born, where she had married Light-Horse Harry Lee, and where Rooney had married Charlotte in 1859, still stood, but had been "plundered" and looted by Federal soldiers. A whole way of life was disintegrating under the pressure of war. Union armies were still too close to Hickory Hill for her husband's comfort, and Lee worried about Mary constantly, but neither he nor the possibility of being captured again by the enemy would persuade her to move until she was good and ready.

Lee did not stay long in Gordonsville—just long enough, in fact, for an afternoon council of war with generals Longstreet and Jackson, in which he played a tactful and conciliatory role, since the two men seem to have disliked each other, perhaps because of Jackson's poor performance during the Seven Days battles. At issue was Jackson's desire to attack Pope at once—he urged an attack in two days' time—while Longstreet argued for a delay long enough to let him bring up the rest of his troops, who were still spread out along the roads and unprovisioned with bread. Lee himself was in favor of an immediate attack, favoring Jackson's opinion, but doubted the cavalry could be brought up in time. Stuart, who was present, would hardly have expressed any concern about the time it would take to bring up his cavalry unless it was realistic, so it was not just Longstreet who was urging a delay on Lee, although after 1865 it became usual among historians in the South to blame Longstreet for anything that went wrong in the Army of Northern Virginia. It is hard to gauge the intensity of the disagreement between the commanders of Lee's "left wing" and his "right wing," and it is possible, even likely, that both of them controlled themselves in Lee's presence; he was not a man who relished noisy arguments, after all. But a noted biographer of Jackson, James L. Robertson Jr., quotes one witness who claims to have seen Jackson leave the meeting and lie down on the ground under a tree groaning "most audibly," prompting Longstreet to complain to Lee that this demonstration was "disrespectful." Certainly, if the account is true, it must have seemed a dramatic show of disapproval for such a normally taciturn man as Jackson to have made.

Lee's strategy depended on speed. He had already informed Longstreet the day before leaving Richmond that "it is all-important that our movement, in whatever direction it is determined, should be as quick as possible." It may well have been galling to him that just as Pope was almost within his reach he was obliged to mark time, but Lee was a professional soldier who respected facts, however unwelcome.

To understand Lee's preoccupation with his cavalry, it is important to realize how ambitious his strategic aim was. On the peninsula the terrain offered little opportunity for maneuver, since everywhere progress was slowed by dense growth, swamps, and intertwining streams, but north of Gordonsville "were long, low ridges, covered with grass or growing crops and broken here and there by rounded eminences, exalted with the name of mountains." In other words, the country before Lee was lightly settled farmland, with good roads, plentiful supplies, and a network of small towns. To the west, the gentle, densely wooded Blue Ridge Mountains, bisected by all-important "gaps" permitting passage of an army, separated the Piedmont from the Shenandoah Valley. To the east there was a series of small prosperous towns, linked by good roads and by the Orange and Alexandria Railroad, leading eighty miles northeast to Washington.

Apart from the railroad, which was Pope's principal line of communication, the two major features were the Rapidan and the Rappahannock rivers, which ran west-east at right angles to the railway, and formed a rough V turned on its side (>). The two rivers were twenty miles apart at the wide end of the > and joined together about ten miles west of Fredericksburg, forming an area shaped like a slice of pie.

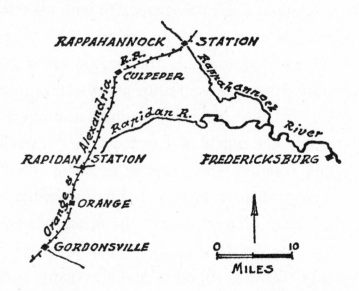

14. *The junction of the Rappahannock and Rapidan rivers.*

Pope had incautiously allowed his army of 60,000 to 70,000 men to concentrate "within the 'V' between the two rivers," a situation made more perilous by the fact that there was only one major bridge over the Rappahannock in the immediate area. If Stuart's cavalry could ride around Pope's army and destroy the bridge at Rappahannock Station, a vigorous attack on Pope's left might cut off him off from being reinforced by McClellan through Fredericksburg and trap him between the two rivers.* Lee could effectively annihilate Pope's army before McClellan's could be brought from the peninsula to join with it—just the decisive victory Lee had failed to achieve over McClellan at Malvern Hill. Lee had 55,000 men, enough to do the job if he struck before Pope and McClellan joined. Here was a window of opportunity if ever there was one, but it would be open only briefly. Jackson was right—an immediate attack was Lee's best opportunity for a victory, but in order to annihilate Pope, Lee would have to wait until Stuart could destroy the vital Rappahannock Station bridge.

And there was the rub: not Longstreet's caution, but the fact that Stuart had only one brigade of cavalry. The rest of his division had been left behind in Richmond; its horses were tired and in desperate need of rest. Lee had foreseen this. "Endeavour to spare your horses as much as possible," he had written to Stuart on July 18, almost a month ago—but the rigors of the war and

---

*Longstreet had proposed attacking Pope's right, at the wide end of the >, but Lee's first priority was to make sure that Pope and McClellan were kept separated. Longstreet did not react as demonstratively as Jackson to having his advice rejected, but like an elephant, he never forgot.

the intense heat had, as always, a greater effect on the horses than on the men, and horses, unlike men, could be pushed only so far before they broke down, and were not spurred on by patriotic sentiment or eagerness for victory. All, therefore, depended on the brigade's commander, Lee's nephew Fitzhugh Lee, a former instructor of cavalry tactics at West Point.* Fitzhugh Lee was cast in the same mold as J. E. B. Stuart—a daring, dashing, high-spirited, fiercely bearded Cavalier—but there is some doubt whether he had been informed that his uncle's whole plan hinged on the speed of his advance.

Stuart had ordered Fitzhugh Lee to advance with his brigade from Beaver Dam, where he was bivouacked, to Raccoon Ford on the Rapidan, a march of sixty-two miles to join Stuart. This would have been a severe challenge for his horses to make in two days. The Rapidan, more so than the Rappahannock, was a river with shallow banks and many well-marked fords at this time of year; most of the fords were shingle and offered an easy crossing to horses and artillery, though infantrymen were likely to have to wade through knee- or waist-high water. As it was, Fitzhugh Lee added to the length of his journey by making a detour to Louisa

---

* And a future major general in the Spanish-American War.

Court House to feed his men and horses and replenish his ammunition—a sensible decision, but one which would seem to indicate that Stuart had failed to impress on him the need to reach Raccoon Ford by the evening of August 17.

This would become one of the more contentious questions about the war. Longstreet would later claim that the war was lost by Fitzhugh Lee's failure to have his brigade in position in time, but by then Longstreet himself had become perhaps the most contentious subject of all. It seems more likely that Fitzhugh Lee had no idea that Lee proposed to attack on August 18, let alone that this attack depended on him. Longstreet censured him in extreme terms, calling the detour "a pleasure ride" and going so far as to write that Fitzhugh Lee "lost the fruits of our summer's work, and lost the Southern cause." In any case Stuart does not seem to have held it against him in the future; Fitzhugh Lee retained his command, and the two men remained friends, even though Fitzhugh Lee's failure to arrive on time was to put Stuart himself in danger.

Stuart had taken command of Jackson's cavalry, amounting to at least another brigade; and Jackson raised no objection, since he had no faith in his own cavalry commander, Brigadier General Beverly Robertson, and had been trying to replace him since the beginning of August, although Lee, deluged with other personnel problems and several courts-martial, had declined to do so. Placing all the cavalry, including Robertson's brigade, under Stuart, was a sensible move on the face of it, but also typical of the kind of compromise Lee often made to solve such problems— Jackson was partially satisfied, and Lee did not have to deal with the unpleasantness of removing Robertson from his command.

On August 17 Stuart rode east from Orange to Verdiersville, a sleepy hamlet a few miles south of Raccoon Ford, where he expected to find Fitzhugh Lee's brigade waiting for him, but there was no trace of it. A cavalry brigade is not easy to miss in comparatively open country, but none of the locals had seen it either, so Stuart sent one of his officers (a major confusingly named Norman Fitzhugh) to search for it, and settled down for the night on the porch of a house. At first light on August 18 he was woken by the "clatter of hooves" and the jingling of bridle chains, clearly signaling the arrival of cavalry, but as he rose from his makeshift bed he heard a voice cry out that it was "Yankee cavalry." Shots rang out, and Stuart quickly mounted his horse, jumped a fence, and—hotly pursued by Federal cavalrymen—galloped into the woods, followed by his staff. The Federals captured Stuart's famous plumed hat and his silk-lined cloak, a loss that he deeply resented; more important, they also captured Major Norman Fitzhugh, who had returned from his vain hunt for Fitzhugh Lee just in time to witness his commander's bold escape. Norman Fitzhugh had on his person a copy of Lee's orders for the attack, so by August 18 Lee's plan was in Pope's hands.*

Lee had already postponed the attack to August 20, with great regret, since it was clear that Fitzhugh Lee's horses would need a day of rest once they actually arrived, but by that time it was too late. Pope was perhaps not the brightest of the Union generals, but once he had read Lee's orders he was quick enough to see that he had fallen into a trap. By the early afternoon on August 18 he was already beginning to withdraw his army to the north of the Rappahannock. Lee and Longstreet rode together to the summit of Clark's Mountain, a large wooded hill just over 1,000 feet high with a spectacular view from the summit toward the northeast, in the late afternoon of August 19, only to see the last of Pope's tents being struck and his rear guard marching toward the Rappahannock, bayonets glinting as they "melted into the bright haze of the afternoon sun,"

---

*Responsibility for leaving Raccoon Ford unguarded fell on Brigadier General Robert Toombs—a vigorous and outspoken critic of President Davis, a successful lawyer, but an amateur soldier. Toombs had countermanded Longstreet's orders and removed the guard, apparently determined to demonstrate his own authority over his men.

and out of Lee's trap. "General," Lee said, according to Longstreet, "we little thought that the enemy would turn his back upon us this early in the campaign."*

One mark of great generalship is the ability to turn on a dime when your plans fail. Lee now faced the problem of what Pope would do next. If Pope turned east he might get between Lee and Richmond, and at the same time join with McClellan's army. If he turned west, he might succeed in recrossing the Rappahannock farther upstream and turning Lee's left.

Clearly, Lee now had to pursue Pope and bring him to bay before McClellan joined him to form an army of some 120,000 men. Early on the morning of August 20 Lee's entire army crossed the Rapidan unopposed over its many fords, "a sight worth seeing," as one soldier observed: 54,500 men in all, including the cavalry— Jackson, with Stuart's cavalry, forming the left; and Longstreet, with Fitzhugh Lee's brigade of cavalry, forming the right. Lee was still determined to fight Pope before he and McClellan could unite, and seems at first to believe that Pope would move east toward

---

*There is no guarantee that these are Lee's exact words. Longstreet was writing many years after the event, and by that time he had become the bête noire of many of Lee's most fervent admirers, and the person responsible, in the minds of many former Confederates, for Lee's defeat at Gettysburg. All the same, it has the formal ring of something Lee might have said, and certainly expresses what must have been his disappointment.

Fredericksburg. Instead Pope began to extend his line toward the west, covering the Rappahannock and moving toward Warrenton, as if he were trying to draw Lee farther and farther from Richmond. Through August 21 and 22 Lee rapidly moved his army upstream from ford to ford along the Rappahannock, from Kelly's Ford to Beverley Ford, looking for a place to cross in force, while Pope ably checked his every move. Late on August 22, Jackson at last managed to get a substantial force across the river at Sulphur Springs Ford, about ten miles north of Rappahannock Station, well beyond the right of Pope's army. Lee sent Stuart with 1,500 horsemen, including the Ninth Virginia, led by Lee's son Rooney, on a daring raid around the Union right all the way to Warrenton, hoping to destroy one of the small railroad bridges at Cattlett's Station, almost twelve miles behind the Union columns along the Rappahannock, and cut off Pope's supply line. Stuart did not arrive at Cattlett's Station until that night, in the middle of a pouring rainstorm that made it impossible to set fire to the timbers of the bridge. His troopers did little damage to it with axes, but it turned out that Stuart had stumbled across General Pope's headquarters. Stuart cut telegraph lines: captured 300 prisoners; perhaps more important, took Pope's dispatch book; and also took—surely a balm to

Stuart's bruised pride—Pope's best uniform coat, as well as his hat. Fitzhugh Lee came very close to capturing his own cousin Colonel Louis Marshall, the son of Lee's beloved sister Anne in Baltimore. Marshall, who was serving on Pope's staff, saved himself at the last moment "by rushing out the rear of his tent, leaving his toddy untouched." Writing about Louis Marshall to Mary, Lee commented, "I am sorry he is in such bad company, but I suppose he could not help it." Stuart was so pleased by his exploit that he sent Pope a letter under a flag of truce offering to return Pope's dress coat in return for his own plumed hat, but Pope does not appear to have shared Stuart's high-spirited sense of humor.

The heavy rain raised the water level of the river instantly—one big storm was all it took to make the fords impassible—and when Stuart arrived back at Sulphur Springs Ford he found that Jackson's engineers were rebuilding a bridge burned by the Federals to "extricate" the forces he had sent across the previous day.

By August 23 Lee had most of Pope's papers in his hands; these gave the exact number of Pope's men and his artillery, and made it clear that Pope's plan was to preserve his line on the Rappahannock until McClellan and his army could advance to Fredericksburg and join him. This was something less than a daring strategy on Pope's part—in effect, he was planning to mark time in place until McClellan, not normally a bold or fast mover himself, arrived. Lee again saw that it was a race for time between himself and McClellan. There was an opportunity, a fleeting one, to defeat Pope, then turn on McClellan, and thereby gain the "annihilating" victory that was, in Lee's view, the only way to win the war.

Because the South eventually lost the war, and because Lee's defeat on the third day of Gettysburg now seems to many people in both the South and the North to have ended the last chance of a Confederate victory, Lee's generalship has been a controversial subject for a century and a half. In the South, Lee's defeats are generally attributed to overwhelming numbers against him—the Union could and did mass more men than the Confederacy, and had a significant advantage in terms of capital and industry, so that Confederates were as a rule not only outnumbered on the battlefield, but also outgunned and outsupplied. There is some truth to this—Lee himself frequently commented on it with a mixture of resignation and mild criticism in his letters to Jefferson Davis: "The army is not properly equipped for the invasion of an enemy's territory. . . . Feeble in transportation . . . animals being much reduced . . . men are poorly provided with clothes, and in thousands of instances destitute of shoes." Nobody could have been more aware than Lee himself of his army's weaknesses, nor of the Confederate government's inability to remedy them. The boldness of his maneuvering and the rapidity with which he fought one great battle after another were in large part a reflection of this—the enemy might gain strength by resting in position and waiting on events (essentially what McClellan wanted to do), but Lee would not. He would lose men he could not replace, from death, wounds, disease, semi-starvation, "straggling," and desertion. The whole Confederacy was a race against time: for Jefferson Davis, to secure the will-o'-the-wisp of foreign recognition and support; for Lee, to inflict on the Union a defeat so complete and humiliating that northerners would lose heart and give up the war.

Criticism of Lee's generalship was muted during his own lifetime, but by no means entirely absent. Longstreet, despite his affection and admiration for his old chief, did not hesitate to voice his criticism of Lee's strategic decisions and battlefield tactics after the war; and Lee deflected it with a certain degree of wry good humor. Once Longstreet committed himself to writing his memoirs, his criticism of Lee became sharper, and at times even personal, and brought down on his own head an avalanche of refutation and indignation by angry southerners. That avalanche is still falling, and is reflected in popular culture by Michael Shaara's Pulitzer Prize–winning novel *The Killer Angels* (1974) and by the film *Gettysburg* that was based on it, for example, and by Alan T. Nolan's more scholarly *Lee Considered: General Robert E. Lee and Civil War History* (1991), all tending to reflect Longstreet's point of view. These views of Lee as a general (and indeed as a man) run counter to those of the southern establishment and tend to be based not just on Longstreet's arguments with Lee about tactics at Sharpsburg and Gettysburg, but on his broader view that Lee should have fought from the beginning a *defensive* war, rather than seeking out and attacking the enemy.

How so large an area as the Confederacy (at just under 800,000 square miles, it represented almost a quarter of the landmass of the United States), with a population of only 9 million people, of whom at least 3.5 million were slaves, was to defend itself, Longstreet did not venture to suggest, either to Lee or to the reader of his memoirs, and for good reason: a *static* defense of the Confederacy was manifestly impossible once war had begun. No army it could raise would be big enough to defend it, and the result would have been history's most emphatic proof of Frederick the Great's famous remark that "he who attempts to defend every-thing, defends nothing." Lee was from the start com-mitted to an offensive defense, in which he maneuvered constantly to survive and fought each battle in the hope that it would be the last.

The case against Lee's generalship was summed up best by Major-General J. F. C. Fuller, CB, CBE, DSO, the influential British strategic thinker and mili-tary historian, in his book *Grant and Lee: A Study in Personality and Generalship* (1933). "Lee was no grand-strategist," Fuller wrote, "for he refused to be influenced by policy or to influence it. His theory of war was based upon the spirit of his army which he considered to be invincible. He understood the valor of his adversaries, though he read like a book the char-acter of many of their generals, and on the whole had the highest contempt for their abilities. His cause was a moral one, and his attacks were also moral ones." (When Fuller writes of Lee's cause being "a moral one," he is, of course, thinking not of slavery or even seces-sion, but of Lee's firm conviction that he was "unwill-ing to do what is wrong at the bidding of the South or the North," and his refusal to acquiesce in the right of the Federal government to raise an army against its own citizens, or, as Lee put it to General Winfield Scott, "to raise my hand against my children.")

Disentangling Lee from his myth is no easy task—even so astute and balanced a military historian as Colonel G. F. R. Henderson, CB, the distinguished nineteenth-century British biographer of Stonewall Jackson, could write, "General Lee [was] one of the greatest, if not *the* greatest soldier who ever spoke the English tongue," thus carefully reserving a place apart for Napoleon, while demoting Wellington to second place among English-speakers. Fuller, despite his admiration for Lee's character, will have none of this. His criticisms of Lee as a general are noteworthy, perhaps because they have become fixed in the minds of northern historians, and echo throughout much of the history of the Civil War. Fuller finds that "the central weakness of [Lee's] character" was that he was unwilling to enforce discipline, and played the role of a saint rather than a commanding general; that his "dread of wounding the feelings of others" prevented him from criticizing or sacking his own generals; that he was unwilling to force his own will on others; that he was poorly served by his staff and unwilling to change them; and that his orders were often unclear and based on insufficient information. Fuller further criticizes Lee for allowing his corps and divisional commanders too much authority, and for not exercising close personal control over his battles.

There is an element of truth in all this. Gentlemanly behavior was perhaps more important to Lee than it should have been; he certainly disliked personal confrontations and went out of his way to avoid them; and his staff, however devoted, was so small that he ended up doing much of the work himself. The fact that he was willing to leave the outcome of a battle in the hands of God was typical of Lee's intense religious faith—Stonewall Jackson often expressed the same belief; in fact he repeated it like a mantra, to the annoyance of many of his generals—but does not mean that Lee abandoned control over his armies once they were on the battlefield, like a rider dropping the reins of his horse.

On the other hand, each of these charges can be refuted. His "lack of thunder," the contrast between Jackson's Old Testament fire-and-brimstone ruthlessness and Lee's polite calm, did not prevent Lee from recommending a much stricter rounding up of stragglers, or from having deserters shot; despite his dislike of confrontations, he managed to move on generals who had failed or disappointed him; his written orders are as detailed and clear as anybody could wish; and his staff diligently carried out his instructions. True, paperwork exhausted and irritated him; even his own patient, faithful aide Walter Taylor noted that "nothing seemed to tax his amiability so much as the necessity for writing a lengthy official communication," but he is not the only general to complain about this (aides said the same thing about Eisenhower). Also true, Lee displayed what might seem to some (and did seem to Fuller) an excessive deference to Jefferson Davis, but Lee was not a politician, nor had he any ambition to become a military dictator and replace Davis; if the Confederacy could have been saved only by Lee's following the examples of Caesar, Cromwell, and Napoleon, Lee would have preferred defeat—he was too much an American for that.

The notion that Lee considered his duty done when he had brought his troops to the right place at the right time, after the model of his old commander in Mexico, General Winfield Scott, may have been something that Lee himself believed, or wanted to believe—yet another example of his modesty—but each of his battles was in fact fought according to his own plan, for better or worse. Of course the battlefield of the mid-nineteenth century was a very different place from that of the eighteenth century; the armies had grown too big for a single man to command, or even see, every detail of an engagement. The portrait beloved of genre painters, showing the commanding general raised on a picturesque knoll surveying the entire battle from horseback, with wounded men and horses in the foreground, raising their worshipful gaze toward him, was over. In real life. Napoleon won the Battle of Austerlitz in 1802 with fewer than 75,000 men, but only eleven years later his army at the Battle of Leipzig comprised over 200,000 men—far more than one man could command without significantly delegating authority to his subordinates. Lee never had a force of that size, of course, but his battlefields were large and were spread out over hilly, forested landscapes that did not necessarily offer him a clear view; and in the absence of any means of communication faster than a man on horseback bearing a written or an oral order, he had no option but to rely on the initiative of his corps commanders and divisional commanders, most of whom understood what Lee wanted done—when they did not, it was not for want of exact orders.

Once Pope escaped from the trap Lee had set for him, Lee's reaction was swift, sure, and sufficiently well planned to satisfy even Major-General Fuller. Lee drew Pope farther and farther away from Fredericksburg, to postpone, or perhaps even prevent the union of McClellan's army with Pope's, then sent Stuart across the Rappahannock to see where Pope's right was located—textbook moves, perfectly executed.

The next move he made was as bold as any ever made in war. On August 24 he sent for Jackson to meet him at Jefferston, where Lee had moved his headquarters, and ordered him to take three divisions, cross the Rappahannock immediately, and circle around Pope's right to cut him off from Washington. This was to ignore every important rule of war—instead of concentrating his forces, Lee split them in two in the face of an enemy with superior numbers, and despite the threat of the imminent arrival of even greater enemy numbers on his right. Retaining only Longstreet's divisions, Lee had no more than 32,000 men to confront the 45,000 men of Pope's army, with the possibility that at least another 75,000 men might soon be joining Pope.

As Lee, Jackson, and Longstreet looked at the map spread out before them on a table, they could hear the constant firing of guns close by. For the last twenty-four hours Confederate artillery had been lined up along the Rappahannock, to engage with Federal artillery across the river. This was partly to discourage any attempt on the part of the Federals to recross the river, and partly to keep Pope's attention fixed to his front, rather than his right. Jackson hoped to proceed upstream until he could cross to the Rappahannock unnoticed, then make a wide half circle, screened by the Bull Run Mountains, until he could cut the Orange and

Alexandria Railroad, with the object of forcing Pope to retreat before McClellan joined him. The Bull Run Mountains are not a formidable natural obstacle in principle (the highest elevation is merely 1,329 feet), but any commander marching against time with three divisions of infantry, a full complement of artillery, and a division of cavalry would sensibly follow the road and cross them through a gap. Lee did not select a point on the railway—he left Jackson free to do that—however, anyone looking at the map could see that to reach the Orange and Alexandria Railroad Jackson would almost certainly have to turn east at Thoroughfare Gap, and that once he did so the roads would bring him naturally to Bristoe Station, within a short reach of Bull Run and the old battlefield at Manassas Junction, just over thirty miles from the center of the District of Columbia. Geography is the firm, unshakable bedrock of strategy—the question was not so much what route Jackson would follow as how long it would take him to reach the railway line. He had to get there before the bulk of McClellan's army could reach Pope's, and he had to cut off Pope's line of communication before Pope realized that Lee had split his forces. By Lee's own reckoning, he had no more than five days in which to defeat Pope and turn on McClellan.

Jackson moved his men at first light on August 25, marching them behind the Bull Run Mountains toward the village of Salem. By the end of the day, Lee ordered Stuart to follow Jackson. Lee himself paused briefly to greet his son Rooney, and took a moment to write to Rooney's wife, Charlotte, reassuring her about her husband's health.

The next day, Lee made an even more momentous decision than splitting his army in the face of the enemy. He would abandon his position on the Rappahannock altogether, and relying on Jackson's speed, concentrate all his forces behind Pope's, leaving Richmond virtually undefended. He was gambling on McClellan's lack of speed, but while Lee felt confident that he knew his man, it was a risk that few other generals would ever have taken.

Lee gave Longstreet a choice: he could force the fords and advance directly north across the river to meet Jackson, or he could follow Jackson's route via Orlean and Salem. Longstreet wisely chose the latter, since Pope was still defending the lower fords. By that evening Lee had broken off contact with the enemy and moved his whole army north of the Rappahannock, effectively abandoning his own line of communications. He left behind only a smattering of artillery to preserve the illusion that the army was still in place. On the evening of August 26 Lee and his staff were dining at the home of the Marshall family in Orlean, on the north side of the river—one of the few occasions when the usually abstemious Lee seems to have been willing forgo his tent and his meager rations for a night indoors, and a dinner served in gracious style. Their hostess, Mrs. Marshall, even served Lee "a sumptuous breakfast" before dawn.

Generally, Lee did not accept such invitations, but Mrs. Marshall seems to have had willpower exceeding his own. Lee's indifference to food and drink was the despair of his staff. Walter Taylor, who was closer than anyone else to him, remarked on his "simplicity of taste." Other generals might have elaborate kits of china and silverware, but in Lee's mess there was only tin, and he "never availed himself of the advantages of his position to obtain dainties for his table or any personal comfort for himself." He avoided "spirituous liquors," and did not encourage others to partake of them, though he kept a supply on hand for important visitors, and was not above an occasional taste of wine when a bottle was sent to him. Taylor remarked that Lee "would have been better off had he taken a little stimulant," but he knew his man better than to suppose that this was likely. On the other hand, Lee was notably vivacious during dinner at Mrs. Marshall's— he was accompanied by General Longstreet, a man who enjoyed a good meal—and "passed an agreeable evening with the ladies," so it is possible he allowed himself a little wine that evening. Colonel A. L. Long, Lee's military secretary, makes it clear that both Lee and Longstreet were in good spirits and at their most entertaining at dinner and afterward, and took formal leave of their hostess after breakfast the next morning.

Lee enjoyed the brief domestic interlude—he was always happiest when surrounded by attentive young women—and his good humor was not spoiled a couple of hours later when he and his staff were almost captured by Federal cavalrymen only a few miles from Orlean. Lee was riding well ahead of Longstreet's column, to enjoy the brief moment of cool air at first light and escape from the clouds of dust raised by thousands of marching men. The men were so hard pressed by heat and thirst that "they drank dry the stagnant mud holes," and Lee asked if there were no alternative routes. There was none, however, and Lee's preoccupation with the comfort of his troops may have slowed his reaction when his staff spotted a squadron of enemy cavalry "moving briskly" toward him. Lee's staff, not more than ten or a dozen men, urged him to retire at once, but he would not do so, wisely deciding that the sight of a single horseman turning and galloping away might alert the Federals that he was somebody of importance. Instead he and his staff quickly formed a line across the road, stirrup to stirrup, and "presuming that it was the head of a considerable troop," the Federal squadron was taken in, halted, wheeled around, and galloped away. Lee's choice of a plain gray uniform no doubt helped to protect him; he wore no gold braid on his sleeves, and from a distance of 100 yards he and his staff would have looked like the vanguard of a Confederate cavalry patrol. No other senior general in either army, except perhaps Grant, would have been riding without a glittering cavalry escort and somebody bearing the flag of his rank.

At some point Lee stopped long enough to console a woman whose pair of matched bay horses had been taken from her carriage by the same Federal cavalrymen who almost captured him. He spent the night encamped near Salem. It is interesting to note that Union cavalry patrols were so active on the west side of the Bull Run Mountains that they had the time to follow to the letter General Pope's much reviled order to seize or destroy the property of Confederate civilians, but at the same time they failed to notice the presence within a mile of them of just over 49,000 Confederate soldiers,* with artillery and a supply train, spread out

---

*Three divisions of Jackson's (17,309 men); three divisions of Longstreet's (16,051 men), with G. T. Anderson's division serving as the rear guard (6,117 men); 2,500 cavalrymen; 2,500 artillerymen; plus at least two more brigades. These figures are from Walter H. Taylor (*Four Years with General Lee*, 61), whose job it was to keep count of these things. One would think all this would be hard to miss.

loosely over thirty miles between the Rappahannock River and Bull Run. It is a measure of the extreme risk that Lee was taking—not only had he split his army; he was moving it widely spread out and vulnerable in open country, in danger of its being attacked in detail, exactly the mistake that all military textbooks warn against. If the Federal cavalry patrol that almost captured Lee had been doing its job instead of stealing horses, and if Pope had not put his headquarters where his hindquarters ought to have been, as southerners joked, he might have wiped out the Army of Northern Virginia; and if McClellan had been moving faster, the vanguard of his troops could have cut off the retreat of the survivors as they attempted to cross the Rappahannock. The war might have been ended in August 1862 with a decisive victory for the North, but Lee showed no sign of concern, if Long and Taylor are to be believed. It was not just a question of Lee's contempt for Pope; it was that he had complete confidence in Jackson's ability to move fast and to take advantage of unexpected opportunities.

And he was right. Early the next morning, as Lee was eating his usual Spartan breakfast outside Salem, a courier arrived to inform him that Jackson had covered an astonishing fifty-four miles in two days and reached Bristoe Station, where he derailed two trains and tore up the tracks. This began a day of triumph for

Jackson. He sent Stuart ahead with the bulk of the cavalry and two infantry regiments seven miles north to
seize Pope's supply base at Manassas Junction. Stuart
captured 300 Federal troops, 8 cannons, 175 horses,
and "some 200 runaway slaves." Late the same morning Jackson reached Manassas Junction himself, after
a sharp engagement with Union troops, to find more
than 100 "bulging freight cars" and a vast supply dump
containing everything from ammunition and shoes to
mustard. Jackson moved his troops out as soon as he
could—he disliked the sight of his men plundering and
pillaging, and worried about the amount of liquor that
was available for the taking. By midnight he had blown
up the ammunition and powder he could not carry and
set a fire whose glow could be seen from Washington,
destroying "50,000 pounds of bacon, 1000 barrels of
corned beef, 200 barrels of salt pork, and 2000 barrels of flour," plus innumerable other stores. Rather
than moving west toward Thoroughfare Gap to join
Longstreet, he moved north, knowing that this would
alarm Lincoln when he learned of it. He also hoped to
draw Pope out of his lines on the Rappahannock. And
in fact Pope, though startled by the loss of the railroad
and his supply depot, still believed he was facing only a
daring raid by Jackson and Stuart, which he was determined to "crush" at Manassas. "If you are prompt and

expeditious," he told one of his generals, "we shall bag the whole crowd."

By the morning of August 27 the pieces of Lee's bold and risky strategy were falling into place. More important even than the destruction of Pope's stores at Manassas Junction, half of Lee's army, under Jackson, was now between Pope's army and Washington, while the other half, under Longstreet, was less than twenty-two miles to the west, its presence apparently still undetected by Pope. If Pope could move north quickly—and perhaps make a junction with the vanguard of McClellan's army—he could certainly "crush" Jackson, but if Lee could reunite the two halves of his army fast enough, and find suitable ground, he could defeat Pope, then turn on McClellan.

Lee's audacity was never on better display. His position was still precarious; he was without any significant cavalry since he had sent Stuart off to protect Jackson's right, and therefore had no way of knowing what his enemy was doing; and his only line of communication back to Richmond was fragile, and dependent on fords over the Rappahannock that a single rainstorm could render impassable.

Lee's vanguard reached Thoroughfare Gap shortly before noon on August 28, after an arduous march in the extreme heat, only to find that it was already in

Union hands. Lee does not seem to have been as dismayed by this as one might have expected, perhaps because couriers had been passing back and forth until quite recently between himself and Jackson during the day, indicating that the Federal force holding the gap was relatively small, and had only just been placed there to contest a retreat by Jackson rather than because Pope had guessed Lee's approach. The "gaps" in the Bull Run Mountains were not romantic Alpine defiles as they are frequently shown in paintings of the time, but they were narrow and rocky enough to discourage a contested frontal attack. Longstreet, displaying a lyrical gift unexpected in such a down-to-earth man, described them as "picturesque," their faces of "basaltic rock . . . relived hither and thither by wild ivy." Because Lee had sent Stuart off with Jackson, he had no idea what lay ahead of him on the far side of the gap. The Federals holding it might have been the advance guard of a division, or even a corps, as in fact they proved to be.

With the serenity of genius, Lee dismounted, examined the gap through his binoculars, and decided that there had to be ways over the rocky, pine-forested heights on either side of it. Breaking his own habit once again, he accepted a dinner invitation for him and his staff from a Mr. Robinson, who lived nearby.

Colonel Long, who accompanied Lee, wrote that "this meal was partaken of with as good an appetite and with as much geniality of manner as if the occasion was an ordinary one, not a moment in which victory or ruin hung in the balance." If Lee was nervous, he hid it well. In addition he had already decided that the Federal position could be turned—in fact before joining his host he gave orders to seek for alternative routes above and below the gap.

Colonel Long makes it clear that by dinner Lee's host meant what we would call lunch—this was still for most people the major meal of the day, the evening meal being lighter, and called supper—and by the end of the meal the sound of fierce fighting could be heard from the gap as the Confederate infantry made its way from rock to rock, firing on the Federals. Toward evening, however, a friendly "woodchopper" showed one of Lee's "reconnaissance parties" an old logging trail that the infantry could use to bypass the Federal position altogether, and by nightfall the Federal troops withdrew, abandoning Thoroughfare Gap to Longstreet's divisions. Throughout the day and night Lee heard the low rumble of gunfire to the east—Jackson was obviously engaged in battle. Although Lee could not have known it, General Pope, anxious to trap Jackson, had ordered Major General Irvin McDowell to move his corps toward Manassas as fast as possible. McDowell had therefore abandoned Thoroughfare Gap, leaving it wide open to Longstreet's divisions, "a tactical error of such magnitude that it could not well be retrieved." When Lee rode through the gap in the early morning it was not to find a large Union force massed there to stop him, but instead to find a clear road ahead.

It was odd that neither the Federal cavalry, which had almost taken Lee prisoner the day before, nor McDowell's troops, which held the gap on August 28, had passed on to Pope the news that they had encountered more than three divisions of Confederate troops. But then again Pope had what we would now call tunnel vision, and was so intent on destroying Jackson that he seems to have "either ignored or forgotten" the possibility that the rest of the Army of Northern Virginia might be on the move; and McDowell had already demonstrated at the First Battle of Manassas (or Bull Run) a fatal combination of high self-regard and inexperience at handling troops in battle. Worse still, he neglected to pass on to Pope the reports of his own subordinates, or to indicate their urgency.

Jackson's march from Manassas Junction was not unopposed. The fierce artillery duel, which Lee heard in the distance, was the sound of Jackson engaging with the Federal forces that were pursuing him. Jackson had found himself in a difficult position for two days. With fewer than 20,000 men, he was being pursued by an enemy more than twice that number. Almost any other general would have hastened to retreat west toward Thoroughfare Gap and join forces with Longstreet. It was less than fifteen miles from Bristoe Station, where he had torn up the tracks, or Manassas Junction, which he had sacked, to the eastern side of the gap, no more than a day's march for Jackson's "foot cavalry." But instead Jackson turned northwest, crossed the Warrenton Turnpike, and halted to concentrate his own forces on higher ground overlooking the hamlet of Groveton, on the wooded eastern slope of "Sudley Mountain," hardly more than a low ridge running parallel to the turnpike and known more accurately as Stony Ridge. Here an unfinished railway cutting provided the equivalent of a ready-made entrenchment, and heavy woods provided an opportunity for concealment.

Jackson's progress on August 27 and 28 might have been designed to further confuse Pope, though it was not. With his usual taste for secrecy and for not letting the left hand know what the right hand was doing, Jackson sent two of his three divisions on roundabout routes on the far side of Bull Run. A. P. Hill marched in a lengthy dogleg as far as Centreville before he joined up again with Ewell and they crossed Stone Bridge to meet Jackson at Groveton. Frustrating as these moves were for Jackson's generals, they presented Pope with a puzzle he was unable to solve: where was Jackson going, and what would he do when got there?

The answer—though it did not occur to Pope—was that Jackson intended to provoke Pope into attacking him on ground of his own choosing. Groveton, though it was hardly more than a speck on the map, was now the point toward which thousands of men on both sides were marching, none of them as yet aware that Jackson was already there. Although invisible to each other, the opposing forces were tantalizingly close. Groveton was only ten miles from Thoroughfare Gap, through which Lee and Longstreet with 25,000 men would emerge the next morning. Manassas Junction, where Pope was trying to decide what to do with over 51,000 Union soldiers scattered across the map, was only seven miles away to the south. The Stone Bridge on Bull Run over which A. P. Hill's division was marching from Centreville was only three miles away. But distances can be deceiving where battles are concerned, and nearness to the enemy is no substitute for a clear picture of his intentions. Close as he was to Jackson in miles, Pope still thought that his quarry was in headlong retreat toward the Bull Run Mountains. He seems to have had no inkling that far from retreating, Jackson was waiting impatiently for him, or that Longstreet was marching as fast as he could to join Jackson, or that Lee himself was less than seventeen miles away from his own headquarters.

Throughout the hot, sultry morning of August 28 Jackson carefully placed his forces where he wanted them, with Major General William B. Taliaferro's division in the center, putting A. P. Hill on his right, in front of Taliaferro's, and Ewell on his left, as they came up during the morning. All three divisions were concealed by the railway cutting and the woods. Jackson's troops rested in whatever shade they could find, while he himself lay down with a saddle for his pillow and went to sleep. He was in a position that would have kept most generals wide awake. True, he had chosen his spot, concentrated his forces there, and carefully overseen the siting of his artillery. Who after all could perform this last task better than the former professor of artillery at VMI? For once he even let Lee know by courier where to find him, and that intercepted intelligence indicated a large part of Pope's army was on the move from Manassas Junction toward Centreville. Jackson realized that he might at any moment find himself fighting a battle in which he was hopelessly outnumbered, and that he had by now sacrificed any possibility of maneuvering or retreat. Before midday he was awake and riding restlessly up and down the tree line on Little Sorrel, alone and apparently determined to avoid conversation with his generals. As usual, he had confided his plans to no one.

It was not until mid-afternoon that a courier, his horse sweating and exhausted, finally arrived from Lee to let Jackson know that Longstreet had reached Thoroughfare Gap. Hearing this, Jackson relaxed a bit, and his expression was actually described as "beaming," an occurrence rare enough to be noticed by those around him. He shook hands with the courier—again an unusual gesture for such a remote and forbidding military figure—drank "a quantity of buttermilk" (his favorite beverage), and surveyed the empty Warrenton-Centreville Turnpike stretching before him. The undulating ground sloped gently down from the tree line to the road, just over a mile away, giving Jackson and his staff a view of it as if they were in a theater, except that for the moment nothing was happening onstage.

Jackson had already ordered Taliaferro and Ewell to advance their divisions closer to the tree line, but it was a false alarm. As the hours went by and the sun began to set, it began to seem to many of the men after their long wait that nothing would happen today. Then, just after five o'clock, Jackson saw the glint of bayonets in the distance, the front ranks of a Federal column marching from Gainesville toward Bull Run and Centreville. As Brigadier General Rufus King's Union division* approached Groveton, Jackson rode out onto the open ground alone to take a closer look, apparently without attracting any attention, though one would have thought the sight of a solitary uniformed horseman, however shabby and indifferently mounted, might have served as a warning that there was a Confederate force nearby, on the eastern slope of Sudley Mountain. Jackson took his time, calmly noted that there were four brigades of Federal infantry marching past him in good order as if he were taking their salute, then rode back into the woods. "Bring out your men, gentlemen," he said. At 6:30 p.m. Confederate artillery began shelling the Union column.

Considering the difficulties facing the Federals— they were taken by surprise, they were marching in a column spread out along a mile and a half of road, and their commanding officer was not present—it is amazing that they reacted so quickly and effectively.

---

*King himself was not present, having suffered an epileptic seizure earlier in the day (Wikipedia, "Second Battle of Bull Run," 4). Brigadier John Porter Hatch replaced King as acting commander of the division.

Just the need to halt, turn ninety degrees to the left, re-form into battle ranks, and advance away from the turnpike and toward the enemy under fire required a remarkable degree of training and discipline. Despite his excellent position, his superior numbers, and the fact that he had successfully "ambushed" the Federal column, the best that can be said for Jackson was that he managed to hold his position until darkness finally put an end to what he described as "a fierce and sanguinary struggle with the enemy." He got only about 6,000 men into the fight, against about 2,100 Federals, and was hampered by thick woods, the encroaching darkness, and what one writer calls "the piecemeal deployment of his forces." Since he held the high ground and had a full day to prepare for a Federal attack, it is hard to understand why Jackson failed to annihilate the Union brigades and send them reeling back to Gainesville in retreat. Instead, they managed to advance over open ground to Brawner's Farm and exchange volleys of musket fire with the Confederates at eighty yards. The result was a bloody "stalemate" with 1,150 Union casualties and 1,250 Confederate. Some units sustained a casualty rate of 70 percent, and General Taliaferro was seriously wounded in the neck and arm. In addition, General Ewell received a musket ball in the leg; it shattered the bone, making amputation necessary the next day, and kept him out of action for almost a year. Nothing much was gained on either side by this "effusion of blood." The Federals, though badly shaken, withdrew toward the turnpike in good order, while Jackson for once betrayed his anxiety by dismounting and putting "his ear to the ground to listen for Longstreet's approach." If Jackson was hoping to hear the rhythmic tread of Longstreet's marching men, he was disappointed. Lee and Longstreet, with the other half of the Army of Northern Virginia, were still at the wrong end of Thoroughfare Gap, from which they had heard the muffled thunder of the guns at Brawner's Farm.

Some historians have argued that the battle was a "strategic" success and that Jackson wanted only to keep Pope's attention fixed on him. Perhaps this is true, but it scarcely required a battle that cost Jackson 1,250 men, including two division commanders, to bewilder Pope, who now knew where Jackson was, and still believing that his enemy was in headlong retreat, hoped to "bag" him the next day. Late that night, Pope withdrew the only forces that stood between Longstreet and Jackson's position at Groveton and ordered them to proceed at once toward Centreville along the Warrenton-Gainesville Turnpike—another fatal mistake.

Certainly one reason why Jackson fought at Groveton was his overriding concern that Pope might cross his army to the northern side of Bull Run and attempt to make a junction with McClellan's army, which was forming up in Alexandria after its voyage from Harrison's Landing. This would have presented Lee with a Union force too numerous for him to meet; but as usual McClellan was moving too slowly, and—typically for him—he was warning Halleck and the president that Lee had perhaps as many as 120,000 troops, more than twice the actual number. On August 28 McClellan was in Washington to urge that Pope, whom he held in contempt even more than Lee did, should "cut his way through and fall back to the capital." He also urged preparing the Chain Bridge over the Potomac for demolition, a precaution that can only have caused dismay in the White House. On the evening of August 28 McClellan could hear the sound of gunfire from Groveton, but he was reluctant to send any of his army to support "that fool Pope." The next day he caused a firestorm by recommending to President Lincoln that it might be best "to leave Pope to get out of his scrape," rather than supporting him. Lincoln took this as a sign of disloyalty, perhaps even treason, on McClellan's part, but it may have been no more than the basic battlefield wisdom embodied in an old British military adage, "Never reinforce failure."★ One of Lee's assets during this campaign was McClellan's pessimism, and his ability to sow alarm and despondency in Washington without even trying. The one thing that Lee feared was the union of McClellan's army and Pope's, which, as it happened, was also the one thing that McClellan was determined to prevent.

Incompetent Pope might be, and looking in the wrong direction, but he could move a lot faster than McClellan when he thought an opportunity had presented itself, and now that he supposed Jackson was trapped, he intended to close on him from the east and the west simultaneously. But Pope's forces were scattered piecemeal all over the map, and most of his generals at this point had no idea where their commander was. Pope had none of McClellan's sense of order or skill at organizing the movements of a large army; but since he had over 60,000 men to bring to bear on the 18,000 effectives remaining to Jackson, none of that should have mattered.

Jackson spent the night at Sudley Springs, alternately praying and napping in a house that had been turned into a makeshift field hospital to the far left of his line. At dawn he rose to reposition his army for the assault

---

★This may be a version of a much older piece of military advice, possibly that of Sun Tzu, who recommended in 500 B.C., "You must reinforce success and starve failure."

he knew was coming. He pulled his troops back to take as much advantage as possible of the unfinished railway cutting, and placed his artillery—forty guns—in the tree line, which would hamper their field of fire but partially conceal them. He anchored his left on Sudley Springs, close to a ford on Bull Run. Only his right was somewhat "in the air," but he counted on Longstreet's arrival with 25,000 men to hold that position once he arrived.

By 10 a.m. the Federal forces, backed up by artillery fire, had begun a series of poorly coordinated attacks—Robertson refers to them as "probes"—intended to reveal the weak spots in Jackson's line. These probes started on the Confederate right, where Jackson was weakest, and then gradually concentrated on his left, where A. P. Hill's division repulsed several stronger Federal attacks; but Pope was hampered by not having a clear picture in his mind of what was actually happening, as well as by his failure to concentrate his overwhelmingly superior forces for a knockout blow against Jackson.

By midmorning on August 29 the leading elements of Longstreet's wing had arrived on the battlefield. Major General John B. Hood's division, with the Texas Brigade in the lead, began to form up on Jackson's right in two lines at "an angle of approximately 160 degrees, strongest at the apex near the Gainesville-Centreville road, looking east." By this time, Lee himself was on the scene, and took command of the battle. He had already performed a feat seldom equaled in the history of warfare: he split his army in the face of a superior enemy; he marched half of it in a wide arc around his enemy's flank; then he rapidly marched the other half forward so that the two forces were united on the battlefield, "a move of extraordinary audacity," as General Fuller, normally not an admirer of Lee, admits. Pope still imagined that Longstreet was miles away on the other side of the Bull Run Mountains, when he was in fact lining up his troops on Jackson's right.

Lee rode forward to survey the scene, his usual impassivity unruffled by the fact that a sharpshooter's bullet grazed his cheek. He found himself not only in possession of the high ground, but also in a position that formed a shallow V from which he could subject Pope's army to enfilade fire if it attacked Lee's center. Pope had been expecting that Porter and McDowell with their corps would arrive on the battlefield from Gainesville and attack Jackson's right, but Longstreet's force was now blocking their advance, his lines extending across the turnpike. Porter and McDowell, who had been harassed by Stuart's cavalry on their march from

Gainesville, had received a contradictory "joint order" from Pope, described by one student of the battle as "a masterpiece of contradiction and obfuscation," and halted in place, uncertain of what to do. McDowell had already demonstrated a certain degree of ineptitude under pressure at First Manassas, but Porter was a competent officer who had fought well on the peninsula, and held Lee at Malvern Hill—it may be that as "McClellan" men, they possibly shared a lack of confidence in General Pope; but in any case, at this crucial point in the battle, they took counsel of their fears. At least Porter, could see that if he advanced against "Jackson's right" his corps would collide with Longstreet's 25,000 men, something that Pope could not or would not see, but in the meantime Pope was left to fight Jackson with only a portion of his potential strength.*

Throughout the late morning and early afternoon Pope threw attack after attack at Jackson's left. Often his troops engaged in volley after volley, sometimes at a distance of only a few paces, as "bodies piled in front of the railroad cut and sprawled over the descending ground to the east," while Longstreet deployed his half of the army. What Lee saw before him was a perfect

---

*Pope charged Porter with disobedience and misconduct, and Porter was court-martialled, found guilty, and dismissed from the army—a controversial decision against which he fought for twenty-three years. Eventually, he was exonerated, and restored to his substantive rank of colonel by President Chester A. Arthur.

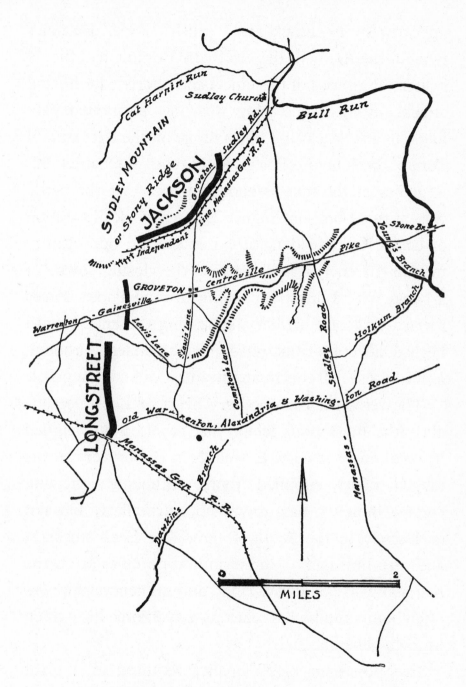

15. Situation at the close of action, August 29, 1862.

opportunity to attack and "crush" Pope. Jackson's wing of the Army of the Northern Virginia had firmly beaten off a series of piecemeal and poorly coordinated attacks; Longstreet's wing was now positioned perfectly to attack, closing like a hinge on the left flank of Pope's forces before Porter could reach the battlefield. A glance at the map is enough to see that the battle was, at that point on August 29, a textbook illustration of classic battlefield tactics. Lee saw an opportunity to trap the enemy as if between the closing covers of a book, with Longstreet's wing driving Pope's forces toward Jackson's artillery, squeezing the enemy until he had no option but retreat or surrender. Although Lee could see all this in an instant, it did not happen.

The reason lay in the very heart of Lee's personality, the mysterious factor that so often outweighed his skill and audacity, as well as in the bravery of his ragged, poorly supplied troops. Although a thriving cottage industry has grown up, particularly but not exclusively in the South, to eradicate Lee's mistakes and turn him into a kind of military secular saint, the real man was not always right, and his generalship was often hampered by his reluctance to enforce his will on his own generals.

Lee possessed every quality required of a great general except the ability to give a direct order to his subordinates and ensure that it was obeyed. He inspired love, admiration, and respect, but not fear. He was not lacking in willpower—he could move an entire army to undertake things that required terrible sacrifices and suffering—but good manners and a remarkable dislike of personal confrontation often hindered the execution of his plans. Of course, as Field Marshal Helmuth Karl von Moltke remarked, "No battle plan ever survives contact with the enemy," but Lee again and again left matters to his corps commanders once battle was engaged, and hesitated to give them a direct order to do what he wanted them to.

The bond between Lee and Jackson, despite the latter's poor showing in the peninsula campaign, came about in large part because Jackson never argued with Lee, and seemed able to divine what Lee wanted with only the barest and politest of suggestions on Lee's part. This was not the case with James Longstreet (called "Old Pete" by his fellow West Pointers), who was stubborn, argumentative, and determined to get his own way—Longstreet was not exactly deaf to Lee's charm, ideas, or suggestions, but unlike Lee he enjoyed an argument and always sought to win one. Longstreet respected Lee but did not worship him and did not hesitate to make a case for what he himself wanted to do—indeed, he was still making it, more stubbornly than ever, in 1896, when he published his memoirs of the war. He disagreed with Lee not just about tactics but about the whole strategy of the Confederacy, and was not shy about expressing his opinion.

This does not mean that the war would have been won had Lee accepted Longstreet's advice—nothing is that simple—but it does mean that Lee, knowing what Longstreet thought, should, if they disagreed, have exerted his authority over the man in whose command he had placed half of his army. Jackson could be trusted to do what Lee wanted him to do on August 29 at Second Manassas, but Longstreet dug in his heels and refused. More important, Longstreet learned what he had no doubt always suspected, which was that Lee would stop short of giving him a direct order and relieving him of his command if he did not obey it; and Lee learned that he would put up with Longstreet's insubordination and not call his bluff. Never mind who was right and who was wrong; this was not a good lesson for either man to learn.

Giving Lee full credit for saintly patience, there might have been nothing wrong with his hearing Longstreet out and then telling him to obey orders—there was no need for Lee to imitate Napoleon's cold fury, as when he told Ney at Waterloo, *"Monsieur, vous m'avez perdu la*

France!"* But at Second Manassas Longstreet declined to attack three times, and Lee let him get away with it, although Longstreet understood perfectly well what Lee wanted him to do—in his own words, "General Lee was inclined to engage as soon as practicable, but did not order." This, in terms of the battlefield, is lawyers' talk. If Longstreet knew what Lee wished, he should not have needed a direct order; at the same time, if Lee noticed Longstreet's reluctance, and he certainly did, it was his duty as commander in chief to give Longstreet a direct order to attack at once or relinquish his command.

Of course one cannot exclude from this the effect of a certain rivalry between Longstreet and Jackson, and on Longstreet's part a degree of resentment about the fame Jackson had accrued despite his poor performance on the peninsula. When Longstreet came to write his memoirs, his comments on Jackson were anything but generous, at a point when Jackson's reputation almost rivaled Lee's. "His [Jackson's] game of hide-and-seek about Bull Run, Centreville and Manassas Plains, was grand, but marred in completeness," Longstreet wrote, dismissing Jackson loftily: "As a leader he was fine; as a wheel-horse, he was not always just to himself. He was fond of the picturesque."

---

* "Monsieur, you have cost me France!" This was after Ney's failed attack at 4 p.m.

A "wheel-horse" describes somebody who is strong, reliable, and a dependable part of a team, which is just what Longstreet prided himself on being. Clearly Longstreet thought that Jackson was something of a prima donna; that he was not a team player, to use a modern term, as he had amply demonstrated on the peninsula; and that while he was up to playing hide-and-seek in the Valley or around Manassas, he was not up to the serious business of war. Part of the problem between the two men was that while Longstreet had ambitions to help direct Confederate strategy—that is, to participate in Lee's decisions as an equal—Jackson was content to command under Lee and had no desire to make policy him-self.

Lee's aide, Colonel Long, makes no secret of the fact that Lee "earnestly" wanted Longstreet to attack as soon as "his command was formed for battle," which happened about noon. Jackson had been under attack by four Federal divisions ("at least thirty thousand men") since early morning, and had just managed to hold on. Federal losses were at least "six to eight thousand in killed and wounded," and the opportunity clearly existed for a decisive blow against the left flank of Pope's army at a critical moment in the first day of the battle. "The question will naturally arise, Why did Longstreet not attack, and so relieve the heavy pressure on Jackson?" Long asks, but declines to answer, leaving it to be understood by the reader that Lee would never override the reluctance of one of his generals to attack "even though his martial instinct and his military judgment alike told him that the thing to do was to attack at once."

Criticism of Longstreet has been widespread for over 150 years, and not just in the South. The distinguished English biographer of Stonewall Jackson, Lieutenant General G. F. R. Henderson, wrote scathingly of Longstreet's behavior on August 29: "Longstreet, with a complacency it is hard to understand, has related how he opposed the wishes of the commander-in-chief. Three times Lee urged him forward. The first time he [Longstreet] rode to the front to reconnoiter, and found that the position, in his own words, was not inviting. Again Lee insisted that the enemy's left might be turned. While the question was under discussion, a heavy force (Porter and McDowell) was reported advancing from Manassas Junction. No attack followed, however, and Lee repeated his instructions. Longstreet was still unwilling. A large portion of the Federal forces on the Manassas road now marched northwards to join Pope, and Lee, for the last time, bade Longstreet attack towards Groveton." Shortly, it was too late in the day to attack, and Longstreet suggested that it would be better to prepare "all things in readiness at daylight for a good day's work." He reports that Lee "hesitated" before accepting what was now inevitable because Longstreet's delays had made it so, but Lee's hesitation suggests that he may have been holding back his temper, or at least his impatience, with some difficulty.

It is impossible to know for sure whether Longstreet was tactically right or not. In his tactful way Taylor, who was there, makes it clear that he thought Longstreet was mistaken; more important, he makes it very clear that Lee did *not* agree with Longstreet and that Lee was "disappointed" at Longstreet's failure to attack. Showing a preference for the defensive that was to cause an even bigger (and fatal) disagreement between the two men at Gettysburg almost a year later, Longstreet wanted to secure the high ground above the turnpike and let Porter attack him. In addition, he did not like the ground before him, over which he would have to advance to support Jackson, and he was concerned that Porter might attack his rear, but Lee had considered all of these things and thought otherwise— and his judgment was certainly as good as Longstreet's.

The important question, with all due respect to Colonel Taylor, is not why Longstreet failed to attack, but why Lee did not simply order him to do so at noon, instead of letting him fritter away the rest of the afternoon. Longstreet was of Dutch descent, a heavyset man who was as stubborn and hard to budge as a rock, but Lee was a commanding presence, already a legendary figure in the Confederacy, and besides commander of the Army of Northern Virginia. Although Lee's deference toward President Jefferson Davis was enormous—even exaggerated, as some thought—he did not hesitate to press his case in military matters when he thought Davis was wrong. Why then did he defer to Longstreet? The answer appears to be that even the greatest of great men have a weakness, and Lee's was a genuine reluctance to enforce his own will on his subordinates. He explained this to a German observer, Captain Justus Scheibert:* "You must know our circumstances, and see that my leading in battle would do more harm than good. It would be a bad thing if I could not then rely on my brigade and divisional commanders. I plan and work with all my might to bring the troops to the right place at the right time; with that I have done my duty. As soon as I order the troops forward into battle, I lay the fate of my army in the hands of God."

---

*Scheibert was a Prussian. Foreign military observers were attached to both the Confederate and the Union armies to report on the lessons of the war to their own army. Perhaps the most famous of them was the (unofficial) British observer Lieutenant-Colonel Arthur Fremantle of the Coldstream Guards, who was present at Gettysburg and wrote a successful book about his experiences in the South.

This is undoubtedly sincere, and what Lee himself believed, but in fact he very often took direct control of his army in battle, rather than leaving matters "in the hands of God." The truth is that Lee had no compunctions about making his wishes known on the battlefield, but he would not overrule a commander who failed to heed them—and Longstreet was as good as tone-deaf to Lee's politely expressed wishes. Probably nobody *but* Longstreet could have resisted Lee's evident desire for an attack throughout a long afternoon, or found more reasons to thwart it.

During all this time the noise of furious battle was heard from the Confederate left, less than half a mile away, where Jackson's brigades were repelling attack after attack, defending with the bayonet when they ran out of ammunition, an engagement such as "even the Army of Northern Virginia had seldom fought." As darkness fell Major General J. B. Hood carried out the "reconnaissance in force" that Longstreet had been demanding, and returned with the "disheartening" news that the Federals held strong positions, and that an attack on them in the morning "would be dangerous." Even *The West Point Atlas of the American Wars*, which is seldom critical, notes, "On three different occasions Lee had wanted Longstreet to attack Pope's south flank, but each time he had reluctantly succumbed to Longstreet's pleas for postponement," and adds that had Lee been insistent, "it is very likely that the Confederates would have gained an important victory" on August 29.

The Army of Northern Virginia was now drawn up in a line facing east toward Bull Run perhaps two miles away. The left wing under Jackson stretched from Sudley Church to the turnpike above Groveton, roughly along the line of the unfinished railway cut at the base of Sudley Mountain, while the right wing under Longstreet, slightly less advanced, stretched from the turnpike to the junction of the Manassas Gap Railroad and the Warrenton, Alexandria, and Washington (Virginia) Railroad. The two wings had not linked up yet, but from left to right they formed a line of about three and a half miles, a secure enough position if Pope could be induced to attack it.

Daylight revealed that Pope had managed to bring up more of his troops during the night—another argument in favor of Lee's desire to have had Longstreet attack at once on the previous afternoon. Apart from desultory artillery fire most of the morning passed quietly. Lee's concern was that Pope might get away and was preparing to retreat, while Pope had convinced himself that the Confederates had been badly beaten the day before and reported to Washington by telegraph that they were now "retreating towards the mountains." He estimated that he had taken 8,000 casualties in yesterday's fighting, and put the number of Confederate casualties at twice that high. Long, however, whose job it was to know such things, put the number of Confederate casualties at 1,507. Although one would have thought that it was hard to hide the presence of Longstreet's 25,000 men, Pope continued to believe that they were still at Thoroughfare Gap.

Around noon Lee summoned Jackson, Longstreet, and Stuart, and they reached a collective decision to wait in expectation of a Federal attack. There seems to have been no friction between Jackson and Longstreet because of Longstreet's failure to support Lee the previous day; certainly neither Longstreet nor Lee's aide Colonel Long makes any mention of it. If Pope did *not* attack, it was Lee's intention "to slip across Bull Run in the vicinity of Sudley Springs" to the extreme left of Jackson's position that night, and place his entire army between Pope and Washington. Sometime after one o'clock in the afternoon, however, Pope at last made his move and attacked Jackson again. Once more, Jackson was hard pressed by the sheer volume and ferocity of the Federal attacks, and some of his brigades were so short of ammunition that they were reduced to throwing rocks at the advancing Union troops. Lee himself was surprised by the attack—he had expected Pope to withdraw—but he quickly realized that the Union commander had presented him with an opportunity. The Federals were now out in the open, advancing across rolling, lightly wooded ground. There was no indication that Pope had noticed Longstreet's 25,000 men on higher ground on his left.

That day Lee's headquarters were "on the Warrenton Pike," almost in the center of the Confederate line and about two miles south of Jackson, whose headquarters were above the pike, in a field full of wheat sheaves. Lee's signals officer Captain J. L. Bartlett briefly summarized the afternoon's action in his record of Lee's signals to Jackson:

> [To] General JACKSON:
>   What is result of movements on your left? LEE
>   Answer. [To] General Lee:
>   So far, enemy appears to be trying to get
> possession of a piece of woods to withdraw out
> of our sight. JACKSON

This rather flippant reply proved optimistic. Six hundred yards away from his position Jackson could now see "some 12,000 Federals—thirty-seven regiments in all—in assault formations that extended a mile and a quarter from Groveton to near Bull Run . . . an awesome sight, battle lines in full array, flags rolling lazily above gleaming bayonets."

Despite the fact that the railway cutting "angled away" from the line of the Federal attack, leaving the Union troops open to volleys of musketry on their right flank as they advanced uphill, they kept coming. Far from trying to withdraw, Pope sent in brigade after brigade against the Confederate far left. At times the Federals were so close to the railway cutting that "the opposing flags were only ten yards apart," and soldiers on both sides used the bayonet, or swung their muskets like clubs as they ran out of ammunition ran out or if they were too close to each other to pause and reload. Even for Jackson's battle-hardened veterans, who had withstood two days of "sanguinary struggle," the pressure was too much. By two o'clock in the afternoon Jackson was obliged to request a division from Longstreet's command. Longstreet's subsequent claim that Jackson "begged for reinforcements" aroused, and continues to incite, bitter quarrels between his supporters and Jackson's—certainly no "begging" was involved. Lee promptly ordered Longstreet to shift a division, which he seems to have been willing enough to do, except that from where he was standing, on higher ground nearer the middle of the Confederate line, he could see that "the left flank of the Federals" was exposed to fire from his artillery, which would "break up [the Federal] attack before he could possibly move a division to Jackson's relief."

Lee may have reached the same conclusion, since his next message to Jackson was:

To General JACKSON:
    Do you still want reinforcements? LEE

By this time, Longstreet's artillery had already opened fire and the Federal attack began "to melt away." Longstreet describes the effect of his "enfilade" fire on the Union troops in his memoirs: "Almost immediately the wounded began to drop off from Porter's ranks; the number seemed to increase with every shot; the masses began to waver, swinging back and forth, showing signs of discomfiture along the left and left centre. In ten or fifteen minutes it crumbled into disorder and turned towards the rear." Half an hour later Jackson signaled to Lee that he no longer needed reinforcements: "No; the enemy are giving way."

Lee, as was his custom, remained an island of calm. As Longstreet's guns were firing, he turned to one of his aides and remarked, "I observe that some of those mules are without shoes. I wish you would see to it that all of the animals are shod at once." This was a perfectly sound observation, but it helps to explain the extraordinary hold Lee had on his men, from generals down to soldiers: he seemed altogether immune to the emotions that buffeted them—excitement, alarm, apprehension, concern. He had perfect control over himself, not by any effort of will, but *naturally,* a very rare thing.

Lee knew he had taken a fearsome risk, split his forces in the face of the enemy, and reunited them in the nick of time; and as Porter's lines began to crumble before Longstreet's well-placed guns, he could hardly have failed to realize that a great victory was within his grasp. He might have been forgiven a moment of exultation, but instead he noticed that a team of passing mules were not shod and politely ordered that this be attended to. Hardly any moment captures Lee's simplicity and greatness better than this.

Next, he gave the order for Longstreet to attack, and then "threw every man in his army against Pope." He sent a further signal to Jackson, telling him that Longstreet was advancing, and to "look out and protect his left flank," for the two wings of the army were now drawn up at an angle of about forty-five degrees, and it was important that Jackson's troops should not open fire on Longstreet's as they advanced through the dense, drifting gun smoke toward each other.

John Brown and Colonel Robert E. Lee.

Lee's mentor,
General Winfield Scott.

Stratford, Lee's birthplace.

Arlington

Lee's rented home at 707 East Franklin Street, Richmond, Virginia.

The president's house, Washington College, Lexington, Virginia.

Mary Custis Lee

Eleanor Agnes Lee

MRS. LEE
AND HER
DAUGHTERS

Mary Anne Custis Lee
and Robert E. Lee, Jr.

Anne Carter Lee

Mildred Childe Lee

Robert E. Lee

William Henry Fitzhugh Lee

ROBERT E. LEE AND HIS SONS

George Washington Custis Lee

Robert E. Lee, Jr.

The "Three Heroes" of the Confederacy: Jackson, Lee, and Stuart.

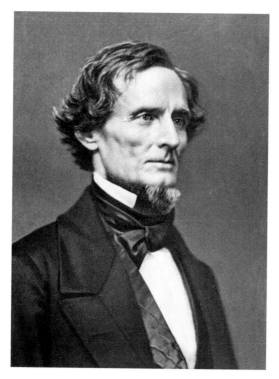

Jefferson Davis, president of the Confederate States of America.

Lee at Fredricksburg.

Chancellorsville

Lee cheered by his
troops after his victory
at Chancellorsville.

Lieutenant-Colonel Fremantle in later years.

Henry Thomas Harrison, General Longstreet's scout, who brought the news to him on the night of June 28, 1863, that General Meade was marching toward Gettysburg.

ROBERT E. LEE AND THE PRINCIPAL GENERALS
OF THE ARMY OF NORTHERN VIRGINIA

J. E. B. Stuart

James A. Longstreet

A. P. Hill

Robert E. Lee

John Bell Hood

T. J. "Stonewall" Jackson

Richard S. Ewell

Confederate dead at the "Bloody Lane," Sharpsburg, 1862.

Sherman's march to Atlanta, 1864.

Lee on Traveller leaving the McLean house, Appomattox Court House, Virginia, after his surrender, followed by his aide, Colonel Marshall.

Lee, photographed by Matthew Brady in Richmond, shortly after the surrender.

Lee's mess kit and field glasses.

Lee on Traveller—the iconic photograph.

Mrs. Lee in old age.   Lee, shortly before his death.

Recumbent statue of Robert E. Lee by Edward Valentine,
the Lee Chapel, Washington and Lee University, Lexington, Virginia.

The two parts of Lee's army were now closing like the jaws of a pair of pliers on the Federal troops advancing toward Jackson's lines, and forcing them back toward Bull Run.

Longstreet's reluctance to attack the previous day was more than compensated for by the precision and the speed of his advance now. His entire wing, nearly 25,000 men in all, moved forward together, surging over the low hills and driving the enemy back, while his artillery rushed forward at a gallop, using every good piece of ground to halt and fire: "The artillery would gallop furiously to the nearest ridge," wrote General Moxley Sorrel, "deliver a few rounds until the enemy was out of range, and then gallop again to the next ridge." As Jackson began to advance, the Federal retreat became a rout. "[The Federals] retreated in confusion," Lee would report, "suffering severely from our artillery, which advanced as [they] retired." Lee added that Federal troops fought "stubbornly" at several "strong points" on the Confederate far right, but Lee's tactics proved to be as effective as his strategy. It was a textbook battle, fought out exactly as planned, though the end result was not everything he had wished.

Unable to remain at his headquarters any longer, Lee himself rode forward to join Longstreet, exposing himself to vigorous artillery fire, until Longstreet "thought to ride through a ravine, and thus throw a traverse between [Lee] and the fire." Lee seems to have shown, unusually for him, a certain polite impatience with Longstreet's concern for his safety. He did not relish attempts to protect him.

His modest belief that it was his job only to bring his army to where it belonged, and not to direct the battle himself, is contradicted by his behavior on August 30. He had placed Longstreet's wing of the army exactly where he wanted it, on ground he had reconnoitered himself, and then decided to wait and see if Pope attacked; he gave an order for Longstreet to transfer one of his divisions to the left wing of the army when Jackson was hard pressed and had asked for reinforcements, then canceled that order when he saw that Longstreet's artillery batteries had made it unnecessary. Finally Lee himself chose the moment for Longstreet to attack, and for Jackson to move forward.

Longstreet pushed his men forward nearly a mile and a half and Lee advanced with them "over the dead-strewn field." He paused for a moment near a Confederate gun to scan the movements of the enemy, once again making himself an easy target—he seems to have shaken off the overprotective Longstreet.

Lee's youngest son, Robbie, was a private in the artillery, and the nearby gun happened to be the one he was serving. "The general," Robbie wrote,

> reined in "Traveller" close by my gun, not fifteen feet from me. I went up . . . and spoke to Captain Mason of the staff, who had not the slightest idea who I was . . . I had been marching night and day for four days, with no opportunity to wash myself, or my clothes; my face and hands were blackened with powder-sweat. . . . When the General, after a moment or two, dropped his glass to his side, and turned to his staff, Captain Mason said:
>
> "General, here is someone who wants to speak to you."
>
> Lee, seeing a much begrimed artillery-man, sponge-staff* in hand, said:
>
> "Well, my man, what can I do for you?" I replied:
>
> "Why, General, don't you know me?" And he, of course, at once recognized me, and was very much amused by my appearance, and glad to see that I was safe and well.

---

* The bore of a muzzle-loading cannon had to be swabbed down with a wet sponge after each round fired, to prevent a spark or burning ember from the last shot from igniting the next charge of powder as it was loaded.

Both wings of the Confederate army were now "driving the enemy from each successive stand made in their sullen retirement," across fields and woodlands carpeted with the dead and wounded from repeated Federal charges, a sight that caused even the battle-hardened Colonel Long to exclaim how sad it all was. The Federals attempted to make a stand at Henry House Hill, which overlooked Bull Run and the vital bridge across it. "Though the fighting [on Henry House Hill] raged until dark, Lee was unable to dislodge the Union forces." By this time it was raining hard, and the Confederate pursuit slowed down, while Pope at last decided to withdraw his army across Bull Run during the night and destroy the bridge behind him, something he had contemplated doing in the morning, before launching an attack that cost him, all told, over 10,000 casualties and sent his defeated army reeling back in chaos toward Centreville. "Thousands of [Union] stragglers," perhaps as many as 20,000, plodded glumly through the rain toward Washington, many having abandoned their units and their weapons. Lincoln was finally convinced that Pope would have to go even if it meant replacing him with McClellan. The state of panic in Washington at the news that Pope was "badly whipped," as McClellan had predicted he would be, can be gauged by the fact that

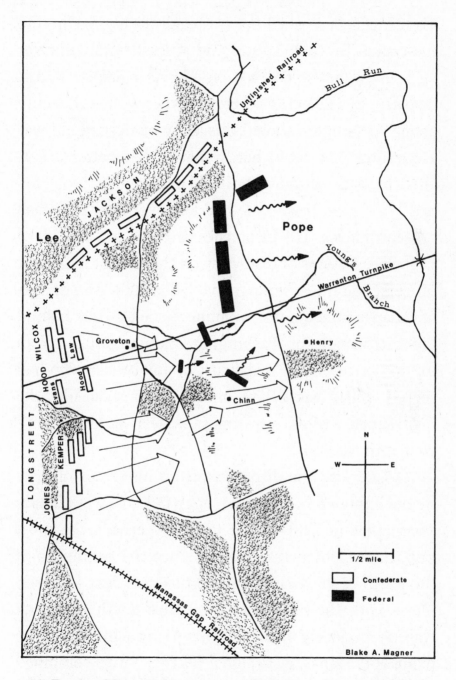

16. Battle of Second Manassas, or Bull Run, August 30, 1862.

Mrs. McClellan asked her husband "to try to slip into the capital [to their house] and at least send the silver off" lest it be stolen by Confederate soldiers. Pope's dispatch to Halleck asking "whether you feel secure about Washington should this army be destroyed" was a question that could hardly have been better calculated to cause dismay at the White House. Not only had Pope been beaten; he had lost overnight his brash self-confidence. His dispatches to Halleck were full of vague accusations of disloyalty on the part of his senior officers, and dire warnings that his army was in danger of collapse unless it was brought to shelter back behind the fortifications of Washington, and reorganized from top to bottom. Pope's mistrust of any officer who had served under McClellan on the peninsula, like the unfortunate Porter, was almost as deep as McClellan's contempt for Pope.

As Lee read the dispatches from his senior officers by the light of a bonfire in a soggy field, he was already aware that he had won a victory, perhaps the most important Confederate victory since the beginning of the war. He wrote late that night to President Jefferson Davis with the news that the entire South had been waiting anxiously to hear: "This Army achieved on the plains of Manassas a signal victory over combined forces of Genls. McClellan and Pope." It is interesting that Lee put McClellan first, although "the Young Napoleon" had in fact been in Alexandria throughout the battle, grinding his teeth over being demoted to a secondary role while portions of his own beloved army were placed under the incompetent and despised Pope, whose defeat he had confidently predicted. Lee carefully gave equal praise to Jackson and Longstreet, although he surely realized by now that Longstreet's repeated refusals to attack on afternoon of August 29 had cost him the decisive victory that he wanted. By the time he wrote his dispatch to Davis on August 30, heavy rain had turned roads to mud, while Bull Run was "rising fast, and in danger of becoming impassible." Since the Federals had destroyed the Stone Bridge behind them, a victory on the twenty-ninth instead of the thirtieth would have given the Confederates the best part of a day of clear weather to pursue the Federal army and perhaps prevent it from crossing Bull Run to safety.

Lee had succeeded in his desire to "suppress" Pope, but at Second Manassas, just as at Malvern Hill, he missed the chance to "annihilate" his opponent's army. The Army of Northern Virginia was a formidable fighting machine, but it was neither big enough, nor sufficiently well supplied to achieve the crushing victory that the Confederacy needed. Even had Lee been able to force Pope to surrender his sword and his army, as Washington forced Cornwallis to surrender at Yorktown, it is by no means certain that the United States would have recognized the Confederacy as a result, since major Union armies were fighting elsewhere. McClellan still had enough men to defend Washington; Lincoln's presidency had another two years to run. The *kind* of victory Lee wanted eluded him at Second Manassas.

He was particularly hampered by the army's constant shortage of food and forage. "An army marches on its stomach,"* of course, but the Army of Northern Virginia's supply line was stretched thin, and the Confederacy was poorly organized to supply it. While Union armies received plentiful supplies and could build up huge depots close to the front, like the one that Jackson had just destroyed at Manassas Junction, the Army of Northern Virginia was forced to keep moving. It lived off the land, consuming food and forage at an alarming rate, and this made it difficult, almost impossible, for the army to remain in place for long, or to retreat over ground it had already picked clean. Time and distance were constantly on Lee's mind, even at the moment of a victory that vali-

---

* This famous remark has been attributed to both Frederick the Great and Napoleon, though the likelihood is that the latter borrowed it from the former.

dated his bold decision to abandon Richmond, cross the Rappahannock, and split his army in the face of the enemy. Lee's wagon train was empty of supplies; the roads before him were turning "nasty and soggy," to quote Longstreet, ever the realist; and the army was hungry, exhausted, and short of every kind of ammunition. Even so, Lee was determined to try once more to cut the bulk of Pope's army off before it could reach the safety of Washington.

At the break of day on the morning of August 31, wearing "rubber overalls and with a rubber poncho over his shoulders" against the steady rain, Lee and Jackson rode out to cross Bull Run, coming under fire from enemy pickets on the far side—proof that the remainder of the Federal army was still around Centreville, behind the lines that the Confederates themselves had dug the year before. Lee made his decision at once. Jackson, being farthest on the left, would move first, cross Bull Run at the Sudley Springs ford, advance north in a wide flanking movement around the right of Pope's army and try to cut off his retreat from Centreville—a repetiton of Lee's strategy at the Rappahannock on August 25. Longstreet would "remain on the battlefield, looking after the wounded and burying the dead, until Jackson had a good start," and would then follow Jackson. Stuart was ordered to cross Bull Run with the cavalry and advance toward Ox Hill and Fairfax Court House, screening Jackson's forces and holding Pope's attention—just the kind of flamboyant display at which Stuart excelled.

Having set Jackson in motion, Lee dismounted briefly near a high railroad embankment to talk to General Longstreet, with Traveller's reins looped loosely over one arm. A party of Federal prisoners under armed guard suddenly surged over the embankment, and Traveller threw up his head and "jumped backwards" in alarm, throwing Lee violently to the ground, spraining both his wrists and breaking a small bone in one hand. A surgeon was summoned, and both of Lee's arms were put in slings, rendering him unable to ride. For some days he would be obliged to accompany his army in an ambulance. Quite apart from the pain, which was considerable, the accident was "a sore trial to the general's patience . . . since inevitably a horse-drawn, wheeled vehicle "could not go into many places where a horse would have carried him."

Time and weather, as well as his own injuries, were now working against Lee. Longstreet followed Jackson at 2 p.m., to the strains of "Dixie" being "cheerfully" played by the army's band in the pouring rain. The troops marched, in Longstreet's words, "over a single-track country road, bad enough on the south side of the river, much worn . . . over quicksand sub-soil on the north side." Longstreet complained—with a certain degree of what sounds very much like petu-lance—that if Jackson "had been followed by enemy whose march he wished to baffle, his gun-carriages could not have made deeper cuts through the mud and quicksand." Hard as it was for Longstreet's army to slog over a muddy road that had already been trampled by Jackson's passage, it would also have made the prog-ress of Lee's ambulance even slower and more uncom-fortable than it would ordinarily have been.★ Enclosed in a small space Lee could have no clear view of what was going on.

During the course of the morning he received a formal request from Pope for a truce to pick up Federal wounded from the battlefield. Lee's response was mea-sured. He would permit Federal ambulances to cross the Confederate line, but he would not agree to a truce. As usual, Lee was practical and hardheaded. He had no wish to swamp his already overburdened medical officers with several thousand Federal wounded, and he also did not want to be slowed by a formal truce.

★ Most "ambulances" of the day were windowless, basically a box with doors at the rear, the rear wheels mounted on springs and the front wheels mounted on a transverse spring, although these merely added a pronounced swaying motion to the bumping up and down on rough roads.

By nightfall Longstreet was still on the wrong side of Bull Run, while Jackson's hungry, weary, rain-soaked troops were still well short of Fairfax Court House. They bivouacked for the night in Pleasant Valley, on Little River Turnpike, almost ten miles from Jackson's goal. The only person who had managed to move quickly was Pope, who had abandoned Centreville and marched his army far enough north so that Jackson could no longer cut off his retreat. By late afternoon of the next day, September 1, Jackson reached the mansion of Chantilly, one of the great houses of Virginia; it had been built by the Stuart family, which intermarried with the Lee family, and was adjacent to the estate of Lee's kinsman Francis Lightfoot Lee. Having realized that he could not get behind Pope, Jackson decided to attack his right flank. This was not a success; a thunderstorm of unprecedented violence "beat in the men's faces" as they advanced to meet the enemy, and the Federals resisted stoutly. Thunder contested with the noise of the guns as the fight continued on until darkness put an end to it. Longstreet, who came up with his army as night fell, commented that the Federals "made a furious attack, driving back the Confederates with some disorder." That may have been due to Lee's absence. His ambulance had arrived too late for him to have taken command of the battle. Doubtless tired and in pain from his injuries, he made his headquarters in a nearby farm-house. Longstreet remarked to Jackson, when he rode up "as the storm of the battle, as well as that of the elements, began to die down," that Jackson's men did not "appear to be working well today," having observed the number of stragglers on the way, a comment that Jackson can hardly have welcomed, especially since Longstreet had not managed to arrive until after the fighting was all but over. Jackson brusquely replied, "No, but I hope that it will prove a victory in the morning."

This did not prove to be the case. The Battle of Ox Hill, as it is known in the South—or Chantilly, as it is known in the North—failed to delay Pope's retreat to the safety of Washington, and cost Lee an additional 1,300 casualties. Although Stuart's cavalry harassed the Federal retreat almost to the Potomac, any hope of annihilating Pope's army was gone.

One of the Union casualties of the battle was Major General Philip Kearny, who had served with Lee in Mexico. He had inadvertently ridden into the Confederate line in the blinding rainstorm as night fell, and realized his mistake too late. He "wheeled his horse and put spurs, preferring the danger of musket-balls to humiliating surrender." Kearny was a *beau sabreur,* who had charged with the French army at the Battle of Solferino, and became the first American to be awarded the *Légion d'Honneur,*★ a wealthy man who had chosen the army as a career, and been obliged to resign after a messy affair and divorce.

Despite the aura of scandal that surrounded Kearny, Lee may have remembered his gallantry at Churubusco, and admired the courage of his last moments. He took the time to write a gracious note to Pope:

September 2, 1862

Major-General John Pope,
United States Army

Sir,—The body of General Philip Kearny was brought from the field last night, and he was reported dead. I send it forward under a flag of truce, thinking that the possession of his remains may be a consolation to his family.

> I am, sir, respectfully,
> your obedient servant,
> R. E. Lee
> General

★ He is also one of only two soldiers whose graves are marked by equestrian statues in Arlington National Cemetery (on ground once owned by Robert E. Lee and his wife), the other being Field Marshal Sir John Dill, CMG, DSO, GCB, former chief of the Imperial General Staff and Britain's senior military representative on the Combined Chiefs of Staff in Washington, 1941–1944.

At times the essential character of Lee appears out of the ferocity of war: formal, unfailingly polite, dignified, and caring. However much Lee despised Pope, he went out of his way to ensure that General Kearny's body was "prepared for burial" and returned to the Union lines with the appropriate ceremony and respect.

Although Lee's victory was greeted with jubilation in Richmond, he was well aware of the difficulties that accompanied it. He had taken over 7,000 Federal prisoners on the plains of Manassas, as well as "about 2,000 Federal wounded left in our hands." In addition, he captured "thirty pieces of artillery, [and] upward of twenty thousand stands of small arms," which caused the luckless Pope to write plaintively to General Halleck, "Unless something can be done to re-store [sic] the tone to this army, it will melt away before you know it." But Lee had neither the number of men needed to attack Washington, having lost nearly 10,000 between crossing the Rappahannock and reaching the Potomac, nor the supplies to carry out a long siege. Years later, when asked why he had failed to pursue Pope farther, Lee would reply simply: "My men had nothing to eat." Victorious they might be, but they were effectively stranded in the muddy shambles of a battlefield, without food for three days. There was no way Lee could ask starving men to assault well-manned fortifications. His army had to move or die.

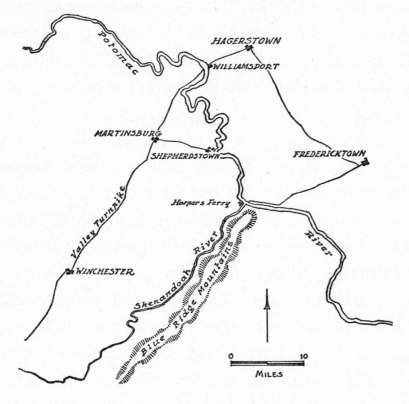

17. Lee's approach to Maryland

He could not fall back—a victorious army does not retreat, and in any case his men had already picked clean the country between Manassas and the Rappahannock; nor did he want to provision it at the expense of his fellow Virginians, who by this time had little left for themselves after the passage of two armies. He had no realistic option except to cross the Potomac and advance north into the rich countryside of Maryland or Pennsylvania, where he could feed his army at the expense of the enemy. Maryland offered many strategic advantages—it was "enemy country," of course, but many of its inhabitants were sympathetic to the southern cause, and he might even hope to acquire recruits.

As usual, Lee made up his mind quickly. He wrote to President Davis only two days after the Battle of Ox Hill: "The present seems to be the most propitious time since the commencement of the war for the Confederate Army to enter Maryland." The danger of carrying out his plan, Lee added, was that his army was "not properly equipped for an invasion . . . is feeble in transportation . . . the men . . . in thousands of instances are destitute of shoes." He did not wait for a reply from Davis. On September 4 he ordered the army to cross the Potomac into Maryland "in the vicinity of Leesburg." By September 7 he had approximately 65,000 men north of the Potomac, marching toward Frederick, Maryland, while Stuart's cavalry, which crossed the Potomac farther east at Edward's Ferry, was spread out from there to New Market, shielding Lee's right flank. As Lee himself crossed the band played "Maryland, My Maryland," inappropriately as it turned out. Seldom has a major military maneuver been decided on so quickly or carried out so rapidly.

One moment, it seemed, his army was just south of Washington, hardly fifteen miles away from the White House; the next it was to the northeast, threatening both Washington and Baltimore. It was a bold move, perhaps the boldest of Lee's career.

His old opponent General Pope had been sent far from the center of events to Minnesota, to fight recalcitrant Indians, and replaced by a reluctant president with General McClellan, after General Burnside, with a realistic view of his own inadequacy for the task, turned the president's offer of command down. McClellan had the confidence of the army. Swiftly, and with his usual competence at organization and logistics, he turned it from a defeated, disgruntled uniformed mob into an efficient fighting machine. Even so, he faced misgivings on the part of Lincoln, and outright hostility from most of Lincoln's cabinet, all of whom doubted whether McClellan could be relied on to *use* the army once he had completed its restoration, and some of whom even feared he would use it to carry out a military putsch, and enforce a deal with the Confederates for a negotiated peace. Typically, McClellan hesitated before accepting what he had wanted in the first place. President Lincoln and General Halleck were obliged to call "unannounced" at McClellan's house, early in the morning on September 5, and spend two hours persuading him to accept the command. Even then he managed to further dismay Lincoln by having the first elements of the army march past his house cheering him on their way out of Washington, instead of past the White House.

For a change, McClellan was seeking a battle, while Lee was not. Lee was more concerned with feeding his army and restoring its strength, and with the political and strategic advantages of moving it to Maryland. So long as he was in place north of Washington, there would be no Federal attempt to renew the advance on Richmond—and so there would be a breathing space for the Confederate government—and Federal troops would have to be deployed in large numbers to defend Washington and Baltimore, as well as to protect Pennsylvania. Lee even contemplated the possibility that the army's presence might inspire Marylanders to join the Confederacy—after all, it was only by a show of strength that Lincoln had kept Maryland in the Union in 1861. Lee issued a lofty proclamation in a rather obvious attempt to portray the invasion of Maryland as a response to "the wish" of its people "to enjoy the inalienable rights of free men, and restore independence and sovereignty to your State." It did not have any effect on the Marylanders, who showed no signs of rising against the United States, joining the Confederate Army in significant numbers, or letting go of their food and forage for Confederate dollars.

On the same day as the proclamation; Lee made a rare attempt to influence politics in Richmond. He wrote a letter to Jefferson Davis urging him to use the invasion of Maryland as the moment to offer a peace proposal to the United States. "Such a proposal coming from us at this time could in no way be regarded as suing for peace," Lee wrote, "but being made when it is in our power to inflict injury upon our adversary, would show conclusively to the world that our sole object is the establishment of our independence and the attainment of an honorable peace."

As it turned out, Lee was about to make several errors of strategy that would undermine, his notion of negotiating from strength, still it is perhaps the clearest statement he ever made of the intention behind his strategy. Once he had taken steps to secure Richmond, he intended to move the fighting out of Virginia and into the North, and to combine battlefield victories with vigorous diplomacy, gambling that the northern public would soon tire of a war fought on their own soil, at a great cost in lives, and with the inevitable destruction of property on a large scale. The victory of Second Manassas may have made him overconfident. He may also have underrated Lincoln's determination or the outrage in the North at the news that the Confederate army had crossed into Maryland. Certainly he could not have guessed that McClellan would replace the ignominious and clumsy Pope as his opponent, still less that McClellan, who had so often retreated before him on the peninsula, had suddenly, and at the last moment, stiffened his spine. McClellan was as hostile as ever toward the president and the secretary of war, but the fact that he had been called on to repair the mess Pope had made, and restored to full command of the Army of the Potomac, boosted his confidence, and convinced him that he had been right all along. He was no longer feeling sorry for himself; there was no more thought about moving the family silver to safety in New York City.

"McClellan has the army with him," Lincoln said in mournful resignation, and he was right. If command of the army had lifted McClellan's spirits, it had an even greater effect on his troops. McClellan loved spit and polish and firm discipline, both of which did much to restore the army's dignity and self-respect, but he also understood the importance of better food and improved sanitation. When he reviewed the Army of the Potomac, cantering past the troops on Daniel Webster, his big, dark bay horse, in full uniform with a gold sash and gleaming gold-and-blue embroidered sword belt, the men cheered him lustily, threw their caps into the air, and told each other that "Little Mac is back!" "Again I have been called upon to save the country," he wrote to Ellen, his self-esteem and complacency restored. His tendency toward paranoia and his contempt for politicians were undiminished, but for the moment held under control. "The march of the Confederates toward the north no longer allowed [McClellan] to confine himself to a mere defense of the capital," noted the ubiquitous Comte de Paris sagely, "but compelled him to undertake an offensive campaign." In fact, McClellan recognized that his return to command depended on one thing, and one thing only: a rapid victory over Robert E. Lee.

As for Lee, if he had truly anticipated an outpouring of support and recruits from Marylanders in response to his proclamation, he was to be disappointed. The state of his army was also a concern. The men were exhausted after continuous fighting and marching for over a month, many were barefoot, most were emaciated, their uniforms were in rags, and the horses were almost as starved as the men. One bystander remembered them as "the dirtiest men I ever saw, a most ragged, lean and hungry set of wolves." Indeed their condition was such as to shock and discourage even the most pro-Confederate of Marylanders.

More seriously still, straggling had become such a problem that Lee was obliged to request from Rihmond a "military commission" and a reinforced "provost-marshal's guard," the nineteenth-century equivalent of military police, to round them up. The paved roads of Maryland were harder for barefoot men to march on than the dirt roads farther south, and many of the men felt they had joined the army to defend the South, not to invade the North. Desertion increased. Lee sent his aide Colonel Long back toward Winchester to see to the problem, and to dissuade President Davis from his proposal to join Lee in Maryland.

The latter mission was all the more important because Lee had decided to move his army from Frederick, where his men had already exhausted the food supply, northwest toward Hagerstown, less than five miles from the Pennsylvania border. This would mean effectively breaking off his line of communication with Richmond in favor of moving farther west. Supplies and ammunition would reach him via Winchester and Martinsburg through the Shenandoah Valley. Admittedly, Lee's line of communications via Culpeper was vulnerable to an attack "from the direction of Washington," but moving it to the Shenandoah Valley, apart from making it longer, was also not without danger. Both Martinsburg and Harpers Ferry were in Union hands, and Lee's new line of communication could be harassed or even altogether cut off from either place. It was Hobson's choice, but he decided on the Shenandoah Valley, although that meant he would have to take Martinsburg and Harpers Ferry. This was a catastrophic decision, since he would have to split his forces to accomplish it. Longstreet, who tends to get the blame for the consequences of most of Lee's bad decisions, argued against splitting the army, and this time he was right.

Lee may have been gambling on McClellan's notorious tendency to wait until everything in his army was perfect before moving,* and even then doing so with extreme caution; but if so, that was also a mistake. For once McClellan seemed aware that his career and his public reputation depended on swift and aggressive movement. He may have been moved by his good fortune in being restored to command of the army after Pope's disgrace, or he may have been reacting to calls from the press in the North urging him to become a military dictator, or to run for the presidency in 1864, or some combination of both—Stephen W. Sears, in his biography of McClellan, cites the *New York Herald*'s call for him "to become an American Cromwell," a role for which McClellan seems singularly ill-suited—but what-

---

*Like General Leboeuf in 1870, McClellan prided himself on having an army that was "ready down to the last button on its gaiters."

ever the reason he seemed to be moving with a firmer step here than on the peninsula, although he had not lost his habit of overestimating his enemy's strength. He now believed that Lee had at least 120,000 men, more than twice the number that Colonel Long gives, from which must be deducted the substantial and growing number of stragglers and deserters since the army had crossed the Rappahannock. Lee had constantly borne in mind the disparity of forces between himself and McClellan—Freeman puts Lee's strength in Maryland at no more than 53,000* men, whereas McClellan had 84,000, with another 75,000 defending Washington.

Lee hoped that when his new line of communication through the Shenandoah Valley was secured, he might reach the Susquehanna bridge of the Pennsylvania Railroad, seventy-one miles west of Harrisburg, Pennsylvania, and cut the East "off from the West," thereby "assuring that no reinforcements could reach his adversary from the West," and making possible a march on Philadelphia, Baltimore, or Washington, and a victorious conclusion of the war for the South.

This is the first but not the last time that Harrisburg would play a vital role in Lee's strategy, but it seems

---

* This would place the number of stragglers and deserters from Lee's army at about 7,000, a alarmingly dangerous figure. Where possible, they were being rounded up and detained at Winchester for return to the army, but in the meantime Lee's units were seriously below strength.

a long reach, and assumes that Lee could maneuver at will in Maryland and Pennsylvania without facing a battle. McClellan was certainly "a deliberate opponent," but not quite so supine as that. In addition, seventy-one miles is a long way to march, particularly for an army that is exhausted and half-starved, and there seems no reason why McClellan could not obtain reinforcements from the North, or even draw on the troops guarding Washington if need be, rather than relying on troops from the West. Finally, at the rate Lee was losing men, would he have enough left to take and—more important—*hold* a large northern city?

In any event, these rosy possibilities, though they dance like sugarplum fairies in many southern accounts of the war, would become possible only when Lee had beaten McClellan *decisively* in the field, and the one way to do that was to concentrate his forces rapidly and strike the Federal army while it was still strung out on the road between Washington and Frederick.

On or around September 9 Lee sent for Jackson. They met in Lee's tent with the tent flap closed, while Lee explained his plan. Jackson was certainly the man best suited to take Harpers Ferry: he knew the place well, and no general North or South could move faster. At some point Lee heard Longstreet's booming voice outside, loud enough so that Lee opened the tent flap and invited him in. As one of Lee's two army commanders, Longstreet cannot have been well pleased to find that his chief was discussing strategy with Jackson behind the equivalent of a closed door. Longstreet notes with a hint of displeasure that the tent flap was not just closed but "tied." Once he learned the subject of their discussion, he was even less happy—this was exactly what Longstreet had been warning against even before Lee crossed the Potomac.

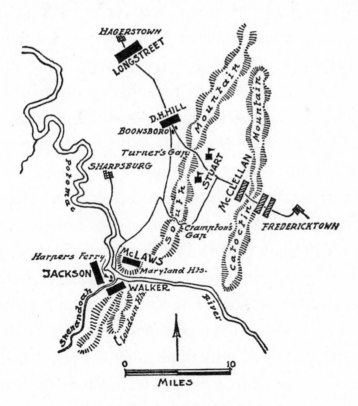

18. *The approach to Sharpsburg.*

Lee's relationship with his two principal subordinates sheds a certain amount of light on his character. Obviously he placed great trust in Jackson, whose religious belief was as strong as Lee's own—though rather more sternly enforced; whose ability to overcome difficulties and keep his army moving was second to none; and who always obeyed Lee's orders without question or hesitation. Yet he had a good deal of affection and respect for Longstreet, an altogether more balky and obstinate character, who not only argued with Lee, but never let go of an argument even when Lee had dismissed it. Lieutenant-Colonel Fremantle of the Coldstream Guards, the shrewd and ubiquitous British observer who attached himself to Lee's headquarters, would remark that "the relationships between [Lee] and Longstreet are quite touching—they are almost always together. . . . It is impossible to please Longstreet more than by praising Lee." Southern historians have often painted a very different picture of the relationship between the two men, but Fremantle was close to both of them, and was no fool. The word "touching" coming from a British military officer of the Victorian age with the stiffest of stiff upper lips suggests not only respect, but a degree of real friendship. No matter how "sulky" Longstreet might be, or how skeptical,

Lee always seems to have heard him out with respect and a degree of affection, even when he had already decided not to follow the advice of the man he called his "Old War Horse."

Longstreet was not the only person to express dismay. Harpers Ferry was not necessarily hard to take—it passed hands many times during the war— but it would have to be attacked from three sides at once to prevent the escape of its garrison of 12,000 men. Lee summoned the commander of one of the three columns to his tent to brief him on his role. Brigadier General John G. Walker's face must have betrayed his astonishment, since Lee said (according to Freeman), "You doubtless regard it hazardous to leave McClellan practically on my line of communication, and to march into the heart of the enemy's country?"

Walker had to admit that this was exactly what he thought.

"Are you acquainted with General McClellan?" Lee asked. "He is an able general, but a very cautious one. His enemies among his own people think him too much so. . . . [He] will not be prepared for offensive operations—or he will not think it so—for three or four weeks. Before that time I hope to be on the Susquehanna."

Lee had not forgotten his intention to demolish the Baltimore and Ohio railroad bridge. He wanted Jackson to accomplish that on his way to Harpers Ferry, as well as to destroy the soaring stone aqueduct of the Chesapeake and Ohio Canal which crossed the Monocacy River, and also to tear up as much of the B&O track as possible. While all this was going on, the rest of the army would proceed toward Hagerstown, where Jackson would rejoin it, so that the whole army would be concentrated before marching into Pennsylvania. All this was spelled out crisply and in much detail in one of Lee's most famous orders, "Special Orders, No. 191," dated September 9, 1862. This is worth reading in full, because it contradicts suggestions that have sometimes been made that Lee's orders were unclear, or that his staff failed to convey them accurately. It might serve, in fact, as the very model of how to draw up orders for an army, were it not for the fact that Major General D. H. Hill received not one but two copies of it, and that the extra copy was used by one of his staff officers "to wrap up three cigars," and place them in an official envelope for safekeeping. Accidentally dropped in "an abandoned Confederate camp" near Frederick, Lee's order was in McClellan's hands four days after it was written, giving an astonished McClellan every detail of Lee's plans.

HEADQUARTERS ARMY OF NORTHERN VIRGINIA,
September 9, 1862.
Special Orders, No. 191.

1. The citizens of Fredericktown being unwilling, while overrun by members of this army, to open their stores in order to give them confidence all officers and men of this army are strictly prohibited from visiting Fredericktown except on business, in which case they will bear evidence of this in writing from division commanders. The provost marshal in Fredericktown will see that his guard rigidly enforces this order.

2. Major Taylor will proceed to Leesburg, Virginia, and arrange for transportation of the sick and those unable to walk to Winchester, securing the transportation of the country for this purpose.

   The route between this and Culpeper Court House east of the mountains being unsafe will no longer be traveled. Those on the way to this army already across the river will move up promptly; all others will proceed to Winchester collectively and under command of officers, at which point, being the general depot of this army, its movements will be known and instructions given by commanding officer regulating further movements.

3. The army will resume its march tomorrow, taking the Hagerstown road. General Jackson's command will form the advance, and after passing Middletown with such portion as he may select, take the route toward Sharpsburg, cross the Potomac at the most convenient point, and by Friday morning take possession of the Baltimore and Ohio Railroad, capture such of the enemy as may be at Martinsburg, and intercept such as may attempt to escape from Harper's Ferry.

4. General Longstreet's command will pursue the main road as far as Boonsborough, where it will halt with reserve, supply, and baggage trains of the army.

5. General McLaws, with his own division and that of General R. H. Anderson, will follow General Longstreet. On reaching Middletown he will take the route to Harper's Ferry, and by Friday morning possess himself of the Maryland Heights and endeavor to capture the enemy at Harper's Ferry and vicinity.

6. General Walker, with his division, after accomplishing the object in which he is now engaged, will cross the Potomac at Cheek's Ford, ascend its right bank to Lovettsville, take possession of Loudon Heights, if practicable, by Friday morning, Keys's Ford on his left, and the road between the end of the mountain and the Potomac on his right. He will, as far as practicable, cooperate with generals McLaws and Jackson, and intercept the retreat of the enemy.

7. General D. H. Hill's division will form the rear-guard of the army, pursuing the road taken by the main body. The reserve artillery, ordnance, and supply-trains, etc., will precede General Hill.

8. General Stuart will detach a squadron of cavalry to accompany the commands of generals Longstreet, Jackson, and McLaws, and, with the main body of the cavalry, will cover the route of the army, bringing up all stragglers that may have been left behind.

9. The commands of generals Jackson, McLaws, and Walker, after accomplishing the objects for which they have been detached, will join the main body of the army at Boonsborough or Hagerstown.

10. Each regiment on the march will habitually carry its axes in regimental ordnance wagons, for use of the men at their encampments, to procure wood, etc.

> By command of General R. E. Lee.
> R. H. CHILTON,
> Assistant adjutant-general.

The fact that Lee's order No. 191 fell into McClellan's hands through spectacular carelessness is only part of its significance. The order presumes an almost uncanny lethargy on the part of McClellan, and violates the first rule of warfare, which is to concentrate one's forces against the enemy. Lee split his army into the three major "columns," and further split Jackson's command into three separate columns, none of them in a position to support the others if the need arose. It is hard to imagine a more dangerous position for an army operating in enemy territory with one very doubtful line of communication and one not yet secured, pursued by an army that was markedly superior in numbers and supplies, as well as in quality and quantity of artillery.

The military historian Major-General J. F. C. Fuller turns positively apoplectic when describing Lee's decision, which he refers to as "a suicidal diversion of force," and goes on to add: "Lee held the enemy in such contempt that he saw no danger in sending half his army in one direction, whilst he proceeded with the remaining half in the other; and this in the face of an enemy which outnumbered his own by nearly two to one!" Fuller is not a writer who uses an exclamation point lightly. Longstreet, who objected to this plan from the beginning, would write, with only a touch more restraint, "The great mistake of the campaign was the division of Lee's army," and it is difficult to disagree. The loss of the order was an accident, a piece of carelessness for which Lee was not responsible, just another of the innumerable hazards of war, but the division of his army was an error, a fatal misreading of the situation.

General Fuller's opinion that "Lee held the enemy in . . . contempt" is surely not the reason for Lee's decision. He was too much a gentleman to either feel or express contempt for anyone, save for General Pope, and that was because of Pope's order threatening punishment for Confederate sympathizers in the areas he controlled. He certainly felt no contempt for General McClellan, whom he described after the war as the ablest Union general he had fought against, and would have been incapable of feeling contempt for the soldiers of the army he had served for most of his adult life. It is much more likely that what Lee felt was a mild euphoria after his recent successes. He had come to rely on the resilience and bravery of Confederate troops even when they were heavily outnumbered, as well as their patient ability to survive near-starvation, lack of boots and decent uniforms, and long, brutal marches day after day. Lee was too humble a man to feel anything so brash as overconfidence in his own skill as a general, but he suffered from overconfidence in his troops, which is almost as dangerous and often leads to rash decisions. What's more, it is contagious—Jackson, and many other Confederate generals, followed Lee's example, and inevitably some of them assumed that even when they made a mistake, their troops would get them out of it. More often than not the troops did so, but even the bravest troops cannot always overcome a serious error on the part of their general. Longstreet's common sense about what Confederate troops could and could *not* do normally acted as a brake on Lee's riskier plans, although on this occasion, as at Gettysburg, it failed to persuade Lee.

The two men reached Hagerstown on September 11, having proceeded via Turner's Gap in South Mountain, where Lee set his troops an example of how he expected them to behave in enemy territory by lifting his hat in salute to a woman who sang "The Star-Spangled Banner" "as he rode through the town."*

Despite Lee's courteous gesture, the good citizens of Hagerstown were as unwilling as those of Frederick to supply the Confederate army (or to accept Confederate dollars for their goods). There was no news from Jackson that Harpers Ferry had fallen; moreover, Lee received the unwelcome news from Stuart that his cavalry scouts had reported Federal troops advancing in force on Frederick, perhaps as many as 90,000. This was the last thing Lee expected—he had been confident that McClellan would be slow and cautious, but instead he was moving rapidly, indeed he was hard on the heels of Lee's army, not more than ten miles from Turner's Gap, which was held loosely by D. H. Hill's division and Stuart's cavalry. Lee's decision to divide his army now began to create a dangerous problem. If McClellan reached Crampton's Gap, only a few miles south of Turner's Gap, he could prevent Jackson's three columns now converging on Harpers Ferry from any chance of rejoining the rest of Lee's army.

---

* This story curiously resembles the famous, but probably apocryphal, incident of Stonewall Jackson and Barbara Fritchie at Frederick, Maryland, which inspired John Greenleaf Whittier's poem, once known by heart by all American schoolchildren (and not a few in England)—" 'Shoot, if you must, this old gray head, / But spare your country's flag!' she said." When Winston Churchill visited Frederick, in 1943, he sought out Barbara Fritchie's house, went upstairs, opened the famous window, and recited the entire poem from memory to those in the street below.

Overnight, Lee's position changed from that of a general advancing into Pennsylvania with a new line of communication opening up via Martinsburg and Harpers Ferry to that of a general with an enemy behind him and no line of communication at all. Rather than advancing into Pennsylvania, Lee now faced the possibility that he might have to turn his scattered army around and retrace his steps.

At this moment of crisis Lee and Longstreet had a major disagreement. Called to Lee's tent on the night of September 13, Longstreet "found him over his map." Lee explained the situation briefly and asked for Longstreet's opinion. Longstreet proposed joining his forces with those of D. H. Hill and taking up a position behind Antietam Creek at Sharpsburg, where the whole army could be concentrated. Longstreet recalled in his memoirs that Lee still suffered from "the hallucination that McClellan was not capable of serious work," and wanted Longstreet to march at daylight the next morning to join with D. H. Hill and defend Turner's Gap. Given the lateness of the hour Longstreet doubted that his men would be ready to march at daybreak and thought that by the time they got to Turner's Gap they would be too tired to defend it, even if they reached it in time. Lee politely rejected this advice, and ordered Longstreet to proceed; but Longstreet's "mind was so disturbed" that he could not rest, so he rose, "made a light," and sat down to write a letter to Lee, once again urging him to concentrate the army at Sharpsburg. Lee ignored this letter, and did not change his plan.

This was not merely a difference of opinion about tactics, as Longstreet supposed, but a much larger question of strategy. If Lee could turn and defeat the enemy at Turner's Gap, he could continue on to the northwest toward Chambersburg, Carlisle, and Harrisburg. If Lee gathered his army at Sharpsburg, as Longstreet wanted him to do, he would have to move south, virtually to the Potomac, with the possibility that McClellan might surround him there, or even make it necessary for him to cross the Potomac back into Virginia—exactly what Lee most wanted to avoid. Following Longstreet's advice would bring to an end the invasion of the North, and with it the chance of threatening one or more of its major cities and enabling the Confederacy to negotiate peace on acceptable terms. Lee had a larger, brighter vision in mind than Longstreet did, and believed he was on the verge of securing it.

Lee may have allowed himself to see, in his mind's eye, the long gray columns capturing Harrisburg and marching on to Baltimore or Washington, battle flags unfurled, but when Longstreet looked at the map he thought it would be more prudent to concentrate the army at Sharpsburg and let McClellan attack it there on ground of Lee's own choosing.

Whatever Lee hoped, at this point, half his troops were twenty miles away near Harpers Ferry, and Lee remained "in the darkest uncertainty" about what had become of them. Nor, of course could he possibly have guessed that McClellan had read his order of September 9. Von Clausewitz's "fog of war" has never been thicker than "at daylight" on the morning of September 14 when Lee and Longstreet rode off—possibly Lee's first time back in the saddle on Traveller since his accident*—toward South Mountain. They did not get very far before they received "a dispatch" from D. H. Hill that he urgently needed reinforcements. He had been holding Turner's Gap since the early morning against overwhelming numbers of Federal troops—two Confederate brigades against eight Federal. Longstreet hurried to send four of his understrength brigades to support Hill. Longstreet respected Lee too much to have said the equivalent of "I told you so," but years later that was certainly on his mind when he came to write his memoirs. As for Lee, he was informed that

---

*Douglas Southall Freeman marks this as Lee's first ride on Traveller since he injured both hands at Second Manassas (*Robert E. Lee*, Vol. 2, 369) but from accounts of Lee's entry into Hagerstown on September 11, when he raised his hat to the woman singing "The Star-Spangled Banner," it sounds as if he was already riding then. However, somebody may have been walking beside Traveller with a lead rope, since Lee could not yet have held the reins.

McClellan had a copy of order No. 191 by ten o'clock that morning. A Confederate sympathizer had been present at McClellan's headquarters while it was being discussed. At last Lee understood why McClellan was moving at such an uncharacteristically rapid pace. In response to this, Lee moved as many brigades as he could toward Turner's Gap, and a growing battle raged there from noon until darkness, restrained only by the cautiousness of the Union's Major General Burnside— McLaws—not surprising in view of McClellan's belief that Lee had at least 120,000 men on the far side of South Mountain.

The Battle of South Mountain cost both sides nearly 2,000 casualties, and by the end of the day it was clear to Lee that the Union attack would be renewed again in the morning; that he could not hold Turner's Gap, or indeed any of the other gaps in South Mountain; and that he also risked losing Major General Lafayette McLaws's division, which was holding Maryland Heights on the north side of the Potomac as part of Jackson's forces besieging Harpers Ferry. Lee now faced a very real risk that the Army of Northern Virginia could be destroyed piecemeal the next day. He decided that he had no option but to order a retreat to Sharpsburg, where he could collect the army, cross the Potomac back to Virginia, and live to fight another day—exactly what Longstreet had advised him to do.

This was reversal of fortune with a vengeance. Lee spent what was, for him, an unusually anxious night, as one general after another informed him that the enemy was "pouring" through the gaps in South Mountain. The next morning, though, there was good news. Harpers Ferry had surrendered. This was hardly surprising, since Jackson had nearly 30,000 men on the heights surrounding a place that *The West Point Atlas of the American Wars* describes as "indefensible." Jackson captured 12,000 Federal troops, 13,000 "stands of arms"* and 73 guns, the biggest Federal surrender of the war.

Lee was relieved by this good news, and his "innate combativeness reasserted itself." His pleasure was only slightly marred by the fact that Colonel Benjamin F. Grimes had led 1,400 Federal cavalrymen out of Harpers Ferry over a narrow pontoon bridge across the Potomac and had accidentally run into a long train of wagons carrying Longstreet's reserve ammunition, capturing forty wagons. The prudent move Lee had contemplated during the night was now banished from his mind by the good news from Jackson. It was only twelve miles from Harpers Ferry to Sharpsburg, and as soon as Jackson had secured his booty and sent his

---

* A "stand of arms" was the complete set of equipment for one soldier: musket, bayonet, belt, cartridge box, sling, etc.

prisoners on to Winchester he could rejoin his three divisions to Lee's army.

Lee himself could still have crossed the Potomac by the Shepherdstown Ford; concentrated his army at Martinsburg, only four miles away; and waited for McClellan to attack him there on high ground of his own choosing—or he could have ordered Jackson to cross to the north bank of the Potomac now that Harpers Ferry had surrendered, march up the Rohrersville Road, and attack the left flank of the Federal forces as they emerged from Cranston Gap. This would surely have slowed down or even stopped McClellan's advance. Instead he chose to move all his forces into the small, hilly stretch of farmland and woodland between the Potomac and Antietam Creek around Sharpsburg, which is at no point wider than three miles. For better or worse, he had decided to put all his eggs in one basket.

Even today Sharpsburg is hardly an imposing town, numbering only 705 inhabitants in the last census. In 1862, however, it was important because it lay astride the road from Shepherdstown on the Potomac; to Centreville, Maryland; and on to Boonsboro, where it joined the main road to Hagerstown and Pennsylvania. The distances are small. It is only three miles from Sharpsburg to the Potomac, and not more

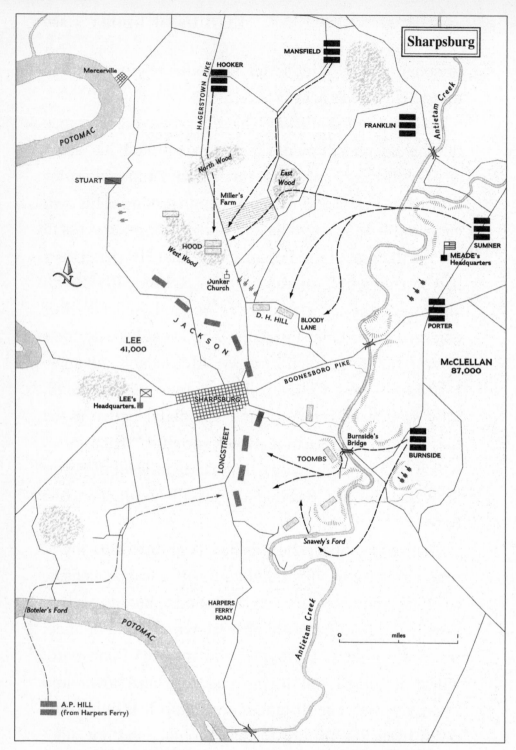

19. Battle of Sharpsburg (or Antietam), September 17, 1862.

than six miles to Hagerstown Pike. Four miles to the south is the meandering Antietam Creek. The distance to the Cranford Gap in South Mountain, through which Federal troops were now "pouring," is only six miles. There would be no room for maneuvering here, and no chance to pull off one of Jackson's brilliant flanking attacks. The battle would be an armed head-on collision, fought in a narrow space. Even the ground was not particularly favorable for Lee to fight a defensive battle against an army almost twice the size of his own.

Lee would be obliged to fight with his back to the Potomac, and only one "deep, rocky" ford (Boteler's Ford) in the rear on the extreme right of his line across which to receive reinforcements and supplies—or to retreat. He placed Longstreet, with half the army, on his right, slightly ahead and south of Sharpsburg, from which gently rolling land stretched down to Antietam Creek about a mile to the east at that point, and directly overlooking one of the bridges across the creek. He would place Jackson when he arrived to the north of the town, farther forward on high ground overlooking Hagerstown Pike and another bridge across Antietam Creek.

This was not a position of great strength. The ground from Antietam Creek to Sharpsburg rolled gently upward, but there were no commanding heights to hold. The east bank of the creek was more elevated than the west one, and in places densely wooded with first growth, which would give McClellan's artillery a number of well covered positions to fire from as Federal troops crossed the creek. Although some of the bloodiest fighting would take place at the lowest of the three bridges, which came to be known as "Burnside's Bridge," after the Union corps commander who sent regiment after regiment across its short, narrow span to attack Lee's right, the troops themselves soon discovered that the creek was easily fordable in several places, which might have saved many lives had General Ambrose Burnside bothered to find out.

On the morning of September 16 Lee woke from a "sound sleep." Although he had only 18,000 men at Sharpsburg until Jackson arrived, and had already observed the enemy coming up "in great strength" through the gaps in South Mountain, raising clouds of dust as they advanced, Lee could not have been more composed "if he had had a well-equipped army of 100,000 veterans at his back," in the words of one observer. This was by no means a pose meant to encourage his officers and troops—Lee was one of those rare generals who *enjoy* battle; underneath the composure was a naturally fierce temperament, all the more impressive because of Lee's ability to conceal it by means of an impenetrable mask.

McClellan was technically every bit as good a general as Lee, perhaps even better, and he was no coward; nor was he afraid of losses. But he did not *enjoy* battle; it did not inspire and thrill him as it did Lee, or for that matter Napoleon. Certainly Lee's cheerfulness as he watched the Union troops, alarming masses of them, advancing over the hills in front of him toward Antietam Creek, can be explained only by his anticipation of a good fight. Everybody remarked on his calm good spirits on September 16, even as there streamed toward Antietam Creek what seemed like endless blue columns of Federal troops.

At noon, a cloud of dust on the road from the Potomac to Sharpsburg announced the arrival of Jackson, fresh from his victory at Harpers Ferry, behind him the ranks of his troops. Even so composed a general as Lee must have felt a certain relief as he shook hands with Jackson that his numbers would soon be doubled, though straggling, casualties, desertion, and sheer exhaustion would mean that he would nevertheless have at most 38,000 men to face 75,000 Federals the next day.

Very fortunately for Lee, McClellan had failed to make any clear plan for attacking, or even to issue a written order to his generals. He expressed only the rather vague intention "to make the main attack on the enemy's left—at least to create a diversion in favor of the main attack, with the hope of something more, by assailing the enemy's right—and as soon as one or both of the flank movements were fully successful, to attack their center with any reserve I might then have in hand." He made no effort to find out if Antietam Creek could be forded, or to see for himself what Lee's positions were. In devising his idea—to attack Lee's left, then his right, and then, if one or both of these attacks succeeded, perhaps to attack Lee's center if any Union troops were available at that point— McClellan woefully underrated Lee's genius and Longstreet and Jackson's competence. If McClellan had made a powerful lunge toward Sharpsburg using his numerical superiority at any time before the afternoon of September 16, when Jackson's troops had only begun to move into position, he might have crushed Lee's forces by the simple weight of numbers; but, overcome once again by caution, McClellan did nothing, and by mid-afternoon Lee had covered his left by placing Jackson's troops on ground that would shortly become famous in military history: North Wood, West Wood, Miller's Farm, "the Cornfield," Dunker Church, "Bloody Lane." Above and behind Jackson's far left Lee placed Stuart's horse artillery. Lee would shortly have a line that extended for nearly five miles, with the sleepy town of Sharpsburg at its center, and a web of roads and country lanes behind it that would enable him to move units quickly from one wing to the other to meet a Federal attack anywhere as it crossed Antietam Creek, possibly canceling out McClellan's superiority in numbers. Shuffling regiments and brigades like a master gambler, Lee was in position to resist anything except a general assault—which, as McClellan's own description of how he intended to fight the battle bears out, was the last thing he had in mind.

Federal artillery was already firing briskly when Lee walked through Sharpsburg, indifferent as always to the explosions bursting around him. "Leading Traveller by the bridle," he paused to warn Confederate gunners "not to waste their ammunition in an idle duel with Federal batteries." He must already have guessed from the direction of the gunfire that the Federal attack was under way on his left. By the time he remounted he heard musketry as the vanguard of Major General Joseph Hooker's corps of three divisions began to approach down Hagerstown Pike exchanging fire with John Bell Hood's division of Texans. It was too late for Hooker to mount a serious attack, but his appearance in strength on the far left of the Confederate line gave Lee an indication of where the fight would start in the morning.

At 4:30 a.m. Lee was awake and warning Brigadier General William Pendleton, his artillery commander, to cover the fords over the Potomac with his reserve artillery in case the army had to retreat. This may have been a reflection of the fact that the divisions of McLaws and Anderson were still strung out on the road from Harpers Ferry. By dawn Lee was going to need every man he could get, however exhausted and footsore. Even then there was a serious chance his forces might not be enough.

The musket fire from Hooker's "skirmishers"* began before first light. By six o'clock in the morning Hooker's corps bore down on the Confederate left, forcing Lee to move more and more men from his center and right to prevent a Federal breakthrough. It is a measure of Lee's willingness to take great risks that he calmly stripped his right to meet the crisis on the left. If McClellan had mounted an attack on Lee's right at the same time as Hooker's troops were pushing Hood's back across the

---

* "Skirmishers" were one of the most ancient traditions of warfare, their function being to precede the mass of infantry formations, using cover to shoot at the front line of the enemy formations and disrupt their cohesion before the main body attacked. By the mid-nineteenth century special units filled this function; examples include the rifle regiments in Britain, with their distinctive dark green uniforms and black buttons instead of the scarlet coats of the rest of the infantry; the *voltigeurs* in France; and the *Jäger* regiments in Germany. In the Union Army during the Civil War dismounted cavalry troopers armed with breech-loading or repeating carbines sometimes played this role; in the Confederate Army they were mostly "sharpshooters," i.e., specially selected natural marksmen (Wikipedia, "Skirmisher").

Cornfield toward Dunker Church, Lee's entire position at Sharpsburg might have collapsed, but perhaps Lee already sensed that McClellan was not exercising complete control over his battle. The numerous swales and ridges of the ground, as well as the sharp bends and wooded banks of the creek, tended to break up the area around Sharpsburg into three separate battlefields. Lee, who rode from one side of the battle to the other taking advantage of interior lines, had a clear picture of the whole battle. McClellan, on the other hand, had chosen to establish fixed headquarters for himself more than a mile behind Antietam Creek. The result was that he allowed his battle to drift into three uncoordinated parts: one on Lee's left in the morning, one on his center around noon, and one on his right in the afternoon. If McClellan had ridden forward and been able to get even two of these powerful attacks to take place at the same time he might have been able to force Lee out of Sharpsburg and back across the Potomac, but by midday he had allowed the opportunity to slip away.

Even so, some of the bloodiest fighting of the war took place early in the morning as artillery fire and massed musketry cut down the cornstalks and trees, and with them row after row of men who lay as neatly as if they had been scythed. Even "Fighting Joe"

Hooker, a heavy drinker and notorious ladies' man,* hardly a poetic soul, whom Grant said was "dangerous" as well as "insubordinate," described the scene with a deep feeling that most people would not have suspected he possessed: "every stalk of corn in the northern and greater part of the field was cut as closely as could have been done with a knife, and the [Confederates] slain lay in rows precisely as they stood in their ranks a few moments before." It was carnage, on both sides, as assault after assault took place across the bodies of the dead and wounded under constant artillery fire at close range and an unending storm of musket fire, all of it in a lurid fog of drifting gun smoke lit by bright flashes of gunfire and shell explosions. Men fired until their weapons became fouled with burned powder or they ran out of ammunition, then fought with the bayonet or used their weapons as clubs. Casualties reached nearly 70 percent in some hard-hit regiments. Even Hood's Texans were eventually driven back as the Federals advanced toward Dunker Church. Around 7:30 a.m., while surveying the scene, Lee was told that without reinforcements "the day

---

* There is some doubt whether the word "hooker" in fact comes from the kind of women who gathered around his headquarters, but even in his own time many people assumed that it did. The nickname "Fighting Joe" was a newspaperman's invention, and Hooker disliked it. When Grant called him "dangerous" he meant to his own men, not the enemy.

might be lost." He replied, gently but firmly, "Don't be excited about it, Colonel; go tell General Hood to hold his ground, reinforcements are now rapidly arriving between Sharpsburg and the ford."

Lee's imperturbability was one of the Army of Northern Virginia's most important weapons—his appearance polite and visibly unafraid, near the firing line, encouraged his soldiers, and no doubt shamed many a soldier who did feel fear into courageous behavior. He did not have Napoleon's flair for the dramatic gesture; instead it was Lee's impassivity that impressed the troops: his calm courage and his confidence in victory. Still, there was one moment during the day when Lee did let his anger slip. He remained anxious about the slowness of the troops marching from Harpers Ferry to the battlefield, and furious at the growing number of stragglers and deserters just when he needed every man. Riding forward toward Dunker Church he encountered a Confederate straggler from Jackson's troops making his way back from the firing line to his camp carrying the carcass of a stolen pig. White-faced, Lee abruptly ordered the man "to be sent to Jackson with orders to have him shot as a warning to the army, and rode on." In the event, Jackson, who knew his own men better than Lee did, ordered the soldier into the hottest part of the battle instead of shooting him. The soldier so distinguished himself that Jackson forgave him. Lee's faithful aide Colonel Long, not normally given to jokes at Lee's expense, remarked: "it may be said that, though [the soldier] lost his pig, he 'saved his bacon.'" Long also recalled that it was one of only two incidents during the entire war when Lee acted in "hot passion." Lee, he noted, with a certain clinical detachment, "was not wanting in temper, but was, on the contrary, a man of decided character and strong passions; yet he had such complete control over himself that few men ever knew him to deviate from his habitual calm dignity of mien."

Although Lee still professed to believe that his job was merely to bring the troops to the right place and leave matters afterward to his generals, Sharpsburg was even more Lee's battle than Second Manassas had been. Lee had brought the army into Maryland, detached Jackson to take Harpers Ferry against Longstreet's advice, and chosen Sharpsburg as the place to concentrate his forces and fight McClellan; he even spent part of the early morning siting artillery batteries where he wanted them—this was the very reverse of hands-off generalship. Perhaps Lee's confidence in his own ability was growing, or he was simply unaware of just how tightly he controlled every aspect of his battles, but both Long's account and Lee's own report of the battle to Richmond make it clear that he was familiar with every unit in his army and all his commanders, and that he was not only the animating spirit of the battle but the man responsible for every decision. Long, who was beside Lee, also makes it clear how great a risk Lee was taking to throw the majority of his forces to the left: "The Confederates, who had advanced about a mile, were gradually borne back to their original position. McClellan now directed his chief attack upon Lee's left, with the hope of forcing it back, so that he might penetrate between it and the river and take the Confederate position in reverse. . . . The entire Confederate force, except D. R. Jones's division, on the far right, was now engaged."

One by one, Lee artfully fed units from his center and right into the fight, dangerously weakening Longstreet's line. Everywhere on the field, row after row of dead and wounded men demonstrated the ferocity of the fight. One Confederate artillery commander called it "Artillery Hell," and a Union commander who was in many of the major battles of the war declared that "the Antietam Turnpike surpassed them all in manifest evidence of slaughter." From 9:30 a.m. to midday D. H. Hill's division clashed with Major General William French's Union division over the sunken road where

Lee's left met his center. The road had served as a shortcut around Sharpsburg for local farmers, and had many zigzagging angles, which acted like the fire bays and traverses of the 1914–1918 trenches and enabled the Confederates to pour fire into the flanks of the Federals each time they attempted to storm it. The road changed hands several times, though it eventually ended up in Union hands, and would become known as "Bloody Lane" because the blood pooled up in the hard-worn hollow of its dried clay surface and literally ran like a river. Three hours of hand-to-hand fighting in this one place cost over 5,000 casualties on both sides.

The morning involved some of the bloodiest fighting of the entire war, in which thousands of men fell in a relatively small area, while scores of field officers and generals on both sides fell leading them. On the Union side Major General Hooker himself was wounded, and Major General Mansfield was killed; on the Confederate side Brigadier General Starke was killed, and three other brigadier generals were seriously wounded, one of whom later died. Throughout the morning, "The roar of musketry and the thunder of artillery proclaimed the deadly conflict that raged. These deafening sounds of battle continued until about twelve o'clock, when they began to abate, and about one they had ceased." McClellan had thrown in four Union corps to break the Confederate left, and failed. The brief, ghastly silence, broken only by the cries of the wounded and dying, signified that the four corps "were so much broken by loss and fatigue that they were unable to renew the contest," which had so far cost both sides more than 13,000 casualties in the course of the morning.

The slaughter in Bloody Lane marked the end of the first phase of the battle. The artillery bombardment resumed, Lee rode back toward the depleted center of his line, where he dismounted on "an eminence" that gave him a view of the whole battlefield to talk to Longstreet, as usual indifferent to the fact that he was fully exposed to enemy fire. D. H. Hill, who had ridden over to report to Lee and remained mounted despite a jocular warning from Longstreet, was thrown to the ground when a Federal cannonball took off both his horse's front legs.

The low hills and farmland to the north of Sharpsburg where the morning fight had been made were now held by the Federals. It was Burnside's turn to make an attack, the time directly on Lee's center and right. But neither he nor McClellan had thought to have Antietam Creek examined for fords, so from one o'clock on he sent brigade after brigade across the narrow stone bridge into a hailstorm of Confederate fire. As the afternoon wore on, one of his brigade commanders finally located Snavely's Ford, about a mile and a half downstream, while many of the soldiers discovered that they could wade across the creek "without getting their waist belts wet in many places," rather than get shot on the bridge. But it took two hours of fierce fighting for Burnside to get his troops across to the west bank of the creek and formed up, giving Lee time to move some of his men from his left, where the Union attacks had subsided, to his center and right. By the time Burnside's attack had reached the southeastern corner of Sharpsburg, Lee played his last card, and sent in A. P. Hill's division, which had been marching at a rapid pace from Harpers Ferry. Hill's unexpected attack against Burnside's left flank drove the Federals back to the bridge they had crossed with such grave losses earlier in the afternoon. McClellan, reluctant to risk his reserves at the end of the day and still believing that Lee outnumbered him, did not attempt another attack, although he had the forces with which to make it. Burnside held onto his bridgehead, Lee still held Sharpsburg, though his position was reduced to a tenuous perimeter, McClellan's army had suffered nearly 12,500 casualties, Lee's more than 10,000, just over 30 percent of his forces. Sharpsburg, or Antietam, was now the bloodiest single day of battle in American history.

As night fell, stretcher bearers and ambulances attempted to pick up the wounded under an informal truce. His headquarters now in the ruined town, Lee was urged by Longstreet and several other of his generals, to retire across the Potomac at once. He just replied, brusquely for him, "Gentlemen, we will not cross the Potomac tonight. . . . If McClellan wants to fight in the morning I will give him battle again. Go!" This was determination indeed, and possibly also pride, the one sin to which Lee was not altogether immune. He had lost nearly a quarter of his army in a single day's fighting—in Longstreet's words, "a struggle of eighteen hours, too fearful to contemplate." In any event, the next day neither army was in a position to renew the battle. On the night of September 18 Lee finally faced reality and withdrew his army across the Potomac. Stuart's aide Heros von Borcke, painted the withdrawal as a Wagnerian scene: "The passage of the Potomac was one of those magnificent spectacles which are only seen in war. The whole landscape was lighted up with a lurid glare from the burning houses of Williamsport, which had been ignited by the enemy's shells. High over the heads of the crossing column and the dark waters of the river, the blazing bombs passed each other in parabolas of flame through the air, and the spectral tress showed their every limb and leaf against the red sky."

Lee moved his shattered army back to Virginia, while McClellan, who should have pursued him, relapsed into immobility, made good his losses, and fended off the efforts of Lincoln and Halleck to make him move. Although Sharpsburg looms large in Lee's legend, it is hard to find much to admire in the Maryland campaign of 1862. Lee certainly had firmer control over his army than he had showed on the peninsula, and his maneuvers from Richmond to First Manassas, and from there to South Mountain, were among the swiftest and most brilliant in the history of warfare, but in the end warfare must be judged by its result. Lee had won a great victory at Manassas, and taken the pressure off Richmond—but his proclamation to the people of Maryland accomplished little; the division of the army after crossing the Potomac into Maryland was, as Longstreet had predicted, disastrous; and the battle at Sharpsburg, into which he had been forced, was at best a costly, if heroic, stalemate, in which neither side could claim victory. Lee escaped by the skin of his teeth, in large part because McClellan refused to renew the battle. Lee never reached Pennsylvania, where he had hoped to resupply his army and then march east to threaten a major city. More seriously, his army was reduced from 50,000 to 38,000 by the time he reached Sharpsburg, which means that he totally underestimated the exhaustion of his men and the fact that so many of them were shoeless. Lee's own determination and ability to endure privation set a noble example for his troops but should not have blinded him to their condition. His pride in them led him again and again to overestimate what they could do, despite the lack of supplies and clothing. There is a point beyond which even the bravest and most devoted of armies can no longer carry out their commander's strategy— one thinks inevitably of Napoleon's *Grand Armée* at Moscow—and Lee's intention to follow Hagerstown Pike into Pennsylvania was a good (though less disastrous) example of this. Longstreet was right—the Battle of Sharpsburg should never have been fought.

It was a political disaster too. Lee's intention had been to bring Maryland into the Confederacy, and by winning a decisive victory to encourage Great Britain or France to recognize the Confederacy. Instead McClellan's fight at Sharpsburg and Lee's subsequent retreat across the Potomac at last convinced President Lincoln to issue the Emancipation Proclamation.

Whether Lee wished it or no, the war was now no longer just about whether the Federal government had the right to coerce Virginia by armed force, as Lee saw it; the issue was slavery. He had inadvertently brought about a shift in politics that, by a supreme irony, was exactly what John Brown had sought to achieve in raiding Harpers Ferry.

Chapter 9

Glory—Fredericksburg and Chancellorsville

"It is well that war is so terrible—we should grow too fond of it."

> —Robert E. Lee, at the
> Battle of Fredericksburg

During the afternoon of September 17, as Lee was preparing to defend his center and right from Burnside's attack at Sharpsburg, he encountered his son Robert again. Robert later described the occasion:

As one of the Army of Northern Virginia, I occasionally saw the commander-in-chief, on the march, or passed the headquarters close enough to recognise him and members of his staff, but a private soldier in Jackson's corps did not have much time, during that campaign, for visiting, and until the battle of Sharpsburg I had no opportunity of speaking to him. On that occasion our battery had been severely handled, losing many men and horses. Having three guns disabled, we were ordered to withdraw, and while moving back we passed General Lee and several of his staff, grouped on a little knoll near the road. Having no definite orders where to go, our captain, seeing the commanding general, halted us and rode over to get some instructions. Some others and myself went along to see and hear. General Lee was dismounted with some of his staff around him, a courier holding his horse. Captain Poague, commanding our battery, the Rockbridge Artillery, saluted, reported our condition, and asked for instructions. The General, listening patiently, looked at us—his eyes passing over me without any sign of recognition— and then ordered Captain Poague to take the most serviceable horses and men, man the uninjured gun, send the disabled part of his command back to refit, and report to the front for duty. As Poague turned to go, I went up to speak to my father. When he found out who I was, he congratulated me on being well and unhurt.

I then said:

"General, are you going to send us in again?"

"Yes, my son," he replied with a smile. "You all must do what you can to drive these people back."

There are conflicting accounts of this meeting, but since Lee and his youngest son were the only people who heard what they said to each other, Robert's is surely the correct one. That Lee once more failed to recognize his son is less surprising if one remembers that commanding generals tend to see their men en masse, rather than as individuals. Lee was focused on the surviving gun, not on the grimy, soot-blackened, tattered gunners who served it, but once he recognized Robert his words were typical of him: patient, kindly, firm. Also typical is the fact that he avoided giving the enemy a name: they were not "Union," or "Federal" troops, still less "Yankees." He always referred to them as "these people," or "those people," as if reluctant to face the fact that he was fighting the U.S. Army, *his* army, in the service of which he had spent most of his adult life.

Even in the midst of great events and heavy responsibilities Lee's family was never far from his mind. His other two boys were also in the army: Rooney, the middle brother, commanding a cavalry brigade under the command of his cousin Fitzhugh Lee; the eldest, Boo, serving as an aide-de-camp to President Jefferson Davis, and eager for a combat command. Lee followed their doings closely, but he scrupulously avoided any hint of favoritism. Rooney was in any case a professional soldier and a first-rate cavalry commander, who would almost certainly have risen to high rank even had his name not been Lee. Of the girls, Annie, Mildred, and Agnes remained in Jones Spring, the spa where Rooney and Charlotte's son had died, while Mrs. Lee and her oldest daughter, Mary, had returned to Richmond to nurse Rooney through a dangerous illness—probably typhoid fever. Lee had advised his wife not to stay there, since by this time it was "one immense hospital . . . [where citizens] breathed the vapors of the charnel house," but Mrs. Lee was no more likely to follow her husband's advice than she had been before. When Rooney was better, she moved to Hickory Hill, north of Richmond on the Pamunkey River, and still only a few miles from the Union lines. Lee, like many another parent, expressed relief when his daughter Mildred agreed reluctantly, after a year's urging on his part, to attend a boarding school out of harm's way in Raleigh, North Carolina, "St. Mary's Academy, the largest church-related seminary for girls in antebellum America," where she would be unhappy and lonely. She does not appear to have made friends there, even though she was treated like a celebrity as the daughter of the South's most famous general.

Worse than Mildred's unhappiness was in store for Lee. The supposed health resort at Jones Spring, which had already claimed the life of Lee's grandchild, now claimed that of his beloved daughter Annie, who succumbed to typhoid fever after three weeks of suffering. Her mother had journeyed down to be with her, keeping Lee informed of Annie's illness, though he did not share his agonizing concern with anyone. When he finally received news of her death, his aide, Colonel Taylor recalled:

> At the usual hour he summoned me to his presence to know if there were any matters of army routine upon which his judgment and action were desired. The papers containing a few such cases were presented to him; he reviewed and gave his orders in regard to them. I then left him, but for some cause returned in a few moments, and with my accustomed freedom entered his tent without announcement or ceremony, when I was startled and shocked to see him overcome with grief, an open letter in his hands. That letter contained the sad intelligence of his daughter's death.

Years later Taylor still marveled at Lee's self-control and dedication to duty:

> He was the father of a tenderly-loved daughter . . . whose sweet presence he was to know no more in this world; but he was also charged with the

command of an important and active army, to whose keeping to a great extent were intrusted the safety and honor of the Southern Confederacy. Lee the man must give way to Lee the soldier. His army demanded his first thought and care. . . . Who can tell with what anguish of soul he endeavoured to control himself, and to maintain a calm exterior, and who can estimate the immense effort necessary to still the heart filled to overflowing with tenderest emotions, and to give attention to the important trusts committed to him, before permitting the more selfish indulgence of private meditation, grief, and prayer? Duty first was the rule of his life, and his every thought, word, and action, was made to square with duty's inexorable demands.

Only in replying to Mary, did Lee let his feelings show: "to know that I shall never see her again on earth, that her place in our circle, which I always hoped one day to enjoy, is forever vacant, is agonizing in the extreme. But God in this, as in all things, has mingled mercy with the blow, in selecting that one best prepared to leave us. May you be able to join me in saying 'His will be done!'" He ended on a bleaker note: "I wish I could give you any comfort, but beyond our hope in the great mercy of God, and that he takes her at the time and place when it is best for her to go, there is none."

Lee could not attend Annie's funeral—he would not take leave for a family tragedy when his soldiers were allowed none—but he selected the lines that would eventually be carved on Annie's granite obelisk, from a hymn which she asked to be sung as she was dying:

Perfect and true are all His ways
Whom Heaven adores and earth obeys.

Lee finally gave his army two months for "Rest, food, refitting, and discipline," the last a gift from General McClellan, who although his own army was soon brought up to full strength, showed no inclination to cross the Potomac and move against Lee. In the meantime Lee was willing to wait—certain that there would be one more campaign before winter set in. He was sure that McClellan would move against Richmond again, and preferred to see from which direction so that he could fight him on ground of his choosing. He took steps to formalize the separation of his army into two wings, promoting both Jackson and Longstreet to the rank of lieutenant general, and did his best to remedy his deficiencies in supply and ordnance—no easy task in the beleaguered Confederacy. The period was not

CLOUDS OF GLORY · 835

without events: Harpers Ferry was retaken by the Federals—no great loss to Lee, since Jackson had already removed the contents of the arsenal—and Lee sent Stuart on another highly publicized raid eighty miles right around McClellan's army all the way into Pennsylvania, recrossing the Potomac with 1,200 Federal horses he had captured along the way.★ Stuart saw no sign of activity on the part of McClellan, nor indeed did the White House, to the growing irritation of the President. Lincoln had taken to referring to the Army of the Potomac unflatteringly as "McClellan's bodyguard." When McClellan complained that he could not contemplate making a move because his cavalry horses were exhausted, Lincoln replied, with unusual waspishness for him, "Will you pardon me for asking what the horses of your army have done since the battle of Antietam that fatigue anything?" At last, on October 26, McClellan began to cross the Potomac in full force. It took over a week for the whole army to cross, during which time Lee, who had moved his headquarters to Culpeper, was uncertain whether the Federals would proceed down the Shenandoah Valley

---

★ One of Stuart's objectives was to destroy the railroad bridge at Chambersburg, but it proved to be made of iron and he was obliged to leave it standing. Unlike T. E. Lawrence in World War I, Confederate cavalry raiders had neither the high explosives nor the demolition skills to destroy bridges unless they were made of wood and could be burned down.

toward Staunton and then turn east toward Richmond, or take the shorter, classic route to the Rappahannock in the hope of reaching Hanover Junction and attacking Richmond from the northwest. If they did the former, Lee could rely on Jackson to hold them back. If the latter, Jackson could attack the Federal forces from the Blue Ridge Mountains, while Longstreet defended Richmond. In either case, Lee would be outnumbered. He now had just over 70,000 men, against about 114,000 Federals, but these were not the kind of odds that gave Lee pause. On November 10, however, electrifying news reached him: Lincoln had at last lost patience with George C. McClellan and replaced him with Major General Ambrose Burnside.

Lee had respect (which President Lincoln did not share) for McClellan's professional ability but also felt that he could usually predict what McClellan, a fellow engineer, would do. He did not have the same certainty about Burnside, who he thought was less able, and probably uncomfortable with his new responsibility. In this he was perfectly right: Burnside had already turned down command of the Army of the Potomac once before on the grounds that he was not qualified for it, and this time it took some argument before he was finally "persuaded . . . to accept," with what appears to have been genuine reluctance. "[Burnside] is as sorry to assume command as I am to give it up," McClellan wrote graciously to Mrs. Burnside.

No less an authority than Ulysses S. Grant thought that Burnside was unfit to command an army; and worse still, Burnside knew it. On the surface, he was jovial, bluff, popular, and good-natured, but his eyes, like those of many fat men, betrayed a certain degree of obstinacy, and perhaps a strong resentment at the possibility that he was not being taken seriously. On the other hand, Burnside was no fool. He had resigned from the army in 1858 to manufacture an ingenious breech-loading carbine of his own design,* gone bankrupt through no fault of his own—a fire destroyed the factory in which the carbines were being manufactured—entered politics in his native Rhode Island only to be defeated in a landslide, and reentered the army at the outbreak of war as a brigadier of the Rhode Island Militia. His appointment to high command was not based on professional ability or any discernible gift for strategy. His qualifications were that he appeared amiable; projected a certain stolid, bulky authority; and, most important of all, was not McClellan.

---

*The Burnside carbine was manufactured in quantity during the Civil War; more than 50,000 reached the army, and despite certain difficulties with the ammunition, it was quite popular among Union cavalrymen, and also among those Confederate cavalrymen who captured one.

Burnside's plan to advance quickly on Richmond by the most direct route was a daring change from McClellan's. He intended to "give up the Orange & Alexandria railroad [to which McClellan had attached much importance], base himself on Aquia Creek, and from Fredericksburg march directly upon Richmond," hoping to race there before Lee could concentrate his forces to stop him. Lincoln, who was by now something of an expert* on the various ways of approaching Richmond, remarked cautiously—and shrewdly—that Burnside's plan might work "if [he] moved very rapidly, otherwise not." The president would have preferred to use the overwhelming strength of the Army of the Potomac, now close to 120,000 men, to attack Lee before Jackson could join him from the Shenandoah Valley instead of trying to take Richmond again, and had little faith in Burnside's elaborate plan to deceive Lee about the direction of his advance by concentrating his army at Warrenton, then making a swift move to the southeast, outflanking Longstreet, and crossing the Rappahannock at Fredericksburg.

It remains hard to understand how Burnside imagined that he could keep Lee and Longstreet focused on Warrenton while he moved the bulk of his forces

---

* Thus demonstrating the truth of Napoleon's comment, "In war as in prostitution, the amateur is often better than the professional."

toward Richmond, particularly since he was in enemy country, where every farmer and villager was a Confederate. Speed was the essence of Burnside's strategy, but whatever other qualities he may have had, he lacked the ability to inspire the War Department to supply his needs quickly. Since the bridges across the Rappahannock where he intended to cross it had been destroyed, he immediately ordered pontoons and bridging material, but neither the pontoons nor the 270 draft horses required to pull them from the Potomac were ready in time. The weather turned bad—hardly surprisingly, since it was now late fall—the roads became muddy, and the pontoons were heavy. Hard as the horses strained, progress was slow; nor would they escape attention. Burnside's intention to cross the Rappahannock at Fredericksburg was quickly made known to Lee, who was never one to move slowly. The pontoons and all the bridging material that accompanied them did not arrive in Falmouth on the north side of the Rappahannock until almost a week after the advance elements of Burnside's army had reached it. This meant there was ample time for Lee to get Longstreet's corps into position, and for Jackson, who been advancing from Winchester by forced marches of over twenty miles a day, to reach there. Burnside lacked the ability to change his plan and seek another place to cross the river—or perhaps he lacked the moral courage required for high command.

What he should have done was to attack Jackson with his full force before Jackson could join Lee, then take on Longstreet; but Burnside's eye, like McClellan's, was fixed on Richmond, not on Lee's army—a huge mistake. No doubt Burnside was also concerned about how further delay would be greeted in Washington; in any case, despite his own doubts about what he was doing and despite the warnings of his generals, he was now committed to an opposed river crossing on improvised bridges against an enemy holding the high ground on the opposite bank, and had given Lee enough time to concentrate the entire Army of Northern Virginia against him there. It would be difficult to find a more a more perilous strategic decision in the annals of military history.

At first Lee seems to have hesitated to believe that Burnside's move toward Fredericksburg was the real attack—he thought it might merely be a diversion for an attack against Jackson toward the Valley, but the sheer weight of numbers (and the lumbering train of pontoons), in addition to the frequent reports from Confederate spies along Burnside's line of march, finally convinced Lee that the improbable was true. He immediately moved his headquarters from Culpeper

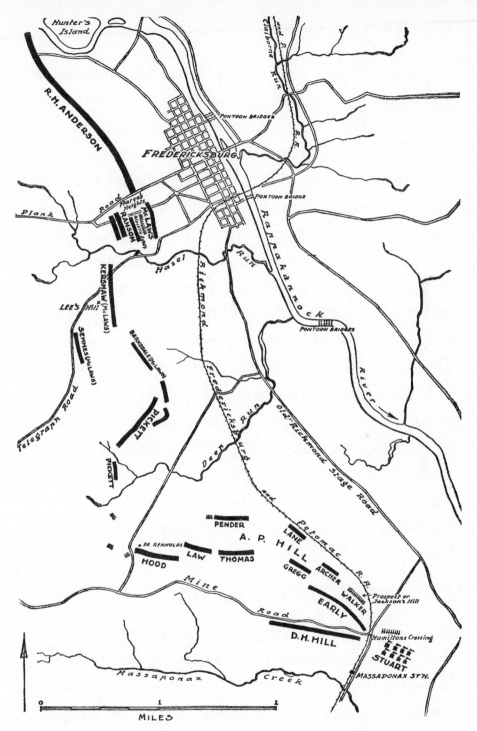

20. Position of the major units of the Army of Northern Virginia at the opening of the battle of Fredericksburg, December 13, 1862.

to Fredericksburg to examine the terrain, and saw at once that despite appearances it was not an ideal place to defend. The town, one of the most graceful and historic in Virginia, would be exposed to artillery fire from the northern bank of the Rappahannock, where Stafford Heights offered an ideal place for Federal batteries. It was estimated that Burnside had almost 400 guns, which in some places would be as close as 500 yards, and which would sweep the narrow area between the southern bank of the river, the town, and the higher ground behind Fredericksburg. It would be difficult, perhaps impossible, to protect Fredericksburg or to prevent Burnside's troops from crossing the river under the cover of his formidable artillery. What is more, Burnside had nearly 120,000 men, while Lee would have fewer than 80,000 even if Jackson joined him (this would be the largest total number of men engaged in any battle of the Civil War).

Fredericksburg, December 13, 1862

When Lee arrived at Fredericksburg on November 20 in a pouring rainstorm he could see the encampments of Burnside's army on Stafford Heights, a few hundred yards away across the river. Any doubts he may have harbored about Burnside's intentions were quickly answered by the quantity of tents, wagon trains, guns, and smoky campfires on the other side of the Rappahannock. A bend in the river placed Fredericksburg in a salient at the center of a kind of natural bowl, exposing it to fire from the north and the east; and even though by now Lee was sure where Burnside was going, he had no way as yet of determining at what points Burnside would try to bridge the river. When Longstreet's corps had arrived on November 25 Lee placed it on the high ground directly behind Fredericksburg. When Jackson arrived on November 29, Lee placed him on Longstreet's right, on high ground overlooking a comparatively flat stretch to the river, between 2,000 and 3,000 yards away. It may be that Lee was trying to spare the town of Fredericksburg, where George Washington had spent part of his boyhood, and which Lee himself had known as a child. He placed Jackson to the south of the town, thinking that this was the most likely place for the Federals to bridge the river, since it narrows considerably there. As for Burnside, he failed to attempt any adequate reconnaissance of Lee's positions, relying solely on two hot-air balloons he had brought along, even though dense brush and woods screened much of the Confederate army.

Had Burnside crossed the river upstream while Jackson was still spread out on the move, the campaign might have had a very different outcome, but he had a kind of elephantine inability to alter a plan once he had made it. Despite Lincoln's doubts—reinforced by a visit from Halleck, the general in chief—Burnside was adamantly determined to proceed with his plan. Inflexibility was his worst weakness, perhaps because he hoped it would look to others like self-assurance and strength.

As the first elements of his army were in place, Burnside's progress slowed. His pontoons lumbered on toward the Rappahannock, but the only significant move from the northern side of the river, apart from a few demonstrations, was a preemptory demand on November 21 from Major General Edwin V. Sumner—Burnside had divided his army into three "Grand Divisions," each consisting of two corps, and Sumner commanded the right Grand Division immediately opposite Fredericksburg—for the immediate surrender of the town, failing which he would commence bombarding it with his long-range artillery at 9 a.m. the next day. When the mayor of Fredericksburg passed this message on to Lee, he expressed astonishment. The deliberate shelling of civilians was not yet the widely accepted practice it became after 1870–1871, when the Germans besieged and shelled Paris mercilessly; but the threat does not appear to have stirred in

Lee the anger he had felt toward General Pope, perhaps because Sumner had forwarded his demand for surrender to the mayor with every possible military civility, under a flag of truce. Anxious to prevent the slaughter of the civilian population, Lee told the mayor that he would not occupy the town or make use of its "manufactories" if the Federals agreed to do the same. Surprisingly, Sumner agreed not to begin shelling the town the next morning, but Lee drew the correct conclusion that Fredericksburg would be impossible to protect once fighting began in earnest, and advised the civilian population to evacuate the town.

Another of Lee's concerns was the coming of winter—his army was in no way prepared for a winter campaign. It was already snowing on November 29, when Jackson arrived ahead of his army, and at least 2,000 or 3,000 men in Lee's army still had no shoes,★ let alone overcoats or blankets. Giving up Fredericksburg, where he could have sheltered his troops, was an act of humanity toward the inhabitants, but it increased the misery of the troops—and of course the number of his sick.

★ This is one of the few subjects on which Lee allowed a certain asperity to show in his letters back to Richmond. "I am informed that there is a large number of shoes now in Richmond in the hands of extortioners, who hold them at an extravagant price," he wrote (*Fuller, Grant and Lee, 170*). Even when he received shoes, there were none that fitted men with particularly large feet.

As the days passed, Lee sought to improve his positions behind and on either side of the town, selecting some of the sites for his artillery himself and making sure that each of his more than 300 pieces were properly ranged in. He did not, however, try to turn Fredericksburg into a fortified camp with elaborate fieldworks, partly because the ground was becoming too frozen to make that practicable, and partly because he did not want to discourage Burnside from attacking him. Of all the places Burnside might have chosen to cross the Rappahannock, Fredericksburg gave Lee the best ground for a successful defensive battle against a larger foe. Forced to wait patiently, while his men "chopped fire wood to keep from freezing." Lee watched as Burnside's pontoon bridges were readied for the assault. At last, just before five o'clock in the morning on December 11, two guns were fired to signal that Federal engineers were beginning to place the pontoons in the water, to build two bridges immediately opposite the town. A third was being built about a mile south of Fredericksburg, where Deep Run Creek empties into the river. Lee could not make use of his artillery to fire on the first two bridges for fear of hitting homes along the river. He relied on sharpshooters to slow down the Federal engineers.

Despite the early morning haze and fog rising from the river, the Union engineers showed extraordinary bravery as they carried one pontoon after another into position, then laid bridging material across them, all the time under constant, heavy, accurate musket fire. When men fell, they were quickly replaced. Inexorably the bridges drew nearer and nearer to the Confederate bank. When the Federal artillery began to fire on the town to suppress Lee's musket fire, he gave vent to a rare outburst at the consequent civilian casualties: "These people delight to destroy the weak and those who can make no defense; it just suits them!"

By early afternoon, dismayed at the slow progress of the bridge builders, Burnside used some of his pontoons to row infantry across the river and form a bridgehead. By nightfall the two pontoon bridges into the town and a double span of pontoon bridges at Deep Run had been completed; Burnside's army began streaming across in force; and Fredericksburg was quickly taken, despite brisk firefights in its narrow streets. Whatever one thinks of Burnside as a general—and in most histories of the Civil War he occupies one of the lowest places among Union commanders—the courage and professional skill of his engineers are beyond question.

On the morning of December 12 heavy fog concealed the Union army from the Confederates, but "up the hillside drifted the echo of phantom voices, the roll of drums, snatches of bugle calls and, ere long, the music of bands in well remembered tunes," reminding the Confederates of their presence as the bulk of the Federal army deployed in full strength unseen in the mist. By that evening 113,000 Federal troops faced just over 78,000* Confederates along a six-mile line, stretching from the bend in the Rappahannock above Fredericksburg, on the Union far right, to Smithfield on the far left, a narrow salient that included the town and was held by two of Burnside's Grand Divisions, as well as part of the third. It was a powerful force, but the position was shallow, at no point more than 1,000 yards deep, and at its back was the river.

The morning of December 13 began with dense fog through which could be heard the eerie sound of bands playing martial music and drumming—clearly an attack was intended. At nine o'clock in the morning the fog lifted, revealing Burnside's army in "martial array," line after line of infantry, their flags streaming in the cold breeze and their swords, buttons, and bayonets reflecting the sun—as impressive a sight as any army has ever presented, the more so given the threadbare appearance of the Confederates. Colonel Long, watching beside Lee, caught the glory of that moment, as he glimpsed the long blue lines stretching "from

---

*Longstreet puts the number a little lower than Long, at 68,000 plus the cavalry, but it was Long's job to know the exact number and inform Lee of it.

the city down the river as far as the eye could reach. All," he wrote, "was bustle and animation in the ranks of the great blue lines. The bright muskets of the men glistened in the sunlight, and countless flags with the stars and stripes floated with the breeze and marked the direction as the troops were maneuvered into line-of-battle formation to the sound of soul-stirring music. No doubt every heart of that mighty host beat high with hope in anticipation of the impending struggle." To Lee, and to every senior Confederate officer present, it was a moment of awe—this, after all, was *their* army, the army that they had attended West Point to serve in, and whose uniform they had worn in Mexico or on the frontier, lined up in perfect formation with a precision that would have satisfied the most demanding of drill sergeants, and about to march straight toward them over open ground, in the face of 306 Confederate cannons, which had been carefully sited, dug in, and ranged to receive them. It can only have been with mixed emotions that Lee watched them dress their lines for an attack he knew must fail.

Both General Jackson, dressed up for once in a spanking new uniform and gold-braided cap, and General Stuart urged Lee to seize the moment and attack the Federal lines, but Lee would not. He had placed his army on higher ground, its artillery and its reserves concealed by woods, and Burnside had done just what Lee had anticipated. Lee would let the Federals charge him and wear them down. The moment the fog began to lift it was clear that they would open their attack on his right, which was held by Jackson's corps. As Lee and his two senior generals stood watching the Federal army emerge from the mist, the disparity between their numbers and those of the Confederates was so startling that Longstreet, who always enjoyed pulling Jackson's leg, asked him what he was going to do with "all those people over there?" Without smiling, Jackson mounted and replied sternly, "Sir, we will give them the bayonet."

At almost that moment the sun came out, "as if the ready war god rang up the curtain on the scene set for slaughter, and against the vast backdrop of the gun-studded hills of Stafford, the whole stage was disclosed, from the upper fringe of Fredericksburg's streets to the distant gray meadows in front of Hamilton's Crossing." There *was* something deeply theatrical about that moment. It was not surprising. Again and again the Civil War produced scenes of grandeur that imprinted themselves on the minds of countless men on both sides of the conflict.

Lee still would not move. His calm was such that as the enemy formed up before him, he was still dictating letters, including a brief refusal to a singularly poorly timed request from the adjutant general in Richmond to "reinforce Wilmington from this army." Lee ended with a stern recommendation: "The people [of Wilmington] must turn out to defend their homes, or they will be taken from them," perhaps a reflection of his implacable, determined mood at the sight of the masses of Federal troops before him.

Lee inadvertently opened the battle at 10:30 a.m. by ordering his batteries on Saint Marye's Heights, "Test the ranges on the left." Thinking that these trial shots were the signal for a Confederate barrage, the Federal batteries responded from across the river. As the smoke drifted from the Confederate guns, Major General William Franklin's Union Grand Division began its advance on the Confederate right, where Jackson's army waited on the wooded slopes of Prospect Hill. Burnside was so poorly informed that he still assumed Jackson had not yet reached Lee, and that he himself was attacking only half of Lee's army. Even so, numbers tell. Franklin's Grand Division at first punched a hole in Jackson's line, then fought its way savagely into the woods at the base of Prospect Hill. On Lee's left Sumner's Grand Division advanced from the streets of Fredericksburg to the base of Saint Marye's Heights, each attack followed by a counterattack. Jackson was barely able to hold his positions, then was halted as he counterattacked by heavy artillery fire from across the river.

On the left an even more dramatic and sanguinary scene was being enacted. Halfway up the gentle slope of Marye's Heights above the town was a partly sunken road, with a thick stone "retaining wall" overlooking the town. No one could have chosen a harder place to attack than Telegraph Road, but that did not stop Burnside, who ordered both Sumner's and Hooker's Grand Divisions, from launching attack after attack there against Longstreet's troops despite massive artillery fire. As lines of Union infantrymen climbed the slope the Confederates shot them down like ducks in a shooting gallery. It was one of the most senseless slaughters in a war that was full of doomed assaults and hopeless attacks. Each time Burnside's men advanced over the bodies of their own dead and wounded, they were shot down.

But Lee looked with growing anxiety on his right, where successive Federal charges were driving Jackson's lines back, and where he could see Confederate prisoners were being taken.

Suddenly an artillery piece near him blew up. It left him unhurt, and then, from a great distance, he heard over the constant roar of cannon and musket fire the unmistakable sound of the rebel yell. Jackson's corps were counterattacking. Turning toward Longstreet, Lee said, "It is well that war is so terrible—we should grow too fond of it!"

This famous quote is usually attributed to Lee's admiration at the disciplined Federal ranks advancing over a field strewn with the bodies of those who had gone before them. Actually Lee said it when he saw A. P. Hill's ragged "butternut"★ troops at Deep Run as they emerged from the woods to counterattack a superior number of Federal troops.

The Federal threat to the Confederate right had been blunted at a terrible cost, but the waves of attacks on Saint Marye's Heights continued unabated, prompting Lee to say to Longstreet, "General, they are massing very heavily, and will break your line, I am afraid." Longstreet replied: "General, if you put every man now on the other side of the Potomac in that field to approach me over the same line, and give me plenty of ammunition, I will kill them all before they reach my line. Look to your right; you are in some danger there, but not on my line."

The futile Federal charges on the right slowly died down into an "artillery duel," which Jackson seemed to

---

★ Although Confederate uniforms were supposed to be gray, they were made with an inferior dye and often faded rapidly to a light khaki color, similar to homespun cloth dyed with bark from the butternut tree (*Juglans cinerea*): hence the appellation "butternut."

be winning. On the right, though, the intensity of the attacks on the sunken road on Saint Marye's Heights increased. Taking advantage of a moment's pause in the battle. Burnside redoubled his attempt to take the road, only to be driven back. Throughout the afternoon, and on into dark, the fight on the Confederate left continued, as Burnside continued to throw forward brigade after brigade, stubbornly defying military wisdom by reinforcing failure. "A series of braver, more desperate charges than those hurled against the troops in the sunken road was never known," wrote the normally reticent Longstreet, "and the piles and cross-piles of dead marked a field such as I never saw before or since."

For the wounded, it was a night of horror, as the temperature dropped and men froze to death in grotesque postures. Although Lee might have relished his victory, it was a night of troubling decisions. He was convinced, as nearly all of his generals were, that Burnside would renew the attack in the morning, probably trying to outflank the Confederate lines rather than attempting another direct assault. Lee worried that his artillery ammunition might be exhausted. He finally reported to the Confederate secretary of war, "About 9 a.m. the enemy attacked our right, and as the fog lifted the battle ran from right to left; raged until 6 p.m.; but thanks to Almighty God, the day closed [with attacks] repulsed along our whole front. Our troops behaved admirably, but, as usual, we have to mourn the loss of many brave men. I expect the battle to be renewed at daylight. Please send to the President."

At dawn the next day, with the battlefield again obscured by heavy morning fog, Lee rode out to urge his men to dig in. But when the sun finally broke through, revealing the ghastly field of dead and wounded, no attack came. He realized that the streets of Fredericksburg had been sealed off with makeshift barricades as if Burnside was preparing to make a desperate last stand there. Meanwhile the long lines of troops on the Confederate right remained motionless, their flags furled as if in mourning. Still the Union divisions were silent, but many noticed that the Union dead were lying "naked and discolored," their clothes having been stripped off by Confederate soldiers in the dark. Neither Lee nor even the venturesome Jackson contemplated a Confederate attack. Stuart's Prussian aide, Major Heros von Borcke however, was critical of this decision. "Our commander-in-chief," Von Borcke wrote, "still objected to a forward movement, for which, in my judgment, the golden opportunity had now passed, had he been inclined to favor it. . . . Not one of our Generals was aware of the magnitude of the victory we had gained, of the injury we had inflicted upon the enemy, and of the degree of demoralization in the hostile army." Even after a victory, the problems of the Army of the Northern Virginia repeated themselves. Lee had no means to pursue the enemy. Food supplies, forage, and ammunition were running low; the men were cold, hungry, and exhausted. Once again Lee had to be content with a victory of numbers: 12,653 Federal casualties against 5,309 Confederate. By any definition it was a great victory, but not one that dispersed the beaten foe. The hapless Burnside asked for and received a truce to bury his dead and collect those of his wounded who had survived. He then withdrew his army across the Rappahannock, pontoons and all, and placed it safely out of Lee's reach.

The Confederate victory at Fredericksburg deeply troubled the North. The Governor of Pennsylvania told President Lincoln, "It was not a battle, it was butchery." On being told the news Lincoln wrote, "If there is a worse place than hell, I am in it." Still, in the end battles must be judged by the effect they have on history, and Fredericksburg, though it demonstrated Lee's ability to choose where and when to fight, changed nothing. The Federal Army of the Potomac was still in Virginia, on the north bank of the Rappahannock, to be sure, but Lee had not driven it out, no foreign government had been moved by his victory to recognize the Confederacy, nor was Lincoln forced to open negotiations for the Confederacy's independence. Both armies soon took up winter quarters to lick their wounds. Major Von Borcke was perfectly right: the "golden opportunity" for a victory like that of Washington at Yorktown had eluded him. Lee was acclaimed universally in the South, and even the North respected his abilities. Burnside, on the other hand, was replaced by "Fighting Joe" Hooker, who was possibly an even more incompetent general, and certainly a less amiable personality.

The onset of winter did not allow Lee much rest. His men did their best to construct makeshift shelters while Lee continued to live in a tent, even though a vacant house was available nearby. His headquarters, according to his youngest son, Robert, recently promoted from artilleryman to a lieutenant on the staff of his brother Rooney, "were very unpretentious, consisting of three or four 'wall-tents' and several more common ones, pitched on the edge of an old pine field, near a group of forest trees from which he drew his supply of fire-wood."

Robert goes on to say that his father's quarters were "rather dismal," but Lee was determined to share his men's discomfort. The short supplies threatened

Lee's army with starvation, and reduced the horses to a heartbreaking condition—a matter of great concern since it threatened to cripple both Lee's cavalry and his artillery.* Despite constant urging from Lee, the Confederate government was unable to organize or maintain supplies of food and forage. Douglas Southall Freeman writes that "Lee's appeals and warnings alike failed to do more than to keep the army alive." The men were lucky indeed if they received "one fourth pound of bacon, 18 ounces of flour, 10 pounds of rice to each 100 men every third day, with some few peas and a small amount of dried fruit occasionally as they can be obtained." The result was that most of the Confederate army suffered from scurvy, dysentery, frostbite, and exhaustion, while many of the horses died of starvation and cold. Major-General Fuller is not wrong in accusing Lee of failing to press his case hard enough: "his pleadings are so tactful that they are disregarded. He never thunders for them." It is true that Lee relied too much on his troops' indomitable spirit than on mundane details of supply. He also shrank from an all-out confrontation with President Davis and the Confederate Congress, who remained lax on this issue.

---

* Every cavalryman needs a horse, of course—in the Confederate Army cavalrymen provided their own—and every gun required twelve horses: six to pull a limber and the gun, six to pull a limber and two caissons of ammunition.

Fredericksburg is only sixty miles from Richmond, and none of Lee's soldiers would have begrudged him a few days to relax with his family. But Lee also took no leave, because his men got none. This was a mistake, as he needed rest to command effectively. He wrote to his daughter Mildred on Christmas day, "I cannot tell you how I long to see you when a little quiet occurs. My thoughts revert to you, your sisters, and your mother; my heart aches for our reunion. Your brothers I see occasionally. This morning Fitzhugh rode by with his young aide-de-camp [Rob] at the head of his brigade, on his way up the Rappahannock."

On the same day he wrote to Mary, "But what a cruel thing is war, to separate and destroy families, and mar the purest joy and happiness God has granted us in this world," and added: "My heart bleeds at the death of every one of our gallant men." Lee's simplicity and sincerity shine through here—as in his decision at this point to proceed with the instructions in his father-in-law's will, and have delivered to all of the Custis slaves "their manumission papers," freeing them as Mr. Custis had wanted. "As regards the liberation of the people, I wish to progress in it as far as I can," he wrote. "I hope they will all do well and behave themselves. I should like, if I could, to attend to their wants and see them placed to best advantage. But that is impossible. All that choose can leave the state before the war closes . . . [These people] are entitled to their freedom and I wish to give it to them." Lincoln's Emancipation Proclamation had in principle freed all slaves in the Confederate states on January 1, 1863, but in practice slavery would continue in those states until the end of the war (except as portions of them were occupied by the Union Army), and the proclamation had no effect on the resolve of both Lees to carry out as exactly as possible the terms of Mr. Custis's will regarding his slaves.

Perhaps the only positive note during the winter was that the War Department followed Lee's sensible suggestion to melt down some of the army's older bronze cannons to make 12-pounder Napoleons, the guns Lee preferred. They would reduce the number of different gun calibers and simplify manufacture.

Meanwhile the weather became crueler and harsher every day. "[The snow] was nearly up to my knees as I stepped out this morning," Lee wrote to Mary, "and our poor horses were enveloped. We have dug them out, and opened our avenues a little, but it will be terrible and the roads impassible. I fear our short rations for man and horse will have to be curtailed." Even when the War Department managed to produce a few animals to feed the men, they were so thin by the time they arrived that Lee could not have them slaughtered. No American army had suffered like this since George Washington's had wintered at Valley Forge.

Lee's own health, usually so robust, failed for a time. He was sleeping poorly, and a persistent throat infection worsened into what was thought to be pericarditis, for which treatment then consisted of rest and painting the chest with iodine. The diagnosis was wrong; Lee was probably suffering from the onset of heart disease, arteriosclerosis, angina, or even a small heart attack. The same symptoms—chest pain, pain in the left arm, and shortness of breath—recurred just before Gettysburg. Even in the winter of 1862 his condition was serious enough that he was persuaded to move out of his tent into a nearby house. Surrounded by strangers, however kind, he yearned for the privacy of his tent. He believed that getting out in the fresh air on Traveller would be better for him than any medicine and complained of "the doctors tapping me all over like an old steam boiler before condemning it." Some historians, including Emory M. Thomas, speculated that Lee may have experienced the first signs of heart trouble as early as his last tour in Texas, but few have considered what effect arteriosclerosis might have on his judgment over the next three years.

Great commanders are usually comparatively young men, while Lee was already fifty-five. He was almost certainly drawing on physical reserves he did not possess. At his age, spending the winter in a tent, with the survival of the Confederacy resting on his shoulders, must have subjected him to enormous strain, however carefully he concealed it.

Much of what happened during the last two years of the war makes more sense if one supposes that Lee was approaching what was then thought of as old age with advanced cardiovascular problems.

By the first week of April he was a little better, although still complaining of fatigue. Spring meant that he was once again facing the renewal of the war, although "Fighting Joe" Hooker gave Lee few clues to what he intended to do. Lee thought the Union commander might attempt to draw him farther up the Rappahannock, so the Federals could strike at Richmond. Or Hooker might make another attempt to cross the Rappahannock at Fredericksburg or farther upstream. He might even be planning to move his army south of the James River by sea and try to take Richmond from the same direction as McClellan. Lee's own hope was to cross the Potomac and try to reach Pennsylvania before Hooker could stop him—a repetition of his last campaign, but without the costly checkmate at Sharpsburg. Apart from Federal cavalry patrols, which suggested that Hooker was asking himself the same questions, the northern army kept several observation balloons in the air.

In the meantime Longstreet and most of his men were foraging in North Carolina for food for the men and their horses. Once Longstreet rejoined him, Lee would have about 60,000 men to Hooker's 138,000, not enough to form a long defensive line, or to prevent the Union Army from crossing the Rappahannock. In any case, Lee would have to wait for Hooker to make the first move.

On April 29 Lee woke up to the sound of distant cannon fire. One of Stuart's aides came up to say that Federal troops were crossing the Rappahannock below

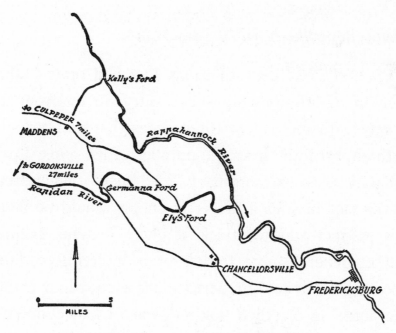

21. The approach to Chancellorsville.

Fredericksburg "in force," while more Federal troops were marching up the northern bank of the river. Although Hooker was approaching Fredericksburg from a new direction, the Battle of Chancellorsville was in fact an attempt to refight the Battle of Fredericksburg by approaching from the west as well as crossing the Rappahannock. Nothing startling was added to Burnside's plan except for a cavalry sweep intended to cut Lee off from Richmond. Lee quickly realized that Hooker's plan was to hold the Confederates at Fredericksburg while crossing the Rapidan and the Rappahannock rivers where there were few of Lee's troops.

Chancellorsville, April 29–May 5, 1863

Without Longstreet's divisions Lee had only 43,000 men in addition to Stuart's cavalry, to confront an enemy with more than three times that number and with almost four times the number of his guns. Lee's audacity was extraordinary. He knew that retreat in the face of such a powerful enemy would be fatal. His instinct was to attack at once. Leaving behind Major General Jubal Early's division, reinforced by one brigade, to hold Fredericksburg against four Union divisions, he marched boldly toward Chancellorsville to meet the three Union corps converging there.

Hooker was by no means as bad a general as he is often considered, although his reputation was not improved by his blustering manner. It was, for example, a mistake for Hooker to inform President Lincoln, "My plans are perfect, and when I start to carry them out, may God have mercy on General Lee, for I will have none." Hooker's bravado, moreover, did not conceal his lack of resolve on the battlefield. His plan was certainly an ambitious if complex one, and his intelligence about the size of Lee's army was relatively accurate—unlike Pinkerton's extravagant estimates, which had virtually immobilized McClellan. Hooker hoped that by attacking Fredericksburg with almost 30,000 men, he would be able to join Lee's army in place. He then would march about 73,000 men straight west and cross the Rappahannock at the United States Ford and the Rapidan at Ely's Ford, and march straight toward Fredericksburg, crushing the Army of Northern Virginia as if it were a nut in the jaws of a nutcracker.

He did not take into account that Lee's first instinct was *always* to maneuver swiftly and attack. Hooker also underrated the difficulty of maintaining his advance across the Wilderness, an area of dense second growth about twelve square miles between the Rapidan and the outskirts of Fredericksburg. Early settlers had felled the trees to make charcoal. When the trees ran out they just abandoned the area to scrub pine, small oak saplings, tangled vines, and thick brush, producing an almost impenetrable thicket with few roads and a large number of meandering creeks with muddy banks. In this dark, depressing, sparsely habited, and largely unmapped region, there was no way to openly deploy large numbers of troops, or to make good use of long-range artillery. Your troops—or the enemy's—might be out of sight only a few yards from where you were standing. Also, in the absence of any visible landmark commanders could get hopelessly lost. Years later General Fuller wrote that "the thickly wooded country" would make it almost impossible to control divided forces.

It turned out that Hooker's plan was simply too ambitious. A competent division or corps commander, he was now responsible for more than 133,000 men spread out over miles of thick forest and tangled brush. He had divided his forces into three powerful columns: one, his far left, advancing along the southern bank of the Rappahannock; and two advancing through the middle of the Wilderness toward Chancellorsville, the small town where Hooker made his headquarters. It was little more than a tavern and a house or two. He then added to his difficulties by sending his entire cavalry, under Major General Stoneman, on "a raid towards Richmond." He intended to disrupt Lee's lines of communication. Not only did this attack fail, but it left Hooker virtually blind in the face of the enemy.

All three of Hooker's columns managed to get through the Wilderness, and Meade's corps, on the far left, advanced within five miles of Fredericksburg, but Hooker had altogether misjudged Lee. Far from clinging to his lines on the heights above Fredericksburg, which his men had been reinforcing all winter, he had already split his army in two and attacked the Federal troops the moment the right and center emerged from the Wilderness onto Orange Plank Road and Orange Turnpike. "The enemy in our front near Fredericksburg," Lee wrote, "continued inactive, and it was apparent that the main attack would be made upon our flank and rear. It was, therefore, determined to leave sufficient troops to hold our lines, and with the main body of our army give battle to the approaching column."

Splitting his army in two in the face of an enemy almost three times larger was one of Lee's typically audacious moves. It threw Hooker badly off balance. Although two of his corps had advanced almost two miles to the east of Chancellorsville into fairly open country, and were well situated to hold their own, Hooker ordered them to withdraw back to

Chancellorsville. Already engaged with the enemy, his commanders were furious, since this order plunged them back into the Wilderness.

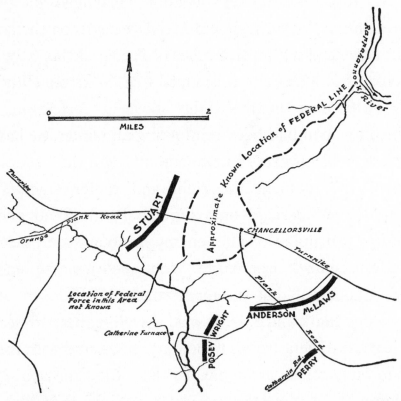

22. Position of the Army of Northern Virginia and assumed position of the Army of the Potomac, about 5 a.m., May 3, 1863.

"The retrograde movement had prepared me for something of the kind," one of them—Major General Darius Couch—wrote later, "but to hear from [Hooker's] own lips that the advantages gained from the successful marches of his lieutenants were to culminate in fighting a defensive battle in the midst of the thickets was too much, and I retired from his presence with the belief that my commanding general was a whipped man."

Major General Couch believed that Hooker had lost confidence in himself before the battle had even begun. Despite Couch's opinion, however, Hooker was not yet whipped. He apparently had second thoughts about his own order, and proceeded to make matters worse by contradicting it, telling his generals to hold their present positions until 5 p.m. Most of them received this new order after they had already abandoned their positions in obedience to the first one. The generals, and their troops who eventually formed up for the night to dig trenches and build log breastworks and abatis★ around the Chancellorsville mansion, were understandably confused and embittered.

Hooker's intention was to force Lee into attacking his army once it was concentrated at Chancellorsville and to inflict the same bloodletting that Lee had inflicted on Burnside. But Hooker's contradictory orders had confused his troops. From the moment on May 1 when Hooker issued his counter order, he lost

---

★ "Branches of trees laid in a row, with the sharpened tops facing outwards" (Wikipedia).

the confidence of his generals, just as Napoleon would have predicted.

Jackson's troops cautiously followed the Union withdrawal. At first there was some suspicion that it might be a trap, but by late afternoon the general informed Lee "he was checked by the enemy." If nothing else, Hooker had created a formidable position, with the bulk of the Union army on higher ground in well-prepared lines. Why Hooker supposed that Lee would attack it head-on, like Burnside at Fredericksburg, remains unclear, but it was wishful thinking.

Lee rode forward to meet Jackson at twilight. Together they went to where Orange Plank Road met a narrower country lane that led to Catherine Furnace, at which point they were less than a mile away from Hooker's headquarters and came under fire from a Federal sharpshooter. They sensibly walked back to the cover of the woods, and quietly discussed the situation. Jackson thought that Hooker would continue to retreat, and would probably recross the Rappahannock in the morning. Lee was less optimistic. He knew the pressure Washington must be putting on Hooker to produce a victory. Just then Lee's nephew Fitzhugh messaged the information that although Hooker's center and left were strongly planted, his right was "in the air"—that is to say, "it did not rest on any natural barrier" and could therefore be turned. In addition there were few signs that Federal cavalry was covering the country beyond Hooker's right. It seemed General Stoneman was still "joyriding" with the bulk of the Federal cavalry toward Richmond.

Lee decided on his favorite tactic—a swift and unexpected flanking attack. Stuart, who had joined him, promised to search for roads that would take a Confederate force around the Federal left undetected. In addition, he would find a local who knew the area and who sympathized with the Confederacy. At some point before midnight, Lee's mind was firmly made up. He asked, "How can we get at those people?" He may have asking Jackson, or he may have simply been thinking out loud as he studied his map, but the sheer audacity of his plan, which has been described by Fuller as his "masterpiece," was breathtaking, even to such daring soldiers as Jackson and Stuart.

Lee, who had already split his army in the face of a larger enemy, was now, on the eve of battle, going to divide it into *three*, leaving only 13,000 men to hold Fredericksburg and protect his rear. He kept 14,000 men under his own direct command "to hold Hooker's 72,000" in the center, and sent Jackson into the Wilderness with 32,000 men to march over fourteen miles on doubtful roads and turn Hooker's right.

It is hard to think of anything further from the principle of "concentration." "Lee's strokes flashed like lightning," said General Fuller.

Stuart, as good as his word, produced a clergyman from his corps, the Reverend B. Tucker Lacy, who had lived in the area and confirmed that the roads Lee had proposed were passable for men and horses. With a grim smile, Jackson said he would get his troops moving at four o'clock in the morning. At that Lee lay down under a tree, unfolding his overcoat for a blanket and using his saddle for a pillow. Within minutes he was asleep.

Jackson was not altogether happy about the route. He thought it was too close to Hooker's right for him to pass unnoticed. He sent Lacy off, together with his topographical genius Major Hotchkiss, to seek a road that would take Jackson's corps farther away from Hooker's right. They located a recent logging trail through the woods, and rousted "the proprietor of [an] iron furnace" who had opened the route and who volunteered his son to serve as a guide if needed. It was a slightly longer and more difficult route than the one Lee had proposed, but it was more likely to produce surprise, and would also bring Jackson's corps closer to Hooker's rear, causing the maximum disruption.

By all reports, Jackson was not feeling well that night. He was shivering in the damp, cool night air, possibly suffering from a cold. He lay down on the ground to rest in the small clearing among the pines that Lee had made his headquarters for the night. One of his staff offered to cover him with his greatcoat but he "politely but firmly declined" it, although he consented to be sheltered with a rain cape. Jackson had unbuckled his sword and placed it, hilt upright, against a tree. At some point while he rested it fell to the ground with a loud clatter, which Lee's aide Colonel Long later decided had been a bad omen—though that does not seem to have occurred to him or anyone else at the time. Jackson's intense faith precluded any belief in superstition, but in any case he did not rest for long.

It was still pitch dark when Hotchkiss returned with the local guide, but Lee and Jackson were already awake and seated on empty cracker boxes, presumably left by the Federal troops, around the dying embers of a campfire. Jackson seemed to have been revived by a hot mug of coffee and listened intently as Hotchkiss drew up another cracker box, sat down beside them, and produced a rough map of the route he proposed. Jackson and Lee discussed it briefly—there was never any argument between the two men, although Longstreet argued with each. "I have but to show him my design, and if it can be done, it will be done," Lee would say of Jackson. "Straight as the needle to the pole he advanced to the execution of my purpose." By way of an order, Lee merely said to Jackson, "Well, go on," and Jackson went off into the darkness to get his men moving.

Lee saw Jackson again for a brief moment as he rode off with his staff, and paused to exchange a few words with him.

Lee would never again see Jackson alive.

Throughout the day on May 2 Lee relied on two assumptions: the first was that Hooker would fail to detect the fact that his center faced 14,000 soldiers, and the second was that Major General John Sedgwick's corps at Fredericksburg would remain inactive. Both were wild gambles, but they paid off. Hooker made no attempt to advance against Lee, and the orders he telegraphed to Sedgwick were so garbled that Sedgwick decided to wait on events. His gift for unfortunate decisions in battle was already well known. He later would meet his end with one of the most famous lines of the Civil War. Chiding his men as they ducked from a sharpshooter's fire, he said, "I'm ashamed of you dodging that way, why they couldn't hit an elephant at this distance," and promptly was killed by a bullet in the forehead. On May 2 Sedgwick's decision that Hooker's ambiguous orders had left it up to him whether or not to attack saved Lee from being overwhelmed from the rear before Jackson's flank had attacked the enemy.

Lee's judgment about his adversary was as correct as Hooker's was wrong. By midmorning, the Union commander was told of the Confederate movement to his far right, but for reasons best known to himself decided that this was proof that the Confederates were retreating. Hooker ordered his troops to attack, but with no sense of urgency, perhaps thinking he would speed up the Confederate retreat. Also by midmorning, an intense, nasty little fight had engulfed Jackson's rear guard, the Twenty-Third Georgia Infantry, at Catherine Furnace. Reinforcements were sent forward to support the Georgians, but not in time to prevent most of them from being surrounded and overwhelmed.

If Hooker had visualized his situation correctly, he might have realized that although his right was in mortal danger, a bold attack on the Confederate center, given its weakness in numbers, might still have carried the day. But he was immobilized by the size and complexity of the battles, and unable to form a clear picture of what was really happening. Although he did warn Major General Oliver Howard that he might be attacked, he did so without conveying any sense of urgency or alarm. He never bothered to ride three-quarters of a mile to the southeast and see for himself what Howard was doing.

At 2 p.m. Fitzhugh Lee reported to Jackson that he had found a hill from which there was a panoramic view of the Union right. Fitzhugh's tone made Jackson aware of the importance of this discovery, because he halted his column and followed "Fitz" through dense woods up to a partly cleared hill. Jackson, to his relief, saw Howard's men resting, their arms neatly stacked, apparently unaware that over 20,000 Confederate troops, as well as most of Stuart's cavalry, were marching past them less than a mile and a half away. Jackson was so pleased at the sight that he decided to march his men two miles farther and attack Howard's troops from behind, which meant that he could not carry out his attack until after five o'clock.

As at Shiloh, the first warning that Howard's men had of the impending attack was the sudden appearance of panicked wildlife emerging from the Wilderness, as the Confederate lines advanced through the forest. Moments later Jackson's men "exploded out of the woods screaming the Rebel Yell." As Lee put it in his report, "Position after position was carried, the guns captured, and every effort of the enemy to rally defeated by the impetuous rush of our troops." At first it was a rout, leading to the virtual collapse of the Union right, but although Jackson hoped to drive the Federal forces in disorder all the way back to the United States Ford four miles away, Union officers finally began to rally their men, while the Confederate troops, exhausted by a fourteen-mile march, were unable to keep up the initial pace of their advance. Although Jackson pushed the Federals back over a mile, he could not take Chancellorsville, nor cut his way through the remaining Union lines to join Lee. Then, despite the genius of his successful flank march—in many ways the military high point of the Confederacy—his victory was compromised by delay. He had optimistically told Lee that he would start out at 4 a.m., but did not, in fact, get under way until after 7 a.m. His decision to follow Fitzhugh's advice and march farther to the west, while it was tactically correct, cost him another two hours. When he did launch his attack there were only two hours of daylight left. As Federal resistance intensified, Jackson worried that his attack was in danger of bogging down and that he was still heavily outnumbered. He rode forward along Plank Road far in front of his men to assess the possibility of a night attack. Jackson had suggested such an attack at Fredericksburg, adding "that we should all strip ourselves perfectly naked," to avoid confusion of identity, which is the bane of all nighttime military assaults. Lee had rejected the idea as too risky and perhaps too eccentric, but the idea of a night attack clearly stayed with him. On May 2 it might have worked, since there was a full moon.

Returning from their reconnaissance, Jackson and his aides were mistaken by his own troops for Federal cavalry, and fired on. Some North Carolina troops had loaded "buck and ball," a .69-caliber ball ahead of which were three buckshot pellets, a formidable load at short to medium distances. Jackson was struck in three places, two of the balls shattering his left arm above and below the elbow. Little Sorrel, reacting to the sudden noise and flash, bolted, and his rider was knocked to the ground by a low-hanging branch. Jackson was only stunned by the fall, and none of his wounds was life-threatening, but his left arm had to be amputated. Pneumonia set in. Eight days later he was dead.

Had Jackson started at 4 a.m., as he told Lee he would, and had he not, at Fitzhugh's suggestion, taken a longer route that added two hours to his march, he might have had more daylight hours to meet up with Lee. This of course would have spared him the need to ride ahead of his own lines in the dark.

For Lee this was "a calamity of the first order": Jackson was by far his best general. A lesser problem was that Jackson, as usual, had not confided his own plan to anyone. Had he intended to advance to the north in the morning and cut off Hooker's army from the United States Ford, or to regroup his scattered units and attack at Orange Pike and then join up again with Lee?

Lee himself spent May 2 making a series of small attacks against Hooker's center to distract Hooker from looking right, and did not hear "the swelling roar of Jackson's attack" until twilight. Volley after volley of artillery fire lit up the night sky, and musketry could be heard until after eleven o'clock. There was no news, however, from the battlefield, so Lee eventually lay down in a small clearing to rest. "Around 2:30" he was woken by Taylor talking to one of Jackson's signal officers, Captain Wilbourn, who described his commander's extraordinary flank march, ending with Jackson's being wounded by his own men.

Neither Wilbourn nor Lee had any reason to suppose that Jackson's wounds would prove fatal, but Wilbourn later wrote that Lee "moaned audibly" at the news, and "seemed about to burst into tears." In the meantime the left wing of his army was without a commander, except for A. P. Hill, with whom Jackson had not shared his plans. Shortly afterward, Hill was wounded and, as the ranking major general on the spot, Jeb Stuart assumed command. At 3 a.m. Lee wrote to Stuart urging him to press forward "with utmost vigor" and to "dispossess" the enemy of Chancellorsville "which will permit the union of the whole army."

It was evident to Lee that the "glorious victory" Jackson had won on May 2 was now in the balance. Hooker had been badly shaken, but he still had 76,000 men to Lee's 43,000; his center and left were well dug in; and any attempt to drive him out was bound to be bloody.

Jackson's wound continued to worry Lee. He called for Traveller, but just as he had mounted, Hotchkiss appeared with a further report. Lee listened patiently until Hotchkiss described Jackson's wound, at which point Lee gently silenced him: "I know all about it, and I [do] not wish to hear more—it is too painful a subject." It was clear to Lee that he and Stuart would have to fight their way forward to join the two wings of the army. Failure to do so would render Jackson's previous victory pointless. Lee was helped at this point by another of Hooker's mistakes, which was to withdraw his artillery batteries from a raised clearing that offered a commanding field of fire to both the west and the east. It would have been difficult or even impossible for the Confederate infantry to take if Hooker had held it with determination.

The Union line now consisted of a horseshoe around Chancellorsville as well as a straight line running from there to the Rappahannock. About five-thirty the next morning Lee and Stuart simultaneously attacked both sides of the horseshoe, in some of the heaviest fighting of the war. Lee remained in the thick of it, though he could not have known that a Confederate cannonball had hit a pillar of the Chancellorsville house against which Hooker was leaning. A large part of it fell "violently" on Hooker's head, knocking him unconscious. Hooker refused to give up command, probably because he disliked his second in command, Major General Couch. It had been Couch who said that Hooker was "whipped" before the battle even begun. Perhaps as a consequence, by ten o'clock that morning he withdrew his artillery batteries from Fairview Hill, effectively giving up any attempt to hold Chancellorsville, and thereby condemned his army to a panicky race for the far side of the Rappahannock. In less than five hours both sides took casualties that were second only to those at Antietam—over 17,000 Union casualties, and over 13,000 Confederate—but Lee had achieved his objective, and won what Fuller has described as his "perfect battle." Also at 10 a.m. the two parts of Lee's army were joined within sight of the Chancellorsville Tavern. Lee rode forward on Traveller to a tumultuous welcome described by Major Charles Marshall, his military secretary:

Lee's presence was the signal for one of those uncontrollable bursts of enthusiasm which no one can appreciate who has not witnessed them. The fierce soldiers, with their faces blackened with the smoke of battle, the wounded crawling with feeble limbs from the fury of the devouring flames, all seemed possessed with a common impulse. One long, unbroken cheer . . . rose high above the roar of battle and hailed the presence of a victorious chief. He sat in the full realization of all that soldiers dream of—triumph; and as I looked at him in the complete fruition of the success which his genius, courage, and confidence in his army had won, I thought it must have been from such a scene that men in ancient days ascended to the glory of the gods.

Marshall was a levelheaded man and a lawyer, but he worshipped Lee, as millions of other men did. As Lee rode through the carnage, a gray man on a gray horse, he appeared the perfect hero.

But once again, the Army of Northern Virginia was in no position to advance and cut the bulk of Hooker's army off from the United States Ford. Dazed and humiliated Hooker might be, but Lee had lost nearly 25 percent of his force. His victory brings to mind the words of King Pyrrhus, "Another such victory and we are undone." Longstreet echoed the thought when he rejoined the army: he considered that by taking the offensive instead of the defensive Lee cost the Confederacy more casualties than it could ever hope to replace. Lee himself took little pleasure from his victory. He dictated the following to the wounded Jackson: "Could I have directed events, I would have chosen for the good of the country to be disabled in your stead."

At this time Lee learned of a Confederate disaster at Fredericksburg, less than ten miles away, where he had left Jubal Early, ordering that if Early was attacked by a much stronger force he was to retreat toward Richmond. Then on May 2 Early received an oral order from a member of Lee's staff sending him to support Lee. After starting his march Early learned that Sedgwick was crossing the Rappahannock to take Fredericksburg. He immediately countermarched back and throughout May 3 fought a desperate battle to prevent Sedgwick from succeeding where Burnside had failed. Owing to a muddled order, Lee found himself having to pay for the same piece of real estate twice, with the additional threat of Union troops coming down Plank Road to attack his rear. Lee at once sent Major General McLaws's division rushing pell-mell for Fredericksburg, again dividing his forces. He quickly followed to make sure there were no further misunderstandings about his orders. May 3 saw intense and bloody fighting, as Sedgwick's troops once again assaulted the Confederate line on Saint Marye's Heights, succeeding at one point in taking the sunken road where so many had been killed in December. By late afternoon the Federal troops had advanced more than four miles until they were halted at Salem Church by a stout, well-organized Confederate defense.

Hooker still remained, unable to decide whether to advance or retreat. He had the manpower for another attack, but neither the will nor the plan. Although fighting continued around Fredericksburg all day on May 4, Hooker was in no position to support Sedgwick, who was already making plans of his own to retreat north of the Rappahannock. On the night of May 5 "Fighting Joe" held a council of war with his commanders, most of whom wanted to renew the battle. By then, however, Hooker had taken counsel of his own fears. Despite his superior strength in numbers and artillery, he chose to end the campaign and retreat to lick his wounds. It was an ignominious end to what had started out as a serious threat to the Army of Northern Virginia, prompting Lincoln to ask, "My God! My God! What will the country say?" Hooker's generals were unanimous in their complaints about him, while he in turn blamed them, undermining whatever little confidence Lincoln and Halleck still had.

Southerners' enthusiasm for Lee's greatest victory was considerably dampened by the death of Stonewall Jackson and by the frightful casualties. The chronology of Lee's battles was almost unique in military history— he fought battle after battle in close succession, without giving himself or his army any time to rest. Since August 1862, he had fought four of the major battles of the Civil War. No Union general had proved to be his equal in boldness and tactical genius. No Federal troops had managed to achieve the level of ferocity and determination in the face of adverse odds as his half-starved, poorly equipped men. All through 1862 the Confederacy faced dire problems—the Federal blockade of southern ports; the loss of New Orleans, its most important city; Grant's relentless descent down the Mississippi River toward Vicksburg and the very heart of the Confederacy; the South's inferiority not only in wealth and numbers, but in terms of all kinds of manufactured goods. The Confederate government had to rely on the hard-won victories of the Army of Northern Virginia as its best means of survival.

Even now, after almost a week of fighting and 13,000 casualties, the best that could be said, strategically, was that Lee had held his ground and forced an enemy more than twice his size to retreat. Now he was planning to resume the northward march into Pennsylvania. The pace of the fighting was astounding—in less than two months, hardly time for his army to recover, Lee would fight the most decisive battle of the war.

Chapter 10
Gettysburg

"If We Do Not Whip Him,
He Will Whip Us"

"General Lee is without exception, the handsomest
man of his age I ever saw. . . . He is a perfect
gentleman in every respect."

—Lieutenant-Colonel Arthur James
Lyon Fremantle, of the Coldstream
Guards, a British observer at
Gettysburg

Although Colonel Fremantle is sometimes described as an official British observer to the Confederate Army in uniform, he was in fact a kind of military tourist who traveled to the United States to visit the Confederacy on leave, rather in the manner of Phileas Fogg, the imperturbable hero of Jules Verne's *Around the World in Eighty Days*. Fremantle resembles Phileas Fogg so strongly that one is inclined to believe Verne must have modeled his hero on him, except that this figure is a familiar mid-nineteenth-century English stereotype: the adventurous, unshockable, curious, courageous world traveler who observes everything from the point of view of an English gentleman. Fremantle had charm and great presence, and along his way he met and won over almost anyone of importance in the Confederacy—it is no surprise that he rose to become a major general and aide-de-camp to H. R. H. Field Marshal the Duke of Cambridge. He was also an acute observer and a first-rate interviewer, the equivalent of a Victorian Alistair Cooke. Nothing escapes Fremantle's notice, from the fact that in Charleston the only difference in dress between Negro women and their mistresses was "that a mulatto woman is not allowed to wear a veil" to the quality of the tea served in President Jefferson Davis's house in Richmond. Fremantle landed "at the miserable village of Bagdad" on the Mexican side of the Rio Grande and traveled from there, often in conditions of excruciating discomfort and some danger, all the way to Gettysburg, where he observed the battle from beside Lee and Longstreet. He paints a vivid picture of what was going on at the western side of the Confederacy, where Grant was about to take Vicksburg, Benjamin Grierson's Union cavalrymen were raiding deep into Mississippi, and crossing the great Mississippi River was already a difficult and hazardous undertaking. Whatever was going on in northern Virginia, the Confederacy was collapsing like a house of cards on the Mississippi, and Fremantle was hardly the only person who noticed it—or remarked on the poverty and misery of people whose homes had been burned, their possessions destroyed, and they themselves turned into penniless refugees in their own country.

Lee's decision to advance into Pennsylvania in search of the grand battle that would bring the United States to the negotiating table with the Confederacy, and would also bring recognition from the major European powers, was not universally approved. General Joseph E. Johnston was against it, as were General Beauregard, Vice President Stephens, and General Longstreet. Stephens wanted to begin peace negotiations at once and thought that invading Pennsylvania was more likely to further antagonize northerners than to turn their minds toward a compromise peace. Generals Johnston, Beauregard, and Longstreet all thought that the South would be better off if Lee went on the defensive along the Rappahannock, where he had proved that he could hold the Union army back, while quickly shifting a good part of his army to the West to prevent Grant from taking Vicksburg, and to attempt to keep

Kentucky, Tennessee, and Mississippi in Confederate hands. The danger that the Confederacy might unravel from west to east, whatever happened between the Rappahannock and the Potomac, was Grant's central strategic idea, and should have been the overriding concern of the Confederate government; but Lee's position as the South's most respected and admired military figure, and the high drama of his rapid marches and his victories against much larger armies, had a profound effect on southern military strategy. Lee himself was too good a general not to be aware of this, but he could never overcome a certain myopia about his native state. He remained a Virginian first and foremost; he had resigned from the U.S. Army to defend Virginia; and while he was committed heart and soul to the Confederacy if only as a matter of honor, his first love remained his own state. His strategic vision was a reflection of his personality—a strong preference for attack over defense, a belief in the superiority of his own troops over Federal troops, and a determination to remove Federal forces as "invaders" from all of Virginia. Moreover, keeping his army in Virginia inevitably meant depriving his fellow Virginians of food, forage, cattle, and horses—the army could be fed only at the expense of civilians—whereas moving it north of the Potomac would enable it to supply itself at the enemy's expense.

Longstreet was sufficiently opposed to this plan that he took his case to Secretary of War James Seddon in Richmond over Lee's head, explaining that the Confederacy's greatest opportunity lay in "the skillful use of our interior lines," and proposing that his corps of the Army of Northern Virginia be sent to join General Braxton Bragg's army so as to attack "in overwhelming numbers" and defeat Major General W. S. Rosecrans's Union army in Tennessee, then "march for Cincinnati and the Ohio River" in order to draw Grant away from Vicksburg.

Longstreet was correct in his opinion that losing Vicksburg would be a severe setback for the South and that perhaps the only way to deflect Grant from his purpose was strike hard enough in the West to threaten a major city. But he failed to convince Seddon, who as a practical politician understood that rightly or wrongly President Davis was committed first and foremost to the aim of obtaining recognition of the Confederacy from Britain or France, and that this would hardly be achieved by a victory over Rosecrans in Tennessee, or even by taking Cincinnati, as opposed to defeating the Army of the Potomac in Pennsylvania and forcing Lincoln to evacuate Washington.

In his patient, stubborn way Longstreet repeated his argument all over again with Lee, who "was averse to having a part of his army so far beyond his reach." Lee made it clear that he still planned "to invade northern soil," and Longstreet backed down, though he did not change his own opinion. "His [Lee's] plan or wishes announced," Longstreet wrote, "it became useless and improper to offer suggestions leading to a different course." Longstreet managed to extract from Lee what he took as a promise that "we should work so as to force the enemy to attack us, in such good positions as we might find in his own country, so well adapted to that purpose"—in other words, to find a way to repeat Fredericksburg, rather than Antietam or Chancellorsville. No doubt Lee was following his usual course in arguments with Longstreet of politely evading the issue, rather than simply telling Longstreet to follow his orders.

Lee's decision on his hearing the news of Jackson's death, to divide his army into three corps and promote R. S. Ewell and A. P. Hill to the rank of lieutenant general to command the two new corps, cannot have pleased Longstreet. Instead of being one of two corps commanders under Lee, he was now one of three, and he did not regard either of the others as his equal in military skill, competence, or vision. At the same time he continued to think of himself as a kind of second in command to Lee, as well as an adviser in the larger realms of strategy. A role as "first among equals" was not what Longstreet had in mind for himself, if the "equals" were going to be Ewell and A. P. Hill.

Over the past century and a half in the work of historians of the "Lost Cause" school, Longstreet has come to appear as the major cause of the Confederates' defeat. Douglas Southall Freeman accuses Longstreet, for example, of being "secretly swollen with the idea that he was the man to redeem the failing fortunes of the Confederacy." These are harsh words, and as much ink as blood has by now been spilled on the subject of Gettysburg and Longstreet's role in the battle, but Lee was not Lear—whatever failings he may have had, nobody has ever accused him of being a poor judge of men, particularly of soldiers. And since Lee trusted Longstreet, we have to assume that he not only valued Longstreet's competence, which nobody denies, but also that he set a certain value on Longstreet's stubborn determination to present him with the facts as he saw them, even at the expense of contradicting or challenging Lee's own views. So long as Jackson was alive he and Longstreet balanced each other, as the ying and yang of subordinates. Jackson was superb at guessing from a few words exactly what Lee wanted done, and setting out to do it immediately without argument or further instructions; Longstreet was as good a soldier, but he was an instinctive contrarian and stubbornly insisted on making Lee think twice, and to separate what was possible from what was not.

Lee was a strong enough personality to bear the presence of a contrarian. Longstreet was a robust, sensible, and solid presence, and Lee had long since come to rely on him considerably. "Although reserved in speech and manner, he learned the value of blunt talk and expressing his opinions in a forthright manner," one of Longstreet's biographers notes; and this too was of some value to Lee, who was himself courteous to the point where "blunt talk" was almost unthinkable from him or, for most of those around him, *to* him. As a gruff, bearish, though kindhearted Georgian in an army where many of his fellow senior generals were Virginians and idolized Lee, Longstreet frequently appointed himself to pronounce on military reality, which is to say that his outlook on war was severely practical rather than romantic. Longstreet's first act when he learned that Lee was not going to follow his advice was typical of him: he sent "a requisition down to Richmond for gold coin for my scout Harrison, gave him what he thought he would need to get along in Washington, and sent him off with secret orders, telling him that I did not care to see him till he could bring information of importance—that he should be the judge of that." "Scout" was a nineteenth-century American euphemism for what we would now call a spy, and it is clear that Longstreet was acting as his own intelligence officer, and perhaps as Lee's as well—indeed Lee had a gentleman's dislike of dealing directly with scouts, and of the whole business of spying in general.

Lee had performed a miracle in the month between his victory at Chancellorsville and the beginning of his move north. "It was now a far stronger army than the one Hooker had faced at Chancellorsville," wrote Colonel Vincent J. Esposito, now consisting of three corps (commanded by Longstreet, Ewell, and A. P. Hill), plus Stuart's "oversize" cavalry division (resembling a Federal cavalry corps), for a total of 76,000 men. Appropriately or not, this was by far the Confederacy's largest army. Bragg had 45,000 men facing 84,000 Union troops in Tennessee; Johnston had 25,000 men in Mississippi; Pemberton had 30,000 men in Vicksburg, by now virtually besieged by Grant; Buckner had 16,000 men holding the vital railway between Richmond and Chattanooga; and Beauregard attempted to defend Savannah and the Atlantic seacoast with a further 16,000 men. Despite shortages of everything needful, an ever more vigilant Federal blockade of southern ports, and an abysmally inefficient supply situation, Lee had restored and increased his army in terms of men, and vastly improved its artillery. He had about 285 guns, still a hodgepodge of types and calibers, but a formidable number—though not the equal of the Army of the Potomac, which had 370 guns and 115,000 men.

Still, what Lee counted on was surprise, swift movement, and the fighting spirit of his men, not numbers or weight of shot. To this end, he developed his plan by small degrees, drawing as little attention to his requests for reinforcement as he could. He was cautious in revealing his plans to the authorities in Richmond: partly to avoid inevitable complaints from other generals as he drew on the severely limited amount of manpower available; and partly because, strange as it may seem, and despite his friendly relationship with President Davis and Secretary of War Seddon, Lee preferred to "disclose his plans little at a time," perhaps out of reluctance to argue about them or simple dislike of the bureaucracy, such as it was, interfering with his broader intentions. He had hoped to take advantage of the "season of the fevers" in the Carolinas to bring Beauregard and his 16,000 men north and "increase the known anxiety of the Washington authorities," tempting them to withdraw troops from the Southwest to defend the capital; but this was too bold a plan for the Confederacy's War Department, which had apparently already heard as much about the value of "interior lines" from Longstreet (whose strategic bee in the bonnet this was) as it wanted to hear.

In the end what Lee intended to do was to keep Hooker's attention fixed on Fredericksburg, while shifting his own army swiftly into the Shenandoah Valley, where Union outposts were few, weak, and scattered, and from there march directly north in the direction of Harrisburg, Pennsylvania. Lee's aide Colonel Walter Taylor, who served as the equivalent of a de facto chief of staff, remarks that Lee's "design was to free the State of Virginia, for a time at least, from the presence of the enemy, to transfer the theater of war to Northern soil," and to choose "a favorable time and place" for a pitched battle. Like Longstreet, Taylor assumed that "the Tycoon,"* as his staff sometimes referred to Lee, would place himself so that the enemy had to attack him on ground of Lee's own choosing, as at Fredericksburg; but Lee had given no guarantees that he would do any such thing, whatever Longstreet may have supposed. His military secretary, Lieutenant Colonel Charles Marshall, who drafted most of Lee's

---

* Taylor used this word, recently introduced into English from the Japanese *taikun*, in the old-fashioned sense of a great leader, rather than the modern sense of a wealthy, powerful businessman.

orders, correspondence, and reports, emphasizes the importance that Lee placed on defending Richmond and "preserving that part of Virginia north of the James and of keeping it free from the presence of the enemy." Lee, in his own report on the Battle of Gettysburg, places foremost his hope that the movement of his army from a defending position south of the Rappahannock at Fredericksburg to an advance into Pennsylvania "might offer a fair opportunity to strike a blow at the army then commanded by General Hooker, and that in any event that army would be compelled to leave Virginia." It is fair to conclude that Lee's view of the war remained, as it had always been, a Virginian's, and that in his order of priorities removing the enemy from Virginia was among the highest, if not *the* highest. Nowhere in describing the objectives of his campaign does he mention any understanding between himself and President Davis that he would so place himself that Hooker would be obliged to attack him on ground of Lee's own choosing, desirable as that might be. Only later on in the report does Lee mention, en passant, "It had not been intended to fight a general battle at such a distance from our base, unless attacked by the enemy"; he then goes on to list the reasons, largely having to do with difficulties of transport and supply, why the battle became "unavoidable." The still hotly debated question of whether Lee should or should not have fought at Gettysburg does not seem to have concerned him deeply—"unavoidable" is a strong word—still less does he seem to have felt that putting his army in a favorable position where the enemy would have to attack him was in any sense an obligation.

On June 3, 1863, Lee began to withdraw his army piece by piece from Fredericksburg. This was exactly a month since his victory at Chancellorsville, and it remains amazing that so soon after a great and costly battle the army was able to embark on such an ambitious flanking march to the west and the north around the right of the Army of the Potomac—or, perhaps more significant, that a man of fifty-six, and possibly not in the best of health, was leading it.

We know that Lee had been very sick toward the end of the winter, and it is possible to suppose, from his symptoms, that he was suffering from arteriosclerosis and what would now be called angina. Neither Taylor nor Marshall, each of whom was close to Lee day and night, mentions his health, but then again Lee was of all men the least likely to complain about it, or allow even those closest to him to see anything beyond his perfect mask of dignity, composure, and self-control. All the same, over the next month he was to undergo enormous and relentless stress, and bear alone the full responsibility for the largest army of the Confederacy and its most daring strategic decision: an invasion of the North intended to provoke the decisive battle that would, at last, win the South independence. Longstreet would later write that Lee was impatient and excitable, and if so, that would be easily understandable, but then Longstreet had a case to make, and wrote long after Lee's death. Nobody else at the time seems to have remarked on Lee's behavior or manner: the "marble face" and dignified composure remained the same as they had always been, in victory and defeat, whatever they may have cost him.

The fact that Lee was "thinning" his forces did not pass unnoticed by General Hooker, who threw a pontoon bridge across the Rappahannock at Deep Run, just over a mile below Fredericksburg, on June 6 and moved a "large force" to the right bank of the river to observe what was happening. Lee ordered A. P. Hill to make "a similar demonstration against Hooker," which persuaded Hooker to withdraw his forces, but he was still concerned that Lee might be there, and sent his cavalry under Major General Alfred Pleasanton across the river to find him.

The result was the largest cavalry battle of the Civil War, which took place on June 9 at Brandy Station, where Stuart had assembled his cavalry corps to be reviewed by Lee. It is difficult to guess which of the two generals was the more surprised: Pleasanton, to find that he had stumbled on 9,500 Confederate troopers; or Stuart, to learn that he was being attacked by 11,000 Federal cavalrymen. By 1863 cavalry was in any case more likely to fight on foot in the role of "mounted infantry" than on horseback, but Brandy Station was a full day of old-fashioned horse-to-horse charges and countercharges, fought mostly with the saber (though infantry and light "horse artillery" were also engaged). Alarmed at the possibility that the Federal cavalry might break through and reach Culpeper, where two-thirds of his army was bivouacked, Lee ordered an infantry brigade forward to support Stuart's horsemen, and rode to the scene of the battle just in time to see his second son, Rooney,* being carried from the field with a severe leg wound. At the end of the day Stuart's men inflicted almost twice as many casualties as they received, but it was something less than a clear-cut victory for Stuart, and this may have left him smarting, with unfortunate consequences. As for Pleasanton, his men managed to cross back over the Rappahannock without reaching Culpeper, only six and a half miles away, where two entire corps of Lee's infantry were encamped, leaving behind them over

---

*A daring and competent cavalry officer, Rooney Lee was then commander of a brigade under Major General J. E. B. Stuart.

900 dead, wounded, and missing, and three guns—not exactly a triumph of reconnaissance.

Hooker's suspicions had in any case already been aroused. He guessed that Lee was moving his army *somewhere*—Lee was not, after all, a man who would waste a whole summer campaigning season guarding Fredericksburg; he was the apostle of the attack—and saw in Lee's move an opportunity. If all of Hooker's intelligence and his own instincts were correct, Lee would be moving west into the Shenandoah Valley, then north across the Potomac screened by the Blue Mountains, leaving Richmond uncovered. If Hooker moved his army quickly south across the Rappahannock, he could not only cut off Lee's lines of communication to the capital but "move directly" against Richmond. This was a daring plan, and might even have worked—the farther away Lee moved his army, the better were Hooker's chances of reaching Richmond—but as it turned out this plan was a good deal too daring for Lincoln and Halleck, both of whom wanted Hooker to cover Washington with his army. Hooker did not take their interference well, nor did he hide his resentment.

It was not until June 12 that Hooker was at last sure Lee was moving the Army of Northern Virginia into the Shenandoah Valley, and began to march his own toward Manassas Junction, with the intention of moving it into Maryland, crossing the Potomac at Conrad's Ferry and Edward's Ferry. It may well have appeared to him that Lee was repeating his advance toward Sharpsburg, this time from the south instead of from the east: one by one, Lee took Federal outposts as he advanced up the Valley: first Berryville, then Winchester, then Martinsburg, until the remaining Federal troops abandoned the valley, withdrew from Harpers Ferry, and concentrated at Maryland Heights, on the northern side of the Potomac, leaving behind them in Confederate hands 4,000 prisoners, "together with 29 pieces of artillery, 300 horses, 270 wagons, and a quantity of supplies of all kinds." For an army short of every kind of supply, these were significant gains, of course, but it is worth noting that Lee could not halt or rest his army—once it was moving, it voraciously devoured food and forage to either side of it. Lee prided himself on preventing plundering by his troops, and frequently issued orders forbidding it and promising prompt and rigorous punishment for those who disobeyed, though this could not always prevent half-starved soldiers from seizing what food they could along their line of march. Moreover, Lee's orders directed the chiefs of his "commissary, quartermaster's, ordnance and medical departments" to "requisition supplies for their respective departments" from "the local authorities or inhabitants," and pay "fair market price" for what they took in Confederate dollars, or vouchers payable by the Confederate government. These would have been accepted most unwillingly by people south of the Potomac, and were worthless to people north of it. Though he did not like to admit it, Lee was "living off the country," in the manner of armies since the beginning of time, but the need to keep his army constantly moving in order to feed it would have serious consequences in the weeks to come.

Of all the many controversies about the Civil War, those that surround the Battle of Gettysburg remain the most long lasting and the most difficult to unravel. There is, of course, nothing much to be learned from speculating on the great what-ifs of history, and this applies particularly to Gettysburg. We do not know and cannot guess what would have happened had Lee followed Longstreet's advice to fight only a defensive battle, or had he paid more attention to Longstreet's opinions during the battle, or had Stuart's orders been clearer before the battle. What we can deduce is that Lee thought he had a good chance to get to Harrisburg, Pennsylvania, without fighting a major battle, and was surprised when this assumption turned out to be wrong. One can see, right from the beginning of the campaign, the various strands that would produce a historic defeat rather than a victory, but Lee could not of course see them. With the hindsight of 150 years and hundreds of books, monographs, theses, television documentaries, and even a successful motion picture, everything is clear—indeed we may know too much, rather than not enough. But none of this was available to Lee on June 21 as he rode into tiny Paris, Virginia, accompanied by his small staff.

The success of Michael Shaara's novel *The Killer Angels* in 1974 (and of the 1993 film *Gettysburg* that was based on it) reignited the long quarrel between Lee's loyalists and General Longstreet that sputtered on after Lee's death, and came to a boil with the publication of Longstreet's memoirs in 1896. Longstreet himself added fuel to the fire by actively supporting the presidential bid of his old friend Ulysses S. Grant, joining the Republican Party, and accepting a number of Federal appointments, ranging from postmaster of Gainesville, Florida, to U.S. ambassador to the Ottoman Empire. The result was that Longstreet came to play the role of Judas in histories of the Lost Cause, as the one who by dragging his heels and disobeying his orders brought about Lee's defeat at Gettysburg.

The problem with this view is first of all that Lee did not share it, and second that Lee was mortal, a fallible human being, not a god—even the best of generals makes mistakes, and Lee was no exception. Lee failed to annihilate McClellan's army at Malvern Hill and again at Second Manassas; he allowed himself to be trapped into a battle he should never have fought at Sharpsburg; he underrated the speed at which Hooker would move the Army of the Potomac north after discovering that the Army of Northern Virginia was marching toward Pennsylvania. This is no criticism of Lee: "War is an option of difficulties," as Major General James Wolfe, the conqueror of Montreal, put it, and not every option leads to the desired result.

The attempt to put all the blame for Gettysburg on Longstreet ignores the facts that Lee, who could have replaced him, set great store by his ability; that they had an affectionate relationship, respectful on Longstreet's part; and that many of the elements leading to defeat at Gettysburg were a fatal consequence of some of Lee's own failings, coupled with the absence of Jackson, whose boldness and inspired skill at flank attacks was in perfect balance with Longstreet's solid competence and caution. Lee had said, when told of Jackson's wounds, that while Jackson had lost his left arm, *he* had lost his right arm, and there was a good deal of truth in this. With the exception of Chancellorsville, Lee had performed best when half his army was commanded by Jackson, and the other half by Longstreet. He knew how to get the best out of both men; they balanced each other and brought out the best in each other even when they disagreed. Now, only six weeks after Chancellorsville, Lee's army was newly divided into three corps (plus Stuart's cavalry); and while two of his three corps commanders—Ewell and A. P. Hill—had served under Jackson, neither of them had a particularly close relationship with Lee. In addition, Ewell was still recovering from the amputation of his left leg after Second Manassas in August 1862.

Compared with most commanders, Lee had always given his generals a good deal more leeway in carrying out his orders, and this had usually worked for him, since both Jackson and Longstreet were used to guessing what he had in mind. He also relied—perhaps too much—on oral orders transmitted by his staff, and in the heat of battle these were sometimes misinterpreted or misunderstood—that had been a serious problem during the peninsula campaign. Then too, Lee's whole style of command, in which he often appeared to offer polite suggestions rather than issue crisp orders, was less well adapted to an army divided into three corps, with two leaders who had never commanded a corps before.

Finally, the victory at Chancellorsville had recon-
firmed in Lee a tendency to rely on the fighting spirit of
Confederate soldiers. Again and again, they had overcome extraordinary hardships, lack of supplies, and
overwhelmingly unfavorable odds to win victories for
Lee over Union troops. They performed miracles, and
Lee had come to expect them to perform miracles,
but this is always a dangerous assumption—even the
bravest of troops cannot do the impossible, or overcome
faulty strategy.

Lee had every reason to feel confident as he rode into
Paris—he had adroitly positioned A. P. Hill to distract
Hooker's attention (and prevent Hooker from risking
a lunge across the Rappahannock toward Richmond),
while moving first Ewell's corps and then Longstreet's
from Culpeper west through the gaps in the Blue
Mountains—he had stolen a march on Hooker, who
so far as Lee knew was still in place on the northern
bank of the Rappahannock. Stuart's cavalry covered
the gaps in the Blue Ridge in case Hooker threatened
them, and by June 17 almost two-thirds of Lee's army
was "strung out over a distance of a hundred miles," in
and beyond the Shenandoah Valley, with Ewell in the
lead already approaching Hagerstown, less than ten
miles from Pennsylvania. To put the matter of distance

in perspective, Ewell's advance brigades had marched almost 120 miles in ten days, partly thanks to the good quality of the roads in the Shenandoah Valley, but still a remarkable achievement for men some of whom had no shoes and each of whom was carrying a musket, a bayonet, and sixty rounds of ammunition. Stonewall Jackson might have pressed them harder, but not by much.

By now Hooker was becoming alert to the danger—and also to the possibility of catching Lee's army strung out and on the move—as was Lincoln, who on June 13 ordered him "to fall back and defend the approaches to Washington," always the president's "default position" whenever Lee moved northward. When Hooker finally did begin to move, on June 15, he withdrew his forces rapidly to the northwest, via Manassas, Aldie, and Leesburg, clearly with the intention of crossing the Potomac and covering Washington, as ordered. His intention was to move the Army of the Potomac toward Frederick, Maryland, where he could be supplied via the Baltimore and Ohio Railroad and confront Lee if Lee moved through the gaps in the South Mountains to attack Washington from the west. In the meantime, Hooker's move enabled Lee to abandon his defense of Fredericksburg, and order A. P. Hill to move his corps into the Shenandoah Valley and follow Longstreet's north. By June 25 the entire Army of Northern Virginia had crossed the Potomac via

Shepherdstown and Williamsport, and was marching through the rich agricultural country of the Cumberland Valley on good roads in the direction of Harrisburg.

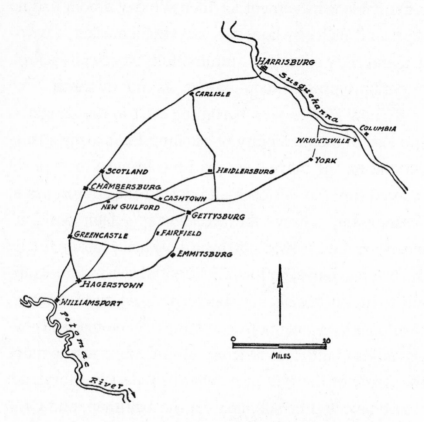

23. *Lines of Confederate advance from Williamsport into Maryland and Pennsylvania, June–July, 1863.*

Fortunately, we have in Lieutenant-Colonel Fremantle's diary an objective professional soldier's assessment of Lee's army and the country through which it was moving. Armed with letters of introduction to generals Longstreet and Lee, Fremantle had set off from Richmond on June 10, and was dismayed to find "an enormous pile of excellent rifles rotting in the open air,"* when he changed trains at Gordonsville— this was his first experience with the haphazard quality of the Confederate supply system.

By June 21, although his borrowed horse had a sore back and had thrown a shoe, Fremantle reached the Shenandoah Valley, and remarked that while the countryside was "really magnificent," it had been "cleaned out" by two years of war. "All fences have been destroyed, and numberless farms burned, their chimneys alone left standing." Procuring feed for his horse proved almost impossible, even for gold—let alone finding a working blacksmith. For two years both armies had been marching back and forth along the Valley and had devastated it. "No animals are grazing and it is almost uncultivated," Fremantle writes, and as he gradually catches up with Lee's army he begins to get a sense of what will become—what is already—a major problem for Lee: he cannot halt his army; he must keep it constantly moving forward to feed his men and his animals, because the inadequacies of the Confederate supply system are such that the army must live off the land, whether its own or the enemy's. At Berryville

---

* These had been captured from the enemy at Chancellorsville, and left to rust.

on June 21 Fremantle gets his first glance at Lee, "a general officer of handsome appearance, who must, I knew from description, be the Commander in Chief," and learns that Ewell's corps is "in front and across the Potomac." On June 25, Fremantle himself fords the Potomac to Williamsport, getting his legs soaked, and rides on to Hagerstown, Maryland, where he observes that the town "is by no means Rebel in its sentiments, for all the houses were shut up, and many apparently abandoned," adding that "the few natives that were about stared at the troops with sulky indifference."

This was the same day that Lee, about to ford the Potomac in the pouring rain on Traveller while a band played "Dixie," was apparently struck by the same sight. He drew the conclusion that neither the Federal government nor the people of the North were as "demoralized" as he had supposed, and wrote to President Davis, from "Opposite Williamsport," suggesting that everything should be done "to promote the pacific feeling" (in the "Federal States") and that "our course ought to be so shaped as not to discourage it." How advancing into Pennsylvania was to shape a "pacific feeling" in the North, Lee does not specify—in fact, for a general embarking on a major invasion with his whole army, his letter is something less than optimistic. He notes that he has "not sufficient troops to maintain my communications, and, therefore, have to abandon them," and repeats an earlier suggestion that General Beauregard be ordered to organize "an army, even in effigy" at Culpeper Court House, presumably to give Lincoln the impression that Washington was to be attacked from the south, as well as cut off from the north by Lee. The time to have proposed this would have been long before the Army of Northern Virginia crossed the Potomac, since by now anyone with a map in hand could see exactly where Lee was going; and once his men were in Maryland or Pennsylvania it did not require a sophisticated spy network to inform Washington of the direction of the Confederate advance or the number of Confederate troops involved—almost every adult civilian was pro-Union, and certain to pass the presence of enemy troops along. Lee ended his letter with a sentence that expresses a certain pessimism about his campaign: "I think I can throw General Hooker's army across the Potomac and draw troops from the south, embarrassing their plan of campaign in a measure, if I can do nothing more and have to return." Of course Lee could not have foreseen that he was only six days away from fighting the biggest and most desperate battle of his life, but even allowing for that, his expectations for the campaign seem curiously modest, as if its whole purpose was merely to draw Hooker away from the Rappahannock, after which Lee might withdraw his army back across the Potomac to Virginia, together with whatever supplies his quartermasters had "requisitioned."

This process too was producing less satisfactory results than had been anticipated. Lee reported to President Davis on June 23 that food, salt, and forage were scarce, and that flour "in Maryland costs $6.50 a barrel; beef, $5 per hundred, gross," adding, "We use Confederate money for all purchases." This is a little disingenuous on Lee's part; he was surely aware that Confederate paper money was regarded as worthless in the North. The Pennsylvania countryside was certainly even more productive than that of Maryland, but there was in both states quiet, stubborn resistance to Confederate requisitions of food and forage, coupled with great reluctance to accept payment in Confederate dollars, still less "vouchers" that could be redeemed in Richmond after the Confederate victory—one imagines that the stout burghers of Maryland and Pennsylvania were hiding away whatever they could, and were not eager to exchange their goods for worthless paper; indeed Colonel Fremantle never fails to note that the only way he could procure corn for his horse and food for himself was by offering to pay in gold coins.

By this time, Lee may already have made a fatal mistake, with consequences so serious that Lee's aide Charles Marshall devotes over twenty pages of his memoirs to explaining how it occurred and why neither Lee nor his staff was responsible for it. Before crossing the Potomac, Lee wrote to Stuart, giving him orders and instructing him "to take position on General Ewell's right . . . guard his flank, keep him informed of the enemy's movements, and collect all the supplies you can for the use of the army." This order was to become one of the most intractable and long lasting of the many controversies surrounding Lee's handling of the Battle of Gettysburg. The importance Lee attached to the instructions to his cavalry commander is underscored by the fact that he repeated them in another letter to Stuart the next day, a sign that he wanted to make sure that Stuart understood them, or was perhaps concerned that his first letter had not been precise enough. In conveying Lee's letter of June 22 to Stuart—who was operating under Longstreet's command—Longstreet added a covering letter of his own with further instructions, another sign of the importance everyone in command attached to the role of the cavalry in the coming days.

Charles Marshall goes to tremendous lengths to unravel this correspondence but avoids the critical question of whether Lee's original orders were clear enough, *considering that they were addressed to Stuart.* Major-General Fuller condemns Lee's orders as being "as usual vague," but the real problem is that they leave too much to Stuart's discretion and set him a whole series of contradictory tasks—"holding the mountain passes south of the Potomac," raiding "round the rear of Hooker's forces," capturing supplies, and eventually taking up a position on Ewell's right as he advanced toward York—without establishing a firm priority among them. Knowing Stuart as well as he did—and Stuart was like another son to him—Lee should have established from the first that Stuart's most important task was to guard Ewell's right and report on the direction of Hooker's advance once Lee crossed the Potomac. The big cavalry battle at Brandy Station had left Stuart smarting—the Richmond newspapers had been unusually critical of him, not only attributing "negligence" and vanity to him but urging him to learn from the experience, and accusing him (unjustly) of "rollicking, frolicking and running after girls." Given Stuart's high spirits and heroic self-image he did not take well to this kind of humiliation, all the less since Brandy Station was a Confederate victory; and it would not have been difficult to guess that given the leeway to do so, he would seek to silence his critics by repeating one of his famous exploits, such as his ride around McClellan's army on the peninsula.

Both Lee and Longstreet were anxious about the exact point at which Stuart would cross the Potomac, although Longstreet, in the postscript on the subject in his covering letter to Stuart, may have unintentionally confused Stuart. The fact was that if Stuart crossed behind Lee's infantry, this would place the cavalry between Lee's army and the enemy, and in a position to guard Ewell's right and warn Lee of Hooker's approach—exactly what Lee expected. On the other hand, if Stuart crossed to the rear of Hooker, the cavalry would be placed between the Federal army and Washington—a position that would enable Stuart to raid Hooker's supply trains, interrupt his line of communications, and ride right around the Federal army to join Ewell near York, a triumphant "joyride" that would bring him within ten miles of Washington. To do Stuart justice he wrote a note to Lee telling him of his position and plans—a note that Lee never received—and then forded the Potomac with considerable difficulty and reached Rockville, Maryland, approximately thirty miles from where Lee expected him to be; there, he and his men fell on an "eight-mile train of 140 wagons." Stuart later boasted that he had taken "more than one hundred and twenty-five best United States model wagons and splendid teams with gay caparisons," containing "foodstuffs, oats, hay . . . bacon, ham, crackers and bread," but his progress was now slowed by his enormous wagon train of captured supplies, horses, and mules, and he did not cross the Pennsylvania state line until June 29. Far from guarding Ewell's right, Stuart was now moving *away* from Ewell, with no idea where Hooker's army might be and no communication at all with Lee, who inquired frequently of his aides, "Can you tell me where General Stuart is?" and was obliged to send out patrols looking for him in vain.

This was the first act of the tragedy that was to take place in Pennsylvania, and which might have been avoided by making it clear to Stuart that his most important task was to remain on Ewell's right. Instead, Stuart would have to make a half circle of more than fifty miles around Gettysburg before arriving at about noon on the second day of the battle, with most of his troopers, his artillery, and his wagon train lumbering along far behind him.

In the meantime, Lee was blind. He did not know that Hooker had crossed the Potomac, nor that the Army of the Potomac was concentrated between Boonsboro and Frederick on June 28, the day Stuart surprised the Federal wagon train at Rockville. At that point, Stuart was well to the east of Hooker's army and unaware of its presence; he was closer to Washington than to Ewell—indeed, had it not been for the burden of his captured wagon train Stuart even contemplated making a quick raid on Washington.

June 28 was an eventful day for both armies. A brigade of Ewell's corps reached the Susquehanna River, overlooking Harrisburg, Pennsylvania, which was guarded by nothing more formidable than the Pennsylvania Militia, while Ewell himself took Carlisle, Pennsylvania, as far north as the Confederacy would ever reach. At about three o'clock in the morning on June 28 a courier from Washington woke Major General George G. Meade and informed him that he was now in command of the Army of the Potomac, Hooker having at last exhausted the patience of Lincoln and Halleck by demanding more and more reinforcements, then threatening to resign if he was not given the garrison on Maryland Heights, overlooking Harpers Ferry. This was a tactical error on Hooker's part—his resignation was quietly, and on Lincoln's part gratefully, accepted, to take effect immediately.

Surprised and unprepared as Meade was, he was in a better position than Lee, had he but known it. His army was spread out from west to east north of the Potomac, his left wing a little below Hagerstown, some of it less than twenty-five miles south of the then insignificant crossroads town of Gettysburg; but at least Meade had a good idea of where Lee's army was—it was hardly a secret to anyone in Pennsylvania who could tell the difference between rebel gray and Union blue—and knew where it was going. The quickest way of reaching him was to march directly on Gettysburg, and from there, if possible, to attack one of Lee's corps before his army was fully concentrated.

Seen from Chambersburg, Pennsylvania, outside which Lee had placed his headquarters, his position looked promising. Ewell had already reached the Susquehanna in two places, opposite Harrisburg and at Wrightsville; farther east, his army was concentrating behind South Mountain, and so far as Lee knew Hooker was still in Virginia. There seemed no reason why Lee should not cross the Susquehanna; advance on Lancaster, Pennsylvania; and march to cut off Baltimore, or Washington, or both from the north. Several members of his staff later reported that he seemed "apprehensive," to quote Charles Marshall, and if that is so it was because he had still heard nothing from Stuart, who was supposed to be close by on Ewell's right, somewhere to the east of South Mountain.

Lee's day, however, was to end with even more startling news than Meade's had begun with. Longstreet, who had gone to bed late, his mind only just beginning to dismiss "the cares and labors of the day," was woken by someone banging on his tent pole. It was the assistant inspector general, Colonel Fairfax, whose pickets had just brought in a well-dressed man asking after General Longstreet. He turned out to be Harrison, Longstreet's scout, or spy, whom Longstreet had paid in gold after Lee had revealed his plan to take the army north. Harrison brought with him the news that General Hooker had been replaced by General Meade, and the even more startling news that Hooker's army, far from still being in Virginia, was already across the Potomac in full force and deployed around Frederick, Maryland, less than forty miles as the crow flies from Lee's own headquarters. Longstreet ordered Fairfax to take Harrison to Lee's headquarters at once, but Lee, whose distaste for the whole subject of espionage was visceral and who "expressed want of faith in reports of scouts" in general, refused to interview Harrison himself, and deputized Fairfax to do so. Harrison, however, was not only brave—he had been gathering information in Washington, and "walked through the lines of the Union Army," then "secured a mount" and rode straight to where Longstreet's corps was bivouacked—but also well-informed and persuasive. Fairfax believed him, and even remarked to Lee that Harrison's information was close to what General Longstreet had predicted, which would seem to indicate that Longstreet, as usual, did not see the army's position in such a rosy light as Lee did.* At any rate, Longstreet sent, along with Fairfax and Harrison, a note to Lee suggesting that Ewell's corps should be halted and brought back from its approach to the Susquehanna in order to concentrate the whole army in the hills of South Mountain, around Chambersburg and Cashtown—thus placing its forward elements less than five miles from Gettysburg, without anyone on either side having planned it. As for Meade, Hooker had not shared his plans with his subordinates, so Meade was completely ignorant of Hooker's intentions. The best he could do was to pursue Lee as quickly as possible, and "fall upon his rear and give him battle," while Lee on his part, hoped to concentrate his army, place it on ground of his own choosing, and let Meade attack him.

As Lee started to concentrate his army which was spread out over thirty miles from Chambersburg to the Susquehanna, and move it to the east of South Mountain (which is actually, despite its name, a series of low hills and ridges), Meade was at the same time moving his army north as fast as he could, both of them advancing in the direction of Gettysburg, where they would collide.

---

*Douglas Southall Freeman describes in some detail a conversation between Lee and Harrison in Lee's tent, but Longstreet, whose scout Harrison was, explicitly denies that it took place (Freeman, *Robert E. Lee*, Vol. 3, 60–61; Longstreet, *From Manassas to Appomattox, 294*).

Lee, when he heard of Meade's assuming command of the Army of the Potomac, remarked that Meade "would commit no blunders on my front, and if I make one he will make haste to take advantage of it," and he was perfectly right: Meade was irritable, sensitive, short-tempered, patrician in manner, and still having trouble coming to grips with his new command, but he was otherwise a calm and well-prepared professional soldier, and unlikely to make a serious blunder. He had one important advantage over Lee—at the head of his army was a cavalry division under the command of Brigadier General John Buford, a supremely competent and tenacious soldier, while Lee, in the continued absence of Stuart, was still virtually blind, and had no idea how many corps Meade had, Harrison having been able to identify only two of them.

Throughout June 29 and June 30 the two armies moved toward each other—a shorter march for Lee than for Meade, but Lee's army was still spread out and could not remotely have been described as "concentrated." Wherever he encountered the Federals, he would have no more than a third of his army with which to meet them—hence the increasing anxiety of his questions about Stuart, from whom he had received no communication since Stuart crossed the

Potomac on June 25. It was not just that Lee desperately needed information about the enemy's position and strength, which Stuart had always excelled at providing, Stuart was also a comforting, cheerful, gallant, ebullient presence, with a contagious confidence and good humor that never failed to lift Lee's spirits even in the most difficult of circumstances. Stuart's absence was to have a profound effect on the battle, even beyond the fact that it rendered Lee "a blinded giant."

There are two schools of thought about Longstreet's presence. Freeman (like the whole "Lost Cause" school of southern historians) holds that Longstreet was "the spirit that inhibits victory": not only was Longstreet argumentative and wrong in his arguments about tactics in the coming battle, and indeed the whole strategy of the Pennsylvania campaign, but his glumness and his stubborn, disloyal opposition to Lee's plans and mulish disruption of them over the next four days would lead inexorably to defeat in the decisive battle for the independence of the South; had Longstreet carried out his orders and done what Lee told him to do, the battle would have been won. "Lee's feelings were gloomy," Freeman writes of June 29, "which had broken dark and stormy" of course, and leaves no doubt whom he holds responsible for the lowering of Lee's spirits. Certainly, Longstreet could be taciturn and argumentative, but the difficulty with this picture of the two men is that it is sharply contradicted by Colonel Fremantle, who was there beside them from June 27 to the end of the battle. "The relations between [Lee] and Longstreet are quite touching," he wrote on June 30; "they are almost always together. Longstreet's corps complain of this sometimes, as they say they seldom get the chance of detached service, which falls to Ewell. It is impossible to please Longstreet more than by praising Lee." Fremantle was a good judge of men, if not of causes— well into 1864, he continued to believe the South would win its independence—and if he found the relationship between the two men "touching," it seems unlikely that Longstreet was full of "sullen resentment" or, worse still, guilty of insubordination, of which Freeman also accuses him. Freeman paints a portrait of Longstreet sulking in his tent like Achilles, but nobody who was there seems to have felt that. Of Lee's staff, Marshall makes no mention of it—Stuart is the man he blames for losing Gettysburg—and Long mostly disputes what Longstreet wrote in his memoirs years after the event, a typical old soldiers' quarrel.* That Longstreet had appealed over Lee's head about the invasion of

---

*These quarrels occur after almost every war. The publication of Field Marshal Montgomery's war memoirs, in which he was sharply critical of Eisenhower, caused no end of heartburn and indignation in the White House.

Pennsylvania is true, and that he thought Lee had agreed to fight a defensive battle once there is also true, but it is a long way from this to the charge that Longstreet sabotaged the battle once it was under way.

Lee was no happier than Longstreet at having to fight at Gettysburg. Indeed, in his report on the battle Lee wrote: "It had not been intended to fight a general battle at such a distance from our base . . . but, finding ourselves unexpectedly confronted by the Federal Army, it became a matter of difficulty to withdraw through the mountains with our large trains. . . . At the same time the country was unfavorable for collecting supplies while in the presence of the enemy's main body. . . . A battle thus became, in a measure, unavoidable."

The word "unavoidable" is exactly the one that Longstreet would have rejected—he wanted to avoid the battle at all costs—but behind all the decisions, misfortunes, and surprises at Gettysburg, and for that matter behind the disagreement between Lee and Longstreet about tactics, lies the simple reality that the Army of Northern Virginia had to keep moving to find food and forage. Lee could not retreat and risk having to abandon his wagon trains, which contained his ammunition; he could not make a long flank march through country his army had already picked clean; he could not look for a better place to fight, where Meade would have to attack him, since Lee's line of communications to Winchester, and from there by railway back to Richmond, was already in jeopardy. Lee was in enemy territory; he could not let his men and his animals starve; and thanks to Stuart, Meade had surprised him, so he had no option but to fight it out where he was.

Longstreet was right to grumble that it was the wrong ground to fight on, but Lee had no other choice from the moment that Harrison brought the news that Meade was only a two-day march behind him. Fremantle, who was temperamentally inclined to see the sunny side of things (no bad quality in a soldier), writes on June 30: "I had a long talk with many officers [including Longstreet, in whose mess Fremantle was a guest] about the approaching battle, which cannot now be delayed long, and which will take place on this road instead of the direction of Harrisburg, as we had supposed. Ewell, who had laid York as well as Carlisle under contribution,* has been ordered to reunite. Everyone, of course, speaks with confidence."

---

* This was the much resented practice, when a Confederate commander captured a northern town, of demanding that those in authority hand over a large sum in U.S. dollars or gold or face the consequences. General Jubal Early demanded $100,000 from the town of York, Pennsylvania, but eventually settled for $28,000 in cash. General R. S. Ewell "requisitioned" from Carlisle, Pennsylvania, 21,000 pounds of bacon, 100 sacks of salt, and 1,300 barrels of flour, in addition to large quantities of molasses, sugar, coffee, potatoes, and dried fruit. Blacks, even if freemen, were liable to be seized as runaway slaves and sent south under guard. This is not to deny that the Federal Army did as bad, or worse, in the South, but Lee's chivalrous Order Number 73 of June 27, 1863, to warn his troops against looting did not represent the reality of Confederate occupation, however brief.

If everybody felt confident (Longstreet may have felt otherwise, but if so he kept his doubts to himself around Fremantle), it was largely due to Lee. First of all, Lee's own presence was an inspiration to those around him, whatever their rank; second, he had total confidence in his own soldiers, who had never failed him even in the most difficult of situations. Ultimately, he believed that his men were unbeatable, and that once he had moved them to the right position, his generals would know what to do. The outcome would be in the hands of God, and would depend on the fighting spirit of the Confederate soldier, in which Lee had almost as profound a belief, though he would have considered it irreligious if not blasphemous to compare the two. Faith can, of course, move mountains, but it is a bad thing to stake a battle on it, which is what Lee did.

On June 30 the whole army was on the move toward Cashtown, which was just over six miles from Gettysburg. Lee still fretted about his lack of cavalry. Stuart's whereabouts were still unknown; Brigadier General John D. Imboden's cavalry brigade, which could certainly have provided enough troopers for a reconnaissance in force, was still to the southwest of Chambersburg, guarding the rear of the army; Brigadier

General Albert G. Jenkins's cavalry brigade was with Ewell's corps, making a forced march toward Cashtown. In the absence of Imboden's cavalry, Lee had left Major General George E. Pickett's division of Longstreet's corps behind to guard Chambersburg—decision that was to have serious repercussions over the next three days. Although Pickett was something of a dandy, who wore his hair "in long ringlets," Colonel Fremantle judged him to be "a desperate character," and he had a reputation as a determined fighter. He was also high-spirited and "mischievous," and this may have been one of the reasons why Longstreet, a taciturn and serious man not given much to humor, enjoyed his company.

Heavy rain slowed the army's march—although it must have come as a relief to men and horses in the sultry heat—and for the moment Lee had no plan except that of "going over and see what General Meade is after." Lee himself spent the night in Greenwood, about fourteen miles from Gettysburg, conscious of the fact that his whole army was on the move now, filling the roads over South Mountain, and that he had not a single cavalryman to scout what was ahead of him. Even the most self-confident of generals might have been dismayed, but Lee seems to have kept his self-composure; at any rate, of his staff, neither Long nor Marshall records anything unusual, though Longstreet notes that "there is no doubt" the absence of the cavalry disturbed Lee's mind. It must have been further disturbed that evening, when A. P. Hill sent word that Brigadier General James Pettigrew, who had heard there was a large supply of shoes in Gettysburg,* had received permission from the commander of his division, Henry Heth, to enter the town and requisition them—acquiring shoes was always a major priority for the Army of Northern Virginia—and was surprised to find Federal cavalry to the southwest of the town, and also to hear the sound of infantry drums from beyond it. Lee does not seem to have shown any concern—this was no doubt partly a result of his firm self-control, but his remark of the previous day about going over to Gettysburg to see what "General Meade is after" would seem to indicate that he had already guessed he might find some of Meade's army there. What he hoped was to get there while most of that Union army was still strung out along the roads from Westminster, Maryland, to Gettysburg.

It is worth bearing in mind that in the mid-nineteenth century most maps were neither topographically accurate nor easily available. Lee had very little idea of what the country ahead of him looked like; even Meade, a

---

*Gettysburg was a thriving center of tanneries and shoe manufacturing of long standing.

Pennsylvanian with Pennsylvanian regiments in his army, had almost no idea of what the country was like around the little town. The average citizen today, with a road map or, more likely, a cell phone and a GPS navigation device in his or her car, would be better informed than was either commanding general. Many of Lee's officers and men knew northern Virginia well, of course, and south of the Potomac local residents would in any case have been eager to point out roads, shortcuts, and important landmarks to the Confederate army; but in Pennsylvania, enemy territory, Lee was on his own: he had little idea of what was in front of him as he and Longstreet's First Corps began to emerge through a gap in South Mountain, "a continuation of the Blue Ridge Mountains," as Fremantle, who wrote admiringly of the scenery, observes. Fremantle was now in the company of the official Austro-Hungarian military observer, Captain Fitzgerald Ross, who gave great amusement to the Confederate soldiers by his carefully waxed moustache tips and elaborate hussar uniform with all the embroidered frogs and trimmings.*

---

*Fremantle himself cut an elegant figure in a gray tweed hacking jacket, well-tailored riding breeches; high boots with spurs; a shiny silk top hat with a jauntily curled brim worn at a rakish angle; and a colorful embroidered poncho or serape with long tassels at the ends, worn over one shoulder, presumably purchased in Texas—a very practical garment for a man on horseback. During part of his journey through the Confederacy he also carried in his saddlebags, like a typical English gentleman, formal black dinner wear should the occasion require it.

Gettysburg: The First Day

July 1 broke as a clear, hot day with a gentle breeze, and by all accounts Lee was "cheerful and composed" as he rode forward and called out to "Old Pete" Longstreet to ride with him. We owe to Fremantle a description of Lee on the day. "He wore a long gray jacket, a high black felt hat, and blue trousers tucked into his Wellington boots," the short ankle length black boots favored by the Duke of Wellington, and carried no sword or pistol, just binoculars in a leather case fastened to the belt of his tunic. "He rides a handsome horse, which is extremely well groomed. He is himself very neat in his dress and his person, and in the most arduous marches he always looks smart and clean."

There were no fewer than five roads leading into Gettysburg from the north and the west—it was a market town, after all—and all of them were packed with Confederate troops from early morning on. Too tightly packed, in fact; more than half of Lee's army and a good part of his artillery were on them, and moving none too fast, for that matter. One senses a certain lack of urgency, perhaps because Lee was not yet aware he was going to have to fight a major battle that day, perhaps because of the absence of Stonewall Jackson scowling from under the brim of his battered cap and growling out, "Press on, press on!" to the troops. In fact, Lee and Longstreet were no sooner on Chambersburg Pike riding toward Gettysburg than Lee had to pause and straighten out what amounted to a traffic jam because a division of Ewell's with all its supply train had "cut in front" of the first elements of Longstreet's corps. Lee had to halt Longstreet's corps and pass on Ewell's supply train, which took long enough for Longstreet to dismount and let his horse Hero graze. Of course a supply train, with its lumbering wagonloads full of ammunition and rations drawn by horses or mules, moved at a slower pace than trained infantry, but one has to observe first of all that it should have been somebody's job to make sure that the infantry's advance was not blocked by wagons, and second that it should not have been up to the commander in chief to sort these matters out on the road. On maps of the battle all these movements are indicated by neat, bold arrows, but one has to picture in one's mind thousands of men and horses—every gun, and every caisson, was drawn by six horses; and most officers above the rank of lieutenant rode a horse—proceeding down narrow roads that were still muddy from yesterday's rain, with stragglers, as always, falling behind, and the pace held down to that of the slowest vehicle. Most of Lee's army was still widely spread out from Chambersburg on the right to

Heidelsburg on the left and in motion by several roads toward Cashtown when two brigades of Heth's division made contact on the outskirts of Gettysburg at 7:30 a.m. with the "vedettes" (the cavalry equivalent of pickets) of Union Brigadier General John Buford's First Division, U.S. Cavalry, Army of the Potomac.

Buford was the steadiest of generals, and almost half of his division consisted of regulars, experienced troopers. He had arrived in Gettysburg the day before, sent by General Meade to scout out the approaches to the town, and it had been his troopers whose presence discouraged General Pettigrew from entering the town to requisition shoes, and whom generals Heth and A.P. Hill had optimistically decided were probably Pennsylvania militiamen.

Buford had seen instantly that the three low, gently sloping ridges to the west of Gettysburg, of which the principal one, called Seminary Ridge after the large Lutheran seminary at its northern end, would be essential to defending the town, and placed his dismounted troopers to hold them. Except for the advantage of good ground it was not a formidable force—Buford had only 1,200 men and a battery of horse artillery deployed behind post-and-rail fences, and while his troopers were armed with breech-loading carbines, giving them a much faster rate of fire than

infantry, one in every four of his men was designated
a "horse holder,"* as was always the case with dismounted cavalry, and could play no active role in the
fight. Still, these were mostly seasoned troops, not the
part-time militiamen General Heth had expected to
find before him.

It took some time for the news that Heth had stumbled on opposition more formidable than local yokels
to make its way back up the crowded Chambersburg
Pike to Cashtown, where Lee, who could hear the
firing of artillery and the rattle of musketry ahead of
him, at last expressed his feelings to Major General
Richard Anderson, whose division was waiting there.
"I cannot think what has become of Stuart," Lee said
to Anderson, as they listened to the sound of firing. "I
ought to have heard from him long before now. He may
have met with disaster, but I hope not. In the absence of
reports from him, I am in ignorance as to what we have
in front of us here. It may be the whole Federal army,
it may be only a detachment. If it is the whole Federal
force, we must fight a battle here. If we do not gain a
victory, those defiles and gorges which we passed will
shelter us from disaster."

---

* The improvements in muskets and artillery had made the full-scale cavalry charge
obsolete (except in the minds of cavalrymen) and the Civil War was closely studied
by foreign observers for its use of cavalry as "mounted infantry."

Anderson, in his account of this conversation, written in a letter to Longstreet, also described Lee as "disturbed and depressed," and speaking more to himself than to Anderson, although Lee's state of mind may have been caused by the fact that A. P. Hill had halted Anderson's division and his reserve artillery at Cashtown, instead of pushing them forward. Anderson does not seem to have been a particularly imaginative man, but Lee had enough confidence in him to consider promoting him to corps commander, so one must assume Anderson was quoting Lee as accurately as he could years after the event.

If the quote is accurate—and it is worth keeping in mind that the two people who make the most of it are Freeman, who was determined to exonerate Lee from any blame for his defeat at Gettysburg; and Longstreet, who was anxious to shift as much of the blame as he could from himself to Stuart—then it is a remarkable thing for a commander in chief to have told one of his own division commanders immediately before a battle. Nobody could have summed up the position he was in better than Lee himself did, or given a more accurate forecast of what was about to happen, although the wisdom of sharing this with General Anderson seems doubtful; nor does it seem likely that Lee, if he was contemplating the possibility of defeat, would have told

Anderson so. But Lee was human, after all, so he may have been doing just what most of us do as we approach a moment of crisis, which is to question whether we made the right decision—to have second thoughts, or doubts, as ordinary human beings call them—though it was a rare phenomenon for Lee. Whatever Lee may have said to Anderson, it would be more typical of him to blame himself rather than Stuart, particularly since the scenario before him was exactly what Longstreet had warned against—Lee had marched his army into enemy territory, put his own line of communication at risk, and was about to collide with the Army of the Potomac in a place he did not know, and with no reliable intelligence about its strength.

In any case, Lee ordered Anderson to resume his march, then rode on himself toward Gettysburg. He seems to have cheered up on the way, perhaps because the prospect of battle always brought out in him a certain excitement beneath the calm exterior—he was a soldier, after all—and perhaps because he preferred to be in the thick of things, rather than stuck on Chambersburg Pike with his staff. Lee was not a commander who was at ease in his headquarters looking at maps and dealing with messages from the front; he preferred to see what was happening for himself; he was like the warhorse in the Book of Job who "*saith among the trumpets, Ha, ha; and . . . smelleth the battle afar off, the thunder of the captains, and the shouting."*

It was not that Lee enjoyed battle—no professional soldier enjoys it—but it was his natural element, as it had been his father's (Light-Horse Harry Lee's political touch was never half as sure as his skill and daring as a soldier); it was what he had been bred for, what he had been trained for, and what he excelled at. Whatever he felt as he approached Gettysburg—perhaps he had been "disturbed and depressed" when talking to Anderson; perhaps even he had felt behind that marble facade the sharp pang of anxiety—we may be sure that the rolling clouds of pungent gun smoke, the deep fiery crash of artillery, the unmistakable sharp crack of musketry cleared his mind and renewed his energy. He had not wanted this fight, not yet, not here, but now that it was before him his tenacity and his will to win took over. Those who saw Robert E. Lee ride out of the woods on Chambersburg Pike and bring Traveller to a stop on a grassy knoll overlooking the battlefield would have felt the sharp anticipation of victory. His very presence was an assurance that this was no skirmish, that a great event would take place here in the gently rolling countryside, with its neat farms, green fields, and carefully tended fencing, under a bright, hot midday summer sky. Those who were near enough cheered him, but

Lee was as indifferent to cheers as he was to danger—
he and Traveller simply halted there, a tall man in gray
on a handsome gray horse, while he unbuckled his
binocular case and brought his field glasses to his eyes.

The morning had gone well for the Confederates,
despite the brave delaying action of Buford's dismounted troopers, which held off two brigades of
Heth's division for nearly three hours, until Major
General John F. Reynolds's I Corps infantry began to
arrive on the scene. The fighting grew in intensity and
numbers—A. P. Hill fed brigade after brigade into the
battle as they emerged from Chambersburg Pike into
the open and deployed against ever larger numbers of
Union troops. Before noon General Reynolds, one of
the best Union generals, was dead, replaced by Major
General Abner Doubleday; and by the early afternoon Federal troops were being pushed back from the
grounds of the Lutheran Seminary into the streets of
Gettysburg itself. This was satisfactory, but in a larger
sense it was also exactly what Lee had wanted to avoid.
Confederate units had been fed into the battle piecemeal as they arrived on the scene, and had taken heavy
casualties without any hope of winning a decisive victory, since three-quarters of the Army of the Potomac
was still on the march toward Gettysburg and Lee had
less than one-third of his own army present.

We do not know whether or to what degree Lee was annoyed by what he saw through his binoculars—his self-control yielded nothing to those around him. Directly ahead of him—he was looking due east—he could see the Lutheran Seminary on the long, low ridge that bore its name; beyond it, in a lower dip, the roofs of the town of Gettysburg just over a mile away; and to the south of the town, indistinct as seen through the haze of gun smoke, a long ledge of steeper, irregular higher ground, with rocky, lightly wooded hills at either end. Baltimore Pike ran straight as an arrow behind the higher ground to the south of Gettysburg, but without Stuart's cavalry Lee had no idea how many Federal corps were marching down it toward the town.

Three of Heth's four brigades had been just about fought out, and Hill was reinforcing them as fast as he could deploy units from Chambersburg Pike. While Lee was pondering what to do, a stir to the right of the Federal line caught his attention. A "long gray line of battle," General Robert Rodes's division, was emerging from the woods to the north of Gettysburg—the first of Ewell's corps marching south down the Carlisle and the Harrisburg roads and beginning to deploy in a position that would overlap the right flank of the Federal line. Freeman writes that this "could not have happened more advantageously if this chance engagement had been a planned battle," but Lee did not think so at the time. When General Heth asked Lee if he had better not attack to support the Confederate assault from the north, Lee replied, "No, I am not prepared to bring on a general engagement today—Longstreet is not up." It is difficult to guess in what tone Lee spoke, or to measure his vehemence, but it was essentially the same message he had conveyed to General Anderson at Cashtown, in shorter form.

"But the very gods of war seemed to wear gray that hot afternoon," Freeman wrote, as Jubal Early's division of Ewell's corps emerged from the woods to the left of Rhodes, forming a gray line nearly a mile long that curved around the Federal line north of Gettysburg. Lee now had four divisions on the field, giving him the opportunity to turn both the Union flanks. Changing his mind swiftly, Lee ordered Major General William Dorsey Pender's division forward, and ordered a general advance, which drove the Federals back. By mid-afternoon the Federal positions, which had formed a kind of salient around the north and west of the town, had collapsed and Union troops were retreating in disorder to the higher ground south and east of town: Culp's Hill, Cemetery Hill, and Cemetery Ridge. It was a victory of sorts, but not the kind that Lee was seeking. Federal troops, however disorganized, now held the high

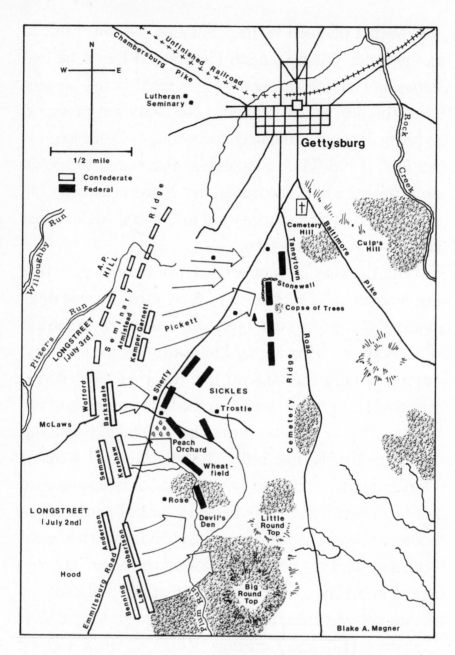

24. Battle of Gettysburg, July 2–3, 1863.

ground. Since General Meade had not yet arrived on the battlefield, he ordered Major General Winfield Scott Hancock to take command and decide if the army's position on the high ground south of Gettysburg could be held. Hancock not only decided that it could be, but was just the man to restore discipline and prepare the ground for the assaults he knew were coming.

Whether "the gods of war" were smiling on Lee or not as he rode over Seminary Ridge to within half a mile of the town, he was now in a perplexing position—although he had won the day, he had pushed the enemy back from a weak and scattered position into a strong and concentrated one. The Confederates held the ridges to the west of Gettysburg, and the town itself; the enemy held the two hills and the high ground to the south of the town, as well as Baltimore Pike, along which their main strength and their supplies were pouring unthreatened and unimpeded. Short of some tactical miracle their strength could only grow rapidly, despite what had happened at Gettysburg so far.

Lee's gaze took in the landscape before him and he immediately realized that Culp's Hill was the key to the situation; it was not all that high; it was roughly conical in form, fairly steep-sided, and heavily wooded; and like all the high ground to the south of Gettysburg, it was dotted with boulders and rocky outcrops dating from the Ice Age. From the top it would be possible to command Cemetery Hill to the east, and the whole long ridge from there to the two hills at the far end of it, almost three miles away, as well as Baltimore Pike, which ran between the two hills as it entered town. Union troops could be seen retreating across Culp's Hill in confusion (Longstreet described their situation at that point as "*Sauve qui peut*," or "Every man for himself"), and taking it as soon as possible would clearly be advantageous. A. P. Hill's men were close to it, but Hill himself was ill—he told Colonel Fremantle that "he had been unwell that day," and Fremantle commented that Hill looked "delicate"—an unusual way to describe a general—and reported back to Lee that his men were "exhausted and disorganized" after a day of desperate fighting in which the two Union corps lost close to 10,000 men, of whom 5,000 were taken prisoner, and the Confederate losses were considerable. One senses in Hill, throughout July 1 a certain listlessness, which Stonewall Jackson would not have tolerated for a moment in any of his generals, particularly Hill, about whom he had always had reservations.

Fremantle managed to make his way through the crowd of Federal prisoners and Confederate wounded moving back up Chambersburg Pike and enter the town of Gettysburg itself, where the fighting had been intense, and where the streets were full "of Yankee dead and wounded." Both he and everyone else seem to have realized that the day was inconclusive and required a final act to affirm and consolidate the hard-won Confederate victory on the ground.

Lee did not, as he might have done, simply order A. P. Hill to pull himself together at once and resume his attack. Instead, he decided to have Ewell take Culp's Hill from the north, although Lee himself was facing the hill from directly to the west of it, and could not therefore have any idea of how it would look from Ewell's point of view. He sent his aide Walter Taylor off posthaste to give Ewell a message that it was necessary "to push those people" off the hill, and that he should do so at once "if practicable."

"Character determines action." Lee's natural politeness, his dislike of confrontation, his preference for letting his corps commanders make their own decisions—none of these a bad thing in a man, even in a general—came together in the afternoon of July 1 to produce a moment of hesitation that would have a fatal effect on the Confederates. Ewell was used to receiving his orders from Stonewall Jackson, and Jackson's orders were famously brief and peremptory. The phrase "if practicable," of which Lee was fond, was a mark of his good manners and his respect for his own commanders; it was not intended as an escape clause. Once Lee had indicated what he wanted done, he expected that it *would* be done, that his generals would find a way to do it their own way, since they were in touch with the situation in front of them, and knew the mood, the condition, and the position of their own troops. It was not, in Lee's mind, up to him to tell Ewell how to take Culp's Hill, it was enough that Ewell knew it was his job to find a way to do it.

It may be that sending Taylor to give Ewell this order was a mistake. Taylor admired Ewell, whom he described as "a gallant soldier and gentleman" and a "chivalric spirit," with "a heart as tender as a woman's, [yet] brave as a lion," although he also noted, with a little less admiration, that Ewell was "nervous in temperament and brusque in manner." It is possible that Taylor, himself a pillar of courtesy, did not make it sufficiently clear to Ewell that Lee expected him to take Culp's Hill before the day was out and while the Union troops on it were still disorganized and in flight; and Taylor himself reports that Ewell, rather than addressing himself to Lee's order, was fussing about the number of Union prisoners he had on his hands "and the embarrassment of looking after them." Ewell may also have felt that it was not up to a comparatively junior staff officer to tell a lieutenant general and corps commander what to do in the middle of a battle.★ In any case, Ewell decided he could do nothing until the arrival of Major General Edward Johnson's division on the battlefield, and in the meantime deemed it "unwise to continue the pursuit." Clearly, if Taylor had carried a written order from Lee, however quickly scrawled or dictated, ordering Ewell to take the hill at once and at all costs before the Federals had time to prepare its defense, that would have made a significant difference. Given the fatal phrase "if practicable" Ewell immediately decided that it was not—he exercised "that discretion . . . which General Lee was accustomed to accord to his lieutenants," as Taylor put it tactfully.

If ever there was a moment when the gentlemanly instincts of three men combined to produce a disaster, this was it. Taylor makes it clear that if Ewell had been given a direct order he would have obeyed it. At least two of Ewell's generals were infuriated at his order to halt when they were in reach of the hill. The enemy was in full retreat, many of them "throwing away their arms," and generals John Brown Gordon and Isaac R. Trimble both believed it could have been "swept" over without difficulty. Trimble, who was

---

★What Lee needed was a chief of staff like Eisenhower's Major General Walter Bedell Smith at SHAEF headquarters during World War II: "Ike's hatchet man," whose job was telling people what they did not want to hear and what Ike did not want to say to them himself. But Lee preferred to act as his own chief of staff, which did not suit his nature and added to the strain on him.

famously outspoken and quick-tempered, later wrote that he had vehemently urged Ewell to let him take the hill. There are many versions of what he said, but in one of them he pointed at Culp's Hill, from which the Union troops were retreating, and said, "There is an eminence of commanding position, and not now occupied, as it ought to be by us or the enemy soon. I advise you to send a brigade and hold it if we are to remain here." In other versions, he volunteered to take the hill himself if Ewell would give him a division, a brigade, or even a regiment—badly wounded at Second Manassas, Trimble had attached himself to Ewell as an aide—and Ewell made an "impatient reply," probably to the effect that when he wanted advice from an officer junior to himself he would ask for it, at which point Trimble is alleged to have thrown down his sword in disgust and walked away without saluting.

Lee was unaware of all this—it was in any case exactly the kind of squabbling that he would most certainly have wanted to ignore—and therefore had every reason to suppose that Ewell was preparing to take Culp's Hill. In mid-afternoon he paused to survey the battle scene from "the top of one of the ridges which form a peculiar feature of the country around Gettysburg," presumably Seminary Ridge, in the company of A. P. Hill and Colonel Fremantle, who could clearly see the enemy retreating from the higher ground beyond the town. It had the appearance of a Confederate victory, though Fremantle, always a careful observer, climbed a tree to get a better view and noticed that the Federals were massing in better order with the town cemetery as their right, and that the position into which they had been driven "was a strong one."

He was not the only person to whom this thought occurred. General Longstreet had arrived—the forward elements of his corps were approaching Gettysburg, though still badly strung out all the way back to Chambersburg—and made a careful survey of the field with his field glasses. To him too the position the Federals were taking seemed "very formidable," as he told Fremantle later that day, but he drew from that a positive conclusion. The ensuing short conversation between Lee and Longstreet has been at the center of a controversy that still sputters on 150 years later and marks the starting point for the whole "Lost Cause" school of southern history, best exemplified by Freeman's three-volume biography of Lee, in which the blame for losing the battle of Gettysburg, and in a larger sense for the defeat of the Confederacy, is assigned primarily to General Longstreet. Longstreet, in this version of the history of the Civil War, is assigned a role comparable to that of the Serpent in the story of Adam and Eve—the man who was single-handedly responsible for depriving Lee of a decisive victory.

Of course the difficulty with this scenario lies in the fact that we have only Longstreet's version of what was said, and over time he added a few embellishments to his story, inserting several touches to emphasize his description of Lee as impatient. That was perhaps a natural failing in anyone writing over the years, for Longstreet did not publish his final version of their conversation until 1896, more than a quarter of a century after Lee's death, and by that time he was sick of being blamed for what went wrong at Gettysburg. Also, Freeman, whose telling of the story is dramatic in the extreme, adds to the problem by his own shading of Longstreet's words, as in "Longstreet retorted sharply. . . ." But in fact we do not know whether Longstreet spoke "sharply" to Lee or not; by his own account he remained extremely respectful of Lee, even though they disagreed. Given that Lee, perhaps mistakenly, retained his respect for Longstreet until the very end of the war, and for some years after its end, it does not seem likely that Longstreet ever spoke "sharply" to him, however little Lee may have wanted to hear what he had to say on the afternoon of July 1, 1863.*

---

*Come to that, we have only Longstreet's account of the conversation that took place between them. It certainly sounds like Lee, but we cannot know whether or not Longstreet remembered his words *exactly* after so many years.

It must be remembered that Longstreet had argued against the invasion of the North in the first place, and when he lost that argument, he thought he had obtained Lee's promise to fight a *defensive* battle, securing ground where the enemy would have to attack him, as at Fredericksburg. Having looked at the ground before them, he reintroduced, with a touch of complacency, and perhaps with an unspoken "I told you so," what he had told Secretary of War Seddon and later Lee while the army was still on the Rappahannock. "We could not call the enemy to a position better suited to our plans," Longstreet said. "All we have to do is to file around his left and secure good ground between him and the capital."

Longstreet was surprised, or claimed to be, when Lee, instead of agreeing with him, struck the air "with his closed hand," and replied: "If he is there tomorrow I will attack him." In describing the exchange, Freeman writes that this was "rather remarkable language for a subordinate to address to the commanding general, ten minutes after his arrival on the field of battle, and when he had not been advised of the strength of the enemy," as if Longstreet's remarks to Lee were a form of lèse-majesté, but nothing Longstreet said was unfamiliar to Lee; he had heard it all before, and he had always allowed Longstreet considerable freedom to express his views.

Longstreet was struck by Lee's "nervous condition" and "uneven temper," and did not realize that the cause might be "the wanderings of the cavalry," though one would have thought that Longstreet ought by now to have been aware of Stuart's absence. In any event, he replied, "If he is there tomorrow it will be because he wants you to attack."

There is no reason to suppose from Longstreet's account that he said this sharply. He also suggested taking "that height," presumably Culp's Hill and the cemetery behind it, immediately, while the Confederates on the field still outnumbered the Federals by nearly two to one. At that point Lee turned to other matters, probably to Longstreet's relief, for he noted that "a little reflection would be better than further discussion," apparently under the impression that Lee would calm down, think things over, and accept Longstreet's recommendations. At any rate, Longstreet realized that further argument at that point would serve no purpose.

Although modern portrayals of Gettysburg— particularly *The Killer Angels* and the film based on it—tend to assume that Longstreet was right and Lee was wrong, the reality is a good deal more complex. Lee still had no cavalry, so he could not be sure how many corps Meade was bringing up or when the bulk of the Army of the Potomac would arrive. The idea of moving his whole army to his right "to secure good ground between [Meade] and Washington" was fraught with risks. Lee's entire army would be exposed for at least two days to flanking attacks as it lumbered around the far end of Cemetery Ridge and off toward— nowhere, since Lee had no idea where this magic "good ground" could be found, and no way to look for it until Stuart arrived with the cavalry.

Besides all that, there was the question of time. Ewell's supply and ammunition train alone was fourteen miles long, and the notion of marching all three corps and their trains down the narrow Emmitsburg Road flanked by the enemy only a few hundred yards away was not one that would appeal to any general. For hours, for days, Lee's army would be vulnerable and exposed to attacks that might cut off one unit from another, reducing the line of march to bloody chaos. What is more, since his army was obliged to live off the country, how was it to find food and forage along the way? Men and animals might starve on a long, flanking march in search of the right place to fight, and the army would be exposed and strung out on the road or roads all the way. Rightly or wrongly, Lee was in the process of concentrating his army at Gettysburg, and considered that his best hope to was to complete that concentration as fast as possible and attack Meade before Meade's whole army was up. Far from being an irresponsible decision, it was the only one he could make.

Clearly Lee *had* already made that decision, whatever Longstreet thought then or later, for almost immediately Lee asked Longstreet where his corps (First Corps) was on the road to Gettysburg. Longstreet replied that McLaws was "about six miles away," but otherwise gave Lee no information about the rest of his divisions. Freeman alleges that this was because Longstreet was angry at Lee's rejection of his plan, but since McLaws was in the lead and Pickett was still, on Lee's orders, guarding Chambersburg until Imboden's troopers arrived to relieve him, it would have told Lee what he needed to know. Although Colonel Long, Lee's principal aide, was present during most of the day, and was later very critical of Longstreet's "tardiness" over the next two days of fighting, he makes no mention of any rudeness or disrespect toward Lee on Longstreet's part, as he surely would have done if he had an example of it. Colonel Charles Marshall, another of Lee's devoted aides, although he gives page after page to Jeb Stuart's failure to support Lee before Gettysburg, does not mention any trace of discourtesy toward Lee on Longstreet's part, let alone any "sullen resentment."

Since Longstreet's corps was not yet up—two of his divisions, those of McLaws and Hood, were on the way, and would arrive during the night; and the third, Pickett's, would not arrive until late on July 2—Lee rode off to see for himself why Ewell had not yet taken Culp's Hill. He found Ewell "in the arbor" of a small stone house on Carlisle Road, and to his dismay the commander of his Second Corps seemed indecisive and confused. "After he had reached Gettysburg [Ewell] had remained passive in the streets awaiting orders," Freeman writes; but this is only partly true, since Colonel Taylor had already delivered Lee's orders to Ewell in person, and Ewell had decided to ignore them on the grounds that advancing on Culp's Hill and the near end of Cemetery Ridge was "impracticable." This cannot have been an easy interview for Lee—all three of his corps commanders were being difficult that afternoon: A. P. Hill was "unwell" and unhelpful; Longstreet had lectured him about a flank move that Lee was in no position to make; and now Ewell was being uncommunicative and had seized on the polite "escape clause" in Lee's orders to avoid doing what Lee wanted him to do—indeed what Lee had assumed was already in progress. It is not difficult to imagine that Lee may have regretted at that moment the absence of Stonewall Jackson, who would probably already have taken Culp's Hill without being ordered to. Lee always rode Traveller on the lightest of reins, without using a whip or spurs, the horse responding instinctively to the gentlest of aids, and his way of dealing with his generals was similar. It was not in his nature to raise his voice, or threaten, or punish; he was used to obedience based on the awe which he produced in others—the story was told, and widely believed, that once when he had taken a nap, a whole division marched past his tent on tiptoe so as not to wake him—so he was at a loss now to know how to deal with all three of his corps commanders, who were behaving like balky or unruly horses at a critical moment in the battle. Even had he been inclined to do so, he could not fire them without endangering the army's esprit de corps and self-confidence, and in any case he had nobody with whom he might replace them.

Ewell scarcely even seemed able to speak for himself. He sent for Major General Jubal Early, one of his division commanders, to explain what was already obvious as the day waned: Ewell "had abandoned all intention of attacking that evening." Early, normally a fiercely thrusting general, and famous even among Confederate commanders for his ferocious beard, scowling expression, and hot temper—Lee often referred to him affectionately as "my bad old man"—now seemed uncharacteristically as cautious as his chief. Perhaps taken aback by Early's reluctance to attack, Lee gave up any remaining hope he may have nurtured that Ewell would try to take Culp's Hill before dark, and turned the conversation to his plans for the next day.

On this subject too Early, still speaking for Ewell, was pessimistic.* He thought that the Federals would be concentrated in front of Ewell's corps in the morning, and that "the approaches were very difficult" to the Federal position around Cemetery Hill; he even suggested that the attack should be made farther to the right, perhaps aimed at two hills, Little Round Top and Round Top, which dominated Cemetery Ridge and were over 6,000 yards away to the south, hardly even visible anymore as the light failed. Neither Early nor his chief Ewell thought Lee's suggestion of moving Second Corps to the right in the morning was practicable.

This was tantamount to saying that the Second Corps would play only a limited role tomorrow, and that the main attack would have to be made by others, farther south against the presumably less challenging ground in the middle of Cemetery Ridge, between Culp's and Cemetery hills and the two Round Tops, for

---

* Ewell's silence while Early spoke for him resembles that of Field Marshal Paul von Hindenburg in World War I, who was known disparagingly as *Marschall "Was Sagst Du?"* for his habit of referring all questions to his chief of staff, General Ludendorff, and asking, "What do you say?"

in the absence of Stuart's cavalry the topography south of Cemetery Hill was still unclear.

The "blame" for what happened at Gettysburg seems already to rest squarely on Lee's shoulders, not Longstreet's—the moment Lee arrived at Ewell's headquarters he should have ordered Ewell to take Culp's Hill, at once, at any cost, or replaced him with somebody who would. Now he had sat in the arbor patiently hearing from Early enough pessimism to depress any commanding general, until it was eventually too dark to accomplish anything. If ever there was a moment when a flash of temper would have been useful this had been it, but Lee remained as courteous and impassive as ever. Why? Ewell, after all, had served under Stonewall Jackson, whose grim, fire-and-brimstone Old Testament wrath toward those who did not follow his orders exactly or who failed to pursue the enemy with enough vigor was notorious, and Jubal Early's bad temper and nit-picking were a source of constant complaint among his own officers and men. A dose of anger was perhaps exactly what was needed to put some backbone into Ewell and get Early out of the arbor and back to leading his troops again, but it was not forthcoming.

A great man's actions are indeed determined, if not foreordained, by his character—not necessarily just the faults in his character, but sometimes, even more tragically, the virtues. Lee was a gentleman, and the need to *behave* like a gentleman was more important to him than anything else, perhaps even victory. He had his father's courage, but not his vanity, nor the combative, fearsome, self-dramatizing, and sometimes unscrupulous side of Light-Horse Harry Lee's expansive nature—perhaps Lee had heard too much about it as a child, or knew the price other people, not just Light-Horse Harry himself, had paid for that angry temper and those sudden rages that led him step by step into disgrace, bankruptcy, and exile. If Lee must have had such feelings, for his aide Colonel Long recalled his repressed fury over some matter and noted, "Lee manifested his ill humor, by a little nervous twist or jerk of the neck and head . . . accompanied by some harshness of manner," apparently not a rare condition for Lee. But he had learned to control them, surely at great cost to himself, for his angina was no doubt at least in part a result of the constant, lifelong effort at self-control that set him apart from other men.

Lee rode back to his headquarters in the dark to draw up his plans for the next day. He had realized at once, talking to Ewell and Early, that the attack would have to be made on the enemy's left, with Ewell's corps playing a supporting role. Since A. P. Hill remained ill, and his corps had been badly mauled in the day's fighting, Longstreet's corps would have to make the main attack. He had contemplated this while he was in the arbor, and Jubal Early would later write that Lee had said, "If I attack from my right, Longstreet will have to make the attack," then added, as if talking to himself, "Longstreet is a very good fighter when he gets in position and gets everything ready, but he is so slow."

This was prophetic, but based on experience— Longstreet's slowness at Second Manassas had very nearly cost Lee the battle. In any case, Lee made Longstreet's attack the linchpin of the next day's battle, Ewell was not to move until he heard Longstreet's guns. The attacks would have to be coordinated over a distance of nearly three miles, from Round Top to Culp's Hill—a plan made more risky by the fact that Stuart's cavalry had not scouted out the ground, so Lee had no clear picture of what was ahead of him.

Still another difficulty was that Longstreet would not only have to move his corps down to Gettysburg, minus Pickett's division, but then move it to the right along Emmitsburg Road behind A. P. Hill's corps before he could attack, leaving Hill on his left. Moving one corps around another was bound to be slow, and much of it was very likely to be in sight of the enemy, who held the high ground, so the element of surprise was almost certain to be lacking. The one piece of good news for Lee was that Stuart had sent word at last that he was on Carlisle Road approaching Gettysburg; but this would have little or no effect on the next day's battle. Had Stuart been there, and able to interrupt or interdict the flow of men and supplies along Baltimore Pike, that would have been helpful, but Lee knew that with every passing hour more Union brigades were marching unthreatened toward Cemetery Ridge. The time of Longstreet's attack was therefore of great importance, and was to give rise to another of the fatal misunderstandings that dogged the Confederates throughout the three days of the battle.

Longstreet had returned to his headquarters in the late afternoon, and presumably over supper had confided to Colonel Fremantle his concern that the enemy would "intrench themselves strongly during the night," which was true enough, as well as the fact that he didn't like fighting without Pickett's division—that it was like going into battle "with one boot off."* Later in the evening he rode off to join Lee—who had just sent Ewell orders not to move to his right, but to attack Culp's Hill when he heard Longstreet's attack begin in

---

* He seems to have said this to several people, including General Hood.

the morning—and made it clear to Longstreet that he wished him to attack as early as possible in the day, before Meade was fully concentrated. Lee did not give Longstreet a specific time when he wanted the attack to begin, perhaps because he was not in the habit of doing so, and Longstreet, writing about it afterward, remarked, "General Lee never, in his life, gave me orders to open an attack at a specific hour. He was perfectly satisfied that, when I had my troops in position, no time was ever lost."

That is very likely true: Lee had always believed in letting his commanders decide for themselves how to fulfill his orders. But it seems unlikely that Lee failed to convey at least that the earlier the attack took place, the better. In any event Lee dismissed the officers present with another fatal instruction: "Gentlemen, we will attack the enemy as early in the morning as practicable." One might have supposed that the words "if practicable" or "as practicable" would have had a cautionary effect on Ewell earlier in the day, but they reappeared, and with similar results. The accusation that Lee set sunrise as the time for Longstreet's attack, and that Longstreet ignored this out of pique because Lee had not followed his advice about strategy—still one of the sharper controversies regarding Gettysburg—is doubtful: in a spirited correspondence long after Lee's death, Long conceded the point to Longstreet. But at the very least it has to be admitted that Longstreet did not spend the night hurrying McLaws and Hood forward, as Jackson might well have done. Lee rode to a small house his staff had found for him to get a few hours of rest, and Longstreet went back to his headquarters to do the same, with whatever reservations or misgivings he had about Lee's plans for the morning.

Gettysburg: The Second Day

Probably no major battle in history has been as minutely studied and described as the three days of Gettysburg, and surely nowhere else is the most important ground of the battle preserved with such devoted care, so it is ironic that much of what happened there remains intensely controversial after a century and a half, and that many accounts of it differ widely. Of all the battle's many puzzles, the most difficult one to resolve, and the most sensitive to southerners, is General Longstreet's behavior on July 2 and July 3. Longstreet himself made matters worse over the years after the war by writing several versions of his account, which differ in detail. The final one was written during a period of five years when he was in his old age, and smarting under attacks from fellow southerners because of his friendship with

his West Point friend Ulysses S. Grant, and his acceptance of a string of lucrative Federal appointments.

There are therefore two competing accounts
of the second and third day of the battle from the
Confederate point of view: one by Longstreet, which
places the blame on Lee; and another, the classic "Lost
Cause" narrative, which places the blame on Longstreet.
Certainly, it would have been better if Longstreet
had attacked early in the morning, as Lee apparently
expected him to do—at daybreak most of the long
ridge between Cemetery Hill and Round Top was still
comparatively bare of Federal troops—but the question remains whether Lee actually ordered Longstreet
to do that, and whether Longstreet ignored Lee's order
and balked and delayed out of sullen resentment.

Longstreet's own view, in *From Manassas to
Appomattox,* was a sharply worded criticism of Lee's
handling of the battle. "Colonel Taylor says that
General Lee urged that the march of my troops should
be hastened and chafed at their non-appearance. Not
one word did he utter to me of their march until he
gave his orders at eleven o'clock for the move to his
right. Orders for the troops to hasten their march of the
1st were sent without even a suggestion from him, but
upon his announcement that he intended to fight the
next day, if the enemy was there. That he was excited

and off his balance was evident on the afternoon of the 1st, and he labored under that oppression until enough blood was shed to appease him."

This is strong stuff, and Longstreet cannot have been surprised that it brought the wrath of many, indeed most, southerners down on his head, though by that time he may not have cared. It must be borne in mind, however, that Longstreet had always, from the very beginning, argued against invading the North, and once he lost that argument, imagined he had won Lee's promise not to seek out a "general engagement" with the enemy, but to place the army on good ground and wait for the Union to attack. Because of Stuart's absence and the lack of reliable intelligence Lee had allowed himself to be placed in a position where he felt himself obliged to do exactly the opposite. Now Meade had been forced into a formidable defensive position, with short interior lines and an unbroken line of communication, which Lee was proposing to attack. It is hardly surprising that Longstreet may have been less than enthusiastic about being the linchpin in a strategy against which he had been arguing for two months. The situation in the early morning of July 1 was exactly the nightmare that he had predicted, and which he still believed could be avoided by moving toward the right and placing the army athwart Meade's line of communication, and between Meade and Washington, so that he would *have* to attack Lee on ground of the latter's own choosing.

The reference to Lee as being "sanguinary," as Colonel Long put it in his spirited reply to Longstreet's assertion, is puzzling, given the respect that Longstreet usually paid to Lee. One sees what he means, and it is in fact a useful corrective to the portrayal of Lee as a plaster saint. Lee was a general, and not only that—he was a singularly fierce and aggressive one, who neither brooded on casualties nor allowed himself to be deterred by them. Yeats's words, *"Cast a cold eye / On life, on death. / Horseman, pass by!"** come to mind when one thinks about Lee's view of casualties. He could be sympathetic when an individual caught his eye: thus after the failure of Pickett's Charge on the third day of Gettysburg he paused to comfort a badly wounded Union soldier lying on the ground who shouted out, "Hurrah for the Union!" as Lee rode past him; Lee dismounted, shook his hand, and said, "My son, I hope you will soon be well." But like Grant he could close off his mind to the inevitable mass horrors of war. Battles were fought at close range in the mid-nineteenth century, and the weapons of the day produced devastating wounds; there was no way

---

* William Butler Yeats, "Under Ben Bulben."

to insulate oneself from the sight and sounds of carnage, nor was Lee a man who commanded from a safe
distance.

None of this, however, means that he either craved
or required bloodshed. What Longstreet seems to have
been saying, though with singularly ill-chosen words,
is that Lee was determined to fight in the early morning of July 2; that he desired a battle, indeed felt he
had no other choice; that he thought he could win it;
and that he had closed off his mind once and for all to
Longstreet's pleas to go around the enemy's left. "The
enemy is here," Lee told General Hood, "and if we do
not whip him, he will whip us." It is hard to disagree
with this judgment, although Longstreet did.

Even the question of time is contradictory in
accounts of the day. Longstreet begins his account
of it by writing. "The stars were shining brightly on
the morning of the 2nd when I reported at General
Lee's head-quarters and asked for orders," which were
not forthcoming. In his old age Longstreet may have
been confounding the time when he arose and break-
fasted with the time when he met Lee. Fremantle, who
was at Longstreet's headquarters and who seldom fails
to consult his pocket watch, notes that "we all got up
around 3:30 a.m.," when indeed the stars may have been
"shining brightly," but it was not until "first light,"

which is to say just before dawn, that Lee, Longstreet, A. P. Hill, Hood, and Heth met on Seminary Ridge, where they were observed from above by Colonel Fremantle, by Fremantle's Austrian colleague with the fancy uniform and waxed moustaches, and by Captain Scheibert of the Prussian army from a perch on a branch of a tree. The observers had climbed the tree to get a better view of the day's events—prematurely, as it turned out. Longstreet and Hood, Fremantle notes, indulged in "the truly American custom of *whittling* sticks." Freeman has Lee eagerly looking "for Longstreet's veterans," but this seems unlikely, since if Longstreet was present, whittling away at his stick, Lee could have asked him when his troops would begin to arrive. Longstreet may again have argued his case for avoiding a frontal attack and trying to turn the enemy's left instead, but if so Lee rejected it.

In any case, no attack could have been made before nine o'clock in the morning, since Longstreet's artillery commander Colonel Edward Porter Alexander did not have his fifty-four guns on the field until that hour. As for Longstreet's infantry, much of it was beginning to be deployed as early as 7 a.m. Colonel Fremantle, having exchanged his tree branch temporarily for a borrowed horse, accompanied Longstreet "over part of the ground," and watched him position General McLaws's division. Fremantle gave as good a description of the battlefield of July 2 as can be found anywhere:

The enemy occupied a series of high ridges, the tops of which were covered with trees, but the intervening valleys these ridges and ours were mostly open, and partly under cultivation. The cemetery was on their right, and their left appeared to rest upon a rocky hill. The enemy's forces, which were supposed to comprise nearly the whole Potomac army, were concentrated into a space apparently not more than a couple of miles in length.

The Confederates inclosed them in a sort of semicircle, and the extreme extent of our position must have been from five to six miles at least. Ewell was on our left, his headquarters in a church★ (with a high cupola) at Gettysburg; Hill in the centre; and Longstreet on the right.

He also points out, "A dead silence reigned till 4:45 p.m., and no one would have imagined that such masses of men and such powerful artillery were about to commence the work of destruction at that hour."

★Lee would probably have hesitated to use a church tower as a vantage point. This is one of Fremantle's rare errors; the building may have been the Gettysburg Alms House, which had a cupola.

The critical question of the historical controversy that still surrounds, and probably always will surround, Lee's strategy at Gettysburg is why he allowed nearly eight hours to elapse between the moment when the bulk of Longstreet's forces reached the field and the time the actual attack took place. It is certainly possible that if the attack had been made earlier it might have succeeded, and also certainly true that with each passing hour the Federal forces on Cemetery Ridge grew stronger and better entrenched; but the delay cannot be blamed entirely on Longstreet, much as he disliked the idea of making the attack in the first place. He may very well have been "in a bad humor," as Freeman puts it, but that does not mean he would have refused to obey a direct order had he been given one.

It is difficult, balancing the various accounts of what happened that morning, not to come away with the impression that the Confederate effort was marked by some ambivalence, doubt, and confusion. The Prussian observer would later remark that Lee looked "careworn" and "was not at his ease," and Longstreet would comment that Lee had "lost the matchless equipoise that usually characterized him." An army depends on the judgment and balance of its commander, and Lee did not show himself at his best in the early hours of July 2. Although he had had all night to think about it, he was still uncertain whether or not to bring about "a general engagement"—that is, to engage his whole army—and whether to make the main attack on his right or his left. It may be that the sight of the ground the enemy now occupied gave him pause, as it should have done, or perhaps he was feeling unwell—certainly he recognized that neither Ewell on his left nor A. P. Hill at his center had been as successful as he would have liked the day before, and that his third corps commander, Longstreet, was showing none of Stonewall Jackson's eagerness for a daring flank march. All those writing about the battle—and not a few of those who commanded brigades and divisions during it—speculate about how different the outcome might have been had Jackson been there.

Sometime before 9 a.m. Lee left Longstreet and rode off to his far left to talk to Ewell again. What he found there was enough to convince him that the main attack would have to be made on his far right, with Ewell in support. When Lee was riding back toward the center, Long has him saying, "What *can* detain Longstreet? He ought to be in position now." But Lee had not in fact given Longstreet his orders yet; he did not actually meet with Longstreet again until 11 a.m. It is just over two miles from the southern end of Seminary Ridge to the center of Gettysburg, and there is nothing difficult or challenging about the landscape, so it seems strange that it took Lee more than two hours to ride into town, see for himself how strong the Federal position was in front of Ewell, confer with Ewell, then ride back to meet Longstreet. Up until that point Lee had not as yet decided to fight "a general engagement," nor had he made the final decision that Longstreet's corps should lead the attack.

After giving Longstreet his oral instructions, Lee rode back to his left, leaving Longstreet to march his troops into position. This took an unconscionably long time. It seems odd that Lee had not urged Longstreet to move quickly, but that was not Lee's way. By the early afternoon, on a day so hot that the troops "were suffering from the lack of water," word was brought to Lee that the Federals were moving troops onto Round Top, which is to say extending their line as far as they could to prevent having their flank turned.

Lee took this news philosophically, and even predicted that Round Top would be in his possession by nightfall; then he rode up a lane to the Pitzer Farm on Seminary Ridge, overlooking the town and the northernmost part of Cemetery Ridge, where he met A. P. Hill. This gave Lee a good view of the battlefield, but if he was concerned about Longstreet, or the passing time, it was a poor place to choose.

Colonel Fremantle, who had made good use of the time by going for a swim and eating "quantities of cherries," went back to the tree where he had been sitting in the early morning, and remarked that Lee would spend the next few hours talking to A. P. Hill and Colonel Long, but "generally sat quite alone on the stump of a tree," and sent only "one message, and only received one report." This is generally mentioned to Lee's credit, since he was putting into practice his own view about what we would now call a hands-off style of command; however, General Fuller is not alone in criticizing it: "When things go wrong," Fuller asks plaintively, "how can subordinates modify a plan? They can only muddle it." What is worse, Lee had not issued any "written operations orders"; he was relying entirely on oral orders, which were open to misunderstanding, particularly when passed on by one of Lee's aides instead of Lee himself.

If Lee's main objective was for Longstreet to carry out a full-scale assault on the Union left, take Round Top and Little Round Top, and turn the Union flank, then he perhaps should have placed himself farther south, possibly on one of the low ridges opposite the Peach Orchard, where Longstreet himself took up his position. Instead, he chose a spot almost 3,000 yards away, with a poor view of Longstreet's corps as it

974 • MICHAEL KORDA

deployed. As for the fact that Lee sent only one message and received only one report, while it is often taken as an indication of his self-control and sangfroid, it does not seem like the best way to control a battle over a front extending for several miles, even allowing for Lee's ideas about letting his corps commanders find their own way to solve their problems. Lee already knew, after all, that Longstreet was pessimistic and disgruntled, yet over the next five or six hours he left Longstreet alone to carry out perhaps the most critical assault in the history of the Confederacy. Lee's presence alone—as well as his authority to shift troops from his center to his right at the moment of crisis—might have been enough to carry the Confederates to the summit of Little Round Top, rather than just halfway up it.

The truth is that Lee had come to "expect the impossible" of his own troops. They had never failed him in the past and he relied on them now to succeed despite the absence of a tight command structure and a well-coordinated battle plan. Colonel Fremantle, had he not been awed by Lee's bearing and gentlemanly qualities, might have recognized this as a manifestation of the British habit of "muddling through," a familiar phrase in the British army right up to the end of World War II, with its implicit preference for the gifted amateur over the stodgy professional, its rejection of "Prussian" efficiency and elaborate staff work, and its reliance instead on courageous personal leadership (Cardigan at Balaclava) and the indomitable spirit of the British Tommy (as in the first day of the First Battle of the Somme) over careful planning.* Since Lee was in fact a consummate professional, whose reputation had been made by brilliant staff work for General Scott in Mexico, it is clear that he was improvising a major engagement. Without Stuart, he still had no precise idea of the enemy's strength, but his view from the cupola in Gettysburg would have been enough to show him the strength of the Union position on Cemetery Ridge, and now, as the afternoon wore on, he could see through his field glasses still more enemy troops and artillery appearing farther south down the ridge, and even in the Peach Orchard opposite Longstreet, where the Union's Major General Daniel Sickles had ordered part of his division, ignoring Meade's orders and creating a salient that would give Longstreet an opening in the Federal line to exploit.

Lee was about to fight a battle he had not wanted, in a place that offered him very little option but an attack over difficult ground on his far right. Unable to

---

*This was exactly the criticism that Field Marshal Sir Bernard Montgomery made about his rival Field Marshal Sir Harold Alexander, though most people, including General Dwight D. Eisenhower, felt that Montgomery spent too much time planning and Alexander not enough.

disengage, Lee had no choice but to fight, and worse still could assault the Federals with only less than one-third of his army, under a general who had already expressed strong doubts about Lee's plan.

Given all this, he may have preferred to observe the battle from closer to his left—when Longstreet's brigades hit the enemy's right hard and swung across the ridge, Lee would have to make sure that Ewell attacked hard at Culp's Hill in support, and that the ailing A. P. Hill's corps struck at the "saddle" of the ridge, ensuring a three-pronged attack that would drive the Federals off Cemetery Ridge and send them in full retreat down Baltimore Pike.

All the same, as the afternoon dragged on, everything was "profoundly still," interrupted only by "occasional skirmishing." In fact, Colonel Fremantle began to "doubt whether a fight was coming off today at all." The heat was intense; there was not even the slightest breeze; men sought even the smallest patch of shade; both sides were motionless, except on Lee's right, where Longstreet struggled to move up his corps and deploy it as he wanted it. He was slowed down by the "reconnoitering officer" who was leading him, then by the discovery that the enemy had placed a signal station on the summit of Little Round Top. His march was being made in full view of it so he was obliged to countermarch: that is, to stop the troops, turn them around, and march back. This inevitably took time and got his divisions mixed up with each other—in other words, it caused confusion, that most dangerous of military conditions—so it was not until 4:45 p.m. that Longstreet's artillery was at last able to open fire in preparation for his attack,* "like the drums of a stirring overture," in Freeman's bravura description. It was accompanied, oddly, by a Confederate band playing "polkas and waltzes" from Gettysburg, to the left of where Lee was sitting on a stump.

The contrast between the long silence and the sudden noise of the cannonade impressed everybody. Ewell's artillery joined in from the left, and the Union artillery soon replied "with at least equal fury." As was always the case in the age of black powder when there was no wind, "dense smoke" covered the whole area of the battlefield, as the guns thundered, projectiles of different types and sizes made their own distinctive noise, shells burst, and an occasional caisson loaded with ammunition was hit and exploded. This was one of the most intense artillery exchanges of the war—even to this day shards of shells and shot from

---

* The time when Longstreet's artillery barrage began varies in different accounts by more than an hour, but I have used Colonel Fremantle's estimate, since he was present and close to Lee, waiting for it to begin.

the battle are still being found in the area around what was then a flourishing peach orchard.

Longstreet, whose mood that day was uncertain, was still moving slowly; indeed one of his own aides was puzzled by his "apathy" on the second day of Gettysburg. As Lee himself had remarked earlier, Longstreet was "slow" and wanted every detail to be correct before he ordered an attack—besides, however much he admired Lee, Longstreet believed he was wrong—not the best frame of mind in which to approach a battle.

Stuart's absence also meant that the terrain on Meade's left was poorly understood, both by Longstreet and, more critically, by Lee. From a modest distance Little Round Top looks like a small, wooded, gentle little hill with a rounded summit, but to approach it from Emmitsburg Road was to realize that its western flank is steeper than it looks and is anchored on a massive, tangled, steep jumble of huge boulders; these, known locally as Devil's Den, were a favorite spot for daring picnickers and for courting couples, difficult to scale, and full of nooks and crannies that would help the defenders. Any attack that involved climbing over the boulders of Devil's Den in order to reach the western slope of Little Round Top was bound to be hazardous unless the objective was undefended—and by the time Longstreet was deployed, he could see with his

own eyes that Meade had extended his left much farther than Lee had assumed, and that the Federal line
now extended beyond his own right.

The attack Lee had wanted Longstreet to make
was to have McLaws's division approach Emmitsburg
Road unseen, then advance straight up it like a knife
thrust *behind* the flank of the Union left, supported by
Hood's division to the right of McLaws. The assault
was intended to drive in the Union left in the midpoint
of Cemetery Ridge; that would be followed by Ewell
attacking the Union right, and Hill the center, thus
collapsing the Federal army before it could be further
reinforced.

Lee had been very emphatic about this to Longstreet
in the early morning, and McLaws described
Longstreet's reaction then as "irritated and annoyed,"
but whatever the truth of this by the late afternoon it
was no longer a practical plan. The Union left was no
longer in the center, or "saddle," of Cemetery Ridge;
it was on Little Round Top. McLaws would have been
advancing with a substantial Federal force on his right;
and attacking straight up Emmitsburg Road would
bring him directly to the Peach Orchard where Sickles
had moved part of his corps. There could be no thrust
that would take McLaws behind the Union line on
Cemetery Ridge; he would have to fight his way there.

General Hood saw this clearly at once. Lee had assumed that Hood could take Little Round Top without any resistance, then take the Union line in reverse on Cemetery Ridge, but Hood now realized that he would have to fight his way over Devil's Den, then up the slope of Little Round Top—an attack that would be costly, slow, and by no means sure. Three times he tried to persuade Longstreet to let him go around Little Round Top and Round Top, but Longstreet refused.

Longstreet gets blamed for what amounts to (in the age-old British Army phrase) "dumb insolence," the equivalent of "silent insolence" in the U. S. Army—which is to say that he was determined now to follow Lee's orders scrupulously, even blindly, although he knew they were no longer relevant and did not correspond to the reality on the ground, rather than use his own initiative to modify them. He did not send an aide to Lee, even though Lee was only two miles* away and easy enough to reach, but Longstreet, always a practical soldier, could see that Hood's plea, while it made sense, was also dangerous. Hood would have a long march around the two hills, all of it observed by Federal troops

---

*In another sharp dig at Longstreet, Freeman criticizes him for writing that too much delay would have been caused by sending "messengers five miles in favor of a move he [Lee] had already rejected," when Lee was only two miles away, "opposite the Pfizer house" (Freeman, *Robert E. Lee, Vol. 2, 98*). But it is clear enough that Longstreet was referring to the distance it would take a messenger to ride there and back.

on Little Round Top, and it was already late afternoon; by the time Hood reached the Union line on Cemetery Ridge it would be growing dark, and during all that time McLaws would be unsupported. Putting Confederate artillery onto Round Top might help, but to do that Hood's gunners would have to chop down woods, make a trail, and haul the guns up by hand to get them into any position where they would be useful, and by that time it would be night. Longstreet was therefore trapped not only by Lee's orders of the morning, but also by the passage of time, partly caused by his own slowness in moving his troops earlier in the day. If he was going to succeed, he needed Hood to take Little Round Top quickly—there was no time to improvise an alternative strategy, which Lee had in any case already dismissed.

In any great battle there is sometimes a moment when doing one's duty and obeying one's orders to the letter may prove fatal to the cause. Longstreet might have reached for a moment of glory as lasting and brilliant as Jackson's flanking attack at Chancellorsville, but he was not Jackson, and in any case he was not about to disobey Lee. Fatally for the Confederates, he told McLaws and Hood to do as they had been ordered—no doubt with a heavy heart because he had never wanted to make this attack in the first place, and he could already see that it was very likely to fail.

The result was that rather than making an angled attack toward the left, McLaws had to fight through Sherfy's Peach Orchard and a wheat field, which were furiously defended by part of Sickles's corps; meanwhile Hood, instead of supporting McLaws and aiming the thrust of his attack toward the Union center, as Lee had envisaged, had to make a grim, head-on, bloody attack straight over Devil's Den and then up the slope of Little Round Top, which was held firmly by Union troops. There was no fancy maneuvering involved here, no element of surprise, no flanking movement—for both divisions it was sheer face-to-face carnage at close range against an enemy that held higher ground. The crest of Cemetery Ridge was reached, briefly, but a fierce counterattack drove the Confederates back, and as darkness fell the major objectives on the Union far left were still in enemy hands—no breakthrough was effected that threatened Meade's position on Cemetery Hill, despite terrible casualties on both sides, which included Hood, who was severely wounded, and on the Federal side, Sickles, who lost a leg to a cannonball.

Ewell's attack, which should have supported Longstreet's, was made late—in some accounts as late as 7 p.m.—and despite heavy fighting in the darkness, failed to dislodge the Federal forces from their positions on Culp's Hill and Cemetery Hill. Ewell's attacks were poorly coordinated and were not made with his full forces, and Meade benefited from the well-known advantages of short interior lines—he was able to move troops quickly to check Longstreet on his left or Ewell on his right, whereas it was nearly six miles from Ewell's position to that of Longstreet, a good part of it in full view of the enemy.

The attack in the center, from A. P. Hill's corps, was gallant and bloody but equally inconclusive, and weakened by confusion about orders. By the end of the day, as firing on both sides died out in the darkness, both Hill and Longstreet had gained some ground, Ewell none. But the Union hold on Cemetery Ridge had not been broken—Meade still held the significant high ground, and benefited from short interior lines and an unbroken line of communication. Lee's army was still scattered from Culp's Hill to Little Round Top. The Federal position on Little Round Top has been described, almost from the time of the battle, as a "fishhook," with the point of the hook to the south of Culp's Hill, the bend of the hook curving around Culp's and Cemetery hills, the shank along the western edge of Cemetery Ridge, and the eye of the hook at Little Round Top; and there is no reason to search for a better or more apt description. Freeman devotes

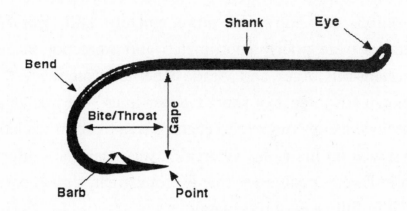

25. *Parts of a hook. Drawing from flytyinginstruction.com.*

nearly thirteen pages to what might have been had one event or another occurred or not occurred, and gives the impression that the second day of Gettysburg was at least a partial Confederate victory, or might have been one, but for Longstreet and Ewell. But anybody who has looked at the ground and studied a map can see that no significant gains had been made, and that there was at the very least a lack of impulsion and leadership on the Confederate side on July 2, for which the blame must rest on Lee's shoulders. Far from galloping from one part of the battlefield to another in order to urge his commanders forward and coordinate their attacks, he stayed in the geographical center of the Confederate line and, as we know, received only one message and sent only one. It is possible that he had come to rely too much on Stonewall Jackson, and assumed that his three corps commanders would demonstrate the same genius and daring, but if so he was guilty of misreading their character.

It is certainly true that the first day of Gettysburg was shaped in part by Stuart's absence, and the fact that Lee did not know where the enemy was and what his strength was. But by late afternoon of the second day this was no longer true—it was clear enough, even without Stuart's cavalry, that the bulk of the Army of the Potomac was present, concentrated, and firmly positioned on Cemetery Ridge, and had been given the time to entrench or fortify itself, thanks to Longstreet's slow deployment of his corps. The sheer ferocity of the fighting on the second day should have brought with it a warning of what might be expected the next. Although that battle lasted only a few hours—it started, after all, late in the day—one estimate is that the Union had 10,000 casualties and the Confederates nearly 7,000, in addition to approximately "9,000 Union and 6,000 Confederate casualties" the day before, which in the case of Lee's army amounts to the loss of over 20 percent in two days of fighting without any significant gain. There was no sign that Meade planned to retreat.

Stuart reappeared late on the second day—Lee may or may not have greeted him by saying, "Well, General, you are here at last," with a pained expression—and Pickett's division arrived, winded but intact, from its guard duties at Chambersburg, but Lee did not expect and would not receive any further reinforcements. He did not need to be told that the army's supply of artillery ammunition was running dangerously low—the Confederate armies had always relied on capturing large quantities of ammunition from the enemy, but this time they had not overrun Federal supply trains or ammunition dumps. A third day's fighting on the same scale as the first two days would exhaust their supply.

In the hot, sultry night, once the firing had died down, the only sound came from the cries and groans of the wounded, while the moonlight picked out in the darkness the uncounted corpses that covered the fields, where they would lie untouched for several days. In the air was the stench of death, not just of men but of horses—as many as 5,000 horses would be killed in the three days of the battle.

Meade, true to the cautious nature that would deprive him of the fruits of victory, held a council of war late that night and asked his generals whether he should retire or stay, and the majority of them urged staying. Lee does not seem to have sought the opinions of his principal officers, no doubt because he had already made up his mind what he intended to do. He would renew the attack in the morning—would make, as Freeman puts it, "the supreme effort" tomorrow, relying once again on the fighting spirit of his troops rather than on any unexpected or brilliant maneuver.

Longstreet had sent a message to Lee by signal at 7 p.m. that he "was doing well," which was technically true—he would bivouac for the night on ground that had been held by the enemy—but was overoptimistic. In fact, Longstreet remarked to the Austrian observer Captain Ross, "We have not been as successful as we wished." Freeman notes critically that Longstreet did not ride over to confer with Lee that night, but this criticism fails to take into account that Longstreet's corps had received heavy casualties, and that he was bringing Pickett's division forward in anticipation of the next morning's battle.

Lee's staff found him a house in which to spend the night—perhaps an indication that he was not feeling well, since he normally insisted on sleeping in his tent—but it is remarkable, given the events of the day, that he did not send for Longstreet, A. P. Hill, and Ewell. Lee was hardly more inclined toward holding councils of war than Jackson had been, but if ever there was a time to gather his corps commanders in one place and explain exactly what he intended to do in the morning, this was it. He was only two miles away from Longstreet, and a mile or less away from Ewell. Hill was a short ride away. Nothing, one would have thought, could be easier; he had only to order them to join him. If he had differences with Longstreet, and felt that Ewell had not done his part on the first and the second day of the battle, now was the moment to confront these issues, and urge his corps commanders to make the "supreme effort," as well as to demand better coordination of the attacks. Long complains that "still there was a lack of accord and cooperation in the different columns of attack, and [therefore] no decisive result," which is exactly right; but assuming that Lee agreed—and as his aide, Long would have known his opinion—then why not point this out forcefully to his commanders, while there was still time to draw up a plan of attack with coordinated timing, and urge on them the importance of adhering to it at all costs? Wellington would certainly have done so, as would Lee's role model General Scott. Thirty-three years later in his memoirs, Longstreet made a detailed and highly critical assessment of Ewell's behavior on the Confederate left at Gettysburg, which he viewed as the critical failure of the battle; but would it not have made more sense to sort out the shortcomings of Confederate command on the second day of battle, before plunging ahead to the third and last day?

But this was not Lee's way—he faced the enemy fearlessly, he had no concern for his own safety, but he recoiled from personal confrontation. He was a gentleman first and foremost, and good manners at some level mattered more to him than victory. Admittedly, the briefest of frowns from that otherwise marble face was reproof enough for most of those around him, but their number did not include Longstreet or Ewell, and A. P. Hill may have been too ill to realize that he too had disappointed the commanding general.

Lee's veiled, polite rebuke of Jeb Stuart, who more than anybody else was responsible for the difficult position of the Army of Northern Virginia at Gettysburg, is typical of the man. It would have done Stuart no harm to "tear a strip off him," in private if not in front of his peers, but Lee was not able to do so, not even later in his official report of the battle. He did not have Napoleon's temper or sardonic cutting edge, but mild irony hardly seems to have been the appropriate way of dealing with his bumptious, glory-seeking cavalry commander.

It was Lee's job, at this critical moment, to knock heads together and produce a perfectly coordinated attack the next day—the spirit of his army was still "superb," "much ground had been taken," and "admirable artillery positions had been won." Pickett's division was now close to the field; there remained enough artillery ammunition for one more day of fighting; but victory would depend on perfect timing between his three commanders, and on an early start to the day while Meade's army was still licking its wounds. Boldness and concerted action might carry the day, over a field still strewn with the dead and dying, against an army still holding higher ground. But it was at just this point when Lee's noble character failed him—he had everything a great commander needs except the willingness to overbear his reluctant commanders and mold them to his will.

Gettysburg: The Third Day

At first light on another scorching day that would torture men and beasts with thirst, Lee mounted Traveller in the dawn to the sound of Ewell's cannons opening fire to his far left—Ewell at least showed signs of obeying his orders—and rode to his right to meet Longstreet. To Lee's disappointment, he saw no signs of Pickett's division, which he had hoped to find deployed and ready for battle. Longstreet he found in a "depressed" and disputatious mood—he had had scouts out all night searching for a way to turn the Union left, and had already begun to move his troops to the right in anticipation of such a move. Whether or not Lee was "weary" of hearing Longstreet's opinion again, as Freeman alleges, he made it very clear that he intended to attack the Union center with the three divisions of Longstreet's corps. It is at this point, in the early morning, that Longstreet looked up from Emmittsburg Road toward the low stone wall at the crest of Cemetery Ridge—just over a mile away across bare, gently rolling ground, offering no cover but shallow swales and bisected only by a post-and-rail fence that would slow the troops down as they scrambled over it—and said, "General, I have been a soldier all my life. I have been with soldiers engaged in fights by couples, by squads, companies, regiments, divisions, and armies, and should know, as well as any one, what soldiers can do. It is my opinion that no fifteen thousand men ever arranged for battle can take that position." Or words to that effect*—Longstreet may have been less eloquent than he remembered later on when he came to write about it—but however he expressed himself, he made his doubts about the proposed attack clear to Lee, no doubt politely, since both of them were gentle-

---

*Longstreet suffered from a certain degree of what the French call *l'esprit de l'escalier,* which means thinking of a witty or telling remark after the event, on the way downstairs as it were; so over the years he may have, to some degree, tidied up his comments to Lee.

men, and Longstreet never failed in his respect for Lee. As the man on the spot, however, he had a practical objection to Lee's plan as well. The divisions of McLaws and Hood had been badly mauled during the previous day's fighting, and were facing superior enemy forces. If they were withdrawn and moved leftward to attack the Union center there would be nothing to prevent the Federals from advancing to attack Longstreet's right flank as he moved forward—his right flank would be "in the air."

This, as it happens, was not a querulous complaint on Longstreet's part; it was a simple statement of fact, as anybody can see who has looked at a map or walked over the Gettysburg battlefield, and it was exactly the kind of thing that should have been thrashed out the night before, had Lee called his corps commanders together.

Lee's intention to attack the Union center using Longstreet's corps carried with it certain risks, and it was even more dangerous because Lee had spent the previous day with A. P. Hill's corps at the center of the Confederate line, and had therefore seen the ground on his far right only through his field glasses. Now that he had seen it with his unaided eyes, he accepted, with whatever reluctance, Longstreet's view. He decided to leave Hood and McLaws where they were, as Longstreet had suggested, and replace them with

Heth's division and two brigades of Pender's division, both from A. P. Hill's corps, perhaps as much to humor Longstreet as because it made good sense. This decision had three disadvantages, however. The first was that placing a divisional or brigade commander under a new corps commander at the last moment is always risky— officers and their men are used to what they know, and to fighting alongside units they are familiar with. They cannot be moved around like chess pieces. The second was that it moved the direction of Longstreet's attack slightly toward the Confederate left, thus exposing it to Union artillery fire on both flanks. The third was that sending out the necessary orders and shuffling units around could only cause delay in an attack that Lee had wished to make as early in the morning as possible. He knew Longstreet was "slow" and that he liked to have everything in order before attacking; now he had given Longstreet a perfectly sound reason for *more* delay.

Even while these changes were being ordered, Longstreet still fretted about the Union artillery, and particularly the batteries on Little Round Top. Although Colonel Long tried to reassure him, Longstreet was—correctly as it turned out—not convinced that Confederate artillery could suppress the fire from the Union guns ahead of him, and was perhaps also unwilling to accept the word of a staff officer on the subject.

Colonel E. P. Alexander, in command of Longstreet's artillery, was less sanguine than Long. All together, Lee had 125 guns to train on Cemetery Ridge for the attack, a formidable number; but only Alexander's 75 guns had been placed well forward of the infantry, where Longstreet wanted them to be. The rest were scattered far behind, most of them along Seminary Ridge at a distance of at least 1,300 yards from the enemy; nor were they placed for the kind of converging fire in which all the guns were aimed at the same point, to create a hole in the enemy's line where the infantry attack should be concentrated. Nobody had understood this kind of thing better than Jackson, the former artillery professor at VMI, but Longstreet too had a thorough knowledge of artillery, and what he saw to the left of him did not give him confidence.

All these things take time and forethought, but since the previous day's battle had been fought late in the day and gone on well into the night, none of these meticulous preparations had been made. It was not an auspicious beginning.

Lee himself seems to have been fretful, perhaps because Longstreet was obstinate. As Longstreet reckoned it, he would be making the attack with about 13,000 men, "the divisions having lost a third of their number the day before," not the 15,000 that Lee was promising him—in any case, his own estimate was that he would need at least 30,000 men to have a chance of succeeding, and even then success was doubtful: "[The] column," he wrote later, "would have to march a mile under concentrating artillery fire, and a thousand yards under long-range musketry."

According to Freeman, Lee rode the entire length of the Confederate line with Longstreet, and then once more without him—the morning was almost gone; a fierce noonday sun was shining down brutally on men who were already thirsty and weary. In the meantime, the consequences of hasty and slipshod staff work were making themselves felt. Lee had sent a message to Ewell that Longstreet's attack had been delayed, and that it would not begin before 10 a.m., an optimistic guess. One of Ewell's division commanders, the fiery Major General Edward Johnson, attacked Culp's Hill before this message was received, and his division was badly cut up—this would inevitably weaken Ewell's corps when he made his attack. One cannot help feeling that Lee's control over his army was not what it should have been on July 3, and that he was allowing the day to slip out of his hands.

Geographically, Lee was in the worst position for a commander: the three corps of his army were spread out loosely over six miles, with Ewell at the bend and the point of the "fishhook" unable to see or guess what might be happening at the center and the left of the line, where Longstreet was preparing his attack very slowly indeed, perhaps, as many of his critics have alleged, in the hope that Lee might still change his mind.

Skirmishing and artillery fire from A. P. Hill's guns on Seminary Ridge sputtered on until noon—for what purpose it is hard to see, particularly since ammunition was scarce, and there was no way of replenishing it. Colonel Fremantle joined Lee and Longstreet and their staffs while they were inspecting the Confederate line together, and was in time to see a random "Yankee" shell hit a building between the two armies. The building was set instantly ablaze, though "filled with wounded, principally Yankee, who, I am afraid, must have perished miserably in the flames," a sinister prelude of what was to come. Fremantle, a good—and, as a noncombatant foreign guest, *objective*—judge of ground, remarked that "the range of heights to be gained was still most formidable, and evidently strongly intrenched," which is pretty much what Longstreet thought, as well as several other officers for whose opinion Lee asked. Fremantle estimated that "the distance between the Confederate guns and the Yankee position—*i.e.* between the woods crowning the opposite ridges—was at least a mile—quite open, gently undulating, and exposed to artillery the whole distance." This is a pretty good description of what was about to become the most famous field of battle in American history. He saw that Longstreet's troops were "lying down in the woods," presumably seeking the shade, and remarked that Longstreet himself "dismounted and went to sleep for a short time," (Longstreet writes that he was not asleep, but simply lay down to think of some way of improving the coming attack). Then Fremantle and his Austrian fellow observer rode off into Gettysburg to find a better place from which to view the attack, possibly the cupola of the seminary, and got caught up in the cross fire of the artillery barrage once it began.

At around noon Lee rode out to the crest of Seminary Ridge to look at the field that rose to the crest of Cemetery Ridge, and chose as the center of the coming attack a "little clump of trees" known to the townspeople of Gettysburg as Ziegler's Grove, more or less at the middle of Cemetery Ridge, facing almost directly west. The grove was compact, highly visible, and situated behind a low, rough, uneven wall of piled stones, typical of the Northeast, where every field had to be cleared of stones before it could be plowed and the easiest way to get rid of them was to pile them up around the edges of the field to prevent cattle from wandering. In the winter these walls tended to collapse, while the frost pushed up more stones, and in the early spring farmers removed the freshly risen stones and added them to the walls more or less piecemeal—an endless process, which Robert Frost described in his famous poem "Mending Wall."

The stone wall on Cemetery Ridge was not a formidable obstacle and varied from two to three feet in height, but for soldiers any wall is better than none—it not only offers some protection but serves as a boundary marker, a more substantial equivalent of a "line drawn in the sand." A company or a regiment can draw up behind a wall and men can say to themselves (or be told) as the enemy approaches, "This far, and no farther." Troops in the mid-nineteenth century were not encouraged to lie prone behind a wall, partly because for a man lying down the long, muzzle-loading musket of the day was almost impossible to reload rapidly; but still a wall, however modest and makeshift, offered at once a line to defend and an illusion of safety. This unimposing wall, which formed a ninety-degree angle enclosing the grove of trees, was to be a far more substantial obstacle than it may have looked from nearly a mile away, as Lee and Longstreet stared at it with their field glasses, the one filled with fierce determination, the other with blackest pessimism.

The portion of the Union line at which Lee intended to direct his attack was less than 1,500 feet long, with a rail fence on the Federal left, the Bryan house and barn on the right, and Ziegler's Grove roughly halfway between. Since the line of Confederate attackers would be roughly a mile in length when it formed, the elements in it would need to converge as they advanced across the open ground toward their objective. Considerable thought had to be given to compressing this long line of troops as it advanced, the object being to deliver a compact, orderly mass of men at "the Angle" of the stone wall to the north side of the grove of trees, but to do so as late as possible, since compressing the line too soon would offer a perfect target for converging Federal artillery fire. Once infantrymen were massed closely together, each round of solid shot, shell, or canister would cause multiple casualties, disabling or killing many men instead of two or three. One Confederate survivor of Second Manassas described the effect: "I heard a thud on my right, as if one had been struck with a heavy fist. Looking around I saw a man at my side standing erect with his head off. . . . As I turned farther around, I saw three others lying on the ground, all killed by this cannon shot." Solid shot would bounce, hitting man after man; an explosive shell was deadly to groups of men clustered close together, each jagged fragment of shell casing sure to find a target; and at close range canister was like a giant shotgun blast.

To some degree the shape of the field, and the rail fence on the western side of it, would in any case force the Confederate infantry closer together as they advanced, like a funnel. In Lee's plan—for it was Lee rather than Longstreet who shaped the plan of the attack—the center brigade (under Colonel B. D. Fry) would advance straight ahead, serving as the marker for the rest, while the brigades of Pickett's division on the Confederate right moved obliquely toward their left, and the brigades of J. Johnston Pettigrew's division moved obliquely toward the right, the forward elements of the formations massing into a single column as they reached the stone wall, their impetus breaking the Union line.

Those who have visited Gettysburg in the warmer months will perhaps have seen small bands of exuberant young men charge from the Virginia State Memorial (which bears the splendid bronze equestrian sculpture of Robert E. Lee on Traveller, looking straight ahead toward Cemetery Ridge with a deeply saddened expression) up the field to the Angle, which is to say reenacting on a small scale Pickett's Charge. Sometimes they carry the Confederate battle flag and wave it, but invariably, however young and fit they are, they are winded and breathing hard when they reach the stone wall at the crest of Cemetery Ridge, although it is a fairly gentle slope. It is important to remember, however, that Pickett's Charge (as it is now called, Pettigrew's role having long since been left out in the interest of simplicity, to the chagrin of North Carolinians) was made at a slow, steady infantry pace, about 120 paces a minute. Doubtless men began to break ranks and run as they approached close enough to the stone wall to see the faces of the men shooting at them, but the whole long approach to it was conducted at the march. This was not just because every man was burdened by his rifle, bayonet, and ammunition in the July heat, but because order, discipline, and the correct alignment of each brigade can be maintained only by *keeping* to a steady pace—men who will run forward might just as easily break and run back. The intention of the infantry attack was to present the enemy with a steady, implacable, formidable mass of men advancing slowly but firmly toward him, not at a run but at a *walk*, conveying the impression that nothing could stop them. An infantry attack was meant to be imposing by its stolid discipline and determination, conveying to the enemy defenders not a ragged mob of armed men out of breath and running as if they were in a footrace, but men who, once they got within range, would bayonet every living soul in front of them.

Lee understood perfectly the shock effect on the enemy of 15,000 or so disciplined troops marching steadily toward them, immediately after a terrifying artillery barrage had sowed death and destruction among the defenders. Napoleon, himself an artillery-man, had called such a concentrated artillery barrage *un feu d'enfer*, or hellfire, and Lee counted on it to break the will of the Federal troops on Cemetery Ridge. It would be followed shortly by the long, steady lines of Confederate infantry advancing straight toward the point at which artillery fire had done the most damage.

The prospect convinced a great many of those around Lee, including the hitherto somewhat apathetic A. P. Hill, who offered to support the attack with his whole corps, a suggestion Lee rejected rather cautiously, since what remained of Hill's corps would be his only reserve "if General Longstreet's attack should fail." One person it did *not* convince was Longstreet himself. At that point, he, Hill, and Lee were sitting together on a log looking at the map, but Longstreet was dismayed, and made no secret of it—so dismayed that he neglected to bring up the critical question of whether the artillery still had enough ammunition to prepare for and support the attack—a question that should have been asked the night before, and to which Lee's staff should have had the answer at their fingertips.

Lee folded up his map and rode off, leaving the disconsolate Longstreet to carry out the attack he didn't want to make, with troops two-thirds of which were not his own. Longstreet is often blamed for his hesitation to give the order, and even for delegating it to Brigadier General E. P. Alexander, the First Corps chief of artillery, but given the importance artillery would play in the coming attack, Longstreet's messages to Alexander seem sensible, rather than any kind of dereliction of duty. He wrote: "If the artillery fire does not have the effect to drive off the enemy or greatly demoralize him, so as to make our effort pretty certain, I would prefer that you should not advise Pickett to make the charge." Alexander was the person best qualified to judge whether his artillery barrage had been successful or not; what is more, he was closer to Pickett than Longstreet was, since the attacking troops were sheltered immediately behind Seminary Ridge and the Confederate artillery. But it is still a puzzling decision. Perhaps Longstreet felt that if the artillery produced the "desired effect" there would be only a brief moment for the attack to begin—certainly not enough time to send a written order.

Alexander's reply was not encouraging. He would be able to judge the effect of his fire only by the enemy's return fire, since the field would be obscured by smoke; moreover, he had only enough ammunition for one full bombardment (or "cannonade") of the Union line, and predicted that even if the attack was "entirely successful, it can only be at very bloody cost." This was exactly what Longstreet thought, but he sent a message to confirm that Alexander should proceed when ready. Alexander then reached Pickett, who was "calm and confident," even eager, and then sent a short message to Longstreet that when his "fire was at its best," he would "advise General Pickett to advance." The element of conditionality perhaps inadvertently suggested in Longstreet's initial message is now missing. Pickett would advance when Alexander's fire was "at its best," not when there was evidence that it had destroyed the Union line to the immediate left of Ziegler's Grove.

At this point there was complete silence over the battlefield, the calm before the storm. The Confederate troops charged with making the attack had not at this point seen the field over which they would be advancing, since they were "under cover" behind the crest of Seminary Ridge, in the woods. This was by design—Lee saw no point in having them brood on the long, uphill, open field before them, rising to the crest of Cemetery Ridge. They would see it for the first time when the artillery in front of them had done its work, and when the excitement and the adrenaline created by the bombardment were still, hopefully, at their highest. The time spent by troops staring at no-man's-land before going over the top in World War I was to be spared them. They would not see the objective until they emerged from the woods, crossed the crest of Seminary Ridge, and advanced toward Emmitsburg Road, deploying as they advanced, and even then it would be shrouded in smoke. Nor did they know that the heavy weight of history rested on their success. Not many of them may have guessed that a great victory here might, at last, bring about negotiations to end the war, as Lee hoped; still fewer that the Confederate vice president, Alexander Stephens, was actually waiting for an expected invitation to meet with President Lincoln to discuss prisoner exchange—a meeting that Stephens hoped might be extended, after a significant Confederate victory, to larger issues. In London, the news of Lee's invasion of Pennsylvania had rekindled flickering interest in the House of Commons for the recognition of the Confederacy. For the Confederacy much—perhaps everything—depended on the outcome of this third day of the battle.

It is the moment captured indelibly by William Faulkner in *Intruder in the Dust*, when the dream of independence, of victory, for the South flickered before the eyes of these tired, sweaty, thirsty, hungry men, as bright as the gunfire they would soon be marching toward:

For every Southern boy fourteen years old, not once but whenever he wants it, there is the instant when it's still not yet two o'clock on that July afternoon in 1863, the brigades are in position behind the rail fence, the guns are laid and ready in the woods and the furled flags are already loosened to break out and Pickett himself with his long oiled ringlets and his hat in one hand probably and his sword in the other looking up the hill waiting for Longstreet to give the word and it's all in the balance, it hasn't happened yet, it hasn't even begun, it not only hasn't begun yet but there is still time for it not to begin against that position and those circumstances which made more men than Garnett and Kemper and Armistead and Wilcox look grave yet it's going to begin, we all know that, we have come too far and with too much at stake and that moment it doesn't need even a fourteen-year-old boy to think This time. Maybe this time with all this much to lose and all this much to gain: Pennsylvania, Maryland, the world, the golden dome of Washington itself to crown with desperate and unbelievable victory the desperate gamble, the cast made two years ago.

We do not know what went on in Lee's head—he was the most private of men; he never wrote his memoirs; he did not confide in his subordinates, or even in members of his own family. We may be sure that he was not moved by personal ambition or thirst for glory—both were completely absent from his character. But he had led his army into the North twice, once in Maryland, now in Pennsylvania; both times he had sought a decisive victory on northern soil and both times he had failed, by the narrowest of margins. He was determined to see the battle at Gettysburg through to the end; whatever Longstreet thought, he was counting on the fighting spirit—the *élan*, as it is called in the French army—of his officers and men to win the day. It would be tempting to describe the two men, Longstreet and Lee, as polar opposites, Sancho Panza and Don Quixote: the one gruff, curmudgeonly, practical; the other tall, polite to a flaw, courtly, and imaginative. But in fact both were serious, well-trained, and experienced professional officers, and neither had any illusions about the glory of war. At bottom, Lee's was the more romantic personality; it shows up in his flowery, flirtatious relationships with women (always held under strict control) and his belief that his men had done and could still do the impossible, and what is more do it with a certain style and panache, that they were simply better soldiers than those of the Union, imbued with a better, a more just cause, and would therefore prevail. He was perhaps not altogether immune to the excitement of battle—it was his one intoxication— and however calm his famous marble face remained, he would have felt the thrill of seeing those long gray lines move out of the woods and into position, the glint of the sun piercing through the smoke on thousands of musket barrels, bayonets, and swords, obliterating at a distance the stained and shabby uniforms, the wide variety of hats and caps, the frayed trousers and occasional bare feet, as the battle flag of each regiment was carefully unfurled before it. Longstreet, who had weighed the odds, and as a practical man decided the assault would fail, may not have been moved by the immense spectacle, except to come as near to tears as a general can get; but Lee, we may be sure, *was*—he did not calculate the odds, and he had complete faith in these men. As a professional, he knew Longstreet may have been right in arguing that the invasion of Pennsylvania was a mistake. But it was wrong to believe the army could make its way around Meade's left and seek better ground for a battle elsewhere; there wasn't enough food, forage, ammunition, or time to do so once the two armies were engaged. Lee had no choice but to fight it out; he would have to whip Meade here, or Meade would whip him, as he put it—it was as simple as that.

In the end, as Lee always believed, it was all in God's hands.

The minutes ticked away as senior officers consulted their pocket watches, and at almost exactly 1 p.m., as had been prearranged, two shots were fired one right after the other, the signal for the beginning of the Confederate artillery barrage. The first salvo from a grand total of 159 guns made a roar that shook the ground, made windows tremble, and could be heard as far away as Pittsburgh. On Cemetery Ridge, outside Meade's headquarters, one Union officer saw "a shell go through six horses standing broadside." Another wrote, "Army headquarters were visited with such a shower of projectiles that sixteen horses belonging to the staff and escort were killed before the officers could get away and 'they stood not upon the order of their going.'" "Shells burst in the air. . . . There was no place of safety. In one regiment twenty-seven were killed or wounded by one shell." The entire length of Cemetery Ridge was a mass of dust, smoke, and explosions, as salvo after salvo of Confederate gunfire hit the Union line from Cemetery Hill to Little Round Top. A reporter from the *New York Tribune* wrote that the shelling "made a very hell of fire that amazed the oldest officers." Soon, the Federals replied, with a line of artillery that stretched along the ridge for two miles, eighteen of the guns firing from around the small grove that was the objective of the Confederate attack. The federal counterfire was less intense than might have been expected—Brigadier General Henry W. Hunt, Meade's artillery commander, was determined to save his ammunition for the Confederate infantry attack to which he knew this was the prelude.

And yet, despite the intensity of the Confederate barrage, it failed to break or scatter the defenders along the crest of Cemetery Ridge. Several reasons are given for this, ranging from defective fuses to Confederate gunners using "too much elevation," so that they "overshot": that is to say their shells fell *behind* the crest, rather than on the men and guns behind the wall—a narrow space, as anyone who has ever visited Gettysburg can attest. One Union officer called it "a waste of powder"; another dismissed it as "a display of fireworks" and "humbug." A Confederate survivor, long after the event, noted that the effect of the "grand cannonade" on the Federal line was "a delusion," since both sides had by then learned that "sheltered lines of infantry cannot be shattered or dislodged when behind breastworks, by field artillery, at the distance of one thousand yards and upwards," which is to say that so long as the infantry lay prone behind a stone wall and didn't try to run, most of them were likely to survive, however terrified they might be by the noise and the blasts directly behind them.

By two o'clock in the afternoon, after he had been firing for the best part of an hour, Colonel Alexander realized that he had used up more than half his ammunition, and that at the rate he was firing he would have nothing left with which to support the Confederate infantry assault when it began; nor did he observe any significant slackening of the Union fire. He sent a hasty note to Pickett, telling him that if he was going to advance at all, he must come at once. The Federal line was wreathed in smoke now, but a few minutes later it lifted enough that Alexander was able to observe that the eighteen guns placed around the grove of trees were being withdrawn. He quickly scribbled another urgent message to Pickett: "For God's sake come quick. The 18 guns have gone. Come quick or my ammunition will not let me support you properly." This is as close to panic as one general is likely to get when communicating to another.

Although Brigadier General Hunt was trying to save his ammunition for the Confederate assault, the Federal fire was still strong enough so that many of Lee's men were more eager to begin the advance than to stay put on the far side of Seminary Ridge under a hail of shell splinters. The fact that what was to come would be known afterward as Pickett's Charge gives the impression of rapidity, a brief moment when the fate of the Confederacy was decided, but in fact events took place at a fairly stately pace. Before Alexander's second message had reached Pickett, the latter was already showing Alexander's first message to Longstreet, behind the crest of Seminary Ridge. Longstreet, as Freeman notes, was dismounted— there was no reason for him to ride over the crest of the ridge for a better look at the field tapering gently uphill toward Cemetery Ridge, since it was a mass of smoke, lit from time to time by bright explosions when a Confederate round set off a Union caisson full of ammunition. Pickett passed Alexander's first message to Longstreet, who read it carefully and stood silently for a moment as if in mourning, unable to give the order. It was by now shortly before three o'clock in the afternoon.

"General, shall I advance?" Pickett asked.

"The effort to speak the order failed, and I could only indicate it by an affirmative bow," Longstreet wrote later. The "affirmative bow" was enough. Pickett galloped off to order the troops forward, while Longstreet mounted his horse and rode away to talk to General Alexander, who was even more disturbed by the prospects for the charge than was Longstreet himself. Lee's artillery chief, General Pendleton, had ordered the wagons of Alexander's ammunition train farther to the rear, fearing for their safety, and withdrew some of the howitzers that Alexander had intended to use "in following up the advance." This seems to have been more of a matter of Pendleton's pulling rank on Alexander than of some deeper tactical plan, and possibly Lee had no idea that Alexander's ammunition was "nearly exhausted." Freeman blames Longstreet for not informing Lee of this, but by then it was too late for Lee to have done anything about it, and it is in any case exactly the kind of question that Lee's staff should have been asking the night before—this is the old problem of the small size of Lee's staff, and the lack of anybody serving as a real, tough-minded chief of staff.

Alexander reported to Longstreet that he was running out of ammunition for his "batteries of position," presumably his remaining howitzers. At this news, Longstreet attempted to stop the advance and ordered Alexander to "fill up his ammunition chests," but Alexander explained that it would take at least an hour to do so, and by now the troops were already in motion. As with many great historical mistakes, it was too late for second thoughts; the mistake was already happening. Whether Longstreet actually told Alexander that he did not "want to make this charge," is uncertain, but this would not have been news to Alexander, who already knew what Longstreet thought, and in any case shared his opinion.

Alexander's guns stopped firing, since the Confederate infantry had to "pass through the batteries" as they advanced over the crest of Seminary Ridge and deployed in the open, so there was a moment in which Longstreet, Alexander, and the gunners looked on as the "grand march moved bravely on." Whatever Longstreet's feelings, he returned "the salute of the officers as they passed, their stern smiles expressing confidence"—a confidence he did not share. As if they were on parade, they dressed their line, almost a mile

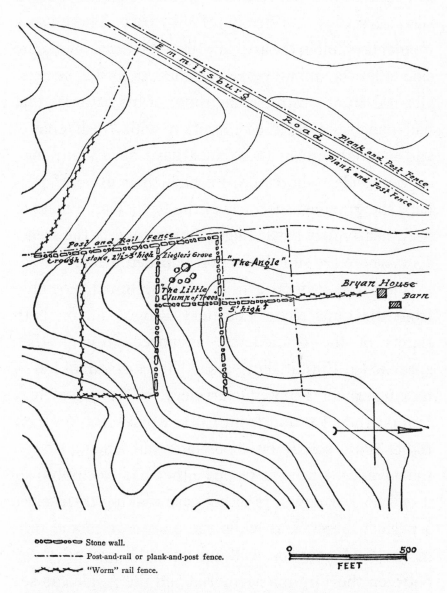

26. Objective of the Confederate assault of July 3, 1863, on the right center at Gettysburg, showing the contours (intervals of four feet) and the nature of the obstructions.

in length at that point, each regiment behind its battle flag, advancing at a steady infantry pace. There was a momentary lull in the artillery fire—on the Confederate side to let the infantry pass, on the Union side because General Hunt was replacing those of his batteries that had exhausted their ammunition with fresh ones— and in this moment there must have been many men on both sides who could not take their eyes off per- haps the grandest spectacle of the Civil War, a mass of gray, nearly fifty battle flags lending color to the scene, everywhere the sun shining off polished metal.

Then the Federal artillery fire resumed, not only from the guns along Cemetery Ridge, but on both flanks of the Confederate advance, since as they approached Emmittsburg Road they formed a kind of moving salient, exposed to artillery fire from Cemetery Hill on their left and from Little Round Top on their right. Stout, solidly built post-and-rail fencing slowed the advance, since the troops either had to climb over it or knock it down, in either case making themselves a perfect target; and while there are swales and dips in the land—anyone walking over the ground today between the Virginia Memorial and the Angle can see them—none of them can have offered significant pro- tection from artillery shells exploding overhead. In any case, even as holes were blown in the Confederate lines by case shot and shells, and soon by carefully aimed volleys of musketry, the gray formations concentrated at a steady pace as the survivors approached the stone wall, and it must have seemed to those watching from the eastern flank of Seminary Ridge that they would prevail.

The indefatigable Colonel Fremantle, at any rate, thought so. He returned from Gettysburg along a road lined with "Yankee dead . . . [who] had been killed on the 1st, the poor fellows had already begun to be very offensive." He noted this in the authentic dead-pan, self-deprecating voice of the British military, but quickly realized that "to see the actual fighting, it was also absolutely necessary to go into the thick of the thing." Never one to hesitate about going into "the thick of the thing," Fremantle rode past Lee and his staff, then through the woods along Seminary Ridge in search of Longstreet. He therefore missed the triumphant but evanescent moment when General Armistead led what remained of his men over the wall, waving his hat on the point of his sword to urge them on, "his colors cut down by a volley against the bristling line of bayonets," only to receive a mortal wound. As the Confederates approached the Angle the Federal gunners "switched to their final choice of ammunition—canister. At three hundred yards, the lanyards were jerked; and instantaneously the barrels spit out their contents to complete the slaughter . . . the tremendous flame spurting out of the blazing cannons, grazing the dead and wounded in its fiery path, scorching and igniting their clothes and flesh in the process." The mass of Confederates who survived canister fired at point-blank range and made it over the wall—a scant handful of them—were enveloped and overwhelmed in moments.

The Confederate tide ebbed; those men who could fell back in an orderly fashion down the field. "I soon began to meet many wounded men returning from the front," Fremantle wrote. "At last I came to a perfect stream of them flocking through the woods in numbers as great as the crowds in Oxford Street in the middle of the day. Some were walking along on crutches composed of two rifles, others were supported by men less badly wounded than themselves. . . . They were still under heavy fire; the shells were continually bringing down great limbs of trees, and carrying further destruction among this melancholy procession." The sight of a regiment in good order marching through the woods gave Fremantle the impression that he was in time to see the main attack, and he remarked breezily to General Longstreet, "I wouldn't have missed this for anything." Longstreet, who had dismounted and was sitting on "a snake fence," looking "perfectly calm and imperturbed," replied: "The devil you wouldn't! I would like to have missed it very much; we've attacked and been repulsed; look there!"

For the first time Fremantle saw the long field rising to Cemetery Ridge, covered now with Confederate dead and wounded, small parties of the walking wounded, still under heavy artillery fire, making their way slowly back to the woods where Longstreet sat. The magnitude of the Confederate defeat was clear at once to Fremantle, but he admired Longstreet's "bulldog" tenacity in the face of disaster, and offered him a drink from his silver flask, which he then presented to Longstreet as a "memorial" of the occasion. Longstreet accepted it gravely.

Fremantle then rode over to join Lee and his staff, and left perhaps the most vivid description of Lee at his best. "If Longstreet's conduct was admirable," he wrote, "that of General Lee was perfectly sublime. He was engaged in rallying and encouraging the broken troops, and was riding about a little in front of the wood, quite alone—the whole of his staff being engaged in a similar manner further to the rear. His face, which is always placid and cheerful, did not show any signs of the slightest disappointment, care or annoyance . . . and I saw many badly wounded men take off their hats and cheer him." Lee paused to talk to Fremantle—they were still under heavy fire, and Lee suggested to the Englishman that he find a safer place—then said, "This has been a sad day for us, Colonel—a sad day; but we can't expect always to gain victories."

Lee's eye for detail, as well as his ever-present gentleness of manner, remained undiminished by the day's tragedy. "When a mounted officer began licking his horse for shying at the bursting of a shell, [Lee] called out, 'Don't whip him, Captain, don't whip him. I've got just such another foolish horse myself, and whipping does no good.'" Lee shook hands with soldiers as they passed by him and said over and over again, "All this has been *my* fault," and then, "It is *I* that have lost this fight, and you must help me out of it in the best way you can." If good behavior under fire in the most trying of circumstances is the measure of a man's grandeur, then Lee was never grander than in the hours that followed Pickett's Charge—indeed one of the reasons for the enduring admiration that still surrounds him, in the North as well as the South, is his dignity and self-control in defeat, his total lack of self-pity, and his willingness to accept responsibility. Rudyard Kipling was not yet born—he would be born in 1865, the year of Lee's surrender at Appomattox Court House, Virginia—but two lines in his most famous poem might have been written with Lee in mind:

If you can meet with Triumph and Disaster
And treat those two imposters just the same . . .

Exhausted, unwell, heartbroken, Lee rode back and forth in the open on Traveller, an easy target, unmindful of shot and shell bursting all around him: consoling his men; taking on all the blame for the failure—which was indeed largely his, but how many great commanders have ever said so to their troops?—telling the wounded Brigadier General Pettigrew to seek help in the rear; pausing to ask after the health of Brigadier General Kemper, who had risen in his stirrups, sword drawn, to urge his men on, shouting, "There are the guns, boys, go for them!" making a conspicuous target of himself, and had been shot in the groin; repeating again and again to one and all, "All will come right in the end," until he was hoarse. Pressed by an immense sadness, Lee did not reach his headquarters and dismount until 1 a.m. on July 4, and stood for a moment, weary, beside Traveller, talking to one of his generals. Then, as he made for his tent, he was heard to whisper to himself, "Too bad! Too bad! Oh, too bad!"

Although everyone, including Lee, had expected a Federal counterattack, it never came. Meade's caution had reasserted itself; then too, both sides were taking full measures of their casualties over the last three days: over 23,000 on the Federal side, as many as 28,000 on the Confederate side, for a total between the two armies of over 50,000—the bloodiest three days in American history. Lee had already made the decision to retreat back across the Potomac. Even had he wished otherwise, Lee had no option but to withdraw; his usual practice had been to replenish his supply of ammunition with that captured from the enemy, but this time the army had captured none, and without it he could not fight. He would move back toward Winchester, where he could be resupplied from Richmond, taking with him his wounded, his prisoners, and the long train of supplies and animals captured by Ewell and Stuart in Pennsylvania—rich booty, but no compensation for his defeat, or for the fact that General Pemberton surrendered Vicksburg, with 30,000 men, to Grant on July 4, ceding to the Union control of the Mississippi from its source to the sea, and effectively splitting the Confederacy into two parts.

The weather turned bad on July 4, preventing Meade from making any attempt to pursue, but turning Lee's retreat into an ordeal almost as terrible as the fighting had been.

The next day, refuting the notion that there was any bad feeling between Lee and Longstreet, Lee paused in the pouring rain at Longstreet's bivouac and told him, "It's all my fault, I thought my men were invincible." It was, and remains the most truthful and convincing explanation for his defeat at Gettysburg, and perhaps the most moving.

Chapter 11
Lee and Grant

"If I had had Stonewall Jackson with me, so far as man can see, I should have won the battle of Gettysburg."
—Robert E. Lee★

The retreat across the Potomac in torrential rain was an epic story of suffering equal to the battle itself. The Potomac flooded, a rickety bridge across it had to be improvised, and the agonies of the wounded were beyond description. Even the horses, most of them lame for want of shoes and with little feed and forage, were in pitiable condition. Throughout this painful march Lee not only led his army, but set his men an example of resilience, confidence, and devotion to duty. Had he taken control of the battle on the second day in the same spirit, he might well have won it. Faced with

---

★Various versions exist of this comment from Lee to a friend shortly before his death, but that quoted in Douglas Southall Freeman, *Robert E. Lee, Vol. 2, 161,* seems the most plausible (and sounds the most like Lee).

defeat, he held the army together and inspired it with his own spirit. A defeated army in full retreat can very easily degenerate into an armed mob, but in the two weeks that followed Gettysburg Lee was praised by North and South. He did not ride ahead, or issue misleading reports, or place the blame on his generals. "I hope," he wrote to President Davis, "Your Excellency will understand that I am not in the least discouraged, or that my faith . . . in the fortitude of this army, is at all shaken." Far from bickering with Longstreet, or criticizing Ewell for having failed to take Culp's Hill, or blaming Stuart for having failed to inform him that Meade had his whole army, not just a portion of it, on Lee's heels, Lee firmly squelched all attempts to blame anyone but himself, and just as firmly ensured that discipline was maintained and orders were obeyed throughout the ranks. He brought a depleted, ragged, defeated army home, but it was an army still, its fighting spirit unbroken.

Whatever he may have thought about Longstreet's performance on July 2, Lee continued to call him "my Old War-Horse," and once Meade had crossed the Potomac, placed Longstreet and his corps around Culpeper in case Meade mounted an attack on Richmond. He never forgot that his family was also suffering. He was particularly worried about

Rooney, his middle son (Brigadier General William Henry Fitzhugh Lee), who had been seriously wounded in the Battle of Brandy Station on June 9. Rooney had been taken to Hickory Hill, the estate of W. F. Wickham, to recuperate, looked after by his wife, Charlotte; his brother Robert Jr., who was on leave; his mother; and two of his sisters, Agnes and Mildred. With a view over the Pamunkey River, Hickory Hill, a plantation of more than 3,000 acres, had been the home of Robert E. Lee's aunt. Now it was perilously close to the Union lines. Lee, who was usually quick to caution his family against this kind of risk, for once does not seem to have been concerned. He sent no warning, perhaps because he assumed that Rooney, as a wounded officer, would be left alone. If so, he was mistaken. On June 26 the family heard shots from the hickory grove beyond the gates. Robert Jr. ran down to investigate, only to see a Federal cavalry patrol galloping toward the mansion. He ran back to the house to warn his brother, but Rooney was in no condition to move quickly, and since he always paroled wounded Federal officers he believed he was in no danger.

He was wrong. Having been informed of Rooney's presence the Federals had come specifically to capture Lee's son. The Union soldiers carried Rooney out of the house on a mattress as his family watched. He was driven under armed guard "in the 'Hickory Hill' carriage," pulled by Mr. Wickham's horses, to a cell at Fort Monroe. His brother Rob managed to escape, hiding behind a box hedge in the formal garden; but Rooney would remain a prisoner of war for nine months, first at Fort Monroe and later in New York state. Finally he was exchanged for a Union officer of equal rank held by the Confederates. "I can appreciate your distress at Fitzhugh's situation," Lee wrote to his daughter-in-law Charlotte. "I deeply sympathize with it, and in the lone hours of the night I groan in sorrow at his captivity and separation from you. . . . You may think of Fitzhugh and love him as much as you please, but do not grieve over him or grow sad." Although Rooney was, as his father predicted, well looked after "in the hands of old army officers and surgeons, most of whom, are men of principle and humanity," Rooney's children died of scarlet fever during his captivity, and his wife, Charlotte, "wasted away" and died "of a broken heart."

Lee was shocked that Rooney had in effect been kidnapped while recovering from his wound. Harsh as the war was, general officers were seldom singled out for such treatment. Lee was also distressed that the capture had been carried out in front of Rooney's wife and children, and appalled to learn that the Federals had savagely beaten an old family servant, "Uncle William," in an attempt to find out where the horses were. "I am very sorry for the injuries done the family at Hickory Hill, and particularly that our dear old Uncle William, in his eightieth year, should be subjected to such treatment," Lee wrote to Mary, urging her "to submit to [God's] almighty will, whatever that may be," though Mary was more inclined to blame the Federal government than accept the situation as God's will.

This was not the only tragedy to touch Lee's family. One of the people who played a long and important role in Robert E. Lee's life was Martha Custis Williams Carter, a cousin of his wife Mary's, and a distant cousin of his. Markie, as she was called, had lived for long periods of time at Arlington and cared for Mary's father, George Washington Parke Custis, after the death of his wife. Indeed Markie thought of Arlington as a second home, though she was a northerner and deeply shocked by southern slave keeping and attitudes toward slave keeping—something which even her affection for Lee could not erase. She was serious-minded and deeply religious, but a portrait of her painted at Arlington shows a buxom, smiling, raven-haired young woman, with a mischievous expression and beguiling eyes. In the picture she wears a glamorous gown, which bares her shoulders, and a straw hat with a ribbon that matches the pink of her sash, and is shown against a background that is clearly the gardens of Arlington, stretching down to the Potomac River. It is, sadly, a portrait of a world that is about to be destroyed, right down to the sailboat in the distance, soon to be replaced by steamboats belching black smoke. Markie corresponded with Lee from 1844 to his death, but although Lee's letters to her were mildly flirtatious, as were his letters to all young women, there was nothing even remotely improper about them—the whole Lee family corresponded with Markie, and her letters to him were read aloud. She was a beloved member of the family.

This correspondence began in 1844 and continued even after the outbreak of war, though Markie and Robert E. Lee were on different sides. Two of her brothers served in the war. One of them, Laurence ("Lolo"), commanded a Union regiment under General McClellan, and in 1862 was briefly placed under arrest, allegedly for displaying too much concern over Mrs. Lee, who at the time found herself living behind Union lines. McClellan quickly released Lolo and wrote to Markie praising his "gallantry and skill," adding that "Mrs. General Lee," her daughter Mary, and her daughter-in-law Charlotte were all in Federal hands, but that "they are well & of course will be kindly taken care of." (It may have been this generosity of spirit that the Lees were counting on when they brought Rooney to Hickory Hill to recuperate, but times had changed by then.)

Another brother, William Orton Williams, called Orton, was dashing, handsome, and rash. Determined to follow a military career—and very impressed by his distant kinsman Robert E. Lee—Orton managed to secure a commission in the U.S. Army, largely by Markie's relentlessly lobbying everybody from the president down. Robert E. Lee, still a colonel in the U.S. Army in 1860, also gave the boy a strong recommendation that obtained for Orton a coveted position on General Winfield Scott's staff in Washington. It was Orton who had ridden to Arlington in May 1861 to warn Mary Lee that the Federal Army intended to occupy her home. Shortly afterward, Orton was placed under arrest for expressing his sympathy for the South, and he was kept under arrest for over a month for fear that he would divulge General Scott's plans. Having fallen "in love with his jailer's daughter," who regarded herself as "engaged" to him, Orton was paroled and after another month allowed to go south, where Lee firmly but tactfully sent him to Tennessee to serve as an aide to General Leonidas Polk.

Lee, for all his family feelings for Markie, could recognize a hothead when he saw one, and no doubt thought Orton would be more useful in battle than in a position that required discretion and good judgment. But if Lee thought he was well rid of the young man, he was wrong. Orton went on to distinguish himself at Shiloh and was promoted to the rank of captain, and eventually colonel. His "quick temper and insistence upon absolute military discipline" led him to shoot one of his own soldiers who failed to show him respect—an incident that greatly damaged Orton's reputation.

He came to visit the Lees at Hickory Hill over Christmas in 1862, where, tall, blond, and handsome in his "képi and hussar jacket," he charmed everyone, and paid particular attention to Lee's daughter Agnes, a friend since their childhood. He had brought "a pair of ladies' riding gauntlets and a riding whip." It should be noted that in those more delicate days, presentation of any article of apparel—say, gloves or a handkerchief—as a gift to a young woman was considered a prelude to an engagement. Agnes and Orton went "on long horseback rides in the woods" unchaperoned, and the entire household seems to have expected that he would ask for her hand. On the last day of his visit he did propose, but to everybody's dismay Agnes declined.

Given his nature Orton probably pressed his suit too hard, and although Agnes could not be described as "worldly," she was able to tell that Orton, however attractive, was not stable enough for marriage. There

1032 · MICHAEL KORDA

is some suggestion that he drank too much, and that he was not only fearless but reckless. At any rate to a daughter of such a pillar of rectitude as Robert E. Lee he may not have seemed like a suitable husband.

For reasons that remain unclear Orton changed his name to Lawrence William Orton, perhaps hoping to escape the blot on his reputation after he had shot one of his own men.★ Perhaps he was also hoping to impress General Lee, and so he set out to perform a great feat of arms. Some continue to contend that Orton was chosen by Judah Benjamin, of President Davis's cabinet, to carry messages to Europe for the Confederacy. However, riding through the Union lines to Canada dressed as a Union officer seems too improbable a scheme for Judah Benjamin to have approved. Orton was six feet tall, with "an indefinable air of distinction and individuality in all that he said and did," as one of his captors put it, so he was hardly a man to pass unnoticed. In any case it would have been unlikely for Benjamin, who was considered extraordinarily clever, to have picked someone as erratic as Orton for an important diplomatic task, or to have suggested such

---

★ The flavor of Orton's somewhat grandiose personality is reflected in his self-justification for the shooting, quoted in *Who Is Markie?* by Frances Scott and Anne Cipriani Webb: "For his ignorance I pitied him; for his insolence I forgave him; for his insubordination, I slew him."

a circuitous route when Confederate blockade runners made frequent voyages to Great Britain and Europe.

In any event, Orton and his cousin Captain Walter G. Peter were apprehended behind the Union lines in Franklin, Tennessee, wearing Federal uniforms, after attempting to borrow money from a Union colonel and pocketing several cigars. Their real names and ranks were inscribed on the headband of their hats, and their documents were quickly recognized as counterfeit. When asked for his opinion, Major General James A. Garfield, a future president, replied by telegraph that they must be tried immediately by "a drum head court martial" as spies, and if found guilty, hanged "before morning without fail." This was draconian punishment, but not unusual on either side. Orton protested that he was not a spy but would not reveal the nature of his mission, and both men were duly convicted and hanged.

Lee was said to be outraged, but although he was concerned about the pain that the execution would cause Markie and Agnes, he could not condone the whole business of espionage, and he would have done the same to Union spies.

Whatever Lee thought about the execution, his greater concern was for Agnes. "Again and again," wrote Mary Coulling in her biography *The Lee Girls*, "she must have wondered whether her refusal of him . . . had propelled him towards such a death-defying scheme." News of Orton's death proved "a shock from which she never recovered"; Agnes never married, and as she lay dying from typhoid fever at the age of thirty-two, she called for the Bible that Orton had given her before the war.

She was as much a victim of it as was Orton.

In August, after the retreat from Gettysburg, Lee offered his resignation to President Davis. This has been regarded by many of his biographers as pro forma, an offer that Lee knew would be refused. Given Lee's honesty, it seems more likely that the combination of defeat, ill health, and his family's woes made him doubt that he was up to the job of defending Virginia, let alone of going west, as Jefferson Davis suggested, to take on the enemy in unfamiliar country. In the end, Lee continued to command the Army of Northern Virginia. His first act was to dispatch Longstreet to reinforce Bragg, reducing that army for the moment to fewer than 50,000 men.

Everywhere Lee looked he saw tragedy: his army was living on scant rations; its animals were dying for want of grain and forage; one of his sons was a prisoner; his daughter-in-law was grief-stricken and dying; his daughter Agnes was heartbroken; his wife was an invalid living in constant pain—the wonder is not that Lee offered to resign, but that he still believed in the cause.

In retrospect, the defeats at Gettysburg and Vicksburg seem to mark the point at which the defeat of the Confederacy became only a matter of time, although there would be almost as many casualties on both sides in the two years after Gettysburg as in the three years preceding it, and vastly more civilian deaths. Lee had twice tried to invade the North, and both times had been defeated, in Maryland and Pennsylvania. After July 1863 the war would be fought only on southern soil. The "defensive" war that Longstreet had urged unsuccessfully on Lee would now become an inevitable reality, although with each battle there would be less to defend. Why, then, go on fighting?

But that is to see the war in hindsight. As if to torment the South, Confederate armies continued to win victories like the one at Chickamauga, when Longstreet distinguished himself by his brave advance through a gap in the Union line. Refusing to surrender soon became an end in itself. No nation is defeated until it believes itself to be so, and in the autumn of 1863 the Confederacy was still determined to fight on. Southerners were also encouraged by the possibility, not by any means unrealistic, that Lincoln and the Republicans might lose the next election and be replaced by the Democrats and a president with a more conciliatory state of mind—McClellan, for instance, to name but one, though he vigorously denied it.

By this time Lee sensed that he was being turned into an object of hero worship, far above any role he could still play as a general. It is part of his greatness that he accepted this role with humility and grace, and that it kindled no political ambition. Southerners had made him into a symbol for which they were fighting, and they recognized his constant, calm acceptance of God's will. A nation besieged needs a powerful national myth to keep it fighting, and Lee became, however unwillingly, the personification of that myth. Jefferson Davis might have his people's respect, but Lee held their trust and affection—he was, and would remain, what they most wanted to see in themselves.

Freeman mentions that soldiers stepped out of the ranks to shake Lee's hand or pat Traveller's neck, and that "he welcomed all visitors, humble in station or exalted in rank." He tells the story of a farmer coming up to Lee: addressing him as "colonel," not guessing Lee's identity; and saying that he had come to see General Lee.* "I am General Lee," Lee replied modestly, "and

---

*What adds credibility to the story is that Lee customarily wore a plain gray uniform with no gold braid on his sleeves, and only the three small stars of a colonel—his last substantive rank in "the Old Army"—on the collar of his coat, and would not therefore have been instantly recognized as a general.

am most happy to meet you." No doubt the story is true, but it has also been told in slightly different forms about other great heroes, including Napoleon, so the point is not so much its truth as that it represents Lee's transformation into a living legend and myth.

He had before him a great and difficult task—the rebuilding of the Army of Northern Virginia, at a time when everything was lacking that was needed, from men to forage. He set about it, aided to no small degree by the inactivity of the Federal Army, though this inactivity could not be expected to last forever. The few skirmishes and battles gave no advantage to either side that fall. It was clear that Meade would not renew the struggle in full force until the spring of 1864. If he had ever enjoyed the confidence of President Lincoln, Meade had lost it by failing to pursue and destroy Lee's army after the Union victory at Gettysburg. The patrician Philadelphian and the Illinois railway lawyer with his folksy stories and canny political skill were not a good mix to begin with. Lincoln was in any case looking for a different kind of general, a self-starter who would "hold on [to Lee] with a bulldog grip, and chew & choke, as much as possible." Despite the stories about his drinking, Lincoln at last chose Major General Ulysses S. Grant, the victor of Fort Donelson, Shiloh, Vicksburg, Chattanooga, and Missionary Ridge.

In March 1864 Grant arrived in Washington, to be made the first lieutenant general since George Washington had been appointed to that rank by Congress, and given command of the whole U.S. Army. Grant's taciturnity, his simplicity, his shyness, his roots in Ohio, and his years as store clerk wrapping packages in Galena, Illinois, all served to increase Lincoln's confidence in him. Lincoln did not interfere in Grant's plans; he did not even ask to know them. From their very first meeting—at a White House soirée when the president had shouted to Mrs. Lincoln, "Why look, mother, here is General Grant," and then asked the general to stand on a sofa so the curious guests could see the man who had taken Vicksburg and 32,000 Confederate prisoners—Lincoln recognized and respected Grant's quiet, firm determination to win the war, and even his reluctance to explain how he intended to do it.

Grant knew Lee, of course—the officers of the Old Army all knew one another—and had served beside him in Mexico. He understood that Lee was a master of maneuver—it had after all been Lee's idea to flank Hooker's right at Chancellorsville, even though Jackson had carried it out—and for that very reason Grant was determined not to let him maneuver. Grant had no interest in Richmond, except that he assumed correctly Lee would feel obliged to defend it as long as he could; nor was he interested in fighting a big set-piece battle that would decide the war. Grant's object was not the Confederate capital, but Lee's army, and he had in mind a three-pronged attack that would wear the Army of Northern Virginia down remorselessly. Grant had more men, more guns, more supplies; he was confident that he could make good his losses more quickly than Lee could, and that if he pushed forward constantly, day after day and never let up the pressure, Lee's casualties would eventually become unsustainable—it was a simple question of mathematics. In addition, Sherman's march through Georgia to the sea would inevitably cut off Lee's supplies from the great southern agricultural heartland, so the Army of Northern Virginia would eventually be reduced, surrounded, and starved into submission. It was only a question of time, and Grant was not in a hurry. He would wear Lee down inexorably, though perhaps not in time for the 1864 election, as Lincoln hoped. Time, pressure, and numbers were Grant's secret weapons— he would fight Lee every day, win or lose; he would go on until the Army of Northern Virginia could fight no more.

Even in his own day people accused Grant of being a "butcher." In fact his casualties were not very different from Lee's, but he had no interest in glory, a firm grasp of the dreadful logic of warfare, and a grim confidence in his own ability to master it—the worse the war was, the more quickly it would be won. Though Grant would have spoken it sadly, rather than triumphantly, *Carthago est delenda* might have been his motto.

After more than three years, Lincoln had at last found the right man for the job.

"Winter of Discontent"

"Blessed be the Lord my strength: who teacheth my hands to war, and my fingers to fight." Freeman quotes this from the most worn and well-fingered page in Lee's copy of the *Book of Common Prayer,* which Lee marked "with a small strip of paper." It is from Psalm 144 and surely indicates how often Lee read and repeated this psalm in his devotions, and his profound belief in the fighting spirit of his troops and in the workings—however difficult to fathom they might be—of the Lord. One imagines that it must have comforted him through a long and difficult winter. His troops were virtually immobilized for want of shoes or the means of repairing them, and many had no blankets—the South had not a single blanket manufacturer—nor were they better off in terms of rations. Lee's troops spent the winter on a daily ration of four ounces of bacon or salt

pork and one pint of cornmeal. Lee himself insisted on sharing their plight—his midday meal was usually cabbage boiled in salt water. As General Fuller points out, with some justice, "Not only did [Lee] refuse to exert his authority to obtain supplies, but instinctively he had a horror of the whole question . . . trading was antipathetic to his aristocratic nature; besides, to compel the people to part with their food stocks was abhorrent to him, he looked upon them as a heroic race, almost as God's chosen people, who must be appealed to only through the heart." He appealed again and again to President Davis, but he recoiled from what might have worked—thunder, anger, a threat to march on Richmond and seize the supplies that were stored there—and as a result his army suffered, even though he suffered with it.

As a result, Lee could not do much with his forces in the winter of 1863–1864 except to hold Meade north of the Rapidan River. Fortunately for Lee, Meade showed little ambition to move. It was typical of Lee that he chose to spend Christmas of 1863 with his army, in his tent, when he might have spent it in Richmond with his family. The day after Christmas he learned that his grief-stricken, ailing daughter-in-law Charlotte had died. "It has pleased God," he wrote to Mary, "to take from us one exceedingly dear to us, and we must be resigned to His holy will. She, I trust, will enjoy peace and happiness forever, while we must patiently struggle on with the ills that may be in store for us. What a glorious thought it is that she has joined her little cherubs and our angel Annie in heaven." Lee's resignation to God's will was a major source of his strength, and of his hold over his own men, though it may not have consoled Mary Lee, who was now living in a cramped rented house in Richmond, and facing, as well as all the other family tribulations, the fact that the Federal government had at last confiscated her beloved Arlington.*

Lee's equanimity in the face of adversity was and would remain remarkable—with no particular effort or sense of sacrifice on his part he was in the process of being turned into a kind of uniformed, secular saint, a remarkable tour de force for a soldier, perhaps unequaled since the days of Joan of Arc. It was clear to him that the Federal Army was being steadily reinforced in preparation for a full-scale assault on northern Virginia as soon as the winter was over, and he devoted a good deal of time to preparing fortifications and earthworks to enable his men to hold their own

---

* This was done under a new law that enabled the Federal government to tax property in areas that were in rebellion. The taxes were not exorbitant, but a wrinkle in the law required that the owner must make the payment in person. Lee obviously could not do this, so Arlington was seized.

against vastly greater numbers. His mastery of the architecture of defense was as impressive as his genius for maneuver. If his troops could not march in the winter of 1863–1864, they could dig, and Lee made them build a line of trenches, redoubts, and forts that would, more than any other single factor, prolong the survival of the Confederacy for nearly a year and a half more.

Lee acted as the Confederacy's secretary of war much of the time, corresponding respectfully but as an equal with President Davis. He urged that conscription be extended and that "more vigorous enforcement" be applied. He also recommended using the utmost severity against deserters. By 1864 conscription in the Confederacy extended to almost every white male from the age of seventeen to fifty-five, but it was still not enough to produce sufficient manpower. At its lowest point, in February 1864, with Longstreet and much of his corps detached to fight in the west, the Army of Northern Virginia was reduced to "no more than 35,000 men," a number ludicrously insufficient to hold off the Army of the Potomac when it finally advanced. The picture of Lee as a benevolent, even saintly figure, sometimes carried to sugary extremes, does not do full justice to his complex character: he *was* kindly; he *did* feel sorrow for the suffering of his men and his animals (the "slow starvation" of the army's horses was particularly painful to him); he *did* regularly include the Union soldiers in his prayers; but he did not flinch from ordering extreme measures of punishment for deserters, or for those who had in any way failed to do their duty by "shirking" or "straggling." His methods of replenishing his ranks were rough-and-ready. They had to be, since the recruiting process in the South was as full of loopholes, exceptions, and what Lee called "partiality" as it was in the North.

Even after Lee's defeat at Gettysburg and Pemberton's surrender at Vicksburg, Lee still did not question the cause he had joined with such reluctance. The strategy of invading the North and seeking out a single major battle in the hope of achieving British or French recognition of the Confederacy failed twice, and it could not be attempted again. What faced the Confederacy now was a war of attrition, which, given the superior numbers and industrial power of the North, could only end in defeat. Seen from 150 years later, this seems inevitable, as does the fact that continuing the war would bring unimaginable destruction in the South once General Sherman introduced what a later generation would call total war, involving the burning of cities, homes, and farms on a wide scale—a "razed earth" policy that would cause untold suffering for generations to come. Admittedly, as the Confederacy shrank it would increasingly enjoy the benefit of shorter interior lines, but even this would be canceled out by the inadequacy of the southern railway system.

Had Lee been willing to contemplate surrender, the last two years of the war need not have been fought, but he was no more able to do that than he could transform himself into the kind of military-political leader that the South needed to overcome its supply and manpower problems. He would not seek or accept dictatorial powers—he was too much of an American for that—and he would not give up his faith in victory, however unlikely it came to seem.

It is symptomatic of the lack of leadership in the Confederacy that President Davis and his major commanders had different ideas about the direction of the Federal attack in the spring, and the best way to prepare for it. General Beauregard wanted to concentrate all the Confederate forces available (a total of about 210,000) against "one decisive point," rather than risk a series of defeats in detail. He suggested an attack in the direction of Knoxville, Tennessee. Lee saw the wisdom of this (he usually admired Beauregard's strategic sense), and foresaw the Federal attack through Georgia, but he was unwilling to take command there himself, or to further weaken the Confederate force in northern Virginia. Longstreet at first suggested moving Confederate forces back to the east for another assault against Washington, then changed his mind and recommended concentrating the army in an attempt to recover Tennessee and Kentucky. Lee, possibly persuaded by Longstreet, thought that recovering "Mississippi and Tennessee . . . would do more to relieve the country and inspire our people than the mere capture of Washington." In the end nothing much came of all this but the transfer back to Lee of Longstreet and his men. The Confederacy remained, despite its loss of territory, too big to be defended by an army of 210,000 men; at the same time its leaders were unable to decide on the right point at which to aim a single, concentrated, decisive attack that would shake public confidence in the North hard enough to bring about a negotiated peace. The old military adage, "When in doubt, do nothing," was in this case fatal to the Confederates, rather than wise; it left the armies in the West too weak to prevent a gradual collapse, and Lee's army too weak to attempt to capture Washington (even had that been a good idea) or in the end to hold on to Richmond.

Lee had spent much of the winter thinking about what Grant would do, finally deciding that he would try to take Richmond, like McClellan, Burnside, and Hooker before him. This was an error on Lee's part. Grant had no interest in Richmond; his aim was to wear down Lee's army, and he guessed correctly that Lee would be forced to *defend* Richmond, and that this would tie him down to a defensive strategy and prevent him from putting his genius for maneuver to use.

At first Lee planned what amounted to a repetition of 1862 and 1863—an advance into the Shenandoah Valley so as to make Grant think he would attack Washington, after which "a great battle would take place on the Rapidan." But Lee was wrong. From his childhood on, Grant always chose to take the shortest and most direct route between two points, and had a marked aversion to retracing his steps. He did not have Lee's skill at maneuver, nor Lee's taste for it; he preferred to plow forward with all his strength, pushing obstacles out of his way.

Lee did not want to wait to be attacked—it was not in his nature. He planned to "give battle" to Grant as soon as possible, foreseeing that Grant would probably cross the Rapidan and advance through the Wilderness, crossing it close to the old battleground of Chancellorsville, with the aim of turning Lee's right and separating him from Richmond.

Having won his greatest victory in this dark, dismal forest, Lee was confident that he could defeat Grant here, as he had defeated Hooker. But Lee woefully underestimated Grant's forces—Grant had 119,000 men to Lee's 64,000.⋆

"The Battle of the Wilderness"

Neither general was well positioned for the battle. Lee's army was spread out too widely to the south and west of the Wilderness, so that he would be forced to launch his attack with only a portion of his forces. He had been obliged to "scatter" his forces during the winter for fear that the army would eat the surrounding countryside into a landscape of starvation. Even his animals were in such poor condition and so reduced in number that he found it hard to concentrate the army quickly. His plan was to launch a full-scale attack on Grant's right as soon as the bulk of the Union forces had crossed the Rapidan and entered the Wilderness. This might have succeeded had Lee

---

⋆ Meade in fact remained in command of the Army of the Potomac, but as general in chief Grant chose to accompany the army rather than remain in Washington. For all practical purposes, Grant directed the strategy of that army and all the other Union armies from the field, and seems to have reached a remarkably good working relationship with Meade, rather like that which existed between Eisenhower and Bradley in 1944–1945. For the reader's convenience I will refer to Grant rather than to Meade in the text.

been able to bring to bear all three of his corps; but Longstreet was still at Gordonsville, over forty miles away, so only Ewell and A. P. Hill were left to attack. As for Grant, he underestimated the difficulty of moving his army rapidly, through such a dense, desolate place, particularly since his army's "wagon train [was] between sixty and seventy miles long," and moving over roads that were poorly marked and even less well maintained.

"The Wilderness," General Fuller writes, ". . . . covered [Lee's] numerical weakness and his administrative deficiencies; his army had so long inhabited it that every cow-path, fastness and ravine was known to his men. Lee's whole strategy now depended upon holding this natural stronghold, . . . entrapping Grant in it and so exhaust[ing] the patience and resources of the North. His idea was to bring his enemy to battle as soon as possible, and his plan was an able one, namely to let Grant cross the Rapidan and get thoroughly entangled in the forest, where numbers, cavalry, and artillery were of little account, and there attack him in flank and force him to retire as he had forced away Hooker."

But Grant was not Hooker. To begin with, while he respected Lee, he was not in awe of him, as almost every other Union general was. He would write later, in his *Memoirs*, "The natural disposition of most people is to clothe a commander of a large army whom they do not know, with almost superhuman abilities. A large part of the National army, for instance, and most of the press of the country, clothed General Lee with just such qualities, but I had known him personally, and knew he was mortal." Grant's refusal to be awed by Lee's "superhuman" skill as a commander was his first step to victory.*

The second advantage was Grant's firm determination to keep his army moving forward—no matter how unpromising the terrain. He intended to keep advancing, inflicting on Lee day by day, mile by mile, casualties the Confederacy could not sustain.

Grant moved swiftly into the "narrow peninsula" that separates the Rappahannock and the Rapidan rivers until they join about three miles north of Chancellorsville. His troops forded the Rapidan at two points beginning at midnight on May 3. Colonel Vincent Esposito speculates that if Grant had crossed the Rapidan at nightfall instead of at midnight he might have emerged from the Wilderness in one

---

* "The problem of overestimating or even hero-worshipping successful enemy commanders in time of war was not, of course, confined to nineteenth-century America" (Michael Korda, *Ulysses S. Grant*, 41). In Great Britain, to the irritation of Winston Churchill, admiration of General (later Field Marshal) Erwin Rommel was widespread until his defeat by General Montgomery at El Alamein proved him to be "mortal."

day and foiled Lee's plan, but considering the size
of Grant's force, his extensive ordnance and supply
train,* and the poor state of the roads running from
north to south through the forest, this may not have
been as feasible as it looks on a map. Grant's supply
train lagged well behind his first two corps, so they
were obliged to bivouac in the Wilderness, waiting for
it to catch up. This gave Lee a perfect opportunity to
attack. All he had to do was push Ewell's corps east
down Orange-Fredericksburg Turnpike and A. P.
Hill's corps down Orange Plank Road so they would
meet at Old Wilderness Tavern, and catch both Federal
corps spread out and off guard in the flank. It helped
him that the roads running from west to east through
the Wilderness were better than those running north
to south.

Fighting began early in the morning of May 5, with
the surprised Federals initially not realizing that they
were facing Ewell's entire corps. In the heavy underbrush and dense pine thickets it was almost impossible for the Union troops to deploy and form coherent
lines or take advantage of their superior artillery,
but the Union generals Gouverneur Kemble Warren
and Winfield Scott Hancock flung in division after

---

* Ammunition and powder for over 300 guns; 4,300 supply wagons; nearly 900 ambulances; and "a herd of cattle for slaughter."

division as each arrived on the field, finally bringing the Confederate advance to a halt in the late afternoon. The fighting was so fierce that many of the men's muskets "became too hot to handle."

Lee established his own headquarters less than a mile behind the front at the Widow Tapp's farmhouse—the Wilderness contained isolated cleared spots for farms, old forges, and, at places where the dirt roads met, simple crossroads stores whose names would pass into history over the next two days. In the middle of the afternoon a party of Union soldiers charged into Widow Tapp's farmyard, forcing Lee, Jeb Stuart, and A. P. Hill to run for the nearby woods just in time to avoid capture, surely a sign that Lee was, as usual, too far forward for a commanding general.

Neither side could claim a victory after a day of desperate fighting at close range in impenetrable second-growth forest and dense undergrowth, split by unmapped, wandering creeks, streams, and swamps, a place where men could not see their own comrades in arms, let alone the enemy, and where volleys of massed musketry and artillery fire seemed to come from nowhere. Even Douglas Southall Freeman, who seldom has a bad word to say about Virginia, calls it a "gloomy maze." The battle has been compared to jungle fighting in World War II, and to Indian fighting in the eighteenth century; and at the end of a bloody and by any standards largely fruitless day, almost any Union general would have withdrawn back to the Rapidan to lick his wounds and start looking for a way around the Wilderness. But Grant did not. He stayed put, to resume the fight the next day.

What took place the following morning was described with a degree of horror by Brigadier General Adam Badeau, an aide of Grant's, as "a wrestle as blind as midnight, a gloom that made maneuvers impracticable, a jungle where regiments stumbled on each other and on the enemy by turns, firing sometimes into their own ranks, and guided only by the crackling of the bushes or the cheers and cries that rose from the depths around." Even Grant's normally unemotional prose becomes incandescent describing the day: "The woods were set on fire by the bursting shells, and the conflagration raged. The wounded who had not strength to move themselves were either suffocated or burned to death. . . . But the battle still raged, our men firing through the flames until it became too hot to remain longer." Photographs of the Wilderness taken after the battle show a thicket of pine saplings shattered by gunfire, and a macabre, gruesome pile of skulls from the Battle of Chancellorsville, left unburied. Accounts of the battle over the next three days remind one of Matthew Arnold's famous lines in "Dover Beach":

And we are here as on a darkling plain
Swept with confused alarms of struggle and flight,
Where ignorant armies clash by night.

Even to hardened veterans, the first day of battle in the Wilderness seemed like Armageddon, full of lurid horrors lit by flames, the clash of hand-to-hand combat, and the screams of the wounded. As the flames spread and engulfed the dry underbrush, the seriously wounded clung to their loaded muskets with fierce determination in case they had no choice but to shoot themselves or be burned alive. It was a portent of things to come.

Lee had counted on Longstreet's corps to arrive by noon on May 5; indeed if Lee had had all three corps deployed that afternoon, the outcome might have been a Confederate victory. Longstreet, however, marched his corps sixteen miles on May 4 and fifteen miles on May 5, and it is difficult to see how he could have arrived on the battlefield in time to join Ewell and A. P. Hill before nightfall. This, like Longstreet's handling of his corps on the second and third days of Gettysburg, has been a subject of fierce controversy over the past century and a half. The only objective conclusion one can draw is that Longstreet may have promised Lee more than he could deliver, and that Lee, given Longstreet's slowness at Second Manassas and Gettysburg, should not have counted on having his whole army concentrated on May 5.

But it is easy to be wise so long after the event—Grant attacked when Lee had only two corps partially deployed, and the day was essentially another long, bloody standoff. Grant did not succeed in getting his army out of the Wilderness into the open country to the southeast, and Lee did not succeed in driving Grant back across the Rapidan.

At dawn on May 6 Grant again attacked first, with an assault down Orange Plank Road intended to shatter Hill's corps. This might have succeeded if Hill's men had not spent the night entrenching their line, and if Burnside had not managed to get lost with most of his corps in two miles of dense, jungle-like second growth—the "grim tangles" between Wilderness Tavern and Widow Tapp's farm.

The previous day, Lee had almost been captured at Widow Tapp's farm. Now, early in the morning of May 6, concerned that his entire line might be driven back before Longstreet was up, Lee attempted to lead a counterattack himself in the same place. Watching as the Confederate line began to crumble, he rode out into the open field to within less than 200 yards of the enemy, while a Confederate battery behind him fired volley after volley of canister into the advancing Union ranks. Surrounded by smoke, explosions, and confusion, Lee saw a few ragged soldiers running forward through the gaps between the guns and cried out, "Who are you, my boys?"

They shouted back that they were Texans, of General Hood's division, the first of Longstreet's corps to arrive. Almost everybody agrees that Lee was "excited," perhaps as much because he was in the front line as because the Texans were proof that Longstreet had arrived at last. He waved his hat, shouting, "Hurrah for Texas!" And after ordering them to form "a line of battle," he led them past the Confederate guns in a swift charge. Although Lee seldom touched wine or liquor, he was not immune to the intoxication of battle: "His face was aflame and his eyes were on the enemy in front." The spectacle of the commander of the Army of Northern Virginia eagerly spurring Traveller ahead of a brigade of Texans toward a Union infantry line now only 150 yards distant apparently attracted the attention of soberer spirits among those infantrymen who suddenly recognized him, and they shouted, "Go back, General Lee, go back!" Beneath the calm exterior, he

hid the spirit of a berserker; the blood of Light-Horse
Harry Lee ran in his veins. Lee's personal courage, his
indifference to danger, and his aggressive nature had
been proved over and over again; still, the sight of their
gray-bearded, fifty-seven-year-old commanding general proposing to lead a "desperate" infantry charge
under fire was enough to startle these hardened veterans, who cried out that they would not go forward
unless he went back. A grizzled sergeant finally seized
Traveller's bridle, and at that moment Colonel Charles
Venable, of Lee's staff, rode up and leaning over close
to Lee's ear shouted to him that Longstreet was now
close at hand and awaiting his orders.

For a moment Lee resisted, as if he had not heard.
Then he regained his calm, waved the Texans on with
his hat, and reined in Traveller. Venable rode off to
bring Longstreet the news that Lee was proposing to
lead a brigade into battle. Longstreet, if his memoirs
are to be believed, asked Venable to return to General
Lee with his compliments and say "that his line would
be recovered in an hour if he would permit me to
handle the troops, but if my services were not needed,
I would like to ride to some place of safety, as it was
not quite comfortable where we were." This reproof
sounds a little too pat, but Longstreet was writing
fourteen years after the event. Freeman is probably

more correct when he writes that when Lee reached Longstreet, the latter told him "bluntly that he should go farther behind the lines." Longstreet ought to have paid attention to this advice himself, in view of what was shortly to happen.

By ten o'clock in the morning Lee had "stabilized" his front, despite ferocious fighting back and forth across an almost "impassible barrier" of scrub, under-growth, and tangled saplings broken by bullets and canister shot, in which it was impossible to move with-out treading on the bodies of the wounded and dead. Casualties had reduced Lee's brigades to one-third of their strength. Of the 800 Texans whom Lee had briefly led forward at Widow Tapp's Farm, fewer than 200 were still alive and unwounded four hours later. Still, Lee could not win a "pounding match," to borrow the Duke of Wellington's description of Waterloo, against superior numbers. He had to find a way to turn Grant's left flank and either cut Grant off from the fords across the Rapidan, or drive him to retreat toward them.

One of Longstreet's staff had discovered an unfin-ished railway cut less than half a mile south of Orange Plank Road. Lee instantly saw the possibility of using it to turn Grant's flank. Before noon he had begun to roll up General Winfield Scott Hancock's Union line, as Hancock put it, "like a wet blanket." A victory like

Chancellorsville must have seemed to be within Lee's grasp as the Union left began to collapse, but Grant did not allow or contemplate a retreat, and held his ground. Longstreet, ignoring his own advice to Lee, rode forward for a closer look as his troops sought to outflank Hancock's corps where Orange Plank Road joined Brock Road and, like Stonewall Jackson, was shot by his own troops, who mistook him and his staff for Federal cavalry. Unlike Jackson, Longstreet survived. The ball pierced his throat and his right shoulder—but as he was carried from the battlefield, he gamely took off his hat, which had been placed over his face to hide his identity, and waved it to prove to his troops that he was still alive. Still, the impetus seemed to drain from the Confederate attack, and the day ended in another stalemate.

That night, an officer warned Grant that he knew Lee's methods from experience, and that Lee would move to cut the army off from the fords across the Rapidan. Grant replied wearily, "Oh, I am heartily tired of hearing about what Lee is going to do. Some of you always seem to think he is suddenly going to turn a double somersault, and land in our rear and on both of our flanks at the same time. Go back to your command and try to think what we are going to do ourselves, instead of what Lee is going to do."

This was a new spirit in which to fight Lee, whose reputation was almost as high in the North as in the South, despite his defeat at Gettysburg. When the next day dawned, Grant did not attack or retreat— he simply broke off the battle and withdrew southeast toward Spotsylvania Court House, where he would be closer than Lee to Richmond. In three days of fighting Grant had taken nearly 18,000* casualties, while Lee's army had suffered only 11,000; but as a proportion of the total Grant's losses were about 17 percent of his force, while Lee's represented about 20 percent— which he could not replace. It is a testimony to Lee's extraordinary skill, and to the powers of recovery of his soldiers, that he managed to reach Spotsylvania before Grant. Thrown on the defensive by Grant's stubborn refusal to retreat, Lee relied on his army's ability to move quickly, in part because of its modest supply train, and on his own "wonderful tactical eye for defensive positions." Wherever Lee went, he sought a place he could defend, and at once set his men to digging. The master of maneuver had again become the master of the spade and shovel. A Union officer serving on Meade's staff, Captain Theodore Lyman, a future overseer of Harvard University, remarked of Lee's skill

---

*Gordon C. Rhea, *The Battles of Wilderness and Spotsylvania*, National Park Service Civil War Series, 435–36, 440.

with earthworks that when the Army of the Potomac advanced it always saw before it "the line of the enemy, nothing showing but the bayonets, and the battle-flags stuck on the top of the works. It is a rule that when the Rebels halt, the first day gives them a good rifle pit; the second a regular infantry parapet with artillery in position; and the third a parapet with an *abattis* in front and entrenched batteries behind. Sometimes they put this three days work into the first twenty-four hours."

Lee had not dozed or dawdled at West Point during the lectures on Vauban and the art of fortification; he never forgot that he was an engineer first, before becoming a cavalry officer; he looked to his earthworks to compensate for the difference in size between the Army of the Potomac and his own—and when one earthwork was no longer tenable, he moved quickly to a new one. As a result, Lyman remarked, "this country is intersected with field works, extending for miles and miles in different directions and marking the different strategic lines taken up by the two armies, as they warily move about each other."

"Warily" is the key word. Grant was determined to swing around Lee's right, and Lee was equally determined not to let him. Lee got to Spotsylvania ahead of Grant, and "ably entrenched himself between the rivers Po and Ny, his entrenchments taking the form of an inverted V," in which position he was able to fight off Grant's greater numbers, and to transfer reinforcements from one side of the V to the other as the situation required. Lee's superb command of his profession and his calm in the face of repeated assaults at Spotsylvania (and bad news from other fronts) serves as a model of generalship to this day. At this point Grant had nearly twice Lee's number of men (120,000 versus about 60,000), and far superior artillery, as well as an abundant and unimpeded supply line. Nevertheless, Lee managed to hold him off, prompting Grant's famous telegraphic message to Halleck: "I propose to fight it out on this line if it takes all summer," a response to growing criticism of his heavy casualties and rumors (incorrect) that he had resumed drinking. Both generals committed errors, Grant's from a rare burst of overconfidence, Lee's from his old habit of letting J. E. B. Stuart choose what to do with his cavalry, thus leaving Lee blind again as he had done at Gettysburg. As for Grant, he sent his cavalry commander Major General Philip Sheridan off on a raid to the outskirts of Richmond, which left *him* blind too. Sheridan had conspicuously failed to screen the army's advance toward Spotsylvania from the Confederate cavalry. Although less of a swashbuckler, Sheridan shared Stuart's preference for the dramatic use of cavalry on a large scale over the less glamorous but vital tasks of screening the infantry's advance, clearing the roads in front of the army, and keeping his commander informed of the enemy's movements. The raid on Richmond was similar to Stuart's ride around McClellan's army on the peninsula in 1862, but it deprived Grant of his cavalry for nearly two weeks and had little effect on the campaign, except to give the Richmond home guard something to do.

The most important effect on the Confederacy was the loss of Major General J. E. B. Stuart, who was severely wounded in a clash at Yellow Tavern on May 11 and died later that day, at the age of thirty-one. "He never brought me a piece of false information," Lee said; then, badly shaken and close to tears, he retired to his tent "to master his grief." He wrote to Mary, "A more zealous, ardent, brave, and devoted soldier than Stuart the Confederacy cannot have"; and announced to the army, "To military capacity of a high order and to the noble virtues of a soldier he added the brighter graces of a pure life, guided and sustained by the Christian's faith and hope." In addition to his bravery and fighting spirit Stuart had the rare ability to amuse and entertain Lee, even in the grimmest moments of the war. Lee had treated Stuart like one of his own sons since the days when he had been superintendent of West Point—"I can scarcely think of him without weeping," he told one of Stuart's officers.

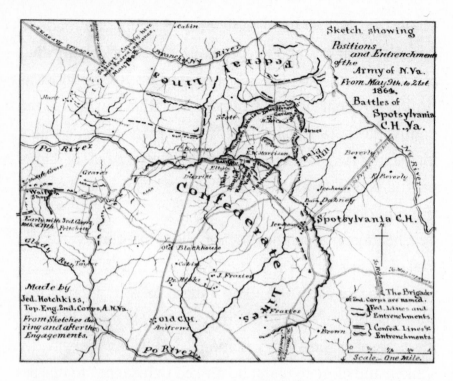

27. Hotchkiss sketch map of the Confederate positions around Spotsylvania Court House, May 1864, after Grant's advance through the Wilderness.

The loss went far beyond that of a gifted cavalry commander, and came at a moment when one by one Lee's closest commanders were being swept away from him— Longstreet recovering slowly from his wounds; A. P. Hill sick and hardly able to lead his corps; Ewell not much better off after the amputation of his leg; Jackson, the man Lee had trusted most, dead.

Lee struggled to handle an amount of work and responsibility that would have kept a deputy commander of the army, a chief of staff, and three corps commanders busy, while his own health, about which he never complained, gave those around him constant anxiety. Widespread as the troubles of the Confederacy might be, they seemed to rest on the shoulders of one man. He had correctly predicted that Grant would strike out for Spotsylvania Court House, and had deftly moved there just in time to thwart him. The Army of Northern Virginia was now firmly established between Grant's army and Richmond, only fifty miles away, and Grant would have to fight for every mile.

The inverted V of the Confederate lines around Spotsylvania grew stronger every hour, but the weakest point was at the apex of the V, which was in effect a salient that could be attacked from, both sides. Grant was determined to break it. From May 8 through May 21 he kept up a series of costly attacks against Lee's lines, sometimes breaking through them, but never quite able to hold or extend his gains. The fighting has been described as "some of the most intense of the Civil War," with a total of almost 32,000 casualties on both sides, along a front that was only four miles long. As one Union officer graphically described it, "the enemy's dead . . . were piled upon each other in some places four layers deep, exhibiting every ghastly phase of mutilation. Below the mass of fast-decaying corpses, the convulsive twitching of limbs and the writhing of bodies showed that there were wounded men still alive and struggling to extricate themselves from the horrid entombment." Grant, like no Union general before him in northern Virginia, managed to disentangle himself from the battle of attrition around Spotsylvania, and tried once again to flank Lee's right, in a series of moves that Lee, like a skilled chess player, managed to parry each time. Each move, however, drove Lee back closer and closer to Richmond. The two armies clashed again at the North Anna River, just over twenty miles from Richmond. From May 23 to 26 Grant moved south along the east bank of the North Anna River, while Lee moved south down the western bank, eventually establishing an entrenched line northeast of Richmond around Mechanicsville and Cold Harbor—exactly where Lee had made his first mark as commander of the Army of Northern Virginia three years ago, in June 1862. This was familiar ground, only eight miles from Richmond; but instead of having the hesitant McClellan facing him, he now had a grimly determined Grant, who arrived on May 28 with four corps, and two more corps due to arrive at White House on May 30. Thus two years of bloody war had brought Lee full circle back to the defense of Richmond, on ground most of which bore the scars and graves of previous battles—an ironic reversal, but not one Lee can have appreciated.

On May 25, Lee was felled by a serious illness. His usually equable temper was frayed, but he remained the animating spirit of his army. What his illness was is hard to tell—it may have been an attack of angina, but it sounds more like dysentery, which was the scourge of all armies in the field and was widespread throughout this army. General Ewell was so ill that he had to surrender command of his corps to General Early. He and Lee had to travel all day on May 28 in their ambulance, something that Lee seldom did, both because he enjoyed riding and because he knew the value to his army's morale of seeing him on Traveller, even from a distance.

Despite his poor health, Lee was still anxious to take the offensive. He was less than ten miles from Richmond; he was receiving such reinforcements as the government could send by stripping divisions from other armies; he had the benefit of short interior lines while Grant's lines of communications were stretched to the breaking point and Grant's men were exhausted by endless marches and daily skirmishes with the enemy. But Lee could not abandon his elaborate defensive works for a set-piece battle against Grant in open country, and Grant remained committed to his strategy of wearing Lee down. Lee's principal aide, Colonel Taylor, accurately describes the actions of the army after Grant disengaged from the Wilderness: "We were in constant contact with the enemy, and every day brought its episodes of excitement and struggling at different points of our line." There was never a moment when cavalry and infantry actions were not taking place, as both armies made their way toward Richmond, where there were elaborate fortifications and earthworks that Lee intended would protect his army from an all-out assault. On the other hand, Lee was acutely aware of the danger of allowing himself to become besieged there. Once he had lost his ability to maneuver, it would become a war of numbers, which favored Grant, with the added danger that the army and the city might be starved into submission. No less an authority than the future Field Marshal Lord Wolseley,* then another British officer observing the war from the Confederate side, wrote, "Lee was opposed to the final defense of Richmond that was urged upon him for political, not military reasons. It was a great strategic error." Wolseley was correct. Lee thought that the policy of defending Richmond to the last man was a mistake, but Jefferson Davis was determined that he do so. As for Grant, while he had no interest in taking Richmond, he was now fighting his

---

*Wolseley's reputation for military knowledge and perfectionism was so great that his name became a late-nineteenth-century British expression for anything done correctly: *"Everything's Sir Garnet Wolseley."*

way toward it day by day, just as McClellan had been two years ago, although more successfully. Neither general was doing what he wanted.

It is remarkable that Lee still retained his optimism and his determination to keep on fighting. As his son Robert remarks, "When [after his illness] we saw him out again, on the lines, riding Traveller as usual, it was as if some great crushing weight had been suddenly lifted from our hearts." Even allowing for a son's natural admiration of his father, the whole army seems to have shared this unyielding belief in its commander—as long as Lee led these men, they would fight on, whatever the odds. With scarcely concealed admiration, Grant wrote of Lee and his army, "The enemy are obstinate, and seem to have found the last ditch."

Grant was determined to put that to the test. Lee had established himself in an ambitious crescent-shaped fortified line near Mechanicsville, using every elaborate feature of Vauban's classic art of fortification; it stretched nearly seven miles in length on the north bank of the Chickahominy River from Atlee's farm on his left, with his right anchored on the river itself. Grant had 108,000 men, Lee about 59,000; and Grant's plan remained to crush the smaller Confederate force, then to swing around Lee's right flank, separate him from Richmond, and give the final coup de grâce to the Army of Northern Virginia once it was driven from its trenches. Grant's temper seems to have been fraying. On the road to Cold Harbor he came across a Union teamster whipping his exhausted horse across the head and face, and, after "an explosion of anger," had the man tied to a tree, with God knows what punishment in mind. Shortly afterward he ordered a full-scale frontal attack against Lee's formidable line, and by noon, scarcely half an hour later, he had taken over 7,000 casualties. By the end of the day, Grant had accomplished nothing, and by some estimates he had taken over 13,000 casualties against 2,500 on the Confederate side. At the very end of his life, as he lay dying, still completing his memoirs, the memory continued to haunt Grant. "I still regret," he wrote, "that the last assault at Cold Harbor was ever made. . . . No advantage was gained for the heavy loss we sustained." It was a day of constant horrors. The Union soldiers, as they dug trenches, were dismayed at uncovering countless human remains from the 1862 battle on the same ground; and after the battle the Union dead and wounded were left between the lines in the broiling sun for two days while Lee and Grant corresponded with each other in a tone of prickly dignity about the conditions for removing them. The dead were grotesquely bloated and "as black as coal," and the wounded were tormented by pain, thirst, and insects, and methodically picked off by Confederate sharpshooters as they lay there helpless. Grant had a brief letter carried under a white flag to Lee proposing that "unarmed men bearing litters" be authorized "to pick up their dead or wounded, without being fired upon by either party."

Lee replied that "he feared such an arrangement would lead to misunderstanding," and proposed instead that removing the wounded be done under a flag of truce, adding, "It will always be my pleasure to comply with such a request as far as circumstances will permit." The next day Grant replied that he would accept what Lee had proposed and collect his wounded and dead between 12 noon and 1 p.m., to which Lee politely replied that without a truce he would be obliged to turn back any parties sent for that purpose. In the end Grant accepted Lee's terms, but it was not until midmorning on June 7, forty-eight hours having elapsed, that the wounded were collected, by which time only two were still alive.

At first sight this correspondence does not reflect well on either general. Grant went to great lengths in his memoirs to make his position seem reasonable and humane—he devoted two and half pages of small type to it. But Lee's view of the situation was professionally correct, and he would not modify it. If Grant wanted to remove his wounded he would have to ask for a formal truce, not merely order a cease-fire of two hours for the purpose. A request for a truce would indicate that Grant had lost the battle, as indeed was the case. Since all but a small number of the wounded were Federals, Lee in his own courteous but stubborn way stuck to his guns.

Grant learned a lesson from the slaughter at Cold Harbor—his most formidable asset was that he was a practical, logical man, unmoved by the chivalry and romantic glory of war. He would not repeat a frontal attack on Lee's lines on the northeast outskirts of Richmond. Instead he would outfox the fox, and continue his attempt to turn Lee's right, this time with one of the most ambitious and spectacular flanking movements in military history. Although Lee was the engineer, Grant had a modern grasp of technology—he had used everything from steam shovels to ironclads to take Vicksburg, and had not hesitated to dig canals and cut through levees in his first attempt to attack it from behind. On the night of June 12 Grant abandoned his trenches at Cold Harbor and moved his whole army southward across the peninsula, exposing it to what might have been a crippling attack while it was on the move, if Lee had guessed what was going on. By June 13 Grant had bridged the Chickahominy

River, and by June 15 he had built a pontoon bridge across the James River over 2,000 feet long, and designed to withstand both the river's strong currents and its tidal rise and fall. He protected the bridge by sinking boats and barges filled with stone upstream to prevent an attack by Confederate ironclads. To speed the transfer of the army Grant had one corps transported from White House, the site of Rooney Lee's ruined home and plantation, down the York River and up the James on steamboats, while his vast wagon train moved south via White House and New Kent Court House, to avoid blocking the roads the army was taking. Even a modern, mechanized army would have been hard pressed to equal Grant's achievement in moving the Army of the Potomac despite poor roads, dense swamps, and two difficult river crossings, as well as a local population that was unsympathetic to his cause and certain to pass information back to Lee. For all that, Grant managed to keep his goal secret for over three days "in a hostile country swarming with spies." By June 16 Grant had his whole army south of the James River facing Petersburg, where two of the railway lines connecting Richmond with the rest of the South passed. Lee would either have to move his army south of Richmond to defend Petersburg, or abandon Richmond and move west.

There is no doubt that Grant took Lee by surprise. It was not until June 13 that Lee realized the Union trenches in front of him were empty. At first he assumed Grant was once again trying to outflank his right by moving to a position between White Oak Swamp and Malvern Hill, exactly the area where Lee had fought McClellan in 1862; but then he realized that Grant had in fact marched his army nearly fifty miles, had bridged and crossed two major rivers, and was now twenty miles south of Richmond, where he could be supplied and reinforced by sea. As early as June 9 Lee had remarked presciently that if Grant got to the James River, "it will become a siege, and then it will become a mere question of time." Now what Lee feared most was happening.

Once Lee realized what Grant had done, he moved with lightning speed to the defense of Petersburg. Despite repeated and costly assaults against the elaborate fortifications Lee had prudently prepared around the town, by June 21 it was clear that old-fashioned siege warfare had set in. Lee's skill at siting and building the redan, a V-shaped wall of two parapets, placed at regular intervals to cover a length of trench with artillery fire in both directions, was as impressive as his speed in maneuver. No sooner had he arrived in Petersburg than he set his men to strengthening every aspect of its fortifications. Inadvertently, Grant by his bold move and Lee by his quick recovery had created a dreadful, static siege that would postpone the end of the war by ten painful months, during which Sherman would march through Georgia, taking Atlanta, marching from there "to the sea," and destroying everything along his way: towns, railway lines, telegraph lines, homes, farms, crops, and livestock.

During this time Lee not only held Richmond and Petersburg with never more than 35,000 men against an army of 150,000, but remained the animating spirit of the Confederacy, "the idol of the South," as his son Robert put it. Indeed, as the Confederacy shrank, he grew, symbolizing the unshakable spirit of resistance, stubborn hope, courage, and honor—beyond criticism, perhaps even beyond reason. Although Grant's control of the James River gave him the ability to shift the balance of his forces from one bank to the other, and attack Lee on his left or his right, Lee's short interior lines enabled him to parry the blow, even though he was now holding a line almost thirty miles long with fewer than 1,000 soldiers to each mile.

Lee's headquarters were now in Petersburg, but he politely rejected all offers of a house, and continued to live in his tent, eating the same spare rations as his troops. "My father's relations with the citizens of Petersburg were of the kindest description," Robert noted. "The ladies were ever trying to make him more comfortable, sending him of their scanty fare more than they could well spare. He always tried to prevent them, and when he could do so without hurting their feelings he would turn over to the hospitals the dainties they sent him—much to the disgust of his mess steward, Bryan." Once when he was presented with a peach—the first he had seen in two years—Lee sent it to the elderly lady in whose yard he had pitched his tents. Shirts, socks, ice cream, bread, vegetables, and milk he invariably gave to the troops, the only exception being two lemons, which he sent on to Mary Lee, who was in Richmond, confined to her "rolling chair." Though it would have been easy enough for Lee to ride into Richmond and see Mary, he would not assume for himself a privilege he could not allow his men. It is part of Lee's role as a kind of martyr-hero that he neither sought nor accepted any alleviation of his condition. When Mary wrote to him, begging him to take better care of himself, Lee replied, "But what care can a man give to himself in the time of war? It is from no desire for exposure or hazard that I live in a tent, but from necessity." This was not altogether true— people offered Lee their homes; he would not accept them—but his role was not only to lead his men, but to share as much as he could their privations. It was a demonstration of his own humility, not so much deliberate as unconscious and natural. Though he did not seek out veneration, and would have regarded it as blasphemous, he was venerated by his men as few generals have ever been. Wherever he went the troops reached out to touch his boots or his horse, as if he were a secular military saint—indeed, contradicting the old French witticism, he was even a hero to his valet.* His aide Colonel Long, who was as close to Lee daily as any man could be, wrote of him at this period, "Never had care for the comfort of an army given rise to greater devotion. . . . He was constantly calling the attention of the authorities to the wants of his soldiers. . . . The feeling for him was one of love, not of awe or dread. They could approach him with the assurance that they would be received with kindness and consideration. . . . There was no condescension in his manner, but he was ever simple, kind, and sympathetic, and his men, while having in him unbounded faith as a leader, almost worshipped him as a man." This is strong praise even for a loyal aide-de-camp, and it captures something of the admiration for Lee's character that held both his army

---

* "No man is a hero to his valet," is attributed variously to Madame Aïssé, a friend of Voltaire's; and to Madame Cornuel, a mistress of Louis XIV.

and his nation together, and inspired the citizens of Petersburg, who suffered all the horrors of a siege for ten months without complaint. His example ennobled their sufferings.

On a practical level, however, Lee could at best hold back the inevitable. Lee had been slow to recognize the boldness of Grant's sudden move across the James. He tried, as he had so often done before, "his old game" of threatening Washington, weakening his own forces by sending generals Breckinridge and Early into the Valley in the hope that Grant might be recalled by the president from his position close to Richmond; but Grant was not Halleck and the Lincoln of 1864 was not the same man as the Lincoln of 1862. Grant remained confident that he could defend the capital however close Early's troops might come to it. The bluff that had been at the heart of Lee's strategy in 1862 and 1863 no longer worked; nor was there any possibility of a new offensive on a large scale across the Potomac since the disaster at Gettysburg. Lee had long since lost hope that the Confederacy might be recognized by the United Kingdom, but he supposed like many people in the South that if the war could be continued until Tuesday, November 8, 1864, northern voters might bring to office a president who favored a negotiated peace, specifically Lee's old antagonist General George

B. McClellan, who, although he was running as a "pro-war" Democrat, was thought to be more open to offering the southern states terms that would bring them back into the Union. This was a faint hope to cling to. McClellan did win the Democratic nomination in August, but carried only three states in the election. To quote the verdict of General Fuller: "from the date that Grant began to lay siege to Petersburg, the end of the Confederacy, like a gathering storm cloud, loomed over the horizon of the war, daily growing greater and more leaden." Only some act of supreme incompetence on the part of Grant could help Lee now.

On July 30 Grant almost presented Lee with one. Although Grant had been contenting himself with sending cavalry raids to the south and west of Petersburg in a constant effort to cut the Confederate railway lines, with mixed results, he still wanted to break through Lee's defenses. In mid-June a former mining engineer proposed digging a mine more than 500 feet long under the Confederate front line and blowing up a fort in the middle of the Confederate First Corps' line. Four tons of gunpowder would open a gap that would allow a full-scale assault to take the enemy trenches from behind. Grant was persuaded—he had a certain fondness for bold schemes involving digging and machinery on a large scale—although in his memoirs he initially plays the plan down somewhat as an attempt to keep a regiment composed of Pennsylvania miners busy. In fact, he carried out an elaborate plan to mislead Lee that involved laying a pontoon bridge across the James River and sending a Union infantry corps and two divisions of cavalry across it to threaten Richmond, and if possible cut the Virginia Central Railroad line connecting Richmond with the Valley. He hoped to force Lee to withdraw troops from around Petersburg—a smaller version of the strategy Lee had used for so long by threatening Washington in order to reduce Federal pressure on Richmond.

President Davis was just as sensitive about the safety of Richmond as President Lincoln was about Washington, so Lee took the bait and thinned his defenses, though the presence of the mine was, by then, an open secret. In fact the Confederates had been vigorously, though unsuccessfully, attempting to dig a countermine and seize the Union mine before the charges could be exploded. The mine was finally set off at five o'clock in the morning on July 30, producing "a crater twenty feet deep and a hundred feet in length." The blast killed over 300 Confederate soldiers instantly. Unfortunately for Grant the preparations for exploiting the explosion were badly bungled. The original plan had called for a division of "United States

Colored Troops" of General Burnside's corps to lead the assault. They had been specially trained for their role, but at the last minute General Meade developed cold feet—he had little confidence in the operation to begin with, and feared that if it failed black soldiers would be blamed.

Instead, Burnside provided another white division from his corps for the task of leading the breakthrough. He allowed his division commanders to draw straws for it, but the unlucky loser commanded a division that had received no training for its mission, and its commander, far from leading it, remained behind and got drunk, having neglected to brief his officers. Instead of making their way *around* the crater and then making a vigorous thrust toward Plank Road, less than half a mile away, which led directly into Petersburg, the leaderless and bewildered troops descended *into* the crater, and found they were unable to climb the steep bank of dirt and debris thrown up in front of them by the explosion. As the dazed Confederates recovered from the shock they began to shoot down into the crater from the rim, "a turkey shoot," as it was later described. The black troops, when they were finally sent in by Burnside, that consistently unlucky general, were attacked on both flanks and virtually slaughtered. Many of their wounded and most of those who attempted to surrender were shot on the spot. It was not only "a tremendous failure," in Grant's words, but "the saddest thing [he] had seen in the war."

Lee rode at once to the spot to make sure the Confederate line was restored. Even the retreat of the surviving Federal troops was a disaster: as Colonel Taylor, who was watching beside Lee, noted, "they were compelled to retreat across the space intervening between the lines, which was commanded by our artillery posted on the right and left of the crater, and the destruction here by musketry fire and the grape and canister poured into the retreating mass was very heavy."

The incident cost Grant about 4,400 casualties for no appreciable gain. The mine was a sensational event, but it did nothing to change the reality of Lee's position. As Colonel Long records, Lee "was sorely tried and beset with difficulties"; he simply did not have enough men to hold such a long line, or to withstand Grant's deft switching of attacks from one place to another. Still, Lee made every effort not to adopt a purely defensive role, and had occasional victories. On August 19, for example, A. P. Hill attacked and "defeated the force opposed to him, capturing twenty-seven hundred prisoners, including a brigadier-general and several field-officers," thus forcing Grant to withdraw his forces "from the north side of the James River." On August 25 Hill attacked again, trying to break the Federal hold on the Weldon Railroad at Reams Station. He took "twelve stands of colors, 2100 prisoners, and 9 pieces of artillery," but left this vital railway line still in Federal hands. During most of this fighting, Lee's army inflicted far more casualties than it received, but as Lee himself recognized, Grant could make good his losses far more easily than the Confederates could.

Colonel Taylor, like many others, refers often to the overwhelming superiority of numbers of the Union Army, and notes, with a detectable sneer, "When patriotism failed soldiers could be bought." In fact the South had introduced conscription before the North, and on both sides exemptions could be sought and substitutes could be had at a price. In the sense that Taylor means it, the Federal troops were no more "mercenaries" than the Confederates, though they were certainly better fed, clothed, and paid. The evils of the Federal draft, which produced the New York City draft riots of July 1863, were mirrored by those of the Confederate system, equally convoluted and skewed in favor of the well-to-do. No doubt a higher proportion of Lee's troops than of Grant's were "volunteers," but after the initial burst of enthusiasm that impelled men to enlist in 1861 and 1862 both sides resorted to conscription, however inefficiently, or unfairly conducted, or enforced by various degrees of coercion. Lee's manpower problem derived not from any unwillingness to recruit forcibly those between the ages of eighteen and thirty-five, but from the fact that the North had a larger population to draw on and from the high rate of desertion and "straggling" in his own army.

The loss and evacuation of Atlanta in September, and its partial destruction on the orders of Lieutenant General John Bell Hood as his troops abandoned the city (the destruction was completed by Major General Sherman after he entered it), inevitably produced a strong impression on "those men in high authority" in Richmond, though it had no apparent effect on Lee's determination to fight on. Colonel Taylor, who accompanied Lee to "a conference" with President Davis the day after Hood evacuated Atlanta, noted (carefully excluding Lee's name) the opinions expressed, which may have been those of President Davis. The Democrats, he wrote, "must have a decided peace candidate to secure the support of the element in opposition to the administration and the war. . . . Let them adhere firmly to their intention to propose an armistice and some good may result to us. . . . My idea of the armistice is that the armies will remain as they are now. There will be no disbanding on either side, nor

will the Federals withdraw from our territory. . . .
We must not claim what it would be unreasonable to
expect."

If this is what President Davis hoped for, he was to be
severely disappointed. When the Democrats nominated
McClellan as their presidential candidate, he rejected
that particular plank in their platform, although had he
been elected he would almost certainly have sought
a negotiated end to the war. But neither Lincoln nor
Grant had the slightest interest in an armistice that
would allow what remained of the Confederacy to survive as a separate nation.

From the account given by Colonel Taylor (not
as a rule a man likely to be critical of his master), it
does not appear that Lee shared Davis's rather cautious
optimism: but then, paperwork was what Lee hated
most, and it was the job of his staff to force it on him.
Although his son Rob had been wounded; his wife,
Mary, was by now a complete invalid, cut off from her
normal round of visits to hot springs to seek relief from
her pain; and both Richmond and Petersburg were suffering the horrors of an ever more vigorously enforced
siege, Lee never lost his singular ability to inspire
his troops with a single, simple gesture, performed
always with perfect serenity and out of a natural and
unself-conscious spirit.

Lee's chaplain, the Reverend J. William Jones, recounts how Lee, under heavy shell fire in an exposed position, ordered those around him to take cover, but himself walked out into the open despite explosions all around him, to pick up from the ground "an unfledged sparrow" that had been blown out of a tree and return it gently to its nest. No other general in history has successfully managed to combine the better qualities of Napoleon with the spirit of Saint Francis of Assisi. There is no better illustration of the special role Lee had already come to play in southern mythology: like the Almighty's, his eye was (literally) on the sparrow. If this story were about anybody else but Lee, we might consider it a myth, like the story of the young George Washington and the cherry tree, but with Lee it rings true. His quick eye and what Colonel Long calls "his love for the lower animals and deep feeling for the helpless," combined with his complete lack of fear and total indifference to danger, make the story about the sparrow ring perfectly true, and help to explain the willingness of his men to follow Lee anywhere and to keep on fighting even when their situation seemed hopeless.

Lee's faith in the Confederate cause did not blind him to the dire reality. Jubal Early's "raid" on Washington, which failed to shake loose Grant's hold on Petersburg, was followed by hard fighting as Early retreated up the Valley—and then by Sheridan's merciless scorched-earth policy there, under which everything from fence posts to barns and houses was set on fire. Meanwhile Sherman's troops not only tore up the railways in Georgia, but heated the rails over open fires and bent them around trees like a steel necklace so they could never be used again. Lee's only hope was to break free of Grant's "strangle-hold, to cut loose from Richmond and transfer the struggle to some other area," where he could once again maneuver his army, and perhaps provision it. But at the same time giving up Richmond, with its arms factories and workshops, would cripple the army and deal a deathblow to the Confederates' morale. Loyally, Lee refused to consider it, conscious perhaps that for him to even raise the issue was to open discussion of surrender. He urged President Davis to transfer officers and men of the "conscript bureau" to the defense of Petersburg and of Wilmington, North Carolina, the last port remaining in southern hands, and to move the Virginia and North Carolina reserves—mostly older men and invalids by now—into the trenches, leaving his own troops "free for active operations." Lee ended his letter with a warning: "It will be too late to do so after our armies meet with disaster."

Yet, like most of the South, Lee fought on. The Army of Northern Virginia had become, to an extraordinary degree, the keystone that held together a disintegrating economy and a shrinking territory. There was a growing belief among many people in the South that this was "a rich man's war and a poor man's fight," as well as doubts about the leadership and wisdom of President Davis, but still there remained a unanimous admiration of Robert E. Lee. He did not have to make noble speeches, or even win great victories, he merely had to be himself. By the autumn of 1864 he had become the symbol of what southerners were fighting for, the essence of courage, courtesy, dignity, and lack of self-interest that they believed separated them from the greedy Yankee hordes who had no respect for the traditions of an older, gentler America. Whether Lee willed it or not—and he clearly did not—his apotheosis was already in progress.

In the meantime, Lee continued to serve in an anomalous position. He was certainly recognized as the "first soldier" of the Confederacy, and his advice was sought on every subject from conscription to the best use of what remained of the Confederate Navy, but his authority extended only to the Army of Northern Virginia. He was not the commander in chief of the whole army, as Grant was, and did not have Grant's ability to plan and carry out a grand strategy involving it. He would eventually become general in chief of the Confederate Army on February 9, 1865, but by then the appointment was an empty honor; "it was too late for him to accomplish anything." The history of the Confederacy might have been quite different had Lee been given full command of the entire army in 1863, but neither Jefferson Davis, who throughout the war saw himself as a military leader more than a political figure, nor the Confederate Congress was eager to give up that power. Lee's exaggerated deference toward Davis and dislike of politics remained unwavering. He would make suggestions about military decisions to Davis, always in the most respectful way, but he would never insist, or threaten. No man was less likely than Robert E. Lee to become the military dictator who alone might have saved the South by taking firm control of all the armies and the economy, and yet no one else had the prestige to fill the role.*

Away from his family, he continued to worry about every detail of their lives. Mrs. Lee, together with two of her daughters, Mildred and Agnes, had accepted the hospitality of friends of the family at their estate on the James River, west of Richmond, leaving her daughter

---

*Missing was the role that General George C. Marshall played vis-à-vis President Roosevelt in World War II. Marshall was the president's trusted military and strategic adviser, as well as the man to whom the two supreme commanders—Eisenhower and MacArthur—reported. President Davis mistakenly attempted to play both roles himself.

Mary Custis behind "to regain strength and weight." Mrs. Lee had no sooner arrived than she slipped on a polished wooden floor and injured herself. Despite pleas from her husband and her doctors, she refused to take to her bed, and in fact seems to have been none the worse for the accident. Lee's letters were always loving and full of good advice, most of which Mrs. Lee ignored, as did, increasingly, her daughters. Though he urged Mildred ("Precious Life") to keep knitting, she spent a good deal of her time playing the piano and reading instead. He urged Mary Custis to join her mother and sisters in the country, but she stayed in Richmond for much of the summer to be with her friends, until the heat finally obliged her to leave. Both Mrs. Lee and the girls knitted a good deal, mostly socks, for which their enthusiasm may have been dampened by the fact that Lee gave these away to soldiers who needed them more than he did. The Lee women were not alone. All over the South women knitted presents and sent them to General Lee, who gave them all away, to the troops or to the wounded in hospitals. To the despair of his mess steward and his aides, he gave away countless gift baskets of delicacies. It is interesting to note that when the general's undergarments needed replacing, new ones were cut and sewn by Mrs. Lee despite her arthritis, although Lee, in his usual mild teasing way, suggested that the more "nimble fingers" of Agnes might have been employed to make them instead, presumably as a preparation to marriage. This too seems to have fallen on deaf ears.

When Lee had meetings in Richmond he always visited 707 Franklin Street, the modest house that his oldest son, Custis ("Boo"), had rented from Mr. John Stewart, and in which his wife Mary and his daughters now usually lived as well. These brief glimpses of domesticity were a great comfort to Lee and, judging from the comments of visitors to the house, even Mrs. Lee, despite her infirmity and the pain of losing Arlington, was in better spirits than before—"she seemed to grow in courage and tranquility as the news from the front grew worse."

The autumn of 1864 brought little good news. Grant had not broken through Lee's lines around Petersburg, but there was now virtually no chance that Lee could break out, nor was there any way to supply enough food and forage to do so. Lee's nephew Major General Fitzhugh Lee★ described his uncle's soldiers as "ragged, gallant fellows . . . whose pinched cheeks told hunger was their portion, and whose shivering forms denoted the absence of proper clothing." Like Richmond, the Army of Northern Virginia was under

---

★ Fitzhugh Lee was not only a brave and brilliant cavalry commander but one of the very few generals of the Confederate Army to be appointed a Union major general in the years after the war.

siege. Defeat was only a matter of time, short of a miracle. In November it became clear that there would be no miracle—Lincoln was reelected with a margin of 400,000 in the popular vote and carried all but three states, the first president to win a second term since Andrew Jackson.

Lee's letters to the secretary of war and to President Davis were full of complaints about the lack of rations and of clothing for his men—in some regiments, he pointed out, "not fifty men" had shoes; and tiny amounts of rancid bacon and moldy cornmeal were all he had to feed his troops. The complete lack of soap, he complained, was a cause of great suffering; and perhaps not surprisingly as winter set in the number of deserters grew "alarmingly." Four days before Christmas, General Sherman completed his march through Georgia to the sea by taking Savannah. It was only a matter of time before he turned his army north to join Grant outside Petersburg. The situation was too critical and the suffering of his troops too great for Lee to spend Christmas Day with his family.

It was not only Lee's troops who deserted. With great reluctance, the Confederacy had agreed to the conscription of slaves as laborers for the army—this was a question not so much of prejudice as of the fact that slaves represented property and wealth, and also that in the absence of so many white men they were the only labor force remaining for many landowners. Not surprisingly those who were conscripted deserted at a far higher rate than white troops. Lee complained that he had requested 5,000 laborers and had received only 2,200 "in small bodies and at different intervals," and by December he had fewer than 1,200 left. The more radical idea of arming slaves to fight for the Confederacy had been raised as early as 1861, but given the desperation of the military situation, it became a more urgent issue in the autumn of 1864. In his masterly study *Conscription and Conflict in the Confederacy*, Albert Burton Moore sums up the "cardinal points" of those opposing this drastic move: "(1) the arming of the slaves would be a repudiation of the theories and traditions of the South; (2) it would mean the abolition of slavery, for 'if the negro was fit to be a soldier, he was not fit to be a slave'; (3) it would be the abandonment of the ground on which the states seceded if they allowed Congress to interfere with the institution of slavery; and (4) it would be an offense to the white soldiers and many of them would lay down their arms." Lee was the "mainstay" of those who advocated this radical step, writing to a member of the Virginia legislature, "We must decide whether slavery shall be extinguished by our enemies and the slaves be used against us, or use them ourselves at the risk of the effects which may be produced upon our social institutions." Lee then cut the Gordian knot by pointing out that any act for enrolling slaves as soldiers must contain a "well digested plan of gradual and general emancipation": the slaves could not be expected to fight well if their service as soldiers was not rewarded by freedom. President Davis was reluctant to confront this most sensitive of issues in the South, and both the Confederate Congress and the southern state legislatures debated and delayed action. Davis not surprisingly preferred to wait "for public opinion to ripen on this subject," but the result was that "the end came before [Negro enlistment] was under way." The remarkable thing is that Lee, by nature the most conservative of men and the most respectful of southern traditions and institutions, in this instance was the most radical voice in favor of enlisting blacks and promising them freedom at the same time as a musket.

On February 4, 1865, Lee was at last nominated "general in chief" of all the Confederate armies. Characteristically, he replied that he was "indebted alone to the kindness of his Excellency the President" for "this high and arduous office," adding, more disturbingly, that he had "received no instructions as to my duties," and did not know what President Davis desired him to undertake.

Lee formally announced that he had "assumed command of the military forces of the Confederate States" on February 9, and immediately drew attention to one of his greatest problems: he gave deserters and those absent without leave twenty days in which to return to their unit or to report to the nearest enrolling officer, after which they would be subject "to such punishment as the courts may impose, and no application for clemency shall be entertained." In theory this meant a pardon for those who returned to the army, and the death penalty for those who did not, but in practice by this time neither the courts of the Confederacy nor the various "home guard" units charged with tracking down and apprehending deserters were up to dealing with over 100,000 deserters. In some cases imprisonment and executions occured, and there was at least one lynching, but the decline in morale, the shortage of supplies, and the anticipation of defeat made it possible for most of the men to slip back into rural life without their neighbors informing on them.

However unshaken Lee appeared before his men, he was not cheerful. Only ten days after accepting his appointment as general in chief he wrote to John C. Breckinridge, the new Confederate secretary of war, that "it may be necessary to abandon all our cities, and preparation should be made for this contingency."

He also urged concentrating "all our armies" in Virginia, "as separately they do not seem able to make head against the enemy." This was a realistic but depressing assessment—events on the ground were now swiftly overtaking the Confederate government's control over what remained of the Confederacy. Lee was already thinking of moving supplies and ordnance from Richmond to Lynchburg, where he might be able to hold the junction of the Southside and Danville railroads "so as to retain communication with North and South as long as practicable, and also with the West." His state of mind can best be inferred from his letter of February 21 to Mrs. Lee: "Should it be necessary to abandon our position to prevent being surrounded, what will you do? Will you remain, or leave the city?" To this, he added, knowing that Mary Lee would almost certainly do just what she wanted to, "You must consider the question and make up your mind."

Just as Lee was considering whether or not to abandon Petersburg, his daughter Agnes, demonstrating the doughty independence of Lee's womenfolk, decided to accept a long-standing invitation to visit the city. Her father feared she had left the visit until too late, but that did not prevent her from taking the train to Petersburg, which was under constant artillery fire, to stay with her friends the Meade family. She remarked on the fact that the citizens of Petersburg seemed to pay no attention to cannon shells exploding in the streets. On her first night, a military band "serenaded the Meade home" to honor the presence of one of Lee's daughters, and "Agnes tossed fresh roses to the gallant musicians." The next day Agnes went to the farmhouse where Lee's headquarters was, only to find that he had been called away in the pouring rain. The next morning he wrote her "a hasty [but loving] note."

> My precious little Agnes,
>
> I was so sorry I was not here to see you yesterday. I might have persuaded you to remain with me. If you had have staid [sic] or come out at four o'clock this morning I could have seen you with my weary sleepy eyes. Now I . . . do not know when I shall have the pleasure of seeing you.

Lee could see all the signs of Grant's preparations to attack the Confederate lines, and knew that at this point there was little he could do to stop the inevitable. Still he was determined to fight on. He had predicted that Grant was going to "draw out by his left with the intent of enveloping me," exactly what Grant had in mind, and urged on his officers the importance of discipline. "The appearance of a steady, unbroken line is more formidable to the enemy and renders his aim less accurate and his fire less effective," Lee wrote, emphasizing that discipline counts for more on the battlefield than "numbers or resources." However, he noted that his ability to move the army rapidly was severely hampered by the fact that "the cavalry and the artillery . . . are still scattered for want of provender, and our supply and ammunition trains, which ought to be with the army in case of sudden movement, are absent collecting provisions and forage." An even more serious problem was that the "state of despondency that now prevails among our people is producing a bad effect upon the troops." There was not much Lee could do about that. On February 24, in a long letter to Governor Vance of North Carolina, he pointed out that the troops were influenced "to a considerable extent by letters . . . written by their friends at home" representing "to their friends in the army that our cause is hopeless, and that they had better provide for themselves." Deserters usually took their weapons with them, often joined large bands of other armed deserters, and in many places were difficult for the home guard to round up. On March 9, in response to Governor Vance's reply, Lee agreed to provide two detachments of troops, with orders "to take no prisoners among those deserters who resist with arms the civil or military authorities."

Lee still hoped that by concentrating all the remaining Confederate forces in Virginia, he might be able to fight one last battle there and defeat Grant, perhaps winning for the Confederacy a new lease on life. This in fact was exactly what Grant feared most. If the protracted campaign around Petersburg and Richmond was not concluded quickly, public opinion in the North might turn against the war, which seemed to many to have been dragging on forever.

Lee's hopes were never fulfilled. Events made it impossible for him to concentrate the number of troops he needed, or to feed them and supply them with ammunition. On March 17 he wrote to Secretary of War Breckinridge that he could no longer "sustain even our small force of cavalry around Richmond," for want of forage. On March 27, he wrote with a touch of bitterness, considering how long he had urged the government to form armed black units, "I have been awaiting the receipt of the order from the Department [of War] for raising and organizing the colored troops before taking any action in the matter. I understand that orders have been published in the newspapers, but have not seen them. In the mean time, I have been informed that a number of recruits may be obtained in Petersburg if suitable persons be employed to get them to enlist."

At 4 a.m. on April 2, Grant began his long-expected attack with "an assault along the whole of the Petersburg front" by 125,000 men against Lee's long, far-stretched line of no more than 33,000 half-starved fighting men. Whether or not Mrs. Lee and her daughters Mary Custis and Mildred could see and hear the preliminary bombardment that turned the early morning sky above Petersburg red, Lee saw it and knew what it portended, and he "dispatched a paroled officer to fetch Agnes from the Meade home and take her to the railroad station." Her father had warned her that she might be trapped in the city, and arranged for her rescue at the last minute, doubtless with a profound sigh of relief on his part that she was on board the last train out of Petersburg. He then turned to the task of writing to Secretary of War Breckinridge. "I see no prospect of doing more than holding our position here till night. I am not certain that I can do that; if I can I shall withdraw tonight north of the Appomattox. . . . Our only chance, then, of concentrating our forces is to do so near the Danville Railroad, which I shall endeavor to do at once. I advise that all preparations be made for leaving Richmond tonight."

On Sunday, April 2, Mrs. Lee and her daughters attended communion service at St. Paul's Church, where they saw the sexton walk down the aisle and respectfully bend over to whisper to President Davis. Davis rose from his pew, followed one after the other by "other important military and government figures." Lee's lines at Petersburg had been broken, and Richmond was lost. By the time Mrs. Lee left church after the service, wagons were already lining up to remove the archives and what remained of the Confederate government's gold bullion. By early afternoon she and her daughters watched as panic spread through the city. The members of the Confederate government were now fugitives, wanted men, in flight to nowhere. "All of Richmond, rich and poor, highborn and lowly, seemed to be scrambling to leave the city. Wagons and carriages piled high with furniture and barrels jostled the endless stream of heavily laden pedestrians, all intent on getting away, somewhere, anywhere, to escape the dreaded Yankees. Through the open casements the family listened to the sounds of flight, the tramping of feet, the creak of wagon wheels, the cries of children, and the whinnies of frightened horses, as 'grim terror spread its wild contagion.'"

By the middle of the afternoon looting and drunkenness swept the city, and by the evening fires spread throughout Richmond as the tobacco warehouses went up in flames, "set by a misapprehension of orders." Soon immense explosions shook the city as the remaining ordnance and naval stores were set off, either by drunken looters or by the retreating troops. Richmond was not destroyed by vengeful Union troops but abandoned to destruction by its own citizens. Just before dawn the city's last remaining powder magazine went up in a huge explosion, and flames moved east toward Franklin Street, engulfing almost everything in their path. April 2 had been, ironically, a perfect spring day, with the scent of budding trees and flowers in the air; but as the sun rose on April 3 it illuminated dimly, through the clouds of acrid smoke and burning debris that filled the air, only the skeletons of its smoldering buildings, and charred, blackened trees. Richmond's public and private buildings were sending up a stream of ashes, burned paper, broken furniture, and carved wood paneling, the bric-a-brac of a century of prosperity and genteel living. Mrs. Lee watched the scene from her window through her lorgnette, "attired," as her biographer Mary P. Coulling tells us, "in her handsomest dress, her best bonnet, veil, and gloves." She was probably not surprised when the firestorm stopped short of her house as if by a miracle. When Tuesday morning dawned she could see, through the clouds of smoke, the "old, familiar" Union flag floating once again above the dome of the capitol, and hear the steady tread of Union troops marching through the streets to put out the remaining fires and restore order. The Union commander offered to evacuate her and her daughters to someplace where they would be more secure, but Mary Lee refused to go. A sentry was posted at her door for her protection—perhaps intentionally the first was a black soldier, but Mary Lee objected to this ultimate humiliation, and he was replaced by a succession of white soldiers. Ration cards were issued to the few civilians remaining, since Confederate money was now worthless, and the girls did what shopping they could. Since Mary Lee was an invalid, she would have missed seeing the ultimate humiliation of all, when, on April 4, only forty-eight hours after her husband had withdrawn his army from the broken Confederate lines around Petersburg, President Lincoln, looking grim and distracted, rode in an open carriage through the ghostly ruins of the former capital of the Confederacy, visiting at last the city that his army had tried to capture for four long, bloody years, and that Lee had so ably defended since June 1, 1862.

The Confederacy had begun its existence as a government without an army; it was ending as an army without a government. Lee's intention had been to concentrate his army at Amelia Court House, and "use the Richmond and Danville Railroad to transfer his army, and hurry south to unite with [General Joseph E.] Johnston and strike Sherman," then return victorious with both armies to strike at Grant.

The failing logistics of the Confederacy thwarted him—the rations he had expected to find there had not arrived, and the resulting delay enabled Grant to cut the railroad to the south. Lee was now trapped, obliged to fight his way along country back roads in the hope of reaching the railway junction at Farmville, where he still hoped to find supplies sent from Lynchburg. In three days of bitter fighting he took over 7,000 casualties, which he could ill afford; and captured over 1,000 Union officers and men, whom he could not feed. By now, exhaustion and starvation were overcoming his own men. On April 6, there took place at Sayler's Creek an event that could not fail to imprint itself on Lee's mind. All the news he received was bad. Federal cavalry was advancing parallel to his own line of march and had attacked his wagon train and set fire to many of the wagons; his flanks were unprotected; Grant and the main body of Union forces were close behind him. Lee was now ahead of most of his army. As he rode along "a high ridge leading northward to the Appomattox" to get a better look at the fighting at Sayler's Creek, he paused and drew rein at the unexpected sight of his men fleeing in panic, soldiers without their guns, groups of men in no formation without their officers—something he had never expected to live to see in the Army of Northern Virginia: a rout. "My God!" Lee exclaimed, "has the army been dissolved?" He sat there motionless on Traveller, holding in the breeze a fluttering Confederate battle flag someone had handed him, surrounded by his men, no longer part of an army, but merely exhausted fugitives halted in their flight only by his commanding presence. Some of them stood around him, perhaps out of shame, even reaching out to touch Traveller's flanks. Major General William Mahone rode up from the battlefield and sought to explain what had happened, and to reassure Lee that there were still men left who would fight—but how many? Lee, his eyes fixed on the battle below, not deigning to look at those who had thrown away their arms and run, waved his hand brusquely to the rear as if to dismiss them, and said, in a rare flash of impatience, "Yes, there are still some true men left. . . . Will you please keep those people back."

It is a pity that no painting has been made of the moment—Lee, on Traveller, holding the battle flag, which streams behind him in the breeze; the smoke of the battle below him; the shamefaced, half-starved soldiers around him. This is in some ways a finer moment than that shown in the famous mural by Charles Hoffbauer in the Virginia Historical Society, where at the center Lee sits erect and dignified on Traveller, surrounded by his generals and lit by the summer sun as if there were a halo around his head. The central panel of the Hoffbauer murals, which is called *Summer of the Confederacy*, is an imaginary scene, since it shows *all* of the South's great generals arranged neatly, mounted or on foot, on a verdant hill around Lee, who is bathed in the light of glory: a painting of an apotheosis rather than a historical moment. But Lee wrapped in the folds of the Confederate battle flag, his eyes fixed on the horizon, determined to fight on—he is reported to have said, with vehemence, "I wish to fight here"—could have been a subject as heroic and visually striking as David's *Napoleon Crossing the Alps*: the fierce old warrior, eyes flashing, clutching that symbolic flag and determined to fight on, in the presence of the ragged veterans who had, for once, failed him.

Lee did not yet know the worst of it. Most of Ewell's corps was surrounded and would surrender, and Ewell himself would be captured by the end of the day, as was Lee's oldest son, Custis, commanding a division. The next day was full of confused and bloody fighting as Lee sought to bring what remained of his army—principally Longstreet's corps and the cavalry, a total of at most 12,000 infantrymen and 3,000 cavalry troopers on horses that were in even worse shape than their riders— to Farmville, where supplies were waiting. When they got there, they found that confusion and poor staff work had prevented the destruction Lee had ordered of the one bridge remaining over the Appomattox River. Federal troops poured over it, and fighting continued into the darkness. At nightfall Lee sought shelter in a cottage near a church, and sometime between nine-thirty and ten that night a courier brought him a message sent through the lines from General Grant.

Headquarters, Armies of the United States
April 7, 1865—5 p.m.

General R. E. Lee
Commanding C. S. Army

General: The results of the last week must convince you of the hopelessness of further resistance on the part of the Army of Northern Virginia in this struggle. I feel that it is so, and regard it as my duty to shift from myself the responsibility for any further effusion of blood, by asking of you to surrender that portion of the C. S. Army known as the Army of Northern Virginia.

> Very respectfully,
> Your obedient servant,
> U. S. Grant
> Lieutenant-General
> Commanding Armies of the United States

Longstreet had joined Lee in the cottage, and Lee handed him the message. Longstreet read it, slowly and carefully, and shook his head. He handed it back. "Not yet," he said.

Considering the abuse to which Longstreet has been subjected over the years, it is interesting that Lee still wanted him close at hand, and still sought his advice. Longstreet would never sugarcoat the truth; nor would he hide his opinion from Lee, even when he knew it would annoy his commander. The Army of Northern Virginia was still fighting. There was still a hope—remote, but not unrealistic—that it might be possible to reach Lynchburg, but Longstreet's comment illustrates very clearly that both men knew by then that surrender was almost inevitable. The casualties and the rate of desertion of the past two days had convinced Lee of that, but so long as what remained of his army was fighting, Lee would not surrender.

Longstreet was the only man with whom Lee shared the letter from Grant, and Longstreet's reaction to it belies the theory that he had been reluctant to fight at Gettysburg. Now, when further resistance was hard to justify except for the sake of honor, Longstreet was determined to continue fighting. He was "competent, wise, forbearing and compassionate, Lee's friend and greatest source of strength." In the final, critical moment of the war, "He was there to back Lee up, not to pull him down," as Longstreet may or may not have said, but as he certainly did. For Lee, now, honor was paramount—not the cause of the Confederacy, which was clearly lost; not victory, which was now unthinkable; but the honor of the army he led, and of course his own, which he could trace back through generations of Lees and Carters. If there was to be an ending, it must be endured with dignity. His concept of honor was not, like that of the Japanese samurai, suicidal or self-sacrificial; nor would he have harbored vainglorious thoughts like Napoleon's* about his future place in history—he was too much a Christian for that. But he had been shocked to the core by the sight of the men—*his* men—running from the enemy. Lee knew his duty, and it is to his credit that Longstreet understood it.

Lee did not reply to Longstreet. It was now his duty to reply to Grant's letter. He wrote the message himself, in a firm, clear hand on a single sheet of paper. He did not ask his aide Marshall to write out a draft for him. Whether he discussed it with Longstreet or Marshall is not known. Marshall claims to have written out Lee's

---

*Even if he had lived long enough to do it, it is hard to imagine Lee being tempted to dictate the equivalent of the eight volumes of Napoleon's *Mémorial de Sainte-Hélène* as a giant literary monument to himself.

reply, but he may have meant that he made a copy of it for Lee's records, since the message is clearly in Lee's handwriting. Marshall also writes that there was "some discussion" of it. If so, it did not involve many people—Lee may have been reluctant to let the news leak out that he was ever so slightly opening the door to surrender, and perhaps too he was simply sure of what he wanted to write, and determined to keep it simple.

7th Apl '65

Genl

I have read your note of this date. Though not entertaining the opinion you express of the hopelessness of further resistance on the part of the Army of N. Va.—I reciprocate your desire to avoid useless effusion of blood, & therefore before considering your proposition, ask the terms you will offer on condition of its surrender

> Very respy your obt. Servt
> R. E. Lee
> Genl
> Lt. Genl. U.S. Grant
> Commd Armies of the U. States

That night the remnants of the army continued to march slowly and painfully toward Lynchburg. The Appomattox River and the Southside Railroad were on his left; the James River was on his right; his movement westward carried him into the point of a narrowing < with the bulk of Grant's army marching parallel to Lee's. Lee was running a risk that he was advancing into a trap, but he was dependent on the supply trains that had been sent on to Appomattox Station and Pamplin's Station. If he could reach those stations before the Federals, feed his men and horses, and advance in good order to Lynchburg, there was still a chance of continuing the fight farther south, and it was his duty to pursue that chance. Those who saw him remarked on his calm, confident expression, but by the afternoon of Saturday, April 8, many of those around Lee were no longer either calm or confident; in fact there seems to have been what is called in Britain a "round robin," in this case an unwritten consensus among some of Lee's generals to persuade him to surrender. Brigadier General William Pendleton was deputized to broach the subject with Lee on behalf of the others.

Longstreet dissociated himself from this attempt, though clearly he was aware of it. Lee in any case declined to accept Pendleton's suggestion, although whether as vehemently as Pendleton remembered when he came to write this conversation down is open to question. Lee may have been more embarrassed than angry—the night before, he had already asked what terms Grant would offer for the surrender of the army, and he would not have wanted to discuss the possibility of surrendering with his senior officers until he knew them. It is also possible that Lee failed to realize that his reply to Grant's letter of April 7, however carefully worded, had opened up what Winston Churchill in a later war would call the "slippery slope" of surrender negotiations.*

The different accounts of what occurred on April 8 undoubtedly derive from the fact that almost all those involved later sought to present their own behavior in the best possible light, except for Lee himself. We know what people said to him—or what they *wrote* that they said to him long after the war—but we cannot be sure what *he* said, and he made no effort to write his own account, or to correct theirs. Lee had already put his foot, however hesitantly, on the bridge Pendleton was asking him to cross, but he did not want to be dictated to by his own generals, and he was not interested in his generals' well-meaning attempt to urge him to

---

*Churchill was arguing in the war cabinet against the case Lord Halifax, then foreign secretary, was making for asking "Signor Mussolini" to inquire from Hitler what terms the *Führer* might offer for a British surrender (May 27, 1940, as quoted in John Lukas, *Five Days in London: May 1940, 149*).

surrender or to share the responsibility for it. On the contrary, he saw it as his moral and military duty to shoulder the full responsibility himself.

This may account for a certain testiness in Lee's behavior on the afternoon of April 8—he did not know what Grant would reply to his letter; he did not want the news that he had written to Grant to spread through the army and further demoralize it; and he was, as always, trying to determine where his duty lay: to fight on at the cost of more "effusion of blood," or to surrender,—and if the latter, on what terms? This may explain the abruptness, so unlike Lee, when he dismissed General Anderson, presumably for his failure at Sayler's Creek. Lee also relieved Pickett of his command, though Lee's order never reached him. Pickett had been unlucky at Gettysburg, and again at Sayler's Creek; Lee may also have felt that Pickett had been too vocal in complaining that Lee was responsible for destroying his regiment at Gettysburg. It was a question not so much of Pickett's opinion as of military discipline. He was *not* entitled to complain about his commanding officer.

On the evening of April 8 Grant's reply to Lee's letter arrived. In it he stated that peace was his great desire, and that he had only one condition: "namely, that the men and officers surrendered shall be disqualified for taking up arms against the Government of the United States, until properly exchanged." Out of courtesy, Grant made the same mistake that General Pendleton had made, by offering "to meet any officers you name" to arrange the surrender of the Army of Northern Virginia, thus sparing Lee the humiliation of surrendering in person. This was a delicate point: General Lord Cornwallis had shrunk from surrendering his army personally at Yorktown, and appointed General O'Hara to represent him. Even then O'Hara ostentatiously tried to hand his sword to the French general Count Rochambeau instead of to Washington, a discourtesy toward the American commander that Rochambeau refused to allow. Lee's father had been present on that famous occasion, and later criticized Cornwallis for deviating "from his general line of conduct, dimming the splendour of his long and brilliant career." In no circumstances would Lee ever do what his father had condemned. If it came to surrender he would do it himself, and hand his sword over to Grant.

Lee still had not made up his mind. He showed the letter to one of his aides, Colonel Charles Venable, and asked, "How would you answer that?" Venable replied, "I would answer no such letter." But that was not the advice Lee had been looking for. There was no way he could bring himself to avoid replying to Grant's letter—it was a matter not only of courtesy, but of duty. "Ah, but it must be answered," he gently reproved Venable, and sat down to do so at once. Again, he wrote in his own hand, leaving it to Marshall to make a copy.

"I received at a late hour your note of today," Lee wrote. "In mine of yesterday I did not intend to propose the surrender of the Army of N. Va—but to ask the terms of your proposition. To be frank, I do not think the emergency has arisen to call for the surrender of this Army, but as the restoration of peace should be the sole object of all, I desired to know whether your proposals would lead to that and I cannot therefore meet you with a view to surrender the Army of N. Va.—but as far as your proposal may affect the C.S. forces under my command & tend to the restoration of peace, I shall be pleased to meet you at 10 a.m. tomorrow on the old stage road to Richmond between the picket lines of the two armies."

This letter is somewhat ambiguous, and seems to have puzzled Grant when he received it. Possibly Lee was having second thoughts, still hoping that he might feed his troops and get them to Lynchburg, yet it also seems to suggest that he was open to a broader peace negotiation, not just a surrender of "the forces under my command." This was a sensitive subject for Grant, who had been rapped gently on the knuckles by Secretary of War Stanton and President Lincoln in March 1865 for passing on Lee's delicately worded suggestion that a meeting between Major General Edward Ord and Longstreet to discuss prisoner exchanges might be extended into one between himself and Grant to discuss "a military convention" with a view to reaching "a satisfactory adjustment of the present unhappy difficulties." Grant had been firmly reminded that he was to have no dealings on the subject of peace with Lee, and that any further communication must be only for the purpose of accepting the surrender of Lee's army.

If Lee was playing for time, his hopes would soon be dashed. That evening the troopers of the twenty-three-year-old Major General George Armstrong Custer reached Appomattox Station. After a fierce but brief fight, his men seized three of the seven trains. Of the others, the Confederates took three back to Farmville and burned the fourth. Thanks to Custer, Lee's hopes of feeding his army as it marched toward Lynchburg were dashed. The three trains that had escaped were now farther away, and there was some doubt that he could reach them. Lee's line was now facing south, his left anchored on a small hill to the east of Appomattox Court House, the tiny town behind his center; and to his right Fitz Lee's cavalry held high ground to the east of the town, just south of the Appomattox River.

By now Grant was ensconced in a Confederate colonel's empty house, stripped for use as a Confederate hospital. He was suffering from one of the severe migraine headaches that plagued him when he was under pressure and removed from the comforting presence of Mrs. Grant, or on occasion the bottle, and which he attempted to cure by a then conventional remedy: sitting with his feet in a tub full of hot water and mustard, and with "a mustard plaster" placed on his wrists and "the back part of his neck."

Still in pain, he roused himself in the early hours of the morning to write to Lee, pointing out that as "he had no authority to treat on the subject of peace, the meeting proposed for ten a.m. to-day could lead to no good. . . . The terms upon which peace can be had are well understood. By the South laying down their arms they will have that most desirable event, save thousands of human lives, and hundreds of millions of property not yet destroyed."

There is a slight tone of asperity in Grant's reply— perhaps as a result of his headache, perhaps because he was simply impatient to get on with the surrender. It was not like Grant to lecture anyone, let alone General Lee, but he no doubt felt he had already made the terms of surrender clear, and by now his own generals were warning him that Lee's letter might be a delaying tactic, that Lee was merely buying time for Johnston's army to arrive from North Carolina. Grant instinctively doubted this—he had a great respect for Lee's sense of honor—and understood the precise military scope of Lee's position. Lee had not yet asked for a truce; he had merely suggested a meeting to discuss the exact terms of surrender he would be offered *if* he decided to surrender. In the meantime, fighting would go on unabated. Grant had negotiated the surrender of Fort Donelson in 1862 and of Vicksburg in 1863, and the niceties of surrender negotiations were familiar to him. He was back in the saddle in the early morning of Sunday, April 9, Palm Sunday, head still throbbing, and rode on "to the head of the column," where the fighting was now intense.

Lee had spent the night bivouacked in the woods, about two miles northeast of the village of Appomattox Court House. His "ambulance and his headquarters wagons were entangled somewhere among the trains" in the chaos of retreat, so he was obliged to do without his tent and camp furniture. The glow from campfires all around him told its own story—he was surrounded by Federals. If it was only Federal cavalry in front of him, there was some hope that his infantry could push through it, and give the army time to reach Lynchburg. Late that night Lee held his last council of war. He stood in front of his own campfire in the chill of the night; Longstreet, silent and pensive, sat on a log smoking his long, curved pipe; and generals Gordon and Fitz Lee sat on a blanket. Lee gave his last orders for an attack: Fitz Lee's cavalry must try to cut a way through the enemy, supported by Gordon's infantry, while the rear guard under Longstreet held the hastily dug trenches for as long as possible against the bulk of the Federal infantry coming up behind them. They all agreed to fight on to the end so long as there remained any glimmer of hope. Longstreet was among those who were most determined to fight on.

At first light Lee rose from a brief nap. General Pendleton, his chief of artillery, was surprised to find him wearing his best uniform, a silk sash wound around his waist, his best sword with a gilded lion's head on its pommel and an ivory grip hanging from a gold-embroidered sword belt. It had been specially commissioned for him in Paris by an admiring Marylander from the swordmaker Louis François Devisme.* His

---

*Lee had numerous swords. He gave one to his youngest son, Robert E. Lee Jr., when the latter received his commission as a Confederate officer; the most elaborate was the one he wore to Appomattox, the blade inlaid in gold on one side with a quotation from Joan of Arc, *Aide-toi, Dieu t'aidera* ("Aid yourself and God will aid you"), and on the other "Gen. Robert E. Lee CSA from a Marylander 1863." Though Lee seldom wore a sword in battle, he did keep one with him throughout the war: it had belonged to George Washington and was left by him to Lee's father-in-law, Mr. Custis. If Lee was going to have to surrender his sword, it would be the fancy French-made one, not the one that had been Washington's.

knee-high cavalry boots were gleaming, he wore gold spurs with rowels, and he carried a new pair of pale gray gauntlets. "If I am to be General Grant's prisoner today I intend to make my best appearance," he said to Pendleton, perhaps in jest. Out of an army that was reduced to about 28,000 men, "the mere skeleton, the ghost of the Army of Northern Virginia," Lee now had fewer than 8,000 exhausted, emaciated infantrymen armed and fit for battle and perhaps 2,100 cavalrymen, with which to confront 80,000 Federal troops, but he was as determined to fight as ever. Fitz Lee began his attack at 5 a.m., but early morning fog concealed the action from Lee, although he could hear intense artillery and musket fire just beyond Appomattox Court House. By 8 a.m. the sounds of battle were intense, but Lee had no word of the results. He sent Colonel Venable forward, and Venable soon rode back with General Gordon's message. "Tell General Lee I have fought my corps to a frazzle, and I fear I can do nothing unless I am heavily supported by Longstreet's corps." Since Longstreet's corps was engaged heavily—and hopelessly—trying to hold off at least two Union corps to the rear, it was instantly apparent to Lee that breaking through the enemy lines was no longer possible: he was surrounded, and the enemy held higher ground on all sides. "Then there is nothing left me to do but go and see General Grant, and I would rather die a thousand deaths." Whether he said this to himself, as some accounts claim, or to his staff is not entirely clear, but there seems no reason for Lee to be talking to himself, or that he would not have been frank with his staff at this point. "Oh, General," one of them said, "what will history say of the surrender of the army in the field?"

Lee's answer was typical: that history would doubtless have "hard things to say of us," though this has not in fact proved to be the case, and that if it was the right thing to do he would "take all the responsibility."

Lee wanted one more opinion: he sent for Longstreet, and briefly explained the situation. The two men were dismounted, standing in front of the embers of a fire built from fence rails. Longstreet later recorded that Lee's "brave bearing failed to conceal his profound depression," but with the blunt common sense that always made his opinion valuable to Lee, Longstreet asked the question nobody else dared to pose. Could "the bloody sacrifice of his army in any way help the cause in other quarters?" Lee thought not, and Longstreet replied, "Then your situation speaks for itself."

Lee was still reluctant to make the final move, and sent for Major General William Mahone. It was a cold morning, and Mahone was shivering. He stirred up the embers with his foot, and said he didn't want

Lee to think that he was scared; he was just chilled. Lee nodded—it probably would never have occurred to him that Mahone might be scared. Mahone was talkative too, and asked Lee more questions than Longstreet thought were necessary. With the menacing, bulky General Longstreet glaring at him to get to the point, Mahone finally gave his opinion. It was time for Lee to see General Grant.

Brigadier General Edward Porter Alexander, Longstreet's young chief of artillery, appeared. Lee took the trouble to peel the bark off a felled oak so as not to soil his best uniform, and sat down with him. Alexander was in favor of fighting on, and when Lee gently disabused him of that idea, he suggested that the men "be ordered to scatter in the woods & bushes & either to rally upon Gen. Johnston in North Carolina, or to make their way, each man to his own state, with his arms & report to the governor." He supposed that two-thirds of the army would do so, "like rabbits and partridges in the bushes, and they [the Union Army] could not scatter to follow us." Lee was not only skeptical of this proposition but actively opposed to it. Though Alexander would later deny that what he had in mind was guerrilla warfare, this was what such a move would have produced. Lee was a supremely well-trained career officer and had the professional's dislike of guerrilla warfare in all its forms; he compared it to "bushwhacking," which would turn the South into a prewar "bloody Kansas" on a much larger scale. The last thing Lee wanted was to see his men scattered in the bushes like rabbits and partridges, taking potshots at Federal troops, and he had no doubt about the bloody reprisals that would follow. The man who had captured John Brown and helped to secure the site of his hanging did not want to spawn hundreds or thousands of southern equivalents of Brown, from which "it would take the country years to recover." Kindly, but firmly, he put the idea out of Alexander's mind altogether. Lee intended to surrender his army in good order, a formal, disciplined surrender of every man, and of every man's weapon. No decision Lee made on April 9 was more important for the future of the South than this—his example would bring the war to an end and put an end to the fighting. No suggestion could have made Lee more determined to get on with what he was so reluctant to do than Alexander's.

Lee had not yet received Grant's message telling him that the meeting Lee had proposed for 10 a.m. "would do no good," since Grant had no authority "to treat on the subject of peace." He mounted Traveller at about half past eight in the morning, and rode toward Longstreet's front line. Sergeant Tucker, the chief courier of the Third Corps, rode in front, followed by Lee's aides colonels Marshall and Taylor, and then, riding alone, Lee. The men cheered him as he passed, though it must have surprised them to see the little party ride through the breastworks that Longstreet's men had built, and then on toward the enemy's line, down "the old stage road to Richmond." After a while, Lee saw a line of Federal skirmishers advancing toward them. Sergeant Tucker raised a white flag and he and Colonel Marshall rode on down the road, expecting to find a member of Grant's staff, or even Grant himself, waiting. Instead, after a pause, a Federal officer appeared and presented them with Grant's letter, which Marshall took back to Lee, who read it carefully.

This was perhaps the most alarming moment of the day for Lee. With every moment that passed his army was being surrounded more tightly, by larger numbers; he had neither asked for nor been granted a truce; and he, the commanding officer, was now half a mile ahead of his own front line, in range of Federal skirmishers. To retreat would be humiliating, to advance an invitation to be shot. He was dictating a reply to Grant when he heard a horse galloping furiously toward him. A Confederate officer, Lieutenant Colonel John Haskell, passed by him, unable to stop his horse, then turned the heaving animal around to give Lee the message from Longstreet that he had found an escape route. But Lee had passed beyond such thoughts. A road that might allow a few cavalrymen to escape would not be large enough for his whole army,* and in any case he was now determined to surrender that army complete and intact, in good order, and with dignity. Lee rebuked the officer for overriding his mare: "Oh, why did you do it?" he asked. "You have killed your beautiful horse." Then he resumed his dictation, hurrying Marshall on as the sound of firing began to increase on all sides. If fighting resumed, Lee knew that given the disparity of forces and the closeness of the enemy, it would be a bloody last stand, from which there was nothing to be gained. He had now dropped his previous hesitation and qualifications. His note to Grant was short, and to the point.

April 9th 1865

General,

I received your note of this morning on the picket line whither I had come to meet you and ascertain definitely what terms were embraced in your proposal of yesterday with reference to the

---

*Lee was right to be doubtful; he soon received a message from Fitz Lee that the previous communication about a route of escape was in error.

surrender of this army. I now request an interview
in accordance with the offer contained in your
letter of yesterday for that purpose.

> Very respectfully,
> Your obt. Servt
> R. E. LEE
> Lt. Gen. U. S. Grant
> Cmmdg U. S. Armies

This was the message that Grant had been waiting
for since Lee's letter of April 7. The moment he received
it, at about eleven o'clock in the morning, his headache
vanished: "the instant I saw the contents of the note
I was cured," he wrote. He quickly dictated a message
back to Lee that he would "push" forward to the front
to meet him, and that Lee should choose the place for
the interview. It was unusually generous, and a breach
of military tradition, to allow the party *requesting* a
surrender to choose the place—but then Grant hardly
knew where he was ("about four miles West of Walker's
Church" was the best he could tell Lee). Appomattox
Court House was behind the Confederate lines, and he
had no clear idea how to get there. Grant, accompanied by a small staff, would have to ride down muddy
back roads while fighting was still going on, in country
where a Confederate sharpshooter would hardly pass

up the opportunity for a shot at the Federal commanding general. One of his staff warned that it would be
a bad idea to shorten the distance by cutting through
fields and lots where he Grant might expose himself to
"men conspicuous in gray," and thought that it would
be "a very awkward condition . . . if Grant became a
prisoner in Lee's lines instead of Lee in his."

None of these thoughts seems to have occurred to
Grant now that his migraine had passed; nor did he
know that Lee was in a similarly dangerous position. Lee was still sitting on Traveller in what would
be called no-man's-land, and it was becoming apparent that the Federals intended to attack toward just
the spot where Lee and his party sat on their horses.
A Union officer rode through his own skirmish line to
ask the Confederate party to withdraw, and Lee used
the opportunity to send another hastily penciled note to
Grant, this time asking for "a suspension of hostilities,"
in other words, a truce. Before it could reach Grant a
Federal officer informed Lee that the attack could not
be delayed and warned him to withdraw. Obliged to
ride back through his own lines, he sent his final note
of the day to Grant. Lee dismounted and lay down to
rest under an apple tree in a small orchard, until his
aide Colonel Taylor finally brought him the news that
Major General Meade had agreed to a formal truce

until two o'clock. Shortly after noon a Federal officer, Colonel Orville E. Babcock of Grant's staff, and his orderly, accompanied by a Confederate officer, rode over and dismounted, handing Lee Grant's letter, which said that Grant was on the way to meet him.

Longstreet thought that Lee had never looked grander or more impressive than he did at that moment. Lee worried that the delay might cause Grant to impose harsher terms, but Longstreet, an old friend of Grant's, thought not. In any case, the next move was up to Lee. He rode to Appomattox Court House, pausing at a small stream to let Traveller drink, accompanied by Marshall, Taylor, Babcock and his orderly, and Sergeant Tucker, in search of an appropriate place for what would become the most famous meeting in American history. Marshall was sent ahead to make a selection—the choice was not a wide one. Major Wilmer McLean showed him around the village. The first place they saw was a bare shell of a house with no furniture, which Marshall thought was unsuitable. McLean then offered his own home, a modest but handsomely furnished little redbrick house with white trim and a big front porch. By an extraordinary coincidence Major Wilmer McLean's farm had been part of the battlefield at the First Battle of Manassas, and he had moved to Appomattox so his family would not be further exposed to the war. Now, as was so often the case, the war had caught up with him. McLean would later remark that the war started in his backyard and ended in his parlor. In any case, Marshall accepted his offer, then rode back to Lee's party.

Colonel Taylor "had no heart for being present at the surrender," and Lee, with his usual magnanimity toward his staff, let him off the hook, taking only Colonel Marshall, who had borrowed a decent sword, a pair of gauntlets, and a clean shirt collar for the occasion. Lee, his orderly, Colonel Marshall, Colonel Babcock, and Sergeant Tucker dismounted in the yard in front of the house, and Tucker took the horses off to let them graze. Lee climbed the six wide wooden steps up to the porch— one can imagine with what reluctance—entered the hall, turned left into the parlor, and nodded his approval.

The McLean house has been painstakingly reconstructed since then—at one time it was taken to pieces, with the idea of reassembling it in Washington, D.C., as a Civil War museum. The parlor, or "front room," is handsome, but very small. Marshall records that he, Lee, and Babcock sat there for about half an hour. Babcock's orderly was sent out to meet Grant on the road outside. Marshall, who was in the room, reports that he, Lee, and Babcock "talked in the most friendly and affable way." There must have been a certain amount of coming and going to create an appropriate mise-en-scène for the surrender. The furniture is heavy, bulky, and overstuffed; a handsome, imposing fold-down desk stands to the right of the big fireplace that dominates the room. The sofa and easy chairs that were grouped around it are missing, both in contemporary prints, drawings, and paintings of the surrender, and in its present form. Somebody—perhaps Major McLean's house servants—must have either removed some of the furniture or pushed it against the walls. Two small tables were placed on either side of the parlor: the one on the left a marble-topped side table, with a handsome wicker armchair behind it; the one on the right a smaller mahogany side table, behind which was placed the large leather upholstered swivel chair taken from the desk. Only a couple of small, formal chairs remain, and neither of them looks comfortable or inviting. Lee may have sat, but it seems unlikely that Marshall and Babcock did.

At about one-thirty they heard the clatter of many hooves. As he rode, Grant had been gathering those whom he wanted to attend the surrender. Lee, Marshall, and Babock rose, and General Grant entered the room, removing his plain, "dark-yellow" string gloves. He was embarrassed by what has been called his "private's uniform," which was creased, rumpled, and splattered with mud, as well as by the fact that he was not wearing a sword, having ridden in straight from the field. In fact, Grant never wore a soldier's uniform, though he stuck to that claim in his memoirs—a natural claim for a general turned politician, who knew more voters were privates than generals.* Grant wore a plain uniform coat with two rows of gilt buttons, worn open, and ending above the knees; a waistcoat with smaller gilt buttons; and a white shirt and collar with a narrow black bow tie. He wore on each shoulder a simple bar, bordered in a single, thin line of gold braid, bearing the three stars of a lieutenant general. His black uniform hat, rather like a modern Stetson, with a gold embroidered hat cord ending in two small gilt "acorns" in front, was standard issue for general officers. Grant, even at his best, was not a "dressy" general, and the contrast between him and Lee in his best uniform must have been striking. At any rate it struck Grant, who apologized for his "rough garb" and lack of a sword. Lee was also at least five inches taller than Grant, with the erect carriage of a cavalry officer, while Grant was a natural "sloucher." From appearances, it might have seemed to a stranger that Grant was about to surren-

---

*General Dwight D. Eisenhower too preferred to wear a simple "battledress," without decorations—in fact, the short waist-length jacket he favored was known as an "Eisenhower jacket" in World War II. It drew a contrast between himself and more "showy" generals like Patton or MacArthur.

der to Lee, rather than the other way around. Grant described the moment perfectly in his memoirs: "What General Lee's feelings were I do not know. As he was a man of much dignity, with an impassible face, it was impossible to say whether he felt inwardly glad that the end had finally come, or felt sad over the result, and was too manly to show it." Another observer wrote that Lee's "demeanor was that of a thoroughly possessed gentleman, who had a very disagreeable duty to perform, but was determined to get through it as well and as soon as he could."

There was a brief moment of embarrassment because while Grant remembered him from the Mexican War, Lee could not "recall a single feature" of Grant's. Nevertheless, they chatted amicably for several minutes, while about a dozen Federal officers entered the parlor and stood against the walls. Some of these Lee knew by sight, including generals Sheridan and Ord. He may have been a little surprised by the presence of Grant's secretary Lieutenant Colonel Ely Parker, a full-blooded Seneca Indian, whom he apparently supposed was black until Parker was introduced to him. "I am glad to see at least one real American here," Lee said politely. Parker replied with equal politeness, "We are all Americans, sir." Lee seems to have had no objection to being put on display, as it were—he and his secretary

Lieutenant Colonel Marshall were the only Confederate officers in the small room.

Grant and Lee continued to chat for some time about Mexico—it may have been a relief for them both to talk about the past, rather than the present. In fact Grant found the conversation so "pleasant" that he almost forgot what they were there for until Lee, in Grant's words, "called [his] attention to the object of our meeting." Grant still seems to have been reluctant to get down to business, but finally said in a soft voice, "The terms I propose are those stated substantially in my letter of yesterday—that is the officers and men surrendered to be paroled and disqualified from taking up arms again until properly exchanged, and all arms, ammunition and supplies to be delivered up as captured property."

Lee nodded, and after a brief exchange, he suggested that Grant "commit to writing" the terms he had proposed. At this point, both men sat down, Lee placed his hat and gloves neatly on the marble-topped table; his military secretary Marshall stood against the fireplace, behind Lee's left shoulder. Grant sat at the smaller of the two tables. The two men did not quite face each other. Lee was seated so as to face directly ahead toward the door; Grant was seated so as to look at Lee's left profile. There was no great space between the two tables, and with the Union officers standing around the two seated men it must have been difficult for Lee to sit motionless before an audience of his enemies, all staring at him, while he looked toward the door with dignity and composure. Grant called for his "order-book"; lit a pipe; scribbled away for a few minutes with pencil, pausing a couple of times to make a correction or add a sentence; then looked up. Lee's sword caught his eye—it was far and away the most handsome one in the room. Grant paused again, added a few lines, then asked Parker to look the draft over. Parker made a few small corrections, and returned it to Grant, who rose and carried the order book over to Lee. Taking his reading glasses from his pocket, Lee polished them carefully with a handkerchief, placed them on his nose, and began to read.

Appomattox C.H., Va.
Apr. 9th, 1865.

Gen. R. E. Lee,
Comd. C. S. A.
Gen.

In accordance with the substance of my letter to you of the 8th instant I propose to receive the surrender of the Army of N. Va. on the following terms, to-wit: Rolls of all the officers and men to be made in duplicate, one copy to be given to an officer designated by me, the other to be retained by such officer or officers as you may designate. The officers to give their individual paroles not to take up arms against the Government of the United States until properly [sic] and each company or regimental commander sign a like parole for the men of their command. . . .

Lee perused the text slowly and carefully. After turning to the second page, he looked up and said to Grant: "After the words 'until properly,' the word 'exchanged' seems to be omitted. You doubtless intended to use that word?"

"Why, yes," answered Grant, "I thought I had put in the word 'exchanged.'"

"I presumed it had been omitted inadvertently, and with your permission I will mark where it should be inserted."

"Certainly."

Lee did not have a pencil on him, or perhaps he had one but could not find it, but Brigadier General Porter, to whom we owe the most accurate version of the surrender, leaned over and handed him his. Lee thanked him, made the correction, and continued reading.

The arms, artillery and public property to be parked and stacked and turned over to the officer appointed by me to receive them.

This will not embrace the side arms of the officers, nor their private horses or baggage. This done each officer and man will be allowed to return to their homes not to be disturbed by United States authority so long as they observe their paroles and the laws in force where they may reside.

Very respectfully,
U. S. GRANT, Lt *Gl*

Having read the terms, Lee became more relaxed. They were what he had hoped for; he could hardly have expected more generous terms. "This will have a very happy effect on my army," he said, referring to the words Grant had added about Confederate officers being allowed to retain their sidearms (pistols and swords), horses and personal property. After a brief hesitation Lee brought up his only objection— Confederate artillerists and cavalrymen owned their own horses, he pointed out. Could the terms be altered so that they too could retain them?

But Grant either could not or would not amend what he had written. He had written the words about

Confederate officers after Lee's sword caught his eye, but he did not want to extend them to soldiers and noncommissioned officers. The idea that "private soldiers" each owned their horse was "new" to him, he said, and as a onetime farmer himself, albeit a failed one, he understood the importance that draft horses would play in resuming agriculture in the South. He understood that most of the men in Lee's army were "small farmers," as he had once been himself, and he agreed that "it was doubtful whether they will be able to put in a crop to carry themselves and their families through the next winter without the aid of the horses they are now riding." Grant said he would not change his text, but he would instruct his officers to let any men who claimed to own a horse or a mule to take it home with them "to work their little farms." Grant could have said nothing more likely to aid the restoration of peace between the North and South, or more gratifying to Lee.

Since Colonel Parker had the best handwriting among the Union officers present—he was a graduate of Rensselaer College, was a civil engineer, and would have been a lawyer too, except that Indians were not yet American citizens—Grant ordered him to write out two copies in ink. In the meantime Lee ordered Colonel Marshall to draft a reply. While he was doing so Grant introduced his officers to Lee, who spoke only to Brevet Major General Seth Williams, an old friend from the Mexican War and from the period when Lee had been superintendent of West Point. By this time there was a crowd of Union officers outside the McLean house, including the "boy general" Brevet Major General George Armstrong Custer.* The McLean house turned out to contain no paper, and the "stoneware inkstand" on Major McLean's desk was empty. Colonel Marshall was obliged to borrow a few sheets of paper from Colonel Parker, and in return produced from his pocket a "small boxwood inkstand." Lee mentioned to Grant that he had 1,000 Union prisoners, and no provisions for them, nor for his own men. He was badly in need "of both rations and forage." It must have cost a man as proud as Lee a lot to make this plea, but Grant responded quickly, offering to make 25,000 rations available immediately, though he had no forage for Lee's horses.

---

*Custer has since been painted into the group in the McLean parlor by several artists, but he was not in fact there. The surrender is not just an iconic moment in American history; it has also become encrusted with legend, and there is even a notable parody, James Thurber's If Grant Had Been Drinking at Appomattox. Not only was Custer not in the room where the surrender was signed; he also did not ride off bearing on his head the table on which Grant signed the fair copy of his letter to Lee, as Evan S. Connell claims in Son of the Morning Star. General Sheridan in fact bought the table for $20 (U.S.) from Wilmer McLean and later gave it to Mrs. Custer. It is known as "the Ark of the Covenant of the Civil War." General Ord paid McClean $40 (U.S.) for the table Lee used. Grant's table is now in the Smithsonian, Lee's in the Chicago Historical Society's Civil War room. Since the collapse of the Confederate dollar left McLean penniless, these were both significant amounts to him.

"I think it will be ample," Lee said. "And it will be a great relief, I assure you."

Lee's sword apparently continued to catch Grant's eye, and he apologized for not wearing his. A little before four o'clock the surrender was complete. Lee shook hands with Grant in the center of the parlor, and the entire room moved out onto the porch, where Lee signaled to Sergeant Tucker to bring up Traveller. "While the animal was being bridled the general stood on the lowest step and gazed sadly in the direction of the valley beyond where his army lay—now an army of prisoners. He smote his hands together a number of times in an absent sort of way; seemed not to see the group of Union officers in the yard who rose respectfully at his approach; and appeared unconscious of everything about him. . . . The approach of his horse seemed to recall him from his reverie, and at once he mounted. General Grant now stepped down from the porch, and moving towards him, saluted him by raising his hat. He was followed in this act of courtesy by all our officers present; Lee raised his hat respectfully, and rode off to break the news to the brave fellows he had so long commanded."

Chapter 12
Apotheosis—
1865–1870

I t seldom happens in history that one man comes
not only to embody but to glorify a defeated cause.
More exceptionally still, Robert E. Lee would become
a *national*, not just a southern hero: a U.S. Navy bal-
listic missile submarine of the *George Washington* class
would be named after him; his face would appear on
a U.S. thirty-cent postage stamp, a U.S. Army tank
(the M3 Lee, very popular with the British Army in
the Western Desert of North Africa in 1941 and 1942)
would be named after him; and his American citizenship would be posthumously restored to him by
President Gerald Ford in 1975.* It is hard to think of

---

*The Virginia Department of Motor Vehicles offers car owners a "Robert E. Lee
Commemorative License Plate" with Lee's picture to the left of the plate, and the
words "The Virginia Gentleman, General Robert E. Lee, 1807–1870" imprinted on it.

any other general who had fought against his own country being so completely reintegrated into national life, or becoming so universally admired even by those who have little or no sympathy toward the cause for which he fought. This process began almost instantly after the surrender.

There was a short period of discomposure when Lee rode through the ranks of his own troops back to the apple orchard outside Appomattox Court House, and dismounted. He was surprised to find himself an object of curiosity, with Federal officers coming forward to introduce themselves, or just to stare at him as if he were "a lion" in a zoo. His staff officers saw that he was in a rage at this invasion of his privacy, and he could not prevent his cheeks from turning red, but he held himself in control until he could make his escape. By the next day, he had recovered his equanimity. He set Colonel Marshall to drafting his farewell address to his army; and hearing that General Grant wished to pay his respects, he mounted Traveller and rode off at once to meet Grant in a field between the two armies—he may not have wanted Grant to see the extent to which the Army of Northern Virginia was lacking in everything from shoes and clothing to food. The two generals talked for over half an hour without dismounting, their staffs at a respectful distance. Grant gently urged

Lee to advise the other armies of the Confederacy to surrender, but this was exactly the political role that Lee never wanted—he politely insisted that he could not do such a thing without first consulting his president, and Grant recognized that "there was no use to urge him to do anything against his ideas of what was right." Both men realized that with Lee's surrender, the war was to all intents and purposes over. The Confederacy had lost its capital and its major army; its president* and its major political figures were in flight; its currency was worthless.

Later that day, General Meade rode over to Lee's camp, and the two opponents at Gettysburg chatted amicably in Lee's tent, Lee joshing Meade about the gray in his beard, and Meade rejoining that Lee was responsible for putting most of it there. Lee seems to have relaxed now that he was back in his own quarters and meeting senior officers and friends from the past, rather than being gawked at by strangers in uniform. Like Grant and Meade, Lee was a product of West Point—rank, seniority, and the respect due to a senior officer were as important to him as to any other West Pointer, never mind what uniform he wore.

---

*Some confusion has been caused in accounts of Lee's surrender by the fact that when he referred to "the president" he was of course referring to Jefferson Davis, not to Lincoln.

Lee signed his parole on April 9, and he remained in camp until April 12 while the army handed over its weapons and disbanded. He then left for Richmond, accompanied for the first few miles by an honor guard of Federal cavalrymen. He spent the night of April 12 camped in the woods a few miles from Buckingham Court House—where a sign on the road now reads "THE HISTORIC VILLAGE at Lee Wayside." He was still not willing to give up his tent and accept invitations to spend the night indoors, and was embarrassed by the attention and gifts of food he received, though he gratefully accepted oats for Traveller. At some point the next day Traveller cast a shoe, so Lee was obliged to spend the night at Flanagan's Mill waiting for his horse to be shod. His "stopping place" is now marked by another roadside historical plaque. The next night he pitched his tent at Windsor, the Powhatan County home of his brother Charles Carter Lee. In the morning, Lee was joined by his son Rooney and his nephew John, and they rode on toward Richmond, in a party of about twenty, followed by Lee's headquarters wagons and ambulance. A witness described Lee as he neared home: "His steed was bespattered with mud . . . the horseman sat his horse like a master; his face was ridged with self-respecting grief; his garments were worn in the service and stained with travel. . . . Even in the fleeting moment of his passing my gate, I was awed by his incomparable dignity." Lee had on his gray campaign uniform, with a plain sword that had once belonged to George Washington. Once he reached home he would never wear a sword again.

The Richmond he rode through was a ruined city, the streets reduced to mere tracks made through the rubble and cinders of the fire that had destroyed so much of it. Passersby cheered him as he rode toward 707 Franklin Street, and he acknowledged their cheers with grave dignity. Before the house, he dismounted and handed Traveller's reins to one of his orderlies, then opened the gate in the wrought iron fence and walked up the steps between the Doric stone porch columns and stepped inside, to start a new life.

He did not give up his uniform, and would not do so for some time. Mathew Brady, the famous photographer, who was a relentless celebrity hunter as well as a great artist, photographed Lee on his back porch only twenty-four hours after his return to Richmond. People had warned Brady that it was "preposterous" to suppose Lee would pose for him at such a moment, but Brady was a man of considerable persuasive powers, and he had photographed Lee before, the first time in 1845. He thought it would be a "historic" image, and apparently Lee agreed: he let Brady take six photographs, in an era when each sitting involved a long period of remaining perfectly motionless. In the mid-nineteenth century having oneself photographed was still a formal and serious occasion. In one of Brady's photographs, Lee stands in the doorway looking defiant, still wearing his colonel's stars and Confederate buttons, but without a sword. In another he sits outside in an upholstered easy chair taken from the house, his gray hat in his lap, his expression distant, perhaps even anguished, with his son Major General Custis ("Boo") Lee standing on his right and his aide Colonel Taylor on his left. It may be that Lee's civilian clothes had long since been lost. Three months later he was still wearing his old Confederate gray uniform, but by then without the stars and the gilt buttons, and with a different hat. His transition to civilian dress evidently took some time, as it did with countless less famous Confederate veterans.

If Lee's expression looks shell-shocked in some of Brady's photographs, it is not surprising. In a matter of days, he had gone from being the commander of all the armies of the Confederacy to a man with nothing to do, besides which he had become an involuntary tourist attraction. Curiosity seekers obliged him to take his walks at night; a constant stream of callers sought his help, blessing, sympathy, or advice. He had already become the symbol of the defeated Confederacy, whether he wished to or not.

Happy as he was to be back among his family, Lee suffered all the privations of that period in the South. The most ordinary of staples, like sugar, tea, and flour, were in short supply or unobtainable; the Confederate currency was (as noted above) worthless; the victorious North was in no hurry to feed the defeated South. Lee's house was crowded; his wife was virtually bedridden; their daughters Mildred and Agnes were exhausted by trying to look after so many people; and Lee himself struggled with self-reproach and grief, his face, as many observed, as deeply marked as if he had aged overnight: "The sorrows of the South were the burden of [the rest of] his life."

Yet Lee was only fifty-eight years old, an active man—his advice to all those who sought it was to find work and begin the process of rebuilding, and he did not exempt himself. He encouraged his son Rooney to return to his ruined plantation, White House, and begin farming. Rooney was soon joined by his brother Rob, and Lee clearly needed to find an occupation for himself. The Lees were fortunate, in the sense that the boys still owned properties, which could be farmed, left to them by their grandfather, and that Lee still retained bonds that produced a modest income, though not enough for the family's needs in Richmond. Their house had been rented by Custis Lee from a Mr. John Stewart—an admiring and sympathetic landlord who urged Lee to remain in the house "as long as your convenience leads you to stay in Richmond," and refused to accept any payment, unless it were "made in Confederate dollars," which in effect made the house rent-free. Lee was not one to accept this kind of generosity, however well meant; nor did he want to stay on in Richmond indefinitely. He was not a city person to begin with, and he felt strongly that Mary Lee would be better off away from the ruins of Richmond and the constant presence of a Federal garrison. She was vastly more embittered by the Union victory than her husband was. Once Lee had surrendered, he accepted Federal rule and its consequences; his "submission to civil authority" was genuine. He took every step that was required of him to seek a pardon, and it was through no fault of his that it was delayed by 110 years, but Mary Lee's feelings toward the North were less forgiving. She still felt that the Confederacy was a holy cause, and Lee feared the consequences of keeping her in what amounted to an occupied city, quite aside from the danger of sickness and contagion there during the summer months.

He thought at first of someplace near White House, but Rooney wrote back to say that the countryside around the charred ruins of the Custis house was devastated by three years of fighting and Federal occupation, not to speak of the effect that the blackened brick chimney, which was all that remained of the house where George Washington had wooed and married Martha Dandridge Custis, would have on his mother. Lee was apparently not convinced, and toward the end of May he decided to see for himself. He rode Traveller past the fields where his army had fought in 1862 and again in 1864, modest places whose names had become famous—Mechanicsville, Gaines's Mill, the Chickahominy River, Cold Harbor. Getting out into the countryside on Traveller was part of Lee's healing process. He may not have known this, but he discovered it en route—the horse, the farms, the familiar roads, the friends who came to see him when he spent the night at the home of his dashing young cousin Colonel Thomas Carter, whose guns had supported Pickett's Charge in 1863, all combined to put the grim reality of Richmond out of his mind for the moment. He had no desire to revisit old battlefields; he enjoyed a sumptuous family dinner in the old antebellum Virginia style, attended by his sons Rooney and Rob, and played with small children for the first time in years; he was among people who wanted nothing from him and did not treat him as a curiosity or an idol. At the same time, he saw at once that Rooney was right: this was not the place to seek a home for himself and Mary. There were too many reminders of the war, too many ghosts, too many battlefields along the Pamunkey River to make this a good choice, but he also understood that his impulse had been right, and that to regain his own balance he must get out of Richmond and seek peace and quiet in which to decide what to do with the rest of his life, for Lee was never a man who could be idle.

While Lee was at Pampatike, Thomas Carter's house, he learned that full amnesty and pardon were to be offered to all except a few former Confederates on the condition that they take an oath to support the government and the constitution of the United States. Lee cannot have been surprised that he was among those excepted, but reading the proclamation he discovered that he was entitled to make an individual application for pardon, and two weeks later he did so, having ascertained that General Grant would be happy to endorse Lee's letter to President Johnson, and bring it to the president's attention. This was a more momentous decision than it sounds. While Lee made no public declaration of the fact that he had sought a pardon, it soon became known. His willingness to submit to Federal authority served as an example, to other Confederates to do likewise. Now that the war was over, he felt strongly that the sooner the Union was fully restored—and accepted in the South—the better for everyone. Once again, in his own quiet way, Lee was acting as a leader for all who had fought for the Confederacy. If *he* could apply for a pardon, few other men could reasonably be so proud as to refuse, and he thus took the first step in bringing about the reconciliation of North and South.

In Lee's case, his application for a special pardon was complicated by the fact that a Federal judge was seeking to indict him for treason—an attempt which Grant tried to "quash," since it was in conflict with the surrender terms he had written—and the outcome was that the application was "spiked" by some bureaucrat. Lee himself had predicted that "we must expect procrastination in measures of relief." He was certainly right—it would take more than 100 years before his pardon was finally signed and his American citizenship restored.

In the meantime, by one of those happy accidents that occurred so frequently in Lee's domestic arrangements, his decision to leave Richmond was solved for him when a wealthy widow offered him a cottage on her extensive 3,000–acre plantation, Oakland, about fifty miles west of the city, on the south bank of the James River. Mrs. Elizabeth Cocke promptly followed up her letter by journeying to Richmond herself to talk to Mrs. Lee, who was quickly won over to the idea, no doubt to Lee's relief. Better still, Oakland could be reached by river and by canal, sparing Mrs. Lee the pain and fatigue of a journey of that length by road. This was a part of the state that had not been fought over by the opposing armies, nor totally denuded of forage and crops, and it seemed to Lee an excellent opportunity to get his wife and his three daughters out of the city.

As usual, Lee did not waste time once he had made up his mind to accept Mrs. Cocke's offer and Mary Lee had agreed to it. He did not, apparently, consult his daughters, whose enthusiasm for the move was a good deal less than their mother's. Mary Coulling, in her book *The Lee Girls*, points out that Lee's daughters, like so many women in the South, had experienced four years of hardship during the virtual absence of their father and their brothers. Whatever Lee might suppose, they were no longer his "little girls." They had nursed their invalid mother; lived through the death of their sister Annie; shared with Agnes the shock of Orton Williams's hanging and their wounded brother Rooney's kidnapping by a Federal raiding party; lost their home; learned to cope with household tasks that for much of their life had been performed without question by slaves; and gone out after the burning of much of Richmond to seek for enough food to sustain the family, through streets that were full of enemy soldiers, angry fleeing Confederates, and freed slaves. They were spared, by their name alone, the extremes of humiliation and desperation that many women experienced on farms that were overrun or burned out by Federal columns, and where the "lady of the house" was left to fend for herself without any adult male to protect her, and with a dwindling workforce of slaves—who were likely to run off or to turn surly and rebellious—to farm the land. Behind the glamorous make-believe of *Gone with the Wind* there was a brutal reality: southern women, rich and poor alike, were left to save what could be saved from the disaster of war and defeat, to scrape out a living from the neglected land, to endure occupation, and to make decisions that had hitherto been made by a husband or a father. Those families who had money in a bank lost it when the Confederate dollar became worthless, and those who had counted slaves as part of their capital could no longer do so. Federal occupation was not as benign as it has been portrayed by many northerners, and even small restrictions grated on southern sensibilities, as a constant reminder of defeat.

Once he returned to Richmond from Appomattox, Lee had been in the habit of giving a uniform button to his daughters' friends who asked for one as a souvenir; but after a Federal order forbade the wearing of Confederate buttons, he stopped, worried that they might get into trouble. He himself thought it necessary to inquire from the Federal provost marshal of Richmond whether he required permission to leave the city. The Federal sentry outside the door of 707 Franklin Street began to seem like an intrusion, rather than a gesture of protection or respect. Coulling properly describes the atmosphere in the city as "oppressive."

The Lee girls were of course better off than many, perhaps better off than most, but the war years had been traumatic for them too, and now they were being taken away from friends and whatever amenities the city still afforded to live in a house they had never seen, with no certain future in view. Nor were they really "girls" any more. Mary Custis, the eldest, was thirty; Agnes was twenty-four; Mildred, was nineteen. The fact that "his girls" were now young women did not change Lee's views about their behavior or his belief that they belonged at home helping their mother and keeping him company until such time as, subject to his approval, they married. As for "the girls," it cannot have escaped their attention that where they were going "there would be an ample supply of fresh vegetables, but few visitors." They were unlikely to find at Derwent, the secluded country cottage Mrs. Cocke had offered Lee, any suitable young men. It is therefore not surprising that no sooner had Mary Custis arrived there than she left for Staunton, to stay with relatives.

Lee had sent his eldest son, Custis, on ahead to ride Traveller to Oakland, while he, Mary, and their three daughters took the James River and Kanawha Canal packet boat, which was hauled by draft horse on the towpath—a slow journey in a day when people had grown used to the speed of a railway train. The canal had been a favorite scheme of the young George Washington, the idea being to link the James River and the Ohio River and thereby open up what was then "the West." It was a major public works project of his presidency, and was still far from completion. It had been dug, at considerable expense, by the labor of slaves, and travel on that part which had been finished was slowed by the number of locks along the way. Washington had left a considerable portion of his shares in the canal company to a then obscure college in Lexington, Virginia, in the Shenandoah Valley, named Liberty Hall Academy, which in gratitude for the gift renamed itself Washington College.

Although travel on the canal boats has sometimes been described as idyllic it seems to have been nothing of the sort. The constant clatter of hooves and snorting of the draft horse, and the frequent, noisy stops as locks were laboriously filled and then opened, made sleep difficult; and the quarters below were cramped and hot (Mary Coulling describes them as "tiny" and "stifling"). After the evening meal a curtain was drawn to separate men and women. It speaks volumes that Lee, who was accustomed to Spartan living, chose to sleep on deck.

The packet arrived at Pemberton Wharf shortly after dawn, and the Lees were met by Custis, riding Traveller; and by one of Mrs. Cocke's sons, Edmund. Mrs. Lee had to be carried off the boat and into a carriage for the short trip to Oakland, where they were to stay for a week while Derwent was being readied for them. Oakland had all the comforts of a Virginia mansion—Federal raiding parties had reached it but had not stripped or vandalized the house—and Lee visibly relaxed there. During that week a revealing incident occurred. While the Lees and the Cocke family were at table, Mrs. Cocke's butler, a former slave, entered the dining room "to say farewell as he was leaving to try his fortune as a freedman." Lee rose from the table and shook the man's hand "cordially," interrupting his meal to give the man advice, and "asked Heaven to bless him."

Not every southerner in those days would have shaken a black man's hand—Lee was to bring a gasp of surprise to onlookers several times by doing so—still less give his blessing to the departure of a man who had been the property of his hostess until only a few weeks ago. In racial relationships, as in other matters, Lee set an example of warmth, sympathy, kindness, and dignity. That did not, it should be noted, change his opinion about blacks. Only a few weeks before, while visiting Colonel Thomas Carter at Pampatike, he had advised his cousin not to depend for labor on his former slaves. "I have always observed," Lee told him, "that wherever you find the Negro, everything is going down around him, and wherever you find the white man, you see everything around him improving." Lee's view of blacks had always been at once benevolent and skeptical. He had not enjoyed owning slaves, either his family's or those Mrs. Lee had inherited from her father, and he had broken what was then Virginia law by setting up a school for them. Following Mr. Custis's will to the letter, Lee had emancipated them in 1862, but his view on their participation in politics remained unchanged. His final word on the subject was made before a congressional committee eight months later: "My own opinion," he replied to a question under oath, "is that, at this time, they cannot vote intelligently, and that giving them the right of suffrage would open the door to a great deal of demagoguism, and lead to embarrassments in various ways. What the future may prove, how intelligent they may become, with what eyes they may look upon the interests of the state in which they may reside, I cannot say more than you can."

Before the war Lee had expressed the belief that slavery was a greater evil for the slave owner than for the slave, and that it was a "moral and political evil." He also thought that slavery was part of God's process for civilizing the blacks and could be ended only when God chose to end it. This opinion was widespread in the South before the war, and would remain so in various forms well into the twentieth century. Lee's belief that the progress of blacks from slavery should have been left in God's hands, rather than legislated or imposed on the South by force, was one he held quietly but firmly throughout his life. He did not modify it, nor apologize for it, and his frankness on the subject before a congressional committee at least has the merit of sincerity. Perhaps the key phrase in Lee's statement to the committee is "*at this time.*" He did not attribute to blacks a permanent inferiority, as many did in the South, but allowed that time (and God) might change their condition in ways he could not foresee or predict. It was, or should be, as he was fond of saying, "all in God's hands." By the standards of many Confederates his opinions were moderate, and efforts on the part of northern congressmen to draw him out further on the subject failed.

The importance of this lies in the increasing and systemized transformation of Lee into a flawless, faultless symbol, in which the real man was rapidly overshadowed by the gleaming marble image. This was no doing of Lee's; he had too much modesty (and robust common sense) to assume the mantle of perfection. The mythic Lee of southern history became in time a man who never made a mistake, and who had no faults: not only the perfect gentleman, but the perfect warrior. Thus the blame for Malvern Hill was transferred to Jackson; the blame for Gettysburg was assigned to Longstreet, or at least to Longstreet, Stuart, and Ewell; and Lee's dislike of the institution of slavery was given more prominence than his pessimism about the future development of the former slaves and freedmen. That Lee was human; that he sometimes made mistakes, even major ones; that his deeply held, sincere views on race do not measure up to contemporary standards, or even the standards of some enlightened northerners in his own time, should not be flinched from. Lee loses nothing by being portrayed as a fallible human being. His strengths were his courage, his sense of duty, his religious belief, his military genius, his constant search to do right, and his natural and instinctive courtesy— he did not hesitate to shake a black man's hand or kneel beside him in prayer—but he did not aspire to saint-hood; indeed the idea would have seemed to him blas-phemous, and he would have been appalled by the fact that he has been elevated to a kind of secular sainthood since his death.

After a week of comfortable living in Mrs. Cocke's home—no doubt a replacement for the departing butler was soon found—the Lees moved into Derwent, a small four-room "tenant's house." Deep in the woods, it was a lonely place—disappointing to Mrs. Lee and the girls, who felt it was "cramped" and poorly furnished. As usual, Lee was forced into the role of "cheerleader," working hard "to keep up the family's spirits," and making light of what his youngest daughter, Mildred, described as "petty trials of wretched service, cooking, marketing—an ugly, meanly-built little house with ordinary surroundings [and] provincial society." For Lee, it was enough to be back with part of his family after four years of living in a tent, to have an opportu-nity to recuperate from the constant stress of high com-mand, and to take an occasional ride on Traveller to the nearest store, where there was an ample supply of fresh vegetables; but none of that would have been likely to sooth the angst of Agnes and Mildred, intensified by a bad scare when Agnes came down with typhoid fever. Then, by another happy coincidence, Mary Custis attended a party in Staunton where she complained that "the people of the South are offering my father everything but work, and that is the one thing he will accept at their hands."

Of all Lee's daughters, Mary Custis was the boldest and most outspoken. Her words were overheard by another guest, Colonel Bolivar Christian of Lexington, Virginia, a trustee of Washington College, the institution to which George Washington had left some of his canal shares. The college had been starved of students during the war and looted by Federal troops (who had also burned down much of the nearby Virginia Military Institute), and it was in the process of seeking a new president, one whose name and reputation would bring in students and donations. Colonel Christian mentioned Mary Custis's comment about Lee at the next meeting of the trustees; they decided to send their rector, Judge Brockenbrough, in person to Derwent to offer Lee the presidency, and as a gesture of their good faith voted unanimously to elect Lee to the office. Lee had been contemplating, without much enthusiasm, a book about his campaigns, and had no warning of Brockenbrough's visit until the judge, a tall, bulky man, appeared at the door and asked to see him. Brockenbrough's appearance was a good example of the penury into which the citizens of Lexington, like so many southern towns, had been plunged. He had been obliged to borrow a decent suit for the trip, as well as the money to make it. Still, what he lacked in worldly goods he made up by his powers of persuasion and his evident sincerity. Nor did he come empty-handed. He carried a letter offering Lee a salary of $1,500 a year, plus a share of the tuition fees and a house and garden. Lee was not unfamiliar with Washington College—his father had been among those who had urged George Washington to make a gift of some of his canal shares to the institution—and the idea of becoming a college president would not have seemed a reach for a man who had once been a successful superintendent of the U.S. Military Academy.

After a short period of reflection, and with the somewhat lukewarm consent of Mary Lee, who felt herself being drawn farther and farther from her friends, Lee wrote to the trustees on August 24, saying that he would accept the presidency, unless they felt that his exclusion from the amnesty of May 29 and the fact that he was "an object of censure to a portion of the country" made him unfit for the post. The trustees felt no such thing, and on September 1 announced that General Robert E. Lee was the new president of

Washington College. On September 15 he set off alone for Lexington on Traveller, his luggage following him by canal. "He prefers that way," Mrs. Lee wrote to a friend, the day before his departure, "and, besides, does not like to part even for a time from his beloved steed, the companion of many a hard fought battle."

A new chapter was beginning in Lee's life, this time as an educator and college administrator and, more important, as a symbol of the desire "to aid in the restoration of peace and harmony," as he wrote in his letter of acceptance, "and in no way to oppose the policy of the State or General Government directed to that object." For the former general in chief of the Confederate Army, who had surrendered his army in the field less than six months ago, this was a bold move. His object had hitherto been to keep what we would now call a low profile, but his rapid transformation into a college president, charged with educating young men, stirred up angry criticism in the North, and fears that his students would be brought up as rebels. That, of course, was to underrate Lee's sincere determination "to set them an example of submission to authority." For the rest of his life he was to achieve the difficult act of striking a balance between his belief in the need to submit to Federal authority and his unrivaled prestige as the Confederacy's most admired military figure.

The president's house at Washington College, where Stonewall Jackson had once lived after marrying the daughter of the then president, was partly occupied and in need of much repair. Arriving in Lexington, Lee found it difficult to avoid being mobbed by admirers—not surprisingly, since he was still wearing his old Confederate gray uniform and riding Traveller, by then almost as famous as his owner. He spent some time at one of the nearby hot springs that surround Lexington and did not return until September 30; he then lodged in a hotel. Despite every effort to speed the work on the house, it was not ready for the Lees to occupy until the beginning of December. They had not had a home of their own since 1861, and their furniture and possessions were scattered. Lee managed to recover the carpets from Arlington; these had been saved and stored at Tudor Place, across the Potomac in Georgetown Heights, by Mrs. Brittania Peter Kinnon, a distant relative who was a descendant of George Washington's. Although they were much too large, even with their edges folded back, for the rooms of "The Presidential Residence on College Hill," they at least provided a touch of luxury and a faint reminder of Arlington. Mrs. Cocke had contributed some of the furniture and an admirer had provided a piano. The Lee family silver, which had providentially been sent to Lexington for safekeeping and buried, was soon unearthed and laboriously cleaned, and on December 2 Mary Lee, accompanied by Rob and Mildred (Agnes was in Richmond), arrived to join her husband, having made the journey from Oakland to Lexington by canal boat. She was, by this time, confined to her "rolling chair," but judging from all accounts, she instantly took charge of the household with firm authority, and of her husband too.

His task at Washington College was an enormous one. The college had at that time "about one hundred students," but its library and its scientific equipment had been pillaged. Reluctant as Lee was to appear in public, the plight of the college made him travel to Richmond in midwinter to appear before "a committee of the general assembly of Virginia," to plead for the state to resume payment of the interest on loans taken out by educational institutions. His brief appearance was greeted by "cheers on all sides." Soon afterward, Lee was summoned to appear before a joint Senate and House subcommittee inquiring into political conditions in Virginia and the Carolinas. Unlike the general assembly of Virginia, this was hostile territory, and Lee was the most conspicuous Confederate figure to appear before it. He journeyed to Washington toward the end of February 1866, his first visit since April 1861, when he had ridden home to write his letter of resignation from the U.S. Army. Now, he was famous, so much so that the subcommittee's questions seem both tame and irrelevant. Asked whether in the event that Great Britain or France declared war against the United States Virginia might join the attacking power, Lee correctly treated the prospect as remote and far-fetched. Later he affirmed his opinion that giving blacks "the right of suffrage" was a mistake "at this time." His replies throughout the lengthy questioning were polite, wary, and uncontroversial. If the members of the subcommittee were hoping to trip him up, they failed.

His administration of Washington College was thorough and painstaking. It involved a huge quantity of correspondence, a task he had always found distasteful, but he pursued it uncomplainingly, with staggering promptitude and attention to detail. His experience in Washington, as well as his inclination, prompted him to stay out of the limelight as much as possible. The one time he stepped out of his role was in the spring of 1866, when, having learned that a horse thief was about to be lynched by an angry mob, he went straight to the town jail to persuade the mob to disperse and let justice take its course. The sight of the victor of Chancellorsville was enough to calm (or possibly shame) the citizens and reaffirm the authority of the aged jail keeper.

Lee had no trouble asserting his authority over the students of Washington College. After all, he had handled the cadets at the U.S. Military Academy. In Lexington as at West Point he was patient, firm, and profoundly respected. He did not attempt to impose any kind of military discipline. This was not VMI (which was only a short distance away), and he was not training young men to become officers. All the same, his vigilant eye and the fact that he knew the strengths and the weaknesses of every one of his students were the same qualities that had made him such an admirable commander at West Point. He was not so much a strict disciplinarian as a wise and enlightened one, but there was no appeal once he made up his mind, and in addition he expected a sustained and maximum effort, absolute truthfulness and the manners of a gentleman, and impressive self-control. Within a year of his accepting the presidency, the student body had increased from about 100 to nearly 400,* the curriculum had been boldly updated and expanded, and the finances of the college were secure.

There was, of course, no way Lee could shield his students from the effects of defeat or from the rising

---

* To put this in context, it was about the number of cadets at West Point in the late nineteenth century, and about half the number of undergraduates at Yale or Harvard in the same period (Freeman, *Robert E. Lee, Vol. 3, 299*).

tide of Reconstruction—inevitably there were "incidents." The passions that had separated North and South persisted, and not even Lee could keep "his young men," a good many of whom were in fact veterans of the Confederate Army, from the occasional conflict with the Federal authorities, or enforce on them the kind of "submission" that he had forced on himself. He managed to defuse the occasional rumor that he would run for governor, and he tried to prevent the expression around him, even in his own home, of opinions that might inflame northerners. Lee's object—like Grant's—was to preserve the peace and restore the Union.

This was not an easy task. Lee's students, like Lee himself, accepted that the war was lost, but they did not accept the right of the Federal government to uproot ancient southern institutions and racial assumptions. Lee had not hesitated to shake a black man's hand, and when another black man had entered St. Paul's Church in Richmond and walked to the chancel rail to receive communion before a shocked, indignant, silent white congregation, Lee rose from his pew, joined the man, and knelt beside him. Lee was determined to treat blacks with the same dignity and courtesy he showed toward everyone else, but that did not mean he accepted full equality for them. He had testified under oath that he did not think they "could vote intelligently," and also that "it would be better for Virginia if she could get rid of them," though he added that he had always believed in "gradual emancipation." The key word here is of course "gradual." Like his students, Lee did not fully accept that the defeat of the South would lead to the destruction of the traditional southern social system, a restructuring that was intended to favor blacks over whites politically and to erase the social barriers between the races, and his students were still less likely to accept this policy than he was. On the other hand "gradual emancipation" was not what northern reconstructionists wanted, nor were they willing to wait for these changes to be brought about incrementally by God in God's own good time, as Lee was.

Under the circumstances, it is hardly surprising that his tenure at Washington College was marked by at least four racial incidents, which received considerable attention in the North. The first involved four students, one of whom was accused of beating a freedman with a pistol during an angry argument—not exactly a student prank. The second and more serious quarrel, known as the "Johnston affair," occurred between a group of students and an armed northerner who had expressed strong sympathy for blacks. The third problem was a complaint from a northern women teaching black children that she had been insulted and hounded by students and called a "damned Yankee bitch of a nigger teacher." The fourth incident stemmed from an accusation that some of the college students had apprehended a "Negro youth" who had shot and wounded one of the sons of Judge Brockenbrough, and marched him to the courthouse with a noose around his neck, with the apparent intent of lynching him.

Lee inquired carefully into all of these incidents—all of which proved to have been exaggerated—and removed those whom he found guilty (the school-teacher's accusation that those insulting her were students of Washington College could not be verified). But he received an unwelcome amount of attention in the northern press. He was accused of running "a school for rebels," and of being unfit to run an institution of learning, by no less a figure than the renowned abolitionist William Lloyd Garrison. Garrison savagely questioned the ability of "the vanquished leader of the rebel armies" to teach his students loyalty to the Union "which he so lately attempted to destroy!" Lee, who might have been a prisoner in Fort Monroe alongside Jefferson Davis, but for the intervention of General Grant, ignored the temptation to reply or to justify himself. Still, the problems illustrate the depth of the bitterness that reigned on both sides between North and South, and the fine line Lee had to walk to keep the college functioning. Lee was indifferent to his own reputation, but his character "as a gentleman and a Christian" was such that it protected the college, and even earned the praise of the abolitionist Henry Ward Beecher, whose sister Harriet Beecher Stowe was the author of *Uncle Tom's Cabin*. Beecher told a New York audience that Lee "was entitled to all honor," and praised him for devoting himself "to the sacred cause of education."

Despite all the pressures on him, Lee testified at the trial of Jefferson Davis in Richmond. He even accepted Grant's invitation to visit him in the White House. Aside from these things Lee seems to have settled back into the kind of quiet domestic life in which he always took the greatest pleasure. Although Mrs. Lee was unable to cross a room without the use of crutches, the house was always full; his daughters were often home to keep him company; he and Mildred, when she was home, went riding together, with Mildred on Lucy Long, the mare Jeb Stuart had given him. The horse had been lost and presumed captured by the Federals in the spring of 1864, but was returned to Lee in 1866. The Lee daughters enjoyed ice-skating when the ponds froze, and there were plenty of gentlemen callers to keep them amused, but no serious suitors to worry their father. Mildred, a born animal lover, collected cats, including Tom the Nipper, who had been reared in the stable next to Traveller's box stall before moving into the house. Tom the Nipper would become a major character in *Traveller*, a novel by Richard Adams, the author of *Watership Down*, 122 years later.

Lee frequently took Mrs. Lee to one of the spas around Lexington, since bathing in the waters was her only relief from constant pain. They both enjoyed the social life. Lee was always happiest in good company, so much so that it seems sad that he spent the best part of his life as a soldier. Despite the catastrophe of the defeat and its consequences for his beloved Virginia, the years from 1866 to 1870 seem among the happiest of his life, and this was the period when the formidable hero thawed into a far less august, less remote figure. He remained a loving father and husband, with a strong interest in agriculture, and a teasing, affectionate sense of humor, very much the man Mary had married. Those who met him then described him as bright and cheerful, and despite the awe in which he was held he seems to have had as good a time as his health would allow. But there was no question that his health was deteriorating, and that the pains in his left arm and his chest which were ascribed to rheumatism were in fact angina, signaling blocked arteries and a failing heart. His decline was so noticeable that the board and the professors of Washington College constantly urged him to take a holiday—a suggestion that he courteously resisted. Even so, Lee was in constant pain, and found walking increasingly difficult. His workload continued to be as formidable as ever—he was completing a revised and corrected edition of his father's book, *Memoirs of the War in the Southern Department*, not so much a labor of love as of duty; running what was now a fast-growing college; and working fitfully at a history of his campaigns, while continuing to deal personally with the moral welfare of his students and maintaining a truly astonishing volume of correspondence, all of it in his own hand.

When he at last consented to take the vacation that everybody had been urging on him for so long, it was a significant choice. Accompanied by his daughter Agnes he decided to visit his daughter Annie's grave, near White Sulphur Springs. This was a pilgrimage he had long wanted to make, and although it was no great distance, it taxed Lee's failing strength. It took him two days to reach Richmond, by canal boat and train. What would once have been an easy trip for him was now fraught with difficulties, and rendered more difficult by the number of people who recognized him. In Lexington, people had grown used to him, but as he approached Richmond his journey started to resemble a Roman triumph or a medieval progress, attracting public attention that tired him still further. The senate of Virginia "unanimously extended to him the privilege of the floor," which he courteously declined; crowds waited outside his hotel; he was deluged with invitations. He accepted a visit from Colonel John S. Mosby, the controversial Confederate cavalry leader★ whose depredation of Union supply lines had once prompted Grant to order Sheridan to hang "without trial" any of Mosby's men not in recognizable uniform. Mosby returned bringing with him a reluctant Pickett. Lee was happy enough to see Mosby, but is said to have greeted Pickett with icy courtesy. As for Pickett, once he was outside Lee's rooms he turned to Mosby and said, "That old man had my division massacred at Gettysburg." Mosby had already made his peace with Grant, and there is some dispute over whether his description of the meeting is correct. It seems likely, however, that Lee had already heard about Pickett's accusation; indeed Pickett made much the same remark directly to Lee shortly after the attack failed, and Lee may well have resented his presence.

Lee and Agnes proceeded to Warrenton, where Lee saw for the first time the truncated obelisk that

---

★ "Mosby's Raiders" (or "Rangers") were accused by the Federals of having crossed the line between uniformed cavalrymen and guerrillas.

had been placed over Annie's grave; at its foot, Agnes placed "white hyacinths and gray moss." From there they proceeded, by slow and ever more tiring stages, and facing ever larger crowds, toward Lee's final destination, his father's grave on Cumberland Island. Lee wrote to Mary that the grave was in good order, but "the house had been burned and the island devastated." As he passed through Augusta and Savannah, Georgia; and Jacksonville, Florida, he was greeted by brass bands playing "Dixie" and "The Bonnie Blue Flag," and by masses of his former soldiers, with cheers, speeches, parades, and rebel yells. Whether he wished it or not, Lee's journey to say good-bye to his daughter Annie and his father turned into a huge, protracted Confederate celebration, which he could neither prevent nor discourage. Yet the purpose of his journey remained clear, at any rate to Lee himself. He was saying farewell to a father whom he had never known all that well, and whose erratic political career and irresponsible personal behavior Lee had sought always to avoid; and to a daughter he had hoped would comfort him in his old age.

Agnes herself fell ill under the strain of the voyage, and Lee felt obliged to return along the coast via Charleston, where he was greeted rapturously. After making another spiritual farewell at Shirley, the great house where his mother had grown up and where she and his father were married, he continued on to White House, where Mary and Markie Williams, for so many years Lee's favorite correspondent, had already joined Rooney. The house itself, to whose front door Mary Lee had pinned a contemptuous note to Federal troops in 1862, had been burned to the ground, and Rooney now lived in the crude, poorly furnished home of the former overseer.

After ten days, Lee returned to Richmond, where, despite his dislike of posing for portraits, he stayed long enough to allow the young artist Edward V. Valentine to take measurements and make sketches for a bust. This was perhaps an example of foresight, for Valentine would be chosen to create a white marble recumbent statue of Robert E. Lee, which was completed in 1875 and placed in its final position in the center of the Lee Chapel in 1883.

In Richmond Lee consulted once again with his physicians, who were no more helpful about his condition than before. Lee may already have guessed from his breathlessness that his heart trouble was more serious than they knew, or were willing to tell him. That was probably why he had decided to undertake the long and tiring trip, aware that he would not have another opportunity of making it.

He returned to Lexington to resume his duties. The previous year, he and Mary had settled into a new house, designed with every possible innovation in terms of heating and plumbing that was available for the day, and built by the college at cost of over $15,000, a considerable amount in the mid-nineteenth century. Lee had accepted the house with many doubts and second thoughts, and in the end agreed only because he thought Mary would be more comfortable there. It had a great veranda where she could sit in her "rolling chair" in good weather. With rare prescience the trustees of the college had agreed that Mrs. Lee should have the use of the "new president's residence" for life, should Lee predecease her, as well as a generous life annuity.

On September 28, 1870, Lee put in a normal day's work. After dinner—what we would call lunch, then still the principal meal of the day—he put on his old blue military cape against the rain and walked to a church meeting. When he returned, half an hour late for supper, something in his expression caught Mrs. Lee's attention, and she asked him if he was chilly. As she poured him a cup of tea, he moved his lips to say grace, but no words came. Clearly, Lee had suffered a severe stroke, or perhaps an aneurysm, and was unable to speak or move.

Doctors were sent for, and he was carried to a couch in the dining room, which would soon be emptied of other furniture to make a sickroom for him. Over the next two weeks he lay there, visited by friends and family, occasionally indicating by an indistinct word or a gesture that his mind was still active. He seemed to dismiss any suggestion that he would recover, or ride Traveller again, with a resigned upward gaze.

By midnight of October 9–10 he seems to have reached a crisis—perhaps another stroke, perhaps the onset of pneumonia, since his breathing was irregular and he suffered "a chill." Those around him— Mrs. Lee was now constantly at his side—claimed that he roused himself to say, "Hill *must* come up!" It is possible that his mind was wandering. Then, after a long pause, at dawn on October 10, he said, firmly and distinctly, as if he were preparing for battle, "Strike the tent." Soon afterward he died.

The announcement was telegraphed to the *Richmond Dispatch*, and from there to the world:

LEXINGTON, VIRGINIA, October 12, 1870
10 a.m.
General Lee died this morning at half past nine o'clock. He began to grow worse on Monday and continued to sink until he breathed his last this morning. He died as he lived, calmly and quietly, and in the full assurance of faith in the Lord Jesus Christ. The places of business are all

closed, the bells are tolling, and the whole community thrown into the deepest grief.

He died with the same stoic dignity that had always defined his character in life. His place in history is unique: "a Caesar without his ambition: a Frederick without his tyranny; a Napoleon without his selfishness; and a Washington without his reward." His character has been best defined by Stephen Vincent Benét, in *John Brown's Body*:

> *Yet—look at the face again—look at it well—*
> *This man was not repose, this man was act.*
> *This man who murmured "It is well that war*
> *Should be so terrible, if it were not*
> *We might become too fond of it—" and showed*
> *Himself, for once, completely as he lived*
> *In the laconic balance of that phrase;*
> *This man could reason, but he was a fighter,*
> *Skilful in every weapon of defence*
> *But never defending when he could assault,*
> *Taking enormous risks again and again,*
> *Never retreating while he still could strike,*
> *Dividing a weak force on dangerous ground*
> *And joining it again to beat a strong,*
> *Mocking at chance and all the odds of war*

With acts that looked like hairbreadth recklessness
—We do not call them reckless, since he won.
We do not see him reckless for the calm
Proportion that controlled the recklessness—
But that attacking quality was there.
He was not mild with life or drugged with justice,
He gripped life like a wrestler with a bull,
Impetuously. It did not come to him
While he stood waiting in a famous cloud,
He went to it and took it by both horns
And threw it down.

Acknowledgments

I would like first of all to thank both my editors, Hugh Van Dusen at HarperCollins, and Phyllis Grann, my colleague for many years at Simon & Schuster, for their invaluable help, support, and *Sitzfleisch*. I also owe special thanks to my agent and dear friend for many decades Lynn Nesbit, without whose belief that I *could* write this book, it would never even have been begun.

Special thanks are owed to my dear friend Mike Hill, whose indefatigable research and optimism have been precious assets over the years, and whom I regard as a partner as much as a researcher. I am grateful too to Kevin Kwan, good friend and peerless art researcher, for his eagle eye and flawless taste. Working with both of them has been one of the major pleasures of writing this book.

I would also like to thank Victoria Wilson, friend and colleague—and author of an even longer biography than this one—for taking the time to read the manuscript of this book and for her unfailing support and enthusiasm throughout; my dear friend Gypsy DaSilva, whose advice has been enormously helpful and unfailingly available day or night; and my assistant Dawn Lafferty, who coped calmly and gently with all the many demands of a book this long with its innumerable details, and whose presence has helped in keeping my daily life in balance.

I am indebted to Robert Krick, the fount of all wisdom on the subject of the Civil War, for pointing out the errors in my chapter on Gettysburg—any that remain are, of course, my own—and for his willingness to answer even the dumbest of questions with patience and supreme common sense.

Finally, the most important thanks of all are due to my beloved wife Margaret, for her patience and understanding as we shared our life together with the constant presence of Robert E. Lee.

Notes

PREFACE   The Portent

xix   "the apostle of the sword": Oswald Garrison Villard, *John Brown: 1800–1859: A Biography Fifty Years After* (New York: Knopf, 1943), 111.

xxi   When he redrafted the Declaration of Independence: Ibid., 334.

xxii   When he struck: Franklin Benjamin Sanborn, *Life and Letters of John Brown: Liberator of Kansas and Martyr of Virginia* (London: Sampson, Low, Marston, Searlef and Rivington, 1885), 40.

xxvii   "that an insurrection was in progress": Villard, *John Brown*, 434.

xxviii   he had lived for fifteen years: Jean H. Baker, *James Buchanan* (New York: New York Times Books, 2004), 75.

xxx   The Arlington property alone: Douglas Southall Freeman, *Robert E. Lee: A Biography* (New York: Scribner, 1934), Vol. 1, 381.

xxxi   Much as Lee: Ibid., 389.

xxxii   "a foe without hate": Benjamin Harvey Hill, *Senator Benjamin Hill of Georgia: His Life, Speeches and Writings* (Atlanta: T.H.P. Bloodworth, 1893), 406.

xxxiii   "the sun was fiery hot": Freeman, *Robert E. Lee,* Vol. 1, 367.

xxxiii   Secretary of War Floyd: Note of J. B. Floyd, secretary of war, to Colonel Drinkard, October 17, 1859, National Archives.

xxxvii   By midnight, Lee, Stuart, Lieutenant Green: *Select Committee of the U.S. Senate, 36th Congress,* 1st Session, Rep. Com. No. 278, June 15, 1860, 41.

xxxviii With exquisite politeness: Freeman, *Robert E. Lee,* Vol. 1, 397, 398.

xxxviii Calmly, Lee surveyed the ground: Ibid., 397.

xl   His mutilated corpse: David S. Reynolds, *John Brown, Abolitionist: The Man Who Killed Slavery, Sparked the Civil War, and Seeded Civil Rights* (New York: Knopf, 2005), 320.

xli   By mid-afternoon, men were falling: Ibid., 317–24; Villard, *John Brown,* 443.

xlii   He sent an elderly civilian: Allan Keller, *Thunder at Harper's Ferry* (Englewood Cliffs, N.J.: Prentice-Hall, 1958), 113.

xliii   Brown took no umbrage: Villard, *John Brown,* 447.

xliv   "Oh, you will get over it": Ibid., 448.

xlvii   "When *Smith* first came to the door": Ibid., 451.

xlviii   "a ragged hole low down": Ibid., 453.

xlviii "With one son dead by his side": Ibid.

xlviii Colonel Washington cried out loudly: Keller, *Thunder at Harper's Ferry*, 149.

xlix The rest "rushed in like tigers": Villard, *John Brown*, 454.

xlix Lee "saw to it that the captured survivors": Ibid.

li "He is a man of clear head": Ibid., 455.

liii "No monument of quarried stone": Susan Cheever, *Louisa May Alcott: A Personal Biography* (New York: Simon and Schuster, 2010), 129.

liv "As it is a matter over which": Robert E. Lee Jr., *Recollections and Letters of Robert E. Lee* (New York: Doubleday, Page, 1924), 21–22.

liv In his majestic biography of Brown: Villard, *John Brown*, 555.

lvii In Philadelphia "a public prayer meeting": Ibid., 559; Elizabeth Preston Allen, *Life and Letters of Margaret Junkin Preston* (Boston: Houghton Mifflin, 1903), 111–17.

lvii "was draped in mourning": Villard, *John Brown*, 559.

lix Southerners were dismayed: Ibid., 496.

lix "He has abolished slavery in Virginia": Ibid., 562.

lx He was as little pleased: Freeman, *Robert E. Lee*, Vol. 1, 417.

lx He regarded secession: Ibid., 421.

lxi "I hope," he wrote: Ibid., 416.

lxii "He had been taught to believe": Ibid., 418.

lxii "Washington," Everett wrote: Quoted ibid., 420.

lxiii "Secession," Lee wrote: Ibid., 421.

CHAPTER 1 "Not Heedless of the Future"

7 By the time of the American Revolution: Richard B. McCaslin, *Lee in the Shadow of Washington* (Baton Rouge: Louisiana State University Press, 2001), 13.

12 The years between 1773 and 1776: Douglas Southall Freeman, *Robert E. Lee: A Biography* (New York: Scribner, 1934), Vol. 1, 2.

14 A year later: Ibid.

14 Washington, recognizing Lee's special skills: Ibid., 3.

15 "much to the horror": Ibid., 66.

16 "sensitive, resentful": Ibid., 4.

17 When Matilda died in 1790: McCaslin, *Lee in the Shadow of Washington,* 17.

18 "Why didn't you come home?": Paul Nagel, *The Lees of Virginia: Seven Generations of an American Family* (New York: Oxford University Press, 2007), 166.

18 In a half-baked scheme: Emory Thomas, *Robert E. Lee* (New York: Norton, 1995), 26.

18 On a visit to Shirley: Freeman, *Robert E. Lee,* Vol. 1, 8.

22 In these modest circumstances: Nagel, *The Lees of Virginia,* 175, 195–96.

26 Henry Lee helped to barricade: Freeman, *Robert E. Lee,* Vol. 1, 14.

26 "Death seemed so certain": Ibid., 15.

26 This proposal was not taken up: Ibid.

27 "Broken in body and spirit": Nagel, *The Lees of Virginia,* 182.

28 He didn't even manage: Freeman, *Robert E. Lee*, Vol. 1, 31.

28 "My dear Sir": Ibid.

28 When it was brought to: McCaslin, *Lee in the Shadow of Washington*, 18.

29 That had been tried before: Freeman, *Robert E. Lee*, Vol. 1, 37.

32 The contrast between her childhood: Thomas L. Connelly, *The Marble Man: Robert E. Lee and His Image in American Society* (New York: Knopf, 1977), 169.

33 For somebody whose health was as frail: Thomas, *Robert E. Lee*, 45.

34 She entrusted him with the keys: Ibid., 39.

34 He accompanied her on drives: Freeman, *Robert E. Lee*, Vol. 1, 34.

35 "Self-denial, self-control": Ibid., 23.

36 When he first went away: Ibid., 30–31.

37 His maternal grandfather: Ibid., 24.

37 Perhaps because Ann Carter Lee: Ibid., 25.

37 As a child he was surrounded: Ibid., 25, 28.

41 At that time there was not as yet: Ibid., 38.

43 Fitzhugh's letter referred: Ibid., 39.

CHAPTER 2 The Education of a Soldier

50 The academy still consisted of only: Douglas Southall Freeman, *Robert E. Lee: A Biography* (New York: Scribner, 1934), Vol. 1, 49.

51 The stone wharf: Bernhard, Duke of Saxe-Weimar Eisenach, *Travels Through North America During the Years 1825 and 1826* (Philadelphia: Carey, Lea and Carey, 1828), 110.

51 An English visitor with an eye for detail: William N. Blane, *An Excursion Through the United States and Canada, 1822–1833 by an English Gentleman* (London: Baldwin, Craddock and Joy, 1824), 352–76.

52 Tent mates were obliged to purchase: Freeman, *Robert E. Lee,* Vol. 1, 51.

52 Meals were ample: Theodore J. Crackel, *West Point: A Centennial History* (Lawrence: University Press of Kansas, 2002), 89.

53 The new cadets were given: Freeman, *Robert E. Lee,* Vol. 1, 52.

54 The marquis was greeted: *Albany* (New York) *Argus,* July 8, 1825.

56 Another roll call and inspection: Freeman, *Robert E. Lee,* Vol. 1, 56–57.

56 The list of things forbidden: Ibid., 52.

56 Unlike third-year cadet Jefferson Davis: Ibid., 55.

57 By the end of his first year: Ibid., 62.

58 One of them later said: Michael Fellman, *The Making of Robert E. Lee* (New York: Random House, 2000), 11.

64 He had no reason to be apprehensive: Freeman, *Robert E. Lee,* Vol. 1, 67.

65 Everywhere they went: Paul Nagel, *The Lees of Virginia: Seven Generations of an American Family* (New York: Oxford University Press, 2007), 232.

66 This is not to say: Ibid., 235.

67 This problem he solved: Ibid., 206.

70 To his credit, perhaps, Henry never denied his guilt: Ibid., 207–14.

70 In a climax worthy of a nineteenth-century romantic novel: Ibid., 218.

74 Perhaps the most intense part of his studies: Freeman, *Robert E. Lee,* Vol. 1, 76–77.

75 Robert's position as adjutant of the corps: Ibid., 80.

75 It is interesting to note: Ibid., 81.

77 Although Douglas Southall Freeman states: Ibid., 84.

78 She was staying at Ravensworth: Ibid., 87.

80 Mrs. Lee was hardly a major slave owner: A. M. Gambone, *Lee at Gettysburg: Commentary on Defeat—The Death of a Myth* (Baltimore, Md.: Butternut and Blue, 2002), 37.

81 He rejoiced in being known: Nagel, *The Lees of Virginia,* 235.

82 In fact two of the older Lee boys: Ibid.

82 Even at the very end of his life: Ibid., 292.

84 Robert was punctual to a fault: Ibid., 236.

87 Lee journeyed north to New York: Emory Thomas, *Robert E. Lee* (New York: Norton, 1995), 57; Freeman, *Robert E. Lee,* Vol. 1, 94.

88 On the other hand, Cockspur Island: Freeman, *Robert E. Lee,* Vol. 1, 95.

88 Major Babcock, to whom Lee: Ibid., 96.

91 In January word finally arrived: Thomas, *Robert E. Lee,* 62.

93 Lee laid siege to Mary's mother: Freeman, *Robert E. Lee,* Vol. 1, 104.

96 Mary was to have no fewer: Ibid., 105; Thomas, *Robert E. Lee,* 64.

96 Nothing except his children: Freeman, *Robert E. Lee,* Vol. 1, 108.

98 Perhaps nothing is more symbolic: Ibid., 109.

CHAPTER 3   The Engineer—1831–1846

103 "I actually could not find time": Emory Thomas, *Robert E. Lee* (New York: Norton, 1995), 65.

103 this is pretty tame stuff: Douglas Southall Freeman, *Robert E. Lee: A Biography* (New York: Scribner, 1934), Vol. 1, 107.

104 During his honeymoon: Ibid., 112–13.

105 The Lees' "apartment": Thomas, *Robert E. Lee,* 66.

107 Convinced that "he was ordained": Tony Horowitz, *Midnight Rising: John Brown and the Raid That Sparked the Civil War* (New York: Henry Holt, 2011), 20.

112 One of the doctors: *William Styron: The Confessions of Nat Turner—A Critical Handbook,* Melvin J. Friedman and Irving Malin, eds. (Belmont, Calif.: Wadsworth, 1970), 43.

112 Fear of further slave insurrections: Freeman, *Robert E. Lee,* Vol. 1, 11–12.

113 He reassured his mother-in-law: Ibid., 111.

114 Notwithstanding his sensible effort to calm: Ibid.

114 "In this enlightened age": Ibid., 372.

116 "My own opinion is that they [blacks]": Michael Fellman, *The Making of Robert E. Lee* (New York: Random House, 2000), 268.

116 "The idea that Southern people": Freeman, *Robert E. Lee,* Vol. 1, 376.

117 In any case, Lee returned to work: Thomas, *Robert E. Lee,* 69.

119 After the boy's birth: Ibid., 71.

120 It was not just a question of neatness: Ibid.

120 "The spirit is willing": Ibid.

122 While she was away: Freeman, *Robert E. Lee,* Vol. 1, 18.

123 At that time, Lee owned: Thomas, *Robert E. Lee,* 72.

123 "an extended mock love affair": Ibid.

123 Whereas the portrait of Mary Custis: Ibid.

124 When Harriet gave birth: Ibid.

124 "How I did strut along": Ibid., 73.

124 "As for the daughters of Eve": Freeman, *Robert E. Lee,* Vol. 1, 118.

125 Owing to Talcott's frequent absences: Ibid., 119.

128 When he took command of the army of Italy: Sir Edward Cust, *Annals of the Wars of the Nineteenth Century* (London: John Murray, 1863), Vol. 3, 260.

132 As a result Mr. Schneider: A. L. Long, *Memoirs of Robert E. Lee* (New York: J. M. Stoddard, 1886), 25.

133 The original boundary line: Thomas, *Robert E. Lee,* 82.

135 "But why do you urge": Ibid., 82–83.

135 The apparent harshness: Ibid., 83; Freeman, *Robert E. Lee,* Vol. 1, 134.

135 In the heroic medical tradition of the day: Thomas, *Robert E. Lee,* 83.

135 Eventually two large "abscesses": Freeman, *Robert E. Lee,* Vol. 1, 134.

136 "I have never seen a man": Ibid.

137 "The country looks very sweet": Ibid., 136.

139 "they wanted a skillful engineer": Ibid., 138.

140 The immediate problem facing Lee: Ibid.

141 Lee's responsibilities included: Ibid.

142 "the dearest and dirtiest": Ibid., 139.

142 His aide and companion on the long trip: Ibid., 140.

143 "The improved condition of the children": Ibid., 141.

144 The problem to which he gave the most immediate attention: Wikipedia, "Mississippi River," 10.

145 When the river was high: Thomas, *Robert E. Lee,* 89.

145 He had planned to survey: Freeman, *Robert E. Lee,* Vol. 1, 143.

146 "in full costume": Elizabeth Pryor, *Reading the Man: A Portrait of Robert E. Lee Through His Private Letters* (New York: Viking, 2007), 114.

149 His solution to the problems: See Stella M. Drumm, "Robert E. Lee and the Mississippi River," *Missouri Historical Society,* Vol. 6, No. 2, February 1929.

150 "The commerce thus made available": Long, *Memoirs of Robert E. Lee,* 28–29.

152 By July 1838, "Lee had pushed": Drumm, "Robert E. Lee and the Mississippi River," 146.

152 On the way home Lee encountered: Freeman, *Robert E. Lee*, Vol. 1, 148.

153 Even so, the Lees left their daughter Mary: Thomas, *Robert E. Lee*, 91–92.

153 Lee boasted that the boys: Ibid., 93.

155 They spent a month: Ibid.

155 Saint Louis was by no means: Pryor, *Reading the Man*, 111; Mary P. Coulling, *The Lee Girls* (Winston-Salem, N.C.: Blair, 1987), 11; Harnett T. Kane, *The Lady of Arlington: A Novel Based on the Life of Mrs. Robert E. Lee* (Garden City, N.Y.: Doubleday, 1953), 91.

156 Although the Lee family: Thomas, *Robert E. Lee*, 94.

156 "brats squalling around": Coulling, *The Lee Girls*, 10.

157 One observer comments on Lee's diligence: Drumm, "Robert E. Lee and the Mississippi River," 170.

158 She was also pregnant: Freeman, *Robert E. Lee*, Vol. 1, 158.

158 "his family was increasing": Ibid., 157.

160 Typically, Lee's correspondence: Drumm, "Robert E. Lee and the Mississippi River."

161 He plunged into Gratiot's defense: Freeman, *Robert E. Lee*, Vol. 1, 158.

161 The improvements Lee had made: Pryor, *Reading the Man*, 116.

161 Fortunately, common sense prevailed: Freeman, *Robert E. Lee*, Vol. 1, 174.

162 After an extended journey: Ibid., 178.

164 The race was won: Pryor, *Reading the Man*, 122.

165 It may be true: Freeman, *Robert E. Lee*, Vol. 1, 185.

167 He took care to praise: Thomas, *Robert E. Lee*, 102.

167 "I receive poor encouragement": Ibid., 103.

169 "He seemed to be weighted down": Freeman, *Robert E. Lee*, Vol. 1, 188.

170 Mary and the children: Ibid., 191.

172 "appointed as a member": Ibid., 194.

173 "horror at the sight of pen": Ibid.

173 It was neither interesting nor demanding: Ibid., 197.

173 "adventuresome young man": Ibid., 196.

174 In a piece of surgery: Ibid.

174 "We must endeavor to assist her": Coulling, *The Lee Girls*, 13.

174 In any event, Lee was the most admirable: Freeman, *Robert E. Lee*, Vol. 1, 196.

174 required a "tight rein": Ibid.

CHAPTER 4 The Perfect Warrior—Mexico, 1846–1848

177 "Generally, the officers": Christopher Conway and Gustavo Pellon, *The U.S.-Mexican War: Binational Reader* (Indianapolis, Ind.: Hackett, 2010), 153.

177 "The Southern rebellion": Joan Waugh, *U.S. Grant: American Hero, American Myth* (Chapel

Hill: University of North Carolina Press, 2009), 203.

178 "better satisfied": Robert E. Lee to Mary Lee, May 12, 1846, Debutts-Ely Papers, Library of Congress; Elizabeth Pryor, *Reading the Man: A Portrait of Robert E. Lee Through His Private Papers* (New York: Viking, 2007), 158.

178 The "Texans": Wikipedia, "Mexican-American War," 3.

179 Provocation was not long in coming: Ibid., 14, n12.

181 "the Sharpening of Swords": Pryor, *Reading the Man,* 158.

181 "If he were left at Fort Hamilton": Douglas Southall Freeman, *Robert E. Lee: A Biography* (New York: Scribner, 1934), Vol. 1, 202.

182 "I reached here last night": Robert E. Lee to Mary Lee, September 21, 1846, Debutts-Ely Letters, Library of Congress.

185 He was accompanied by his "faithful": Robert E. Lee Jr., *Recollections and Letters of Robert E. Lee* (New York: Doubleday, Page, 1924), 5.

185 Connally took care: Ibid.; Reverend J. William Jones, *Life and Letters of Robert E. Lee: Soldier and Man* (New York: Neale, 1906), 50.

188 This was cautious, but unnecessary: Freeman, *Robert E. Lee,* Vol. 1, 208; Wikipedia, "Mexican-American War," 8.

189 To Wool's dismay: Freeman, *Robert E. Lee,* Vol. 1, 211.

194 Worth was a fiery hero: Ibid., 53.

200 "the largest amphibious invasion yet attempted": John Eisenhower, *So Far from God: The U.S. War in Mexico, 1846–1848* (New York: Anchor, 1990), 255.

200 His incredibly detailed plans: Ibid., 253–54.

201 They were "the first specially built": K. Jack Bauer, *Surfboats and Horse Marines: U.S. Naval Operations in the Mexican War 1846–1848* (Annapolis, Md.: U.S. Naval Institute Press, 1969), 66.

205 Dust clouds in the distance: Freeman, *Robert E. Lee*, Vol. 1, 214.

205 Lee picked "the son": Ibid., 215.

206 Lee's cavalry escort: Ibid.

206 "on a hill not far away": Ibid.

207 "This Mexican was the most delighted": Ibid., 216.

207 Lee had ridden: Ibid.

207 The incident apparently: Ibid.

209 Although Scott couched his demand: Winfield Scott, *Memoirs of Lieut.-General Scott, LL.D. Written by Himself* (New York: Sheldon, 1864), Vol. 2, 403.

209 A second problem was that Scott: Ibid., 402.

210 "a great disappointment": Ibid.

210 "I had now": Ibid., 403.

212 For the moment: Freeman, *Robert E. Lee*, Vol. 1, 219.

213 From the sea Tampico: Ibid., 220.

214 Scott had been informed: Scott, *Memoirs*, Vol. 2, 413.

214 Lee was one of the few: Freeman, *Robert E. Lee*, Vol. 1, 221.

215 "a gently curving strip": Bauer, *Surfboats and Horse Marines*, 77.

215 The landing was scheduled: Ibid., 78.

216 Lee witnessed the landing: Scott, *Memoirs*, Vol. 2, 419.

217 "were considered . . . to be among the strongest": Bauer, *Surfboats and Horse Marines*, 83.

217 The wall around: Ibid.

218 As "Scott's protégé": Allan Peskin, *Winfield Scott and the Profession of Arms* (Kent, Ohio: Kent State University Press, 2003), 155, 156.

219 "a lurid glare": Ibid., 157.

220 "but hidden from its view": Ibid.

220 Lee built the battery: Bauer, *Surfboats and Horse Marines*, 92.

220 Lee found the sailors: Freeman, *Robert E. Lee*, Vol. 1, 230.

221 "unconscious of personal danger": Ibid., 231.

221 "No matter where I turned": Fitzhugh Lee, *General Lee* (New York: Appleton, 1913), 36–37; Freeman, *Robert E. Lee*, Vol. 1, 231.

221 The hellish exchange: Peskin, *Winfield Scott*, 158.

221 On March 25 the city's: Scott, *Memoirs*, Vol. 2, 427; Eisenhower, *So Far from God*, 264.

222 Mexico's "principal port": Scott, *Memoirs*, Vol. 2, 428.

222 "It was awful": Freeman, *Robert E. Lee*, Vol. 1, 231.

223 As Lee looked: Peskin, *Winfield Scott*, 159.

223 Of these, the better road: Ibid., 162.

224 This road crossed: Ibid.

224 In Washington, President Polk: Ibid., 174.

225 Worth's behavior: Ethan Allen Hitchcock, *Fifty Years in Camp and Field* (New York: Putnam, 1909), 130.

227 Two days out of Vera Cruz: Justin H. Smith, *The War with Mexico* (St. Petersburg, Fla.: Red and Black, 2011), 47; Peskin, *Winfield Scott*, 162.

227 The troops applauded: Scott, *Memoirs*, Vol. 2, 432.

228 "that indefatigable engineer": Smith, *The War with Mexico*, 50.

230 "The right of the Mexican line": Freeman, *Robert E. Lee*, Vol. 1, 239.

231 One of Twiggs's engineers: Peskin, *Winfield Scott*, 163.

231 there were Mexican troops: Freeman, *Robert E. Lee*, Vol. 1, 239.

231 More soldiers came and went: Ibid., 240.

232 "He did not reach": Ibid., 241.

233 Worth was still sulking: Peskin, *Winfield Scott*, 149.

233 The spirit of the senior officers: Ibid.

234 It was a grueling: Smith, *The War with Mexico*, 51.

234 The intention had been: Freeman, *Robert E. Lee*, Vol. 1, 242–43.

234 "You infernal scoundrel": Ibid., 243.

235 "Charge them to hell": Ibid.

235 Twiggs had sacrificed: Peskin, *Winfield Scott*, 148.

237 "Her plaintive tone": Freeman, *Robert E. Lee*, 291.

238 The only part of Scott's plan: Peskin, *Winfield Scott*, 167.

238 Over 1,000 Mexican soldiers: Ibid.; Freeman, *Robert E. Lee,* Vol. 1, 246.

239 "Nor was he less conspicuous": Freeman, *Robert E. Lee,* Vol. 1, 248.

240 The landscape delighted: *The Robert E. Lee Reader,* Stanley F. Horn, ed. (Indianapolis, Ind.: Bobbs-Merrill, 1949), 58.

240 Lee busied himself: Freeman, *Robert E. Lee,* Vol. 1, 250.

240 "strongly occupied": Ibid.

242 In desperation, Scott determined: Scott, *Memoirs,* Vol. 2, 460.

243 "the gorgeous seat": Ibid., 466–67.

243 More important: Ibid., 469.

246 "passable for infantry": Freeman, *Robert E. Lee,* Vol. 1, 256.

247 Lee concluded that if the Mexicans: Peskin, *Winfield Scott,* 178.

247 Again serving as a kind of trailblazer: Ibid., 179.

248 Lee stayed with the artillery: Freeman, *Robert E. Lee,* Vol. 1, 260.

248 "screw [their] courage": Shakespeare, *Macbeth,* I, vii, 59.

249 He was among the first to recognize: Freeman, *Robert E. Lee,* Vol. 1, 260.

249 The attacks against General Valencia's center: Ibid., 261.

251 Lee set out at eight o'clock: Ibid., 263.

251 "drenched and sore": Ibid., 264.

252 For several minutes: Peskin, *Winfield Scott,* 181.

252 "the greatest feat": Ibid., 180.

253 The center of the Mexican position: Freeman, *Robert E. Lee,* Vol. 1, 267.

254 "Our troops being now hotly": Henry Alexander White, *Robert E. Lee* (New York: Greenwood, 1969), 42; Freeman, *Robert E. Lee,* Vol. 1, 269.

254 The fight at the fortified convent: Timothy Johnson, *A Gallant Little Army: The Mexico City Campaign* (Lawrence: University Press of Kansas, 2007), 180.

255 He had lost over: Peskin, *Winfield Scott,* 182.

256 The general made his headquarters: Freeman, *Robert E. Lee,* Vol. 1, 273.

257 "on slightly elevated ground": Ibid., 274.

258 Accompanied by two other engineering officers: Ibid., 276.

259 He spent September 9: Ibid.

260 The volunteers had been formed: Ibid., 279.

262 "wild, looting and hunting": Peskin, *Winfield Scott,* 188.

264 He made his way back: Freeman, *Robert E. Lee,* Vol. 1, 285.

265 Lee never lost confidence: Ibid., 292.

266 No fewer than seventy-eight: Johnson, *A Gallant Little Army,* 291.

266 He returned home: Freeman, *Robert E. Lee,* 294.

CHAPTER 5   A Long Peace—1848–1860

268 The family dog Spec: Douglas Southall Freeman, *Robert E. Lee: A Biography* (New York: Scribner, 1934), Vol. 1, 301.

269 "After a moment's greeting": Robert E. Lee Jr., *Recollections and Letters of Robert E. Lee* (Garden City, N.Y.: Doubleday, Page, 1924), 4.

269 "as much annoyance": Ibid., 6.

269 "always petting her": Ibid.

270 "From that early time": Ibid.

274 He was influenced: Elizabeth Brown Pryor, *Reading the Man: A Portrait of Robert E. Lee Through His Private Letters* (New York: Viking, 2007), 229.

279 He *felt* anger: Gamaliel Bradford, *Lee the American* (Boston: Houghton Mifflin, 1927), 225.

279 "Lee not only loved": Ibid., 214; Reverend J. William Jones, *Life and Letters of Robert E. Lee: Soldier and Man* (New York: Neale, 1906), 94.

280 *"My heart quails within me":* Bradford, *Lee the American*, 212.

281 "frugal and thrifty": Ibid.

282 Lee's duties at the War Department: Freeman, *Robert E. Lee*, Vol. 1, 302.

284 As usual, his work progressed: Ibid., 306.

284 "The Cuban revolutionary junta": Ibid.

285 Daily labor overseeing: Ibid.

288 "We must not for our own pleasure": Robert E. Lee to Mary Lee, January 2, 1851, quoted in Emory Thomas, *Robert E. Lee* (New York: Norton, 1995), 148.

288 Baltimore was full of Lee: Freeman, *Robert E. Lee*, Vol. 1, 309.

288 The Lees participated: Lee, *Recollections and Letters of Robert E. Lee*, 10.

289 Lee had in fact gone to a good deal: Freeman, *Robert E. Lee,* Vol. 1, 309.

289 Here, at last, was an area: Ibid.

289 At first his grades: Ibid., 310.

290 "deeply humiliated": Ibid.

290 Lee wrote to his son, "Dearest Mr. Boo": *New York Times,* April 14, 1918, sec. VII, 5.

292 "We came home on a Wednesday": Robert E. Lee to G.W. C. Lee, December 28, 1851, Jones, *Life and Letters of Robert E. Lee,* 76–77.

293 "Nothing was needed to assure": Freeman, *Robert E. Lee,* Vol. 1, 314.

294 "I learn with much regret": Henry Alexander White, *Robert E. Lee* (New York: Greenwood, 1969), 48.

297 "to receive a packet of socks": Freeman, *Robert E. Lee,* Vol. 1, 321.

298 "It was built of stone": Lee, *Recollections and Letters of Robert E. Lee,* 11–12.

300 A letter he wrote to *"My Precious Annie":* Ibid., 15.

301 The cadets, seeing Lee: Ibid., 13.

304 Lee was spared any such trouble: Freeman, *Robert E. Lee,* Vol. 1, 333.

304 Lee may have wished: Ibid., 334.

306 "I fear the Genl": Robert E. Lee to Markie, June 29, 1854, quoted in Thomas, *Robert E. Lee,* 158.

306 The joke here: Allan Peskin, *Winfield Scott and the Profession of Arms* (Kent, Ohio: Kent State University Press, 2003), 140–1.

310 "What is the excuse": William Montgomery Meigs, *The Life of Thomas Hart Benton* (Philadelphia: Lippincott, 1904), 429.

312 He had called Mrs. Custis "Mother": Freeman, *Robert E. Lee*, Vol. 1, 328.

312 "May God give you strength": Lee, *Life and Letters of Robert E. Lee*, 18–19.

313 It is surely no accident: Paul Nagel, *The Lees of Virginia: Seven Generations of an American Family* (New York: Oxford University Press, 2007), 252.

314 "inculcating those principles": Freeman, *Robert E. Lee*, Vol. 1, 325.

314 "You must not infer": Ibid., 341.

314 Lee considered discharging cadets: Ibid., 344, n24.

314 His pride in inspecting the first graduating class: Ibid., 329.

315 She brought several of the familiar: Mary P. Coulling, *The Lee Girls* (Winston-Salem, N.C.: Blair, 1987), 40.

316 The grounds and gardens: Ibid., 34.

316 The board of visitors: Freeman, *Robert E. Lee*, Vol. 1, 347.

317 Again and again small detachments: Ibid., 348–49.

319 "with his dying breath": Ibid., 350.

319 Lee gained nothing: Thomas, *Robert E. Lee*, 159.

321 The sheer tedium: Freeman, *Robert E. Lee*, Vol. 1, 362.

323 "These people give a world": Freeman, *Robert E. Lee*, Vol. 1, 364.

324 "Yesterday I returned": Ibid.

326 "my feelings for my country": Robert E. Lee to Mary Lee, August 4, 1856, Freeman, *Robert E. Lee*, Vol. 1, 367.

326 "I saw nothing": Ibid.

327 Mildred, who was four years younger: Nagel, *The Lees of Virginia*, 233.

327 That Edward Childe: Ibid., 234.

327 "The news came to me": Robert E. Lee to Mary Lee, August 11, 1856, Jones, *Life and Letters of Robert E. Lee*, 80.

332 "I was much pleased": Robert E. Lee to Mary Lee, December 27, 1856, Virginia Historical Society, Richmond.

336 "I have been out four days": Robert E. Lee to Mary Lee, June 29, 1857, Virginia Historical Society, Richmond.

337 "In the day, the houses": Robert E. Lee to Annie Lee, August 8, 1857, Virginia Historical Society, Richmond.

338 "adds more than years": Nagel, *The Lees of Virginia*, 258.

339 "I can see that": Thomas, *Robert E. Lee*, 174, quoting a letter from Robert E. Lee to A. S. Johnston, Howard-Tilton Library, Tulane University, New Orleans, Louisiana.

341 He had already had the thankless task: Thomas, *Robert E. Lee*, 164.

342 Each of these places: Ibid., 175.

343 "I can see little prospect": Pryor, *Reading the Man*, 262.

345 Custis generously sent his father: Freeman, *Robert E. Lee,* Vol. 1, 384.

348 Slaves were no longer needed: Lisa Kraus, John Bedell, and Charles LeeDecker, "Joseph Bruin and the Slave Trade," June 2007, 1–5, 17.

350 "the general impression": Pryor, *Reading the Man,* 260.

351 The Lees themselves complained: Ibid., 268.

353 "were apprehended and thrown into prison": Pryor, *Reading the Man,* 260.

356 Although these letters: Robert E. Lee to Custis Lee, July 2, 1859, Jones, *Life and Letters of Robert E. Lee,* 102.

357 After Norris's account appeared: Pryor, *Reading the Man,* 272; Robert E. Lee to E. S. Quirk, April 13, 1866, quoted in Michael Fellman, *The Making of Robert E. Lee* (New York: Random House, 2000), 67.

358 far from being unusual: Pryor, *Reading the Man,* 273.

359 "by the French Minister at Washington": Ibid., 261.

359 His military career: Freeman, *Robert E. Lee: A Biography,* Vol. 1, 393.

361 He left Arlington: Ibid., 405.

CHAPTER 6   1861—"The Thunder of the Captains and the Shouting"

362 "The thunder of the captains": Job 39:25.

363 "He was a United States officer": Douglas Southall Freeman, *Robert E. Lee: A Biography* (New York: Scribner, 1934), Vol. 1, 404.

364   "gain the affection of your people": Emory Thomas, *Robert E. Lee* (New York: Norton, 1995), 178.

365   From San Antonio: Freeman, *Robert E. Lee,* Vol. 1, 388.

366   His chief concern: Ibid., 405.

366   Another of Lee's concerns: Ibid., 407.

366   Lee was perfectly willing: Freeman, *Robert E. Lee,* Vol. 1, 407.

367   "For the attainment of this object": Reverend J. William Jones, *Life and Letters of Robert E. Lee: Soldier and Man* (New York: Neale, 1906), 112.

368   "A divided heart": Freeman, *Robert E. Lee,* Vol. 1, 411.

368   "You know I was very much": Robert E. Lee to Annie Lee, August 27, 1860, quoted in Thomas, *Robert E. Lee,* 184

369   This was not exactly a midlife crisis: Ibid., 185.

369   "leave politics to the politicians": Freeman, *Robert E. Lee,* Vol. 1, 412.

370   Many of Lee's own officers: Ibid., 413.

370   "Politicians," Lee concluded: Robert E. Lee to Major Van Dorn, July 3, 1860, Debutts-Ely Collection, Library of Congress.

372   Four days after Lincoln's election: Freeman, *Robert E. Lee,* Vol. 1, 413.

372   "Let me tell you": Wikipedia, "Sam Houston," 5.

373   "I hope, however, the wisdom": Robert E. Lee to Custis Lee, December 14, 1860, Jones, *Life and Letters of Robert E. Lee,* 118–19.

376   "hold on to specie": Freeman, *Robert E. Lee,* Vol. 1, 417.

377 "to suffer these *Views*": Ibid., 418.

377 "a man's first allegiance": Ibid.

377 replied abruptly: Ibid.

378 "I will not, however": Robert E. Lee in letter home, January 23, 1861, Freeman, *Robert E. Lee,* Vol. 1, 420.

379 To Custis, he wrote almost in despair: Jones, *Life and Letters of Robert E. Lee,* 120–1.

380 On January 26 Louisiana seceded: Freeman, *Robert E. Lee,* Vol. 1, 426.

380 Rightly assuming that he would: Ibid., 425.

380 "On the right of the entrance": Robert E. Lee to Agnes Lee, August 4, 1856, Debutts-Ely Collection, Library of Congress.

382 "I cannot be moved": Freeman, *Robert E. Lee,* Vol. 1, 429.

384 Though travel was excruciatingly difficult: Mary P. Coulling, *The Lee Girls* (Winston-Salem, N.C.: Blair, 1987), 76.

384 "I am told": Ibid.

385 she returned at the end of the summer: Ibid., 77.

385 She was appalled: Ibid., 78.

385 Even when Mary Lee: Ibid., 80.

385 As state after state: Jones, *Life and Letters of Robert E. Lee,* 119–21.

385 He was determined to remain: Coulling, *The Lee Girls,* 90.

385 Mary Chesnut: C. Vann Woodward, ed., *Mary Chesnut's Civil War* (New Haven, Conn.: Yale University Press, 1981), 26.

387 On April 4: Freeman, *Robert E. Lee,* Vol. 1, 434.

388 "Now they have intercepted": Woodward, *Mary Chestnut's Civil War*, 45.

389 Two days later Fort Sumter surrendered: Freeman, *Robert E. Lee*, Vol. 1, 435.

390 Francis P. Blair had already: John Nicolay and John Hay, *Abraham Lincoln: A History* (New York: Century, 1980), Vol. 4, 498.

391 Early in the morning: Freeman, *Robert E. Lee*, Vol. 1, 436.

391 "to enforce Federal law." Ibid.

392 "I declined the offer": Robert E. Lee to Reverdy Johnson, February 25, 1868, Robert E. Lee Jr., *Recollections and Letters of Robert E. Lee* (Garden City, N.Y.: Doubleday, Page, 1924), 27–28.

392 "There are times": Freeman, *Robert E. Lee, A Biography*, Vol. 1, 28n.

393 "I must say that I am": John S. Mosby, *Memoirs of John S. Mosby*, Charles S. Russell, ed. (Boston: Little, Brown, 1917), 379.

393 "I am unable to realize": Frances Scott and Anne C. Webb, *Who Is Markie? The Life of Martha Custis Williams Carter, Cousin and Confidante of Robert E. Lee* (Berwyn Heights, Md.: Heritage, 2007), 132.

395 "I have the honor": Freeman, *Robert E. Lee*, Vol. 1, 440.

395 "Save in defense": Ibid., 442.

395 When he was done: Ibid.

396 "I know you will blame me": Lee, *Recollections and Letters of Robert E. Lee*, 25–26.

397 "There is no man": Michael Fellman, *The Making of Robert E. Lee* (New York: Random House, 2000), 90.

398 Never one to waste a minute: Freeman, *Robert E. Lee,* Vol. 1, 448.

399 "bald-headed, florid, and bottle-nosed": Ibid., 463.

399 His letter to Lee: *Ordinances Adopted by the Convention of Virginia in Secret Session in April and May, 1861,* 9.

401 "Its foundations are laid": Benjamin Quarles, *The Negro in the Civil War* (New York: Da Capo, 1953), 43.

401 "his official rank or *personal* position": Freeman, *Robert E. Lee,* Vol. 1, 70.

404 Lee was given a small office: Thomas, *Robert E. Lee,* 191.

404 four members: Ibid., 464.

405 "I hope we have heard": Mosby, *Memoirs of John S. Mosby,* 379.

405 Finally, the doors were opened: Freeman, *Robert E. Lee,* Vol. 1, 465.

406 The Federal arsenal: Ibid., 473.

407 the Norfolk Navy Yard: Ibid., 474.

410 "40,000 troops": Thomas, *Robert E. Lee,* 194.

411 Although both he and Custis: Coulling, *The Lee Girls,* 85.

411 "You *have to move*": Ibid., 86.

411 In the morning he rode over: Ibid.

411 The silver of the Lee and Custis families: Thomas, *Robert E. Lee,* 61; Edmund Jennings Lee, *Lee of*

Virginia, 1642–1892 (Philadelphia, 1895), 409–10; Coulling, *The Lee Girls*, 87.

412 The dashing Lieutenant: Scott and Webb, *Who Is Markie?* 133.

413 There is no question: Coulling, *The Lee Girls*, 87.

413 even at Ravensworth: Lee, *Recollections and Letters of Robert E. Lee*, 30.

414 Her oldest son, Custis: Coulling, *The Lee Girls*, 89.

414 She went on at some length: Ibid., 88–89.

415 Sanford was sensible: Thomas, *Robert E. Lee*, 195.

415 All homes would henceforth seem: Lee, *Recollections and Letters of Robert E. Lee*, 32.

415 Deep and sincere: Coulling, *The Lee Girls*, 89.

417 "last ten years": Robert E. Lee to Mary Lee, April 30, 1861, Fitzhugh Lee, *General Lee* (New York: University Society, 1894), 93.

417 A flurry of complaints: Thomas, *Robert E. Lee*, 196; *Boston Daily Advertiser*, May 4, 1861; *New York Times*, May 4, 1861.

417 Even Mary Chesnut: Woodward, *Mary Chesnut's Civil War*, 70–71.

417 "FOR SALVATION OF OUR CAUSE": Thomas, *Robert E. Lee*, 197.

419 Not everyone who saw him: Woodward, *Mary Chesnut's Civil War*, 116.

420 At first Lee refused: Thomas, *Robert E. Lee*, 197, quoting the *Richmond Whig* of June 7, 1861.

422 "I was at once attracted": Walter Herron Taylor, *General Lee: His Campaigns in Virginia,*

1861–1865 (Lincoln: University of Nebraska Press, 1994), 21–22.

423 Lee, Taylor commented: Ibid., 25.

424 Taylor's admiration for Lee: Ibid., 6.

425 Governor Letcher and the convention: Freeman, *Robert E. Lee*, Vol. 1, 492.

429 "COLONEL: Under authority": *The War of the Rebellion: A Compilation of the Official Records of the Union and Confederate Armies.* Series I, Vol. LI, Part 2 (Washington, D.C.: U.S. Government Printing Office, 1897), 92.

431 sound military advice: *The War of the Rebellion: A Compilation of the Official Records of the Union and Confederate Armies.* Series I, Vol. II (Washington, D.C.: U.S. Government Printing Office, 1880), 793–94.

433 Keeping a firm rein: Freeman, *Robert E. Lee*, Vol. 1, 518.

433 The defense of Richmond: Ibid., 519.

434 From Richmond, Garnett's job: Le Comte de Paris, *History of the Civil War in America* (Philadelphia: Porter and Coates, 1886), Vol. 1, 221.

436 In less than a month: Freeman, *Robert E. Lee*, Vol. 1, 522.

437 "I should like to retire": Robert E. Lee to Mary Lee, June 8, 1861, quoted in Freeman, *Robert E. Lee*, Vol. 1, 527.

439 Although Davis held Lee in "esteem": Ibid., 516.

441 There has been conjecture: Ibid., 527.

442 "in a miserable condition": *The War of the Rebellion*, Series I, Vol. II, 236.

442 Garnett had fewer than 5,000 men: Freeman, *Robert E. Lee*, Vol. 1, 532–33.

443 He carried out a textbook attack: Ibid., 533.

444 McClellan's victory: Ibid., 535.

444 The *New York Herald:* Carl Sandburg, *Storm over the Land: A Profile of the Civil War Taken Mainly from Abraham Lincoln: The War Years* (New York: Harcourt Brace, 1942), 62.

446 "My movements are very uncertain": Robert E. Lee to Mary Lee, Lee, *Recollections and Letters of Robert E. Lee*, 36.

446 Eighteen days later: Ibid.

447 From Kinloch: Coulling, *The Lee Girls*, 89.

448 Lee sent a young man: Lee, *Recollections and Letters of Robert E. Lee*, 36.

448 Her daughter Mildred: Coulling, *The Lee Girls*, 90.

448 Mary's maid Selina: Scott and Webb, *Who Is Markie?* 134–35.

450 And true to form: Colonel Vincent J. Esposito, *The West Point Atlas of the American Wars, 1689–1900* (New York: Praeger, 1959), Vol. 1, see text accompanying map 19.

452 "You are green": Edwin C. Bearrs, *Fields of Honor* (Washington, D.C.: National Geographic, 2006), 35.

452 McDowell himself had never: Wikipedia, "Irvin McDowell," 1.

453 Even the date of McDowell's advance: Bearrs, *Fields of Honor*, 35.

454 Apart from that: Ibid.

455 McDowell's first mistake: *Confederate Military History: A Library of Confederate States History*, Clement Anselm Evans, ed. (Atlanta, Ga.: Confederate Publishing, 1899), Vol. 3, 107.

456 Flowing from west: Barbara Tuchman, *The Guns of August* (New York: Library of America, 2012), 29.

458 Bee, impressed by Jackson's: Sarah Nicholas Randolph, *The Life of Stonewall Jackson* (Philadelphia: Lippincott, 1876), 86.

460 "We have whipped them": Hunter McGuire, M.D., "An Address at the Dedication of Jackson Memorial Hall, Virginia Military Institute, July 9, 1897" (R. E. Lee Camp, No. 1, 1897), 6.

460 "no preparations whatever": David Detzer, *Donnybrook: The Battle of Bull Run* (Orlando, Fla.: Harcourt, 2004), 486.

461 Even Secretary of War Edwin M. Stanton: Frank Abial Flower, *Edwin McMasters Stanton: The Autocrat of Rebellion* (Akron, Ohio: Saalfield, 1905), 109.

461 "pouring through this place": John G. Nicolay and John Hay, "Abraham Lincoln: A History," *Century Illustrated Magazine* (New York: Century, 1888), Vol. 36, 288.

462 All that was missing: George Francis Robert Henderson, *Stonewall Jackson and the American Civil War* (New York: Longmans, Green, 1900), Vol. 1, 154.

463 Mary Lee and her girls: Coulling, *The Lee Girls*, 91.

463 The next day, in the pouring rain: Ibid.

465 "The empty saddle": Woodward, *Mary Chesnut's Civil War*, 106–7.

465 He also broke the news: Lee, *Recollections and Letters of Robert E. Lee*, 37.

466 The military situation: R. Lockwood Tower, ed., *Lee's Adjutant: The Wartime Letters of Colonel Walter Herron Taylor, 1862–1865* (Columbia: University of South Carolina Press, 1995), 7.

466 Lee's own position: Freeman, *Robert E. Lee*, Vol. 1, 541.

468 He would write to Mary: Robert E. Lee to Mary Lee, August 4, 1861, Lee, *Recollections and Letters of Robert E. Lee*, 38–39.

468 Brigadier General Henry R. Jackson: Freeman, *Robert E. Lee*, Vol. 1, 543–44.

468 "jaded and galled": Ibid., 544.

473 "Our troops, I know": Ibid., 556, n5.

474 "had lived with gentle people": Ibid., 552.

478 The attack was set: Ibid., 565.

480 "the right branch of the Elkwater Fork": Ibid., 568.

480 Curiously enough: Lee, *Recollections and Letters of Robert E. Lee*, 46–47.

481 On September 19 Lee rode: Taylor, *General Lee: His Campaigns in Virginia*, 31.

483 The *Richmond Examiner* dismissed: James McPherson, *Battle Cry of Freedom: The Civil War Era* (New York: Oxford University Press, 1988), 302.

484 "I am sorry, as you say": Lee, *Recollections and Letters of Robert E. Lee*, 51.

488 His original name was: "General Robert E. Lee's War Horses: Traveller and Lucy Long," *Southern Historical Society Papers,* Vol. 18, January–December 1890, 388–91.

489 The Broun brothers: Ibid.

489 Lee had several horses: Lee, *Recollections and Letters of Robert E. Lee,* 54.

490 Even Jefferson Davis: Ibid., 53.

491 "the best man available": Freeman, *Robert E. Lee,* Vol. 1, 607.

492 Lee quickly set about: Ibid., 615, 614.

492 "an unromantic routine": Ibid., 614.

493 "Had some old English cathedral crypt": Ibid., 612.

495 "achievement . . . unworthy of any": Ibid., 618.

496 "As to our old home": Lee, *Recollections and Letters of Robert E. Lee,* 59.

497 Lee did not gloat: Robert E. Lee to Mary Lee, February 8, 1862, Ibid., 64.

498 "If circumstances will": Freeman, *Robert E. Lee,* Vol. 1, 628.

CHAPTER 7 The Seven Days—"The Power of the Sword"

499 "The power of the sword": Job 5:20.

499 There was a movement: Douglas Southall reeman, *Robert E. Lee: A Biography* (New York: Scribner, 1934), Vol. 1, 2, 6.

499 "the conduct of military operations": *The War of the Rebellion: A Compilation of the Official*

Records of the Union and Confederate Armies, Series I, Vol. V (Washington, D.C.: U.S. Government Printing Office, 1881), 1099; *National Intelligencer* (Washington, D.C.), April 14, 1861.

502 The ostensible reason: Freeman, *Robert E. Lee: A Biography,* Vol. 1, 2, 3.

502 Of course what nobody: Stephen W. Sears, *George B. McClellan: The Young Napoleon* (New York: Ticknor and Fields, 1988), 108–9.

503 "cautious and weak": Ibid., 180; George B. McClellan to Abraham Lincoln, April 20, 1862, Lincoln Papers, Library of Congress.

503 "There was no hesitation": A. L. Long, *Memoirs of Robert E. Lee* (New York: J. M. Stoddard, 1886), 435.

503 "In audacity": J. F. C. Fuller, *Grant and Lee: A Study in Personality and Generalship* (London: Eyre and Spottiswoode, 1933), 267.

503 Lee himself found some consolation: Mary P. Coulling, *The Lee Girls* (Winston-Salem, N.C.: Blair, 1987), 98.

504 Even though White House was: Ibid., 101.

505 In two of the blank pages: Ibid., 99–101.

515 Although Confederate knowledge: Colonel Vincent J. Esposito, *The West Point Atlas of the American Wars, 1689–1900* (New York: Praeger, 1959), Vol. 1, text accompanying map 39.

519 He understood at once: Peter Cozzens, *Shenandoah 1862: Stonewall Jackson's Valley Campaign* (Chapel Hill: University of North Carolina Press, 2013), 23–25.

519 If one thinks of the Valley Pike: Ibid., 22.

520 "with the serenest faith": C. Vann Woodward, ed., *Mary Chesnut's Civil War* (New Haven, Conn.: Yale University Press, 1981), 361.

522 "a constant supervision": Walter H. Taylor, *Four Years with General Lee* (New York: Appleton, 1878), 38.

523 By April 9: Sears, *George B. McClellan: The Young Napoleon*, 172.

523 This was an unparalleled: Ibid., 168.

524 "No one but McClellan": Ibid., 180.

525 He arrived there on April 13: Douglas Southall Freeman, *Robert E. Lee: A Biography* (New York: Scribner, 1934), Vol. 2, 21.

526 "War of posts": Letter to John Hancock, September 8, 1776, *Papers of George Washington, Revolutionary War Series*, Dorothy Twohig, ed. (Charlottesville: University of Virginia Press, 1994), Vol. 6, 249.

528 "exhibited . . . a patient persistence": Freeman, *Robert E. Lee*, Vol. 2, 17.

528 He advised Magruder: Ibid., 19.

529 On April 21: James Robertson, *Stonewall Jackson: The Man, the Soldier, the Legend* (New York: Macmillan, 1997), 364.

531 "I cannot pretend": *The War of the Rebellion: A Compilation of the Official Records of the Union and Confederate Armies*, Series I, Vol. XII, Part 3, 866.

535 It was an extraordinary achievement: *Shenandoah, 1862* (New York: Time-Life Books, 1997), 9.

537 He had warned Mary: Coulling, *The Lee Girls*, 101.

538 "the Confederate army had disappeared": Le Comte de Paris, *History of the Civil War in America* (Philadelphia: Porter and Coates, 1886), Vol. 2, 12.

539 He had preserved his army: Freeman, *Robert E. Lee: A Biography*, Vol. 2, 46.

539 a complaint obviously directed: Ibid., 45.

540 Lee tactfully deflected: *The War of the Rebellion: A Compilation of the Official Records of the Union and Confederate Armies*, Series 1, Vol. XI, Part III (Washington, D.C.: U.S. Government Printing Office, 1884), 500.

541 "Northern soldiers who profess": Coulling, *The Lee Girls*, 102.

542 Lee managed to send two aides: Freeman, *Robert E. Lee*, Vol. 2, 251–55.

543 "against General McClellan's orders": Coulling, *The Lee Girls*, 104–7.

547 Lee apparently answered: Freeman, *Robert E. Lee*, Vol. 2, 48.

547 "tears ran down his cheeks": J. H. Reagan, *Memoirs: With Special Reference to Secession and the Civil War* (New York: Neale, 1906), 139.

548 Although "the fate of the Confederacy": Ibid.

549 "if he was not going to give battle": Ibid.

549 McClellan was advancing "cautiously": Freeman, *Robert E. Lee*, Vol. 2, 58.

549 He still believed: Sears, *George B. McClellan*, 189.

552 "If Lee was the Jove of the war": Walter Herron Taylor, *General Lee: His Campaigns in Virginia, 1861–1865* (Lincoln: University of Nebraska Press, 1994), 46.

552 On May 30: Freeman, *Robert E. Lee,* Vol. 2, 66.

553 At the junction: Ibid., 68.

553 "witnessed the advance": Reagan, *Memoirs,* 141.

555 "I protested": Ibid.

555 Johnston had replied: Freeman, *Robert E. Lee,* Vol. 2, 72.

555 Shortly after this news: Reagan, *Memoirs,* 141.

556 For the moment: Colonel Vincent J. Esposito, *The West Point Atlas of the American Wars, 1689–1900* (New York: Praeger, 1959), Vol. 1, text accompanying map 43.

556 "as much mud": Charles Dickens, *Bleak House,* in *The Works of Charles Dickens* (New York: Scribner, 1899), Vol. XVI, 1.

556 Davis and Lee rode back: *Freeman, Robert E. Lee,* Vol. 2, 74.

557 In the judgment of J. F. C. Fuller: Fuller, *Grant and Lee,* 156.

560 bayonets were responsible for less: Wikipedia, "Bayonet."

561 "in a state of utter exhaustion": Sears, *George B. McClellan,* 196.

561 "his communications and the immense park": Le Comte de Paris, *History of the Civil War in America,* Vol. 2, 69.

561   he left things as they were: Freeman, *Robert E. Lee,* Vol. 2, 77.

562   "feeble and accomplished nothing": Esposito, *The West Point Atlas of the American Wars, 1689–1900,* Vol. 1, text accompanying map 43.

563   "After much reflection I think": Robert E. Lee, *Lee's Dispatches: Unpublished Letters of Robert E. Lee* (New York: Putnam, 1915), 5.

568   "conducted with your usual skill": *The War of the Rebellion: A Compilation of the Official Records of the Union and Confederate Armies,* Series I, Vol. XII, Part 3 (Washington, D.C.: U.S. Government Printing Office, 1885), 908.

569   "Leave your enfeebled troops": Ibid., 910.

570   "In moving your troops": Ibid., 913.

571   He put J. E. B. Stuart: Ibid., 916.

572   McClellan's left was anchored: Freeman, *Robert E. Lee,* Vol. 2, 96.

572   Stuart set off: Jeffrey D. Wert, *Cavalryman of the Lost Cause: A Biography of J. E. B. Stuart* (New York: Simon and Schuster, 2008), 103.

573   "a tasseled yellow sash": Ibid., 94.

576   "That will depend on the time": Freeman, *Robert E. Lee,* Vol. 2, 102.

580   "Honest A has again fallen": Sears, *George B. McClellan,* 200–1.

580   "I will then have them": Ibid., 201, 204.

580   Jackson spent that day: Robertson, *Stonewall Jackson,* 460–61.

580   He wore no badges: Ibid., 461.

581 In the mid-afternoon: Freeman, *Robert E. Lee,* Vol. 2, 107.

581 Hill shepherded: Ibid., 109.

581 Jackson was thirty-eight: Ibid.

582 Like Lee, Longstreet: Ibid.

584 When asked when his army: Robertson, *Stonewall Jackson,* 466.

587 He ordered General Samuel P. Heintzelman: Sears, *George B. McClellan,* 204.

588 "If there is one man": Emory Thomas, *Robert E. Lee* (New York: Norton, 1995), 226.

589 Though Lee could not have: Sears, *George B. McClellan,* 205.

590 "Stonewall is coming up": C. Vann Woodward, ed., *Mary Chesnut's Civil War,* 395.

590 Had McClellan chosen: Sears, *George B. McClellan,* 205–6.

594 He had willed himself: Coulling, *The Lee Girls,* 104.

594 "The four divisions": *The War of the Rebellion: A Compilation of the Official Records of the Union and Confederate Armies,* Series I, Vol. XI, Part 2 (Washington, D.C.: U.S. Government Printing Office, 1884), 499.

595 "In your march": Robertson, *Stonewall Jackson,* 469.

595 In the days when roads: Taylor, *General Lee: His Campaigns in Virginia,* 66.

595 Even the faithful Walter Taylor: Ibid., 65.

596 "The Confederate commanders": Richard Taylor, *Destruction and Reconstruction: Personal*

Experiences of the Late War, Richard B. Harwell, ed. (New York: Longmans Green, 1955), 107–8.

597 Jackson had given himself: Robertson, *Stonewall Jackson,* 476.

597 On June 24: Ibid., 467.

597 His assistant adjutant general: Ibid., 360.

598 Dabney had no military experience: Ibid., 467.

600 It may have been that: Ibid., 469.

600 "underway" by 2:30 a.m.: Ibid., 470.

602 Stuart and his cavalry: Ibid., 471.

602 Jackson had accepted: Ibid., 470.

606 As Jackson understood his orders: Douglas Southall Freeman, *Lee's Lieutenants: A Study in Command* (New York: Scribner, 1942), Vol. 1, 513.

606 From here, he could see: Freeman, *Robert E. Lee,* Vol. 2, 125.

607 If Lee felt any anxiety: Ibid., 127.

608 Even before then Lee: Ibid., 129.

609 It was after 5 p.m.: Ibid., 130.

610 "It is not my army": Ibid., 132.

610 He dictated an order: Ibid.

611 Instead, McClellan: Sears, *George B. McClellan,* 209.

612 "to think we are invincible": Ibid., 208–10.

615 Porter was too busy: Ibid., 210.

617 "the seedy appearance": Robertson, *Stonewall Jackson,* 476.

618 "This position, three miles": Taylor, *Destruction and Reconstruction,* 87.

619 Lee's plan was that Jackson: Freeman, *Robert E. Lee,* Vol. 2, 142.

619   It was 11 a.m.: Robertson, *Stonewall Jackson*, 476.

620   " 'Gentlemen,' Lee said to his staff": Freeman, *Robert E. Lee*, Vol. 2, 144.

621   At 2:30 p.m. A.P. Hill attacked: Ibid., 146.

622   He had deployed his men: Ibid., 148.

622   The Confederate soldiers from A. P. Hill's division: Ibid., 146–47.

623   A Union war correspondent: Charles A. Page, *Letters of a War Correspondent*, James R. Gilmore, ed. (Boston: L. C. Page, 1899), 5–6.

623   "brutally repulsed": Freeman, *Robert E. Lee*.

624   The Timberlake family's farm: Robertson, *Stonewall Jackson*, 477.

625   Jackson ordered the twenty-six-year-old: Ibid., 476.

626   Private Timberlake began to explain: Freeman, *Lee's Lieutenants*, Vol. 1, 524.

628   Though Private Timberlake could not have known it: Robert Lewis Dabney, *Life and Campaigns of Lieut. General Thomas J. Jackson* (New York: Blelock, 1866), 443.

630   "No, let us trust": Ibid., 444.

630   The Federals were not retreating: Freeman, *Robert E. Lee*, Vol. 2, 149.

631   There was no time: Taylor, *Destruction and Reconstruction*, 88.

631   Just before six o'clock: Freeman, *Robert E. Lee*, Vol. 2, 153.

632   The sound of firing: Ibid.

633   "Sweep the field with the bayonet!": Dabney, *Life and Campaigns of Lieut. General Thomas J.*

Jackson, 163; Robertson, *Stonewall Jackson,* 481 and 875 n62.

634 "the incessant roar of musketry": Page, *Letters of a War Correspondent,* 5.

634 "The men were within twenty yards": Freeman, *Robert E. Lee,* Vol. 2, 155.

634 Lee's aide Major Taylor: Taylor, *General Lee: His Campaigns in Virginia,* 69.

635 "A motley mob": Page, *Letters of a War Correspondent,* 7.

635 "Scores of riderless": Ibid.

637 "I have lost this battle": George Francis Robert, Henderson, *Stonewall Jackson and the American Civil War* (New York: Longmans, Green, 1900), Vol. 2, 239; Sears, *George B. McClellan,* 213–14.

638 With commendable restraint Lincoln: Walter H. Taylor, *Four Years with General Lee* (New York: Appleton, 1878), 47.

638 "Jackson's whole force": "General Estimates of the Rebel Forces in Virginia," ibid., 71.

639 "A train was heard approaching": Taylor, *Destruction and Reconstruction,* 89.

642 Magruder was anxious: Freeman, *Robert E. Lee,* Vol. 2, 165.

643 The rough-and-ready reconstruction: Robertson, *Stonewall Jackson,* 489.

645 The result was a bloody draw: Wikipedia, "Battle of Savage's Station."

647 "I regret much that": Gary W. Gallagher, *Lee and His Generals in War and Memory* (Baton Rouge:

Louisiana State University Press, 1998), 129; Robertson, *Stonewall Jackson*, 490.

648 "A heavy rain came down": Taylor, *Destruction and Reconstruction*, 89.

649 As for McClellan himself: Sears, *George B. McClellan*, 218–19, 217.

650 Jackson reached Magruder's headquarters: Robertson, *Stonewall Jackson*, 491.

651 "to pursue the enemy on the road": Freeman, *Robert E. Lee*, Vol. 2, 180.

652 Major Dabney describes the ground: Dabney, *Life and Campaigns of Stonewall Jackson*, 465–66.

652 He adds that "the remainder of the afternoon": Ibid., 466–67.

653 Indeed, Jackson was so exhausted: Ibid., 467.

653 Even Dabney, who was there: Ibid., 466.

654 "a little clearing of broom straw": Freeman, *Robert E. Lee*, Vol. 2, 181.

655 Lee's plan, which had called for: Wikipedia, "Battle of Glendale," 2.

657 Jackson, who had at last retired: Dabney, *Life and Campaigns of Stonewall Jackson*, 473.

657 "No, I think he will clear out": Ibid.

658 In short, the whole army of McClellan: Ibid., 469.

659 "a natural fortress": Freeman, *Robert E. Lee*, Vol. 2, 204.

660 "His temper": Ibid., 200.

660 Longstreet was bluffly optimistic: Ibid.

660 "If General McClellan is there": James Longstreet, *From Manassas to Appomattox: Memoirs of the*

Civil War in America (Bloomington: Indiana University Press, 1960), 143.

660 "Don't get scared": General D. H. Hill, "McClellan's Change of Base," *Century Magazine*, Vol. 30, 1885, 450.

660 When Brigadier General Jubal A. Early: John Goode, *Recollections of a Lifetime* (New York: Neale, 1906), 58.

663 On the right, pioneers: Freeman, *Robert E. Lee*, Vol. 2, 206.

666 "Batteries have been established": Thomas, *Robert E. Lee*, 242.

667 "When the hunt was up": Longstreet, *From Manassas to Appomattox*, xxii.

668 Lee feared that: Ibid., 116.

669 "It was not war": William C. Davis, *The Battlefields of the Civil War* (Norman: University of Oklahoma Press, 1996), 69.

669 "grandly heroic": Freeman, *Robert E. Lee*, Vol. 2, 218.

669 A Union soldier wrote home: Sears, *George B. McClellan*, 222.

669 Malvern Hill was remembered: Freeman, *Robert E. Lee*, Vol. 2, 218.

670 "The result of the battle": Longstreet, *From Manassas to Appomattox*, 116.

671 "The strategy displayed": Taylor, *Destruction and Reconstruction*, 92–93.

672 That night, when Lee rode: Freeman, *Robert E. Lee*, Vol. 2, 218.

672 "In obedience to your orders": Ibid.

673 In just one week: Ibid., 230.

673 The *New York Times* noted: *New York Times*, June 3, 1862.

CHAPTER 8 Triumph and Tragedy—Second Manassas and Sharpsburg

678 A further Federal "column": Douglas Southall Freeman, *Robert E. Lee: A Biography* (New York: Scribner, 1934), Vol. 2, 258.

679 "from the West, where we have always seen": David Herbert Donald, *Lincoln* (New York: Simon and Schuster, 1995), 361.

680 Lincoln, who had appointed him: Ibid., 369.

681 Perhaps under the circumstances: Colonel Vincent J. Esposito, *The West Point Atlas of American Wars, 1689–1900* (New York: Praeger, 1959), text accompanying map 55.

682 To his east McClellan's army: Walter H. Taylor, *Four Years with General Lee* (New York: Appleton, 1878), 63.

682 Lee was thus caught: Ibid., 59.

684 He gave himself ten days: Esposito, *The West Point Atlas of American Wars*, text accompanying map 56.

684 Hill "was high spirited": James Robertson, *Stonewall Jackson: The Man, the Soldier, the Legend* (New York: Macmillan, 1997), 518.

685 "A. P. Hill you will find": *War of the Rebellion: Official Records of the Union and Confederate*

Armies (Wilmington, N.C.: National Historical Society, Broadfoot, 1971), 919.

686 "None of his Division commanders": Robertson, *Stonewall Jackson,* 519.

687 "We cannot afford to be idle": Jeffrey D. Wert, *Cavalryman of the Lost Cause: A Biography of J. E. B. Stuart* (New York: Simon and Schuster, 2008), 139.

690 At the same time Lee simplified: Taylor, *Four Years with General Lee,* 91.

691 "It required great confidence": Ibid., 86.

691 "if practicable to Gordonsville": *Papers of the Military Historical Society of Massachusetts* (Boston: Military Historical Society of Massachusetts, 1990), 402.

691 Typically, Lee urged Stuart: *War of the Rebellion, Official Records of the Union and Confederate Armies,* Series I, Vol. XII, Part III (Washington, D.C.: U.S. Government Printing Office, 1885), 916.

692 "headquarters in the grove": Robertson, *Stonewall Jackson,* 519.

694 urged him to "turn the enemy's position": Gamaliel Bradford, *Lee the American* (Boston: Houghton Mifflin, 1929), 95.

694 He had already been warned: Freeman, *Robert E. Lee,* Vol. 2, 269.

695 Bit by bit, he began the process: Ibid., 271.

697 This time Jackson once again had: Robertson, *Stonewall Jackson,* 525.

698 "nightfall found the Confederate army": Ibid.

699 On August 9 Jackson had his army: Ibid., 526.

700 At this moment Jackson: Ibid., 527.

700 By early afternoon the artillery duel: Ibid., 531, 528.

701 Jackson knew that there was a moment: Robert Lewis Dabney, *Life and Campaigns of Lieut. General Thomas J. Jackson* (New York: Blelock, 1866), 500.

701 Undeterred, Jackson unfastened: Ibid., 501.

701 These may not have been: Ibid.

702 "his blood was up": Ibid., 502.

703 "as if the troops were preparing": Robertson, *Stonewall Jackson*, 538.

704 He and his staff: Emory Thomas, *Robert E. Lee* (New York: Norton, 1995), 250.

705 In her book about the Lee daughters: Mary P. Coulling, *The Lee Girls* (Winston-Salem, N.C.: Blair, 1987), 105.

706 "He was the same loving father": Robert E. Lee, *Recollections and Letters of Robert E. Lee* (Garden City, N.Y.: Doubleday, Page, 1924), 74.

706 Mrs. Lee cannot have been cheered: Coulling, *The Lee Girls*, 112, 105.

706 War had scarcely touched Hickory Hill: Ibid., 206.

708 Lee himself was in favor: Robertson, *Stonewall Jackson*, 540–1.

708 groaning "most audibly": Ibid., 541.

709 "it is all-important that our movement": *War of the Rebellion, Official Records of the Union and Confederate Armies*, Series I, Vol. XI, Part III

(Washington, D.C.: U.S. Government Printing Office, 1884), 676.

709 On the peninsula the terrain: Freeman, *Robert E. Lee*, Vol. 2, 279.

710 Pope had incautiously allowed: Ibid., 280.

712 Stuart had ordered: Ibid., 284; Wert, *Cavalryman of the Lost Cause*, 123–24.

713 Longstreet censured him: James Longstreet, *From Manassas to Appomattox: Memoirs of the Civil War in America* (Bloomington: Indiana University Press, 1960), 159.

714 "clatter of hooves": Freeman, *Robert E. Lee*, Vol. 2, 284.

715 Lee and Longstreet rode together: Longstreet, *From Manassas to Appomattox*, 131; Freeman, *Robert E. Lee*, Vol. 2, 287, n35.

716 Early on the morning of August 20: Wert, *Cavalryman of the Lost Cause*, 126.

717 Stuart did not arrive at Cattlett's Station: Ibid., 127–28.

717 Stuart cut telegraph lines: Ibid., 128.

718 "by rushing out the rear of his tent": Reverend J. William Jones, *Life and Letters of Robert E. Lee: Soldier and Man* (New York: Neale, 1906), 192.

718 "I am sorry he is in such bad company": Ibid.

718 The heavy rain raised: Wert, *Cavalryman of the Lost Cause*, 128.

719 "The army is not properly": Robert E. Lee to Jefferson Davis, September 3, 1862, *Papers of*

Jefferson Davis, Lynda Lasswell Crist, ed. (Baton Rouge: Louisiana State University Press, 1995), Vol. 8, 373.

722 "Lee was no grand-strategist": J. F. C. Fuller, *Grant and Lee: A Study in Personality and Generalship* (New York: Scribner, 1933), 126.

722 When Fuller writes: Jones, *Life and Letters of Robert E. Lee*, 118; Fuller, *Grant and Lee*, 97.

724 "lack of thunder": Fuller, *Grant and Lee*, 125.

724 True, paperwork exhausted and irritated him: Walter Herron Taylor, *General Lee: His Campaigns in Virginia, 1861–1865* (Lincoln: University of Nebraska Press, 1994), 25.

730 Their hostess, Mrs. Marshall: A. L. Long, *Memoirs of Robert E. Lee* (New York: J. M. Stoddard, 1886), 116.

730 Other generals might have: Taylor, *General Lee: His Campaigns in Virginia*, 157–58.

730 Lee "would have been better off": Ibid., 158.

730 On the other hand: Long, *Memoirs of Robert E. Lee*, 116.

731 "they drank dry": Freeman, *Robert E. Lee*, Vol. 2, 309.

731 There was none, however: Long, *Memoirs of Robert E. Lee*, 116.

733 Early the next morning: Ibid., 117; Freeman, *Robert E. Lee*, Vol. 2, 309.

733 This began a day: Robertson, *Stonewall Jackson*, 554.

734 "bulging freight cars": Ibid., 556.

734   Jackson moved his troops: Long, *Memoirs of Robert E. Lee,* 507.

734   "If you are prompt": Emory Upton, *Military Policy of the United States* (Washington, D.C.: U.S. Government Printing Office, 1917), 334.

735   Lee's vanguard reached: Long, *Memoirs of Robert E. Lee,* 117.

736   Longstreet, displaying a lyrical gift: Longstreet, *From Manassas to Appomattox,* 141.

737   "this meal was partaken of": Long, *Memoirs of Robert E. Lee,* 117.

738   "a tactical error": Ibid., 118.

738   It was odd that neither: Esposito, *The West Point Atlas of American Wars,* text accompanying map 60.

739   It was less than fifteen miles: Robertson, *Stonewall Jackson,* 559.

742   Hearing this, Jackson relaxed a bit: Ibid., 560.

742   He shook hands with the courier: Ibid.

743   As Brigadier General Rufus King's Union division approached Groveton: Ibid., 561.

744   He got only about 6,000 men: Wikipedia, "Battle of Groveton," 6.

744   a bloody "stalemate": Ibid., 5.

745   "effusion of blood": Grant to Lee, April 7, 1865, L. T. Remlap, *Grant and His Desscriptive Account of His Tour Around the World* (New York: Hurst, 1885), Vol. 1, 177.

745   "his ear to the ground": Robertson, *Stonewall Jackson,* 563.

746 McClellan was in Washington: Stephen W. Sears, *George B. McClellan: The Young Napoleon* (New York: Ticknor and Fields, 1988), 252.

746 "that fool Pope": Ibid., 253–54.

747 Jackson spent the night: Robertson, *Stonewall Jackson,* 564.

748 By 10 a.m. the Federal forces: Ibid., 565.

748 By midmorning on August 29: Freeman, *Robert E. Lee,* Vol. 2, 322.

749 He had already performed: Fuller, *Grant and Lee,* 164.

749 Lee rode forward to survey the scene: Thomas, *Robert E. Lee,* 253.

750 "a masterpiece of contradiction": John J. Hennessey, *Return to Bull Run: The Campaign and Battle of Second Manassas* (Norman: University of Oklahoma Press, 1999), 232.

750 Throughout the late morning: Robertson, *Stonewall Jackson,* 566.

755 "General Lee was inclined": Longstreet, *From Manassas to Appomattox,* 147.

756 Lee's aide, Colonel Long: Taylor, *General Lee: His Campaigns in Virginia,* 107.

756 "The question will naturally arise": Ibid.

757 "even though his martial instinct": Freeman, *Robert E. Lee,* Vol. 2, 322.

759 "You must know our circumstances": Ibid., 347.

760 During all this time: Ibid., 325.

760 As darkness fell: Ibid., 328.

760 Even *The West Point Atlas:* Esposito, *The West Point Atlas of American Wars,* text accompanying map 62.

762 If Pope did *not* attack: Freeman, *Robert E. Lee,* Vol. 2, 330.

763 Six hundred yards away: Robertson, *Stonewall Jackson,* 572.

764 "the opposing flags": Freeman, *Robert E. Lee,* Vol. 2, 351.

764 Even for Jackson's battle-hardened veterans: Robertson, *Stonewall Jackson,* 890.

764 Lee promptly ordered Longstreet: Freeman, *Robert E. Lee,* Vol. 2, 332.

765 began "to melt away": Ibid.

765 "Almost immediately": Longstreet, *From Manassas to Appomattox,* 152.

765 As Longstreet's guns were firing: Freeman, *Robert E. Lee,* Vol. 2, 332.

766 "threw every man in his army": Ibid.

767 "The artillery would gallop": Gilbert Moxley Sorrel, *Recollections of a Confederate Staff Officer* (New York: Neale, 1905), 98, quoted in Freeman, *Robert E. Lee,* Vol. 2, 334.

767 As Jackson began to advance: Long, *Memoirs of Robert E. Lee,* 510.

767 Lee himself rode forward: Longstreet, *From Manassas to Appomattox,* 154.

768 Longstreet pushed his men: Freeman, *Robert E. Lee,* Vol. 2, 335.

769 "Why, General": Robert E. Lee, *Recollections and Letters of Robert E. Lee,* 76–77.

770 Both wings of the Confederate army: Taylor, *General Lee: His Campaigns in Virginia,* 114.

770 "Though the fighting": Esposito, *The West Point Atlas of American Wars*, text accompanying map 63.

770 By this time it was raining: Sears, *George B. McClellan*, 256.

770 The state of panic: Ibid., 257.

772 He wrote late that night: Robert E. Lee, *Lee's Dispatches: Unpublished Letters of General Robert E. Lee, C.S.A., to Jefferson Davis and the War Department of the Confederate States of America, 1862* (New York: Putnam, 1957), 59–60.

773 Lee carefully gave: Freeman, *Robert E. Lee*, Vol. 2, 338.

775 At the break of day: Ibid.

775 Longstreet would "remain on the battlefield": Ibid., 339.

776 Having set Jackson in motion: Taylor, *General Lee: His Campaigns in Virginia*, 115.

776 Quite apart from the pain: Ibid.

776 Longstreet followed Jackson at 2 p.m.: Freeman, *Robert E. Lee*, Vol. 2, 340.

777 Longstreet complained: Longstreet, *From Manassas to Appomattox*, 157.

778 This was not a success: Freeman, *Robert E. Lee*, Vol. 2, 341.

778 Longstreet, who came up: Longstreet, *From Manassas to Appomattox*, 158.

779 "as the storm of the battle": Ibid.

779 One of the Union casualties of the battle: Ibid., 159.

781 However much Lee despised Pope: Freeman, *Robert E. Lee*, Vol. 2, 342.

781 He had taken over 7,000: Taylor, *General Lee: His Campaigns in Virginia,* 117.

781 "Unless something can be done": Ibid.

781 "My men had nothing to eat": Fuller, *Grant and Lee,* 304.

781 Victorious they might be: Freeman, *Robert E. Lee,* Vol. 2, 349.

783 Maryland offered many strategic advantages: Fuller, *Grant and Lee,* 166.

783 "The present seems to be": *War of the Rebellion, A Compilation of the Official Records of the Union and Confederate Armies,* Series 1, Vol. XIX, Part II (Washington, D.C.: U.S. Government Printing Office, 1887), 590–1.

783 "not properly equipped": Ibid., 590.

783 On September 4 he ordered: Fuller, *Grant and Lee,* 167.

784 President Lincoln and General Halleck were obliged: Sears, *George B. McClellan,* 263.

785 Even then he managed: Ibid., 268–69.

786 Lee wrote, "but being made": *War of the Rebellion, A Compilation of the Official Records of the Union and Confederate Armies,* Series 1, Vol. XIX, Part II, 600.

787 "McClellan has the army with him": Sears, *George B. McClellan,* 262.

787 When he reviewed: Ibid.

788 "The march of the Confederates": Le Comte de Paris, *History of the Civil War in America* (Philadelphia: Porter and Coates, 1886), Vol. 2, 317–18.

788   The state of his army: Freeman, *Robert E. Lee*, Vol. 2, 359, n22.

789   More seriously still: Ibid., 359.

789   Admittedly, Lee's line of communications: Ibid.

791   Lee had constantly borne in mind: Ibid., 360–61.

791   cut the East "off from the West": Ibid.

791   This is the first but not the last time: Ibid., 359.

792   Lee heard Longstreet's booming voice: Ibid., 361, n46.

793   As one of Lee's two army commanders: Ibid.

794   Lieutenant-Colonel Fremantle: Lt. Col. Arthur James Lyon Fremantle, *Three Months in the Southern States, April–June, 1863* (New York: John Bradburn, 1864), 249.

795   "He is an able general": Freeman, *Robert E. Lee*, Vol. 2, 362.

796   It might serve: Ibid., 363.

796   Accidentally dropped in "an abandoned Confederate camp": Fuller, *Grant and Lee*, 168.

800   Mayor-General J. F. C. Fuller turns positively apoplectic: Ibid., 168.

802   The two men reached Hagerstown: Freeman, *Robert E. Lee*, Vol. 2, 366.

804   At this moment of crisis: Longstreet, *From Manassas to Appomattox*, 179.

806   Whatever Lee hoped, at this point: Freeman, *Robert E. Lee*, Vol. 2, 369.

806   "at daylight": Longstreet, *From Manassas to Appomattox*, 179.

808   This was hardly surprising: Wikipedia, "Battle of Harpers Ferry," 6.

808 Lee was relieved by this good news: Esposito, *The West Point Atlas of American Wars*, text accompanying map 67.

808 It was only twelve miles: Wikipedia, "Battle of Harpers Ferry," 6.

811 Lee would be obliged to fight: Esposito, *The West Point Atlas of American Wars*, text accompanying map 67.

812 On the morning of September 16: Freeman, *Robert E. Lee*, Vol. 2, 381.

812 "if he had had a well-equipped": Ibid.

813 He expressed only the rather vague intention: Esposito, *The West Point Atlas of American Wars*, text accompanying map 67.

815 Federal artillery was already firing: Freeman, *Robert E. Lee*, Vol. 2, 382.

816 At 4:30 a.m. Lee was awake: Ibid., 387.

818 Even "Fighting Joe" Hooker: Ronald H. Bailey, *Antietam: The Bloodiest Day* (New York: Time-Life Books, 1984), 70.

818 Around 7:30 a.m.: Freeman, *Robert E. Lee*, Vol. 2, 391.

819 "to be sent to Jackson": Ibid., 390.

820 Lee's faithful aide: Long, *Memoirs of Robert E. Lee*, 134.

821 Long, who was beside Lee: Ibid., 131.

821 Everywhere on the field: Rufus Robinson Dawes, *Service with the Sixth Wisconsin Volunteers* (Marietta, Ohio: E. R. Alderman, 1890), 95.

822 "The roar of musketry": Long, *Memoirs of Robert E. Lee*, 132.

823 The slaughter in Bloody Lane: Freeman, *Robert E. Lee,* Vol. 2, 392.

824 "without getting their waist belts": Henry Kyd Douglas, *I Rode with Stonewall* (Chapel Hill: University of North Carolina Press, 1940), 172.

825 "Gentlemen, we will not cross": Henry Alexander White, *Robert E. Lee* (New York: Greenwood, 1969), 224–25.

825 This was determination indeed: Longstreet, *From Manassas to Appomattox,* 214.

825 "The passage of the Potomac": Heros von Borcke, *Memoirs of the Confederate War of Independence* (Edinburgh: William Blackwood, 1866), Vol. I, 255.

CHAPTER 9   Glory—Fredericksburg and Chancellorsville

829 "Yes, my son": Robert E. Lee Jr., *Recollections and Letters of Robert E. Lee* (Garden City, N.Y.: Doubleday, Page, 1924), 77–98.

831 Lee had advised his wife: Mary P. Coulling, *The Lee Girls* (Winston-Salem, N.C.: Blair, 1987), 105.

831 Lee, like many another parent: Ibid., 106.

832 "At the usual hour": Walter H. Taylor, *Four Years with General Lee* (New York: Appleton, 1878), 76.

832 "He was the father of a tenderly-loved daughter": Ibid., 76–77.

833 He ended on a bleaker note: Lee, *Recollections and Letters of Robert E. Lee,* 79–80.

834 "Perfect and true are all His ways": Ibid., 80–81.

834 Lee finally gave his army two months: Douglas Southall Freeman, *Robert E. Lee: A Biography* (New York: Scribner, 1934), Vol. 2, 415.

835 "Will you pardon me": Stephen W. Sears, *George B. McClellan: The Young Napoleon* (New York: Ticknor and Fields, 1988), 334.

836 In this he was perfectly right: Ibid., 340.

836 "[Burnside] is as sorry": Ibid., 341.

838 He intended to "give up": J. F. C. Fuller, *Grant and Lee: A Study in Personality and Generalship* (New York: Scribner, 1933), 170.

838 Lincoln, who was by now: Ibid., 170.

842 When Lee arrived at Fredericksburg: Freeman, *Robert E. Lee*, Vol. 2, 433.

845 Anxious to prevent the slaughter: Ibid., 434.

846 Forced to wait patiently: Ibid., 442.

847 "These people delight to destroy": Ibid., 446.

847 heavy fog concealed: Ibid., 452.

848 The morning of December 13: Walter Herron Taylor, *General Lee: His Campaigns in Virginia, 1861–1865* (Lincoln: University of Nebraska Press, 1994), 146.

849 "No doubt every heart": Ibid., 150–51.

850 Without smiling, Jackson mounted: Gilbert Moxley Sorrel, *Recollections of a Confederate Staff Officer* (New York: Neale, 1905), 128.

850 "as if the ready war god": Freeman, *Robert E. Lee*, Vol. 2, 456.

851 "The people [of Wilmington]": *War of the Rebellion: A Compilation of the Official Records of the Union and Confederate Armies*, Series I,

Vol. XXI (Washington, D.C.: U.S. Government Printing Office, 1888), 1061.

851 On the left: Freeman, *Robert E. Lee*, Vol. 2, 458.

853 "It is well that war": Ibid., 462.

853 "General, they are massing": Jeffrey Wert, *General James Longstreet: The Confederacy's Most Controversial Soldier* (New York: Simon and Schuster, 1993), 221.

854 "A series of braver": James Longstreet, *From Manassas to Appomattox: Memoirs of the Civil War in America* (Bloomington: Indiana University Press, 1960), 265.

854 "About 9 a.m.": *War of the Rebellion: Formal Reports, Both Union and Confederate, The First Seizures of United States Property in the Southern States* (Washington, D.C.: U.S. War Department, 1985), Vol. 53, 523.

855 "naked and discolored": Freeman, *Robert E. Lee*, Vol. 2, 470.

855 "Our commander-in-chief": J. F. C. Fuller, *Grant and Lee*, 173.

856 "It was not a battle": Patrick Hook and Steve Smith, *The Stonewall Brigade* (Minneapolis, Minn.: Zenith, 2008), 65.

856 "If there is a worse place": Wikipedia, "Battle of Fredericksburg," 14.

857 His headquarters: Lee, *Recollections and Letters of Robert E. Lee*, 85.

858 "one fourth pound of bacon": *War of the Rebellion: A Compilation of the Official Records of the Union and Confederate Armies*, Series I, Vol. XXV,

Part II (Washington, D.C.: Government Printing Office, 1889), 730, quoted in Freeman, *Robert E. Lee*, Vol. 2, 494.

858 "his pleadings": Fuller, *Grant and Lee*, 124.

859 "My thoughts revert": Lee, *Recollections and Letters of Robert E. Lee*, 87.

859 "My heart bleeds": Ibid., 89.

859 "As regards the liberation of the people": Ibid., 90.

860 "[The snow] was nearly": Ibid., 93.

861 "the doctors tapping me": Freeman, *Robert E. Lee*, Vol. 2, 503.

865 "My plans are perfect": Edwin C. Bearss, *Fields of Honor* (Washington, D.C.: National Geographic, 2006), 124.

866 there was no way to openly deploy: Fuller, *Grant and Lee*, 185.

866 He then added to his difficulties: Ibid., 186.

867 "The enemy in our front": *The Rebellion Record*, Frank Moore, ed. (New York: Van Nostrand, 1867), Vol. 10, 254.

868 "The retrograde movement": Curt Anders, *Henry Halleck's War: A Fresh Look at Lincoln's Controversial General-in-Chief* (copyright Curt Anders, 1999), 422.

870 Just then Lee's nephew Fitzhugh: Freeman, *Robert E. Lee*, Vol. 2, 520.

871 "to hold Hooker's 72,000": Fuller, *Grant and Lee*, 187.

872 Stuart, as good as his word: Sears, *George B. McClellan*, 129.

872 They located a recent logging trail: Freeman, *Robert E. Lee*, Vol. 2, 522–23.

873 One of his staff: James Robertson, *Stonewall Jackson: The Man, the Soldier, the Legend* (New York: Macmillan, 1997), 712.

873 Jackson had unbuckled his sword: Ibid., 913.

873 "I have but to show him my design": Freeman, *Robert E. Lee*, Vol. 2, 524.

876 Jackson, to his relief: Robertson, *Stonewall Jackson*, 719.

876 "exploded out of the woods": Wikipedia, "Battle of Chancellorsville," 13.

876 "Position after position": *War of the Rebellion: A Compilation of the Official Records of the Union and Confederate Armies*, Series I, Vol. XXV, Part I (Washington, D.C.: U.S. Government Printing Office, 1889), 798.

877 "that we should all strip": Fuller, *Grant and Lee*, 173.

878 "a calamity of the first order": Ibid., 189.

879 Lee himself spent May 2: Freeman, *Robert E. Lee*, Vol. 2, 531.

879 "moaned audibly": Ibid., 533.

879 "with utmost vigor": *War of the Rebellion*, Series I, Vol. XXV, Part I, 769.

880 "I know all about it": Freeman, *Robert E. Lee*, Vol. 2, 535.

881 "Lee's presence": Henry Alexander White, *Robert E. Lee* (New York: Greenwood, 1969), 273.

882 Dazed and humiliated: Fuller, *Grant and Lee*, 191.

884 "My God!": Michael Burlingame, *Abraham Lincoln: A Life* (Baltimore: Johns Hopkins University Press, 2008), 498.

CHAPTER 10   Gettysburg—"If We Do Not Whip Him, He Will Whip Us"

891 Longstreet was sufficiently opposed: James Longstreet, *From Manassas to Appomattox: Memoirs of the Civil War in America* (Bloomington: Indiana University Press, 1960), 277.

891 In his patient, stubborn way: Ibid., 280.

892 Lee made it clear: Ibid.

892 Longstreet managed to extract: Ibid., 280–81.

893 "secretly swollen with the idea": Douglas Southall Freeman, *Robert E. Lee: A Biography* (New York: Scribner, 1935), Vol. 3, 15.

894 "Although reserved in speech": Jeffrey Wert, *General James Longstreet: The Confederacy's Most Controversial Soldier* (New York: Simon and Schuster, 1993), 21.

894 Longstreet's first act: Longstreet, *From Manassas to Appomattox*, 282.

895 "It was now a far stronger army": Colonel Vincent J. Esposito, *The West Point Atlas of American Wars, 1689–1900* (New York: Praeger, 1959), text accompanying map 92.

896 He was cautious in revealing: Longstreet, *From Manassas to Appomattox*, 285.

896 He had hoped to take advantage: Ibid.

897 Colonel Walter Taylor: Walter Herron Taylor, *General Lee: His Campaigns in Virginia, 1861–1865* (Lincoln: University of Nebraska Press, 1994), 180.

897 His military secretary: Charles Marshall, *An Aide-de-Camp of Lee* (Boston: Little Brown, 1927), 182.

898 "might offer a fair opportunity": Jeffrey D. Wert, *A Glorious Army: Robert E. Lee's Triumph, 1862–1863* (New York: Simon and Schuster, 2011), 213.

900 The fact that Lee was "thinning": Longstreet, *From Manassas to Appomattox*, 286.

900 Lee ordered A.P. Hill: Ibid.

902 If Hooker moved his army: Esposito, *The West Point Atlas of American Wars*, text accompanying map 93.

903 It may well have appeared: Taylor, *General Lee: His Campaigns in Virginia*, 182.

908 Stuart's cavalry covered the gaps: Esposito, *The West Point Atlas of American Wars*, text accompanying map 93.

909 By now Hooker: J. F. C. Fuller, *Grant and Lee: A Study in Personality and Generalship* (New York: Scribner, 1933), 195.

911 "All fences have been destroyed": Douglas Southall Freeman, *Robert E. Lee: A Biography* (New York: Scribner, 1934), Vol. 2, 178.

912 At Berryville on June 21: Lieutenant-Colonel Arthur James Lyon Fremantle, *Three Months in the Southern States, April–June, 1863* (New York: John Bradburn, 1864), 249.

912 On June 25, Fremantle: Ibid., 236.

912 This was the same day: Fuller, *Grant and Lee*, 195.

913 "I think I can throw": *The Papers of Jefferson Davis*, Lynda Lasswell Crist, ed. (Baton Rouge: Louisiana State University Press, 1997), Vol. 9, 244.

914 "We use Confederate money": Robert E. Lee to Jefferson Davis, June 23, 1863, ibid., 238.

915 "to take position": Fitzhugh Lee, *General Lee* (New York: Appleton, 1894), 265.

916 Major-General Fuller condemns: Fuller, *Grant and Lee*, 195.

916 The big cavalry battle at Brandy Station: Wert, *A Glorious Army*, 251.

917 "eight-mile train": Ibid., 271.

917 Stuart later boasted: Ibid.

918 "Can you tell me": Ibid., 273.

921 Longstreet ordered Fairfax: Longstreet, *From Manassas to Appomattox*, 294.

924 Stuart's absence was to have: Freeman, *Robert E. Lee*, Vol. 3, 105.

924 "the spirit that inhibits victory": Ibid., 68.

925 Longstreet's corps complain: Fremantle, *Three Months in the Southern States*, 249.

926 "It had not been intended": *Three Days at Gettysburg: Essays on Confederate and Union Leadership*, Gary W. Gallagher, ed. (Kent, Ohio: Kent State University Press, 1999), 18.

927 "I had a long talk": Fremantle, *Three Months in the Southern States*, 250.

929 Although Pickett was something of a dandy: Ibid., 247.

929 Heavy rain slowed: Freeman, *Robert E. Lee*, Vol. 3, 64.

932 "He wore a long gray jacket": Fremantle, 198.

934 Except for the advantage: Edwin C. Bearss, *Fields of Honor* (Washington, D.C.: National Geographic, 2006), 158.

935 "I cannot think": Longstreet, *From Manassas to Appomattox*, 303.

938 *"saith among the trumpets"*: Job 39:25.

940 A "long gray line": Freeman, *Robert E. Lee*, Vol. 3, 69–70.

941 When General Heth: Ibid.

944 "exhausted and disorganized": Robert K. Krick, *Stonewall Jackson at Cedar Mountain* (Chapel Hill: University of North Carolina Press, 1990), 284.

944 Fremantle managed to make his way: Fremantle, *Three Months in the Southern States*, 255.

946 Taylor admired Ewell: Taylor, *General Lee: His Campaigns in Virginia*, 182.

946 It is possible that Taylor: Ibid., 190.

947 Given the fatal phrase: Ibid.

948 In other versions: Gallagher, *Three Days at Gettysburg*, 28.

948 In mid-afternoon he paused: Fremantle, *Three Months in the Southern States*, 254.

951 Longstreet was surprised: Longstreet, *From Manassas to Appomattox*, 304.

953 Besides all that: Ibid., 306.

954   Longstreet replied that McLaws: Freeman, *Robert E. Lee*, Vol. 3, 76.

955   Since Longstreet's corps was not yet up: Ibid., 77.

955   "After he had reached Gettysburg": Ibid.

956   It was not in his nature: Lieutenant-Colonel Arthur James Lyon Fremantle, *The Fremantle Diary*, Walter Lord, ed. (New York: Capricorn, 1960), 292, n3.

956   He sent for Major General Jubal Early: Freeman, *Robert E. Lee*, Vol. 3, 78.

957   He thought that the Federals: Ibid., 79.

959   Lee must have had such feelings: Taylor, *General Lee: His Campaigns in Virginia*, 156.

960   "If I attack from my right": Ibid, 80.

961   "intrench themselves strongly": Fremantle, *Three Months in the Southern States*, 256.

962   "General Lee never, in his life": Douglas Southall Freeman, *Lee's Lieutenants: A Study in Command, Gettysburg to Appomattox* (New York: Simon and Schuster, 1997), Vol. 3, 110.

962   "Gentlemen, we will attack": "The Gettysburg Campaign," in *Southern Historical Society Papers*, Robert Alonzo Brock, ed. (Richmond, Va.: W.M. Ellis Jones Sons, September 1915), New Series, No. 2, Vol. 40, 275.

966   "My son, I hope you will soon": Freeman, *Robert E. Lee*, Vol. 3, 131.

967   "The enemy is here": Ibid., 89.

967   "The stars were shining": Longstreet, *From Manassas to Appomattox*, 307.

968 "the truly American custom": Fremantle, *Three Months in the Southern States*, 257.

968 Freeman has Lee eagerly looking: Freeman, *Robert E. Lee*, Vol. 3, 86.

968 In any case, no attack: Wert, *General James Longstreet*, 272.

969 "The enemy occupied a series of high ridges": Fremantle, *Three Months in the Southern States*, 257.

969 "A dead silence": Ibid., 258.

970 He may very well: Freeman, *Robert E. Lee*, Vol. 3, 87.

970 The Prussian observer: Ibid., 90.

971 "What can detain Longstreet": Gallagher, *Three Days at Gettysburg*, 159.

972 "were suffering from the lack": Freeman, *Robert E. Lee*, Vol. 3, 94.

973 "quantities of cherries": Fremantle, *Three Months in the Southern States*, 258.

973 "When things go wrong": Fuller, *Grant and Lee*, 198.

976 "profoundly still": Fremantle, *Three Months in the Southern States*, 259.

977 "polkas and waltzes": Ibid., 260.

978 "apathy": Gilbert Moxley Sorrel, *Recollections of a Confederate Staff Officer* (New York: Neale, 1905), 164.

979 "irritated and annoyed": Freeman, *Robert E. Lee*, Vol. 3, 89.

985 Although that battle lasted: Noah Trudeau, *The Second Day: A Testing of Courage* (New York: HarperCollins, 2002), 272.

986 "Well, General, you are here": Wert, *General James Longstreet*, 282.

987 "was doing well": Fremantle, *Three Months in the Southern States*, 260.

987 "We have not been as successful": Wert, *General James Longstreet*, 282.

989 It was Lee's job: Freeman, *Robert E. Lee*, Vol. 3, 105.

991 "General, I have been": Wert, *General James Longstreet*, 283.

994 All together, Lee had 125: Freeman, *Robert E. Lee*, Vol. 3, 109–10.

994 The rest were scattered: Ibid.

994 As Longstreet reckoned: Longstreet, *From Manassas to Appomattox*, 325.

996 "filled with wounded": Fremantle, *Three Months in the Southern States*, 262.

996 "the range of heights": Ibid., 263.

997 "little clump of trees": Freeman, *Robert E. Lee*, Vol. 3, 111.

999 "I heard a thud on my right": John H. Worsham, *One of Jackson's Foot Cavalry* (New York: Neale, 1912), 129.

1002 "if General Longstreet's attack should fail": Freeman, *Robert E. Lee*, Vol. 3, 114.

1003 Lee folded up his map: Ibid.

1003 "If the artillery": Ibid., 115.

1004 "entirely successful": Edward Porter Alexander, *Military Memoirs of a Confederate: A Critical Narrative* (New York: Scribner, 1914), 421.

1004 "calm and confident": Freeman, *Robert E. Lee*, Vol. 3, 116.

1006 "For every Southern boy": From William Faulkner's *Intruder in the Dust*. See Charles Shelton Aiken, *William Faulkner and the Southern Landscape* (Athens: University of Georgia Press, 2009), 115.

1009 The first salvo: Bearss, *Fields of Honor*, 197.

1009 saw "a shell go through six horses": Earl J. Hess, *Pickett's Charge: The Last Attack at Gettysburg* (Chapel Hill: University of North Carolina Press, 2001), 149.

1010 "Shells burst in the air": *War of the Rebellion: A Compilation of the Official Records of the Union and Confederate Armies*, Series I, Vol. 27, Part I (Washington, D.C.: U.S. Government Printing Office, 1889), 706.

1010 "made a very hell": Jacob Hoke, *Historical Reminiscences of the War* (Chambersburg, Pa.: M.A. Foltz Printer, 1884), 81.

1010 "too much elevation": Bearss, *Fields of Honor*, 196.

1011 "a display of fireworks": Jeffrey D. Wert, *Gettysburg: Day Three* (New York: Touchstone, 2001), 182.

1011 "sheltered lines of infantry": "Review of the Gettysburg Campaign," in *Southern Historical Society Papers*, R.A. Brock, ed. (Richmond, Va.: Southern Historical Society, 1909), Vol. 37, 137.

1012 "For God's sake come quick": Wert, *General James Longstreet*, 290.

1012 Although Brigadier General Hunt was trying: Freeman, *Robert E. Lee*, Vol. 3, 120.

1013 Lee's artillery chief: Ibid., 121.

1013 "nearly exhausted": Ibid.

1014 Alexander reported to Longstreet: Longstreet, *From Manassas to Appomattox*, 350.

1014 "fill up his ammunition chests": Ibid., 351.

1014 "grand march moved bravely on": Ibid.

1014 "the salute of the officers": Ibid., 350.

1017 "Yankee dead": Fremantle, *Three Months in the Southern States*, 264.

1017 "his colors cut down": Longstreet, *From Manassas to Appomattox*, 332.

1017 As the Confederates approached: Philip M. Cole, *Civil War Artillery at Gettysburg: Organization, Equipment, Ammunition and Tactics* (New York: Da Capo, 2002), 132.

1018 "I soon began to meet": Fremantle, *Three Months in the Southern States*, 265.

1020 "When a mounted officer began": Ibid., 268.

2021 "There are the guns, boys": Freeman, *Robert E. Lee*, Vol. 3, 128.

2021 "Too bad!": Ibid., 133–34.

1023 "It's all my fault": Ibid., 136.

CHAPTER 11   Lee and Grant

1025 "I hope," he wrote: Robert E. Lee to Jefferson Davis, July 8, 1863, *Papers of Jefferson Davis*, Lynda Lasswell Crist, ed. (Baton Rouge: Louisiana State University Press, 1997), Vol. 9, 266.

1027 "I deeply sympathize": Robert E. Lee, Jr., *Recollections and Letters of Robert E. Lee* (Garden City, N.Y.: Doubleday, Page, 1924), 100.

1029 Markie corresponded with Lee: Frances Scott and Anne C. Webb, *Who Is Markie? The Life of Martha Custis Williams Carter, Cousin and Confidante of Robert E. Lee* (Berwyn Heights, Md.: Heritage, 2007), 41.

1030 Having fallen "in love": Ibid., 133.

1031 But if Lee thought he was well rid: Mary P. Coulling, *The Lee Girls* (Winston-Salem, N.C.: Blair, 1987), 114.

1031 He came to visit the Lees: Scott and Webb. *Who Is Markie?* 148.

1031 Agnes and Orton: Ibid.

1032 "an indefinable air": Ibid., 151.

1033 When asked for his opinion: Ibid., 152–53.

1033 Lee was said to be outraged: Douglas Southall Freeman, *Robert E. Lee: A Biography* (New York: Scribner, 1934), Vol. 3, 213.

1033 "Again and again": Coulling, *The Lee Girls*, 125.

1036 Freeman mentions that soldiers: Freeman, *Robert E. Lee*, Vol. 3, 243.

1040 *"Blessed be the Lord"*: Ibid., 242.

1040 a daily ration: Ibid., 248.

1041 "Not only did [Lee] refuse": J. F. C. Fuller, *Grant and Lee: A Study in Personality and Generalship* (New York: Scribner, 1933), 125.

1041 "It has pleased God": Freeman, *Robert E. Lee*, Vol. 3, 217.

1043 "more vigorous enforcement": Ibid., 254.

1043 At its lowest point: Ibid., 253.

1045 General Beauregard wanted to concentrate: Fuller, *Grant and Lee*, 210.

1046 Lee, possibly persuaded: Ibid., 211.

1047 At first Lee planned: Ibid., 212.

1048 Lee woefully underestimated: Colonel Vincent J. Esposito, *The West Point Atlas of the American Wars, 1689–1900* (New York: Praeger, 1959), Vol. 1, text accompanying map 120.

1048 Lee's army was spread: Ibid., map 121.

1049 As for Grant: Ibid.

1049 "The Wilderness": Fuller, *Grant and Lee*, 212.

1050 Colonel Vincent Esposito speculates: Esposito, *The West Point Atlas of the American Wars*, Vol. 1, text accompanying map 121.

1052 The fighting was so fierce: Freeman, *Robert E. Lee*, Vol. 3, 280–81.

1053 "a wrestle as blind as midnight": Adam Badeau, *Military History of Ulysses S. Grant: From April, 1861 to April, 1865* (New York: Appleton, 1882), Vol. 2, 113.

1053 "The woods were set on fire": Ulysses Grant, *Personal Memoirs of U. S. Grant* (New York: Charles L. Webster, 1894), 457.

1054 As the flames spread: Mark Grimsley, *And Keep Moving On: The Virginia Campaign, May–June, 1864* (Lincoln: University of Nebraska Press, 2002), 38.

1055 This might have succeeded: Freeman, *Robert E. Lee*, Vol. 3, 284.

1056 "His face was aflame": Ibid., 287.

1056 Beneath the calm exterior: James Longstreet, *From Manassas to Appomattox: Memoirs of the Civil War in America* (Bloomington: Indiana University Press, 1960), 480.

1057 "that his line would be recovered": Ibid.

1058 Freeman is probably more correct: Freeman, *Robert E. Lee*, Vol. 3, 288.

1058 By ten o'clock in the morning: Ibid., 290.

1059 "Oh, I am heartily tired": Brooks D. Simpson, *Ulysses S. Grant: Triumph over Adversity* (New York: Houghton Mifflin, 2000), 298.

1060 Thrown on the defensive: Fuller, *Grant and Lee*, 216.

1061 "Sometimes they put this three days": Ibid.; Theodore Lyman, *Meade's Army: The Private Notebooks of Lt. Col. Theodore Lyman*, David W. Lowe, ed. (Kent, Ohio: Kent State University Press, 2007), 99–100.

1061 "this country is intersected": Ibid.

1061 "ably entrenched himself": Fuller, *Grant and Lee*, 218.

1063 "He never brought me a piece of false information": Freeman, *Robert E. Lee*, Vol. 3, 327.

1063 "A more zealous": Lee, *Recollections and Letters of Robert E. Lee*, 125.

1063 "I can scarcely think of him": Freeman, *Robert E. Lee*, Vol. 3, 327.

1065 As one Union officer graphically described: Horace Porter, *Campaigning with Grant* (New York: Century, 1897), 111.

1068 "We were in constant contact": Walter Herron Taylor, *General Lee: His Campaigns in Virginia, 1861–1865* (Lincoln: University of Nebraska Press, 1994), 245.

1068 "Lee was opposed to the final defense": Lee, *Recollections and Letters of Robert E. Lee*, 130.

1069 It is remarkable that Lee: Ibid., 127.

1070 The dead were grotesquely bloated: Grimsley, *And Keep Moving On*, 38.

1071 "he feared such an arrangement": Grant, *Personal Memoirs of U. S. Grant*, 343.

1072 By June 13 Grant had bridged: Esposito, *The West Point Atlas of the American Wars*, Vol. 1, text accompanying map 137.

1073 For all that, Grant managed: Fuller, *Grant and Lee*, 224.

1074 "it will become a siege": Freeman, *Robert E. Lee*, Vol. 3, 398.

1076 "He always tried to prevent them": Lee, *Recollections and Letters of Robert E. Lee*, 132.

1076 "But what care can a man": Ibid., 140.

1077 His aide Colonel Long: Ibid., 138.

1078 Lee had been slow to recognize: Fuller, *Grant and Lee*, 222.

1079 To quote the verdict: Ibid., 228.

1080 "a crater twenty feet deep": Grant, *Personal Memoirs of U. S. Grant*, 612.

1082 It was not only "a tremendous failure": Frances H. Kennedy, ed., *The Civil War Battlefield Guide* (Boston: Houghton Mifflin, 1998), 356.

1082 Even the retreat: Taylor, *General Lee: His Campaigns in Virginia,* 260.

1082 "was sorely tried and beset": Ibid., 261–62.

1083 "from the north side of the James River": Ibid., 261.

1083 On August 25 Hill attacked: Ibid., 262.

1083 Colonel Taylor, like many others: Ibid.

1084 "must have a decided peace candidate": Ibid., 262–63.

1086 Lee's chaplain: A. L. Long, *Memoirs of Robert E. Lee* (New York: J. M. Stoddard, 1886), 387–88.

1086 "his love for the lower animals": Ibid., 388.

1087 Lee's only hope was to break free: Fuller, *Grant and Lee,* 228.

1087 "It will be too late": *War of the Rebellion: A Compilation of the Official Records of the Union and Confederate Armies,* Series 1, Vol. 42, Part 2 (Washington, D.C.: U.S. Government Printing Office, 1893), 1230.

1088 "a rich man's war": Gary W. Gallagher, *The Confederate War* (Cambridge, Mass.: Harvard University Press, 1999), 18.

1088 He would eventually become: Long, *Memoirs of Robert E. Lee,* 346.

1090 "to regain strength and weight": Coulling, *The Lee Girls,* 139.

1090 Though he urged Mildred: Ibid., 140.

1090 It is interesting to note: Ibid.

1091 These brief glimpses: Ibid.

1091 Lee's nephew Major General Fitzhugh Lee: Lee, *Recollections and Letters of Robert E. Lee,* 141.

1093   Lee complained that he had requested: Long, *Memoirs of Robert E. Lee*, 345.

1093   In his masterly study: Albert Burton Moore, *Conscription and Conflict in the Confederacy* (New York: Macmillan, 1924), 345.

1093   "We must decide whether slavery": Ibid., 346.

1094   President Davis was reluctant: Ibid., 348.

1094   On February 4, 1865: Long, *Memoirs of Robert E. Lee*, 351.

1095   "to such punishment as": Ibid., 354.

1095   "it may be necessary to abandon": Ibid., 355.

1096   Lee was already thinking: Ibid.

1096   "You must consider the question": Ibid., 348.

1096   Just as Lee was considering: Coulling, *The Lee Girls*, 149.

1097   "serenaded the Meade home": Ibid., 142.

1097   "My precious little Agnes": Ibid.

1097   "draw out by his left": Long, *Memoirs of Robert E. Lee*, 356.

1097   "The appearance of a steady": Ibid., 357.

1098   he noted that his ability: Ibid.

1098   An even more serious problem: Ibid., 359.

1098   On February 24, in a long letter: Ibid.

1098   Deserters usually took: Ibid., 360.

1099   "sustain even our small force": Ibid., 362.

1100   At 4 a.m. on April 2: Fuller, *Grant and Lee*, 239.

1100   Whether or not Mrs. Lee: Coulling, *The Lee Girls*, 143.

1100   "I see no prospect": Long, *Memoirs of Robert E. Lee*, 364.

1101 Davis rose from his pew: Coulling, *The Lee Girls*, 144.

1101 "Through the open casements": Ibid., 145.

1101 By the middle of the afternoon: Long, *Memoirs of Robert E. Lee*, 366.

1102 Mrs. Lee watched the scene: Coulling, *The Lee Girls*, 146.

1103 Lee's intention had been to concentrate: Long, *Memoirs of Robert E. Lee*, 367.

1105 "My God!" Lee exclaimed: Douglas Southall Freeman, *Robert E. Lee: A Biography* (New York: Scribner, 1935), Vol. 4, 84.

1106 The central panel of the Hoffbauer murals: Keith D. Dickson, *Sustaining Southern Identity: Douglas Southall Freeman and Memory in the Modern South* (Baton Rouge: Louisiana State University Press, 2011), xiv.

1106 Lee did not yet know the worst: Freeman, *Robert E. Lee*, Vol. 4, 86.

1108 "competent, wise, forbearing": William Garrett Piston, *Marked in Bronze: James Longstreet and Southern History* (New York: De Capo, 1998), 219.

1109 "He was there to back Lee up": Jeffrey Wert, *General James Longstreet: The Confederacy's Most Controversial Soldier* (New York: Simon and Schuster, 1993), 401.

1111 Those who saw him: Freeman, *Robert E. Lee*, Vol. 4, 109.

1114 Lee's father had been present: Charles Marshall, *An Aide-de-Camp of Lee* (Boston: Little Brown, 1927), 258.

1118 His "ambulance and his headquarters": Freeman, *Robert E. Lee*, Vol. 4, 114.

1120 "If I am to be General Grant's prisoner": Reverend John William Jones, *Personal Reminiscences of General Robert E. Lee* (New York: D. Appleton, 1874), 147.

1120 "Tell General Lee I have fought": Freeman, *Robert E. Lee*, Vol. 4, 120.

1120 "Then there is nothing left me to do": Ibid.

1121 "hard things to say of us": Ibid., 121.

1121 "Then your situation": James Longstreet, *From Manassas to Appomattox: Memoirs of the Civil War in America* (Bloomington: Indiana University Press, 1960), 538.

1122 Alexander was in favor: Edward Porter Alexander, *Fighting for the Confederacy: The Personal Recollections of General Edward Porter Alexander*, Gary W. Gallagher, ed., (Chapel Hill: University of North Carolina Press, 1898), 531–33.

1125 "You have killed your beautiful horse": Freeman, *Robert E. Lee*, Vol. 3, 126.

1129 Colonel Taylor "had no heart": Ibid., 133.

1129 "talked in the most friendly": Marshall, *An Aide-de-Camp of Lee*, 269.

1132 Another observer wrote: Reverend J. William Jones, *Life and Letters of Robert E. Lee: Soldier and Man* (New York: Neale, 1906), 375.

1133 Grant and Lee continued to chat: Grant, *Personal Memoirs of U. S. Grant*, 736.

1134 Parker made a few small corrections: This represents a combination of the accounts of Douglas Southall Freeman, Marshall, General Grant, and Brigadier General Horace Porter of Grant's staff. Marshall, Grant, and Porter were close to Lee in the small room during the surrender.

1138 The McLean house turned out to contain: Porter, *Campaigning with Grant*, 480.

CHAPTER 12   Apotheosis—1865–1870

1141 There was a short period of discomposure: Douglas Southall Freeman, *Robert E. Lee: A Biography*, (New York: Scribner, 1934), Vol. 3, 145–46.

1141 The two generals talked: Ulysses Grant, *Personal Memoirs of U. S. Grant* (New York: Charles L. Webster, 1894), 744.

1143 "His steed was bespattered": Freeman, *Robert E. Lee*, Vol. 3, 161.

1146 "The sorrows of the South": Ibid., 194.

1147 Their house had been rented: Reverend J. William Jones, *Life and Letters of Robert E. Lee: Soldier and Man* (New York: Neale, 1906), 383.

1147 Once Lee had surrendered: Freeman, *Robert E. Lee*, Vol. 3, 205.

1150 In Lee's case: Ibid., 206–7.

1150 "we must expect procrastination": Ibid., 207.

1152 Once he returned to Richmond: Ibid., 209–10.

1153   As for "the girls": Mary P. Coulling, *The Lee Girls* (Winston-Salem, N.C.: Blair, 1987), 152.

1153   They were unlikely to find: Ibid., 153.

1155   Lee rose from the table: Freeman, *Robert E. Lee,* Vol. 3, 211.

1156   "I have always observed": Ibid., 199.

1156   "My own opinion": *Reports of the Joint Committee on Reconstruction,* 39th Congress, Part 2 (Washington, D.C.: U.S. Government Printing Office, 1866), 7, 121, 126.

1159   After a week of comfortable living: Coulling, *The Lee Girls,* 154.

1160   "the people of the South": Ibid., 156.

1160   Colonel Christian mentioned: Ibid., 156–57.

1162   "He prefers that way": Freeman, *Robert E. Lee,* Vol. 3, 226.

1163   Mrs. Brittania Peter Kinnon: Ibid., 160.

1163   "The Presidential Residence": Coulling, *The Lee Girls,* 160.

1164   His brief appearance: Freeman, *Robert E. Lee,* Vol. 3, 246.

1165   The one time he stepped out of his role: Ibid., 261.

1167   Lee had not hesitated: Emory M. Thomas, *Robert E. Lee* (New York: Norton, 1995), 372.

1167   He had testified under oath: Ibid., 382.

1168   The first involved four students: Ibid., 388.

1169   "a school for rebels": Freeman, *Robert E. Lee,* Vol. 3, 354.

1169   "which he so lately attempted to destroy": *New York Independent,* April 2, 1868, 4, column 5.

1170   Lee was indifferent to his own reputation: Freeman, *Robert E. Lee*, Vol. 3, 350–51.

1173   The senate of Virginia: Ibid., 444.

1173   He accepted a visit: Mark E. Neely, *The Fate of Liberty; Abraham Lincoln and Civil Liberties* (New York: Oxford University Press, 1991), 79.

1173   Lee was happy enough: John Singleton Mosby, *The Memoirs of John Singleton Mosby* (Boston: Little Brown, 1917), 380–81; Freeman, *Robert E. Lee*, Vol. 3, 445.

1173   Lee and Agnes proceeded: Coulling, *The Lee Girls*, 173.

1174   From there they proceeded: Robert E. Lee, *Recollections and Letters of Robert E. Lee* (Garden City, N.Y.: Doubleday, Page, 1924), 398.

1178   He died with the same stoic dignity: Reverend John William Jones, *Personal Reminiscences of General Robert E. Lee* (New York: D. Appleton, 1874), 158.

Bibliography

Adams, Richard. *Traveller.* New York: Dell, 1988.

Alexander, Edward Porter. *Fighting for the Confederacy: The Personal Recollections of Gen. Ed. Porter,* G. W. Gallagher, ed. Chapel Hill: University of North Carolina Press, 1898.

———. *Military Memoirs of a Confederate: A Critical Narrative.* New York: Scribner, 1914.

Allen, Elizabeth Preston. *Life and Letters of Margaret Junkin Preston.* Boston: Houghton Mifflin, 1903.

Ambrose, Stephen E. *Duty, Honor, Country.* Baltimore: Johns Hopkins University Press, 1999.

Anders, Curt. *Henry Halleck's War: A Fresh Look at Lincoln's Controversial General-in-Chief.* Carmel: Guild Press of Indiana, 1999.

Badeau, Adam. *Military History of Ulysses S. Grant: From April, 1861, to April, 1865,* Vol. 2. New York: Appleton, 1882.

Baker, Jean H. *James Buchanan.* New York: Times Books, 2004.

Bailey, Ronald H. *Antietam: The Bloodiest Day.* New York: Time-Life Books, 1984.

Bauer, K. Jack. *Surfboats and Horse Marines: U.S. Naval Operations in the Mexican War, 1846–48.* Annapolis: U.S. Naval Institute Press, 1969.

Bearss, Edwin C. *Fields of Honor.* Washington, D.C.: National Geographic Society, 2006.

Benét, Stephen Vincent. *John Brown's Body.* Chicago: Elephant Paperbacks, 1990.

Bernhard, Duke of Saxe-Weimar-Eisenach. *Travels Through North America During the Years 1825 and 1826.* Philadelphia: Carey, Lea and Carey, 1828.

Blair, Francis P. *Abraham Lincoln: A History,* Vol. 4. New York: Century, 1980.

Blane, William N. *An Excursion Through the United States and Canada, 1822–1833, by an English Gentleman.* London: Baldwin, Craddock and Joy, 1824.

Blotner, Joseph, et al. *Faulkner.* New York: Library of America, 1994.

Bradford, Gamaliel. *Lee the American.* Boston: Houghton Mifflin, 1929.

Bradley, Michael R. *It Happened in the Civil War.* Guilford, Conn.: Morris, 2002.

Brands, H. W. *The Man Who Saved the Union.* New York: Doubleday, 2012.

Burlingame, Michael. *Abraham Lincoln: A Life.* Baltimore: Johns Hopkins University Press, 2008.

Catton, Bruce. *The American Heritage Picture History of the Civil War*. New York: Bonanza Books, 1982.

Cheever, Susan. *American Bloomsbury*. New York: Simon and Schuster, 2006.

———. *Louisa May Alcott: A Personal Biography*. New York: Simon and Schuster, 2010.

Cheney, Captain Charles Cornwallis. *A Military View of Recent Campaigns in Virginia and Maryland*. London: Smith, Edler, 1863–1865.

Cole, Philip M. *Civil War Artillery at Gettysburg: Organization, Equipment, Ammunition and Tactics*. New York: Da Capo, 2002.

Clinton, Catherine. *Fanny Kemble's Civil Wars*. New York: Oxford University Press, 2001.

Comte de Paris. *History of the Civil War in America*, Vol. 1. Philadelphia: Porter and Coates, 1875.

———. *History of the Civil War in America*, Vol. 2. Philadelphia: Porter and Coates, 1876.

———. *History of the Civil War in America*, Vol. 3. Philadelphia: Porter and Coates, 1888.

———. *History of the Civil War in America*, Vol. 4. Philadelphia: Porter and Coates, 1888.

Connelly, Thomas L. *The Marble Man: Robert E. Lee and His Image in American Society*. New York: Knopf, 1977.

Conner, Philip Syng Physick. *The Home Squadron Under Commodore Conner in the War with Mexico*. Kessinger Publishing's Legacy reprints, 2007.

Conway, Christopher, and Gustavo Pellon. *The U.S.-Mexican War: Binational Reader*. Indianapolis, Ind.: Hackett, 2010.

Coulling, Mary P. *The Lee Girls.* Winston-Salem, N.C.: Blair, 1987.

Cozzens, Peter. *Battlefields of the Civil War.* New York: Sterling, 2011.

————. *Shenandoah 1862: Stonewall Jackson's Valley Campaign.* Chapel Hill: University of North Carolina Press, 2013.

Crackel, Theodore J. *West Point: A Centennial History.* Lawrence: University Press of Kansas, 2002.

Crist, Lynda Lasswell, ed. *The Papers of Jefferson Davis,* Vol. 9. Baton Rouge: Louisiana State University Press, 1997.

Cust, Sir Edward. *Annals of the Wars of the Nineteenth Century,* Vol. 3. London: John Murray, 1863.

Dabney, Robert Lewis. *Life and Campaigns of Lieut. Gen. Thomas. J. Jackson.* New York: Blelock, 1866.

Davis, William C. *The Battlefields of the Civil War.* Norman: University of Oklahoma Press, 1996.

Davis, William C., et al., eds. *Civil War Journal—The Battles.* Nashville: Rutledge Hill, 1998.

————. *Civil War Journal—The Leaders.* Nashville: Rutledge Hill, 1997.

————. *Civil War Journal—The Legacies.* Nashville: Rutledge Hill, 1999.

Dawes, Rufus Robinson. *Service with the Sixth Wisconsin Volunteers.* Marietta, Ohio: E. R. Alderman and Sons, 1890.

DeButts, Mary Custis Lee. *Growing Up in the 1850's.* Chapel Hill: University of North Carolina Press, 1984.

Detzer, David. *Donnybrook: The Battle of Bull Run.* Orlando, Fl.: Harcourt, 2004.

Dickens, Charles. *The Works of Charles Dickens,* Vol. 16. New York: Scribner, 1899.

Dickson, Keith D. *Sustaining Southern Identity.* Baton Rouge: Louisiana State University Press, 2011.

DiNardo, R. L., and Albert A. Nofi, eds. *James Longstreet.* New York: Da Capo, 2001.

Donald, David Herbert. *Lincoln.* New York: Simon and Schuster, 1995.

Douglas, Henry Kyd. *I Rode with Stonewall.* Chapel Hill: University of North Carolina Press, 1940.

Drumm, Stella M., "Robert E. Lee and the Mississippi River," *Missouri Historical Society,* Vol. 6, No. 2, February 1929.

East, Charles. *Sarah Morgan: The Civil War Diary of a Southern Woman.* New York: Touchstone, 1992.

Eisenhower, John S. D. *So Far from God: The U.S. War in Mexico, 1846–1848.* New York: Anchor, 1990.

Esposito, Colonel Vincent J. *The West Point Atlas of American Wars, 1689–1900,* Vol. 1. New York: Praeger, 1959.

Faulkner, William. *Sanctuary.* New York: Vintage International, 1993.

———. *Snopes.* New York: Modern Library, 1994.

Fellman, Michael. *The Making of Robert E. Lee.* New York: Random House, 2000.

Flower, Frank Abial. *Edwin McMasters Stanton: The Autocrat of Rebellion.* Akron, Ohio: Saalfield, 1905.

Flood, Charles Bracelen. *Lee—The Last Years.* Boston: Houghton Mifflin, 1981.

Foote, Shelby. *The Civil War,* Vol. 1. New York: Random House, 1958.

———. *The Civil War,* Vol. 2. New York: Random House, 1963.

———. *The Civil War,* Vol. 3. New York: Random House, 1974.

Foreman, Amanda. *A World on Fire.* New York: Random House, 2010.

Fraser, George MacDonald. *Flashman and the Angel of the Lord.* New York: Plume, 1996.

Freeman, Douglas Southall. *Lee's Lieutenants: A Study in Command,* Vol. 1. New York: Scribner, 1942.

———. *Lee's Lieutenants,* Vol. 2. New York: Scribner Macmillan Hudson River Editions, 1943.

———. *Lee's Lieutenants,* Vol. 3. New York: Simon and Schuster, 1997.

———. *Robert E. Lee: A Biography,* Vol. 1. New York: Scribner, 1934.

———. *Robert E. Lee: A Biography,* Vol. 2. New York: Scribner, 1934.

———. *Robert E. Lee: A Biography,* Vol. 3. New York: Scribner, 1935.

———. *Robert E. Lee: A Biography,* Vol. 4. New York: Scribner, 1935.

Fremantle, Lieutenant-Colonel Arthur James Lyon. *Three Months in the Southern States, April-June, 1863.* New York: John Bradburn, 1864.

———. *The Fremantle Diary.* Walter Lord, ed. New York: Capricorn, 1960.

Friedman, Melvin J., and Irving Malin, eds. *William Styron: The Confessions of Nat Turner—A Critical Handbook.* Belmont, Calif.: Wadsworth, 1970.

Fuller, Major-General J. F. C. *Grant and Lee: A Study in Personality and Generalship.* London: Eyre and Spottiswoode, 1933.

Furgurson, Ernest B. *Ashes of Glory.* New York: Knopf, 1996.

Gallagher, Gary W. *The Confederate War.* Cambridge, Mass.: Harvard University Press, 1999.

———. *Lee.* Chapel Hill: University of North Carolina Press, 2001.

———. *Lee and His Generals in War and Memory.* Baton Rouge: Louisiana Sate University Press, 1998.

———. *Marshall: Lee's Aide-de-Camp.* Boston: Little, Brown, 1927.

———. *The Union War.* Cambridge, Mass.: Harvard University Press, 2011.

Gallagher, Gary W., ed. *Three Days at Gettysburg: Essays on Confederate and Union Leadership.* Kent, Ohio: Kent State University Press, 1999.

Gallagher, Gary W., and Alan T. Nolan, eds. *The Myth of the Lost Cause and Civil War History.* Bloomington: Indiana University Press, 2010.

Gambone, A. M. *Lee at Gettysburg: Commentary on Defeat—The Death of a Myth.* Baltimore: Butternut and Blue, 2002.

Gatrell, V. A. C. *The Hanging Tree: Execution and the English People 1770–1868.* Oxford: Oxford University Press, 1994.

Gilman, Priscilla. *The Anti-Romantic Child*. New York: HarperCollins, 2011.

Goode, John. *Recollections of a Lifetime*. New York: Neale, 1906.

Grant, Ulysses S. *Personal Memoirs of U.S. Grant*. New York: Charles L. Webster, 1894.

Grimsley, Mark. *And Keep Moving On: The Virginia Campaign, May-June, 1864*. Lincoln: University of Nebraska Press, 2002.

Harwell, Richard Barksdale, ed. *Cities and Camps of the Confederate States*. Chicago: University of Illinois Press, 1997.

Henderson, George Francis Robert. *Stonewall Jackson and the American Civil War*, Vol. 1. New York: Longmans, Green, 1900.

Hennessey, John J. *Return to Bull Run*. Norman: University of Oklahoma Press, 1999.

Hess, Earl J. *Pickett's Charge: The Last Attack at Gettysburg*. Chapel Hill: University of North Carolina Press, 2001.

Hill, Benjamin Harvey. *Senator Benjamin Hill of Georgia: His Life, Speeches and Writings*. Atlanta: T. H. P. Bloodworth, 1893.

Hitchcock, Ethan Allen. *Fifty Years in Camp and Field*. New York: Putnam, 1909.

Hoke, Jacob. *Historical Reminiscences of the War*. Chambersburg, Pa.: M. A. Foltz Printer, 1884.

Hook, Patrick, and Steve Smith. *The Stonewall Brigade*. Minneapolis: Zenith, 2008.

Horn, Stanley F., ed. *The Robert E. Lee Reader*. Indianapolis: Bobbs-Merrill, 1949.

Horowitz, Tony. *Midnight Rising: John Brown and the Raid That Sparked the Civil War.* New York: Henry Holt, 2011.

Hurst, Jack. *Nathan Bedford Forrest.* New York: Vintage Civil War Library, 1994.

Johnson, Timothy D. *A Gallant Little Army: The Mexico City Campaign.* Lawrence: University Press of Kansas, 2007.

Jones, Charles C. *Reminiscences of the Last Days, Death and Burial of General Henry Lee.* Albany, N.Y.: J. Munsell, 1870.

Jones, Reverend John William. *Life and Letters of Gen. Robert E. Lee: Soldier and Man.* New York: Neale, 1906.

——. *Personal Reminiscences of General Robert E. Lee.* New York: Appleton, 1874.

Kane, Harnett T. *The Lady of Arlington: A Novel Based on the Life of Mrs. Robert E. Lee.* Garden City, N.Y.: Doubleday, 1953.

Keller, Allan. *Thunder at Harper's Ferry.* Englewood Cliffs, N.J.: Prentice-Hall, 1958.

Kemble, Fanny. *Journal of a Residence on a Georgian Plantation 1838–1839.* New York: Harper, 1864.

Kennedy, Frances H., ed. *The Civil War Battlefield Guide.* Boston: Houghton Mifflin, 1998.

Ketchum, Richard M., ed. in charge. *The American Heritage.* New York: American Heritage, 1960.

Korda, Michael. *Ulysses S. Grant.* New York: Harper Perennial, 2009.

Krick, Robert K. *Stonewall Jackson at Cedar Mountain.* Chapel Hill: University of North Carolina Press, 1990.

Kunhardt, Philip B., Jr., et al. *Lincoln*. New York: Knopf, 1992.

Le Comte de Paris. *History of the Civil War in America,* Vol. 1. Philadelphia: Porter and Coates, 1886.

———. *History of the Civil War in America,* Vol. 2. Philadelphia: Porter and Coates, 1886.

Lee, Edmund Jennings. *Lee of Virginia, 1642–1892.* Philadelphia, 1895.

Lee, Fitzhugh. *General Lee*. New York: Appleton, 1913.

———. *General Lee*. New York: University Society, 1894.

Lee, Robert E., Jr. *Lee's Dispatches: Unpublished Letters of Robert E. Lee*. New York: Putnam, 1915.

———. *Recollections and Letters of Robert E. Lee*. New York: Doubleday, Page, 1924.

Livermore, Thomas L. *Numbers and Losses in the Civil War in America 1861–65*. Whitefish, Mo.: Kessinger Publishing-Rare Reprints, 2006.

Long, Armistead Lindsay. *Memoirs of Robert E. Lee*. New York: J. M. Stoddart, 1886.

Long, E. B., with Barbara Long. *The Civil War Day by Day*. New York: Da Capo, 1971.

Longstreet, James. *From Manassas to Appomattox: Memoirs of the Civil War in America*. Bloomington: Indiana University Press, 1960.

Lyman, Theodore. *Meade's Army: The Private Notebooks of Lt. Col. Theodore Lyman*. David W. Lowe, ed. Kent, Ohio: Kent State University Press, 2007.

Marshall, Charles. *An Aide-de-Camp of Lee*. Boston: Little, Brown, 1927.

McCaslin, Richard B. *Lee in the Shadow of Washington*. Baton Rouge: Louisiana State University Press, 2001.

McFeely, Mary Drake, et al. *Grant,* Vol. 1. New York: Library of America, 1990.

McPherson, James M. *Battle Cry of Freedom.* New York: Oxford University Press, 1988.

———. *This Mighty Scourge.* New York: Oxford University Press, 2009.

Meigs, William Montgomery. *The Life of Thomas Hart Benton.* Philadelphia: Lippincott, 1904.

Mensch, Pamela. *The Landmark Arrian.* New York: Pantheon, 2010.

Merry, Robert T. *A Country of Vast Designs.* New York: Simon and Schuster, 2009.

Moore, Albert Burton. *Conscription and Conflict in the Confederacy.* New York: Macmillan, 1924.

Moore, Frank, ed. *The Rebellion Record,* Vol. 10. New York: Van Nostrand, 1867.

Mosby, John S. *Memoirs of John S. Mosby.* Charles Wells Russell, ed. Boston: Little, Brown, 1917.

Nagel, Paul C. *The Lees of Virginia: Seven Generations of an American Family.* New York: Oxford University Press, 2007.

Neely, Mark E. *The Fate of Liberty: Abraham Lincoln and Civil Liberties.* New York: Oxford University Press, 1991.

Nolan, Alan T. *Lee Considered.* Chapel Hill: University of North Carolina Press, 1991.

Oates, Stephen B. *The Approaching Fury.* New York: Harper Perennial, 1997.

———. *To Purge This Land with Blood.* Amherst: University of Massachusetts Press, 1984.

Page, Charles A. *Letters of a War Correspondent.* James R. Gilmore, ed. Boston: L. C. Page, 1899.

Page, Thomas Nelson. *Robert E. Lee, the Southerner.* New York: Scribner, 1908.

Patterson, Benton Rain. *The Great American Steamboat Race.* Jefferson, N.C.: McFarland, 2009.

Peskin, Allan. *Winfield Scott and the Profession of Arms.* Kent, Ohio: Kent State University Press, 2003.

Piston, William Garrett. *From Manassas to Appomattox: Memoirs of the Civil War in America.* Barnes and Noble, 2004.

———. *Marked in Bronze: James Longstreet and Southern History.* New York: Da Capo, 1998.

Porter, Horace. *Campaigning with Grant.* New York: Century, 1897.

Post, Lydia Minturn, ed. *Soldier's Letters, from Camp, Battlefield and Prison.* Michigan: Michigan Historical Reprint Series, 2005.

Powell, Jim. *Greatest Emancipations: How the West Abolished Slavery.* New York: Palgrave Macmillan, 2008.

Preston, Walter Creigh. *Lee, West Point and Lexington.* Whitefish, Mo.: Kessinger Legacy Reprints, 2011.

Pryor, Elizabeth Brown. *Reading the Man: A Portrait of Robert E. Lee Through His Private Letters.* New York: Viking, 2007.

Quarles, Benjamin. *The Negro in the Civil War.* New York: Da Capo, 1953.

Randolph, Sarah Nicholas. *The Life of Stonewall Jackson.* Philadelphia: Lippincott, 1876.

Reagan, J. H. *Memoirs: With Special Reference to Secession and the Civil War.* New York: Neale, 1906.

Reardon, Carol, and Tom Vossler. *A Field Guide to Gettysburg.* Chapel Hill: University of North Carolina Press, 2013.

Remlap, L. T. *Grant and His Descriptive Account of His Tour Around the World,* Vol. 1. New York: Hurst, 1885.

Reynolds, David S. *John Brown, Abolitionist: The Man Who Killed Slavery, Sparked the Civil War, and Seeded Civil Rights.* New York: Knopf, 2005.

———. *Mightier Than the Sword.* New York: Norton, 2011.

Robertson, James I., Jr. *Stonewall Jackson: The Man, the Soldier, the Legend.* New York: Macmillan, 1997.

Royster, Charles. *Sherman,* Vol. 2. New York: Library of America, 1990.

Sanborn, Franklin Benjamin. *The Life and Letters of John Brown: Liberator of Kansas and Martyr of Virginia.* London: Sampson, Low, Marston, Searlef and Rivington, 1885.

Sandburg, Carl. *Storm over the Land: A Profile of the Civil War Taken Mainly from A. Lincoln—The War Years.* New York: Harcourt Brace, 1942.

Scott, Frances, and Anne Cipriani Webb. *Who Is Markie? The Life of Martha Custis Williams Carter, Cousin and Confidante of Robert E. Lee.* Berwyn Heights, Md.: Heritage, 2007.

Scott, Winfield. *Memoirs of Lieut.-Gen. Scott, LL.D., Written by Himself,* Vol. 2. New York: Sheldon, 1864.

Sears, Stephen W. *George B. McClellan—The Young Napoleon.* New York: Ticknor and Fields, 1988.

———. *Landscape Turned Red.* New York: Houghton Mifflin, 1983.

Shaara, Michael. *The Killer Angels.* New York: Ballantine, 1975.

Simpson, Brooks D. *Ulysses S. Grant: Triumph over Adversity.* New York: Houghton Mifflin, 2000.

Simson, Jay W. *Custer and the Front Royal Executions of 1864.* Jefferson, N.C.: McFarland, 2009.

Smith, Justin H. *The War with Mexico.* Saint Petersburg, Fl.: Red and Black, 2011.

Sorrel, Gilbert Moxley. *Recollections of a Confederate Staff Officer.* New York: Neale, 1905.

Stern, Philip Van Doren. *Robert E. Lee: The Man and the Soldier.* New York: Bonanza, 1963.

Stowe, Harriet Beecher. *Three Novels.* New York: Library of America, 1982.

———. *Uncle Tom's Cabin.* New York: Oxford University Press, 2011.

Taylor, Richard. *Destruction and Reconstruction: Personal Experiences of the Late War.* Richard B. Harwell, ed. New York: Longmans, Green, 1955.

Taylor, Walter H. *Four Years with General Lee.* New York: Appleton, 1878.

———. *General Lee: His Campaigns in Virginia, 1861–1865.* Lincoln: University of Nebraska Press, 1994.

Thomas, Emory M. *Robert E. Lee.* New York: Norton, 1995.

Time-Life Books, eds. *Shenandoah, 1862.* New York: Time-Life Books, 1997.

Tower, R. Lockwood, ed. *Lee's Adjutant: The Wartime Letters of Colonel Walter Herron Taylor, 1862–1865.* Columbia: University of South Carolina Press, 1995.

Traas, Adrian George. *From the Golden Gate to Mexico City.* Washington, D.C.: Office of History, Corps of Engineers, 1993.

Trudeau, Noah. *The Second Day: A Testing of Courage.* New York: HarperCollins, 2002.

Twain, Mark. *Mississippi Writings.* New York: Library of America, 1982.

Twohig, Dorothy, ed. *Papers of George Washington, Revolutionary War Series,* Vol. 6. Charlottesville: University of Virginia Press, 1994.

Upton, Emory. *Military Policy of the United States.* Washington, D.C.: U.S. Government Printing Office, 1917.

Vandiver, Frank E. *Civil War Battlefields and Landmarks.* New York: Random House, 1996.

Villard, Oswald Garrison. *John Brown, 1800–1859: A Biography Fifty Years After.* New York: Knopf, 1943.

Von Borcke, Heros. *Memoirs of the Confederate War of Independence,* Vol. 1. Edinburgh: William Blackwood, 1866.

Von Briesen, Martha. *The Letters of Elijah Fletcher.* Charlottesville: University Press of Virginia, 1965.

Ward, Geoffrey C., et al. *The Civil War.* New York: Knopf, 1990.

Warren, Robert Penn. *The Legacy of the Civil War.* Lincoln, Neb.: Bison, 1998.

Waugh, Joan. *U. S. Grant: American Hero, American Myth*. Chapel Hill: University of North Carolina Press, 2009.

Wert, Jeffrey D. *Cavalryman of the Lost Cause: A Biography of J. E. B. Stuart*. New York: Simon and Schuster Paperbacks, 2008.

———. *General James Longstreet*. New York: Simon and Schuster, 1993.

———. *Gettysburg: Day Three*. New York: Touchstone, 2001.

———. *A Glorious Army: Robert E. Lee's Triumph, 1862–1863*. New York: Simon and Schuster, 2011.

Wheeler, Richard. *Witness to Gettysburg*. New York: New American Library, 1987.

White, Henry Alexander. *Robert E. Lee*. New York: Greenwood, 1969.

Wilson, Edmund. *Patriotic Gore*. New York: Oxford University Press, 1962.

Woodhead, Henry. *Echoes of Glory*, Vol. 1. Alexandria, Va.: Time-Life Books, 1991.

Woodward, C. Vann, ed. *Mary Chesnut's Civil War*. New Haven: Yale University Press, 1981.

Worsham, John H. *One of Jackson's Foot Cavalry*. New York: Neale, 1912.

Map and Art Credits

BLACK & WHITE PHOTO INSERT:Portrait of John Brown—Photo credit: National Portrait Gallery, Smithsonian Institution / Art Resource, NY

Colonel Robert E. Lee—Photo credit: Prints & Photographs Division, Library of Congress, LC-DIG-ds-04730

General Winfield Scott—Photo credit: Culver Pictures / The Art Archive at Art Resource, NY

Stratford—Photo credit: © G.E. Kidder Smith / Corbis

Arlington—Photo credit: Library of Congress, Prints & Photographs Division, HABS VA,7-ARL,1-2 (CT)

707 East Franklin Street, Richmond—Photo credit: Detroit Publishing Co., Prints & Photographs Division, Library of Congress, LC-DIG-det-4a12504

President's House, Washington College—Photo credit: Dennis Johnson / Getty Images

Mary Custis Lee—Photo credit: Lee Papers, Special Collections, Leyburn Library, Washington and Lee University

Eleanor Agnes Lee—Photo credit: Virginia Historical Society

Mary Anne Custis Lee & Robert E. Lee, Jr.—Photo credit: Virginia Historical Society

Anne Carter Lee—Photo credit: Courtesy of Arlington House, The Robert E. Lee Memorial

Mildred Childe Lee in 1870—Photo credit: Virginia Historical Society

Robert E. Lee Standing with Sword—Photo credit: Getty Images

William Henry Fitzhugh Lee—Photo credit: Lee Papers, Special Collections, Leyburn Library, Washington and Lee University

George Washington Custis Lee—Photo credit: Lee Papers, Special Collections, Leyburn Library, Washington and Lee University

Robert Edward Lee, Jr.—Photo credit: Virginia Historical Society

Three Heroes Sketch—Photo credit: F.C. Buroughs, Prints & Photographs Division, Library of Congress, LC-DIG-ppmsca-22750

Jefferson Davis—Photo credit: Prints & Photographs Division, Library of Congress, LC-DIG-cwpbh-00879

Lee at Fredericksburg—Photo credit: Henry Alexander Ogden, Prints & Photographs Division, Library of Congress, LC-DIG-pga-01927

Lee at Chancellorsville—Photo credit: Prints & Photographs Division, Library of Congress, LC-USZ62–118168

Lee on Horseback at Chancellorsville—Photo credit: Henry Alexander Ogden, copyrighted by F.E. Wright, Prints & Photographs Division, Library of Congress, LC-USZ62–51832

Lt.-Colonel Fremantle—Photo credit: Author's Collection

Henry Thomas Harrison—Photo credit: Author's collection

J.E.B. Stuart—Photo credit: © 2014 Stock Sales WGBH / Scala / Art Resource, NY

James A. Longstreet—Photo credit: SSPL via Getty Images

A.P. Hill—Photo credit: Author's collection

Robert E. Lee—Photo credit: Prints & Photographs Division, Library of Congress, LC-DIG-cwpb-07494

John Bell Hood—Photo credit: SSPL via Getty Images

T.J. Stonewall Jackson—Photo credit: The Art Archive at Art Resource, NY

Richard S. Ewell—Photo credit: © 2014 Stock Sales WGBH / Scala / Art Resource, NY

"Bloody Lane, Confederate Dead, Antietam"—Photo credit: Alexander Gardner, American (1821–1882),

"Bloody Lane, Confederate Dead, Antietam," September 19, 1862, Albumen Print, 3⅛ x 3¾ in. Chrysler Museum of Art, Norfolk, VA, Gift of David L. Hack and by exchange Walter P. Chrysler, Jr. 98.32.137

Sherman's March to Atlanta, 1864—Photo credit: Alexander Hay Ritchie, Prints & Photographs Division, Library of Congress, LC-DIG-ppmsca-09326

Lee on Traveller Leaving McLean House—Photo credit: Alfred R. Waud, Morgan collection of Civil War drawings, Prints & Photographs Division, Library of Congress, LC-DIG-ppmsca-21320

Lee, photographed by Matthew Brady—Photo credit: Prints & Photographs Division, Library of Congress, LC-DIG-cwpbh-03115

Lee's mess kit & field glasses—Photo credit: Author's collection

Lee on Traveller—Photo credit: Oversize Collection, Special Collections, Leyburn Library, Washington and Lee University

Mrs. Lee in old age—Photo credit: Christian F. Schwerdt, © Chicago History Museum/The Bridgeman Art Library

Robert E. Lee shortly before his death—Photo credit: Time & Life Pictures / Getty Images

Tomb of Robert E. Lee—Photo credit: Photographs in the Carol M. Highsmith Archive, Prints & Photographs Division, Library of Congress, LC-DIG-highsm-11812

COLOR PHOTO INSERT:

Anne Hill Carter Lee—Photo credit: Washington-
Custis-Lee Collection, Washington and Lee University,
Lexington, VA

Henry Lee—Photo credit: National Portrait Gallery,
Smithsonian Institution / Art Resource, NY

George Washington Custis Family—Photo credit:
Christian Schussele, Colored mezzotint c.1864 after
painting / Universal History Archive/ UIG / The
Bridgeman Art Library

Mrs. Robert E. Lee—Photo credit: William Edward West,
"Mary Anna Randolph Custis Lee (Mrs. Robert E. Lee),
1838," Washington-Custis-Lee Collection, Washington and
Lee University, Lexington, VA_LC1959.10.2

Robert E. Lee—Photo credit: William Edward West,
"Robert E. Lee in the Dress Uniform of a Lt. of Engineers,
1839," Washington-Custis-Lee Collection, Washington and
Lee University, Lexington, VA LC1959.10.1

"The Spring of the Confederacy" Hoffbauer Mural—
Photo credit: Hoffbauer, Charles, "Four Seasons of the
Confederacy," Virginia Historical Society

Eye of the Storm—Photo credit: Painting by Don Troiani,
Historical Art Prints

"The Last Meeting of Lee and Jackson"—Photo credit:
Everett D. B. Julio (1843–79) (after), Brown University
Library / The Bridgeman Art Library

"Decision at Dawn"—Photo credit: Painting by Don Troiani, Historical Art Prints

Little Round Top from Below—Photo credit: Edwin Forbes, Morgan collection of Civil War drawings, Prints & Photographs Division, Library of Congress, LC-DIG-ppmsca-22564

Little Round Top from Above—Photo credit: Edwin Forbes, Morgan collection of Civil War drawings, Prints & Photographs Division, Library of Congress, LC-DIG-ppmsca-22565

Winslow Homer's "Prisoners from the Front"—Photo credit: © The Metropolitan Museum of Art, Image source: Art Resource, NY

General Grant and General Lee in the parlor of McClean House—Jean Leon Gerome Ferris, "Let Us Have Peace"—Photo credit: Virginia Historical Society

Lee's sword—Photo credit: The Museum of the Confederacy, Richmond, Virginia, Photography by Katherine Wetzel

Lee's frock coat—Photo credit: The Museum of the Confederacy, Richmond, Virginia, Photography by Katherine Wetzel

Lee Monument Gettysburg—Photo credit: Images Etc Ltd / Getty Images

Lee Monument, Richmond—Photo credit: © Buddy Mays / Corbis

Stone Mountain Monument—Photo credit: © Walter Bibikow / JAI / Corbis

About the Author

M ichael Korda is the author of *Ulysses S. Grant,
Ike, Hero,* and *Charmed Lives.* Educated at Le
Rosey in Switzerland and at Magdalen College, Oxford,
he served in the Royal Air Force. He took part in the
Hungarian Revolution of 1956 and on its fiftieth anni-
versary was awarded the Order of Merit of the People's
Republic of Hungary. He and his wife, Margaret, make
their home in Dutchess County, New York.

HARPER LUXE

THE NEW LUXURY IN READING

We hope you enjoyed reading
our new, comfortable print size and found it
an experience you would like to repeat.

Well — you're in luck!

HarperLuxe offers the finest in fiction and
nonfiction books in this same larger print size and
paperback format. Light and easy to read, HarperLuxe
paperbacks are for book lovers who want to see
what they are reading without the strain.

For a full listing of titles and
new releases to come, please visit our website:

www.HarperLuxe.com

SEEING IS BELIEVING!